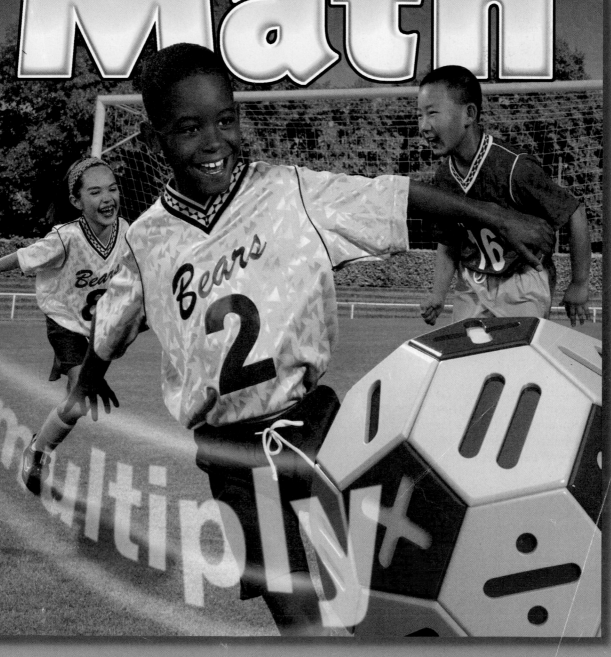

Houghton Mifflin
California
Math

 HOUGHTON MIFFLIN   BOSTON

Printed in the U.S.A.

ISBN-13: 978-0-618-82739-8

ISBN-10: 0-618-82739-0

3 4 5 6 7 8 9 - DOW - 15 14 13 12 11 10 09 08

Houghton Mifflin
California Math

Authors & Consultants

Authors

Renee Hill
Mathematics Specialist
Riverside Unified School District
Riverside, CA

Matt Larson
Curriculum Specialist for
Mathematics
Lincoln Public Schools
Lincoln, NE

Miriam A. Leiva
Bonnie E. Cone Distinguished
Professor Emerita
Professor of Mathematics Emerita
University of North Carolina
Charlotte, NC

Jean M. Shaw
Professor Emerita of Curriculum
and Instruction
University of Mississippi
Oxford, MS

Dr. Lee Stiff
Professor of Mathematics Education
North Carolina State University
Raleigh, NC

Dr. Bruce Vogeli
Clifford Brewster Upton Professor
of Mathematics
Teachers College, Columbia
University
New York, NY

Consultants

Mental Math Strategies

Greg Tang
Author and Mathematics
Consultant
Belmont, MA

English Learners

Dr. Russell M. Gersten
Executive Director, Institutional
Research Group & Professor
Emeritus
College of Education, University of
Oregon
Long Beach, CA

Lisette Estrella-Henderson
Director of District and School
Support
Solano County Office of Education
Fairfield, CA

Language and Vocabulary

Dr. Shane Templeton
Foundation Professor, Department
of Educational Specialties
University of Nevada at Reno
Reno, NV

Strategic Consultant

Dr. Liping Ma
Senior Scholar
Carnegie Foundation for the
Advancement of Technology
Palo Alto, CA

Special Projects

Catherine Valentino
Author-in-Residence
Houghton Mifflin
West Kingston, RI

Content Reviewers

Dr. W. Stephen Wilson
(Grades K–2)
Professor of Mathematics
Johns Hopkins University
Baltimore, MD

Dr. Kurt Kreith
(Grades 3–4)
Emeritus Professor of Mathematics
University of California at Davis
Davis, CA

Dr. Solomon Friedberg
(Grade 5)
Professor of Mathematics
Boston College
Chestnut Hill, MA

Dr. Bert Fristedt
(Grade 6)
Professor of Mathematics
University of Minnesota
Minneapolis, MN

California Reviewers

Grade K

Cynthia Dominguez
Highlands Elementary School
Saugus, CA

Dana Hight
Royal Oaks Elementary School
Visalia, CA

Patricia Mahoney
John Adams Elementary School
Madera, CA

Teresa Rogers
Skyline North Elementary
School
Barstow, CA

Schelly Solko
Roy W. Loudon Elementary
School
Bakersfield, CA

Julie Towne
Jurupa Vista Elementary School
Fontana, CA

Grade 1

Kirsten Marsh
Edgemont Elementary School
Moreno Valley, CA

Jill McCarthy
Edgemont Elementary School
Moreno Valley, CA

Brandee Ramirez
Myford Elementary School
Tustin, CA

Rebecca Solares
Cerritos Elementary School
Glendale, CA

Leanne Thomas
Scott Lane Elementary School
Santa Clara, CA

Sheila Vann
Folsom Hills Elementary School
Folsom, CA

Grade 2

Deborah Nelson
North Park Elementary School
Valencia, CA

Kathryn Smith
Quail Run Elementary School
San Ramon, CA

Angelica Yates
Allen at Steinbeck
Elementary School
San José, CA

Grade 3

Pamela Aurangzeb
Grapeland Elementary School
Etiwanda, CA

Veronica Fowler
Challenger School of Sports &
Fitness
Victorville, CA

Nancy Hayes
Toro Park School
Salinas, CA

Megan Heavens
North Park Elementary School
Valencia, CA

Caryl Lyons
Manuel L. Real Elementary
School
Perris, CA

Stacey McKay
Glenn E. Murdock Elementary
School
La Mesa, CA

Peggy Morrill
Grapeland Elementary School
Etiwanda, CA

Kristine Salomonson
Freedom Elementary School
Clovis, CA

Susan Steubing
Folsom Hills Elementary School
Folsom, CA

The reviewers work with the authors, consultants, and publisher to be sure that problems are correct, instructions work, and this book is the best it can be.

California Reviewers

Grade 4

Cheryl Robertson
McPherson Magnet School
Orange, CA

JoAnna Trafecanty
North Park Elementary School
Valencia, CA

Grade 5

Karen Clarke
Manuel L. Real Elementary
School
Perris, CA

Bonita DeAmicis
Highlands Elementary School
Saugus, CA

Gretchen Oberg
Ralph Dailard Elementary
School
San Diego, CA

Grade 6

Judy Denenny
McPherson Magnet School
Orange, CA

Terri Parker
Leo B. Hart Elementary School
Bakersfield, CA

George Ratcliff
Joseph Casillas Elementary
School
Chula Vista, CA

Patricia Wenzel
Cloverly Elementary School
Temple City, CA

Across Grade

Gina Chavez
California State University, Los
Angeles
Los Angeles, CA

Catherine De Leon
Washington Elementary School
Madera, CA

Cindy Ellis
Madera Unified School District
Madera, CA

Jenny Maguire
Orinda Union School District
Orinda, CA

Ernest Minelli
Selby Lane School
Redwood City, CA

Barbara Page
Modesto City Schools
Modesto, CA

Ian Tablit
Delano Union Elementary
School District
Delano, CA

Jeannie Tavolazzi
Grapeland Elementary School
Etiwanda, CA

Dina Tews
John J. Pershing Elementary
School
Madera, CA

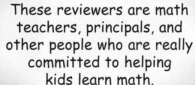

These reviewers are math teachers, principals, and other people who are really committed to helping kids learn math.

California Mathematics

Content Standards

What are Key Standards ?

- The standards are goals for what you will learn in math.

- The standards have five strands: Number Sense; Measurement and Geometry; Algebra and Functions; Statistics, Data Analysis, and Probability; and Mathematical Reasoning.

- The symbol  means it is a KEY to success this year.

- Knowing the content standards means you can do well on tests.

How will this book help you succeed?

It's as easy as one, two, three.

1. Look for **Key Standards** in this book.

2. Do your best work. Ask questions.

3. Use the Key Standards Handbook.

Doing well feels teriffic!

Number Sense

	Standards You Will Learn	Some Places to Look
1.0	Students understand the place value of whole numbers:	Lessons 1.1, 1.2, 1.3, 1.4, 2.1, 2.2, 2.3, 2.4, 2.5, 4.5, 20.3, 20.4, 21.1
1.1	Count, read, and write whole numbers to 10,000.	Lessons 1.1, 1.2, 1.3, 1.4, 1.5, 2.1, Chapter 1 Standards-Based Extra Practice
1.2	Compare and order whole numbers to 10,000.	Lessons 2.1, 2.2, 2.5, 3.6, 12.5, Chapter 1, 2 Standards-Based Extra Practice; Chapter 2 Vocabulary; Chapter 3 Math Works!
KEY 1.3	Identify the place value for each digit in numbers to 10,000.	Lessons 1.1, 1.2, 1.4, 2.1, 2.2, 2.3, 2.4, 2.5, 5.5, 21.1 Key Standards Handbook, pp. KSH2–KSH3; Chapter 1 Standards-Based Extra Practice; Chapters 3, 12 Key Standards Review
1.4	Round off numbers to 10,000 to the nearest ten, hundred, and thousand.	Lessons 2.3, 2.4, 4.5, 4.6, 5.5, 9.5, 19.3, 20.3, 20.4, 23.5 Chapter 2 Extra Practice; Chapter 3 Challenge
KEY 1.5	Use expanded notation to represent numbers (e.g., 3,206 = 3,000 + 200 + 6).	Lessons 1.2, 1.4, 5.5, 9.5, 23.5 Key Standards Handbook, pp. KSH4–KSH5; Chapters 2, 3, 12 Key Standards Review
2.0	Students calculate and solve problems involving addition, subtraction, multiplication, and division:	Lessons 3.1, 3.3, 3.4, 3.5, 3.6, 4.1, 4.2, 4.3, 4.4, 4.5, 4.6, 5.1, 5.2, 5.4, 5.5, 6.1, 6.5, 7.2, 7.3, 7.4, 7.5, 8.5, 12.1, 12.3, 12.4, 12.5, 13.1, 13.2, 13.3, 13.4, 13.5, 14.2, 14.3, 14.4, 14.5, 16.5, 19.1, 19.2, 19.4, 20.1, 20.2, 21.3, 21.5, 24.1, 24.2, 24.3, 24.4, 25.1, 25.3, 25.4, 26.1, 26.2, 26.3, 26.4, 28.4 Chapters 13, 24 Standards-Based Extra Practice
KEY 2.1	Find the sum or difference of two whole numbers between 0 and 10,000.	Lessons 3.1, 3.3, 3.5, 3.6, 4.1, 4.2, 4.3, 4.4, 4.5, 4.6, 5.5, 7.5, 8.5, 14.5, 16.5, 20.5, 28.4 Key Standards Handbook, pp. KSH6–KSH7; Chapter 3 Vocabulary; Chapter 3 Math Works!; Chapter 4 Standards-Based Extra Practice; Chapters 5, 17 Key Standards Review; Unit 2 Get Ready Game
KEY 2.2	Memorize to automaticity the multiplication table for numbers between 1 and 10.	Lessons 5.3, 5.4, 6.2, 6.3, 6.4, 7.2, 7.3, 7.5 Key Standards Handbook, pp. KSH8–KSH9; Chapters 5, 6, 7 Standards-Based Extra Practice; Chapters 7, 8, 9, 24 Key Standards Review; Unit 7 Get Ready Game
KEY 2.3	Use the inverse relationship of multiplication and division to compute and check results.	Lessons 12.2, 12.3, 12.4, 13.1, 13.2, 13.3, 13.4, 13.5, 14.2, 14.3, 14.4, 24.3, 25.3, 26.1, 26.2, 26.3, 26.4 Key Standards Handbook, pp. KSH10–KSH11; Chapter 15 Key Standards Review; Chapters 12, 13, 24 Extra Practice

Number Sense (continued)

	Standards You Will Learn	Some Places to Look
KEY 2.4	Solve simple problems involving multiplication of multidigit numbers by one-digit numbers ($3{,}671 \times 3 =$ __).	Lessons 19.1, 19.2, 19.3, 19.4, 20.1, 20.2, 20.3, 20.4, 20.5, 21.1, 21.2, 21.3, 21.4, 21.5, 25.4 Key Standards Handbook, pp. KSH12–KSH13; Chapters 19, 20, 21 Standards-Based Extra Practice; Chapter 21 Key Standards Review
2.5	Solve division problems in which a multidigit number is evenly divided by a one-digit number ($135 \div 5 =$ __).	Lessons 25.1, 25.2, 25.3, 26.1, 26.2, 26.4 Chapters 25, 26 Standards-Based Extra Practice
2.6	Understand the special properties of 0 and 1 in multiplication and division.	Lessons 6.1, 7.1, 7.4, 14.1, 20.2,
2.7	Determine the unit cost when given the total cost and number of units.	Lessons 24.4, 26.3, 26.5, 27.6 Chapter 26 Standards-Based Extra Practice
2.8	Solve problems that require two or more of the skills mentioned above.	Lessons 1.5, 4.4, 5.4, 6.5, 7.5, 8.5, 9.6, 11.5, 12.5, 13.5, 14.5, 18.5, 20.2, 20.5, 22.6, 24.3, 24.4, 25.3, 26.5, 27.6 Chapter 3 Math Works!; Chapter 20 Challenge
3.0	Students understand the relationship between whole numbers, simple fractions, and decimals:	Lessons 15.1, 15.2, 15.3, 15.4, 15.5, 15.6, 16.5, 17.2, 17.3, 17.4, 17.5, 19.4 Chapters 15, 17 Standards-Based Extra Practice; Chapter 17 Challenge
3.1	Compare fractions represented by drawings or concrete materials to show equivalency and to add and subtract simple fractions in context (e.g., $\frac{1}{2}$ of a pizza is the same amount as $\frac{2}{4}$ of another pizza that is the same size; show that $\frac{3}{8}$ is larger than $\frac{1}{4}$).	Lessons 15.3, 15.4, 15.5, 16.1, 16.2, 16.3, 17.1 Chapter 15 Standards-Based Extra Practice; Unit 6 Get Ready Game
KEY 3.2	Add and subtract simple fractions (e.g., determine that $\frac{1}{8} + \frac{3}{8}$ is the same as $\frac{1}{2}$).	Lessons 16.1, 16.2, 16.3, 16.4, 16.5, 19.4 Key Standards Handbook, KSH14–KSH15; Chapter 16 Standards-Based Extra Practice; Chapters 17, 19 Key Standards Review
KEY 3.3	Solve problems involving addition, subtraction, multiplication, and division of money amounts in decimal notation and multiply and divide money amounts in decimal notation by using whole-number multipliers and divisors.	Lessons 18.1, 18.2, 18.3, 18.5, 21.4, 23.5, 26.3, 26.5, 27.6 Key Standards Handbook, pp. KSH16–KSH17; Chapters 18, 21, 26 Standards-Based Extra Practice; Chapters 19, 22, 27, 28 Key Standards Review
3.4	Know and understand that fractions and decimals are two different representations of the same concept (e.g., 50 cents is $\frac{1}{2}$ of a dollar, 75 cents is $\frac{3}{4}$ of a dollar).	Lessons 17.2, 17.3, 17.4, 17.5 Chapter 17 Standards-Based Extra Practice

Algebra and Functions

	Standards You Will Learn	Some Places to Look
1.0	Students select appropriate symbols, operations, and properties to represent, describe, simplify, and solve simple number relationships:	Lessons 3.2, 3.3, 3.4, 3.5, 18.5, 20.1, 28.3
KEY 1.1	Represent relationships of quantities in the form of mathematical expressions, equations, or inequalities.	Lessons 3.2, 5.1, 5.3, 7.3, 12.5, 13.5, 16.5, 18.5, 25.4, 26.3, 27.6, 28.3 Key Standards Handbook, pp. KSH18–KSH19; Chapter 3 Standards-Based Extra Practice; Chapters 4, 5, 9, 21, 22, 24 Key Standards Review
1.2	Solve problems involving numeric equations or inequalities.	Lessons 3.2, 3.3, 5.2, 7.3, 7.4, 13.2, 13.3, 13.4, 14.4, 16.2, 18.5, 26.3 Chapter 14 Challenge
1.3	Select appropriate operational and relational symbols to make an expression true (e.g., if 4 __ 3 = 12, what operational symbol goes in the blank?).	Lessons 3.2, 3.5, 13.2, 13.4, 14.3, 25.3, 26.2 Chapter 6 Challenge
1.4	Express simple unit conversions in symbolic form (e.g., __ inches = __ feet × 12).	Lessons 8.2, 14.4, 19.1, 27.5, 27.6, 28.3 Chapters 27, 28 Extra Practice
1.5	Recognize and use the commutative and associative properties of multiplication (e.g., if 5 × 7 = 35, then what is 7 × 5? and if 5 × 7 × 3 = 105, then what is 7 × 3 × 5?).	Lessons 5.2, 6.1, 7.2, 7.3, 7.4, 20.1 Chapters 5, 7 Standards-Based Extra Practice; Chapter 6 Challenge; Chapter 7 Vocabulary
2.0	Students represent simple functional relationships:	Lessons 1.5, 10.5, 12.5, 13.4, 21.5, 27.5
KEY 2.1	Solve simple problems involving a functional relationship between two quantities (e.g., find the total cost of multiple items given the cost per unit).	Lessons 12.5, 18.4, 21.4, 21.5, 24.4, 27.5, 27.6 Key Standards Handbook, pp. KSH20–KSH21; Chapters 20, 28 Key Standards Review
2.2	Extend and recognize a linear pattern by its rules (e.g., the number of legs on a given number of horses may be calculated by counting by 4s or by multiplying the number of horses by 4).	Lessons 1.5, 5.2, 5.5, 7.3, 8.2, 10.5, 18.4

Measurement and Geometry

	Standards You Will Learn	Some Places to Look
1.0	Students choose and use appropriate units and measurement tools to quantify the properties of objects:	Lessons 8.1, 8.2, 8.3, 8.4, 10.1, 10.2, 10.3, 10.4, 11.3, 11.4, 27.1, 27.4, 28.1, 28.2, 28.4 Chapter 27 Standards-Based Extra Practice; Unit 4 Game
1.1	Choose the appropriate tools and units (metric and U.S.) and estimate and measure the length, liquid volume, and weight/mass of given objects.	Lessons 8.1, 8.2, 8.3, 8.4, 8.5, 10.1, 27.1, 27.2, 27.3, 27.4, 28.1, 28.2, 28.4 Chapters 8, 27, 28 Standards-Based Extra Practice
KEY 1.2	Estimate or determine the area and volume of solid figures by covering them with squares or by counting the number of cubes that would fill them.	Lessons 10.3, 10.4, 10.5, 11.3, 11.4, 11.5 Key Standards Handbook, pp. KSH22–KSH23; Chapter 10 Standards-Based Extra Practice; Chapter 14 Key Standards Review
KEY 1.3	Find the perimeter of a polygon with integer sides.	Lessons 10.1, 10.2, 10.4, 10.5, 11.5, 16.5, 25.3 Key Standards Handbook, pp. KSH24–KSH25; Chapter 10 Standards-Based Extra Practice; Chapters 14, 16 Key Standards Review; Challenge pp. 433, 529, 547
1.4	Carry out simple unit conversions within a system of measurement (e.g., centimeters and meters, hours and minutes).	Lessons 8.2, 8.4, 12.5, 14.4, 19.1, 27.1, 27.2, 27.5, 27.6, 28.2, 28.3 Chapter 25 Standards-Based Extra Practice
2.0	Students describe and compare the attributes of plane and solid geometric figures and use their understanding to show relationships and solve problems:	Lessons 9.1, 9.2, 9.3, 9.4, 9.5, 11.1, 11.2
KEY 2.1	Identify, describe, and classify polygons (including pentagons, hexagons, and octagons).	Lessons 9.2, 9.4, 9.5 Key Standards Handbook, pp. KSH26–KSH27; Chapter 9 Standards-Based Extra Practice; Chapters 10, 11, 18 Key Standards Review; Challenge p. 547
KEY 2.2	Identify attributes of triangles (e.g., two equal sides for the isosceles triangle, three equal sides for the equilateral triangle, right angle for the right triangle).	Lessons 9.3, 9.4, 9.6, 10.1, 25.3, 26.4 Key Standards Handbook, pp. KSH28–KSH29; Chapter 9 Standards-Based Extra Practice; Chapters 10, 11 Key Standards Review
KEY 2.3	Identify attributes of quadrilaterals (e.g., parallel sides for the parallelogram, right angles for the rectangle, equal sides and right angles for the square).	Lessons 9.3, 9.5, 9.6, 10.1, 10.2, 25.3 Key Standards Handbook, pp. KSH30–KSH31; Chapter 9 Extra Practice; Chapters 13, 18 Key Standards Review
2.4	Identify right angles in geometric figures or in appropriate objects and determine whether other angles are greater or less than a right angle.	Lessons 9.1, 9.3, 9.4, 9.5

Measurement and Geometry (continued)

	Standards You Will Learn	**Some Places to Look**
2.5	Identify, describe, and classify common three-dimensional geometric objects (e.g., cube, rectangular solid, sphere, prism, pyramid, cone, cylinder).	Lessons 11.1, 11.2 Chapter 11 Standards-Based Extra Practice; Chapter 11 Wrap Up
2.6	Identify common solid objects that are the components needed to make a more complex solid object.	Lessons 11.2, 11.4 Chapter 11 Vocabulary; Chapter 11 Game; Chapter 11 Wrap Up

Statistics, Data Analysis, and Probability

Standards You Will Learn	Some Places to Look
1.0 Students conduct simple probability experiments by determining the number of possible outcomes and make simple predictions:	Lessons 23.1, 23.2, 23.3, 23.4 Chapter 23 Game
1.1 Identify whether common events are certain, likely, unlikely, or improbable.	Lessons 23.2, 23.3, 23.4, 23.5 Chapter 23 Vocabulary; Chapter 23 Standards-Based Extra Practice
KEY 1.2 Record the possible outcomes for a simple event (e.g., tossing a coin) and systematically keep track of the outcomes when the event is repeated many times.	Lessons 23.1, 23.3 Key Standard Handbook, p. KSH32; Chapter 23 Standards-Based Extra Practice; Chapter 26 Key Standards Review
KEY 1.3 Summarize and display the results of probability experiments in a clear and organized way (e.g., use a bar graph or a line plot).	Lessons 23.1, 23.3, 23.4 Key Standard Handbook, pp. KSH33–KSH34; Chapters 22, 23 Standards-Based Extra Practice; Chapter 25 Key Standards Review
1.4 Use the results of probability experiments to predict future events (e.g., use a line plot to predict the temperature forecast for the next day).	Lessons 22.1, 22.2, 23.3, 23.4 Chapters 22, 23 Standards-Based Extra Practice

Mathematical Reasoning

	Standards You Will Learn	**Some Places to Look**
1.0	Students make decisions about how to approach problems:	Lessons 2.5, 3.6, 4.6, 5.5, 8.5, 11.5, 12.4, 12.5, 13.5, 19.4, 22.5, 23.2, 23.4, 23.5, 24.4, 25.4, 28.4
1.1	Analyze problems by identifying relationships, distinguishing relevant from irrelevant information, sequencing and prioritizing information, and observing patterns.	Lessons 1.5, 2.5, 3.6, 5.5, 6.5, 7.5, 8.5, 10.5, 11.1, 11.2, 11.5, 12.5, 13.5, 14.5, 15.6, 16.5, 17.5, 18.5, 19.1, 19.4, 20.5, 22.6, 23.5, 24.4, 25.4, 26.5, 27.6
1.2	Determine when and how to break a problem into simpler parts.	Lessons 6.5, 7.4, 7.5, 8.5, 9.6, 11.5, 12.5, 13.4, 13.5, 14.5, 16.4, 19.4, 20.2, 20.5, 22.6, 24.4, 25.3
2.0	Students use strategies, skills, and concepts in finding solutions:	Lessons 1.5, 2.2, 2.5, 3.6, 4.6, 5.2, 5.5, 6.5, 7.4, 7.5, 8.5, 8.4, 10.5, 11.5, 12.5, 13.5, 14.5, 15.6, 16.5, 17.5, 18.5, 19.4, 20.5, 21.5, 22.3, 23.5, 24.4, 26.5, 27.6, 28.4
2.1	Use estimation to verify the reasonableness of calculated results.	Lessons 4.5, 20.3, 20.4, 21.2, 21.5, 25.4
2.2	Apply strategies and results from simpler problems to more complex problems.	Lessons 3.4, 3.5, 18.1, 24.1, 25.1, 25.4, 26.2
2.3	Use a variety of methods, such as words, numbers, symbols, charts, graphs, tables, diagrams, and models, to explain mathematical reasoning.	Lessons 1.1, 1.5, 2.1, 3.1, 4.6, 5.1, 5.3, 5.4, 6.5, 7.5, 8.5, 9.4, 9.6, 10.5, 14.5, 15.6, 17.5, 18.5, 20.5, 21.5, 23.4, 24.1, 24.4, 26.1, 27.6
2.4	Express the solution clearly and logically by using the appropriate mathematical notation and terms and clear language; support solutions with evidence in both verbal and symbolic work.	Lessons 1.5, 2.5, 3.6, 6.5, 7.5, 9.6, 10.5, 11.5, 13.5, 14.5, 15.6, 17.5, 19.4, 24.1, 24.4, 25.4, 26.5
2.5	Indicate the relative advantages of exact and approximate solutions to problems and give answers to a specified degree of accuracy.	Lessons 2.3, 2.4, 19.3, 21.2, 21.4, 28.4 Chapter 19 Standards-Based Extra Practice
2.6	Make precise calculations and check the validity of the results from the context of the problem.	Lessons 3.4, 6.5, 8.5, 10.5, 16.2, 16.5, 20.2, 21.2, 24.4, 26.5

Mathematical Reasoning (continued)

	Standards You Will Learn	**Some Places to Look**
3.0	Students move beyond a particular problem by generalizing to other situations:	Lessons 1.5, 4.6, 6.5, 7.2, 7.4, 7.5, 9.6, 10.5, 11.5, 13.5, 14.1, 14.5, 15.6, 17.5, 18.5, 20.5, 21.5, 23.2, 25.2, 26.3, 26.5, 27.6, 28.4
3.1	Evaluate the reasonableness of the solution in the context of the original situation.	Lessons 1.5, 4.4, 6.5, 7.5, 9.6, 10.5, 13.5, 14.5, 15.6, 18.5, 21.5, 24.4, 26.5, 27.6
3.2	Note the method of deriving the solution and demonstrate a conceptual understanding of the derivation by solving similar problems.	Lessons 1.5, 4.6, 6.5, 7.4, 7.5, 9.6, 10.5, 11.5, 12.2, 13.5, 14.5, 15.6, 16.4, 17.5, 18.5, 20.5, 21.5, 23.2, 24.2, 24.4, 25.2, 26.5, 27.6
3.3	Develop generalizations of the results obtained and apply them in other circumstances.	Lessons 1.5, 4.6, 6.1, 6.5, 7.1, 7.2, 7.4, 7.5, 9.6, 10.5, 11.5, 13.2, 13.5, 15.6, 17.5, 20.5, 21.5, 22.2, 23.2, 25.2, 26.3, 26.5, 27.6, 28.4

Key Standards Handbook

The key standards will help me meet my goals in math.

These are my goals in math this year.

I can add, subtract, multiply, and divide.

$2 \times 3 = 6$

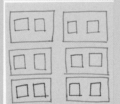

I share mathematical ideas with others.

I know that different strands of math are related.

I can think logically about a problem and analyze ideas.

I find math in everyday life.

Math is important to me and everyone around me!

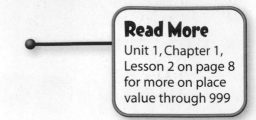
How do you identify the place value of a digit in a 3-digit number?

Read More
Unit 1, Chapter 1, Lesson 2 on page 8 for more on place value through 999

▶ **Connect It**

A place-value chart shows the **place value** of each digit in a number.

EXAMPLE:

What is the value of each digit in 256?

Hundreds	Tens	Ones
2	5	6

The value of 2 is 200.   The value of 5 is 50.   The value of 6 is 6.

USE YOUR SKILLS

Write the place value of each underlined digit. Then write its value.

1. 6<u>5</u>7

2. 3<u>0</u>

3. 4<u>2</u>8

4. <u>9</u>05

5. Compare Is the value of the digit 8 the same in 482 and 814? Why or why not?

KEY **NS 1.3** Identify the place value for each digit in numbers to 10,000.

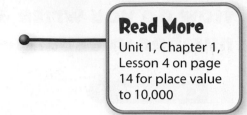
How do you identify the place value of digits in numbers to 10,000?

Read More
Unit 1, Chapter 1, Lesson 4 on page 14 for place value to 10,000

▶ Connect It

A place-value chart can be used to show the place value of each digit in larger numbers, too.

EXAMPLE:

What is the place value of the digits in 9,256?

Thousands	Hundreds	Tens	Ones
9	2	5	6

The value of the 9 is 9,000.   The value of the 2 is 200.   The value of the 5 is 50.   The value of the 6 is 6.

USE YOUR SKILLS

Write the place value of the underlined digit. Then write its value.

1. 1,8<u>9</u>7

2. <u>6</u>,172

3. 3,<u>6</u>73

4. 8,<u>9</u>57

5. Contrast How is the value of the digit 3 different in 3,002 than in 5,347?

How do you write a 3-digit number in expanded form?

Read More
Unit 1, Chapter 1, Lesson 2 on page 8 for more on writing numbers in expanded notation

▶ **Connect It**

You can write a number in a way that shows the place value of each digit. This way is called **expanded form**.

EXAMPLE:

How do you write 479 in expanded form?

Hundreds	Tens	Ones
4	7	9

The value of the 4 is 400.   The value of the 7 is 70.   The value of the 9 is 9.

In expanded form, 479 is written as:

$400 + 70 + 9$

USE YOUR SKILLS

Write each number in expanded form.

1. 345

2. 687

3. 508

4. 442

5. Generalize What patterns do you notice when writing a number in expanded form?

KEY **NS 1.5** Use expanded notation to represent numbers (e.g., 3,206 = 3,000 + 200 + 6).

How do you write a 4-digit number in expanded form?

Read More

Unit 1, Chapter 1, Lesson 4 on page 14 for more on writing numbers to 10,000 in expanded notation

▶ **Connect It**

You can write a number in a way that shows the place value of each digit. This way is called expanded form.

EXAMPLE:

How do you write 7,698 in expanded form?

Thousands	Hundreds	Tens	Ones
7	6	9	8

The value of the 7 is 7,000.　　The value of the 6 is 600.　　The value of the 9 is 90.　　The value of the 8 is 8.

In expanded form, 7,698 is written as:

7,000 + 600 + 90 + 8

USE YOUR SKILLS

Write each number in expanded form.

1. 3,490
2. 2,578
3. 5,606
4. 5,882
5. **Summarize** How does the digit 0 affect how a number is written in expanded form?

KEY **NS 1.5** Use expanded notation to represent numbers (e.g., 3,206 = 3,000 + 200 + 6).

How do you add larger numbers?

Read More
Unit 2, Chapter 3, Lessons 1 through 5 on pages 50 though 62 for more on adding whole numbers

▶ **Connect It**

Add.

998 + 1,025 = ?

Step 1: Add the ones. 8 + 5 = 13	**Step 2:** Add the tens. 1 + 9 + 2 = 12	**Step 3:** Add the hundreds. 1 + 9 + 0 = 10	**Step 4:** Add the thousands. 1 + 1 = 2
¹ 998 +1,025 — 3	¹ ¹ 998 +1,025 — 23	¹ ¹ ¹ 998 +1,025 — 023	¹ ¹ ¹ 998 +1,025 — 2,023
Regroup 13 ones as 1 ten and 3 ones.	Regroup 12 tens as 1 hundred and 2 tens.	Regroup 10 hundreds as 1 thousand and 0 hundreds.	

So, 998 + 1,025 = 2,023.

USE YOUR SKILLS

Find each sum. Regroup when necessary.

1. 4,506
    + 3,256

2. 2,030
    + 5,664

3. 3,087
    + 5,945

4. 3,888
    + 321

5. Explain Why is it helpful to solve addition problems in a column format?

KEY NS 2.1 Find the sum or difference of two whole numbers between 0 and 10,000.

KSH6

How do you subtract larger numbers?

Read More
Unit 2, Chapter 4, Lessons 1 through 4 on pages 72 through 82 for more on subtracting numbers

▶ **Connect It**

Subtract.

525 − 380 = ?

Step 1: Place the larger number on the top. Subtract the ones.	Step 2: Subtract the tens; because 8 > 2, you will regroup 1 hundred as 10 tens. Subtract.	Step 3: Subtract the hundreds.	Step 4: Check your subtraction using addition. Is 380 + 145 = 525? Yes!
525 − 380 5	4 12 5̶2̶5̶ − 380 45	4 12 5̶2̶5̶ − 380 145	1 380 + 145 525

So, 525 − 380 = 145.

USE YOUR SKILLS

Subtract. Check by adding.

1. 1,445
   − 392

2. 3,765
   − 1,920

3. 8,125
   − 2,784

4. 4,003
   − 1,992

5. **Create** Write a subtraction problem in which you need to regroup twice. How do you know your problem requires regrouping? Solve, then check by adding.

KEY NS 2.1 Find the sum or difference of two whole numbers between 0 and 10,000.

How do you use a multiplication table?

▶ Connect It

You can use a multiplication table to find **products** .

Read More
Unit 3, Chapter 7, Lesson 1 on page 142 for more on using the multiplication table

EXAMPLE:

What is 4×8?

×	0	1	2	3	4	5	6	7	8	9	10
0	0	0	0	0	0	0	0	0	0	0	0
1	0	1	2	3	4	5	6	7	8	9	10
2	0	2	4	6	8	10	12	14	16	18	20
3	0	3	6	9	12	15	18	21	24	27	30
4	0	4	8	12	16	20	24	28	(32)	36	40
5	0	5	10	15	20	25	30	35	40	45	50
6	0	6	12	18	24	30	36	42	48	54	60
7	0	7	14	21	28	35	42	49	56	63	70
8	0	8	16	24	32	40	48	56	64	72	80
9	0	9	18	27	36	45	54	63	72	81	90
10	0	10	20	30	40	50	60	70	80	90	100

Step 1 Find the row for 4.

Step 2 Find the column for 8.

Step 3 Find the box where the row and column meet. The number in that box is the product of 4×8.

So, $4 \times 8 = 32$

USE YOUR SKILLS

Use the multiplication table to find the products.

1. 4×7 **2.** 9×3

3. 6×7 **4.** 8×8

5. Justify Would a multiplication table be a good tool to use to find the products of greater numbers? Explain.

KEY **NS 2.2** Memorize to automaticity the multiplication table for numbers between 1 and 10.

How do you use a multiplication table to find patterns?

Read More
Unit 3, Chapter 7, Lesson 1 on page 142 for more on using the multiplication table

▶ **Connect It**

You can use a multiplication table to find patterns.

EXAMPLE:

Look at Row 6. What pattern do you see?

×	0	1	2	3	4	5	6	7	8	9	10
0	0	0	0	0	0	0	0	0	0	0	0
1	0	1	2	3	4	5	6	7	8	9	10
2	0	2	4	6	8	10	12	14	16	18	20
3	0	3	6	9	12	15	18	21	24	27	30
4	0	4	8	12	16	20	24	28	32	36	40
5	0	5	10	15	20	25	30	35	40	45	50
6	0	6	12	18	24	30	36	42	48	54	60
7	0	7	14	21	28	35	42	49	56	63	70
8	0	8	16	24	32	40	48	56	64	72	80
9	0	9	18	27	36	45	54	63	72	81	90
10	0	10	20	30	40	50	60	70	80	90	100

All the numbers increase by 6.

USE YOUR SKILLS

Below are rows of a multiplication table. In which row or column is each part found?

1.

8	16	24	32

2.

15	20	25	30

3. **Describe** Is the pattern the same from Row 8 and Column 8? Why or why not?

KEY **NS 2.2** Memorize to automaticity the multiplication table for numbers between 1 and 10.

How are multiplication and division related?

Read More
Unit 5, Chapter 12, Lesson 2 on page 262 to learn about the relationship between multiplication and division

▶ **Connect It**

Multiplication and **division** are opposite operations. You can use arrays to see how multiplication and division are related.

Multiplication

5 groups of 7 = 35

Division

35 divided into 5 equal groups = 7 in each group

USE YOUR SKILLS

Use the array to complete each number sentence.

1.
```
●● ●● ●●
●● ●● ●●
●● ●● ●●
●● ●● ●●
```

___ × 4 = 24   ___ ÷ 4 = 6

2.
```
●●●●●●●
●●●●●●●
```

2 × ___ = 14   14 ÷ ___ = 7

3.
```
○○○○○○
○○○○○○
○○○○○○
```

18 ÷ ___ = 6   3 × ___ = 18

4. **Apply** Write a multiplication and division sentence for this array.

```
○○○○○○○○○○
○○○○○○○○○○
○○○○○○○○○○
○○○○○○○○○○
```

KEY **NS 2.3** Use the inverse relationship of multiplication and division to compute and check results.

How can you use multiplication to check answers in division?

Read More
Unit 5, Chapter 12, Lesson 2 on page 262 to learn about the relationship between multiplication and division

▶ **Connect It**

Multiplication and division are opposite operations. That means you can multiply to check your division answer.

EXAMPLE:

Divide. Use multiplication to check your answer.

$$112 \div 2 = 56$$
$$\text{dividend} \div \text{divisor} = \text{quotient}$$

$$\begin{array}{r} \overset{1}{5}6 \\ \times\,2 \\ \hline 112 \end{array}$$ factor (quotient)
factor (divisor)
product (dividend)

The product is the same as the dividend. The answer is correct.

USE YOUR SKILLS

Divide. Use multiplication to check your answer.

1. $125 \div 5$ **2.** $164 \div 4$

3. $160 \div 2$ **4.** $130 \div 10$

5. Summarize Write the steps you need to use when checking a division problem using multiplication. Use an example to help explain your answer.

KEY **NS 2.3** Use the inverse relationship of multiplication and division to compute and check results.

How do you multiply 3-digit numbers by 1-digit numbers?

Read More

Unit 7, Chapter 21, Lessons 2 on page 450 for more on multiplying 3-digit numbers by 1-digit numbers

▶ Connect It

Multiplication can help solve some problems more easily than addition.

EXAMPLE:

The soccer team raised $115. The basketball team raised 3 times as much money. How much money did the basketball team raise?

Step 1:	Step 2:	Step 3:
Multiply the ones.	Multiply the tens.	Multiply the hundreds.
$5 \times 3 = 15$	$1 \times 3 = 3$	$1 \times 3 = 3$
Regroup 15 ones as 1 ten and 5 ones.	Add the regrouped ten. $3 + 1 = 4$.	
$\begin{array}{r} \overset{1}{\$1}15 \\ \times\ \ \ 3 \\ \hline 5 \end{array}$	$\begin{array}{r} \overset{1}{\$1}15 \\ \times\ \ \ 3 \\ \hline 45 \end{array}$	$\begin{array}{r} \overset{1}{\$1}15 \\ \times\ \ \ 3 \\ \hline \$345 \end{array}$

So, the basketball team raised $345.

USE YOUR SKILLS

Find each product.

1. 234×2

2. 321×4

3. 293×3

4. 465×7

5. **Relate:** How does regrouping in multiplying problems relate to regrouping in addition problems?

KEY NS 2.4 Solve simple problems involving multiplication of multidigit numbers by one-digit numbers $(3{,}671 \times 3 = \_\_\_\_)$.

How do you multiply 4-digit numbers by 1-digit numbers with more than one regrouping?

Read More
Unit 7, Chapter 21, Lessons 2 and 3 on pages 450 through 455 for more on multiplying multidigit numbers

▶ Connect It

Some multiplication problems involve multidigit numbers that require you to regroup several times.

EXAMPLE:

The zoo had 3,475 visitors this month. Next month, it plans to have twice as many visitors. How many visitors are predicted to come to the zoo next month?

Step 1:	Step 2:	Step 3:	Step 4:
Multiply the ones. 5 x 2 = 10 Regroup 10 ones as 1 ten and 0 ones.	Multiply the tens. 7 x 2 = 14 Regroup 14 tens as 1 hundred and 4 tens. Add the regrouped ten. 4 + 1 = 5	Multiply the hundreds. 4 x 2 = 8 Add the regrouped hundred. 8 + 1 = 9	Multiply the thousands. 3 x 2 = 6
$\overset{1}{\$3,4}75$ x 2 ——— 0	$\$3,\overset{1}{4}\overset{1}{7}5$ x 2 ——— 50	$\$3,\overset{1}{4}\overset{1}{7}5$ x 2 ——— 950	$\$3,\overset{1}{4}\overset{1}{7}5$ x 2 ——— 6,950

The zoo predicts there will be 6,950 visitors next month.

USE YOUR SKILLS

Find the product.

1. 2,345 × 4

2. 3,827 × 2

3. 1,214 × 6

4. Jordan travels 2,445 miles round trip to visit her grandmother. If she makes the trip 3 times a year, how many miles does she travel?

5. Create Write a word problem in which a 4-digit number is multiplied by a 1-digit number. Switch problems with a friend and solve each other's problems.

KEY NS 2.4 Solve simple problems involving multiplication of multidigit numbers by one-digit numbers (3,671 × 3 = ____).

How do you add fractions with like denominators?

Read More

Unit 6, Chapters 16, Lesson 2 on page 348 for more on adding fractions

▶ Connect It

When the denominators are the same, you can just add the numerators. The denominator stays the same.

$$\frac{2}{5} + \frac{1}{5} = \frac{3}{5}$$ Add the numerators.
Denominator stays the same.

USE YOUR SKILLS

Add.

1. $\frac{1}{4} + \frac{2}{4}$

2. $\frac{4}{9} + \frac{1}{9}$

3. $\frac{4}{5} + \frac{2}{5}$

4. $\frac{3}{8} + \frac{3}{8}$

5. Illustrate Miguel is making a pizza with 8 slices. He decides to put pepperoni on $\frac{2}{8}$ of the pizza. He puts mushrooms on $\frac{3}{8}$ of the pizza. He left the rest of the pizza plain. How much of the pizza has toppings? Draw a picture to show how you added.

KEY **NS 3.2** Add and subtract simple fractions (e.g., determine that $\frac{1}{8} + \frac{3}{8}$ is the same as $\frac{1}{2}$).

How do you subtract fractions with like denominators?

Read More

Unit 6, Chapters 16, Lesson 3 on page 352 for more on subtracting fractions

▶ **Connect It**

When the denominators are the same, you can just subtract the numerators. The denominator remains the same.

$$\frac{5}{8} - \frac{2}{8} = \frac{3}{8}$$ Subtract the numerators. Denominator stays the same.

USE YOUR SKILLS

Subtract.

1. $\frac{8}{9} - \frac{2}{9}$

2. $\frac{4}{7} - \frac{1}{7}$

3. $\frac{5}{5} - \frac{1}{5}$

4. $\frac{6}{8} - \frac{4}{8}$

5. Connect How could you use addition to check your work on these problems? Use Exercise 4 to explain your ideas.

KEY **NS 3.2** Add and subtract simple fractions (e.g., determine that $\frac{1}{8} + \frac{3}{8}$ is the same as $\frac{1}{2}$).

How can you solve problems involving money?

Read More
Unit 6, Chapter 18, Lessons 2 and 3 on pages 386 through 392 for more on adding and subtracting money Unit 7, Chapter 21, Lesson 4 on page 456 for more on multiplying money

▶ **Connect It**

Some problems involving money require more than one step to solve. Read the problem. Decide what you need to find and what operations you need to use. Then solve.

EXAMPLE:

Jason ordered 3 orange smoothies and 1 apple juice for his friends. Each smoothie cost $1.65 and the juice cost $0.85. If he paid with a $10 bill, how much change should he get?

Step 1: Find the cost of 3 orange smoothies.	Step 2: Add the cost of the smoothies to the cost of the apple juice.	Step 3: Subtract the total cost from the $10 bill. Write the $10 with a decimal and 2 zeros.
$1.65 x 3 ――― $4.95	$4.95 + 0.85 ――― $5.80	$10.00 − 5.80 ――― $4.20

So, Jason will get $4.20 as change.

USE YOUR SKILLS

Solve each problem.

1. Megan saves $3.50 each week. At the end of 4 weeks, how much money will she still need to have $25.00?

2. Rosa wants to buy 4 pens that cost 70¢ each and one folder that cost $1.25. If she gives the clerk a $5 bill, how much change will she receive?

3. At the fair, it costs $2.50 to enter and 75¢ for each ride. If Ryan rides 6 rides and brought $10 to the fair, how much money will he have left?

4. **Explain** How do you know when to multiply when solving a word problem?

KEY **NS 3.3** Solve problems involving addition, subtraction, multiplication, and division of money amounts in decimal notation and multiply and divide money amounts in decimal notation by using whole-number multipliers and divisors.

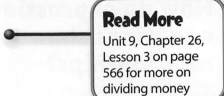
How can you solve problems that involve division with money?

Read More
Unit 9, Chapter 26, Lesson 3 on page 566 for more on dividing money

 **Connect It**

Some problems involving money require division to solve. Read the problem. Then solve.

EXAMPLE:

Michael needs to save $84 to buy a new bike. He has already saved $20. If he saves $8 each week, how many weeks will he need to save?

Step 1: Find out how much more Michael needs to save.	**Step 2:** Find out how many more weeks Michael needs to save.
$84.00 − 20.00 $64.00	$64.00 ÷ $8.00 = 8

So, Michael needs to save for 8 weeks.

USE YOUR SKILLS

Solve.

1. Mindy had $110.00. At one store, she spent $60.00 on a jacket. At another store, she wanted to spend the rest of her money on shirts that cost $10.00 each. How many shirts can Mindy buy?

2. Logan has $20.00. He bought 8 card packs for $2.25 each and then decided to spend the rest of his money on erasers that cost $0.50 each. How many erasers can he buy?

3. The soccer club raised $120.00. They spent $40.00 on new shirts. The club also wants new soccer balls. How many soccer balls can they buy if each ball costs $8.00?

4. **Compare and Contrast** How were the steps for Exercise 2 different from Exercise 3? How were they alike?

KEY **NS 3.3** Solve problems involving addition, subtraction, multiplication, and division of money amounts in decimal notation and multiply and divide money amounts in decimal notation by using whole-number multipliers and divisors.

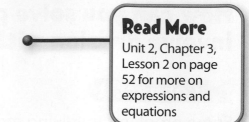
How do expressions and equations show mathematical relationships?

Read More
Unit 2, Chapter 3, Lesson 2 on page 52 for more on expressions and equations

▶ Connect It

An **expression** is a number or a group of numbers with an operational symbol. 4, 16 + 4, and 16 ÷ 4 are all examples of expressions.

An **equation** is a mathematical sentence with an equal sign that shows that two expressions have the same value. 20 = 20 and 2 + 18 = 16 + 4 are examples of equations.

EXAMPLE:

You can write an equation.

12 plus 18 is the same as 6 times 5.

$\quad +\qquad\qquad =$

$12 + 18 = 6 \times 5$

USE YOUR SKILLS

Write an equation for each sentence.

1. 24 split equally by 6 is the same as 32 minus 28.

2. The product of 3 and 6 equals 9 times 2.

3. 16 increased by 4 means 20.

4. **Apply** Mark has 42 cards he needs to share equally with 6 friends. How many cards will each friend get? Write and solve an equation for this problem.

KEY **AF 1.1** Represent relationships of quantities in the form of mathematical expressions, equations, or inequalities.

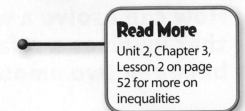

How can you write inequalities to show mathematical relationships?

Read More
Unit 2, Chapter 3, Lesson 2 on page 52 for more on inequalities

▶ **Connect It**

Inequalities compare expressions using > or <.

EXAMPLE:

You can write inequalities.

17 <u>minus</u> 6 is <u>less than</u> 20.
     −   <
      17 − 6 < 20

18 is <u>greater than</u> 10 <u>times</u> 1.
      >   ×
    18 > 10 × 1

USE YOUR SKILLS

Write an inequality for each statement.

1. 16 is less than 2 times 30.

2. 8 times 3 is greater than four increased by 8.

3. 9 plus 7 is less than 20 minus 2.

4. Create Write an inequality statement using words that include the phrase greater than. Then write your phrase using math symbols.

KEY **AF 1.1** Represent relationships of quantities in the form of mathematical expressions, equations, or inequalities.

How can I solve a word problem that involves a relationship between two amounts?

Read More
Unit 6, Chapter 18, Lesson 4 on page 394 for more on functions

▶ Connect It

Sometimes you need to find a relationship between two numbers, or a **function**, to solve a problem. You can make a **function table** to help you solve the problem.

EXAMPLE:

Ben is buying 10 treats for his dog. At Pretty Pets, the treats are 5 for $1.25. At Happy Pets, the same treats are 2 for 40 cents. Which store offers the cheaper treats?

Step 1: Make a table to show how much 10 treats cost at Pretty Pets.	**Step 2:** Make a table to show how much 10 treats cost at Happy Pets.	**Step 3:** Compare the prices.

Number of treats	Cost
5	$1.25
10	$2.50

Number of treats	Cost
2	$0.40
4	$0.80
6	$1.20
8	$1.60
10	$2.00

Ten treats at Pretty Pets will cost $2.50.

Ten treats at Happy Pets will cost $2.00.

Happy Pets offers the cheaper treats.

USE YOUR SKILLS

Solve.

1. Andrea needs 12 cans of juice for a camping trip. Bea's Market is selling 6 cans of juice for $5.50 and Gordon's Grocery has 4 cans of juice for $3.00. Which market offers the best price for juice?

2. Jose is selling 15 cookies. He offered Sam 3 cookies for $1.50. He offered Mike 5 cookies for $2.00. Who will pay the most money for 15 cookies?

3. **Apply** The Fitness Club is sponsoring all its members who join the Walk-a-thon. They will give $3 for every 2 miles walked. Make a function table to show how much money the club would sponsor to a member who walked 10 miles.

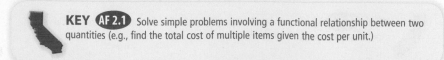

KEY AF 2.1 Solve simple problems involving a functional relationship between two quantities (e.g., find the total cost of multiple items given the cost per unit.)

How can you solve a word problem that involves a pattern?

Read More
Unit 6, Chapter 18, Lesson 4 on page 394 for more on functions

▶ **Connect It**

Some word problems can be solved by finding a pattern. You can make a function table to find a pattern.

EXAMPLE:

Joe can read 1 page in two minutes, 2 pages in four minutes, and 3 pages in six minutes. If he continues to read at the same rate, how long will it take him to read 5 pages?

The pattern is that it takes 2 minutes to read one page. Multiply the number of pages read by 2. Make a function table to show the results.

Number of pages read	Number of minutes
1	2
2	4
3	6
4	8
5	10

It will take Joe 10 minutes to read 5 pages.

USE YOUR SKILLS

Solve.

1. Tracy can buy 1 milk for 35 cents, 2 milks for 70 cents and 3 milks for $1.05. If the cost of the milk does not change, what would be the cost of 6 milks?

2. Shyla hit 10 golf balls in 5 minutes, 20 golf balls in 10 minutes, and 30 golf balls in 15 minutes. If she keeps the same pace of hitting golf balls, how many golf balls will she hit in 40 minutes?

3. **Formulate** Chris can build 3 cubes in 9 minutes, 4 cubes in 12 minutes, and 5 cubes in 15 minutes. How long will it take him to build 2 cubes? Make a table to help you find a pattern rule.

KEY **AF 2.1** Solve simple problems involving a functional relationship between two quantities (e.g., find the total cost of multiple items given the cost per unit).

How can you determine the surface area?

Read More

Unit 4, Chapter 10, Lessons 3 and 4 on pages 218 through 222 for more on area

▶ **Connect It**

Area is the number of square units needed to cover a figure.

Each ☐ = 1 **square unit**. To find the area, count the number of square units.

EXAMPLE:

What is the area of this figure?

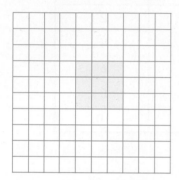

The area of this figure is 9 square units.

USE YOUR SKILLS

Find the area of each figure. Each ☐ = 1 square unit.

1.

2.

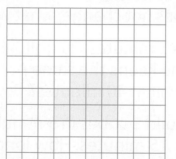

3.

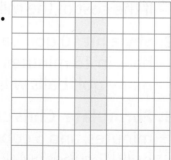

4. Extend One side of a cube has a surface area of 9 square units. How can you determine the total surface area of a cube that has a side showing 9 squares?

KEY **MG 1.2** Estimate or determine the area and volume of solid figures by covering them with squares or by counting the number of cubes that would fill them.

How can you determine the volume of a solid figure?

Read More
Unit 4, Chapter 11, Lessons 3 and 4 on pages 238 through 242 for more on volume

▶ **Connect It**

Volume is the number of cubic units it takes to fill a **solid figure**. The area of each side of a **cubic unit** is equal to one square unit. To find the volume of a solid, count the cubic units that make up the figure.

EXAMPLE:

What is the volume of this figure?

Remember to count the cubes that are hidden.

This figure has a volume of 10 cubic units.

USE YOUR SKILLS

Find the volume of each figure. Each ▪ = 1 cubic unit.

1.
2.
3.

4. **Explain** How can you find the volume of any solid figure made with cubes?

KEY **MG 1.2** Estimate or determine the area and volume of solid figures by covering them with squares or by counting the number of cubes that would fill them.

Key Standards Handbook **23**

How can you find the perimeter of a polygon?

Read More
Unit 4, Chapter 10, Lessons 1 and 2 on pages 212 through 216 for more on perimeter

▶ **Connect It**

The distance around a figure is its **perimeter**. To find perimeter, add the length of all of the sides.

EXAMPLE:

What is the perimeter of this triangle?

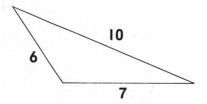

$7 + 10 + 6 = 23$ units

The perimeter of this triangle is 23 units.

USE YOUR SKILLS

Find the perimeter.

1.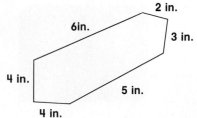
8 in.
6 in.
6 in.
8 in.

2.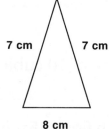
7 cm   7 cm
8 cm

3.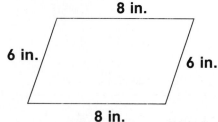
2 in.
6in.
3 in.
4 in.
5 in.
4 in.

4.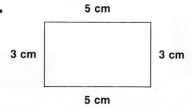
5 cm
3 cm   3 cm
5 cm

5. **Apply** The perimeter of a pentagon is 42 centimeters. Two of the sides are each 9 centimeters, one side is 10 centimeters, and one side is 6 centimeters. What is the length of the remaining side?

KEY **MG 1.3** Find the perimeter of a polygon with integer sides.

How can you find the perimeter of a polygon that has equal sides?

Read More
Unit 4, Chapter 10, Lessons 1 and 2 on pages 212 through 216 for more on perimeter

▶ **Connect It**

Some **polygons** have all sides the same length. If you know the length of one side in a polygon with all the sides the same length, you can determine the perimeter of the polygon.

EXAMPLE:

What is the perimeter of this square?

5 inches

$5 + 5 + 5 + 5 = 20$ inches

So, the perimeter of this square is 20 inches.

USE YOUR SKILLS

Find the perimeter.

1.

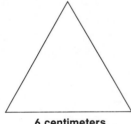

6 centimeters

2.

10 inches

3.

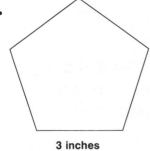

3 inches

4.

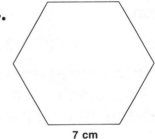

7 cm

5. **Formulate** Find another way to determine the perimeter of a polygon with all equal sides that does not use adding.

 KEY MG 1.3 Find the perimeter of a polygon with integer sides.

How can you classify polygons?

▶ Connect It

Read More

Unit 4, Chapter 9, Lesson 2 on page 192 for more on plane figures and polygons

Polygons are closed **plane figures**. They are made up of three or more **line segments**.

You can classify polygons by the number of sides they have.

Types of Polygons		
Name of Polygon	**Number of Sides**	**Example**
Triangle	3	△
Quadrilateral	4	▭
Pentagon	5	⬠
Hexagon	6	⬡
Octagon	8	⯃

EXAMPLE:

What type of polygon is this?

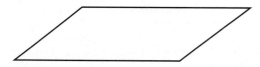

This polygon has 4 sides, so it is a quadrilateral.

USE YOUR SKILLS

Name each polygon.

1. **2.** **3.** **4.**

KEY **MG 2.1** Identify, describe, and classify polygons (including pentagons, hexagons, and octagons).

How can you describe polygons?

▶ Connect It

You can use what you know about classifying polygons to help you describe them.

Read More
Unit 4, Chapter 9, Lesson 2 on page 192 for more on plane figures and polygons

EXAMPLE:

Here is a **hexagon** .

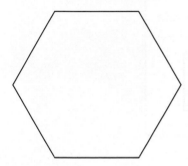

What do you know about a hexagon?

It is a polygon with 6 sides.

So a good description of a hexagon is: A hexagon is a polygon with 6 sides.

USE YOUR SKILLS

Name the figure that could be described as:

1. a polygon with 5 sides

2. a polygon with 3 sides that are all the same length

3. a quadrilateral with parallel opposite sides

4. a polygon with 8 sides

5. Extend Write a description of a square. Be sure to say how a square is a special type of quadrilateral.

KEY **MG 2.1** Identify, describe, and classify polygons (including pentagons, hexagons, and octagons).

What are ways to describe a triangle?

Read More
Unit 4, Chapter 9, Lesson 4 on page 198 for more on triangles

▶ **Connect It**

Each **triangle** has special characteristics. When you describe a triangle, look at both the sides and the **angles** of the triangle.

No equal sides	Two equal sides	Three equal sides	One right angle

USE YOUR SKILLS

Describe the sides of these triangles. Also, determine if any of these triangles have a right angle.

1.

2.

3.
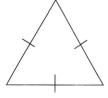

4.

5. Decide Can a triangle have 3 equal sides with a right angle? Use drawings to help you decide.

KEY **MG 2.2** Identify attributes of triangles (e.g., two equal sides for the isosceles triangle, three equal sides for the equilateral triangle, right angle for the right triangle).

What are the different types of triangles?

Read More
Unit 4, Chapter 9, Lesson 4 on page 198 for more on triangles

▶ **Connect It**

Each type of triangle has a special name. If you know the name of a triangle, you can identify the special qualities of that triangle.

Types of Triangles				
Name of Triangle	Scalene	Isosceles	Equilateral	Right Triangle
Description of Attributes	no equal sides	two equal sides	three equal sides	one right angle
Picture of Triangle				

USE YOUR SKILLS

Name the kind of triangle shown. Write *scalene*, *isosceles*, *equilateral*, or *right*.

1.

2.

3.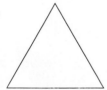

4.

5. Predict Draw an equilateral triangle. What do you think is true about the angles of an equilateral triangle?

What are quadrilaterals?

▶ Connect It

Quadrilaterals are polygons with 4 sides.
Squares and rectangles are just two types of
quadrilaterals.

Read More
Unit 4, Chapter 9,
Lesson 5 on page
200 for more on
quadrilaterals

EXAMPLE:

Which of the following are NOT quadrilaterals? How do you know?

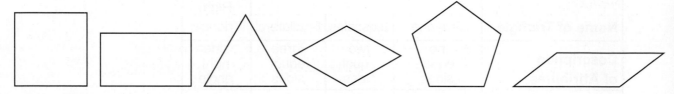

The triangle and pentagon are not quadrilaterals because they
do not have 4 sides.

USE YOUR SKILLS

Tell whether the figure is a quadrilateral.

1.

2.

3.

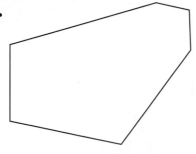

4. **Illustrate** Does every quadrilateral have four right
   angles? Use a drawing to illustrate your answer.

KEY **MG 2.3** Identify attributes of quadrilaterals (e.g., parallel sides for the
parallelogram, right angles for the rectangle, equal sides and right angles for the square.)

What are the different types of quadrilaterals?

Read More
Unit 4, Chapter 9, Lesson 5 on page 200 for more on quadrilaterals

 **Connect It**

Some quadrilaterals have a special name. If you know the name of a quadrilateral, you can identify the special qualities of that quadrilateral.

Quadrilaterals

Name of Figure	Rectangle	Square	Parallelogram
Description	a quadrilateral with four right angles	a quadrilateral with four equal sides and four right angles	a quadrilateral with opposite sides parallel
Picture			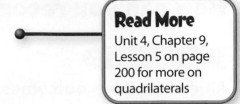

USE YOUR SKILLS

Name the kind of quadrilateral shown. Write *rectangle*, *square*, or *parallelogram*.

1.

2.

3.

4. Justify Can a square have other names besides *square*? Use an example to justify your answer.

KEY **MG 2.3** Identify attributes of quadrilaterals (e.g., parallel sides for the parallelogram, right angles for the rectangle, equal sides and right angles for the square.)

How can you record outcomes?

Read More
Unit 8, Chapter 23, Lesson 1 on page 496 for more on recording outcomes

All **events** have **outcomes**. You can keep track of outcomes by making a chart. A **tally chart** will help record outcomes for events that are repeated several times.

EXAMPLE:

Luis is spinning this spinner. There are three possible outcomes.

Luis spun the spinner 10 times. The tally chart shows the outcome.

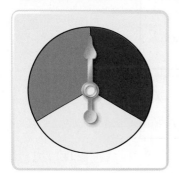

Luis's Spinner Outcomes		
Outcome	**Tally Mark**	**Number**
Red	ⅢⅠ	5
Blue	|||	3
Yellow	||	2

How many times did Luis spin red?

Luis spun red 5 times.

USE YOUR SKILLS

1. Flip a coin 20 times. Record the outcomes in the chart.

Coin-Toss Experiment		
Outcome	**Tally Mark**	**Number**
Heads		
Tails		

2. **Predict** Based on your results, what do you think would happen if you flipped the coin 10 more times?

KEY **SDAP 1.2** Record the possible outcomes for a simple event (e.g., tossing a coin) and systematically keep track of the outcomes when the event is repeated many times.

How do you make a bar graph?

Read More
Unit 8, Chapter 22, Lesson 4 on page 482 for more on bar graphs

 **Connect It**

A **bar graph** is a good way to show outcomes.

EXAMPLE:
Four friends were tossing a coin to see how many times they could land on heads. Use the table to make a bar graph.

Number of Times Landed on Heads

Student	Number of Heads
Leah	6
Andrea	8
John	4
Marco	10

Step 1: Draw an outline of the graph. Include the title, labels, and the scale.

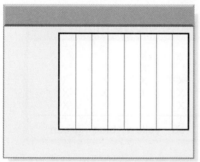

Step 2: Draw the bars.

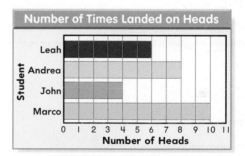

USE YOUR SKILLS

1. Use the table to make a bar graph.

2. **Justify** What scale did you use to show the number of times each color of marble was drawn? Why did you choose that scale?

Colors of Marbles Drawn

Color	Number
red	10
yellow	15
blue	20
purple	10

KEY **SDAP 1.3** Summarize and display the results of probability experiments in a clear and organized way (e.g., use a bar graph or a line plot).

How do you make a line plot?

▶ **Connect It**

Read More
Unit 8, Chapter 22, Lesson 2 on page 476 for more on line plots

A **line plot** is a good way to show data.

EXAMPLE:

Miss Sanderson's class was spinning a spinner. Use the data to make a line plot.

Color on Spinner

Angela red	Tim blue	Matt green
Lauren yellow	Andrew yellow	Kate red
Missy blue	Nadia yellow	Dora yellow
Lincoln green	Doug green	Julie blue
Owen red	Hannah blue	Bill yellow

Step 1: Draw the outline of the line plot.

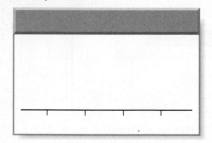

Step 2: Fill in the data.

Color on Spinner

```
              X
              X      X
       X      X      X      X
       X      X      X      X
       X      X      X      X
     _____
       red  yellow  blue  green
```

USE YOUR SKILLS

1. Use the data to make a line plot.

Number Rolled on Number Cube

Megan 1	Nancy 4	Joseph 4
Miguel 5	Frank 5	Anna 6
Joan 5	Hayden 3	Diego 4
Vanessa 3	Beth 3	Amy 1
Patrick 2	Sam 6	Luisa 1

2. Extend What is the range of the data?

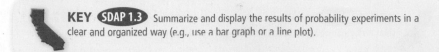

Using the Table of Contents

A table of contents helps you find special features in your math book.

It's a good habit to look here first. It saves a lot of time.

Each unit teaches big ideas in math in 2 to 4 chapters. You get ready for the unit with a game.

All chapters have hands on and problem solving lessons.

Reading and writing can help you learn math.

Field Trips let you do math in special places in California.

Table of Contents

Unit 1 Numbers to 10,000

BIG IDEAS!

- You can use standard form, expanded form, or word form to write any number.

- No matter how large the number, each digit has its own place value.

- When you round a number, you estimate about how many by finding the nearest ten, hundred, or thousand.

CHAPTER 1 Place Value

Order and Round Whole Numbers

Contents

Maintaining California Standards	**Reading & Writing Math**	**Science, History-Social Science, and Data**
Key Standards Review, pages 11, 33	**Reading and Writing Math,** pages 3, 20, 38	**Problem Solving Field Trip,** page 36
Problem Solving on Tests, page 37	**Vocabulary,** pages 5, 25	**Science Link,** page 29
Spiral Review and Test Practice, pages 23, 41		**Real World Data,** pages 10, 35

Unit 2 # Addition and Subtraction

California Living Museum

Contents

Unit 3 **Multiplication Facts**

 BIG IDEAS!
- You can use arrays, patterns, skip counting, and other strategies to learn the multiplication facts.
- The Commutative and Associative Properties help you multiply.

 CHAPTER 5

Multiplication Concepts

CHAPTER 6

Multiplication Patterns

CHAPTER
7

Multiplication Patterns and Practice

Maintaining California Standards	Reading & Writing Math	Science, History-Social Science, and Data
Key Standards Review, pages 105, 127, 147 **Problem Solving on Tests,** page 115 **Spiral Review and Test Practice,** pages 119, 139, 161	**Reading and Writing Math,** pages 97, 116, 136, 158 **Vocabulary,** pages 99, 121, 141	**Problem Solving Field Trip,** page 114 **Science Link,** pages 104, 130, 146 **History-Social Science Link,** page 108 **Real World Data,** pages 126, 149, 154

Unit 4 Geometry and Measurement

BIG IDEAS!

- There are different units to measure length.
- You can tell one type of polygon from another by counting the sides and angles.
- Perimeter is the sum of the lengths of the sides of a shape and area is the number of square units that cover a shape.
- Volume is the number of unit cubes that make up a solid figure.

CHAPTER 8 — Length

CHAPTER 9 — Shapes and Angles

Contents

Maintaining California Standards	Reading & Writing Math	Science, History-Social Science, and Data
Key Standards Review, pages 175, 195, 217, 237 **Problem Solving on Tests,** page 183 **Spiral Review and Test Practice,** pages 187, 209, 229, 251	**Reading and Writing Math,** pages 167, 184, 206, 226, 246 **Vocabulary,** pages 169, 189, 211, 231	**Problem Solving Field Trip,** page 182 **Science Link,** pages 174, 202, 216, 242 **History-Social Science Link,** page 236 **Real World Data,** pages 180, 194, 222

Unit 5 **Division Facts**

BIG IDEAS!
- You can find a division fact by thinking about a related multiplication fact.
- You can divide by making equal groups, drawing arrays, using repeated subtraction, and looking for patterns.

Division Concepts

Division Patterns

CHAPTER 14 Division Patterns and Practice

Maintaining California Standards	**Reading & Writing Math**	**Science, History-Social Science, and Data**
Key Standards Review, pages 265, 285, 305	**Reading and Writing Math,** pages 257, 274, 294, 314	**Problem Solving Field Trip,** page 272
Problem Solving on Tests, page 273	**Vocabulary,** pages 259, 279, 299	**Science Link,** pages 270, 290, 310
Spiral Review and Test Practice, pages 277, 297, 317		**History-Social Science Link,** page 304
		Real World Data, pages 264, 284

Unit 6 # Fractions, Decimals, and Money

BIG IDEAS!
- Fractions that show the same part of a whole are equivalent.
- A decimal is another way to show a fraction.
- You can add and subtract fractions using fraction tiles.
- You can add and subtract money by lining up the digits by place value.

CHAPTER 15

Fraction Concepts

CHAPTER 16

Addition and Subtraction of Fractions

Maintaining California Standards	Reading & Writing Math	Science, History-Social Science, and Data
Key Standards Review, pages 337, 351, 373, 393 **Problem Solving on Tests,** page 359 **Spiral Review and Test Practice,** pages 343, 363, 383, 403	**Reading and Writing Math,** pages 323, 340, 360, 380, 400 **Vocabulary,** pages 325, 345, 365, 385	**Problem Solving Field Trip,** page 358 **Science Link,** pages 336, 350, 372, 396 **History-Social Science Link,** page 356 **Real World Data,** pages 329, 333, 376, 389, 392

Contents

Contents

The Gardens of Hakone

Unit 8 Data and Probability

BIG IDEAS!

● Line plots and bar graphs are good ways to show the results of probability experiments.

● You can do probability experiments and use the results to make predictions.

CHAPTER 22

Data and Graphs

Maintaining California Standards	Reading & Writing Math	Science, History-Social Science, and Data
Key Standards Review, pages 479, 501 **Problem Solving on Tests,** page 509 **Spiral Review and Test Practice,** pages 493, 515	**Reading and Writing Math,** pages 471, 490, 510 **Vocabulary,** pages 473, 495	**Problem Solving Field Trip,** page 508 **Science Link,** pages 486, 500 **Real World Data,** pages 478, 506

Bodie State Historic Park

Unit 9 **Divide Greater Numbers**

BIG IDEAS!

- You can use multiplication to check division.

- When you divide multidigit numbers, you divide one place value at a time.

- You can divide money the same way as whole numbers, putting the decimal point in the same place in the quotient.

CHAPTER 24

Get Ready for Multidigit Division

CHAPTER 25

Divide 2-Digit Numbers

CHAPTER 26

Divide 3- and 4-Digit Numbers

Contents

Maintaining California Standards	Reading & Writing Math	Science, History-Social Science, and Data
Key Standards Review, pages 529, 547, 565 **Problem Solving on Tests,** page 553 **Spiral Review and Test Practice,** pages 539, 557, 577	**Reading and Writing Math,** pages 521, 536, 554, 574 **Vocabulary,** pages 523, 541, 559	**Problem Solving Field Trip,** page 552 **Science Link,** pages 532, 546, 564 **History-Social Science Link,** page 528 **Real World Data,** pages 550, 568

Unit 10 Weight, Mass, and Capacity

BIG IDEAS!

- Weight, mass, and capacity can be estimated and measured using customary or metric units.

- You can multiply, divide, or use patterns to change from one unit to another unit.

CHAPTER 27 Customary Units

Contents

Metric Units

Maintaining California Standards	Reading & Writing Math	Science, History-Social Science, and Data
Key Standards Review, pages 591, 615 **Problem Solving on Tests,** page 617 **Spiral Review and Test Practice,** pages 605, 621	**Reading and Writing Math,** pages 583, 602, 618 **Vocabulary,** pages 585, 607	**Problem Solving Field Trip,** page 616 **Science Link,** pages 598, 614 **Real World Data,** pages 590, 595, 611

Back to School

Welcome!

This year in math you'll learn about numbers, patterns, shapes, and different ways to measure. Scientists, cooks, builders, and artists all use math every day— and you will too. You'll use the mathematics you know to solve problems and describe objects and patterns you see. You can get started by finding out about yourself as a mathematician and about the other students in your class.

Real World Connection
Collecting Data

About Me

Write your math autobiography by writing two or three things about each question. You can also draw a picture of yourself doing math, if you want.

- What do you like best about math class?
- What are you good at in math class?
- What would you like to know more about?
- How do you (or how does someone in your family) use math outside of math class?

About My Class

Your classmates may be just like you in some ways but different in other ways. You can collect data to find out something about the whole class.

- Think of one topic you'd like to know about all your classmates.
- Write a survey question for your topic.
- Take a survey among your classmates. Use tally marks to collect the data.
- Make a bar graph or picture graph to show your results.
- Use your graph and data to write what you learned about your class.

Relate Addition and Subtraction

Objective Learn how addition and subtraction are related.

▶ Review and Remember

A school bus makes 10 stops on the way to school. The bus has already made 4 stops. How many more stops will the bus make?

Addition and subtraction are related. You can use either operation to find the answer.

Different Ways to Find the Difference Between 10 and 4

Way 1 **Write an addition sentence. Find the missing addend.**

$$4 + 6 = 10$$

- 4 → stops made
- 6 → remaining stops
- 10 → total stops (sum)

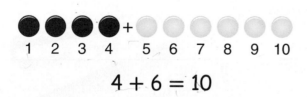

| 1 | 2 | 3 | 4 | 5 | 6 | 7 | 8 | 9 | 10 |

$$4 + 6 = 10$$

Way 2 **Write a subtraction sentence. Find the difference.**

$$10 - 4 = 6$$

- 10 → total stops
- 4 → stops made
- 6 → remaining stops (difference)

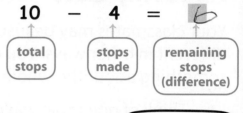

| 1 | 2 | 3 | 4 | 5 | 6 | 7 | 8 | 9 | 10 |

$$10 - 4 = 6$$

Solution: The bus will make 6 more stops.

A **fact family** is a group of number sentences that use the same numbers.

Fact families show how addition and subtraction are related.

Fact Family for 4, 6, and 10

$$4 + 6 = 10 \qquad 10 - 4 = 6$$
$$6 + 4 = 10 \qquad 10 - 6 = 4$$

▶ Guided Practice

Use counters to find each missing number.

1. 3 + 4 = 7
   7 − 3 = 4

2. 12 + 10 = 22
   22 − 10 = 12

3. 40 + 20 = 60
   60 − 40 = 20

(123) Math Talk There are only two facts in the fact family for 3, 3, and 6. Explain why.

Ask Yourself
- How can the given fact help me find the missing number?
- Do I need to find a missing addend or the difference?

▶ Practice and Problem Solving

Use counters to find each missing number.

4. 5 + 3 = 8
   8 − 3 = 5

5. 8 + 7 = 15
   15 − 7 = 8

6. 14 + 10 = 24
   24 − 14 = 10

Complete each fact family.

7. 6 + 8 = 14
   8 + 6 = 14
   14 − 8 = 6
   14 − 6 = 8

8. 7 + 9 = 16
   9 + 7 = 16
   16 − 9 = 7
   16 − 7 = 9

9. 2 + 8 = 10
   8 + 2 = 10
   10 − 2 = 8
   10 − 8 = 2

Solve.

10. Represent Twenty-eight students take the bus to school. Nineteen students take the bus home. Write an addition sentence to find how many more students take the bus to school.

11. Write a simple word problem that can be modeled by using the counters shown below.

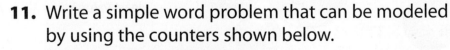

✓ Spiral Review and Test Practice

Open Response

Round each to the nearest ten.

(Grade 2)

12. 76   **13.** 116   **14.** 82

15. Antonio wrote 39 − 18 = 21. What addition sentence could he use to check his answer?

(Grade 2)

Problem Solving and Money

Objective Review basic money and problem-solving skills.

▶ Review and Remember

You know a lot about money. On this page, you will review money concepts.

Look at the coins at the right. Is their value less than (<) or greater than (>) one dollar?

One way to find out is to put the coins in order of their value. Then count on to find the total value.

| 25¢ | 50¢ | 75¢ | 85¢ | 95¢ | 96¢ |

96¢ is less than $1.00. 96¢ < $1.00

▶ Guided Practice

Find the value of each group of coins.

1.

2.

Ask Yourself
- What is the value of each coin?
- Did I count the money in order from greatest to least value?

3. Use < or > to compare the values of the groups of coins in Exercises 1 and 2.

4. If you combine the coins in Exercises 1 and 2, how much money would you have?

123 Math Talk Suppose you pay for a pencil that costs 32¢ with 2 quarters. Explain two different ways to find how much change you should get.

Back to School

Find the value of each group of coins.

5.

6.

7. Use < or > to compare the values of the groups of coins in Exercises 5 and 6.

8. Suppose you combine the coins in Exercises 5 and 6. How much money would you have?

Use the pictures at the right.
Solve each problem.

9. How much would it cost to buy a pencil and a ruler?

10. You pay for a pencil with a quarter. How much change should you get?

11. How much more does a notebook cost than a pencil?

12. **Create Your Own** Write a problem about money. Trade problems with a classmate and solve.

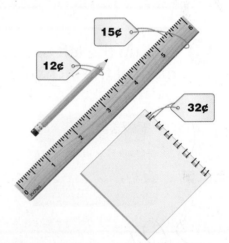

Spiral Review and Test Practice

Open Response

Write the next 3 numbers to continue each pattern. (Grade 2)

13. 5 10 15 20 25 30 ___, ___, ___

14. 50 48 46 44 42 ___, ___, ___

Multiple Choice

15. How much money do you need to buy one of each of the three items shown above? (Grade 2)

A 47¢   C 79¢

B 59¢   D 95¢

Measurement

Objective Review basic measurement skills needed to start third grade.

 **Explore**

Materials
inch ruler

In some lessons, you will learn as you do an activity. In this activity you will work with a partner to measure objects in the classroom.

1 Estimate. Then measure the length of the pencil above to the nearest inch.

2 Line up the left end of the pencil with the zero mark of the inch ruler.

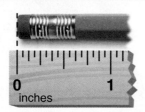 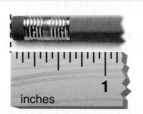

On some rulers there is no zero mark. The left end of the ruler is zero.

3 Find the inch mark closest to the right end of the pencil.

- What is the length of the pencil to the nearest inch?

- How close is your measurement to your estimate?

Extend

Estimate the length of each pencil. Then measure to the nearest inch.

1.

2.

Use an inch ruler to solve.

3. Collect 5 pencils from people in your class. Measure each to the nearest inch.

4. Write the lengths from Exercise 3 in order from shortest to longest.

5. Find an object that you estimate is about 6 inches long. Measure the object. Write the name and length of the object.

6. Draw a line segment that is 4 inches long.

Writing Math

7. **What's Wrong?** Jacob says that the pencil below is about 5 inches long. What did he do wrong? Explain your answer.

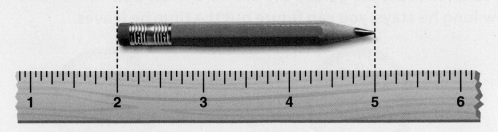

8. A yardstick is 36 inches long. List 3 things in your classroom that would be easier to measure with a yardstick than with a 12-inch ruler.

Elapsed Time

Objective Use a clock to help you tell how long an activity will last.

Gavin volunteers with his mom at an animal shelter every Wednesday. He arrives at 4:00 P.M. and leaves at 5:30 P.M. How long is he at the animal shelter?

If you know the starting time and the ending time, you can figure out how long Gavin volunteers.

Start at 4:00.

Count the hours.
4:00 to 5:00 is 1 hour.

Then count the minutes.
5:00 to 5:30 is 30 minutes.

Solution: Gavin is at the animal shelter for 1 hour and 30 minutes.

Suppose Gavin gets to the animal shelter at 4:15 P.M. and stays for 40 minutes. What time does he leave?

If you know when he gets to the animal shelter and how long he stays, you can figure out the time he leaves.

Start at 4:15.

Count ahead 40 minutes to 4:55.

Solution: He leaves at 4:55 P.M.

Back to School

Tell what time it will be.

1. in 3 hours   **2.** in 20 minutes   **3.** in 45 minutes

123 Math Talk Visiting hours at the animal shelter are from 9:00 A.M. to 11:30 A.M. on Saturday. How long is that?

 Practice and Problem Solving

Tell what time it will be.

4. in 5 minutes   **5.** in 35 minutes   **6.** in 1 hour   **7.** in 3 hours

      11:40

Solve.

8. It took Gavin 6 minutes to walk from school to the animal shelter. If he left at 3:37, what time did he get to the shelter?

9. Andy groomed 3 dogs starting at 4:00 and ending at 4:45. Each dog took 15 minutes to groom. What times did Andy begin grooming each dog?

✓ Spiral Review and Test Practice

Open Response

Tell whether the number is even or odd. (Grade 2)

10. 9   **11.** 25   **12.** 34

Multiple Choice

13. A baseball game began at 20 minutes before 3. Avery arrived at two fifty-five. Was he on time? Explain your answer. (Grade 2)

Back to School

Visual Thinking
Going Geometric

What looks like a bus, but is not a bus? The answer is a trolley coach! It runs on electricity instead of gasoline. Some cities use trolleys to take people from place to place.

Many different shapes are used in the picture above.

1. Look at the shapes with 4 sides. Write the names of as many of those shapes as you can. If you cannot name one, then just draw the shape.

2. Name or draw any shapes you know that have more or fewer than 4 sides.

3. Look at the door of the trolley. The artist used rectangles to draw the door. How many rectangles do you see in the door?

4. In Exercises 1–3 you worked with plane shapes. Now look at the drawing and name any solid shapes you see.

1

Numbers to 10,000

BIG IDEAS!

- You can use standard form, expanded form, or word form to write any number.
- No matter how large the number, each digit has its own place value.
- When you round a number, you estimate about how many by finding the nearest ten, hundred, or thousand.

Chapter 1
Place Value

Chapter 2
Order and Round Whole Numbers

Songs and Games

Math Music Track 1: *Many Ways to Show Numbers*

eGames at
www.eduplace.com/camap/

Math Readers

Soccer Bash
Congratulations
STEEL TOES

Concert Halls of the World

Bicyclists wait for the start of the Garrett Lemire Memorial Grand Prix in Ojai, CA.

Game

Greatest to Least

Object of the Game Make the greatest possible two-digit number using number cubes.

Materials
- number cube labeled 1–6
- number cube labeled 4–9

Number of Players 4

How to Play

1 Player 1 rolls both number cubes. He or she makes the greatest possible two-digit number from the digits on the cubes and records the number.

2 Players take turns repeating Step 1.

3 The player with the greatest number after a round wins 4 points, the next greatest number is worth 3 points, the next number is worth 2 points, and the least number is worth 1 point.

4 Play continues until one player gets 25 points. That player is the winner.

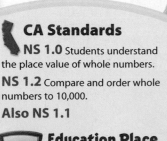

Reading Before reading a story or article, you can preview it to get an idea of what it is about and how it is organized. You can also preview a math lesson.

Mark previewed Lesson 1 on pages 6–7. This is what he found.

This is a hands-on lesson about numbers. I'll follow the numbered steps to learn what to do.

Lesson 1 Preview

✓ **Lesson title:** Model Numbers

✓ **Special kind of lesson:** Hands On

✓ **Objective (what you will learn):** Use base-ten blocks to show the value of each digit in a 3-digit number.

✓ **Vocabulary (highlighted words):** place value, digit

✓ **Main headings:** Explore, Extend

✓ **Special sections:** Writing Math

✓ **Special features:** drawings, numbered steps, base-ten blocks, place-value chart

---

Writing Use the checklist to preview another lesson. See if the lesson includes the items listed in red type. Then write a sentence or two telling what you think the lesson is about or what you expect to do or learn.

Place Value

Saturn's rings are made of gases
and small pieces of ice.

Check What You Know

Word Bank

digits

hundreds

ones

tens

thousands

Vocabulary and Concepts GRADE 2 KEY NS 1.1

Choose the best word to complete each sentence.

1. The number 35 has 3 ____.

2. The number 357 has 7 ____.

3. The number 754 has three ____.

Skills GRADE 2 NS 1.2

Write the number for each model.

4.

5.

6.

Show each number a different way.

7. 2 tens 7 ones

8. 66

9. $800 + 50 + 4$

Problem Solving and Reasoning GRADE 2 NS 1.2

10. Andrea's secret number has 2 hundreds, 3 ones, and 1 ten. What is the number?

Vocabulary

Visualize It!

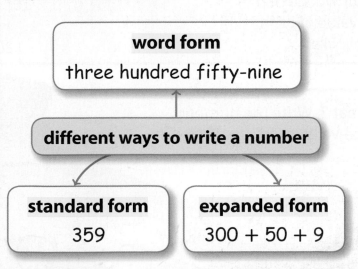

word form

three hundred fifty-nine

different ways to write a number

standard form

359

expanded form

$300 + 50 + 9$

Language Tips

The word *digit* can mean a finger or a toe. In mathematics, *digit* refers to any of the number symbols 0, 1, 2, 3, 4, 5, 6, 7, 8, 9.

Some words are similar in Spanish and English.

English	Spanish
digit	dígito
form	forma

See **English-Spanish Glossary** pages 628–646.

Education Place Visit www.eduplace.com/camap/ for the **eGlossary** and **eGames**.

CA Standards MR 2.3 Use a variety of methods, such as words, numbers, symbols, charts, graphs, tables, diagrams, and models, to explain mathematical reasoning. **Also NS 1.0, NS 1.1**

Chapter 1   5

CA Standards

KEY **NS 1.3** Identify the place value for each digit in numbers to 10,000.

Also NS 1.0, NS 1.1, MR 1.1, MR 2.3, MR 2.4

Vocabulary

place value

digit

Materials
- Base-ten blocks
- Workmat 3
- eManipulatives (optional) www.eduplace.com/camap/

Hands On
Model Numbers

Objective Use base-ten blocks to show the value of each digit in a 3-digit number.

▶ **Explore**

Question How can base-ten blocks help you understand **place value**?

Rose has a 320-piece jigsaw puzzle. She checks to see if she has all the pieces. She counts 203 pieces. She knows 320 and 203 are not the same. Use blocks to show the value of each **digit** in 320.

1 Show the number using blocks.

There are 3 hundreds, 2 tens, and 0 ones.

2 Draw a quick picture to record your work. Then write the value of each group of blocks.

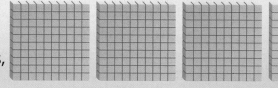

300   20

3 Use Workmat 3. Write the number in the place-value chart.

THOUSANDS			ONES		
hundred thousands	ten thousands	thousands	hundreds	tens	ones
			3	2	0

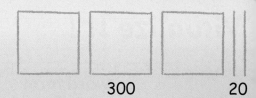

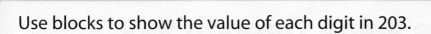

Use blocks to show the value of each digit in 203.

1 Show the number using blocks.

2 Draw a quick picture to record your work. Then write the value of each group of blocks.

3 Use Workmat 3. Write the number in the place-value chart.

▶ **Extend**

Work in groups. Follow these steps for each number:

• Show the number using blocks.
• Draw a quick picture to record your work.
• Write the value of each group of blocks.
• Write the number in the place-value chart.

1. 176   **2.** 893   **3.** 310   **4.** 407   **5.** 551

Write the number for each quick picture.

6.    **7.**    **8.**

Write the value of the underlined digit.

9. 26<u>7</u>   **10.** <u>3</u>56   **11.** 9<u>2</u>8   **12.** 6<u>4</u>0   **13.** <u>4</u>07

14. Challenge What is the greatest possible value for a digit in the hundreds place? Explain.

Writing Math

Right or Wrong? Ben says that Rose's puzzle is missing some pieces because 320 is greater than 203. Is he right or wrong? Use words and models to explain.

CA Standards
KEY NS 1.5 Use expanded notation to represent numbers (e.g., 3,206 = 3,000 + 200 + 6).

KEY NS 1.3 Identify the place value for each digit in numbers to 10,000.

Also AF 1.2, NS 1.0, NS 1.1, MR 2.3

Vocabulary

standard form

expanded form

word form

Place Value Through 999

Objective Write numbers through 999 in standard form, expanded form, and word form.

▶ Learn by Example

The space suits worn by NASA Shuttle astronauts weigh about 315 pounds each.

You can show 315 on a place-value chart.

ONES		
hundreds	tens	ones
3	1	5

You can show 315 using blocks.

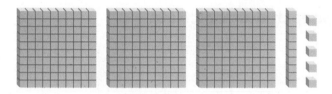

You can **write** 315 in different ways.

Vocabulary Tip
Standard form is sometimes called **standard notation**.

Different Ways to Write a Number	
Way 1 You can use **standard form**.	315
Way 2 You can use **expanded form**.	300 + 10 + 5
Way 3 You can use **word form**.	three hundred fifteen

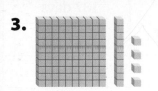

Guided Practice

Ask Yourself
- What is the value of each digit?
- Do any places have zeros?

Write the number in two other ways. Use standard form, expanded form, and word form.

1. 700 + 10 + 7   **2.** two hundred four

Write the number in standard form.

3.   **4.** 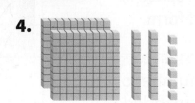   **5.**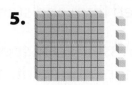

Algebra Equations
Find the value of ▪ .

6. 100 + 30 + ▪ = 136   **7.** 200 + ▪ + 5 = 245   **8.** ▪ + 20 + 9 = 929

(123) Math Talk In the number 507, what is the meaning of the zero in the tens place?

Practice and Problem Solving

Write the number in two other ways. Use standard form, expanded form, and word form.

9. 300 + 90 + 6   **10.** six hundred eight   **11.** 672

12. one hundred seventeen   **13.** 200 + 30   **14.** 185

Write the number in standard form.

15. 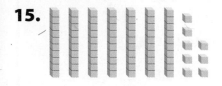   **16.** 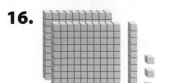   **17.**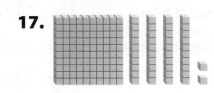

Algebra Equations
Find the value of ▪ .

18. 300 + 60 + ▪ = 367   **19.** 700 + ▪ + 3 = 713   **20.** ▪ + 70 + 9 = 579

Real World Data

Use the table for Problems 21–24.

Time in Orbit on the International Space Station	
Mission	**Days**
Mission 9	187 days
Mission 10	192 days
Mission 11	179 days
Mission 12	189 days

21. Which mission crew spent one hundred seventy-nine days in orbit? Write the number of days they spent in space in expanded form and standard form.

22. Which mission crew spent closest to 200 days in orbit? Write the number of days they spent in space in expanded form and word form.

23. Jane wrote $100 + \blacksquare + 7 = 187$ to show the total number of days Mission 9 spent in orbit. What is the value of $\blacksquare$?

24. **Challenge** Nick says that Mission 10 spent the fewest days in orbit because there is a 2 in the ones place. Is he right or wrong? Explain.

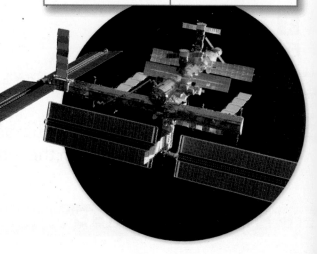

 Spiral Review and Test Practice

Write the missing numbers. Grade 2, KEY NS 1.3

25. 149, _____, 151, 152, _____, 154

Compare the numbers. Write <, >, or = for the ⬭. Grade 2, KEY NS 1.3

26. 99 ⬭ 10   **27.** 35 ⬭ 29   **28.** 15 ⬭ 73   **29.** 25 ⬭ 25

Write the letter of the correct answer. KEY NS 1.5

30. Ed has 305 buttons. Which of these equals 305?

   A $3 + 0 + 5$ **B** $300 + 5$ **C** $30 + 5$ **D** $3 + 5$

Extra Practice See page 21, Set A.

Key Standards Review

Need Help?
See Key Standards Handbook.

Write a fraction to name the shaded part of the figure.
GRADE 2 KEY NS 4.1

1.

2.

3.

4.

Solve. GRADE 2 KEY NS 5.1

5. Kim has 1 penny, 1 nickel, and 1 dime.
How much money does Kim have?

6. Pat has these coins.   Ken has these coins.

Who has more money? Explain.

Challenge
Number Sense

Many Ways to Write a Number

Here are 4 ways to write 350.

- • 3 hundreds + 5 tens
- • 2 hundreds + 15 tens
- • 1 hundred + 25 tens
- • 35 tens

Write each of these numbers in four different ways. KEY NS 1.3, KEY NS 1.5

1. 65
   a. 6 tens + 5 ones
   b. _____ tens + 15 ones
   c. _____ tens _____ ones
   d. _____ ones

2. 104
   a. 10 hundreds + _____ ones
   b. _____ tens + 14 ones
   c. _____ tens _____ ones
   d. _____ ones

CA Standards
NS 1.1 Count, read, and write whole numbers to 10,000.

NS 1.0 Students understand the place value of whole numbers.

Also NS 1.2, MR 2.3, MR 3.0, MR 3.2

Vocabulary

thousand

Materials

• Learning Tools 9, 10 (Paper-Square Strips and Recording Sheet)
• Crayons
• Scissors
• Tape

Hands On
How Big Is 1,000?

Objective Relate a thousand to hundreds and tens.

▶ **Explore**

You have modeled 3-digit numbers. In this lesson, your class will divide into 10 teams to model one **thousand** using paper squares.

Question How can you use models to compare 10, 100, and 1,000?

Paper Square

1 Choose a team color. Use it to color a strip of 10 squares. Cut out the strip. Then color and cut out 9 more strips of 10 squares.

2 Look at your strips.

• How many strips do you have?

• How many squares do you have?

Use Learning Tool 10. Fill in the first row of the table.

Think
Be sure not to overlap any squares.

3 Tape your team's 10 strips end to end. Join another team. Tape both teams' strips together. Then fill in the second row of your table.

4 Work as a class to tape all of the strips together. Then complete your table.

▶ **Extend**

Use your completed table to answer the question.

1. How many squares are in each strip?

2. How many strips of 10 squares does each team have?

3. How many squares does each team have in all?

4. How many strips do all 10 teams have together?

5. How many squares are there in all?

Tell if the amount is greater than, less than, or equal to 1,000.

6. 8 boxes of 100 pencils

7. 9 boxes of 1,000 craft sticks

8. 10 trays of 10 muffins

9. 10 bags of 100 letters

10. **Analyze** Look at the table you completed. What pattern do you notice in each row? In each column?

11. **Challenge** Look at the long strip for 1,000. How many of these long strips would you need to show 10,000?

Writing Math

Explain How many bags of 100 pennies would you need to have 1,000 pennies? How many bags of 10 pennies would you need to have 1,000 pennies? Use your table or the model to explain.

Vocabulary

standard form

expanded form

word form

Materials
Workmat 3 (optional)

Place Value to 10,000

Objective Identify values of digits in numbers to 10,000.

▶ **Learn by Example**

In this lesson, you will use what you know about 3-digit numbers to understand larger numbers.

When the Space Shuttle returns to Earth, it gets very hot. That is why the shuttle is made of materials that can stand temperatures of more than 2,390° Fahrenheit! Write this number in different ways.

THOUSANDS			ONES		
hundred thousands	ten thousands	thousands	hundreds	tens	ones
		2	3	9	0

A place-value chart can help you find the value of each digit.

Different Ways to Write a Number	
Way 1 You can use **standard form**.	2,390
Way 2 You can use **expanded form**.	2,000 + 300 + 90
Way 3 You can use **word form**.	two thousand, three hundred ninety

Ask Yourself

• What is the value of each digit in the number?

• Do any places have zeros?

▶ **Guided Practice**

Write the place of the underlined digit. Then write its value. Use Workmat 3 if you need help.

1. <u>4</u>,150   **2.** 2,<u>3</u>98   **3.** 7,5<u>8</u>1   **4.** 1,32<u>1</u>

Write the number in two other ways. Use standard form, expanded form, and word form.

5. 1,000 + 700 + 8   **6.** 2,039   **7.** ten thousand

Guided Problem Solving

Use the clues to solve this problem.

8. Use these clues to find the year that the first Space Shuttle launched.

   - The value of the thousands digit is 1,000.

   - The ones digit is the same as the thousands digit.

   - It has an 8 in the tens place.

   - The hundreds digit is greater than the tens digit.

   a. **Understand** What is the question?

   b. **Plan** What information do you have?

   c. **Solve** Use the clues, one at a time. Write the answer.

   d. **Look Back** Why do you think your answer should not have a comma?

 Math Talk What is the largest 4-digit number? What number comes next?

▶ Practice and Problem Solving

Write the place of the underlined digit. Then write its value. Use Workmat 3 if you need help.

9. <u>3</u>,650

10. 1,0<u>9</u>8

11. 5,7<u>5</u>1

12. 6,70<u>9</u>

13. 4,<u>1</u>84

14. <u>9</u>,276

15. 7,53<u>7</u>

16. <u>1</u>0,000

17. 6,<u>0</u>02

18. 7,2<u>8</u>0

19. 2,46<u>5</u>

20. 8,<u>1</u>37

Write the number in two other ways.

21. 8,000 + 7

22. five thousand, one hundred thirty

23. 4,916

24. 2,000 + 100 + 30 + 2

25. six thousand, ninety-four

26. 9,000 + 700 + 6

Choose the number or numbers that match the statement.

27. There is a 2 in the hundreds place.
2,487 1,240 234

28. There is a 5 in the tens place.
4,525 4,050 532

29. There is a 4 in the thousands place.
4,086 4,004 459

Make the greatest possible number using the set of digits. Then make the least possible number.

30. 1, 8, 6, 5

31. 3, 5, 2, 6

32. 3, 5, 9, 6

33. 4, 7, 9, 0

Solve.

34. Sally Ride was born in Los Angeles, CA. She was an astronaut aboard the Space Shuttle *Challenger*.

Use these clues to find the year that Sally Ride became the first American woman in outer space.

- The value of the thousands digit is 1,000.
- It has an 8 in the tens place.
- The ones digit is 2 more than the thousands digit.
- The hundreds digit is the largest digit possible in the hundreds place.

Sally Ride

Spiral Review and Test Practice

Solve. Grade 2, KEY NS 3.3

35. 3 × 5 = ▢

36. 2 × 10 = ▢

Test Tip
Sometimes you will see thousands written without a comma.

Write the letter of the correct answer. KEY NS 1.3

37. Which digit is in the thousands place in the number 4239?

A 2 **B** 3 **C** 4 **D** 9

Extra Practice See page 21, Set C.

By the Numbers

Maria is a volunteer at the local museum. The museum has many different exhibit spaces. Today, Maria is working in the space shuttle exhibit.

A group of first-graders could not read the big numbers. Maria helped out by reading the numbers to them.

Use the data in the table above to answer the questions. Write the number in words, as you would read the number aloud.

Space Shuttle Facts
In the space shuttle, they used:
230 miles of wire.
over 1,060 plumbing valves and connections.
over 1,440 circuit breakers.
more than 27,000 special tiles to keep the shuttle from getting too hot or cold.

1. How many miles of wire are used?

2. How many plumbing valves and connections are used?

3. How many circuit breakers are used?

4. **Challenge** About how many special tiles are used?

NASA Space Camp

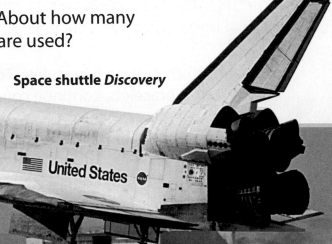

Space shuttle *Discovery*

CA Standards
NS 1.0, NS 1.1

CA Standards

MR 1.1 Analyze problems by identifying relationships, distinguishing relevant from irrelevant information, sequencing and prioritizing information, and observing patterns.

AF 2.2 Extend and recognize a linear pattern by its rules (e.g., the number of legs on a given number of horses may be calculated by counting by 4s or by multiplying the number of horses by 4).

Also NS 1.1, KEY **NS 2.1**, NS 2.8, AF 2.0, MR 1.2, MR 2.0, MR 2.3, MR 2.4, MR 3.0, MR 3.1, MR 3.2, MR 3.3

Problem Solving Strategy
Number Patterns

Objective Use number patterns to solve problems.

▶ Learn by Example

In this lesson, you will find patterns to solve problems.

Iliana is making charm bracelets. Each bracelet has 4 charms. How many charms are on 5 bracelets? 12 bracelets?

UNDERSTAND

Each bracelet has 4 charms.
Find the number of charms on 5 and 12 bracelets.

PLAN

Look for a pattern.

1 bracelet	2 bracelets	3 bracelets	4 bracelets	5 bracelets
4 charms	8 charms	12 charms	16 charms	20 charms

+4   +4   +4   +4

SOLVE

There are 20 charms on 5 bracelets. To find the number of charms on 12 bracelets, continue counting by 4.

4, 8, 12, 16, 20, 24, 28, 32, 36, 40, 44, 48
+4 +4 +4 +4 +4 +4 +4

There are 48 charms on 12 bracelets.

LOOK BACK

How can you use counting by 2s to check counting by 4s?

Guided Problem Solving

Solve using the Ask Yourself questions.

Ask Yourself
• What is the number pattern?
• How can I use the pattern to answer the question?

1. A jacket has a space patch on each sleeve and a patch on the pocket. How many patches are on 1 jacket? 9 jackets?

   123 Math Talk Do you think the numbers 3000, 3003, and 3006 are part of the pattern in Problem 1? Explain.

Independent Problem Solving

Solve. Explain why your answer makes sense.

2. Todd made a plastic model of the NASA Space Shuttle. The model has two booster rockets. How many booster rockets are on 20 space shuttle models?

3. One charm necklace has 10 space charms. How many charms are in 10 identical necklaces? 100 necklaces?

4. There are 7 houses on Jim's street. The first four house numbers are 9004, 9008, 9012, and 9016. If the pattern continues, what are the numbers on the next 3 houses likely to be?

5. **Multistep** A Space Food Sampler contains 2 Astronaut Ice Creams, 2 Food Sticks, and 1 Freeze-dried Apple. What is the total number of items in 8 samplers?

6. **Challenge** One sheet of spaceship stickers has 8 stickers on it. How many sheets of stickers will have a total of 56 stickers?

7. **Create and Solve** Write and solve a problem that uses a number pattern.

Reading & Writing Math

Vocabulary

A **place-value** chart can help explain what a number means.

Look at the number in the place-value chart. Use this number to complete each exercise in the word web.

THOUSANDS			ONES		
hundred thousands	ten thousands	thousands	hundreds	tens	ones
		3 ,	6	2	7

Expanded form shows the value of each digit in the number.

1. Write the expanded form of the number.

Ways to Write a Number

Word form uses words to write a number.

2. Write the word form of the number.

Standard form is the simplest way to write a number using digits.

3. Write the standard form of the number.

4. Find the number of students in your school. Make a place-value chart that shows that number.

Writing
Use the number of students in your school. Write the number in word form, in standard form, and in expanded form.

Reading
Check out this book in your library.

• *How Much, How Many, How Far, How Heavy, How Long, How Tall is 1000?* by Helen Nolan

CA Standards

MR 2.3 Use a variety of methods, such as words, numbers, symbols, charts, graphs, tables, diagrams, and models, to explain mathematical reasoning.
Also NS 1.0, NS 1.1, KEY NS 1.3, KEY NS 1.5

Standards-Based Extra Practice

Set A
KEY NS 1.5 page 8

Write each number in two other ways. Use standard form, expanded form, and word form.

1. 957

2. three hundred sixty-two

3. 800 + 20 + 1

4. 354

5. four hundred thirty-seven

6. 200 + 90 + 1

7. 108

8. nine hundred fifty-six

9. 500 + 70 + 3

10. 677

11. two hundred two

12. 700 + 60 + 5

13. At a dinner party 300 people wanted chicken, 50 people wanted steak, and 8 people wanted the vegetarian meal. Write the total number of meals in standard form and word form.

Set B
NS 1.2 page 12

Tell if each is greater than, less than, or equal to 1,000.

1. 10 packs of 100 staples

2. 3 boxes of 1,000 shirts

3. 100 bags of 100 peanuts

4. 6 cases of 100 juice boxes

5. Ed works at a grocery store. He needs to put away 9 boxes of 100 apples. Is he putting away more or less than 1,000 apples?

Set C
KEY NS 1.3 page 14

Write the place of the underlined digit. Then write its value.

1. 8,<u>7</u>88

2. <u>6</u>,481

3. 1,<u>2</u>34

4. 3,51<u>4</u>

5. 4,66<u>8</u>

6. 1,5<u>8</u>1

7. 9,25<u>0</u>

8. 2,6<u>7</u>7

9. Jamal goes to the beach every summer and collects seashells. He has collected 1,584 seashells. What place is the digit 5 in? What is the value of the digit 5?

Education Place
Visit www.eduplace.com/camap/
for more **Extra Practice.**

Chapter Review/Test

Vocabulary and Concepts ———————————— KEY NS 1.3, NS 1.1

Choose the best word to complete each sentence.

1. In the number 958, the digit 9 is in the hundreds _____.

2. Eight hundred thirty-two is the _____ of the number 832.

3. Ten hundreds has the same value as one _____.

> **Word Bank**
> word form
> place
> thousand

Skills ———————————————————— KEY NS 1.3, NS 1.1, KEY NS 1.5

Write each number in two other ways.

4. $600 + 90 + 3$ 5. 381 6. eight hundred seventy-four 7. $500 + 30 + 5$

Tell if each is greater than, less than, or equal to 1,000.

8. 10 boxes of 1,000 paper clips

9. 6 bags of 100 erasers

10. 10 tanks of 100 goldfish

Write the place of the underlined digit. Then write its value.

11. 8,3<u>5</u>4

12. <u>7</u>,216

13. 3,<u>5</u>35

14. 4,57<u>6</u>

15. 2,1<u>4</u>2

16. 3,<u>8</u>76

17. 1,61<u>5</u>

18. <u>5</u>,350

Problem Solving and Reasoning ———————— KEY NS 1.3, NS 1.1, MR 2.3

Solve.

19. Write the standard form for the number that has 8 hundreds, 2 thousands, 4 tens and 0 ones.

20. Sue has 1,000 pennies. She put them in bags of 100 each. How many bags of pennies does Sue have?

Writing Math Jane says that 6,432 is the standard form for $60 + 400 + 3 + 2,000$. What did she do wrong?

Spiral Review and Test Practice

1.   243
     + 162

(A) 305

B 321

C 405

D 3105

Grade 2 **KEY** NS 2.2

2. Reginald has more than 163 coins in his collection. Which could be the number of coins Reginald has?

A 136

(B) 165

C 162

D 137

Grade 2 **KEY** NS 1.3

3. Which number is likely to come next in this pattern?

45, 50, 55, 60

(A) 61

B 65

C 70

D 75

> **Test Tip**
> Try finding the difference between the numbers.

Grade 2 **SDAP 2.1**

4. Which is a way to write five hundred sixty?

A 56

B 506

C 560

D 5060

NS 1.1 page 8

5. Todd has 9 packages of 100 napkins. Which number shows the number of napkins he has?

A 9

B 90

C 900

D 9000

> **Test Tip**
> You can use patterns to help you solve.

NS 1.0 page 12

6. Which is another way to write six thousand, four hundred nine?

A 60,004,009

(B) 600,049

C 6409

D 6049

KEY NS 1.3 page 14

 Education Place
Visit www.eduplace.com/camap/ for
Test-Taking Tips and **Extra Practice.**

Chapter 2

Order and Round Whole Numbers

Vocabulary and Concepts KEY NS 1.3, KEY NS 1.5, MR 2.3

Choose the best term to complete each sentence. page 8

1. In the number 56, 5 is in the _____ place.

2. The number 300 + 20 + 7 is written in _____.

Skills KEY NS 1.3

Write the place of the underlined digit. Then write its value. page 14

3. 4̲3

4. 18̲5

5. 6̲7̲2

6. 1,3̲48

Use the number line for Questions 7–8. GRADE 2 KEY NS 1.3

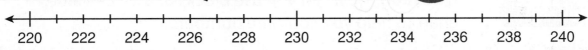

220 222 224 226 228 230 232 234 236 238 240

7. What number comes after 220?

8. What number is between 224 and 226?

Problem Solving and Reasoning KEY NS 1.3

9. Sammy is thinking of the number 4,750. What digit is in the hundreds place?

Vocabulary

Visualize It!

Five is greater than three.
5 > 3
★ ★ ★ ★ ★ > ★ ★ ★

Two is less than three.
2 < 3
☀ ☀ < ☀ ☀ ☀

compare

Examine the value of numbers to find if they are greater than, less than, or equal to one another.

Language Tips

When you *order* a sandwich, you ask a waitperson to bring it to you. In mathematics, when you *order* numbers, you arrange them from greatest to least, or from least to greatest.

Some words are similar in Spanish and English.

English	Spanish
compare	comparar
order	ordenar

See **English-Spanish Glossary** pages 628–646.

 Education Place Visit www.eduplace.com/camap/ for the **eGlossary** and **eGames**.

CA Standards **MR 2.3** Use a variety of methods, such as words, numbers, symbols, charts, graphs, tables, diagrams, and models, to explain mathematical reasoning. **Also NS 1.2**

Chapter 2   25

LESSON 1

CA Standards
NS 1.2 Compare and order whole numbers to 10,000.

KEY NS 1.3 Identify the place value for each digit in numbers to 10,000.

Also NS 1.0, NS 1.1, MR 2.3, MR 2.4

Vocabulary

greater than (>)

less than (<)

compare

Materials
• Workmat 3
• Base-ten blocks
• eManipulatives (optional)
  www.eduplace.com/camap/

Hands On
Compare Numbers

Objective Use base-ten blocks or a place-value chart to compare numbers to 10,000.

▶ **Explore**

In Chapter 1, you learned about place value. In this lesson, you will use place value to **compare** numbers.

Question How can you use blocks or a place-value chart to help you compare numbers?

It is time for the yearly dance recital. There are 124 ballet dancers and 128 hip-hop dancers in the recital. Which group has the greater number of dancers?

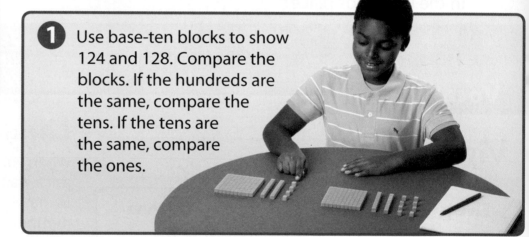

1 Use base-ten blocks to show 124 and 128. Compare the blocks. If the hundreds are the same, compare the tens. If the tens are the same, compare the ones.

Hint
The tip of symbol points to the smaller number.

2 Write the number sentences.

124 < 128	124 is **less than** 128.
128 > 124	128 is **greater than** 124.

Solution: The hip-hop group has the greater number of dancers.

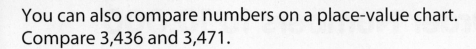
You can also compare numbers on a place-value chart.
Compare 3,436 and 3,471.

Think

If the digits are the same, move to the next greatest place.

1 Write both numbers on the place-value chart.
Compare the digits. Begin with the greatest place.

THOUSANDS			ONES		
hundred thousands	ten thousands	thousands	hundreds	tens	ones
		3	4	3	6
		3	4	7	1

           ↑   ↑   ↑

      same   same 3 tens < 7 tens

2 Write the number sentences.

$3,471 > 3,436$ 3,471 is **greater than** 3,436.

$3,436 < 3,471$ 3,436 is **less than** 3,471.

▶ **Extend**

Compare. Write >, <, or = for the ⬤.

1. 213 ⬤ 211

2. 89 ⬤ 347

3. 612 ⬤ 612

4. 976 ⬤ 1,283

5. 509 ⬤ 403

6. 830 ⬤ 819

7. 2,401 ⬤ 2,401

8. 10,000 ⬤ 8,907

9. 5,683 ⬤ 5,683

10. 8,559 ⬤ 10,000

11. 1,231 ⬤ 2,134

12. 9,489 ⬤ 4,989

13. How can you use a number line to show that
4,782 < 4,786?

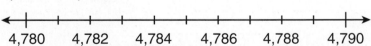

  4,780   4,782   4,784   4,786   4,788   4,790

14. Challenge Draw a number line that you could use to
compare 3,950 and 3,956. Then compare the numbers.

Math Journal

Writing Math

Julio wrote this number sentence.
Is he correct? Explain.

> 309 < 390

LESSON 2

CA Standards
NS 1.2 Compare and order whole numbers to 10,000.

KEY **NS 1.3** Identify the place value for each digit in numbers to 10,000.

Also NS 1.0, MR 2.0, MR 2.3, MR 2.4

Order Numbers to 10,000

Objective Use place value to order numbers to 10,000.

▶ Learn by Example

In Lesson 1, you learned how to **compare** two numbers. In this lesson, you will **order** 3 or more numbers.

A theater group sold these tickets. Write the numbers from the chart in order from greatest to least.

Day	Tickets
Thursday	978
Friday	1,212
Saturday	907

1 Write the numbers in the place-value chart. Compare the digits. Begin with the greatest place.

THOUSANDS			ONES		
hundred thousands	ten thousands	thousands	hundreds	tens	ones
			9	7	8
		1	2	1	2
			9	0	7

4-digit numbers are greater than 3-digit numbers.

So 1,212 is the greatest number.

9 = 9 so compare tens.

7 > 0 so 978 > 907.

2 Write the numbers in order from greatest to least.

1,212   978   907

Solution: The numbers in order from greatest to least are: 1,212 978 907

▶ Guided Practice

Write the numbers in order from greatest to least.

1. 1,400 10,000 1,578   **2.** 165 1,257 309

 Math Talk Why is 1,752 greater than 564?

Vocabulary

compare

order

Materials
• Workmat 3 (optional)
• Workmat 5 (optional)

Ask Yourself
• Which place should I look at first?
• Which number is greatest?

Practice and Problem Solving

Write the numbers in order from greatest to least.

3. 3,117 3,111 3,317

4. 7,402 7,204 7,220

5. 771 780 7,800

6. 683 592 714

7. 6,116 6,611 6,161 1,661 10,000

Write the numbers in order from least to greatest.

8. 1,089 10,000 1,103

9. 1,348 5,790 1,484

10. 5,491 4,951 5,995

Science Link

Use the Fun Facts to solve Problems 11–12.

11. Order the years from the earliest to the most recent.

12. The first sound radio was invented in 1907. Write a number sentence comparing this year to the year radio waves were discovered.

Scientists Discover Wave Energy

Energy can be carried from one place to another by waves.

- Electric current was discovered in 1820.
- Radio waves were discovered in 1888.
- A theory of light waves was published in 1690.

Science PS 1.d

Spiral Review and Test Practice

Write the number in two other ways. KEY **NS 1.5** page 14

13. 2,356

14. 9,000 + 500 + 80 + 3

Test Tip
Sometimes 4-digit numbers are written without the comma.

Write the letter of the correct answer. NS 1.2

15. Which set of numbers is in order from least to greatest?

    A 2576, 1750, 1243, 986

    C 986, 1243, 1750, 2576

    B 1750, 1243, 2576, 986

    D 1243, 1750, 2576, 986

Extra Practice See page 39, Set A.

LESSON 3

CA Standards

NS 1.4 Round off numbers to 10,000 to the nearest ten, hundred, and thousand.

NS 1.0 Students understand the place value of whole numbers.

Also KEY NS 1.3, MR 1.1, MR 2.3, MR 2.4, MR 2.5

Vocabulary

round

estimate

Round 2-Digit and 3-Digit Numbers

Objective Round 2-digit and 3-digit numbers to the nearest ten or hundred.

▶ Learn by Example

You can use what you know about place value to **round** numbers and **estimate** quantities.

A theater company performed 154 shows. Give an estimate of the number of shows by rounding to the nearest hundred.

Different Ways to Round

Way 1   Use rounding rules.

1 Underline the digit in the place you are rounding to.

<u>1</u>54

↑ hundreds place

2 Circle the digit to the right of the underlined digit.

1⑤4

↑ circled digit

3 If the circled digit is 5 or greater, increase the underlined digit by 1.

1⑤4 ⟶ 200

↑ 154 rounds to 200.

If the circled digit is less than 5, leave the underlined digit unchanged.

Then replace the digits to the right of the underlined digits with zeros.

30

Way 2 Use a number line.

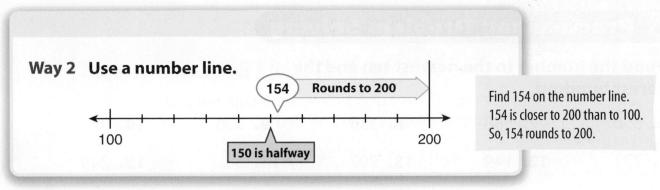

154 Rounds to 200

100   150 is halfway   200

Find 154 on the number line.
154 is closer to 200 than to 100.
So, 154 rounds to 200.

Solution: The theater company performed about 200 shows.

Another Example

Round 263 to the nearest ten.   26③ Rounds to 260. ← 3 is less than 5. So, 263 rounds to 260.

▶ **Guided Practice**

Round the number to the nearest ten and the nearest hundred.

Ask Yourself

To what place am I rounding?

1. 466   **2.** 765   **3.** 45   **4.** 71

Guided Problem Solving

Use the questions to solve this problem.

5. The show is about to start. There are 273 people to be seated. Estimate to the nearest ten the number of people waiting.

a. **Understand** What are you asked to find?

b. **Plan** Choose a way to solve the problem.

c. **Solve** Round and show your work.

d. **Look Back** Solve the problem another way. Did you get the same answer?

 Math Talk Will says that 395 rounded to the nearest ten is the same as 395 rounded to the nearest hundred. Is he right or wrong? Explain your answer.

Round the number to the nearest ten and the nearest hundred.

6. 856   **7.** 588   **8.** 333   **9.** 306   **10.** 97

11. 731   **12.** 149   **13.** 992   **14.** 36   **15.** 245

16. 461   **17.** 72   **18.** 619   **19.** 555   **20.** 184

Solve.

21. Mr. Adams has 185 movie posters and 212 music posters.

   a. To the nearest ten, how many movie posters does he have?

   b. Mr. Adams says that he has about 200 of each type of poster. Why does he use the same estimate for each type of poster?

22. Challenge Rounded to the nearest ten, the number of shows given by a puppet theater was 120. According to this estimate, what is the least number of shows that could have been given? Explain.

 Spiral Review and Test Practice

Write the place of the underlined digit. Then write its value. KEY **NS 1.3**   page 14

23. <u>3</u>,150   **24.** 7,<u>1</u>98   **25.** 1,3<u>0</u>5   **26.** 4,<u>2</u>60

Write the letter of the correct answer. NS 1.4

27. What is 798 rounded to the nearest ten?

   A 790   **B** 800   **C** 900   **D** 1,000

Extra Practice See page 39, Set B.

Key Standards Review

Need Help?
See Key Standards Handbook.

Write each number in expanded form. KEY NS 1.5

1. 259

2. 1,793

3. 6,015

4. 3,507

5. 7,306

6. 4,008

Write each number in standard form. NS 1.1

7. $1{,}000 + 3 + 60$

8. $5 + 10 + 800$

9. $100 + 4{,}000 + 20 + 4$

10. $70 + 5{,}000$

Write the place of the underlined digit.
Then write its value. KEY NS 1.3

11. 20<u>8</u>

12. 1,<u>9</u>84

13. 5,2<u>0</u>8

14. <u>1</u>,720

15. 7,<u>4</u>92

16. 6,25<u>0</u>

17. 2,<u>0</u>06

18. <u>1</u>0,000

Number Sense

Brain Teasers NS 1.4

Use the clues. Find all the numbers that match.

1. Ken is thinking of a number.

- Rounded to the nearest ten, it is 250.

- Rounded to the nearest hundred, it is 300.

What could Ken's number be?

2. Yumi is thinking of a number.

- Rounded to the nearest ten thousand it is 10,000.

- Rounded to the nearest thousand, it is 9,000.

What could Yumi's number be?

CA Standards

NS 1.4 Round off numbers to 10,000 to the nearest ten, hundred, and thousand.

NS 1.0 Students understand the place value of whole numbers.

Also KEY NS 1.3, MR 2.3, MR 2.4, MR 2.5

Round 4-Digit Numbers

Objective Round 4-digit numbers to the nearest ten, hundred, or thousand.

▶ **Learn by Example**

You can use what you know about rounding 2- and 3-digit numbers to help you round 4-digit numbers.

The musical *Cats* was one of the longest-running shows on Broadway. It ran almost 20 years with 7,485 performances. What is 7,485 rounded to the nearest thousand?

Think

Round up means to increase the underlined digit by 1.

Round down means to leave the underlined digit unchanged.

1 Underline the digit in the place you are rounding to.

$$\underline{7}, 4\ 8\ 5$$

↑

(thousands place)

2 Circle the digit to the right of the underlined digit.

$$\underline{7}, ④\ 8\ 5$$

↑

(circled digit)

3 If the circled digit is 5 or greater, round up. If the circled digit is less than 5, round down.

$$\underline{7}, ④\ 8\ 5$$ ← (4 is less than 5, so round down.)

↓

$$7, 0\ 0\ 0$$

Solution: 7,485 rounded to the nearest thousand is 7,000.

Other Examples

A Round 7,485 to the nearest ten.

7,48 ⑤ rounds to 7,490.

B Round 7,485 to the nearest hundred.

7,4 ⑧ 5 rounds to 7,500.

Round to the nearest thousand, the nearest hundred, and the nearest ten.

1. 3,267   **2.** 7,434   **3.** 9,720   **4.** 1,465

 Math Talk Is it possible for a four-digit number to round to a three-digit number? Explain.

► **Practice and Problem Solving**

Round to the nearest thousand, the nearest hundred, and the nearest ten.

5. 7,803   **6.** 4,434   **7.** 8,944   **8.** 6,329   **9.** 9,601

 Real World Data

Use the table for Problems 10–11.

10. How many performances of *Annie* were there, rounded to the nearest ten?

11. Challenge Felix said there were about 7,000 performances of *Cats*. Sam said there were about 7,500. Whose estimate was closer to the exact number? Explain.

Broadway Musical	Number of Performances
Cats	7,485
Oklahoma!	2,212
Les Misérables	6,680
Annie	2,377

 Spiral Review and Test Practice

Write the numbers in order from greatest to least. NS 1.2 page 28

12. 2,400 10,000 1,793   **13.** 795 3,247 1,654

Write the letter of the correct answer. NS 1.4

14. What is 8489 rounded to the nearest thousand?

  A 8000   **B** 8400   **C** 8500   **D** 9000

Field Trip...

San
Francisco, CA

CA Standards
MR 1.0, MR 1.1,
MR 2.0, MR 2.4,
NS 1.0, NS 1.2,
KEY NS 1.3, NS 1.4,
NS 2.0, KEY NS 2.1

Problem Solving

Objective Use skills and strategies to solve word problems.

The San Francisco Symphony performs in Davies Symphony Hall.

The Louise M. Davies Symphony Hall is home to the San Francisco Symphony Orchestra and Chorus and the Youth Symphony Orchestra.

Solve. Use the table for Problems 1–3. Tell which strategy or method you used.

String Instrument	Total Number
Bass	9
Cello	12
Harp	1
Viola	14
Violin	34

1. How many more violins than violas are in the string section?

2. Look at the number of cellos and the number of harps. What is the value of the digit 1 in each number?

3. Make a new table that shows the number of string instruments in order from greatest to least.

4. **Analyze** About 9,000 people went to the symphony. If the exact number was rounded to the nearest thousand, could the exact number be 9,136? 8,427? What is the greatest number it could be? Explain.

Problem Solving On Tests

1. Ali chose a number that is less than 248 and greater than 198. Which number can it be?

A 95   **C** 215

B 128   **D** 250

> **Test Tip**
> Test each number by comparing it to 248 and 198.

GRADE 2 KEY NS 1.3

2. Carlos has 38 stamps, and 26 are U.S. stamps. He says that 12 stamps are from foreign countries. Which number sentence will show if Carlos subtracted correctly?

A 12   **B** 12   **C** 26   **D** 26
+ 38   + 26   + 38   + 26

GRADE 2 KEY NS 2.1

3. A farmer sold 434 pumpkins and 226 squash. How many pumpkins and squash is this?

A 652   **B** 650   **C** 660   **D** 612

GRADE 2 KEY NS 2.2

4. Bea is making a poster and needs to write numbers in standard form. How is seven hundred six written in standard form?

A 76   **B** 706   **C** 760   **D** 7006

NS 1.1 page 8

```
  4 34          38
+ 2 26        + 2 6
 ─────
   660
```

5. Shing buys an item that costs $1.40. Which is a way that he can pay with the correct change?

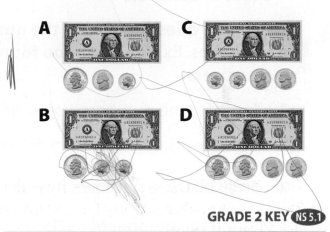

A   B   C   D

GRADE 2 KEY NS 5.1

6. Sheila wrote this number sentence.

$$5 + 3 + 1 = 9$$

Which number sentence has the same answer as Sheila's number sentence?

A $5 + 4 + 1 = $ ▓

B $9 + 1 + 3 = $ ▓

C $3 + 5 + 9 = $ ▓

D $1 + 5 + 3 = $ ▓

> **Test Tip**
> Which sentences cannot be correct? You can solve the number sentences to check.

GRADE 2 KEY AF 1.1

Education Place
Visit www.eduplace.com/camap/ for
Test-Taking Tips and **Extra Practice**.

Chapter 2 Lesson 5   **37**

Reading & Writing **Math**

Vocabulary

When working with numbers, you can **round** them, **compare** them, or **order** them.

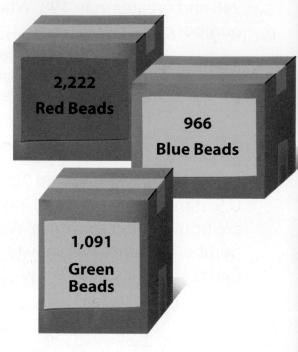

2,222 Red Beads

966 Blue Beads

1,091 Green Beads

Marta is making beaded bracelets for her friends. She bought a box of red beads, a box of blue beads, and a box of green beads. There are a different number of beads in each box.

Answer the questions using the numbers on the boxes. Explain how you found your answers.

1. Compare the numbers. Use < or >.

   966 ⬤ 1,091   2,222 ⬤ 1,091

2. Order all three numbers from greatest to least.

3. Round the number of red beads to the nearest ten.

4. Complete the number sentences.

   2,222 is _____ 966 (greater than, less than)

   966 is _____ 1,091 (greater than, less than)

   1,091 _____ 2,222 (< >)

Writing Find three products that are sold in boxes, such as cereal, pencils, or toys. Look for numbers on the boxes. Write three problems using the numbers.

Reading Check out this book in your library.
- *Math Appeal*, by Greg Tang

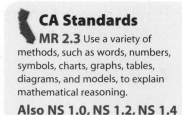
CA Standards
MR 2.3 Use a variety of methods, such as words, numbers, symbols, charts, graphs, tables, diagrams, and models, to explain mathematical reasoning.
Also NS 1.0, NS 1.2, NS 1.4

Standards-Based Extra Practice

Set A
NS 1.2 page 28

Write the numbers in order from least to greatest.

1. 685   473   576

2. 748   1,275   795

3. 1,310   4,040   944

4. 7,500   6,538   7,697

Write the numbers in order from greatest to least.

5. 574   515   4,564

6. 6,810   6,587   8,123

7. 326   831   366

8. 8,741   6,584   9,714

9. In a forest there are 234 maple trees, 410 pine trees, and 243 oak trees. Put the number of trees in order from greatest to least.

Set B
NS 1.4 page 30

Round to the nearest ten and the nearest hundred.

1. 567

2. 888

3. 123

4. 245

5. 841

6. 581

7. 947

8. 568

9. Michelle is on the dance team at school. During her warm-up she does 152 crunches. To the nearest ten and the nearest hundred, how many crunches does she do?

Set C
NS 1.4 page 34

Round to the nearest thousand, the nearest hundred, and the nearest ten.

1. 3,878

2. 6,807

3. 4,468

4. 1,069

5. 9,512

6. 7,418

7. 8,764

8. 2,489

9. Marta sent out 1,818 flyers for a fundraiser. To the nearest thousand, the nearest hundred, and the nearest ten, how many flyers did she send out?

Education Place
Visit www.eduplace.com/camap/
for more **Extra Practice.**

Chapter Review/Test

Vocabulary and Concepts ———————————————— NS 1.2

Choose the best word to complete each sentence.

1. 495 is _____ 594.

2. The symbols < and > are used to _____ numbers.

> **Word Bank**
> compare
> less than

Skills ————————————————— NS 1.2, KEY NS 1.3, NS 1.4

Write the numbers in order from least to greatest.

3. 635 297 1,547

4. 862 2,671 294

5. 164 3,588 1,427

6. 9,247 568 5,581

7. 4,481 927 2,631

8. 872 827 8,246

Compare. Write >, <, or = for the ⬤.

9. 874 ⬤ 784

10. 659 ⬤ 926

11. 8,816 ⬤ 1,524

12. 247 ⬤ 247

13. 1,217 ⬤ 1,765

14. 2,342 ⬤ 2,342

Round to the nearest ten, hundred, and thousand.

15. 1,574

16. 3,651

17. 7,255

18. 5,868

Problem Solving and Reasoning ——————— KEY NS 1.3, NS 1.4, MR 1.0, MR 2.3

Solve.

19. There are 852 people waiting in line for a concert. To the nearest hundred, how many people are waiting in line?

20. The Dawson family picked 2,398 cherries. To the nearest thousand, how many cherries did they pick?

Writing Math Use place value to explain why nine hundred six is greater than six hundred nine.

Spiral Review and Test Practice

1. The Muñoz family traveled 386 miles. Which of these equals 386?

   A $300 + 800 + 60$

   B $300 + 80 + 6$

   C $3 + 80 + 600$

   D $3 + 8 + 6$

> **Test Tip**
> Add the numbers in each answer choice. Is their sum 386?

               KEY NS 1.5 page 8

2. In standard form, what number does the model show?

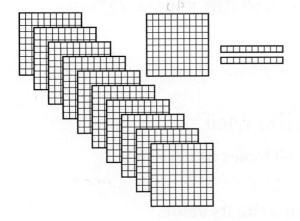

   A 1120   **C** 1102

   B 1012   **D** 112

               NS 1.1 page 12

3. Which number, rounded to the nearest ten, is 90?

   A 95   **C** 86

   B 98   **D** 84

               NS 1.4 page 30

4. Which set of numbers is in order from greatest to least?

   A 965, 5649, 5469, 4569

   B 5469, 5649, 4569, 965

   C 965, 4569, 5469, 5649

   D 5649, 5469, 4569, 965

               NS 1.2 page 28

5. Which number has a 5 in the ones place and a 5 in the thousands place?

   A 9595

   B 5959

   C 9955

   D 5995

> **Test Tip**
> First, check the digit in the thousands place. It should be 5.

             KEY NS 1.3 page 14

6. What is 6,784 rounded to the nearest thousand?

   A 6800

   B 6700

   C 7000

   D 6000

               NS 1.4 page 34

Education Place
Visit www.eduplace.com/camap/ for
Test-Taking Tips and **Extra Practice**.

Unit 1 Review/Test

Vocabulary and Concepts ———————————— MR 2.3 Chapters 1–2

Choose the best word to complete each sentence.

1. You always _____ up if the digit is 5 or greater.

2. The symbols < (less than) or > (greater than) are used to _____ numbers.

3. In the number 627, the _____ 2 has a _____ of 20.

4. You can _____ numbers from greatest to least, or least to greatest.

> **Word Bank**
> value
> order
> digit
> round
> compare
> add

Skills ——————————— NS 1.1, NS 1.2, KEY NS 1.3, NS 1.4, KEY NS 1.5 Chapter 1, Lessons 1–4

Write the number in two other ways.

5. 500 + 70 + 3   6. four hundred fifty-two   7. 837

Tell if each is greater than, less than, or equal to 1,000.

8. 10 boxes of 100 markers   9. 60 tables of 10 people

Write the place of the underlined digit. Then write its value.

10. 2,<u>1</u>49   11. <u>3</u>,765   12. 1,97<u>8</u>   13. 4,<u>3</u>07

Write the numbers in order from least to greatest. Chapter 2, Lesson 2

14. 241   947   653   15. 8,261   1,837   942

Round to the nearest thousand, the nearest hundred, and the nearest ten. Chapter 2, Lessons 3–4

16. 2,459   17. 8,361   18. 5,627

Problem Solving and Reasoning

NS 1.1, KEY **NS 1.3**, NS 1.4 Chapters 1–2

Solve.

19. The soccer team sold cookies to raise money for new uniforms. Benito sold 1,845 cookies. Will sold 1,795 cookies. Tanya sold 1,725 cookies. Rounded to the nearest hundred, who sold 1,800 cookies?

20. Jessica says that her favorite number has a one in the tens place, a nine in the thousands place, a zero in the hundreds place, and an eight in the ones place. What is Jessica's favorite number?

BIG IDEA!

Writing Math What is the greatest 4-digit number you can make using the digits 0–9 and using each digit only once? How does place value help you decide?

Performance Assessment

Guessing Game

NS 1.4, MR 1.0, MR 1.1, MR 2.3, MR 2.4, MR 2.6

The Eastside Pep Club is raising money for charity. They are holding a contest in which people have to guess the number of marbles in a jar.

Task	Information You Need
As a club member, you need to decide how many marbles to put in the jar. Use the information to help you. Then write the clues for the contest.	One clue gives the number rounded to the nearest hundred.
	One clue gives the number rounded to the nearest ten.
	One clue uses a greater than or less than statement.

Partial Sums

Partial sums are fast to do.
First break each number into two!

Partial sums make adding easy!
Break the numbers into pieces, then
add. Look at Problem 1. Because
$30 + 20 = 50$ and $5 + 4 = 9$, the
answer is $50 + 9 = 59$.

1. $35 + 24 = \boxed{50} + \boxed{9} = \boxed{59}$ **2.** $24 + 71 = \boxed{90} + \square = \square$

3. $46 + 32 = \square + \square = \square$ **4.** $73 + 25 = \square + \square = \square$

Keep up the good work!

5. $51 + 37 = \square + \square = \square$ **6.** $42 + 43 = \square + \square = \square$

7. $25 + 42 = \square + \square = \square$ **8.** $72 + 26 = \square + \square = \square$

Take It Further!

Now try doing all the steps in your head!

9. $36 + 42$ **10.** $61 + 25$ **11.** $54 + 45$ **12.** $43 + 36$

Doing Great!

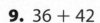

44

Unit

Addition and Subtraction

BIG IDEAS!

- You can show number relationships by writing expressions, equations, or inequalities.

- Knowing properties will help you add.

- If you know how to regroup with smaller numbers, you can add and subtract any size whole numbers.

Chapter 3
Addition

Chapter 4
Subtraction

Songs and Games

 Math Music Track 2: *I Can Estimate*

eGames at
www.eduplace.com/camap/

Math Readers

Add It Up!

Object of the Game Make two-digit addends so that
the sum has a large number in the ones place.

Materials
- number cube labeled 1–6
- number cube labeled 4–9

Number of Players 2

How to Play

1 Player 1 rolls both number cubes and writes a two-digit number using the rolled numbers. Then he or she rolls both cubes again and writes another two-digit number.

2 Player 1 adds the two numbers. Player 2 checks the addition. The ones digit of the sum is the number of points that Player 1 earns.

3 Players take turns repeating Steps 1 and 2. Each player keeps a record of his or her total number of points. The first player to reach 50 points wins.

4 Repeat the game again with Player 2 going first.

CA Standards
KEY NS 2.1 Find the sum or difference of two whole numbers between 0 and 10,000.
Also NS 1.1

 Education Place
Visit www.eduplace.com/camap/ for
Brain Teasers and **eGames** to play.

Reading
It can be helpful to show the information and numbers in a word problem in a different way. You can make a list, write a number sentence, make notes, or draw a picture or diagram.

Read the word problem.	Study the drawing.
Problem 1 On Friday, 185 parents and friends bought tickets for the school fair. On Saturday, 325 people bought tickets. How many people in all bought tickets for the fair?	**Total Tickets Sold** Friday 185 | Saturday 325

In Problem 1, you know the parts, but not the whole. You can see that you need to add to find the total.

Writing
Read Problem 2. Then show the information in a different way.

Here is how I showed the information in the problem.

Problem 2

On Thursday, 185 people bought tickets for the school play. By Friday night, 510 people had bought tickets. How many people bought tickets on Friday?

Addition

These colorful birds are called Rainbow Lorikeets.

Check What You Know

Word Bank

compare

greater than

less than

Vocabulary and Concepts NS 1.2, MR 2.3

Choose the best term to complete each sentence. page 26

1. The number 765 is _____ the number 567.

2. You _____ to find which of two numbers is greater.

Skills KEY NS 1.5

Write each number in expanded form. page 8

3. 81   **4.** 347   **5.** 603

Problem Solving and Reasoning NS 1.1

6. What is the smallest number that can be made from the digits 3, 2, and 7?

Vocabulary

Visualize It!

regroup
12 ones equals
1 ten and 2 ones.

$$\begin{array}{r} 1 \\ 27 \\ +\ 5 \\ \hline 32 \end{array}$$

addend
A number to be added in an addition expression.

sum
The result of addition.

Language Tip

Some words are similar in Spanish and English.

English	Spanish
regroup	**reagrupar**
sum	**suma**

See **English-Spanish Glossary** pages 628–646.

Education Place Visit www.eduplace.com/camap/ for the **eGlossary** and **eGames**.

CA Standards MR 2.3 Use a variety of methods, such as words, numbers, symbols, charts, graphs, tables, diagrams, and models, to explain mathematical reasoning. **KEY NS 2.1**

Chapter 3   49

CA Standards

KEY **NS 2.1** Find the sum or difference of two whole numbers between 0 and 10,000.

MR 2.3 Use a variety of methods, such as words, numbers, symbols, charts, graphs, tables, diagrams, and models, to explain mathematical reasoning.

Also NS 2.0, MR 2.4

Vocabulary

regroup

addend

Materials
- Base-ten blocks
- Workmat 1
- eManipulatives
  www.eduplace.com/camap/

Hands On
Addition with Regrouping

Objective Regroup to add 3-digit numbers.

▶ **Explore**

Last year the bird-watching club had 179 members. This year, 158 new members joined. How many members are in the club now?

Question How can you use base-ten blocks to show addition with **regrouping**?

$$179 + 158 = \bigcirc$$

1 Show each **addend**. Record.

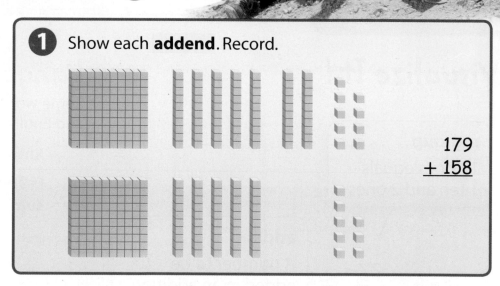

$$\begin{array}{r} 179 \\ + 158 \\ \hline \end{array}$$

2 Add the ones. Regroup 10 ones as 1 ten. Record.

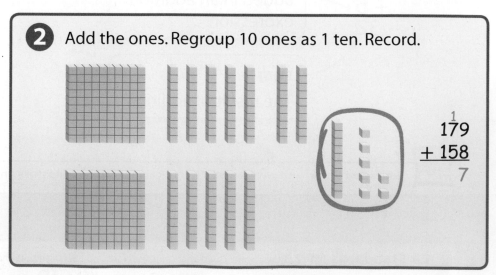

$$\begin{array}{r} \overset{1}{1}79 \\ + 158 \\ \hline 7 \end{array}$$

Think

9 ones + 8 ones = 17 ones

Regroup 17 ones as 1 ten and 7 ones.

3 Add the tens. Regroup 10 tens as 1 hundred. Record.

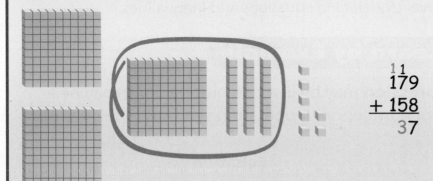

$$\begin{array}{r} \overset{1\ 1}{179} \\ +\ 158 \\ \hline 37 \end{array}$$

> **Think**
>
> 1 ten + 7 tens + 5 tens = 13 tens
>
> Regroup 13 tens as 1 hundred and 3 tens.

4 Add the hundreds. $179 + 158 = 337$

Solution: The club has 337 members.

▶ **Extend**

Work with a partner. Use blocks to solve each problem. Tell whether you regrouped tens, ones, or both.

1. $\begin{array}{r}446\\+235\\\hline\end{array}$	**2.** $\begin{array}{r}258\\+114\\\hline\end{array}$	**3.** $\begin{array}{r}135\\+\ 27\\\hline\end{array}$	**4.** $\begin{array}{r}67\\+75\\\hline\end{array}$
5. $\begin{array}{r}294\\+676\\\hline\end{array}$	**6.** $\begin{array}{r}428\\+179\\\hline\end{array}$	**7.** $\begin{array}{r}574\\+352\\\hline\end{array}$	**8.** $\begin{array}{r}236\\+129\\\hline\end{array}$
9. $\begin{array}{r}484\\+392\\\hline\end{array}$	**10.** $\begin{array}{r}442\\+\ 77\\\hline\end{array}$	**11.** $\begin{array}{r}517\\+295\\\hline\end{array}$	**12.** $\begin{array}{r}371\\+\ 59\\\hline\end{array}$

13. Create and Solve Write an addition problem that you need to regroup tens and ones to solve.

Writing Math

What's Wrong? Freddie adds 674 and 281 and says that the sum is 855. What is the correct sum? Explain the mistake that Freddie made.

LESSON 2

CA Standards
KEY **AF 1.1** Represent relationships of quantities in the form of mathematical expressions, equations, or inequalities.
Also AF 1.0, AF 1.2, AF 1.3, MR 2.3, MR 2.4

Equations and Inequalities

Objective Understand equations and inequalities.

▶ Learn by Example

An **expression** may be just one number, or it may be a group of numbers with operation symbols $(+, -, \times, \div)$.

Vocabulary

expression
$6 + 4$
$6 - 4$
10

equation or **equality**
$6 + 4 = 10$
$10 = 6 + 4$
$12 - 2 = 9 + 1$

inequality
$6 + 4 > 9$
$6 - 4 < 12$
$10 + 2 > 10 + 1$

Equation

Two expressions that have the same value can form an **equation** or **equality**. Use $=$ to show an equation.

$$5 + 4 = 6 + 3$$ ← 5 plus 4 is equal to 6 plus 3.
or
$$6 + 3 = 5 + 4$$ ← 6 plus 3 is equal to 5 plus 4.

Inequality

Two expressions that do not have the same value can form an **inequality**. Use $>$ or $<$ to show an inequality.

$$5 + 1 < 2 + 6$$ ← 5 plus 1 is less than 2 plus 6.
or
$$2 + 6 > 5 + 1$$ ← 2 plus 6 is greater than 5 plus 1.

Ask Yourself

- What is the value of each expression?
- Are the values of each expression equal? not equal?

▶ Guided Practice

Write $>$, $<$, or $=$ for the ⬤. Tell if the number sentence is an *equation* or an *inequality*.

1. $12 + 10$ ⬤ 22 **2.** $19 - 16$ ⬤ $16 - 12$

Choose the numbers that make the number sentence true.

3. $25 - \blacksquare > 17 + 2$

| 7 | 0 | 5 | 9 | 2 |

 Math Talk For Exercise 3, why is there more than one correct answer?

Practice and Problem Solving

Write $>$, $<$, or $=$ for ⬭. Tell if the number sentence is an *equation* or an *inequality*.

4. $23 + 29$ ⬭ 52

5. $52 + 23$ ⬭ $55 + 23$

6. $24 + 16$ ⬭ $27 + 12$

7. $37 - 16$ ⬭ $29 - 5$

8. $26 + 18$ ⬭ $34 + 9$

9. $42 - 21$ ⬭ $55 - 34$

Choose the number or numbers that make the sentence true.

10. $12 + \blacksquare = 20$

11. $6 + 2 < 11$

12. $7 + \blacksquare > 17$

13. $32 - \blacksquare > 12 + 16$

14. $4 + 30 = \blacksquare + 29$

15. $6 + 11 > \blacksquare + 0$

8	14
1	5
4	12
2	

Write the letter of the number sentence that matches the story.

16. One goose and 5 goslings were walking on the grass. Six geese were flying overhead. Which compares the number of geese walking to the number of geese flying?

A $1 + 6 > 5$

B $1 + 5 = 6$

> **Vocabulary Tip**
> A **gosling** is a baby goose. The plural of goose is geese.

Spiral Review and Test Practice

Order each set of numbers from least to greatest. NS 1.2 page 28

17. 8,764 3,899 7,605

18. 4,025 4,089 4,008

Write the letter of the correct answer. AF 1.2

19. What number makes this number sentence true?
$7 + 4 = \blacksquare + 6$

A 11   **B** 17   **C** 5   **D** 3

CA Standards

KEY NS 2.1 Find the sum or difference of two whole numbers between 0 and 10,000.

AF 1.0 Students select appropriate symbols, operations, and properties to represent, describe, simplify, and solve simple number relationships.

Also NS 2.0, AF 1.2, MR 2.3, MR 2.4

Vocabulary

Commutative Property of Addition
$2 + 7 = 7 + 2$

Zero Property of Addition
$9 = 0 + 9$

Associative Property of Addition
$(3 + 5) + 2 = 3 + (5 + 2)$

Addition Properties

Objective Use the Commutative Property, the Zero Property, and the Associative Property to add.

▶ **Learn by Example**

The three addition properties listed below are important rules that can also help you add.

Addition Properties

Commutative Property

Changing the order in which numbers are added does not change the sum.

$$5 \quad + \quad 3 \quad = \quad 8$$
addend   addend   sum

$$3 \quad + \quad 5 \quad = \quad 8$$
addend   addend   sum

$$\begin{array}{r} 5 \\ + 3 \\ \hline 8 \end{array}$$
You can add down.

$$\begin{array}{r} 3 \\ + 5 \\ \hline 8 \end{array}$$
You can add up.

Zero Property

The sum of any number and zero is the number.

$$4 \quad + \quad 0 \quad = \quad 4$$

Associative Property

Changing the way in which addends are grouped does not change the sum.

Parentheses show which numbers to add first.

$$(6 + 4) + 3 \qquad 6 + (4 + 3)$$
$$10 + 3 = 13 \qquad 6 + 7 = 13$$

Write the number that makes the number sentence true. Tell which property you used.

1. $15 + 3 = \boxed{} + 15$

2. $0 + \boxed{} = 32$

3. $(73 + 14) + \boxed{} = 73 + (14 + 2)$

Ask Yourself
What number will make the two expressions have the same value?

 Math Talk Describe three ways to find $8 + 2 + 6$. Is one way easier than the others? Explain.

► **Practice and Problem Solving**

Write the number that makes the number sentence true. Tell which property you used.

4. $4 + 16 = 16 + \boxed{}$

5. $9 + \boxed{} = 9$

6. $5 + (61 + 32) = (5 + \boxed{}) + 32$

7. $57 + 32 = \boxed{} + 57$

8. $0 + \boxed{} = 7$

9. $(7 + 4) + 2 = 7 + (\boxed{} + 2)$

Solve.

10. **Analyze** Ken's family caught 6 trout, 5 bass, and 4 pike on their fishing trip. Find the total number of fish. Which two numbers did you add first? Explain.

11. **Right or Wrong?** Rosa caught 104 fish last year. This year, she caught 26 more fish than last year. Rosa said she caught 78 fish this year. Is Rosa right? Explain.

 Spiral Review and Test Practice

Write the place of the underlined digit. Then write its value. **KEY NS 1.3** page 14

12. 9,<u>8</u>02

13. <u>1</u>0,000

14. <u>4</u>,921

15. 5,6<u>6</u>2

Write the letter of the correct answer. **AF 1.2**

16. What number makes the number sentence true?
$3 + (2 + 8) = (\boxed{} + 2) + 8$

A 23   **B** 14   **C** 13   **D** 3

CA Standards

KEY NS 2.1 Find the sum or difference of two whole numbers between 0 and 10,000.

MR 2.2 Apply strategies and results from simpler problems to more complex problems.

Also NS 2.0, AF 1.0, MR 1.0, MR 1.1, MR 1.2, MR 2.3, MR 2.4, MR 2.6, MR 3.0, MR 3.2, MR 3.3

Vocabulary

sum

Column Addition

Objective Add 3 or more addends (2-digit or 3-digit numbers).

▶ **Learn by Example**

You can use what you know about adding two numbers to add three or more numbers.

Desert Rosy Boa

At a reptile exhibit there are 124 snakes, 78 lizards, and 52 turtles. How many reptiles are there in all?

Find the **sum** of 124 + 78 + 52.

1 Add the ones.

$4 + 8 + 2 = 14$ ones

$$
\begin{array}{r}
\overset{1}{1}24 \\
78 \\
+\ \ 52 \\
\hline
4
\end{array}
$$

Regroup 14 ones as 1 ten 4 ones.

Hint

Be sure to line up the numbers correctly.

2 Add the tens.

$1 + 2 + 7 + 5 = 15$ tens

$$
\begin{array}{r}
\overset{11}{1}24 \\
78 \\
+\ \ 52 \\
\hline
54
\end{array}
$$

Regroup 15 tens as 1 hundred 5 tens.

3 Add the hundreds.

$1 + 1 = 2$ hundreds

$$
\begin{array}{r}
\overset{11}{1}24 \\
78 \\
+\ \ 52 \\
\hline
254
\end{array}
$$

4 Check your work. You can check by adding upward.

$$
\begin{array}{r}
\overset{11}{1}24 \\
78 \\
+\ 152 \\
\hline
254
\end{array}
$$

Solution: There are 254 reptiles in the exhibit.

Guided Practice

Find the sum. Check by adding in a different order.

Ask Yourself
• Did I line up the numbers correctly?
• Do I need to regroup?

1.
```
   62
   15
 + 17
```

2.
```
  154
  218
+ 463
```

3.
```
   18
  243
 + 71
```

4.
```
  245
  101
  319
+ 172
```

Guided Problem Solving

Use the questions to solve the problem.

Green Anaconda

5. The zoo has a boa constrictor that is 96 inches long. The python is 204 inches longer than the boa. The anaconda is 36 inches longer than the python. How long is the anaconda?

a. Understand Which picture can you use to solve the problem?

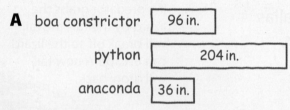

A
boa constrictor	96 in.
python	204 in.
anaconda	36 in.

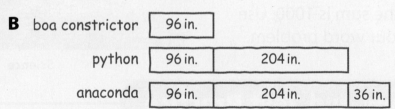

B
boa constrictor	96 in.
python	96 in.	204 in.
anaconda	96 in.	204 in.	36 in.

b. Plan What do you need to do to find the length of the anaconda?

c. Solve Write the equation.

d. Look Back Does your answer make sense? Why?

Fun Fact

Reptiles are cold-blooded animals that use the sun's heat to stay warm.

Science PS 1.a

Math Talk What is the greatest number of ones that you could regroup when adding three one-digit numbers?

Find the sum. Check by adding in a different order.

6.   2
    549
    335
  + 76
    100

7.   1
    504
    372
  + 118
    994

8.   ✗
    112
    231
  + 422
    765

9. $146 + 68 + 16$ 10. $184 + 15 + 79 + 12$

 Science Link

Use the Fun Facts to solve Problem 11.

11. **Multistep** A snapping turtle can live 32 years longer than a chuckwalla. A giant tortoise can live 95 years longer than a snapping turtle. How many years can a giant tortoise live?

12. Order the mass of three chuckwallas from greatest to least: 543 grams, 482 grams, and 620 grams.

13. **Create and Solve** Write a word problem in which the sum is 1000. Use three addends in your word problem.

Chuckwallas

- Chuckwallas are found in the Sonoran and Mojave deserts.

- A chuckwalla can live up to 25 years.

- A chuckwalla can puff up its body to wedge itself between rocks for protection.

- If a predator grabs the lizard by the tail, the tail will break off so the lizard can escape. A new tail will grow back.

Science LS 3.b

 Spiral Review and Test Practice

Write the numbers in order from least to greatest. NS 1.2 page 28

14. 609   415   280   965   15. 4,751   8,909   3,002   4,334

Write the letter of the correct answer. KEY **NS 2.1**

16. Last year, Jan read 131 picture books, 14 novels, 12 nonfiction books, and 24 magazines. How many books and magazines did Jan read?

   A 81   **B** 171   **C** 180   **D** 181

Extra Practice See page 67, Set C.

Key Standards Review

Need Help?
See Key Standards Handbook.

**Name the place of the underlined digit.
Then write its value.** KEY NS 1.3

1. 5<u>1</u>4   **2.** <u>9</u>23   **3.** 6<u>0</u>7   **4.** 82<u>0</u>

5. 5,<u>2</u>80   **6.** <u>1</u>,720   **7.** 9,<u>0</u>00   **8.** 6,22<u>9</u>

**Write the number. Read the clues carefully to identify
the correct place.** KEY NS 1.3

9. 9 in the hundreds place, 3 in the ones place, 7 in the
tens place

10. 1 in the hundreds place, 5 in the tens place, 0 in the
ones place, 8 in the thousands place

11. 0 in the tens and hundreds place, 6 in the thousands
place, 7 in the ones place

**Write each number in two other ways. Use standard form,
expanded form, and word form.** KEY NS 1.5

12. 372   **13.** 2,000 + 90 + 5

14. eight thousand fifteen

Number Sense

Rounding Riddles

Solve. KEY NS 1.3, NS 1.4

1. Ken is thinking of a number. Rounded to the nearest ten,
it is 250. Rounded to the nearest hundred, it is 300. What
could Ken's number be? List all of the possible answers.

2. Make up your own rounding riddle. Exchange with
a partner and solve.

LESSON 5

CA Standards

KEY NS 2.1 Find the sum or difference of two whole numbers between 0 and 10,000.

AF 1.0 Students select appropriate symbols, operations, and properties to represent, describe, simplify, and solve simple number relationships.

Also NS 2.0, AF 1.3, MR 2.0, MR 2.2, MR 2.3, MR 2.4

Add Greater Numbers

Objective Find the sum of two 4-digit numbers.

▶ Learn by Example

You can use what you know about adding smaller numbers to add larger numbers.

If one little brown bat ate 1,248 insects and another bat ate 1,664 insects, how many insects did they eat in all?

$1,248 + 1,664 = \bigcirc$

---

1 Add the ones.

$8 + 4 = 12$ ones

$$\begin{array}{r} \overset{1}{1,248} \\ + 1,664 \\ \hline 2 \end{array}$$

Regroup 12 ones as 1 ten 2 ones.

2 Add the tens.

$1 + 4 + 6 = 11$ tens

$$\begin{array}{r} \overset{11}{1,248} \\ + 1,664 \\ \hline 12 \end{array}$$

Regroup 11 tens as 1 hundred 1 ten.

3 Add the hundreds.

$1 + 2 + 6 = 9$ hundreds

$$\begin{array}{r} \overset{11}{1,248} \\ + 1,664 \\ \hline 912 \end{array}$$

4 Add the thousands.

$1 + 1 = 2$ thousands

$$\begin{array}{r} \overset{11}{1,248} \\ + 1,664 \\ \hline 2,912 \end{array}$$

Solution: The two bats ate 2,912 insects.

Albino Brown Bat

Other Examples

A.
$$\begin{array}{r} \overset{1}{1,}\overset{1}{603} \\ + 3,509 \\ \hline 5,112 \end{array}$$

The only ten is the regrouped ten.

B.
$$\begin{array}{r} \overset{1}{5,}\overset{11}{678} \\ + 4,322 \\ \hline 10,000 \end{array}$$

10 thousands are regrouped as 1 ten thousand.

60

Find the sum.

Ask Yourself
• What is the sum of the digits in each column?
• Do I need to regroup?

1.	7,925
	+ 54

2.	3,838
	+ 2,165

3.	4,025
	+ 3,082

4.	5,312
	+ 866

5.	3,215
	+ 4,927

6.	8,023
	+ 1,977

7. $6,750 + 325$ 8. $1,948 + 57$

(123) Math Talk Why can you add numbers in a different order to check that the sum is correct?

► **Practice and Problem Solving**

Find the sum.

9.	354
	+ 215

10.	3,223
	+ 1,211

11.	3,192
	+ 5,466

12.	5,380
	+ 1,046

13.	3,103
	+ 1,903

14.	1,599
	+ 325

15.	2,468
	+ 7,532

16.	2,999
	+ 4,025

17.	4,514
	+ 97

18.	6,032
	+ 2,784

19.	5,437
	+ 899

20.	2,980
	+ 5,020

21. $1,479 + 7,521$ 22. $3,038 + 6,962$

✗ Algebra Number Sentences **Compare. Use $<$, $>$ or $=$** for each ⬤. **Tell what addition property you used.**

23. $48 + 60$ ⬤ $60 + 48$ 24. $35 + 20 + 20$ ⬤ $35 + 40$

25. $81 + 0$ ⬤ $81 + 1$ 26. $(150 + 25) + 10$ ⬤ $150 + (25 + 10)$

Write the letter of the sentence that matches the story.

27. Seven baby river otters and 4 adult river otters were on a rock. Twelve baby river otters and 7 adult river otters were in the water. Compare the number of river otters on the rock to the number of river otters in the water.
    A $7 + 4 < 12 + 7$ **B** $7 + 4 + 12 > 7$

Solve.

28. Black bears live in Yosemite National Park. In August, 489 people reported seeing a bear. In September, 637 people reported seeing a bear, and in October, only 49 people reported seeing a bear. In all, how many bear sightings were reported?

29. One year, California rangers tracked 3,492 wild horses. The following year, they tracked 4,123 more horses. How many horses were tracked in all?

 Real World Data

Use the table to answer Problems 30–33.

30. Which sea lion has a weight closest to 1,000 pounds?

31. Which sea lion has a weight closest to 400 pounds?

32. Challenge If Corky's weight was doubled, would he weigh more or less than Flip?

33. Jumper weighs 1,122 pounds. Willy weighs 109 more pounds than Jumper. How many pounds does Willy weigh?

Weight of Sea Lions

Bar graph showing Weight (in Pounds) on the y-axis from 0 to 2,000, for sea lions Corky, Jumper, Squeaky, and Flip on the x-axis (Sea Lions).

 Spiral Review and Test Practice

Round to the place of the underlined digit. NS 1.4 pages 30, 34

34. 5̲76   **35.** 8̲0̲2   **36.** 1̲,780   **37.** 5,4̲9̲6

Write the letter of the correct answer. KEY NS 2.1

38. $1,316 + 7,805 =$ ⬤

   A 9,101   **B** 9,111   **C** 9,121   **D** 9,211

Feeding Time

Carla is an aquarium worker. She cares for and feeds the animals, making sure each animal is healthy. The table shows the amount of fish that Carla feeds to different groups of animals each week.

1. Order the number of pounds of fish eaten by each group of animals from greatest to least. Which group eats the most fish?

2. How many pounds of fish does Carla need in order to feed all four groups of animals each week?

Animal	Pounds of Fish Eaten (per week)
Orcas	3,390
Dolphins	2,238
Sea Otters	1,045
Sea Lions	2,826

3. **Multistep** This week, the zoo receives two shipments of fish. One shipment weighs 4,365 pounds and the other weighs 5,142 pounds. Will Carla have enough fish to feed all four groups of animals this week? Explain.

CA Standards
NS 1.2, KEY NS 2.1,
NS 2.8

LESSON 6

Field Trip...

Bakersfield, CA

CA Standards
MR 1.0, MR 1.1,
MR 2.0, MR 2.4,
NS 1.2, NS 2.0,
KEY **NS 2.1**, KEY **AF 1.1**

Problem Solving

Objective Use skills and strategies to solve word problems.

Black bears are the only bears that live in California.

The California Living Museum displays plants and animals from California, including black bears.

Solve. Tell which strategy or method you used.

1. **Compare** Look at the pictures of the bear tracks. Tell if each statement is true or false.

   a. length of front paw > length of hind paw

   b. width of front paw = width of hind paw

2. A black bear cub stays with its mother until it is 18 months old. If a black bear cub left its mother 16 months ago, how old is it now?

3. On her first visit, Sara counted 4 bears in the exhibit. By her second visit, 3 bears had been added. By her third visit, 2 bears had been moved to a different zoo. Write an equation to show how many bears were in the exhibit on Sarah's third visit.

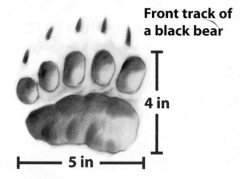

Front track of a black bear

4 in

5 in

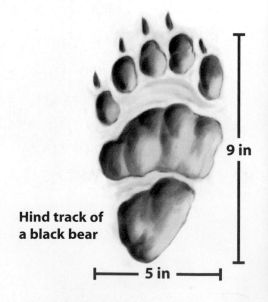

9 in

Hind track of a black bear

5 in

Problem Solving On Tests

Select a Strategy
- Draw a Picture
- Make an Organized List
- Make a Table

1. Katie wrote a number with a 3 in the tens place and a 5 in the hundreds place. Which could be Katie's number?

A 3355

B 3553

C 5335

D 5535

> **Test Tip**
> Draw a picture of a number with a 3 in the tens place and a 5 in the hundreds place.

KEY **NS 1.3** page 14

2. Nelson wrote the number seven thousand, fifty-three in standard form. Which number did he write?

A 70,053

B 7053

C 7530

D 753

NS 1.1 page 8

3. The set of numbers shows attendance at four basketball games. Which set of numbers is ordered from greatest to least?

A 1250   1127   1023   1018

B 1018   1023   1127   1250

C 1018   1023   1250   1127

D 1250   1018   1127   1023

NS 1.2 page 28

4. Lakisha wrote a number with the digit 4 in the tens place and in the thousands place. Which is Lakisha's number?

A 4247   **C** 7244

B 4472   **D** 7424

KEY **NS 1.3** page 14

5. On Monday, 542 people went to the park. On Tuesday, 483 people went to the park. How many people went to the park in all?

A 1025 people   **C** 1000 people

B 59 people   **D** 925 people

KEY **NS 2.1** page 60

6. There were 3861 people at a concert. Rounded to the nearest hundred, how many people were at the concert?

A 4000   **C** 3900

B 3000   **D** 3800

NS 1.4 page 34

Education Place
Visit www.eduplace.com/camap/ for
Test-Taking Tips and **Extra Practice**.

Chapter 3 Lesson 6   **65**

Reading & Writing Math

Vocabulary

The **Commutative Property**, the **Zero Property**, and the **Associative Property** are important rules that can help you add.

Copy the word map. Complete it by explaining each property.

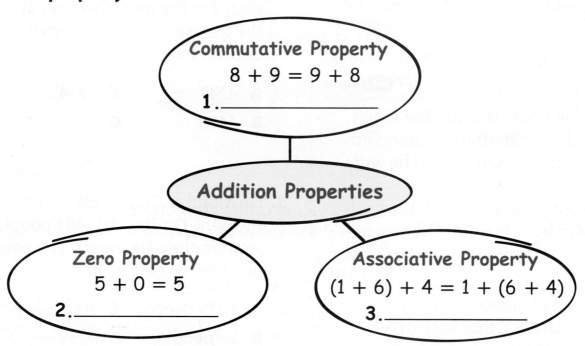

Commutative Property
$8 + 9 = 9 + 8$
1. _____

Addition Properties

Zero Property
$5 + 0 = 5$
2. _____

Associative Property
$(1 + 6) + 4 = 1 + (6 + 4)$
3. _____

Write the number that makes the number sentence true. Tell which property you used.

4. $8 + 0 = \blacksquare$

5. $(3 + 8) + 2 = 3 + (\blacksquare + 2)$

6. $11 + 3 = 3 + \blacksquare$

7. $13 + \blacksquare = 13$

8. $4 + 6 = \blacksquare + 4$

9. $9 + (2 + 7) = (\blacksquare + 2) + 7$

Writing Can you use more than one property to solve an addition problem? Give an example.

Reading Look for this book in your library.

• *Dealing with Addition*, by Lynette Long

CA Standards
MR 2.3 Use a variety of methods, such as words, numbers, symbols, charts, graphs, tables, diagrams, and models, to explain mathematical reasoning.

Also KEY NS 2.1, AF 1.0, AF 1.2

Standards-Based Extra Practice

Set A ———————————————————— KEY **AF 1.1**, AF 1.2, AF 1.3 page 52

Write >, <, or = for each ⬭. Tell if the number sentence is
an equation or an inequality.

1. 45 + 51 ⬭ 76 + 20

2. 12 + 63 ⬭ 46 + 32

3. 56 − 48 ⬭ 12 − 5

4. 47 + 2 ⬭ 59 + 8

Choose the number or numbers that make the number
sentence true.

5. 15 + 7 = 12 + ▨

6. 3 + 24 > 24 + ▨

7. 18 − 12 < 10 − ▨

> | 10 | 1 |
> | 2 | |
> | 0 | 3 |

8. Two otters and their 6 babies were eating clams. Four otters
were eating fish. Which compares the number of otters
eating clams to the number of otters eating fish?

   a. 2 + 6 > 4   **b.** 2 + 6 = 4

Set B ———————————————————— AF 1.2, AF 1.0 page 54

Write the number that makes the number sentence true.
Tell which property you used.

1. 20 + 8 = ▨ + 20

2. 11 + 0 = ▨

3. (31 + 4) + ▨ = 31 + (▨ + 12)

4. (▨ + 23) + 3 = 23 + (4 + ▨)

Set C ———————————————————— NS 2.0 page 56

Add. Check by adding in a different order.

1.   64
     17
  + 19

2.   21
   246
 + 74

3. 158
  222
+ 467

4. 250
 106
 324
+ 177

5. Julia is 34 inches tall. Raoul is 19 inches taller than Julia.
Lee is 18 inches taller than Raoul. How tall is Lee?

Education Place
Visit www.eduplace.com/camap/
for more **Extra Practice**.

Chapter Review/Test

Vocabulary and Concepts
KEY **AF 1.1**, AF 1.0

Choose the best word to complete each sentence.

> **Word Bank**
> Commutative Property
> Zero Property

1. We know that $12 + 0 = 12$ because of the _____.

2. The _____ says that $8 + 6 = 14$ and $6 + 8 = 14$.

Skills
KEY **AF 1.1**, AF 1.0, KEY **NS 2.1**

Write >, <, or = for each **.**

3. $48 + 54$ ⬭ $80 + 23$

4. $65 - 53$ ⬭ $17 - 9$

Write the number that makes the number sentence true.

5. $25 + $ ▨ $= 30 + 9$

6. $9 - $ ▨ $> 4 + 3$

7. $58 + 11 = 87 - $ ▨

Write the number that makes the number sentence true.
Tell which property you used.

8. $6 + 25 = $ ▨ $+ 6$

9. $(5 + 13) + $ ▨ $= 5 + ($ ▨ $+ 41)$

Add.

10.
```
  528
  142
+ 276
```

11.
```
   25
  354
+  82
```

12.
```
  6,818
+ 1,279
```

13.
```
  1,597
+ 3,481
```

Problem Solving and Reasoning
KEY **NS 2.1**, MR 1.1, MR 1.2, MR 2.3, MR 3.1

Solve.

14. Jay and Vanessa climbed 1,965 feet in one day. The next day they climbed 1,277 feet. How many feet did they climb in all?

15. Right or Wrong? Aaron says that the sum of 384 and 159 is 443. Is he right? Explain.

Writing Math Tom says $11 + 15 + 9 = 35$. Would his answer change if he added in a different order? Why or why not?

Spiral Review and Test Practice

1. What is the greatest whole number that can be made with the digits 2, 7, 9, and 8? Use each digit only once.

A 2789

B 2987

C 9872

D 9782

> **Test Tip**
> Find the digit with the greatest value. Place it first.

KEY **NS 1.3** page 14

2. Which is another way to write four thousand, five hundred sixty?

A $4000 + 500 + 60$

B 450,060

C $400 + 500 + 6$

D 4516

KEY **NS 1.5** page 14

3. Which set of numbers is in order from least to greatest?

A 1541, 1514, 1415, 1145

B 1514, 1541, 1415, 1145

C 1145, 1415, 1541, 1514

D 1145, 1415, 1514, 1541

NS 1.2 page 28

4. Which shows 485 rounded to the nearest ten?

A 500

B 490

C 480

D 400

NS 1.4 page 30

5. What is 5,493 rounded to the nearest thousand?

A 6000

B 5500

C 5490

D 5000

NS 1.4 page 34

6. What number makes this number sentence true?

$$8 + 5 = \square + 7$$

A 6

B 12

C 13

D 20

> **Test Tip**
> Check your work by using your answer in place of the box in the equation.

AF 1.2 page 52

Education Place
Visit www.eduplace.com/camap/ for
Test-Taking Tips and **Extra Practice**.

Chapter 3 Spiral Review and Test Practice **69**

Subtraction

Vocabulary and Concepts KEY NS 2.1, MR 2.3
Choose the best word to complete each sentence. page 50

1. When you add 4 and 9, the _____ is 13.

2. You can _____ 10 ones as 1 ten when you add.

Skills NS 1.4, KEY NS 2.1, AF 1.2
Find the missing number. page 50

3. $8 + \rule{1cm}{0.3cm} = 12$ 4. $11 + \rule{1cm}{0.3cm} = 20$ 5. $5 + \rule{1cm}{0.3cm} = 12$ 6. $7 + \rule{1cm}{0.3cm} = 15$

Round each number to the greatest place. page 30

7. 89   8. 852   9. 305

Problem Solving and Reasoning KEY NS 2.1

10. Jason has 15 baseball cards. His older brother gives him 3 more. How many cards does he have now?

Vocabulary

Visualize It!

subtraction
An operation that shows the difference of two numbers or quantities.

$$
\begin{array}{r}
43 \\
-\ 22 \\
\hline
?
\end{array}
$$

difference
The result of subtraction.

$43 - 22 = 21$

Language Tip
Some words are similar in Spanish and English.

English	Spanish
difference	diferencia
result	resultado

See **English-Spanish Glossary** pages 628–646.

Education Place Visit www.eduplace.com/camap/ for the **eGlossary** and **eGames**.

CA Standards MR 2.3 Use a variety of methods, such as words, numbers, symbols, charts, graphs, tables, diagrams, and models, to explain mathematical reasoning. **KEY NS 2.1**

Chapter 4   71

LESSON 1

CA Standards
KEY **NS 2.1** Find the sum or difference of two whole numbers between 0 and 10,000.

MR 2.3 Use a variety of methods, such as words, numbers, symbols, charts, graphs, tables, diagrams, and models, to explain mathematical reasoning.

Also NS 2.0, MR 2.4

Vocabulary

regroup

Materials
• Base-ten blocks
• Workmat 1 (optional)
• eManipulatives (optional)
  www.eduplace.com/camap/

Hands On
Model Subtraction

Objective Use base-ten blocks to regroup tens and hundreds to subtract.

▶ **Explore**

Question How can you use base-ten blocks to subtract with regrouping?

$145 - 37 = \bigcirc$

1 Use base-ten blocks to show 145.

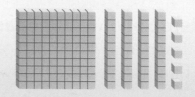

2 You cannot subtract the ones. Regroup 1 ten as 10 ones.

> 5 < 7, so I need to regroup before I can subtract.
> 10 ones + 5 ones = 15 ones.

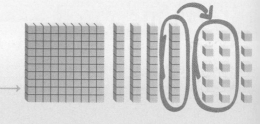

3 Subtract the ones.

15 ones − 7 ones = 8 ones.

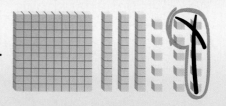

4 Subtract the tens.

3 tens − 3 tens = 0 tens.

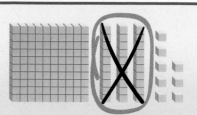

> **5** Subtract the hundreds.
>
> 1 hundred − 0 hundreds = 1 hundred.

Solution: 145 − 37 = 108

Sometimes you need to regroup tens and hundreds.

353 − 164 = ◯

1 Use base-ten blocks to show 353.

2 Subtract the ones. Regroup if you need to.

3 Subtract the tens. Regroup if you need to.

4 Subtract the hundreds.

▶ Extend

Use models to solve the problem. Tell whether you regrouped once or twice.

| **1.** 123
 − 99 | **2.** 152
 − 36 | **3.** 239
 − 47 | **4.** 261
 − 129 | **5.** 325
 − 176 |

6. Challenge A ferry is carrying 300 people. If 137 people get off the ferry, how many people are still on the ferry?

Writing Math

Right or Wrong? Hana wants to use base-ten blocks to subtract 43 from 234. She says that there are not enough ones to subtract without regrouping. Is Hana right or wrong? Explain.

LESSON 2

CA Standards
KEY **NS 2.1** Find the sum or difference of two whole numbers between 0 and 10,000.
Also NS 2.0, MR 2.3, MR 2.4

Vocabulary

regroup

Materials
• Base-ten blocks
• Workmat 1 (optional)
• eManipulatives (optional)
  www.eduplace.com/camap/

Hands On
Subtract with Regrouping

Objective Regroup tens and hundreds to subtract 3-digit numbers.

▶ **Learn With Manipulatives**

The Martinez family is driving to visit Aunt Martha who lives 234 miles away. They have gone 158 miles. How much farther do they have to drive?

$234 - 158 = \bigcirc$

Model It	**Write It**
1 Use blocks to show 234. 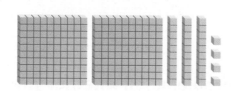	$\begin{array}{r} 234 \\ -158 \\ \hline \end{array}$
2 Look at the ones place. 4 < 8, so you need to regroup 1 ten as 10 ones. 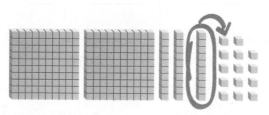	$\begin{array}{r} {\scriptstyle 2\ 14} \\ 2\,3\!\!\!/\,4 \\ -158 \\ \hline \end{array}$
3 Now you can subtract the ones. 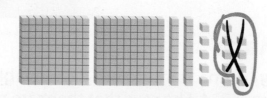	$\begin{array}{r} {\scriptstyle 2\ 14} \\ 2\,3\!\!\!/\,4 \\ -158 \\ \hline 6 \end{array}$

4 Look at the tens place.
2 < 5, so you need to regroup
1 hundred as 10 tens.

```
      12
    1 2 14
    2 3 4
  − 1 5 8
        6
```

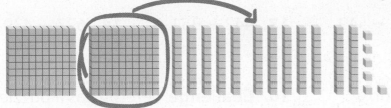

5 Subtract the tens.

```
      12
    1 2 14
    2 3 4
  − 1 5 8
      7 6
```

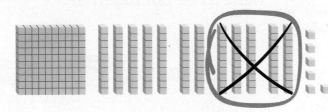

6 Subtract the hundreds.

```
      12
    1 2 14
    2 3 4
  − 1 5 8
      7 6
```

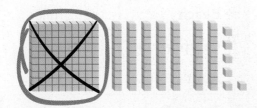

Check
Addition and subtraction are related.
Use addition to check subtraction.

```
   2 3 4        1 5 8
 − 1 5 8      +   7 6
     7 6        2 3 4
```

▶ **Guided Practice**

Subtract. Check using addition.

1. 772
− 214

2. 642
− 353

3. 728
− 349

4. 315 − 248   **5.** 432 − 316   **6.** 534 − 465

Ask Yourself
• Are there enough ones to subtract?
• Are there enough tens to subtract?

123 Math Talk How can you tell if you need to regroup a ten as 10 ones by just looking at an exercise?

Practice and Problem Solving

Subtract. Check using addition.

7. 834
− 676

8. 682
− 453

9. 328
− 247

10. 756
− 427

11. 542 − 351

12. 928 − 549

13. 442 − 351

14. 627 − 439

Solve.

15. Lily will travel 439 miles on a train. She has traveled 157 miles so far. How many more miles will she travel?

16. Challenge Jeremy has a puzzle with 420 pieces. So far he has put together 287 pieces. How many pieces still need to be put together?

 Real World Data

Use the table for Problems 17–19. Show your work.

17. How much farther from home is the beach than the campground?

18. The Martinez family visits a cousin 394 miles away. How much farther away is their cousin than their aunt?

19. Create and Solve Use the information from the table to write a problem with the answer 183 miles.

Martinez Family Summer Trips	
Place	**Miles from Home**
Beach	292 miles
Campground	218 miles
Aunt's House	178 miles
Theme Park	109 miles

 Spiral Review and Test Practice

Round the number to the nearest ten and nearest hundred. NS 1.4 pages 30, 34

20. 663

21. 2,539

22. 2,096

Write the letter of the correct answer. KEY NS 2.1

23. 564 − 237 =

A 207 **B** 227 **C** 327 **D** 801

Extra Practice See page 89, Set A.

Key Standards Review

Need Help?
See Key Standards Handbook.

Write an equation or inequality to show each relationship. KEY **AF 1.1**

1. 15 minus a number is less than 30.

2. 26 plus a number is equal to 40.

3. 30 minus a number is equal to 2.

4. 7 plus 3 is greater than a number.

5. 139 minus 50 is greater than 40 plus a number.

Add. Check by adding in a different order. NS 2.0

6.
```
   75
  125
+ 367
```

7.
```
  130
  561
+  71
```

8.
```
  451
  149
+ 263
```

9.
```
 1,009
   775
+   30
```

10.
```
  2,580
    120
+ 3,045
```

Challenge

Mathematical Reasoning

Guess and Check

Solve. Explain how you solved the problem. KEY **AF 2.1**

1. Three numbers in a row (such as 3, 4, 5 or 25, 26, 27) add up to 705. What are the numbers?

2. Romero's aunt is three times as old as he is. The sum of their ages is 36. How old are Romero and his aunt?

CA Standards
KEY **NS 2.1** Find the sum or difference of two whole numbers between 0 and 10,000.
Also NS 2.0, NS 2.8, MR 1.2, MR 2.2, MR 2.3

Vocabulary

difference

$$9 - 5 = 4$$

↑
difference

Subtract Greater Numbers

Objective Subtract 4-digit numbers.

▶ **Learn by Example**

In Lessons 1 and 2, you subtracted 3-digit numbers. You can use the same steps when you subtract 4-digit numbers.

Three jumbo jets land at Los Angeles airport. The jets carry a total of 1,445 passengers and 2,932 pieces of luggage. How many more pieces of luggage than passengers are on the jets?

$2,932 - 1,445 = \bigcirc$

1 2 < 5, so you need to regroup 1 ten as 10 ones.

$$\begin{array}{r} \overset{2\ 12}{2,9\cancel{3}\cancel{2}} \\ -1,4\ 4\ 5 \\ \hline \end{array}$$

2 Subtract the ones.

$$\begin{array}{r} \overset{2\ 12}{2,9\cancel{3}\cancel{2}} \\ -1,4\ 4\ 5 \\ \hline 7 \end{array}$$

3 2 < 4, so you need to regroup 1 hundred as 10 tens.

$$\begin{array}{r} \overset{12}{\underset{8\ \cancel{9}\ 12}{2,\cancel{9}\cancel{3}\cancel{2}}} \\ -1,4\ 4\ 5 \\ \hline 7 \end{array}$$

4 Subtract the tens.

$$\begin{array}{r} \overset{12}{\underset{8\ \cancel{9}\ 12}{2,\cancel{9}\cancel{3}\cancel{2}}} \\ -1,4\ 4\ 5 \\ \hline 8\ 7 \end{array}$$

5 Subtract the hundreds.

$$\begin{array}{r} \overset{12}{\underset{8\ \cancel{9}\ 12}{2,\cancel{9}\cancel{3}\cancel{2}}} \\ -1,4\ 4\ 5 \\ \hline 4\ 8\ 7 \end{array}$$

6 Subtract the thousands.

$$\begin{array}{r} \overset{12}{\underset{8\ \cancel{9}\ 12}{2,\cancel{9}\cancel{3}\cancel{2}}} \\ -1,4\ 4\ 5 \\ \hline 1,4\ 8\ 7 \end{array}$$

Solution: There are 1,487 more pieces of luggage than passengers.

Ask Yourself
- Do I need to regroup?
- Did I subtract ones, tens, hundreds, and thousands in that order?

Find the difference.

1.   7,918
   − 7,426
	2. 8,482
	   − 2,845
		3. 6,194
		   − 3,467

 Math Talk   Why doesn't the value of a number change when you regroup?

▶ **Practice and Problem Solving**

Find the difference.

4.   4,828
   − 1,476
	5. 8,726
	   − 3,579
		6. 5,682
		   − 1,941
			7. 5,388
			   − 4,679

8. 3,594 − 1,678   **9.** 6,725 − 2,839   **10.** 9,824 − 6,912

Solve.

11. There were 1,149 people at the air show on Friday. On Saturday, there were 3,428 people. How many more people were at the air show on Saturday than Friday?

12. Challenge 1,500 girls, 679 boys, and 1,623 adults were at the show. How many more children than adults were at the show?

Spiral Review and Test Practice

Complete. Write >, <, or = for the ⬤. AF 1.3 page 52

13. 64 + 58 ⬤ 96   **14.** 36 + 29 ⬤ 65   **15.** 25 + 42 ⬤ 76

Write the letter of the correct answer. KEY NS 2.1

16. 6435 − 2179 =

   A 3256   **C** 4356

   B 4256   **D** 8614

Test Tip
Sometimes you may see 4-digit numbers written without a comma.

LESSON 4

CA Standards
KEY **NS 2.1** Find the sum or difference of two whole numbers between 0 and 10,000.
Also NS 2.0, NS 2.8, MR 1.2, MR 2.2, MR 2.3, MR 2.4, MR 3.1

Subtract Across Zeros

Objective Subtract from numbers with one or more zeros.

▶ **Learn by Example**

You have learned to subtract 3- and 4-digit numbers. In this lesson, you will learn how to subtract across zeros. Sometimes you have to regroup more than once before you begin to subtract from numbers with zeros.

A taxi company owns and operates 4,302 taxis. There are 1,155 taxis on duty today. How many taxis are not on duty today?

$4{,}302 - 1{,}155 =$ ◯

Example

1 2 < 5, so you need to regroup. There are no tens to regroup. Regroup 3 hundreds as 2 hundreds and 10 tens.

$$\begin{array}{r} \overset{2\ \ 10}{4,\cancel{3}\,\cancel{0}\,2} \\ -\ 1,1\,5\,5 \end{array}$$

2 Regroup 10 tens as 9 tens and 10 ones.

$$\begin{array}{r} \overset{\ \ 9}{\underset{}{}} \\ \overset{2\ \cancel{10}\ 12}{4,\cancel{3}\,\cancel{0}\,\cancel{2}} \\ -\ 1,1\,5\,5 \end{array}$$

3 Subtract ones, tens, hundreds, and thousands.

$$\begin{array}{r} \overset{\ \ 9}{\underset{}{}} \\ \overset{2\ \cancel{10}\ 12}{4,\cancel{3}\,\cancel{0}\,\cancel{2}} \\ -\ 1,1\,5\,5 \\ \hline 3,1\,4\,7 \end{array}$$

Solution: 3,147 taxis are not on duty today.

Another Example

To subtract from 10,000, you must regroup.

$$
\begin{array}{r}
\overset{\scriptscriptstyle 9\ \ \ 9\ \ \ 9}{\underset{\scriptscriptstyle 10\ 10\ 10\ 10}{10,0\,0\,0}} \\
-\ 5,7\,3\,2 \\
\hline
4,2\,6\,8
\end{array}
$$

1 Regroup a ten thousand into 10 thousands.

2 Regroup 10 thousands.

3 Regroup 10 hundreds.

4 Regroup 10 tens

▶ Guided Practice

Find the difference.

1. 840 − 49

2. 4,000 − 3,258

3. 3,405 − 1,267

Ask Yourself

• Did I subtract correctly?

• Is my answer reasonable?

Guided Problem Solving

Use the questions to solve this problem.

4. A helicopter is flying at a height of 450 feet. If its height decreases by 134 feet, at what height will it be flying?

  a. Understand Which picture could you use to help you solve the problem?

  b. Plan Use the picture to decide. Should you add or subtract?

  c. Solve Solve the problem and write the answer.

  d. Look Back Look at the picture you chose. Does your answer make sense?

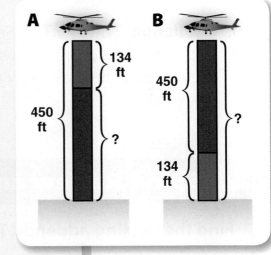

123 Math Talk How is regrouping to find 450 − 134 different from regrouping to find 400 − 134?

Find the difference.

5. 901
    − 667

6. 802
    − 577

7. 700
    − 353

8. 400
    − 271

9. 1,900
    − 1,652

10. 4,702
    − 1,436

11. 2,089
    − 1,451

12. 8,713
    − 8,627

13. 504 − 97

14. 300 − 254

15. 10,000 − 2,164

16. 9,032 − 5,637

Solve.

17. A helicopter pilot flies no higher than 1,000 feet. If she is currently flying at 224 feet, how many feet higher can she fly?

18. There are 205 packages in the truck. If 128 are delivered, how many are still in the truck?

19. **Multistep** A taxi company has 1,065 cabs. It buys 1,035 more cabs. If 255 cabs are then sold, how many cabs will the company have left?

20. **Challenge** The City Taxi Service made 6,543 trips this week. This is 3,256 fewer trips than the number they made last week. How many trips did they make last week?

> **Hint**
>
> In which week were there more trips?
>
> Should your answer be more or less than 6,543?

Spiral Review and Test Practice

Find the missing addends. Tell what property you used. AF 1.2 page 54

21. 4 + 3 = 3 + ▨

22. 8 + ▨ = 8

23. (3 + 4) + 5 = 3 + (▨ + 5)

24. ▨ + 0 = 12

25. (2 + 7) + ▨ = 2 + (▨ + 9)

26. 8 + ▨ = 6 + 8

Write the letter of the correct answer. KEY NS 2.1

27. What number is 6 less than 10,000?

    A 4,000   **B** 9,994   **C** 10,006   **D** 10,994

Extra Practice See page 89, Set C.

World Traveler

Yukio is a pilot. He is based in Los Angeles and flies to major cities all over the world.

The table shows the flying distances from Los Angeles to several cities.

City	Flying Distance from Los Angeles
New York	2,450 miles
Mexico City	1,540 miles
Tokyo	5,470 miles
Honolulu	2,560 miles

Use the table to solve the problems below.

1. Which city is the greatest distance from Los Angeles?

2. How much farther is it to fly from Los Angeles to New York than from Los Angeles to Mexico City?

3. Yukio is flying from Los Angeles to Tokyo. He has flown 2,982 miles so far. How many more miles does he have left to fly?

4. Last week, Yukio flew from Los Angeles to Melbourne, Australia. To get to Melbourne, he had to stop in Honolulu. If it is 5,510 miles from Honolulu to Melbourne, how many miles did Yukio fly in all?

CA Standards
NS 2.0, KEY NS 2.1

CA Standards

NS 1.4 Round off numbers to 10,000 to the nearest ten, hundred, and thousand.

KEY NS 2.1 Find the sum or difference of two whole numbers between 0 and 10,000.

Also NS 1.0, NS 2.0, MR 2.1, MR 2.4

Vocabulary

estimate

Estimate Sums and Differences

Objective Estimate sums and differences by rounding numbers.

▶ **Learn by Example**

Sometimes you do not need an exact answer to a problem.

Use the map. Sandra is traveling from Sacramento to San Diego. About how many miles does she travel in all?

The word **about** asks you to **estimate**. Round each number to the greatest place. Then add.

The greatest place is the place with the highest value.

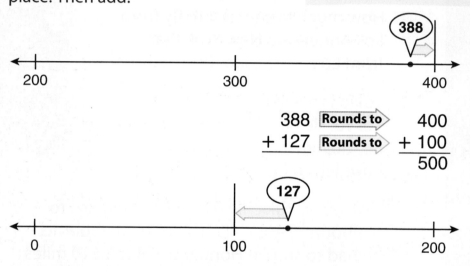

$$388 \text{ Rounds to } 400$$
$$+127 \text{ Rounds to } +100$$
$$\overline{500}$$

Solution: Sandra travels *about* 500 miles in all.

▶ **Guided Practice**

Estimate the sum or difference by rounding each number to the greatest place.

1. 756
  + 117

2. 483
  − 409

3. 5,015
  + 2,877

4. 6,314
  − 739

Ask Yourself

• What place should I round each number to?

• How many zeros should my estimate have?

 Math Talk Look back at the estimate of how far Sandra travels. What would the estimate be if both numbers were rounded to the nearest ten?

84

Practice and Problem Solving

Estimate the sum or difference by rounding each number to the greatest place.

5.   4,019
       + 3,802

6.   6,755
       − 4,392

7.   5,045
       − 212

8.   7,716
       + 807

9.   4,620
       − 613

Science Link

Solve.

10. The California State Railroad Museum's Excursion Train has 225 seats. The Museum's Theater has 135 seats.
   a. How many more seats are in the Excursion train?

   b. Use estimation to check if your answer is reasonable.

11. Challenge An auto museum has 5 more displays on the first floor than on the second floor. Together the two floors have 23 displays. How many displays are on each floor?

A Steam Locomotive

This steam locomotive could use the energy from 16 tons of coal and 14,000 gallons of water to pull 15 passenger cars 150 miles at 80 miles per hour.

Science PS 1.c

Spiral Review and Test Practice

Find the sum. KEY **NS 2.1** page 56

12. 215 + 167 + 43

13. 1,314 + 3,405 + 2,557

Write the letter of the correct answer. NS 1.4, KEY **NS 2.1**

14. Last week, 2,117 students went to the zoo. This week, 3,708 students went. About how many students went to the zoo in these 2 weeks?

   A 2,000   **B** 4,000   **C** 5,000   **D** 6,000

CA Standards

MR 2.5 Indicate the relative advantages of exact and approximate solutions to problems and give answers to a specified degree of accuracy.

MR 2.4 Express the solution clearly and logically by using the appropriate mathematical notation and terms and clear language; support solutions with evidence in both verbal and symbolic work.

Also NS 1.4, NS 2.0, KEY NS 2.1, MR 1.0, MR 2.0, MR 2.3, MR 3.0, MR 3.2, MR 3.3

Problem Solving Plan
Estimate or Exact Amount?

Objective Decide if an estimate or an exact answer is needed to solve a problem.

▶ **Learn Through Reasoning**

Before you solve a problem, you must first decide whether you need an estimate or an exact answer.

The Coast Starlight train runs between Los Angeles and Seattle, Washington. The distance from Los Angeles to Santa Barbara is 104 miles. The distance from Los Angeles to Redding is 720 miles.

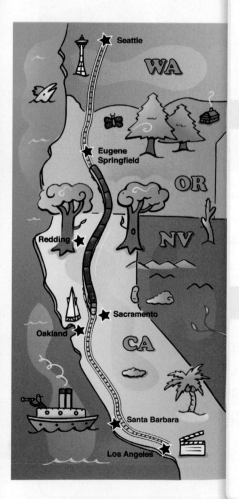

EXACT ANSWER

How far it is from Santa Barbara to Redding?

Since the question asks for the exact distance, you need to find an exact answer.

$$\begin{array}{r} \overset{1\,10}{72\cancel{0}} \\ -\ 104 \\ \hline 616 \end{array}$$

It is 616 miles from Santa Barbara to Redding.

ESTIMATE

About how far it is from Santa Barbara to Redding?

Since the question asks "about how far," you can estimate the answer to solve the problem.

$$\begin{array}{r} 720 \\ -\ 104 \\ \hline 616 \end{array} \quad \begin{array}{l} \text{rounds to} \\ \text{rounds to} \end{array} \quad \begin{array}{r} 700 \\ -\ 100 \\ \hline 600 \end{array}$$

It is about 600 miles from Santa Barbara to Redding.

ESTIMATE TO SOLVE PROBLEM

A student ticket to the railroad museum costs $4.25. Can Steve buy 5 tickets with a $20 bill?

> $4.25 rounds to $4.00
> $4.00 + $4.00 + $4.00 + $4.00 + $4.00 = $20.00

Each ticket costs more than $4.00. So the total cost is more than $20.00. Steve cannot buy 5 tickets.

Guided Problem Solving

Solve using the Ask Yourself questions. Did you use an estimate or an exact answer?

Ask Yourself
• Does the problem ask for an exact amount?
• Will an estimate work for this problem?

1. The California Zephyr train runs 2,438 miles between Emeryville and Chicago. The distance from Chicago to Provo is 1,563 miles. To the nearest hundred miles, what is the distance between Provo and Emeryville?

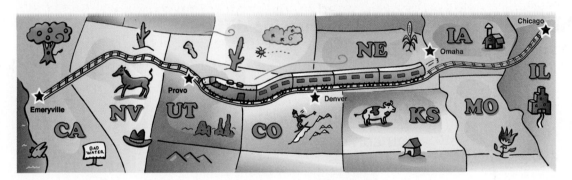

 Math Talk When is an estimate good enough? When might it be better to give an exact answer? Give examples to explain your thinking.

Independent Problem Solving

Solve. Did you use an estimate or an exact answer?

2. A college student is taking a train trip. One round-trip train fare is $434. The student discount is $65. What is the student price for a round trip ticket?

3. Rita took the train to the airport. The trip took 11 minutes. Henry drove, and the trip took 41 minutes. About how many more minutes did the trip take Henry?

4. Aretha is a bus driver on the route from Sacramento to Redding. The total distance is 217 miles. She has already driven 68 miles. How much farther must she drive?

5. **Challenge** Carlos took 225 pictures at the zoo and 85 on the train. Will his pictures fit in 2 photo albums that each hold 150 pictures?

6. **Create and Solve** Write and solve two problems— one that needs an exact answer and one that can be solved by estimating.

Vocabulary

There are different ways to show **subtraction**.

Mario is doing his math homework. He is getting ready to start his first subtraction problem. "I can solve this problem in several ways," he says.

Copy the word map. Complete it by showing different ways to subtract 117 from 245.

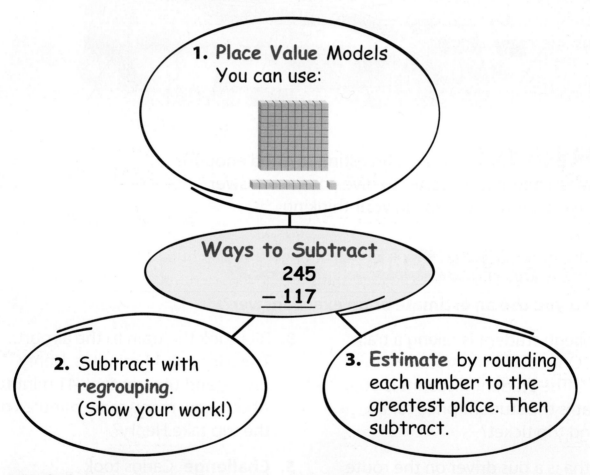

1. Place Value Models
You can use:

Ways to Subtract
245
− 117

2. Subtract with **regrouping**.
(Show your work!)

3. Estimate by rounding each number to the greatest place. Then subtract.

Writing What if you didn't have paper or a pencil? Tell how you would use mental math to solve this problem.

Reading Check out this book in your library.

• *One Less Fish*, by Kim Michelle Toft and Allan Sheather

CA Standards
MR 2.3 Use a variety of methods, such as words, numbers, symbols, charts, graphs, tables, diagrams, and models, to explain mathematical reasoning.

Also KEY NS 2.1

Standards-Based Extra Practice

Set A ───────────────────────────── KEY **NS 2.1** page 74

Subtract. Check using addition. Regroup if you need to.

1.   234
       − 144

2.   780
       − 222

3.   565
       − 434

4. 548 − 497

5. 787 − 598

6. 688 − 452

7. Jack worked as a sheepherder on his father's ranch. He was in charge of 684 sheep. One day he sold 136 of them. How many sheep did Jack have left?

Set B ───────────────────────────── KEY **NS 2.1** page 78

Subtract.

1.   7,848
       − 4,568

2.   5,125
       − 1,247

3.   8,974
       − 3,544

4. 9,999 − 4,564

5. 9,432 − 6,871

6. 7,538 − 2,314

7. Sarah's almond orchard is on 2,582 acres. She wants to clear out 1,301 acres for walnuts. How many acres will she have left for her almonds?

Set C ───────────────────────────── KEY **NS 2.1** page 80

Find the difference.

1.   5,105
       − 1,247

2.   1,560
       −   234

3.   10,000
       −   4,564

4. 950 − 68

5. 3,000 − 2,147

6. 3,078 − 2,367

7. A store has 540 cans of soup. It sells 312 cans. How many cans are left?

8. A library has 9,000 books and 259 magazines. How many more books than magazines does the library have?

Education Place
Visit www.eduplace.com/camap/
for more **Extra Practice**.

Chapter 4 Extra Practice   **89**

Chapter Review/Test

Vocabulary and Concepts —————————————— KEY **NS 2.1**, NS 1.4

Choose the best word to complete each sentence.

> **Word Bank**
> regroup
> difference
> estimate

1. When you round a number, you are giving an _____ of its value.

2. You can _____ 10 tens as 1 hundred.

3. The _____ of 9 − 3 is 6.

Skills ——————————————————————————— KEY **NS 2.1**, NS 1.4

Subtract. Check using addition.

4. 657 − 589   **5.** 324 − 137   **6.** 824 − 437   **7.** 7,932 − 644

8. 3,636 − 1,358   **9.** 8,974 − 3,982   **10.** 5,429 − 3,162   **11.** 8,321 − 4,747

Estimate the sum or difference. Round to the greatest place.

12.
$$957$$
$$+\ 138$$

13.
$$924$$
$$-\ 578$$

14.
$$88$$
$$+\ 78$$

15.
$$8,483$$
$$-\ 3,529$$

16.
$$324$$
$$+\ 57$$

Problem Solving and Reasoning ————— NS 2.0, KEY **NS 2.1**, MR 1.0, MR 1.2, MR 2.3

Solve.

17. A cruise ship has 500 passengers. If 354 of them get off in Los Angeles, how many passengers are left on the ship?

18. Rebecca is flying 425 miles to go to Maine. She has traveled 187 miles so far. How many more miles will she travel?

19. There were 1,987 people at the play on Saturday. On Sunday, there were 2,314 people. How many more people were at the play on Sunday?

20. Multistep Drew has 1,569 sheep at his farm. He bought 1,014 more sheep. If 758 sheep are then sold, how many sheep will Drew have left?

Writing Math For Exercise 18, how did you choose the operation?

Spiral Review and Test Practice

1. Which number has a 5 in the tens place and a 6 in the hundreds place?

A 561 **C** 651

B 6150 **D** 6510

KEY **NS 1.3** page 14

2. Which set of numbers is in order from greatest to least?

> **Test Tip**
> How many digits are in the least number?

A 998, 9089, 9809, 9908

B 998, 9809, 9089, 9908

C 9908, 9809, 9089, 998

D 9908, 998, 9809, 9089

NS 1.2 page 28

3. Which shows 251 rounded to the nearest ten?

A 300 **C** 260

B 250 **D** 200

NS 1.4 page 30

4. 164
 + 108

A 156

B 168

C 172

D 272

KEY **NS 2.1** page 50

5. Beth has 14 gold buttons, 124 pearl buttons, 78 silver buttons, and 32 crystal buttons. How many buttons is this in all?

A 138

B 148

C 238

D 248

> **Test Tip**
> Write the numbers in a column and line them up by place value.

KEY **NS 2.1** page 56

6. $873 - 456 =$

A 417 **C** 423

B 427 **D** 1329

KEY **NS 2.1** page 74

Education Place
Visit www.eduplace.com/camap/ for
Test-Taking Tips and **Extra Practice**.

Unit 2 Review/Test

Vocabulary and Concepts ———————————— MR 2.3 Chapters 3–4

Choose the best word to complete each sentence.

> **Word Bank**
> equation
> regroup
> inequality
> estimate
> expression

1. A number sentence that says that two expressions have the same value is an _____.

2. A number sentence that says that two expressions do not have the same value is an _____.

3. You can _____ 10 tens as 1 hundred.

4. You can _____ to find *about how much*.

Skills ———————————— NS 1.4, KEY NS 2.1, AF 1.0, KEY AF 1.1, AF 1.2, AF 1.3 Chapter 3, Lesson 2

Write >, <, or = for the ⬭. Tell if the number sentence is an equation or an inequality.

5. $51 + 33$ ⬭ 84 6. $22 + 13$ ⬭ $27 + 18$ 7. $34 - 21$ ⬭ $31 - 17$

Write the number that makes the equation true. Tell which property you used. Chapter 3, Lesson 3

8. $16 + 0 =$ ▨   9. $(9 + 24) +$ ▨ $= 9 + ($ ▨ $+ 5)$ 10. $38 + 17 = 17 +$ ▨

Add or subtract. Chapter 3, Lesson 4; Chapter 4, Lessons 1–4

11.
$$\begin{array}{r} 873 \\ -\ 30 \\ \hline \end{array}$$

12.
$$\begin{array}{r} 249 \\ 156 \\ 83 \\ +\ 15 \\ \hline \end{array}$$

13.
$$\begin{array}{r} 543 \\ -\ 405 \\ \hline \end{array}$$

14.
$$\begin{array}{r} 374 \\ 260 \\ +\ 121 \\ \hline \end{array}$$

15.
$$\begin{array}{r} 1,354 \\ +\ 4,291 \\ \hline \end{array}$$

16.
$$\begin{array}{r} 5,000 \\ -\ 4,768 \\ \hline \end{array}$$

Estimate the sum or difference by rounding each number to the greatest place. Chapter 4, Lesson 5

17. $665 + 125$

18. $4,126 - 2,561$

Problem Solving and Reasoning

NS 2.0, KEY **NS 2.1** Chapters 3–4

Solve.

19. One year, Tamika and Sara read a total of 1,242 books. Tamika read 629 books. How many books did Sara read?

20. Jo has 105 stamps. Sue has 267 stamps. Sue's mom gave her 49 more stamps. Do the 2 girls have more than 400 stamps together? Explain.

BIG IDEA!

Writing Math Show how you can use addition to check your answer to 500 − 192?

Performance Assessment

Symphony Field Trip

NS 2.0, KEY **NS 2.1**, MR 1.0, MR 1.1, MR 2.0

A symphony orchestra is offering free concerts for students.

Population by Grade Level of Smith County	
Grade 3: 1,416	Grade 4: 1,439
Grade 5: 1,493	Grade 6: 1,471
Grade 7: 1,428	Grade 8: 1,387

Task	Information You Need
Use the table and the information to the right. • In what combinations should the grades be sent to hear the concerts? • How many concerts will be needed? • How many students will be at each concert? Explain your thinking.	The entire grade must attend a concert together. All children in grades 3–8 will go to the concert.
	The concert hall has 2,900 seats.
	At least 2,750 seats must be filled for each performance.
	All grades will go.

Go Fast, Go Far

Unit 2 Mental Math Strategies

Partial Differences

Partial differences are quick. Subtracting pieces is the trick!

Partial differences make subtracting easier! Break the numbers into pieces, then subtract the pieces. Look at Problem 1. Because $40 - 10 = 30$ and $6 - 5 = 1$, the answer is $30 + 1 = 31$.

1. $46 - 15 = \boxed{30} + \boxed{1} = \boxed{31}$

2. $45 - 12 = \boxed{30} + \boxed{} = \boxed{}$

3. $67 - 27 = \boxed{} + \boxed{0} = \boxed{}$

4. $86 - 35 = \boxed{} + \boxed{} = \boxed{}$

Good work! Keep on going!

5. $36 - 24 = \boxed{} + \boxed{} = \boxed{}$

6. $79 - 12 = \boxed{} + \boxed{} = \boxed{}$

7. $84 - 63 = \boxed{} + \boxed{} = \boxed{}$

8. $93 - 31 = \boxed{} + \boxed{} = \boxed{}$

Go Faster!

Take It Further!

Now try doing all the steps in your head!

9. $57 - 32$ **10.** $98 - 54$ **11.** $68 - 32$ **12.** $78 - 47$

3

Multiplication Facts

BIG IDEAS!

- You can use arrays, patterns, skip counting, and other strategies to learn the multiplication facts.
- The Commutative and Associative Properties help you multiply.

Chapter 5
Multiplication Concepts

Chapter 6
Multiplication Patterns

Chapter 7
Multiplication Patterns and Practice

Songs and Games

Math Music Track 3: *Multiplication*

eGames at
www.eduplace.com/camap/

Math Readers

Collections Times Four

The Workshop

Here's What I Do

Block Out

Object of the Game Make arrays to cover more squares than the other player.

Materials
- Learning Tool 11: Centimeter Grid
- 2 number cubes labeled 1–6
- crayons

Number of Players 2

How to Play

1 Player 1 rolls the number cubes. One cube shows the number of rows. One cube shows the number of columns.

2 Player 1 colors an array on grid paper using the numbers rolled.

The array can be 3 rows of 5 or 5 rows of 3.

3 Player 2 repeats Steps 1–2. The players take turns rolling the number cubes and coloring their arrays.

4 Play continues until each player has had 5 turns. The player with more squares colored is the winner.

CA Standards

KEY NS 2.2 Memorize to automaticity the multiplication table for numbers between 1 and 10.

MR 2.3 Use a variety of methods, such as words, numbers, symbols, charts, graphs, tables, diagrams, and models, to explain mathematical reasoning.

 Education Place
Visit www.eduplace.com/camap/ for **Brain Teasers** and **eGames** to play.

Reading In both reading and math, you should ask yourself, "What's the point?" or "What is this all about?" If you can answer the question, you know the big idea.

As Camila works through her math textbook, she takes notes to help her understand the big ideas. These are the notes she took on Chapter 5, Lesson 1.

Big Idea	Notes/Examples
• You can use equal groups, skip counting, and other strategies to model multiplication.	Example: 3 groups of 5 1. Draw equal groups 2. Skip count 5, 10, 15 3. Repeated addition $5 + 5 + 5 = 15$ 4. Multiplication sentence $3 \times 5 = 15$
• Multiplication can help you find the total number of items when you have equal groups.	

The examples show the big ideas.

Writing Copy the Big Idea Chart for Unit 3. Take notes as you work through the unit.

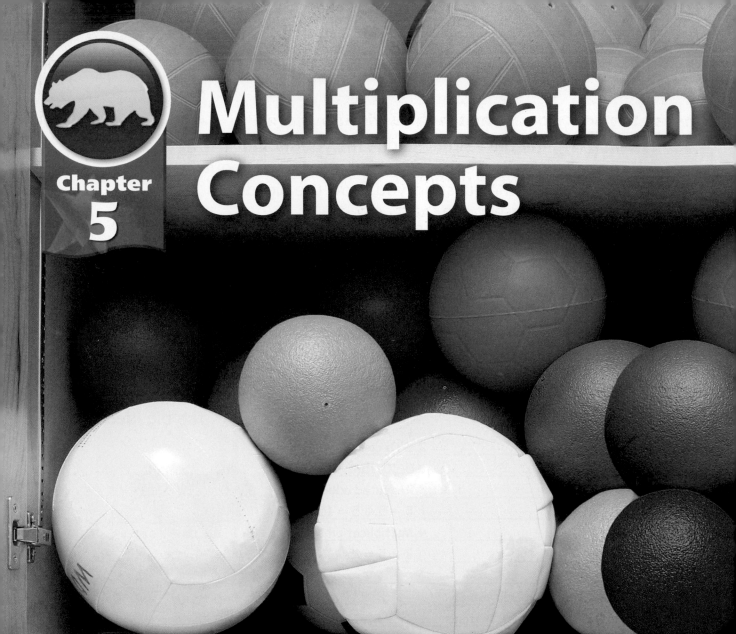

Multiplication Concepts

Vocabulary and Concepts NS 2.0, KEY NS 2.1, MR 2.3
Choose the best word to match the definition. pages 48, 70, 84

1. An operation on two or more numbers that gives a sum.

2. An operation that gives a difference.

3. An answer that is close to the exact answer.

Skills AF 1.0, NS 2.0

Find the sum. page 50

4. $5 + 5 + 5 + 5$ 5. $2 + 2 + 2 + 2 + 2 + 2$ 6. $10 + 10 + 10 + 10 + 10$

**Complete each equation. Use the Commutative Property
of Addition or the Associative Property of Addition.** page 54

7. $34 + 45 = 45 + \underline{\quad}$ 8. $(83 + 51) + 23 = 83 + (51 + \underline{\quad})$

Problem Solving and Reasoning NS 2.0, AF 1.0

9. Ricardo counted how many students were in three classrooms.
He told Marcos that he would get a different number if he
counted in a different order. Was Ricardo correct? Explain.

Vocabulary

Visualize It !

$$3 \times 3 = 9$$

multiply
To combine
equal groups.

product
The result of
multiplication.

Language Tip
Some words are similar in Spanish
and English.

English	Spanish
product	producto
multiply	multiplicar

See **English-Spanish Glossary** pages 628–646.

You can **skip count** to find the total.   3, 6, 9

You can **add** to find the total. $3 + 3 + 3 = 9$

Education Place Visit www.eduplace.com/camap/ for the **eGlossary** and **eGames**.

CA Standards MR 2.3 Use a variety of methods, such as words, numbers, symbols, charts,
graphs, tables, diagrams, and models, to explain mathematical reasoning. **KEY NS 2.2**

Hands On
Model Multiplication

Objective Use models to solve multiplication problems.

 **Explore**

You can use **multiplication** when you add equal groups.

Question How can you model multiplication in different ways?

Kim has 3 strips of stickers. There are 5 stickers on each strip. How many stickers does Kim have in all?

Model **equal groups**. Draw 3 circles to stand for the strips. Use counters to stand for the stickers.

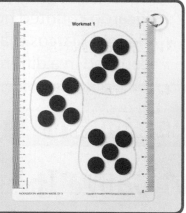

There are 3 groups of 5. Skip count to find the total.

5, 10, (15)

Use **repeated addition** to find the total.

$5 + 5 + 5 = (15)$

Write a multiplication sentence to find the total.

$3 \times 5 = (15)$

Solution: Kim has 15 stickers in all.

What if Kim had 4 strips of stickers with 3 on each strip?
How many would she have in all?

1 Model equal groups.

2 Skip count.

3 Use repeated addition.

4 Write a multiplication sentence.

▶ **Extend**

**Copy and complete the table. Use counters
to model each problem.**

		Draw Equal Groups	Skip Count	Addition Sentence	Multiplication Sentence
1.	3 groups of 2		2, 4, 6	$2 + 2 + 2 = 6$	$3 \times 2 = 6$
2.	3 groups of 6				
3.	2 groups of 10				
4.	5 groups of 4				
5.	2 groups of 7				
6.	5 groups of 2				
7.	1 group of 4				
8.	4 groups of 1				

Math Journal

Writing Math

Explain Can you write a multiplication sentence
to describe this picture? Explain why or why not.

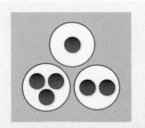

CA Standards
AF 1.5 Recognize and use the commutative and associative properties of multiplication (e.g., if 5 × 7 = 35, then what is 7 × 5? and if 5 × 7 × 3 = 105, then what is 7 × 3 × 5?)

AF 2.2 Extend and recognize a linear pattern by its rules (e.g., the number of legs on a given number of horses may be calculated by counting by 4s or by multiplying the number of horses by 4).

Also NS 2.0, KEY NS 2.2, NS 2.8, AF 1.0, AF 1.2, MR 1.2, MR 2.0, MR 2.3, MR 2.4

Vocabulary

array

column

Commutative Property of Multiplication

factor

product

row

Arrays and the Commutative Property

Objective Use arrays to multiply numbers in any order.

▶ **Learn by Example**

A rectangular **array** shows objects arranged in equal **rows** and equal **columns**. Look at the arrays below. Do the two arrays have the same number of stamps?

1 Multiply to find the total number of stamps.

3 columns

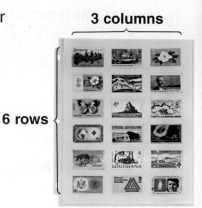

6 rows

6 × 3 = 18

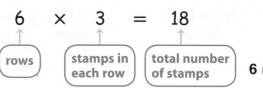

rows | stamps in each row | total number of stamps

2 Turn the page of stamps. The total stays the same.

6 columns

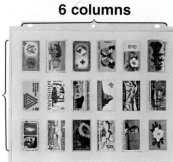

3 rows

3 × 6 = 18

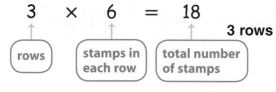

rows | stamps in each row | total number of stamps

Solution: Both arrays have 18 stamps.

Commutative Property of Multiplication

Changing the order of the **factors** does not change the **product**.

6 × 3 = 18   3 × 6 = 18

factor factor product   factor factor product

Write two multiplication sentences for the array.

1. ★ ★ ★ ★
   ★ ★ ★ ★
   ★ ★ ★ ★

2. ★ ★ ★ ★ ★ ★
   ★ ★ ★ ★ ★ ★

Ask Yourself
• How many rows are there?
• How many objects are in each row?
• How can I use the Commutative Property?

Find the missing number.

3. $2 \times 3 = 6$
   $3 \times \blacksquare = 6$

4. $24 = 8 \times 3$
   $\blacksquare = 3 \times 8$

5. $18 = 6 \times 3$
   $18 = 3 \times \blacksquare$

 Math Talk How can knowing $4 \times 6 = 24$ help you find 6×4?

► **Practice and Problem Solving**

Write two multiplication sentences for the array.

6. ♥ ♥ ♥
   ♥ ♥ ♥

7. ▲ ▲ ▲ ▲
   ▲ ▲ ▲ ▲

8. ✹ ✹ ✹ ✹ ✹
   ✹ ✹ ✹ ✹ ✹
   ✹ ✹ ✹ ✹ ✹

Find the missing number.

9. $2 \times 6 = 12$
   $6 \times \blacksquare = 12$

10. $8 = 4 \times 2$
    $\blacksquare = 2 \times 4$

11. $21 = 7 \times 3$
    $21 = 3 \times \blacksquare$

12. $3 \times 4 = 12$
    $4 \times \blacksquare = 12$

Solve.

13. Alyssa has a scrapbook with 4 rows of 5 photos. How many photos does she have?

14. **Justify** Horace has 12 cards. Why can't he put them in an array that has 4 rows of 4 cards in each row?

15. **Analyze** Sara has 2 rows of 5 stickers. Can she give 1 sticker to each of 12 friends? Explain.

16. **Challenge** Ken has 12 marbles. Jack has 20 marbles. What rectangular arrays can they make if they use all the marbles?

Science Link

17. Copy and complete the table.

Number of Starfish	Number of Arms
1	5
2	10
3	
4	
5	
6	
7	
8	
9	
10	

Solve.

18. Tell what strategy you used to complete the table.

19. How many arms do 8 starfish have all together?

20. How can you use the table to find the number of arms when there are 15 starfish?

Spiral Review and Test Practice

Subtract. KEY NS 2.1 page 80

21. 205 − 175

22. 300 − 53

23. 1,000 − 998

24. 4,003 − 999

25. 10,000 − 7,523

26. 9,009 − 1,809

Write the letter of the correct answer. AF 1.5

27. If 6 × 8 = 48, then what is 8 × 6?

A 14   **B** 48   **C** 68   **D** 86

Extra Practice See page 117, Set A.

Key Standards Review

Need Help?
See Key Standards Handbook.

Solve. KEY **NS 2.1**

1. $8003 + 375 =$

2. $783 + 999 =$ ▓

3. $543 + 809 =$ ▓

4.
```
   312
   505
 + 739
```

5.
```
   546
   679
 |  90
```

6.
```
   249
   453
 +  78
```

7.
```
    67
   547
 + 892
```

8.
```
   703
    97
 + 300
```

Write an inequality or an equation to show each. KEY **AF 1.1**

9. 5 plus 4 is less than 10.

10. 2 plus 3 is equal to 5.

11. 12 plus 2 is less than 10 plus 7.

12. 20 is equal to 4 plus 16.

13. 50 is greater than 30 plus 10.

Challenge Problem Solving

Math Reasoning NS 2.0, MR 2.3

1. Jane chose two different one-digit numbers. She multiplied one of them by 10. She multiplied the other one by 2. Then she added the products. Her answer was 78. What two numbers did Jane choose?

2. Roy has an array of star stickers. He writes a multiplication sentence for the total number of stickers. No matter which way he turns the array, his sentence stays the same. Explain the relationship between the rows and colums in Roy's array.

CA Standards

KEY NS 2.2 Memorize to automaticity the multiplication table for numbers between 1 and 10.

KEY AF 1.1 Represent relationships of quantities in the form of mathematical expressions, equations, or inequalities.

Also NS 2.0, AF 1.5, MR 2.0, MR 2.3, MR 2.4

Multiplication Review: 2, 5, and 10

Objective Use different ways to multiply with 2, 5, or 10 as a factor.

▶ **Learn by Example**

Yuji collects different kinds of rocks. He has 5 boxes with 2 rocks in each box. How many rocks does Yuji have in all?

$5 \times 2 = \bigcirc$

Pyrite

Talc

Galena

Mica

Quartz

Different Ways to Multiply
Way 1 Skip count.   2, 4, 6, 8, ⑩
Way 2 Use repeated addition. $2 + 2 + 2 + 2 + 2 = ⑩$
Way 3 Make equal groups. Draw 5 circles to stand for the boxes. Put 2 counters in each circle to stand for the rocks.
Way 4 Draw an array.     $5 \times 2 = 10$ $2 \times 5 = 10$

Remember that the array for 2×5 has the same value as the array for 5×2.

Solution: Yuji has 10 rocks in all.

▶ Guided Practice

Find the product.

1.   2
    × 8

2. 6 × 2

3.   2
    × 4

4. 3 × 2

5.   10
    × 9

6. 6 × 10

7.   5
    × 9

8. 6 × 5

9. Look at your answers for Exercises 1–4. How does knowing how to add doubles help you to multiply by 2?

10. Look at your answers for Exercises 5–6. Can you find a shortcut for multiplying by 10?

Guided Problem Solving

Use the questions to solve this problem.

11. Julie collects baseball caps. She hangs them on a wall. She makes 3 rows with 5 caps in each row. How many caps does she have in all?

  a. Understand How many rows of caps are there? How many are in each row?

  b. Plan Explain why you can multiply to solve this problem.

  c. Solve Write the answer to the problem. Julie has ◯ caps.

  d. Look Back Show another way to solve the problem.

 Math Talk Kim uses 7 + 7 to find 2 × 7, and Ella uses 2 + 2 + 2 + 2 + 2 + 2 + 2. Rosa says they both will get the right answer. Is Rosa correct?

Ask Yourself
• Can I multiply in my head?
• Can I draw a picture or an array?

Practice and Problem Solving

Find the product.

12. 2
×7
14

13. 2
×5
10

14. 9
×2
18

15. 2
×2
4

16. 10
×2
20

17. 10
×7
70

18. 10
×5
50

19. 2
×10
20

20. 10
×10
720

21. 10
×3
30

22. 5
×8
40

23. 3
×5
13

24. 5
×10
15

25. 5
×1
5

26. 5
×6
30

27. 8 × 10 *80* **28.** 5 × 2 *10* **29.** 5 × 4 *20* **30.** 5 × 9 *45* **31.** 5 × 5 *25*

History-Social Science Link

Solve.

32. The *Eureka* has 2 paddlewheels that help it to move in the water. If each paddlewheel has 10 spokes, how many spokes are there in all?

33. Challenge On one trip, the *Eureka* carries 120 cars. If the cars are lined up in 10 rows on the ship, how many cars will be in each row?

Eureka Steamer

This paddle steamboat, built in 1890, is a national historical landmark in San Francisco.

Length	300 feet
Width	78 feet
Passengers	2,300
Automobiles	120

History-Social Science 3.4.3

Spiral Review and Test Practice

Order the numbers from greatest to least. NS 1.2 page 28

34. 3,712   3,801   3,799

35. 8,008   8,800   8,080

Write the letter of the correct answer. NS 2.0

36. A bicycle has 2 tires. How many tires do 7 bicycles have in all?

A 2   **B** 7   **C** 9   **D** 14

Extra Practice See page 117, Set B.

Make It to the Top!

Mount Whitney is the tallest mountain in California. It is 14,495 feet above sea level. Many people use the many hiking trails. Some experienced hikers go all the way to the top.

1. While climbing up the peak, 5 climbers each carried 3 bottles of water. How many bottles did they carry in all? Draw a picture or an array to help find the answer.

2. The five climbers carry flashlights for safety. Each flashlight uses two batteries. Use two different ways to show how many batteries they have in all.

3. Justin is putting photos from his mountain climbing trip in an album. There are 10 pages in the album and 4 photos fit on each page. How many photos are there in all?

4. Two hikers each carried 9 pounds of gear. How much did the hikers carry together?

California's Mount Whitney

CA Standards
KEY NS 2.2

CA Standards

KEY NS 2.2 Memorize to automaticity the multiplication table for numbers between 1 and 10.

MR 2.3 Use a variety of methods such as words, symbols, charts, graphs, tables, diagrams, and models, to explain mathematical reasoning.

Also NS 2.0, NS 2.8, MR 1.2, MR 2.4

Vocabulary

double

Multiply with 4

Objective Use different ways to multiply when 4 is a factor.

▶ **Learn by Example**

You can draw equal groups, use repeated addition, make an array, or skip count to multiply. In this lesson, you will learn another way to multiply when 4 is a factor.

A group of 4 friends wants to share their sports cards. Each friend has 3 cards. How many cards do they have in all?

$4 \times 3 = \bigcirc$

Think

4 is double 2, so 4 × 3 is double 2 × 3.

① Multiply by 2 instead of by 4. Then **double** the product.

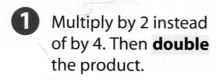

$2 \times 3 = 6 \qquad 2 \times 3 = 6$

$6 + 6 = 12$

② Write the multiplication sentence. $4 \times 3 = 12$

Solution: The friends have 12 cards in all.

Ask Yourself

• How can multiplying by 2 help me?
• Did I add to double?

▶ **Guided Practice**

Find the product.

1. $2 \times 4 = 8$ **2.** $4 \times 5 = 25$ **3.** $7 \times 4 = 29$

4. 4   **5.** 6   **6.** 3   **7.** 10
   $\times 9$ $\times 4$ $\times 4$ $\times 4$
    16   24   12   40

123 **Math Talk** How can knowing $2 \times 8 = 16$ help you to find 4×8?

Find the product.

8. $2 \times 4 = 8$ **9.** $4 \times 3 =$ **10.** $10 \times 4 = 12$ **11.** $4 \times 4 =$ **12.** $7 \times 4 =$

13. $\begin{array}{r} 4 \\ \times\, 8 \\ \hline 32 \end{array}$ **14.** $\begin{array}{r} 5 \\ \times\, 4 \\ \hline 20 \end{array}$ **15.** $\begin{array}{r} 4 \\ \times\, 9 \\ \hline \end{array}$ **16.** $\begin{array}{r} 6 \\ \times\, 4 \\ \hline \end{array}$ **17.** $\begin{array}{r} 4 \\ \times\, 2 \\ \hline \end{array}$

Solve.

18. Randy stores his collection of football cards in an album. Each page in his album holds 4 cards. How many cards can 9 pages hold?

19. Multistep Michelle makes 6 stacks of cards. Two stacks have 3 cards each. The other 4 stacks have 5 cards each. How many cards does she have?

20. Jesse has 7 packs of baseball cards. There are 4 cards in each pack. How many cards does Jesse have?

21. Challenge On each of 4 days, Kate put 6 more soccer cards in her album than the day before. She put in 15 cards on the third day. How many cards in all did Kate put in her album during those 4 days?

✓ Spiral Review and Test Practice

Compare. Write $>$, $<$, or $=$ for the ●. Tell whether the number sentence is an equation or an inequality. AF 1.3 page 52

22. 71 ● 82

23. $61 + 37$ ● $59 + 29$

24. $4{,}610 + 33$ ● $4{,}527 + 116$

25. 99 ● 201

Write the letter of the correct answer. NS 2.0

26. Max is having friends over for dinner. If he puts 2 chairs on each of 4 sides of a square table, how many chairs will he need?

    A 2   **B** 4   **C** 6   **D** 8

Multiplication Facts Practice

Be sure you have memorized your facts. Then find each product as quickly as you can. **KEY NS 2.2**

1. $\begin{array}{r} 2 \\ \times\,4 \\ \hline 8 \end{array}$

2. $\begin{array}{r} 2 \\ \times\,1 \\ \hline 2 \end{array}$

3. $\begin{array}{r} 10 \\ \times\,2 \\ \hline 20 \end{array}$

4. $\begin{array}{r} 1 \\ \times\,5 \\ \hline 5 \end{array}$

5. $\begin{array}{r} 7 \\ \times\,2 \\ \hline 14 \end{array}$

6. $\begin{array}{r} 5 \\ \times\,7 \\ \hline 35 \end{array}$

7. $\begin{array}{r} 3 \\ \times\,4 \\ \hline 12 \end{array}$

8. $\begin{array}{r} 2 \\ \times\,9 \\ \hline 18 \end{array}$

9. $\begin{array}{r} 5 \\ \times\,4 \\ \hline 20 \end{array}$

10. $\begin{array}{r} 10 \\ \times\,5 \\ \hline 50 \end{array}$

11. $\begin{array}{r} 2 \\ \times\,7 \\ \hline 14 \end{array}$

12. $\begin{array}{r} 5 \\ \times\,9 \\ \hline \end{array}$

13. $\begin{array}{r} 2 \\ \times\,2 \\ \hline \end{array}$

14. $\begin{array}{r} 4 \\ \times\,5 \\ \hline 20 \end{array}$

15. $\begin{array}{r} 2 \\ \times\,3 \\ \hline 6 \end{array}$

16. $\begin{array}{r} 10 \\ \times\,6 \\ \hline 60 \end{array}$

17. $\begin{array}{r} 9 \\ \times\,2 \\ \hline \end{array}$

18. $\begin{array}{r} 2 \\ \times\,5 \\ \hline \end{array}$

19. $\begin{array}{r} 1 \\ \times\,4 \\ \hline 4 \end{array}$

20. $\begin{array}{r} 8 \\ \times\,5 \\ \hline \end{array}$

21. $\begin{array}{r} 5 \\ \times\,5 \\ \hline 25 \end{array}$

22. $\begin{array}{r} 4 \\ \times\,9 \\ \hline \end{array}$

23. $\begin{array}{r} 10 \\ \times\,1 \\ \hline \end{array}$

24. $\begin{array}{r} 4 \\ \times\,4 \\ \hline \end{array}$

25. $\begin{array}{r} 2 \\ \times\,6 \\ \hline \end{array}$

26. $\begin{array}{r} 8 \\ \times\,4 \\ \hline 32 \end{array}$

27. $\begin{array}{r} 8 \\ \times\,10 \\ \hline \end{array}$

28. $\begin{array}{r} 5 \\ \times\,3 \\ \hline \end{array}$

29. $\begin{array}{r} 9 \\ \times\,4 \\ \hline \end{array}$

30. $\begin{array}{r} 3 \\ \times\,2 \\ \hline \end{array}$

31. $5 \times 2 = 10$

32. 6×5

33. 10×3

34. 4×3

35. 8×2

36. 9×2

37. 6×10

38. 6×2

39. 4×10

40. 2×9

41. 10×5

42. 7×4

43. 8×5

44. 1×5

45. 2×5

46. 2×2

47. 2×1

48. 7×5

49. 2×6

50. 10×10

Copy and complete each table. AF 2.2

51.

number of chickens	1	2	3	4	5	6	7	8	9	10
number of legs	2	4								

52.

number of hands	1	2	3	4	5	6	7	8	9	10
number of fingers	5	10								

Multiplying Dots

Object of the Game Practice multiplication by playing this game with a partner. Try to get the most dots by the end of the game!

Materials
- Number cube labeled 2, 2, 4, 5, 5, 10
- 2 sheets of paper, each divided into 4 equal spaces

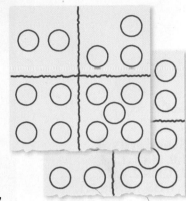

How to Play

1 On their sheets of paper, players draw 2 large circles in the first space, 3 in the second space, 4 in the third space, and 5 in the fourth space.

2 The first player rolls the number cube and chooses a square on his or her paper. The player then multiplies the number rolled by the number of circles in the chosen space. He or she records the multiplication by making dots in each circle, equal to the number rolled.

3 Players take turns repeating Step 2 until all the spaces on their papers have been used. The player with more dots wins!

Analyze
If you roll a low number, is it better to choose a space that has many circles or few circles?

CA Standards
NS 2.0, KEY **NS 2.2**, MR 2.0

Education Place
Visit www.eduplace.com/camap/ for **Brain Teasers** and **eGames** to play.

LESSON 5

Field Trip...

Los Angeles, CA

CA Standards
MR 1.0, MR 1.1,
MR 2.0, MR 2.4,
MR 3.1, NS 1.0, NS 1.1,
KEY NS 1.3, NS 1.4,
KEY NS 1.5, NS 2.0,
KEY NS 2.1, AF 2.2

Problem Solving

Objective Use skills and strategies to solve word problems.

Natural History Museum of Los Angeles County

The Natural History Museum of Los Angeles County has more than 33 million items in its collections!

At the Natural History Museum, visitors can learn about Native American culture and California history, as well as animals, fossils, gems, and minerals.

Solve. Tell which strategy or method you used.

1. A Megamouth shark at the museum is 449 cm long. What is the length of the shark rounded to the nearest ten cm? to the nearest hundred cm?

2. **Explain** The museum has 300 pounds of gold. If the museum moved 86 pounds to a new exhibit, how many pounds would be left?

3. The Insect Zoo at the museum displays insects from around the world. The table shows that an ant has 6 legs. Copy and complete the table.

number of ants	1	2	5	10
number of legs	6			

4. On one day, 3,425 people visited the museum.

   a. Write this number in expanded form.

   b. What is the value of the digit 4 in the number?

> **Hint**
> Read the problem again. Does your answer make sense?

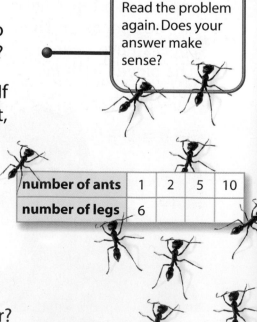

114

Problem Solving On Tests

Select a Strategy
- Estimate
- Guess and Check
- Choose the Operation

1. At an outdoor concert, 1286 people sat on chairs. Another 2324 people sat on the grass. How many people were at the concert?

A 3500 **B** 3510 **C** 3600 **D** 3610

KEY NS 2.1 page 60

2. Ms. Simon bought these items for her art students: 98 packages of glitter, 8 glue sticks, 12 colored pencils, and 4 pieces of poster board. How many items did she buy?

A 122 **B** 110 **C** 102 **D** 24

NS 2.0 page 56

3. Al bought 5 packages of pencils. Each package has 10 pencils. How many pencils did he buy?

A 5 **B** 10 **C** 50 **D** 20

KEY NS 2.2 page 106

4. Tran has 6 + 8 model cars. Otis has 5 model cars. The boys want to have equal numbers of cars. How many more cars does Otis need?

$6 + 8 = 5 +$

A 14 **C** 9
B 10 **D** 3

AF 1.2 page 52

5. Mr. Barton's class made 219 paper cranes. Ms. Jackson's class made 196 paper cranes. How many more paper cranes did Mr. Barton's class make?

A 14
B 23
C 183
D 415

Test Tip
Read the problem carefully to help you decide which operation to use.

KEY NS 2.1 page 74

6. Janet and Carl went canoeing. They paddled 3257 yards and took a break. Then they paddled another 4729 yards. How far did they paddle in all?

A 8986 yards **C** 7986 yards
B 8016 yards **D** 7976 yards

KEY NS 2.1 page 60

7. Kay has 423 photos in her album. Todd has 502 photos in his album. How many more photos does Todd have than Kay?

A 79 **B** 125 **C** 121 **D** 910

KEY NS 2.1 page 80

Education Place
Visit www.eduplace.com/camap/ for
Test-Taking Tips and **Extra Practice**.

Chapter 5 Lesson 5 **115**

Vocabulary

Using an **array** is a good way to show **multiplication**. Look at the arrays below. The **product** of 4 × 7 is the same as the **product** of 7 × 4.

4 × 7
4 groups of seven
4 × 7 = 28

7 × 4
7 groups of four
7 × 4 = 28

Write two multiplication sentences for each array.

1.

2.

3.

4.

5.

6.

Writing Reread the example at the top of the page. How does this example show the **Commutative Property of Multiplication?**

Reading Check out this book in your library.

• *Amanda Bean's Amazing Dream: A Mathematical Story*, by Cindy Neuschwander and Marilyn Burns

CA Standards

MR 2.3 Use a variety of methods, such as words, numbers, symbols, charts, graphs, tables, diagrams, and models, to explain mathematical reasoning.

Also KEY NS 2.2 , AF 1.5

Standards-Based Extra Practice

Set A ─────────────────────────────────── KEY **NS 2.2**, **AF 1.5** page 102

Write two multiplication sentences for the array.

1. ★ ★ ★
★ ★ ★
★ ★ ★
★ ★ ★
★ ★ ★

2. ● ● ● ●
● ● ● ●

3. (array of flowers, 4 rows of 6)

Find the missing number.

4. $13 \times \blacksquare = 52$
$4 \times 13 = 52$

5. $5 \times \blacksquare = 30$
$6 \times 5 = 30$

6. $9 \times 7 = 63$
$\blacksquare \times 9 = 63$

7. Ramon has 28 stamps. He puts them in 7 groups of 4 stamps each. Sally also has 28 stamps. She put them in 4 equal groups. How many stamps are in each of Sally's groups?

Set B ─────────────────────────────────── KEY **NS 2.2** page 106

Find the product.

1. $\begin{array}{r} 4 \\ \times\ 2 \\ \hline \end{array}$
2. $\begin{array}{r} 2 \\ \times\ 8 \\ \hline \end{array}$
3. $\begin{array}{r} 2 \\ \times\ 3 \\ \hline \end{array}$
4. $\begin{array}{r} 8 \\ \times\ 5 \\ \hline \end{array}$
5. $\begin{array}{r} 3 \\ \times\ 5 \\ \hline \end{array}$

6. Sarah made a display of all the postcards she has collected. She made 4 rows with 10 postcards in each row. How many postcards does Sarah have in all?

Set C ─────────────────────────────────── KEY **NS 2.2** page 110

Find the product.

1. $\begin{array}{r} 4 \\ \times\ 2 \\ \hline \end{array}$
2. $\begin{array}{r} 10 \\ \times\ 4 \\ \hline \end{array}$
3. $\begin{array}{r} 3 \\ \times\ 4 \\ \hline \end{array}$
4. $\begin{array}{r} 4 \\ \times\ 9 \\ \hline \end{array}$

5. Melissa is giving a surprise party for her friend. The room she is using for the party can hold 8 tables. If 4 people can sit at each table, how many people can she invite?

Education Place
Visit www.eduplace.com/camap/
for more **Extra Practice**.

Chapter Review/Test

Vocabulary and Concepts ———————————— NS 2.0, AF 1.5

Choose the best term to complete each sentence.

1. The _____ says that the product will be the same no matter what order the factors are in.

2. The answer to a multiplication sentence is the _____.

3. When you solve the problem 4 × 3 by adding 4 three times, you are using _____.

> **Word Bank**
> Commutative Property of Multiplication
> repeated addition
> product

Skills ———————————— NS 2.0, AF 1.5, KEY NS 2.2, AF 1.2

Write two multiplication sentences for the array.

4.

5.

6.

Find the missing number.

7. $14 = 7 \times 2$
   $\blacksquare = 2 \times 7$

8. $9 \times 3 = 27$
   $3 \times \blacksquare = 27$

9. $\blacksquare \times 8 = 40$
   $8 \times 5 = 40$

10. $12 \times 4 = 48$
    $4 \times \blacksquare = 48$

Find the product.

11. 9×10

12. 5×6

13. 6×7

Problem Solving and Reasoning —— NS 2.0, MR 1.0, MR 2.3, MR 2.6, KEY AF 2.1, MR 3.1

Solve.

14. Ming ran 2 miles every day for a week. How many miles did he run?

15. Alice has 12 shells. Can she put them in 5 groups of 3 shells each?

Writing Math How can you use an array to explain the Commutative Property of Multiplication?

Spiral Review and Test Practice

1. Which is a way to write two hundred nine?

A 2009

B 290

C 209

D 29

KEY **NS 1.3** page 8

2. Which number, rounded to the nearest hundred, is zero?

A 95

B 60

C 55

D 37

Test Tip
You can use rounding rules.

NS 1.4 page 30

3. What is 7950 rounded to the nearest hundred?

A 8000

B 7950

C 7900

D 7000

NS 1.4 page 34

4. $1635 + 2583 =$

A 3118

B 3218

C 4118

D 4218

KEY **NS 2.1** page 60

5. A charity collected $2,266 on Thursday and $1,965 on Friday. How much more did the group collect on Thursday than on Friday?

A $201

B $301

C $1,301

D $4,231

KEY **NS 2.1** page 78

6. If $2 \times 8 \times 4 = 64$, then what is $8 \times 2 \times 4$?

A 8

B 16

C 32

D 64

Test Tip
Remember the properties of multiplication.

AF 1.5 page 102

Education Place
Visit www.eduplace.com/camap/ for
Test-Taking Tips and **Extra Practice**.

Chapter 6

Multiplication Patterns

Ring-tailed Lemurs

Word Bank

equal
   groups
factor
product
skip count
times

Vocabulary and Concepts NS 2.0, MR 2.3
Choose the best term to complete each sentence. page 106

1. When you multiply two numbers, the answer is the ____.

2. One way to solve a multiplication sentence is to ____.

3. You multiply ____ to find the product.

Skills NS 2.0, KEY NS 2.2, KEY AF 1.1
Write a multiplication sentence for each. page 100

4. $2 + 2 + 2 + 2 = 8$
5. $5 + 5 + 5 = 15$
6. $1 + 1 + 1 + 1 + 1 = 5$

Multiply. page 100

7. 2×3
8. 3×2
9. 3×10

Problem Solving and Reasoning NS 2.0

10. Keiko has a favorite number. When she adds the number to itself, the answer is the same as when she multiplies the number by itself. What is Keiko's favorite number?

Vocabulary

Visualize It !

array

An arrangement of objects or pictures in equal columns and rows.

3 rows

4 columns

$3 \times 4 = 12$

$$\begin{array}{r} 3 \\ \times\,4 \\ \hline 12 \end{array}$$ **factors** / **product**

Language Tip
Some words are similar in Spanish and English.

English	Spanish
factor	factor
product	producto

See **English-Spanish Glossary** pages 628–646.

CA Standards **MR 2.3** Use a variety of methods, such as words, numbers, symbols, charts, graphs, tables, diagrams, and models, to explain mathematical reasoning. **KEY** NS 2.2

CA Standards

NS 2.6 Understand the special properties of 0 and 1 in multiplication and division.

MR 3.3 Develop generalizations of the results obtained and apply them in other circumstances.

Also NS 2.0, AF 1.2, AF 1.5, MR 2.3, MR 3.0

Vocabulary

Identity Property of Multiplication
$6 \times 1 = 6$ or $1 \times 6 = 6$

Zero Property of Multiplication
$8 \times 0 = 0$ or $0 \times 8 = 0$

Materials
• Workmat 1
• Counters

Hands On
Multiply with 0 and 1

Objective Use the special properties of 1 and 0 in multiplication.

▶ **Explore**

Identity Property of Multiplication The product of 1 and any number is that number.

Zero Property of Multiplication The product of any number and 0 is 0.

Question How can you use counters and equal groups to show multiplication by 1 or 0?

Maya has 8 plates. She puts one mango on each plate. How many mangos are there?

1 Draw 8 circles to show the 8 plates.

Put 1 counter in each circle to show the mangos.

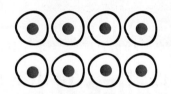

2 Write a multiplication sentence to show the total.

$$8 \times 1 = 8$$
$$1 \times 8 = 8$$

Solution: There are 8 mangos on the plates.

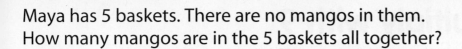

Maya has 5 baskets. There are no mangos in them.
How many mangos are in the 5 baskets all together?

1 Draw circles to show the baskets.

2 Use counters to show the mangos. How many counters do you need?

3 Write a multiplication sentence to show the total.

▶ **Extend**

**Multiply. Tell which property you used.
Write *Identity* or *Zero*.**

Hint
Remember, 0×1 and 1×0 have the same product.

1. 1×6 **2.** 0×7 **3.** 0×9 **4.** 1×5

Find the missing number.

5. ▧ $\times 1 = 5$ **6.** $46 \times 0 =$ ▧ **7.** $459 \times 1 =$ ▧ **8.** $7{,}811 \times$ ▧ $= 0$

Solve the problems below.

9. Generalize Is it easier to find 5×0 than 598×0?
Explain.

10. Analyze What number or numbers make this number
sentence true? Explain.

▧ $\times 0 = 7 \times 0$

Writing Math

What's Wrong? Marly wrote the number
sentence $4 \times 0 = 0$ to describe her picture.
What did she do wrong?

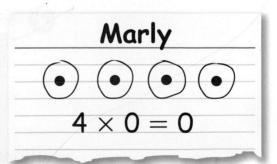

Marly

$4 \times 0 = 0$

CA Standards

KEY NS 2.2 Memorize to automaticity the multiplication table for numbers between 1 and 10.

AF 1.2 Solve problems involving numeric equations or inequalities.

Also NS 2.0, KEY AF 2.1, MR 1.1

Multiply with 9

Objective Use patterns to multiply when 9 is a factor.

▶ Learn by Example

This chart shows the 9s facts. The yellow boxes show the facts you already know.

These facts follow a special pattern that can help you learn and remember them.

Factors	Product
$\underline{1} \times 9 =$	9
$\underline{2} \times 9 =$	18
$\underline{3} \times 9 =$	27
$\underline{4} \times 9 =$	36
$\underline{5} \times 9 =$	45
$\underline{6} \times 9 =$	54
$\underline{7} \times 9 =$	63
$\underline{8} \times 9 =$	■
$\underline{9} \times 9 =$	■
$\underline{10} \times 9 =$	■

- Look at each row in the chart. Notice that the tens digit of the product is always 1 less than the underlined factor.

$$\underline{7} \times 9 = 63$$

- Look at each product in the chart. Notice that the sum of the digits in the product is always 9.

$$7 \times 9 = 63 \longrightarrow 6 + 3 = 9$$

Find the next product in the chart: $8 \times 9 = \bigcirc$.

1 What number is 1 less than 8? Write 7 in the tens place of the product.

$$\underline{8} \times 9 = \underline{7}\_$$

> The tens digit in the product is 1 less than the factor you are multiplying by 9.

2 Seven plus what number is 9? Write 2 in the ones place of the product.

$$8 \times 9 = \underline{7}\underline{2}$$

> The sum of the digits in the product is 9.

Solution: $8 \times 9 = 72$

Guided Practice

Multiply.

Ask Yourself
- How can I find the tens digit in the product?
- How can I find the ones digit in the product?

1. 3
    × 9

2. 9
    × 7

3. 2
    × 9

4. 9
    × 5

5. 4
    × 9

6. 9
    × 1

7. 6
    × 9

8. 9
    × 10

9. 9
    × 8

10. 9
    × 3

11. 9
    × 9

12. 7
    × 9

Guided Problem Solving

Use the questions to solve this problem.

13. Yoon Ki visited the Olympic National Park rainforest for 9 days. She bought 3 postcards each day. How many postcards did she buy in all?

    a. **Understand** How many days was Yoon Ki's trip? How many postcards did she buy each day?

    b. **Plan** Choose a way to solve the problem.

    c. **Solve** Use your plan. Write the answer.

    d. **Look Back** Solve the problem a different way. Did you get the same answer?

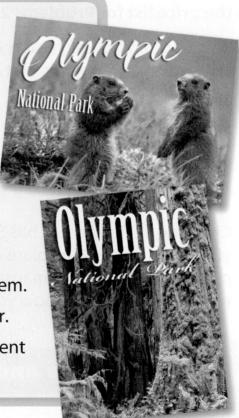

Solve.

14. Look back at Problem 13. If Yoon Ki bought 6 postcards each day instead of 3, how many postcards would she have in all?

123 Math Talk How can you use patterns to help you find 9 × 9?

Multiply.

15. 4
×9

16. 3
×9

17. 1
×9

18. 9
×5

19. 9
×2

20. 8
×9

21. 2
×9

22. 9
×3

23. 9
×10

24. 9
×9

25. 6
×9

26. 7
×9

 Real World Data

Use the price list for Problems 27–30.

27. There are 9 different posters of the rainforest. How much do 9 posters cost?

28. Estimate About how much more does a video cost than a map?

29. Compare Key chains normally cost $5. How much money do you save if you buy 4 on sale?

30. Challenge Mrs. Gomez has $37 to spend on science-fair prizes. She plans to spend all of the money on posters and maps. How many prizes will she have? Explain how you found your answer.

SALE

Rainforest Poster	$5
Key Chain	$3
Map	$9
Video	$18
Book	$22

 Spiral Review and Test Practice

Multiply. NS 2.6 page 122

31. 9×0

32. 6×1

33. 11×0

34. 722×1

Write the letter of the correct answer. KEY NS 2.2, AF 1.2

35. What number makes this number sentence true?
$2 \times 9 < 3 \times \blacksquare$

A 4
B 5
C 6
D 7

Extra Practice See page 137, Set A.

Key Standards Review

Need Help?
See Key Standards Handbook.

Write the place of the underlined digit. Then write its value. KEY **NS 1.3**

1. <u>3</u>06 **2.** 8<u>5</u>2 **3.** 6,<u>0</u>98 **4.** <u>4</u>,771 **5.** 8,<u>2</u>07

Multiply. KEY **NS 2.2**

6. 5
  ×8

7. 2
  ×9

8. 10
  ×4

9. 6
  ×1

10. 3
  ×9

11. 5
  ×3

12. 8
  ×0

13. 4
  ×4

14. 10
  ×2

15. 9
  ×7

Algebra and Functions

Looking for Signs AF 1.0, AF 1.3

Write the correct sign to complete the number sentence. Choose +, −, or ×.

1. 3 ⬭ 2 = 5 **2.** 4 = 1 ⬭ 4 **3.** 9 ⬭ 8 = 72

4. 10 ⬭ 4 = 6 **5.** 0 ⬭ 8 = 8 **6.** 4 = 6 ⬭ 2

7. 5 ⬭ 3 = 15 **8.** 9 = 3 ⬭ 3 **9.** 16 = 4 ⬭ 4

Getting Into Shapes AF 1.2

**Different shapes stand for different numbers.
The same shapes stand for the same numbers.
Find the value of each shape.**

10. ■ − ▲ = 1
  ■ × ▲ = 6
  ■ = ? ▲ = ?

11. ◆ − ● = 8
  ◆ × ● = 20
  ◆ = ? ● = ?

CA Standards
KEY NS 2.2 Memorize to automaticity the multiplication table for numbers between 1 and 10.

MR 2.3 Use a variety of methods, such as words, numbers, symbols, charts, graphs, tables, diagrams, and models, to explain reasoning.

Also NS 2.0, KEY AF 2.1, **MR 1.0**

Vocabulary

The product of a whole number multiplied by itself is a **square number**.

$$3 \times 3 = 9$$

Materials
Learning Tool 11
(Centimeter Grid Paper)

Square Arrays

Objective Use square arrays to multiply 2 factors that are the same. Identify square numbers.

▶ **Learn by Example**

In this lesson, we will look at multiplication facts that have special arrays. The arrays are squares.

Model It	Write It
1 $3 \times 3 = \bigcirc$	$3 \times 3 = 9$
	9 is a **square number**.
2 $5 \times 5 = \bigcirc$ 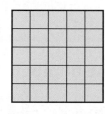	$5 \times 5 = 25$
	25 is a square number.

Ask Yourself
Does my array have the same number of rows and columns?

▶ **Guided Practice**

Draw an array to find the product. Use grid paper.

1. 9×9 **2.** 8×8 **3.** 1×1

Does the array show a square number? If not, how many squares could be added to make it a square number?

4.    **5.**   **6.**

Guided Problem Solving

Use the questions to solve the problem.

7. Chris is hanging pictures in a gallery, in a square array. There are 4 rows of 4 pictures. How many pictures are there in all?

   a. **Understand** What do you know? What do you want to find out?

   b. **Plan** You can draw an array. Will the array be a square?

   c. **Solve** Draw the array. Use the array to solve the problem.

   There are ◯ pictures in all.

   d. **Look Back** Use another multiplication strategy to solve the problem. Did you get the same answer?

 **Math Talk** How can knowing $4 \times 2 = 8$ help you to find 4×4?

 **Practice and Problem Solving**

Draw an array to find the product. Use grid paper.

8. 2×2 **9.** 6×6 **10.** 7×7 **11.** 9×9 **12.** 10×10

Does the array show a square number? If not, how many squares could be added to make it a square number?

13.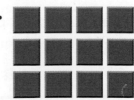

14.

15.

Solve.

16. Alex is making a model of the rainforest. The model has 3 groups of 5 Kapok trees, which can be 150 feet tall or more. How many Kapok trees are in the model?

17. Tarantulas, spiders with 8 legs, live in the rainforest. Alex makes 8 tarantulas for his model. How many legs does Alex make in all?

Science Link

Solve.

18. Six groups of 6 students saw a film about the rainforest. How many students saw the film?

19. Juan, Emily, and Jack are working on a report about rainforest animals. If each student finds information on 3 animals, how many animals in all will be in the report?

Sun Conure

Rainforest

- Tropical rainforests have four layered zones.
- Different plants and animals live in each zone.

emergents

canopy

understory

forest floor

Science LS 3.b

✓ Spiral Review and Test Practice

Round each number to the greatest place. Then add or subtract to find an estimated answer. NS 1.4, KEY **NS 2.1** page 84

20. 5,431 − 3,807   **21.** 87 + 61   **22.** 855 + 237   **23.** 85 − 47

Write the letter of the correct answer. KEY **NS 2.2**, KEY **AF 2.1**

24. Mr. Jones bought 6 books for $6 each. How much did he pay for all of the books?

   A $1   **B** $12   **C** $32   **D** $36

Extra Practice See page 137, Set B.

Looking for Signs

Addition and multiplication have special properties. These properties can be very helpful when you are doing these operations.

The *Commutative Property* states that order does not matter. This means that

$$a + b = b + a$$ and $$a \times b = b \times a$$.

The *Associative Property* states that the way the numbers are grouped does not affect the result. This means that

$$a + (b + c) = (a + b) + c$$ and $$a \times (b \times c) = (a \times b) \times c$$.

Subtraction does not have a commutative or associative property.

Write the correct operation signs to complete the number sentences. Choose +, −, or ×.

1. 17 ⬤ 5 = 12

2. 4 ⬤ 4 = 16

3. 0 ⬤ 8 = 4 ⬤ 2

4. 12 ⬤ 3 = 5 ⬤ 4

5. 3 ⬤ (2 ⬤ 1) = 6

6. 6 = (3 ⬤ 2) ⬤ 1

7. 10 ⬤ 2 = 2 ⬤ 6

8. 2 ⬤ 10 = 3 ⬤ 4

9. 24 = 6 ⬤ 4

10. 4 ⬤ 6 = 24

11. 14 ⬤ 9 = 23 = 9 ⬤ 14

12. (10 ⬤ 16) ⬤ 7 = 33 = 10 ⬤ (16 ⬤ 7)

13. 2 ⬤ 7 = 14 = 7 ⬤ 2

CA Standards
AF 1.3, AF 1.5

Multiply with 3

Objective Use strategies to learn and memorize facts with 3.

▶ Learn by Example

The nature club is going on a hike. Each person brings 4 bottles of water. How many bottles in all will 3 people bring?

You can use doubles facts to help learn the 3s facts. Since multiplying by 3 is like adding a number 3 times, you can double the number and add one more group.

$4 \times 3 = \bigcirc$

Think

- I know a doubles fact for 4.
- Now I'll add another group of 4.

1 Multiply 4 by 2.

$$\begin{array}{r} 4 \\ \times 2 \\ \hline 8 \end{array}$$

$4 \times 2 = 8$

2 Then add a third group of 4.

$8 + 4 = 12$

3 Write the multiplication equation. $4 \times 3 = 12$

Solution: Three people will bring 12 bottles of water.

▶ Guided Practice

Find the product.

1.   3
    $\times 9$

2.   6
    $\times 3$

3.   3
    $\times 3$

4.   5
    $\times 3$

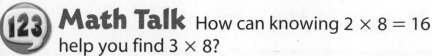 **Math Talk** How can knowing $2 \times 8 = 16$ help you find 3×8?

Practice and Problem Solving

Find the product.

5. 3
   × 4

6. 3
   × 8

7. 9
   × 3

8. 7
   × 3

9. 3
   × 1

10. 5
    × 3

11. 3
    × 3

12. 2
    × 3

13. 10
    × 3

14. 3
    × 0

Solve the problems below.

15. A park ranger led 3 groups of hikers. There were 4 people in each group. How many hikers did she lead?

16. **Multistep** Ty planted 3 seeds every day for 5 days. Mina planted 12 seeds. Who planted more seeds? How many more?

17. Lucia buys 3 sheets of nature stickers. Each sheet has 8 stickers. Does she have 24 stickers? Use words, pictures, or numbers to explain.

18. **Challenge** If 7 sets of triplets and 9 sets of twins go to a picnic, are there more twins or more triplets at the picnic? How many more?

Hikers at Yosemite National Park

Spiral Review and Test Practice

Draw an array to show the product. Write the product. KEY **NS 2.2** pages 102, 106, 110

19. 6 × 5

20. 9 × 4

21. 10 × 7

22. 7 × 2

Write the letter of the correct answer. KEY **NS 2.2**, KEY **AF 2.1**

23. At Keesha's party there are 3 tables. Each table seats 7 people. How many people are at the party?

    A 10   **B** 14   **C** 21   **D** 27

CA Standards

MR 1.2 Determine when and how to break a problem into simpler parts.

NS 2.8 Solve problems that require two or more of the skills mentioned above.

Also NS 2.0, MR 1.1, MR 2.0, MR 2.3, MR 2.4, MR 2.6, MR 3.0, MR 3.1, MR 3.2, MR 3.3

Problem Solving Plan
Multistep Problems

Objective Solve problems that have more than one step.

▶ Learn by Example

Rosa's uncle sends her a postcard every week.

> Rosa has 3 postcards of fish. She has 9 times as many postcards of birds. How many postcards of fish and birds does she have?

UNDERSTAND

The problem asks how many postcards of fish and birds Rosa has. Rosa has 3 fish postcards. She has 9 times as many bird postcards.

PLAN

It takes more than one step to solve this problem. Break the problem into parts.

- First, find the number of bird postcards.
- Then find the sum of the bird and fish postcards.

SOLVE

1 Find the number of bird postcards.

$$
\begin{array}{r}
3 \leftarrow \text{fish postcards} \\
\times\ 9 \\
\hline
27 \leftarrow \text{bird postcards}
\end{array}
$$

2 Add to find the total.

$$
\begin{array}{r}
27 \leftarrow \text{bird postcards} \\
+\ 3 \leftarrow \text{fish postcards} \\
\hline
30 \leftarrow \text{total postcards}
\end{array}
$$

Rosa has 30 postcards of fish and birds.

LOOK BACK

Did you answer the question that was asked?

Piranha – South America

White-Bellied Parrot – South America

▶ Guided Problem Solving

Solve using the Ask Yourself questions.

Ask Yourself
- How can I break the problem into parts?
- Did I answer the question that was asked?

1. Rosa received 6 postcards of mammals and 3 postcards of frogs each month for 3 months. How many postcards is that?

 Math Talk Look back at Problem 1. Did you multiply and then add or add and then multiply? Will both work?

▶ Independent Problem Solving

Solve. Explain why your answer makes sense.

2. Maria saw 7 butterflies at the greenhouse. André saw 3 times as many butterflies. What was the total number of butterflies the two friends saw?

3. At a Save the Rainforest fundraiser, Ms. Brown's class sold 9 pencils. They sold 3 times as many erasers. How many more erasers than pencils did the class sell?

Use the price list for Problems 4–7.

4. Mr. Watkins bought 4 key chains and 3 erasers at the fundraiser. How much did he spend?

5. Each pack of pencils contains 8 pencils. Sari bought 3 packs. She gave away 10 pencils to her friends. How many pencils does Sari have left?

6. **Challenge** Yuri had $20 to spend at the fundraiser. He bought 2 packs of pencils, 5 erasers, and a key chain. How much change should he receive?

7. **Create and Solve** Use the price list to create and solve a multistep problem.

Rainforest Fundraiser	
Item	**Costs**
Pack of pencils	$4
Pack of postcards	$2
Key chain	$5
Eraser	$1

Reading & Writing **Math**

Vocabulary

You have learned about the special properties of 1 and 0 in multiplication. You have also learned about **square numbers**.

The **Identity Property of Multiplication** says that the product of 1 and any number is that number.

The **Zero Property of Multiplication** says that the product of any number and 0 is 0.

Multiply. Tell which property you used. Write *Identity* or *Zero*.

1. 1×8 **2.** 0×7

3. 1×2 **4.** 3×0

Write a multiplication sentence for each array. Does the array model a square number? Write *yes* or *no*.

5.

6.

7.

8.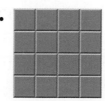

Writing

Can you draw an array to show 6×0? Explain why or why not.

Reading

Look for this book in your library.

- *Anno's Mysterious Multiplying Jar,* by Masaichiro Anno and Mitsumasa Anno

CA Standards
MR 2.3 Use a variety of methods, such as words, numbers, symbols, charts, graphs, tables, diagrams, and models, to explain mathematical reasoning.
Also KEY NS 2.2, NS 2.6

Standards-Based Extra Practice

Set A ───────────────────────────────────── KEY **NS 2.2** page 124

Multiply.

1. 9
     × 9

2. 2
     × 9

3. 9
     × 6

4. 1
     × 9

5. Marissa has 4 baskets of peaches. There are 9 peaches in each basket. How many peaches does she have in all?

Set B ───────────────────────────────────── KEY **NS 2.2** page 128

Draw an array to find the product. Use grid paper.

1. 6 × 6   **2.** 3 × 3   **3.** 9 × 9   **4.** 2 × 2   **5.** 4 × 4

Write whether the array shows a square number. If not, write how many squares could be added to make it show a square number.

6.

7.

8.

9. There are 8 different lemon trees. George picked 8 lemons from each tree. How many lemons did he pick in all?

Set C ───────────────────────────────────── KEY **NS 2.2** page 132

Find the product.

1. 3
     × 0

2. 3
     × 7

3. 6
     × 3

4. 5
     × 3

5. 3 × 1   **6.** 9 × 3   **7.** 8 × 3   **8.** 3 × 4

9. Mrs. Ruiz baked 3 trays of muffins. There are 6 muffins on each tray. How many muffins did she bake in all?

Education Place
Visit www.eduplace.com/camap/
for more **Extra Practice.**

Chapter 6 Extra Practice   **137**

Chapter Review/Test

Vocabulary and Concepts

NS 2.6, KEY **NS 2.2**

Choose the best word to complete each sentence.

Word Bank
Zero Property of Multiplication
square numbers

1. The numbers 4, 9, and 16 are all _____.

2. The _____ says that the product of any number multiplied by 0 is 0.

Skills

KEY **NS 2.2**, NS 2.0

Multiply.

3. 8×9 **4.** 6×9 **5.** 9×2 **6.** 9×3 **7.** 4×9

Draw an array to show the product. Write the product.

8. 5×5 **9.** 8×8 **10.** 1×1 **11.** 7×7 **12.** 4×4

Does the array show a square number? If not, how many squares could be added to make it a square number?

13.   **14.**    **15.**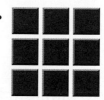

Find the product.

16.   3
       $\times 9$

17.   3
       $\times 5$

18.   8
       $\times 3$

Problem Solving and Reasoning

KEY **NS 2.2**, MR 1.1, MR 2.3, MR 3.1

Solve.

19. Lisa has 2 boxes with 24 crayons in each box. How many crayons does Lisa have?

20. Dylan played 4 soccer games each month for 3 months. How many games did he play in all?

Writing Math Emmet hung 36 photos in an array of 6 rows of 6 pictures. Tell another way to hang the pictures.

Spiral Review and Test Practice

1. What number makes this number sentence true?

$$5 + 9 = 10 + \square$$

A 4   **C** 14

B 19   **D** 24

AF 1.2 page 52

2. Which number makes the number sentence true?

$$5 + (3 + 6) = (\square + 3) + 6$$

A 23

B 15

C 14

D 5

KEY **AF 1.1** page 54

3. What number is 14 less than 10,000?

A 9086

B 9986

C 10,006

D 10,086

Test Tip

First, identify the answer choices that are greater than 10,000.

KEY **NS 2.1** page 80

4. More than 4825 people attended a fair on Saturday. Nearly 3350 people attended on Sunday. About how many thousand people attended the fair?

A 6000

B 7000

C 8000

D 9000

Test Tip

First, round each number to the thousands place.

NS 1.4 page 84

5. Which number sentence is true?

A $5 \times 30 = 15$

B $5 \times 4 = 20$

C $5 \times 4 = 25$

D $5 \times 6 = 11$

KEY **NS 2.2** page 106

6. Mrs. King bought 6 candles for $6 each. How much did she pay for all the candles?

A $36   **C** $30

B $12   **D** $1

KEY **NS 2.2** page 128

Chapter 7

Multiplication Patterns and Practice

These homes on Alamo Square in San Francisco, CA are known as painted ladies.

Vocabulary and Concepts AF 1.5, MR 2.3
Choose the best term to complete each sentence. page 102

1. An _____ shows equal groups in rows and columns.

2. The _____ tells us that changing the order of the factors does not change the product.

3. A _____ sentence includes a times sign and an equals sign.

Skills GRADE 2 KEY NS 3.1
Write the missing number. GRADE 2

4. 3, 6, ▨ , 12, 15

5. 7, ▨ , 21, 28, 35

6. $6 + 6 + 6 + 6 =$ ▨

7. $8 + 8 + 8 =$ ▨

8. $5 \times 9 =$ ▨

9. $6 \times 2 =$ ▨

Problem Solving and Reasoning NS 2.0, MR 2.0

10. Josephine knows that 4×10 equals 40. How can she find 4×11, without having to multiply?

Vocabulary

Visualize It!

multiplication

An operation that finds the total number of items (the product) in several equal groups.

Associative Property of Multiplication

Changing the grouping of factors does not change the product.

$$(3 \times 4) \times 2 \qquad = \qquad 3 \times (4 \times 2)$$

 Education Place Visit www.eduplace.com/camap/ for the **eGlossary** and **eGames**.

CA Standards MR 2.3 Use a variety of methods, such as words, numbers, symbols, charts, graphs, tables, diagrams, and models, to explain mathematical reasoning. **Also AF 1.5**

Chapter 7   141

CA Standards
KEY **NS 2.2** Memorize to automaticity the multiplication table for numbers between 1 and 10.

Also NS 2.6, MR 1.1, MR 2.3, MR 3.3

Vocabulary

factor

row

column

product

Materials
Learning Tool 12
(Multiplication Table)

Hands On
Use a Multiplication Table

Objective Find patterns in a multiplication table.

▶ **Explore**

You can use the multiplication facts you know to make a multiplication table. The patterns in the table will help you remember the multiplication facts.

Question How are factors and products represented on a multiplication table?

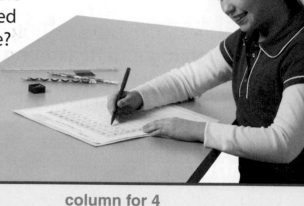

1 The numbers along the top and side are **factors**. Find the **row** for 2 and the **column** for 4. Then find the square where the row and column meet. Write the **product** of 2 × 4 in that square.

column for 4
↓

row for 2

×	0	1	2	3	4	5	6	7	8	9	10
0											
1											
2					⑧						
3											
4											
5											
6											
7											
8											
9											
10											

2 × 4 = 8

2 Fill in other squares that have products you know.

3 Use the patterns in the table to complete the chart.

▶ **Extend**

Use your multiplication table to answer the question.

1. When you multiply a number by 1, what is the product?

2. Where do you find the square numbers?

3. What do all the products in the column for 10 have in common?

4. Look for other patterns in the table. Describe two patterns that you find.

Look at the section from a multiplication table. Identify the row or column where the section is found.

5.

6.

7.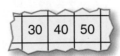

8.

9.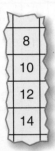

10.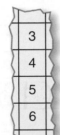

11.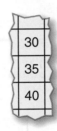

12.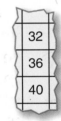

Write *true* or *false* for the statement. Give an example to support your answer.

13. The product will always be 1 when you multiply by 1.

14. Each product appears at least two times in the table.

Writing Math

Connect How could you use the products in the row for 2 to help you find the products in the row for 4?

CA Standards

KEY **NS 2.2** Memorize to automaticity the multiplication table for numbers between 1 and 10.

AF 1.5 Recognize and use the commutative and associative properties of multiplication (e.g., if 5 × 7 = 35, then what is 7 × 5? and if 5 × 7 × 3 = 105, then what is 7 × 3 × 5?).

Also NS 2.0, NS 2.6, MR 2.0, MR 2.3, MR 2.4, MR 3.0, MR 3.2, MR 3.3

Use What You Know to Multiply with 6, 7, and 8

Objective Use strategies to learn and memorize multiplication facts with 6, 7, and 8.

▶ Learn by Example

The table shows the facts for 6, 7, and 8. The numbers in the yellow boxes show the facts you already know. The other numbers show the facts you still need to learn.

These are the facts you need to learn.

6 × 7 = 42
7 × 6 = 42

6 × 8 = 48
8 × 6 = 48

7 × 8 = 56
8 × 7 = 56

If you know the Commutative Property, you only need to learn 3 new facts.

×	0	1	2	3	4	5	6	7	8	9	10
0							0	0	0		
1							6	7	8		
2							12	14	16		
3							18	21	24		
4							24	28	32		
5							30	35	40		
6	0	6	12	18	24	30	36	42	48	54	60
7	0	7	14	21	28	35	42	49	56	63	70
8	0	8	16	24	32	40	48	56	64	72	80
9							54	63	72		
10							60	70	80		

Here are some ways to help you learn these facts.

Different Ways to Multiply

Way 1 Use a fact you know.

5 × 7 = 35
+ 7
6 × 7 = 42 ◀

5 × 7 plus one more set makes 6 × 7, or 42

Way 2 Use doubling.

6 is double 3, so 6 × 7 is double 3 × 7.

3 × 7 = 21
6 × 7 = 21 + 21
21 + 21 = 42, so 6 × 7 = 42.

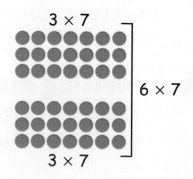

3 × 7

6 × 7

3 × 7

Multiply.

1. 7   2. 6   3. 8   4. 7
   × 6   × 8   × 6   × 8

5. Draw a picture to show how you can use doubling to find 8 × 6.

6. You know that 5 × 8 = 40. How can you use this fact to find 6 × 8?

Guided Problem Solving

Use the questions to solve this problem.

7. The city council voted to have a 6-day street fair. The fair goes on for 8 hours each day. How many hours long is the fair?

   a. **Understand** What do you know?

   b. **Plan** What are you trying to find? What operation can you use to find the answer?

   c. **Solve** Use your plan and write the answer. The fair lasted ◯ hours.

   d. **Look Back** Solve the problem in a different way. Did you get the same answer?

8. Look back at Problem 7. What if there was an 8-day street fair that lasted 6 hours each day? How many hours long would this fair be?

123 Math Talk Why is it useful to know that you can multiply factors in any order?

Multiply.

9. 8
     ×7

10. 7
      ×6

11. 6
      ×8

12. 7
      ×8

13. 6
      ×7

14. 8
      ×6

15. Leah has 8 strips of stickers. There are 7 stickers on each strip. How many stickers does Leah have?

16. Challenge Carol bought 90 stickers on strips. Some strips have 8 stickers and some have 6. What is one possibility for the number of strips Carol bought?

Science Link

Solve.

17. Predict Dr. Kwan usually collects between 5 and 10 animal fossils each month. What is the greatest number of fossils Dr. Kwan can collect in 7 months? the least number?

18. Estimate Scientists found 138 fossils, 261 fossils, and 322 fossils over three months. About how many fossils did they find in all?

The La Brea Tar Pits

- The La Brea Tar Pits are in Los Angeles, CA.
- The fossils of over 660 types of animals and plants are found in the tar pits.
- Mammoths lived in the Los Angeles area during the Ice Age. They are now extinct, and their fossils are found in the La Brea Tar Pits.

Science   LS 3.b

Spiral Review and Test Practice

Find the difference. KEY NS 2.1 pages 74, 78, 80

19.   309
       − 147

20.   4,273
       − 2,428

21.   7,000
       − 3,667

22.   5,012
       − 2,405

Write the letter of the correct answer. NS 2.0

23. Coley needs 7 cups of blueberries to make a batch of muffins. How many cups does she need for 8 batches?

  A 15   **B** 48   **C** 56   **D** 42

Extra Practice See page 159, Set A.

Key Standards Review

Need Help?
See Key Standards Handbook.

Solve. KEY NS 2.2

1. 3 $\times$ 7	**2.** 6 $\times$ 4	**3.** 9 $\times$ 4	**4.** 5 $\times$ 8	**5.** 8 $\times$ 10	**6.** 10 $\times$ 3
7. 7 $\times$ 6	**8.** 6 $\times$ 9	**9.** 6 $\times$ 7	**10.** 9 $\times$ 3	**11.** 1 $\times$ 7	**12.** 8 $\times$ 6
13. 7 $\times$ 4	**14.** 7 $\times$ 3	**15.** 6 $\times$ 5	**16.** 9 $\times$ 9	**17.** 7 $\times$ 7	**18.** 8 $\times$ 8

Write an equation and solve. KEY AF 1.1, KEY AF 2.1

19. A spider has 8 legs. What is the number of legs on 5 spiders?

20. A truck has 6 wheels. What is the number of wheels on ten trucks?

21. A table seats 4 people. How many people can be seated at 6 tables?

22. There are 3 feet in 1 yard. How many feet are in 7 yards?

23. Sam has 3 baseball caps. Sue has 2 fewer caps than Sam. How many baseball caps does Sue have?

24. Lao read 54 pages in his book. Kim read 9 more pages than Lao. How many pages did Kim read?

Number Sense

Number Riddles NS 2.0, MR 1.0, MR 2.4

Solve.

1. Tina is thinking of two numbers that are both less than 10. If she multiplies the numbers, the answer is 34 more than if she adds them. What are the numbers? Explain how you found your answer.

2. Make up another number riddle like Tina's. Exchange riddles with a partner to solve.

CA Standards

KEY **NS 2.2** Memorize to automaticity the multiplication table for numbers between 1 and 10.

AF 1.5 Recognize and use the commutative and associative properties of multiplication (e.g., if 5 × 7 = 35, then what is 7 × 5? and if 5 × 7 × 3 = 105, then what is 7 × 3 × 5?).

Also NS 2.0, NS 2.8, KEY AF 1.1, AF 1.2, MR 1.2, MR 2.0, MR 2.3, MR 2.4

Practice Multiplying with 6, 7, and 8

Objective Use strategies to practice multiplication facts with 6, 7, and 8.

▶ Learn Through Reasoning

You know different ways to multiply. You can use these ways to practice multiplying with 6, 7, and 8 as factors.

$8 \times 6 = \bigcirc$

Different Ways to Multiply	
Way 1 **Use doubling.**	**Way 1** **Use a fact you know.**
8 is double 4, so 8 × 6 is double 4 × 6. $4 \times 6 = 24$ $8 \times 6 = 24 + 24$ $24 + 24 = 48$, so $8 \times 6 = 48$	$8 \times 5 = 40$ $\underline{+\ 8}$ $8 \times 6 = 48$ 8 × 5 plus one more 8 makes 8 × 6, or 48

Other Strategies
• Use repeated addition.
• Use skip counting.
• Make equal groups.
• Use a multiplication table.

Ask Yourself
• Have I memorized this fact?
• Can I use a strategy to find the fact?

▶ Guided Practice

Find the product.

1. 7×5 **2.** 9×7 **3.** 4×6 **4.** 5×8

5. 4×7 **6.** 8×6 **7.** 7×8 **8.** 6×7

 Math Talk How are the multiplication facts for 6 related to the facts for 3?

Find the product.

9. 4×8 **10.** 7×7 **11.** 8×9 **12.** 6×9

13. 8×8 **14.** 7×4 **15.** 7×8 **16.** 7×9

 Algebra Properties **Find the missing factor.**
Tell which property you used.

17. $8 \times \boxed{} = 4 \times 8$ **18.** $1 \times \boxed{} = 6$ **19.** $\boxed{} \times 7 = 0$

20. $9 \times 8 = \boxed{} \times 9$ **21.** $8 \times \boxed{} = 0$ **22.** $3 \times \boxed{} = 7 \times 3$

 Real World Data

Use the pictograph for Problems 23–25.

23. How many students have visited Los Angeles?

24. Multistep How many more students have visited Los Angeles than San Diego?

25. Challenge Write an inequality that shows that the number of students who visited San Francisco is less than the number of students who visited Sacramento.
$8 \times 4 \bigoplus 8 \times \boxed{}$

Cities Visited

San Francisco	🚗 🚗 🚗 🚗
San Diego	🚗
Sacramento	🚗 🚗 🚗 🚗 🚗

Los Angeles 🚗 🚗 🚗

Each 🚗 stands for 8 students

✔ **Spiral Review and Test Practice**

Multiply. KEY **NS 2.2** pages 106, 110

26. 2×8 **27.** 5×5 **28.** 10×6 **29.** 4×9

Write the letter of the correct answer. NS 2.0

30. Ants have 6 legs. There are 8 ants on the table. How many legs is this in all?

   A 14   **B** 48   **C** 42   **D** 56

Multiplication Facts Practice

Be sure you have memorized your facts. Then find each product as quickly as you can. KEY **NS 2.2**

1. 3
×1

2. 4
×2

3. 6
×3

4. 9
×8

5. 3
×3

6. 4
×5

7. 7
×7

8. 5
×7

9. 6
×7

10. 6
×4

11. 4
×9

12. 6
×8

13. 6
×10

14. 8
×8

15. 3
×7

16. 6
×6

17. 8
×4

18. 0
×6

19. 5
×8

20. 6
×9

21. 10
×9

22. 3
×8

23. 9
×9

24. 7
×8

25. 8
×10

26. 9
×6

27. 9
×0

28. 7
×5

29. 5
×6

30. 1
×1

31. 8 × 9

32. 2 × 1

33. 6 × 7

34. 3 × 3

35. 1 × 10

36. 3 × 10

37. 5 × 4

38. 5 × 5

39. 8 × 7

40. 6 × 8

41. 7 × 7

42. 7 × 5

43. 9 × 6

44. 7 × 0

45. 3 × 9

46. 10 × 4

47. 6 × 6

48. 9 × 8

49. 2 × 4

50. 9 × 9

Copy and complete each table. AF 2.2

51.

number of weeks	1	2	3	4	5	6	7	8	9	10
number of days	7	14								

52.

number of baseball games	1	2	3	4	5	6	7	8	9	10
number of innings		9	18							

To answer the riddle, match the letter with the product in the code below. KEY **NS 2.2**

Riddle 1: What clothing does a house wear?

Multiply.

1. $9 \times 4 = A$

2. $5 \times 6 = D$

3. $7 \times 8 = N$

4. $6 \times 3 = S$

5. $6 \times 6 = A$

6. $7 \times 3 = R$

7. $8 \times 5 = E$

8. $2 \times 9 = S$

9. $3 \times 10 = D$

36 56 36 30 30 21 40 18 18

A N A D D R E S S

Riddle 2: Why can't you feed teddy bears?

Multiply.

10. $3 \times 4 = A$

11. $2 \times 5 = H$

12. $5 \times 4 = E$

13. $8 \times 3 = D$

14. $7 \times 9 = L$

15. $1 \times 8 = F$

16. $6 \times 2 = A$

17. $4 \times 4 = T$

18. $10 \times 2 = E$

19. $2 \times 3 = R$

20. $6 \times 4 = D$

21. $3 \times 3 = Y$

22. $6 \times 7 = S$

23. $2 \times 6 = A$

24. $8 \times 2 = T$

25. $2 \times 10 = E$

26. $5 \times 5 = U$

27. $6 \times 1 = R$

28. $2 \times 4 = F$

29. $5 \times 4 = E$

30. $1 \times 9 = Y$

16 10 20 9   12 6 20

12 63 6 20 12 24 9   42 16 25 8 8 20 24

CA Standards
AF 1.5 Recognize and use the commutative and associative properties of multiplication (e.g., if 5 × 7 = 35, then what is 7 × 5? And if 5 × 7 × 3 = 105, then what is 7 × 3 × 5?).

Also NS 2.0, NS 2.6, NS 2.8, AF 1.0, AF 1.2, MR 1.2, MR 2.0, MR 2.3, MR 2.4, MR 3.0, MR 3.2, MR 3.3

Vocabulary

Associative Property of Multiplication

Use the Associative Property

Objective Use the Associative Property for multiplication.

▶ Learn by Example

Mr. Ramsey's class went to a sushi restaurant. There were 2 trays on each table and 5 pieces of sushi on each tray. There were 4 tables in all. How many pieces of sushi did they have in all?

$$5 \times 2 \times 4 = \bigcirc$$

- 5 → pieces of sushi
- 2 → number of trays
- 4 → number of tables

Associative Property of Multiplication

The way factors are grouped does not change the product.

You can multiply 5 × 2 first.

$$(5 \times 2) \times 4 = \bigcirc$$
$$10 \times 4 = 40$$

You can multiply 2 × 4 first.

$$5 \times (2 \times 4) = \bigcirc$$
$$5 \times 8 = 40$$

The parentheses ( ) tell you which factors to multiply first.

Solution: Mr. Ramsey's class had 40 pieces of sushi in all.

Ask Yourself
Which two numbers will I multiply first?

▶ Guided Practice

Find the product. Multiply factors in parentheses first.

1. 6 × (1 × 7) = ▮
   (6 × 1) × 7 = ▮

2. 3 × (2 × 2) = ▮
   (3 × 2) × 2 = ▮

Use parentheses. Find the product in two different ways.

3. 3 × 2 × 4 = ▮   **4.** 2 × 5 × 2 = ▮   **5.** 9 × 0 × 9 = ▮

Guided Problem Solving

Use the questions to solve this problem.

6. Five students each make 2 posters about their city's recycling program. Each poster has 3 graphs. How many graphs are there in all?

   a. **Understand** What is the question?

   b. **Plan** Why would you multiply to find the answer?

   c. **Solve** Complete the number sentence.

   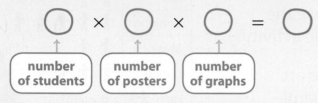

   ◯ × ◯ × ◯ = ◯

   number of students   number of posters   number of graphs

   d. **Look Back** How can a picture help check?

7. Look back at Problem 6. What if there were 3 students who each made 2 posters and each poster had 5 graphs. Would there be the same number of graphs in all? Explain.

123 Math Talk In which order would you multiply 3 × 2 × 6? Explain why.

▶ Practice and Problem Solving

Find the product. Multiply factors in parentheses first.

8. (3 × 1) × 2 = ▮
   3 × (1 × 2) = ▮

9. 4 × (9 × 0) = ▮
   (4 × 9) × 0 = ▮

10. 3 × (3 × 2) = ▮
    (3 × 3) × 2 = ▮

Use parentheses. Find the product in two different ways.

11. 4 × 2 × 1 = ▮

12. 4 × 2 × 3 = ▮

13. 7 × 0 × 6 = ▮

14. 1 × 1 × 1 = ▮

15. 3 × 3 × 2 = ▮

16. 2 × 2 × 4 = ▮

Solve.

17. If $3 \times 9 \times 4 = 108$, then what is $9 \times 4 \times 3$?

18. If $4 \times 7 \times 8 = 224$, then what is $8 \times 4 \times 7$?

 Algebra Properties **Use the Associative Property to find each missing factor.**

19. $1 \times (2 \times \blacksquare) = 10$

20. $(\blacksquare \times 2) \times 6 = 48$

Real World Data

Use the pictograph for Problems 21–23.

21. How many more students chose the cooking activity than the music activity?

22. Multistep Each student in the art group used 2 packages of origami paper. Each package had 7 sheets of paper. How many sheets of paper did the group use in all?

23. Each student signed up for only 1 activity. How many students signed up in all? Explain how you know.

After School Program Activity Sign-up

Art	🚶🚶
Cooking	🚶🚶🚶🚶
Music	🚶🚶
Dance	🚶🚶

Each 🚶 = 2 students.

Spiral Review and Test Practice

How many are in the array? KEY **NS 2.2** page 102

24. ▪▪
▪▪

25. ▪▪▪▪▪▪▪
▪▪▪▪▪▪▪

26. ◆◆◆◆◆
◆◆◆◆◆

Write the letter of the correct answer. AF 1.5

27. If $7 \times 10 \times 8 = 560$, then what is $10 \times 7 \times 8$?

A 25 **B** 78 **C** 560 **D** 780

  **Extra Practice** See page 159, Set C.

Ride Safely!

Lola's older sister works at an amusement park. Her job is to make sure that the ride she is running is safe. If too many people get on a ride, it will not be safe.

Complete the table to find out how many people Lola's sister can let onto the ride at one time.

1.

Balloon Ride					
number of balloons	2	4		7	8
number of riders	10		25		40

2.

Blast Off					
number of rockets	1		5	8	9
number of riders	4	8		32	

3.

Ferris Wheel					
number of cars	1		5		9
number of riders	3	9		21	27

4.

Safari Boats					
number of boats		2	5	8	12
number of riders	6	12		48	

5. Invent your own amusement park ride. Make a table showing the number of people that could ride safely on 1, 3, 5, 7, and 9 cars of your ride.

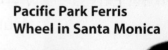

Pacific Park Ferris Wheel in Santa Monica

CA Standards
AF 2.2

CA Standards

MR 2.0 Students use strategies, skills, and concepts in finding solutions.

NS 2.0 Students calculate and solve problems involving addition, subtraction, multiplication, and division.

Also KEY NS 2.1, KEY NS 2.2, NS 2.8, MR 1.1, MR 1.2, MR 2.3, MR 2.4, MR 3.0, MR 3.1, MR 3.2, MR 3.3

Problem Solving Strategy
Guess and Check

Objective Use the guess and check strategy to solve problems.

▶ **Learn by Example**

Lin and Farha took a trip to Chinatown. Lin took 6 times the number of photos that Farha did. If they took a total of 28 photos, how many photos did they each take?

UNDERSTAND

You need to find the number of photos each girl took.

The girls took 28 photos. Lin took 6 times as many photos as Farha did.

PLAN

You can guess and check to find the answer.

Guess the number of pictures Farha took. If your guess does not work, use it to make a better guess.

SOLVE

1st Guess: 6	2nd Guess: 3
Multiply: $6 \times 6 = 36$	Multiply: $3 \times 6 = 18$
Check: $6 + 36 = 42$	Check: $3 + 18 = 21$
$\qquad 42 > 28$	$\qquad 21 < 28$
Guess again.	Guess again.
Use a smaller number.	Use a larger number.

3rd Guess: 4

Multiply: $4 \times 6 = 24$

Check: $4 + 24 = 28$

This guess is correct. Farha took 4 pictures and Lin took 24 pictures.

LOOK BACK

Check: 24 is 6 times the number of pictures Farha took.
$\qquad 4 + 24 = 28$, the total number of pictures taken.

Guided Problem Solving

Solve using the Ask Yourself questions.

1. Mato went to a butterfly festival at the San Diego Zoo. He saw these pictures of the butterfly and the moth with the greatest wingspans. The total length of their wingspans is 58 centimeters. The moth's wingspan is 2 centimeters longer than the butterfly's wingspan. What is the wingspan of each?

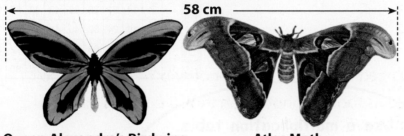
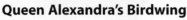

58 cm

Queen Alexandra's Birdwing   **Atlas Moth**

Math Talk
How can you use your first guess to make a better second guess?

Independent Problem Solving

Solve. Explain why your answer makes sense.

2. Emily and Jacob found 18 books about the Capitol Building in Sacramento. Emily found 4 more books than Jacob. How many books did they each find?

3. **Multistep** Leo saw 8 times more snails than starfish at the aquarium. He saw 10 more sea horses than starfish. Leo saw 70 animals. How many of each did he see?

4. Lydia and Dipak walked a total of 50 blocks. Lydia walked 9 times as many blocks. How many blocks did they each walk?

5. One bike trail is 7 times longer than another trail. Their combined length is 24 miles. What is the length of each trail?

6. **Challenge** The total of two numbers is 572. The expression 8×6 represents the difference between the two numbers. What are the two numbers?

7. **Create and Solve** Write a problem that can be solved using the guess and check method.

Reading & Writing Math

Vocabulary

You have learned many multiplication fact strategies. Solve this problem in 3 ways.

Sam has six model racers. Each racer has four wheels. How many wheels are there altogether?

×	0	1	2	3	4	5	6	7	8	9	10
0	0	0	0	0	0	0	0	0	0	0	0
1	0	1	2	3	4	5	6	7	8	9	10
2	0	2	4	6	8	10	12	14	16	18	20
3	0	3	6	9	12	15	18	21	24	27	30
4	0	4	8	12	16	20	24	28	32	36	40
5	0	5	10	15	20	25	30	35	40	45	50
6	0	6	12	18	24	30	36	42	48	54	60
7	0	7	14	21	28	35	42	49	56	63	70
8	0	8	16	24	32	40	48	56	64	72	80
9	0	9	18	27	36	45	54	63	72	81	90
10	0	10	20	30	40	50	60	70	80	90	100

1. **Use a multiplication table.**
   Find the row for 6.
   Find the column for 4.
   The row and the column meet at the number ____.

Different Ways to Multiply 6 × 4

2. **Use doubling.**
   6 is double 3
   3 × 4 = 12
   So 6 × 4 is double 12, or _____.

3. **Use a fact you know.**
   5 × 4 = 20
   1 × 4 = 4
   6 × 4 = 20 + 4 = ___.

Writing Write a word problem for this multiplication sentence: 8 × 7. Then explain how to solve it using the three different strategies.

Reading Look for this book in your library.

• *Henry and the Boy Who Thought Numbers Were Fleas*, by Marjorie Kaplan

CA Standards

MR 2.3 Use a variety of methods, such as words, numbers, symbols, charts, graphs, tables, diagrams, and models, to explain mathematical reasoning.

Also NS 2.0, KEY NS 2.2

Standards-Based Extra Practice

Set A
KEY NS 2.2 page144

Multiply.

1. 6×7 **2.** 8×6 **3.** 8×7 **4.** 6×8

5. 7×7 **6.** 7×8 **7.** 7×6 **8.** 8×8

9. Andrew and his dad go fishing every year for 8 days. If Andrew catches 3 fish each day of the trip, how many fish does he catch in all?

Set B
KEY NS 2.2 page 148

Find the product.

1. 6×8 **2.** 9×7 **3.** 7×8 **4.** 6×9

5. 7×6 **6.** 4×7 **7.** 8×3 **8.** 6×2

9. Samantha reads one whole shelf of books a month from her grandfather's library. If there are 9 books on a shelf, how many books will she read in 6 months?

Set C
AF 1.5 page 152

Find the product. Multiply the factors in parentheses first.

1. $(2 \times 1) \times 9 =$ ▨
$2 \times (1 \times 9) =$ ▨

2. $5 \times (3 \times 1) =$ ▨
$(5 \times 3) \times 1 =$ ▨

3. $4 \times (2 \times 2) =$ ▨
$(4 \times 2) \times 2 =$ ▨

4. $5 \times (2 \times 0) =$ ▨
$(5 \times 2) \times 0 =$ ▨

5. $3 \times (2 \times 3) =$ ▨
$(3 \times 2) \times 3 =$ ▨

6. $1 \times (4 \times 1) =$ ▨
$(1 \times 4) \times 1 =$ ▨

Use parentheses. Find the product in two different ways.

7. $2 \times 5 \times 2 =$ ▨   **8.** $8 \times 2 \times 1 =$ ▨   **9.** $3 \times 4 \times 5 =$ ▨

10. $6 \times 3 \times 2 =$ ▨   **11.** $5 \times 0 \times 8 =$ ▨   **12.** $7 \times 1 \times 4 =$ ▨

13. Three students eat 2 slices of pizza each. Each slice has 5 mushrooms. How many mushrooms were eaten in all?

Education Place
Visit www.eduplace.com/camap/
for more **Extra Practice**.

Chapter Review/Test

Vocabulary and Concepts ———————————— KEY NS 2.2, AF 1.5, MR 1.1

Choose the best term to complete each sentence.

> **Word Bank**
> **multiplication**
> **factors**
> **Associative Property of Multiplication**

1. The _____ of 10 are 5 and 2.

2. We know that $(2 \times 4) \times 1 = 2 \times (4 \times 1)$ because of the _____.

3. You use _____ to find the product of two numbers.

Skills ———————————————————— KEY NS 2.2, NS 2.0, AF 1.5

Multiply.

4. 8×6 5. 7×6 6. 8×7 7. 6×8 8. 7×7

Find the product. Multiply factors in parentheses first.

9. $4 \times (4 \times 2) = \blacksquare$
   $(4 \times 4) \times 2 = \blacksquare$

10. $(8 \times 1) \times 6 = \blacksquare$
    $8 \times (1 \times 6) = \blacksquare$

11. $3 \times (7 \times 2) = \blacksquare$
    $(3 \times 7) \times 2 = \blacksquare$

Use parentheses. Find the product in two different ways.

12. $8 \times 1 \times 2$ 13. $2 \times 9 \times 3$ 14. $5 \times 3 \times 5$ 15. $7 \times 2 \times 3$ 16. $6 \times 2 \times 2$

Problem Solving and Reasoning ——————— NS 2.0, MR 1.2, MR 2.3, MR 3.1

Solve. Show how to check your answer.

17. Javier has 3 goldfish bowls. He puts 9 fish in each bowl. How many fish does he have?

18. Phillip has 6 bananas, 4 oranges, and 2 apples. How many pieces of fruit does he have?

19. Marissa tried on 4 pairs of shoes in each of 6 stores. How many pairs of shoes did she try on in all?

20. Raquel practiced singing 6 days a week for 7 weeks. How many days did she practice?

Writing Math How did you decide which operation to use for Exercise 18?

Spiral Review and Test Practice

1. Which set of numbers is in order from least to greatest?

> **Test Tip**
> How many digits are in the first number in the set?

A 4786, 786, 8678, 874

B 8678, 4786, 874, 786

C 786, 874, 4786, 8678

D 786, 874, 8678, 4786

NS 1.2 page 28

2. Mei collected cans to recycle. She collected 310 cans one week, 76 cans the next week, and 216 cans the third week. How many cans did Mei collect?

A 386   **C** 526

B 592   **D** 602

KEY NS 2.1 page 56

3. 681 − 457 =

A 1,138   **C** 224

B 234   **D** 134

KEY NS 2.1 page 74

4. Jeff is sorting his rock collection. He puts 9 rocks in each of 4 display boxes. How many rocks is Jeff displaying?

A 5

B 13

C 32

D 36

> **Test Tip**
> Drawing an array may help you solve a problem.

KEY NS 2.2 page 110

5. What number can be multiplied by 6351 to give the answer 6351?

A 0

B 1

C 10

D 100

NS 2.6 page 122

6. Mr. Wilson set up tables in a restaurant. He puts 8 chairs at each of 7 tables. How many chairs is this in all?

A 56   **C** 42

B 15   **D** 1

KEY NS 2.2 page 144

Education Place
Visit www.eduplace.com/camap/ for
Test-Taking Tips and **Extra Practice**.

Chapter 7 Spiral Review and Test Practice   **161**

Unit 3 Review/Test

Vocabulary and Concepts ———————— MR 2.3 Chapters 5–7

Choose the best term to complete each sentence.

1. The product of a whole number multiplied by itself is a _____.

2. We know that $(3 \times 2) \times 2 = 3 \times (2 \times 2)$ because of the _____.

3. The _____ says that changing the order of the factors does not change the product.

> **Word Bank**
> **Commutative Property**
> **factor**
> **Associative Property**
> **square number**

Skills ———————— KEY NS 2.2, NS 2.6, AF 1.2, AF 1.5 Chapter 5, Lesson 2

Find the missing number.

4. $12 = 6 \times 2$
$\blacksquare = 2 \times 6$

5. $10 \times 3 = 30$
$3 \times \blacksquare = 30$

6. $\blacksquare \times 8 = 32$
$8 \times 4 = 32$

Find the product. Chapters 5–7

7. $\begin{array}{r} 2 \\ \times\,6 \\ \hline \end{array}$

8. $\begin{array}{r} 5 \\ \times\,9 \\ \hline \end{array}$

9. $\begin{array}{r} 10 \\ \times\,4 \\ \hline \end{array}$

10. $\begin{array}{r} 4 \\ \times\,3 \\ \hline \end{array}$

11. 9×2

12. 8×3

13. 6×5

14. 7×8

Draw an array to find the product of the square number.
Use grid paper. Chapter 6, Lesson 3

15. 9×9

16. 7×7

17. 2×2

Find the missing factor. Tell which property you used. Chapter 6, Lesson 1

18. $8 \times \blacksquare = 0$

19. $\blacksquare \times 6 = 6$

20. $3 \times 4 = \blacksquare \times 3$

Find the product. Multiply factors in parentheses first. Chapter 7, Lesson 4

21. $5 \times (3 \times 1) = \blacksquare$
$(5 \times 3) \times 1 = \blacksquare$

22. $6 \times (4 \times 2) = \blacksquare$
$(6 \times 4) \times 2 = \blacksquare$

23. $9 \times (2 \times 4) = \blacksquare$
$(9 \times 2) \times 4 = \blacksquare$

Problem Solving and Reasoning

Solve.

24. Joe had 24 roses. He gave an equal number to his mother, aunt, and cousin. How many roses did he give to each person?

25. Beth has 8 red beads and 6 white beads. She has 4 times as many blue beads as red beads. How many beads does Beth have?

Writing Math How does knowing the Commutative and Associative Properties make multiplication easier?

Performance Assessment

Party Planning

KEY **NS 2.2**, NS 2.8, MR 1.2

Marisa and her mom are planning to make 12 party bags.

PARTY BAGS	High-Bounce Balls	Bubbles	MINI YO-YO's	FUNNY GLASSES	Crazy Straws
6 for $1	4 for $3	4 for $1	6 for $4	3 for $2	6 for $2

Task	Information You Need
Use the prices above and the information to the right. List the 3 toys you think they should buy. Find the total cost of the 12 filled party bags, including the cost of the bags. Explain your thinking.	They want to put 3 toys in each bag.
	They would like each of the 12 party bags to be exactly alike.
	They want the total cost of the 12 party bags (including the bags) to be under $25.

Multiply by 6

A group of 6 is quick to see, if you think in groups of 3!

Multiplication is just repeated addition—see how! Look at Problem 1. Because it's just 6 groups of 4, add 3 groups of 4 to another 3 groups of 4 and get 12 + 12 = 24.

1. $6 \times 4 = \boxed{12} + \boxed{12} = \boxed{24}$
  3×4 3×4

2. $6 \times 6 = \boxed{18} + \boxed{} = \boxed{}$
  3×6 3×6

3. $6 \times 5 = \boxed{} + \boxed{} = \boxed{}$
  3×5 3×5

4. $6 \times 9 = \boxed{} + \boxed{} = \boxed{}$
  3×9 3×9

You are doing fine!

5. $6 \times 3 = \boxed{} + \boxed{} = \boxed{}$
  3×3 3×3

6. $6 \times 8 = \boxed{} + \boxed{} = \boxed{}$
  3×8 3×8

7. $6 \times 10 = \boxed{} + \boxed{} = \boxed{}$
  3×10 3×10

8. $6 \times 7 = \boxed{} + \boxed{} = \boxed{}$
  3×7 3×7

Take It Further!
Now try doing all the steps in your head!

9. 6×2

10. 6×11

11. 6×12

12. 6×20

Good For You!

Geometry and Measurement

BIG IDEAS!

- There are different units to measure length.
- You can tell one type of polygon from another by counting the sides and angles.
- Perimeter is the sum of the lengths of the sides of a shape and area is the number of square units that cover a shape.
- Volume is the number of unit cubes that make up a solid figure.

Chapter 8
Length

Chapter 9
Shapes and Angles

Chapter 10
Perimeter and Area

Chapter 11
Solids and Volume

Songs and Games

 Math Music Track 4: *Polygons*

eGames at
www.eduplace.com/camap/

Math Readers

The desert tortoise, the subject of this sign, lives in the Mojave and Sonoran deserts of southern California.

Measurement Hunt

Object of the Game Make estimates about the length of an object.

Materials
- 20 paper clips (per team)

Number of Players
2 teams of 2 players

How to Play

1 Each team makes a game sheet like the one shown below.

Then each team finds 5 objects to measure that they think match the target lengths given on the game sheets.

Target Length	Object	Actual Length
2 paper clips		
5 paper clips		
10 paper clips		
15 paper clips		
20 paper clips		

2 Teams measure the objects they found and record the actual lengths on the game sheets. If the actual length of an object does not match the target length given, the team must find another object.

The first team to find 5 objects that match the target lengths, wins.

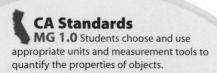

CA Standards
MG 1.0 Students choose and use appropriate units and measurement tools to quantify the properties of objects.

Education Place
Visit www.eduplace.com/camap/ for **Brain Teasers** and **eGames** to play.

Reading In reading, thinking about what you already know helps you to understand a new topic. You already know a lot about math. You can use what you know to move ahead.

Before beginning a lesson on plane figures, Ricky lists five things he already knows.

Topic: Plane Figures

What do I already know?

1. Plane figures are flat shapes.
2. A circle is a flat shape.
3. A circle is round.
4. Triangles are flat shapes with 3 sides and 3 vertices.
5. The number of sides and vertices can help you name shapes.

> I remember making shapes with pattern blocks.

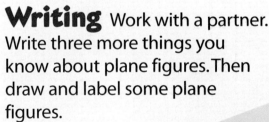

Writing Work with a partner. Write three more things you know about plane figures. Then draw and label some plane figures.

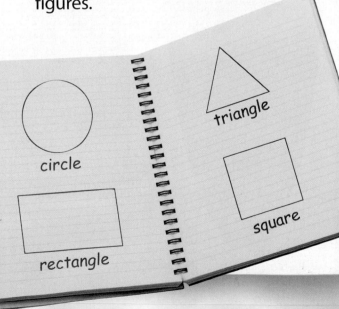

circle

triangle

rectangle

square

Length

Surfing is a popular sport at many locations along the California coast.

Vocabulary and Concepts GRADE 2 MG 1.0
Choose the best word to complete each sentence.

1. An _____ is a customary unit of measure.

2. To find the width of an object you would _____ it.

3. A _____ is a metric unit of measure.

Skills GRADE 2 MG 1.0
Which object is longer?

4. a sock or a scarf
5. a road or a hallway
6. a horse or a cat

Which object is shorter?

7. a chair or a door
8. a tree or a flower
9. a table or a man

Problem Solving and Reasoning KEY NS 2.2

10. In a set of 6 colored pencils, each pencil is 9 centimeters long. If you place the pencils end-to-end in a row, how long will the row be?

Vocabulary

Visualize It!

centimeter

2 cm

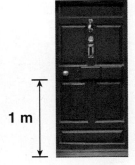

1 m

meter

1 meter = 100 centimeters

kilometer

Language Tips

You can use the prefix of words to help you understand their meanings. For example *cent* or *centi* refers to one hundred and *kil* or *kilo* refers to one thousand.

Some words are similar in Spanish and English.

English	Spanish
meter	metro
centimeter	centímetro
kilometer	kilómetro

See **English-Spanish Glossary** pages 628–646.

Education Place Visit www.eduplace.com/camap/ for the **eGlossary** and **eGames**.

CA Standards MR 2.3 Use a variety of methods, such as words, numbers, symbols, charts, graphs, tables, diagrams, and models, to explain mathematical reasoning. **Also MG 1.1**

Chapter 8 169

CA Standards

MG 1.1 Choose the appropriate tools and units (metric and U.S.) and estimate and measure the length, liquid volume, and weight/mass of given objects.

Also MG 1.0, MR 2.3, MR 2.5

Vocabulary

estimate

inch (in.)

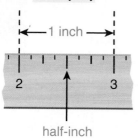

half-inch mark

Materials
• Inch ruler
• Pencil
• Classroom objects

Hands On
Measure to the Nearest Inch

Objective Estimate and measure length to the nearest inch.

▶ **Explore**

In this lesson you will **estimate** and measure length in inches. An **inch (in.)** is a standard unit used to measure length in the customary measurement system.

Question How can you estimate and measure the length of everyday objects in inches?

1 Look at your pencil. Estimate the length in inches.

1 inch

2 Line up one end of your pencil with the left end of your ruler.

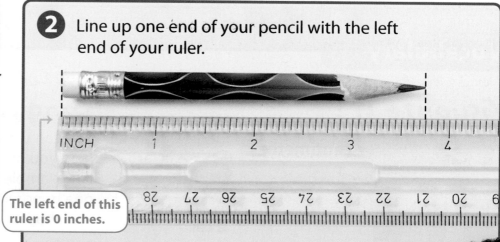

The left end of this ruler is 0 inches.

3 Find the inch mark that is closest to the other end of your pencil.

What is the length of your pencil to the nearest inch? Is this measurement exact? Explain.

What is the length of the pencil in the picture? Is this measurement exact? Explain.

 **Extend**

Estimate and measure.

1. Find 5 classroom objects to measure. Estimate and measure the length of each object to the nearest inch. Record your work in a table like the one below.

Object	My Estimate	Length to the Nearest Inch

Measure each object below to the nearest inch.

2.

3.

Use a ruler. Draw a line of each length.

4. 3 inches

5. 10 inches

6. 6 inches

7. **Estimate** Name three objects that are about 1 inch long or wide.

8. **Challenge** Find objects in the classroom that are about 6 inches long. Measure the objects to check your estimates.

 Writing Math

What's Wrong? Mary said the pencil below is about 4 inches long. What did she do wrong when she measured?

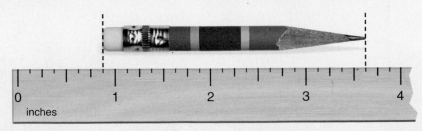

Vocabulary

foot (ft)

yard (yd)

mile (mi)

Convert Customary Units of Length

Objective Choose the appropriate unit to estimate and measure objects. Convert between units.

▶ **Learn by Example**

In Lesson 1, you learned how to measure an object to the nearest inch. To measure longer lengths, you can use units such as **foot (ft)**, **yard (yd)**, and **mile (mi)**.

Question How can you decide which unit to use to measure an object?

Choose a unit to measure the length of the Golden Gate Bridge.

Customary Units of Length
1 foot = 12 inches
1 yard = 3 feet
1 yard = 36 inches
1 mile = 1,760 yards
1 mile = 5,280 feet

Hint

Using a larger unit gives you a number that is smaller and easier to work with.

The Golden Gate Bridge connects San Francisco and Sausalito.

The length of the Golden Gate Bridge is:

• 107,772 inches

• 8,981 feet

• about 3,000 yards

• about 2 miles

Solution: Measure the Golden Gate Bridge in mile units because the bridge is long.

Guided Practice

**Choose the unit you would use to measure each.
Choose *inches*, *feet*, *yards*, or *miles*.**

> **Ask Yourself**
>
> Do I need to use a small, medium, or large unit of measure?

1. distance from your home to an airport

2. length of a soccer field

Choose the better estimate.

3. width of your desk

   a. 3 miles   **b.** 3 feet

4. length of a classroom

   a. 10 yards   **b.** 10 inches

Find a pattern. Then copy and complete the table.

5.

Feet	1	2	3	4	5
Inches	12	24			

6.

Yards	1	2	3	4	5
Feet	3	6			

 Math Talk Why would a person use miles instead of feet to measure the distance from Los Angeles to New York City?

Practice and Problem Solving

**Choose the unit you would use to measure each.
Write *inches*, *feet*, *yards*, or *miles*.**

7. the width of your bed

8. the distance from your school to a hospital

Choose the better estimate.

9. the height of a mountain
   a. 5,000 inches   **b.** 5,000 feet

10. the width of a door
   a. 30 inches   **b.** 30 yards

11. the height of a tall building
   a. 50 feet   **b.** 50 inches

12. the length of a dollar bill
   a. 6 inches   **b.** 6 yards

13. the length of a car
   a. 8 feet   **b.** 8 yards

14. the height of your chair
   a. 2 inches   **b.** 2 feet

Find a pattern. Then copy and complete the table.

15.

12 inches = 1 foot
 inches = 2 feet
36 inches =  feet

16.

3 feet = 1 yard
▢ feet = 2 yards
9 feet = ▢ yards
12 feet = ▢ yards

 Science Link

Solve.

17. One sunflower head has 1,750 flowers. Another sunflower head has 1,180 flowers. How many more flowers does the first sunflower have?

18. **Explain** Paul's sunflower plant is 4 feet tall. Paul is 48 inches tall. Is Paul taller than his plant?

19. **Challenge** Sunflower A is 8 feet tall. Sunflower B is 100 inches tall. Which sunflower is taller? Explain.

Spiral Review and Test Practice

Round each number to the greatest place. Then add or subtract. NS 2.0, NS 1.4 page 84

20. $312 + 287$ 21. $893 - 705$ 22. $4,561 + 480$ 23. $6,921 - 2,032$

Write the letter of the correct answer. MG 1.4

24. There are 36 inches in 1 yard. How many inches are in 3 yards?

    A 9 inches   **B** 72 inches   **C** 108 inches   **D** 144 inches

Extra Practice See page 185, Set A.

Key Standards Review

Need Help?
See Key Standards Handbook.

**Write the place of the underlined digit.
Then write its value.** KEY NS 1.3

1. 8<u>0</u>4   **2.** <u>5</u>19   **3.** <u>3</u>,357   **4.** 4,12<u>8</u>

Write the number.

5. 2 in the thousands place, 3 in the hundreds place, 4 in the tens place, 9 in the ones place

6. 7 in the thousands place, 6 in the tens place, 5 in the hundreds place, 0 in the ones place

7. 1 in the ones place, 4 in the tens place, 8 in the thousands place, 0 in the hundreds place

8. 0 in the tens place, 9 in the thousands place, 7 in the ones place, 0 in the hundreds place

Multiply. KEY NS 2.2

9. 7 × 9   **10.** 6 × 8   **11.** 6 × 7   **12.** 9 × 6   **13.** 1 × 5   **14.** 8 × 4

15. 4 × 9   **16.** 7 × 4   **17.** 6 × 9   **18.** 4 × 6   **19.** 8 × 9   **20.** 10 × 6

Challenge — Algebra

Make It True! KEY AF 1.1

Pick two different measurement units from the box to complete each number sentence.

in.
ft
yd

1. 1 ___ > 2 ___   **2.** 12 ___ = 1 ___   **3.** 2 ___ > 5 ___

4. 4 ___ < 2 ___   **5.** 3 ___ = 9 ___   **6.** 32 ___ < 3 ___

CA Standards
MG 1.1 Choose the appropriate tools and units (metric and U.S.) and estimate and measure the length, liquid volume, and weight/mass of given objects.

MR 2.5 Indicate the relative advantages of exact and approximate solutions to problems and give answers to a specified degree of accuracy.

Also MG 1.0, MR 2.3

Vocabulary

millimeter (mm)

centimeter (cm)

Materials
Centimeter ruler

Hands On
Centimeters and Millimeters

Objective Estimate and measure length in metric units.

▶ **Explore**

Millimeters (mm) and **centimeters (cm)** are metric units of length used to measure small objects.

Question How do you measure the lengths of small objects in centimeters and millimeters?

Metric Units of Length
1 cm = 10 mm

---

1 Estimate the length of the shell.

How many finger widths do you think it is? Check your estimate.

---

2 Now measure the length of the shell in centimeters. Line up one end of the shell with the zero mark on the ruler.

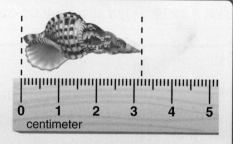

---

3 Find the centimeter mark closest to the other end of the shell. The shell is about 3 cm long.

Hint
Millimeters are smaller and allow the measurement to be more exact.

4 Look at the ruler again. The smaller marks in between the centimeter marks are called millimeters. Measure the length of the shell in millimeters. The shell is about 32 mm long.

▶ **Extend**

Estimate. Then measure to the nearest centimeter and the nearest millimeter.

1.

2.

3.

Choose the better estimate.

4. width of your thumb
   a. 1 cm   **b.** 1 mm

5. width of your foot
   a. 60 mm   **b.** 60 cm

6. length of your leg
   a. 50 mm   **b.** 50 cm

7. length of a dollar bill
   a. 15 cm   **b.** 15 mm

8. length of a key
   a. 6 cm   **b.** 60 cm

9. thickness of a penny
   a. 1 cm   **b.** 1 mm

Use a ruler. Draw a line of each length.

10. 3 cm

11. 12 mm

12. 6 cm

13. Estimate Name two objects that are about 1 cm long.

14. Challenge Find objects in the classroom that are about 5 cm long. Measure the objects to check your estimates.

Writing Math

Explain Is the length more exact if it is measured to the nearest millimeter or nearest centimeter? When might this be important?

CA Standards
MG 1.1 Choose the appropriate tools and units (metric and U.S.) and estimate and measure the length, liquid volume, and weight/mass of given objects.

MG 1.4 Carry out simple unit conversions within a system of measurement (e.g., centimeters and meters, hours and minutes).

Also AF 1.4, AF 2.0, KEY AF2.1, MG 1.0, MR 2.0, MR 2.3, MR 2.4, MR 3.1

Vocabulary

meter (m)

kilometer (km)

Convert Metric Units of Length

Objective Choose the appropriate unit and convert between units of metric length.

▶ Learn Through Reasoning

In Lesson 3, you learned about measuring to the nearest millimeter (mm) and centimeter (cm). You can measure longer lengths in **meters (m)** and **kilometers (km)**.

Metric Units of Length
1 centimeter = 10 millimeters
1 meter = 100 centimeters
1 kilometer = 1,000 meters

The door to Fran's house is about 1 meter wide.

Her house is about 1 kilometer from the beach. It takes Fran about 10 minutes to walk 1 kilometer to the beach.

▶ Guided Practice

Ask Yourself
- Do I need a small or large unit?
- Which is the smaller unit? the larger unit?

Choose the unit you would use to measure each. Write *mm*, *cm*, *m*, or *km*.

1. how far you can throw a ball

2. distance to the Moon

Choose the better estimate.

3. length of an airplane

   a. 70 m   **b.** 70 km

4. height of a horse

   a. 6 m   **b.** 2 m

5. length of a car

   a. 5 m   **b.** 2 km

6. distance from California to New York

   a. 4,000 m   **b.** 4,000 km

Guided Problem Solving

Use the questions to solve this problem.

7. Diana sailed a 3-kilometer race one week and a 2,500-meter race the next week. How many meters did Diana sail in all?

   a. **Understand** What do you know? What do you need to find out?

   b. **Plan** Can you add 3 kilometers and 2,500 meters? If not, what should you do?

   c. **Solve** 3 kilometers = ◯ meters.
      ◯ meters + 2,500 meters = ◯ meters.

   d. **Look Back** Does your answer make sense? Why or why not?

 Math Talk Would you measure the distance from your home to school in meters or kilometers? Explain.

Practice and Problem Solving

Choose the better estimate.

8. height of a person

   a. 2 m   **b.** 20 m

9. length of bridge

   a. 100 km   **b.** 1 km

 Algebra Functions **Find a pattern.
Then copy and complete the table.**

10.

Meters	1	2	3	4	5
Centimeters	100	200			

11.

Kilometers	1	2	3	4	5
Meters	1,000	2,000			

 Real World Data

Use the table to answer Problems 12–13.

12. Right or Wrong? Ming says he is 1 meter and 36 centimeters tall. Is he correct? Explain.

13. Challenge If all the students lie down head to toe in a line, will their length be more or less than 1 kilometer? Explain your thinking.

Name	Height
Cheryl	135 cm
Janelle	132 cm
Dominick	135 cm
Eduardo	133 cm
Ming	136 cm
Bridget	134 cm

Spiral Review and Test Practice

Find the product. KEY **NS 2.2** pages 144, 148

14. 6×5 **15.** 7×9 **16.** 8×7 **17.** 6×8

Write the letter of the correct answer. MG 1.4

18. There are 1000 meters in a kilometer. How many meters are in 3 kilometers?

   A 3 meters   **B** 30 meters   **C** 300 meters   **D** 3000 meters

Extra Practice See page 185, Set B.

The Cubit

Long before tape measures and rulers were invented, people needed a way to measure things. One of the earliest ways to measure was developed by the Egyptians around 3000 B.C. It was called a *cubit*. A *cubit* is the length from your elbow to the tip of your outstretched hand. Egyptians also used many smaller measurements. Spread your fingers out as far as possible. You have made a *large span*. The *large span* is the distance from the tip of your thumb to the tip of your little finger.

Using ancient Egyptian measuring tools, the *cubit* and the *large span*, solve Problems 1–5.

1. Measure your desk. How many cubits is it? How many large spans is it?

2. Measure your teacher's desk. How many cubits long is it? How many large spans is it?

3. Measure another object in the room. What did you measure? How many cubits was it? How many large spans long was it?

4. Look back at your answers to Problems 1–3. Do you notice anything about the number of large spans and the number of cubits?

5. Did all of your classmates get the same answers as you? Why or why not?

Pyramids at Giza

CA Standards
MG 1.0

LESSON **5**

Field Trip...

Santa
Barbara, CA

CA Standards
MR 1.0, MR 1.1,
MR 1.2, MR 2.0,
MR 2.3, MR 2.6,
NS 2.0, KEY **NS 2.1**,
NS 2.8, MG 1.1

Problem Solving

Objective Use skills and strategies to solve word problems.

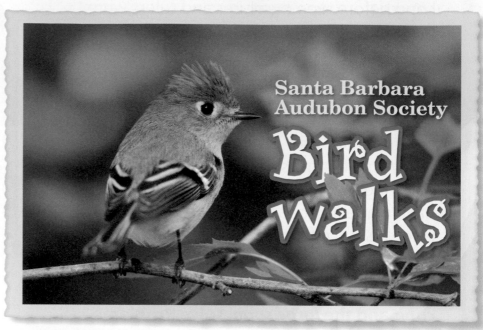

Santa Barbara
Audubon Society

Bird
walks

On a bird walk you can see birds in their natural habitats.

The Santa Barbara Audubon Society teaches people
about birds and their habitats.

Solve. Tell which strategy or method you used.

1. There are bird walks twice each month. If Ed went on
   every bird walk for 8 months, how many bird walks
   did he take? Explain why your answer makes sense.

2. What would be a reasonable estimate for the
   length of a bird walk trail?

   A 1 mile   **B** 1 yard   **C** 1 inch   **D** 1 foot

3. **Multistep** After walking along a creek for
   67 meters, Mark saw a wren. He walked
   469 more meters along the creek and saw a
   woodpecker. Then he turned to walk back to
   his starting point. On his way back, he saw a vulture
   230 meters from where he saw the woodpecker.
   How far is the vulture from his starting point?

Problem Solving On Tests

Select a Strategy
- Estimate
- Choose the Operation
- Draw a Picture

1. Which of the following objects is longer than 1 foot?

A

C

B

D

MG **1.1** page 172

2. Brett has this number card. Which digit is in the hundreds place?

6923

A 2 **B** 3 **C** 6 **D** 9

KEY **NS 1.3** page 14

3. In 2006, the population of Emeryville was 8537. What was the population to the nearest thousand?

A 9000

B 8540

C 8500

D 8000

Test Tip
Look at the place to the right of the rounding place. Is it <5, 5, or >5?

NS **1.4** page 34

4. The Nile River is 4160 miles long. The Mississippi River is 2340 miles long. How much longer is the Nile River than the Mississippi River?

A 1820 miles **C** 2820 miles

B 2220 miles **D** 6500 miles

KEY **NS 2.1** page 78

5. Kelly has a jar with 235 pennies in it. Which of these equals 235?

A 2 + 3 + 5

B 200 + 30 + 5

C 20 + 30 + 50

D 3 + 50 + 200

KEY **NS 1.5** page 8

6. There are 156 places in after-school activities. Twenty-eight students have signed up. How many places are left for other students?

A 28 **B** 128 **C** 138 **D** 184

KEY **NS 2.1** page 74

Education Place
Visit www.eduplace.com/camap/ for
Test-Taking Tips and **Extra Practice**.

Chapter 8 Lesson 5 **183**

Reading & Writing Math

Vocabulary

When you find how long or tall something is, you find its **length**. There are different ways to measure length.

You will need:

• inch ruler

• centimeter ruler

Inches and **centimeters** are units used to measure **length**.

Use an inch ruler to measure the length of each line.

1. _____

2. _____

3. _____

4. _____

Use a centimeter ruler to draw a line for each measurement.

5. 1 cm

6. 7 cm

7. 11 cm

8. 14 cm

Writing Make a list of things that are about 1 inch long. Then make a list of things that are about 1 cm long.

Reading Check out this book in your library.

• *Measuring Penny*, by Loreen Leedy

CA Standards
MR 2.3 Use a variety of methods, such as words, numbers, symbols, charts, graphs, tables, diagrams, and models, to explain mathematical reasoning.
Also MG 1.0, MG 1.1

Standards-Based Extra Practice

Set A ————————————————————— MG 1.1 page 172

Choose the unit you would use to measure each.
Write *inches*, *feet*, *yards*, or *miles*.

1. height of a television

2. width of your math book

3. distance across the ocean

4. length of a crayon

Choose the better estimate.

5. length of a car
   a. 10 feet   **b.** 10 inches

6. length of a football field
   a. 100 miles   **b.** 100 yards

7. height of an adult
   a. 6 feet   **b.** 6 miles

8. height of your door
   a. 7 inches   **b.** 7 feet

9. Matthew and Karen are drawing pictures of dogs. Matthew's picture is 13 inches wide. Karen's picture is 1 foot wide. Who's picture is wider? Explain.

Set B ————————————————————— MG 1.1 page 178

Choose the unit you would use to measure each.
Write *mm*, *cm*, *m*, or *km*.

1. width of your finger

2. depth of a swimming pool

3. width of a pencil

4. thickness of a penny

Choose the better estimate.

5. height of a mountain
   a. 4 m   **b.** 4 km

6. length of a piece of spaghetti
   a. 15 mm   **b.** 15 cm

7. width of a computer
   a. 30 cm   **b.** 30 km

8. height of a tree
   a. 10 m   **b.** 10 km

9. A soccer field is about 100 meters long. About how many soccer fields laid end-to-end would be 1 km long? Explain.

Education Place
Visit www.eduplace.com/camap/
for more **Extra Practice.**

Chapter Review/Test

Vocabulary and Concepts ——————————— MG 1.0, MG 1.1

Choose the best word to complete each sentence.

1. The distance from California to New York is measured in _____.

2. A more accurate _____ of length is made with smaller units of measurement.

> **Word Bank**
> estimate
> miles

Skills ——————————————————————— MG 1.0, MG 1.1

Choose the customary unit you would use to measure each.

3. height of a door   **4.** width of a coffee table   **5.** length of a fish tank

Choose the better estimate.

6. width of a frying pan   **7.** length of a boat   **8.** distance across a lake

   a. 12 feet   **b.** 12 inches   **a.** 20 feet   **b.** 20 miles   **a.** 4 yards   **b.** 4 miles

Choose the metric unit you would use to measure each.

9. height of an elephant   **10.** width of a maple leaf   **11.** length of a trail

Problem Solving and Reasoning —— MG 1.0, MG 1.1, MR 1.0, MR 2.1, MR 2.3, MR 3.1

Solve.

12. Sudan has a dollar bill and a paper clip in his pocket. Which one is approximately 1 inch long?

13. Susanne estimates that the tree in her backyard is 6 miles tall. Is this a reasonable estimate? Explain.

14. Ricky says his notebook is about 18 cm wide. Trina measured it and found that it was 182 mm wide. Whose answer is more accurate?

15. At a store, 1147 desks are each 1 meter long. Is the total length of all the desks more or less than one kilometer? Explain.

Writing Math Sarah said that 30 centimeters is about 3 millimeters. Do you agree? Why or why not?

Spiral Review and Test Practice

1. What is the value of the digit 5 in the number 5046?

   A 5000

   B 500

   C 50

   D 5

   KEY **NS 1.3** page 14

2. What is 2855 rounded to the nearest ten?

   A 2850

   B 2860

   C 2900

   D 3000

   NS 1.4 page 34

3. What number makes the number sentence true?

   $4 + \square = 5 + 8$

   A 17

   B 13

   C 9

   D 8

   Test Tip
   Remember, the sums on both sides should be equal.

   AF 1.2 page 52

4. Which number sentence is true?

   A $5 \times 8 = 3 \times 10$

   B $5 \times 8 = 4 \times 10$

   C $5 \times 8 = 5 \times 10$

   D $5 \times 8 = 6 \times 10$

   KEY **NS 2.2** page 106

5. There are 8 napkins in one set of napkins. If Janice buys 6 sets of napkins, how many napkins does she buy?

   A 14

   B 18

   C 42

   D 48

   KEY **NS 2.2** page 148

6. There are 36 inches in 1 yard. How many inches are in 4 yards?

   A 12

   B 32

   C 138

   D 144

   Test Tip
   Think: Will your answer be less than or greater than 36?

   MG 1.4 page 172

Education Place
Visit www.eduplace.com/camap/ for **Test-Taking Tips** and **Extra Practice.**

Shapes and Angles

This building is made from recycled shipping containers.

Vocabulary and Concepts GRADE 2 KEY MG 2.1

Choose the best word to complete each sentence. GRADE 2

1. A sail on a sailboat has 3 straight sides like a ____.

2. A penny looks like a ____.

Skill GRADE 2 KEY MG 2.1

Use the list below. Write the name of each figure. GRADE 2

circle   rectangle   triangle   square   pyramid

3.

4.

5.

Problem Solving and Reasoning GRADE 2 KEY MG 2.1

6. Allyson wants to draw a plane shape with 4 straight sides. Why wouldn't she draw a triangle?

Vocabulary

Visualize It!

polygons
- two-dimensional **figure**
- sides are line segments

Triangles: 3 sides

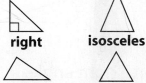

right   isosceles

scalene   equilateral

Quadrilaterals: 4 sides

parallelogram

square   rectangle

More than 4 sides:

pentagon   hexagon   octagon

Language Tip

Some words are similar in Spanish and English.

English	Spanish
polygon	polígono
quadrilateral	cuadrilátero
triangle	triángulo
hexagon	hexágono
pentagon	pentágono
figure	figura

See **English-Spanish Glossary** pages 628–646.

Education Place Visit www.eduplace.com/camap/ for the **eGlossary** and **eGames**.

CA Standards MR 2.3 Use a variety of methods, such as words, numbers, symbols, charts, graphs, tables, diagrams, and models, to explain mathematical reasoning. **Also KEY** MG 2.1

Chapter 9   189

CA Standards
MG 2.0 Students describe and compare the attributes of plane and solid geometric figures and use their understanding to show relationships and solve problems.

MG 2.4 Identify right angles in geometric figures or in appropriate objects and determine whether other angles are greater or less than a right angle.

Also MR 1.1, MR 2.3

Vocabulary

parallel line segments

right angle

Materials
2 toothpicks (blunt edges)

Hands On
Line Segments and Angles

Objective Identify parallel line segments and right angles.

 **Explore**

Question How can you model line segments and angles?

1 These appear to be **parallel line segments**. Parallel line segments are parts of parallel lines. Parallel lines will never meet.

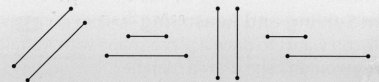

Use 2 toothpicks to show parallel line segments.

2 These appear to be **right angles**. A right angle has a square corner.

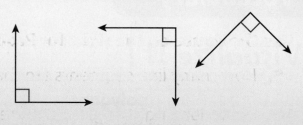

Now show a right angle.

3 These angles appear to be less than right angles.

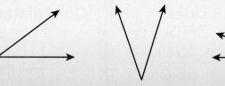

Now show an angle that is less than a right angle.

4 These angles appear to be greater than right angles.

Now show an angle that is greater than a right angle.

▶ **Extend**

Tell whether the pair of line segments appears to be
parallel or not parallel.

1.   2.  3. 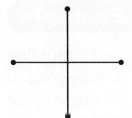 4.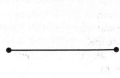

Tell whether the angle appears to be a right angle,
less than a right angle, or greater than a right angle.

5.  6.   7.  8.

Use the figure on the right for Problems 9–12.

9. How many line segments are there?

10. How many right angles do there appear to be?

11. How many angles greater than a right angle
do there appear to be?

12. How many angles less than a right angle do there
appear to be?

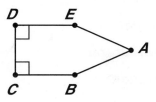

13. **Analyze** At what hours do the hands on a clock
form right angles?

Writing Math

Explain Mori says that parallel line segments can never
form a right angle. Do you agree or disagree? Explain your
thinking.

CA Standards
MG 2.0 Students describe and compare the attributes of plane and solid geometric figures and use their understanding to show relationships and solve problems.

KEY MG 2.1 Identify, describe, and classify polygons (including pentagons, hexagons, and octagons).

Also MR 1.0, MR 2.4, MR 3.0, MR 3.3

Vocabulary

- **plane figure**
- **circle**
- **polygon**
- **side**
- **vertex**
- **triangle**
- **quadrilateral**
- **pentagon**
- **hexagon**
- **octagon**

Plane Figures

Objective Identify, describe, and classify plane figures.

> ## Learn by Example

In Lesson 1, you learned about line segments and angles. **Polygons** are **plane figures** that are made up of line segments and angles.

Plane figures are flat figures. They can be closed or not closed. A **circle** is a closed plane figure.

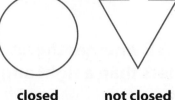

closed   **not closed**

Polygons

Polygons are closed plane figures that have three or more sides.

The name of a polygon tells the number of sides.

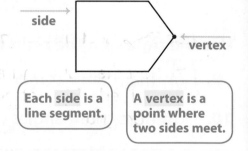

side   **vertex**

| Each side is a line segment. | A vertex is a point where two sides meet. |

Triangle
3 sides

Quadrilateral
4 sides

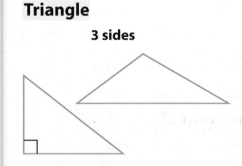

Pentagon
5 sides

Hexagon
6 sides

Octagon
8 sides

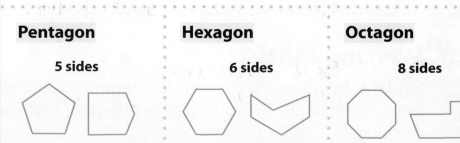

Tell whether the figure is a polygon. If it is, write its name.

Ask Yourself
• Is the figure closed?
• How many sides does the figure have?

1.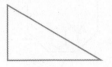

2.

3.

4.

5.

6.

Guided Problem Solving

Use the questions to solve this problem.

7. Sort the plane figures that are marked with a letter into two or more groups.

  a. Understand What are you asked to do?

  b. Plan How can you sort the figures?

  c. Solve Use your rule. Sort the figures.

  d. Look Back How can you check that you included all the figures?

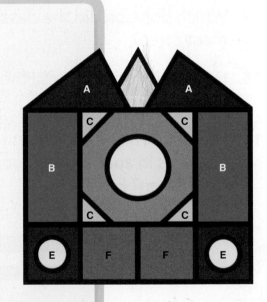

8. Look back at Problem 7. Sort the figures in another way.

123 Math Talk Is a circle a polygon? Explain why or why not.

Tell whether the figure is a polygon. If it is, write its name.

9.

10.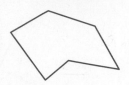

11.

12.

 Real World Data

Use the graph to solve Problems 13–16.

Ms. Diaz asked her class to record the kinds of polygons they found in their classroom. The graph at the right shows the results.

13. How many pentagons did the class find?

14. Which polygon did the class find most often?

15. How many polygons did the class find in all?

16. **Predict** Which shape might the students in another classroom find most often? Explain.

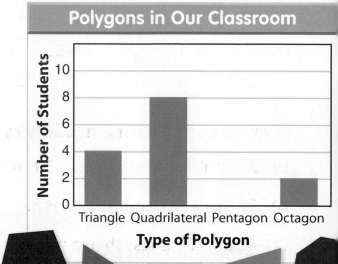

Spiral Review and Test Practice

Complete the number sentence using >, <, or =. AF 1.3 page 52

17. 22 + 39 ▇ 44 + 17   **18.** 25 + 16 ▇ 32 + 8   **19.** 43 + 24 ▇ 34 + 34

Write the letter of the correct answer. KEY MG 2.1

20. Which of these is a hexagon?

A   B   C   D

Extra Practice See page 207, Set A.

Key Standards Review

Need Help?
See Key Standards Handbook.

Multiply. KEY NS 2.2

1.	6 × 7	2.	1 × 8	3.	7 × 10	4.	7 × 9	5.	8 × 6	6.	9 × 6

7.	6 × 3	8.	3 × 7	9.	8 × 0	10.	3 × 6	11.	6 × 6	12.	7 × 4

13.	7 × 8	14.	9 × 4	15.	9 × 8	16.	5 × 4	17.	5 × 8	18.	8 × 7

Write an equation or inequality to show each relationship. KEY AF 1.1

19. A number times 2 equals 3 times 4.

20. 20 minus a number equals 8.

21. 42 plus 21 is less than a number plus 13.

Visual Thinking

Sign Shapes

Use the sign for Problems 1–4. MG 2.0

ROCK AND ROLL
HALL OF FAME

1. How many line segments are in the word "FAME"?

2. How many right angles are in the word "HALL"?

3. How many angles greater than a right angle are in the word "FAME"?

4. How many angles less than a right angle are in the word "HALL"?

CA Standards
KEY **MG 2.2** Identify attributes of triangles (e.g., two equal sides for the isosceles triangle, three equal sides for the equilateral triangle, right angle for the right triangle).

KEY **MG 2.3** Identify attributes of quadrilaterals (e.g., parallel sides for the parallelogram, right angles for the rectangle, equal sides and right angles for the square).

Also MG 2.0, MG 2.4, MR 1.1

Vocabulary

triangle

quadrilateral

Materials
- Learning Tools 13, 14 (Triangles and Quadrilaterals)
- Scissors
- Ruler

Hands On
Sort Triangles and Quadrilaterals

Objective Describe, sort, and classify triangles and quadrilaterals.

 **Explore**

In Lesson 2 you learned about different plane figures. In this lesson you will use attributes to sort triangles and quadrilaterals.

Question How can you sort triangles and quadrilaterals?

---

1 Cut out the triangles from the Learning Tool. Sort the triangles into two groups.

Set A
Triangles with 1 right angle

Set B
Triangles with no right angles

---

2 Sort the triangles again. Use a ruler to help you.

Set A
Triangles with all sides the same length

Set B
Triangles with all sides not the same length

---

3 Cut out the quadrilaterals from the Learning Tool. Sort the quadrilaterals.

Set A
Quadrilaterals with 1 right angle

Set B
Quadrilaterals with no right angles

④ Sort the quadrilaterals again. Use a ruler to help you.

Set A
Quadrilaterals with all
sides the same length

Set B
Quadrilaterals with all
sides not the same length

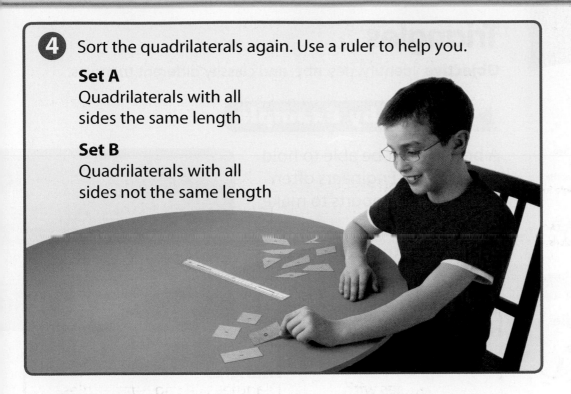

▶  **Extend**

Draw a figure to match the description. Use a ruler to help you. If you cannot draw the figure, write *impossible*.

1. Triangle with 1 right angle

2. Triangle with 3 equal sides

3. Quadrilateral with 4 right angles

4. Triangle with 2 right angles

5. Quadrilateral with 1 right angle

6. Quadrilateral with 1 pair of parallel sides

7. **Challenge** Draw a quadrilateral with no equal sides

> **Vocabulary Tip**
> • The prefix
>   *tri-* means 3.
> • The prefix
>   *quad-* means 4.
> • Think about a
>   *tri*cycle, *tri*plets,
>   and *quad*ruplets.

 Writing Math

Sort the triangles from the Learning Tool. Write the letters of the triangles to tell which triangles are in each set. Tell the sorting rule you used. Tell two other sorting rules you could have used.

CA Standards
KEY **MG 2.2** Identify
attributes of triangles (e.g., two
equal sides for the isosceles
triangle, three equal sides for the
equilateral triangle, right angle for
the right triangle).

**Also MG 2.0, KEY MG 2.1,
MG 2.4, MR 2.3, MR 2.4**

Vocabulary

equilateral triangle

isosceles triangle

right triangle

scalene triangle

Materials
Ruler

Triangles

Objective Identify, describe, and classify different triangles.

▶ **Learn by Example**

A bridge must be able to hold
heavy loads. Engineers often
use triangle supports to make
bridges strong.

Can you see the different kinds
of triangles in this bridge?

Some triangles have special
names.

Triangles

Equilateral Triangle

All of the sides
have equal lengths.

Isosceles Triangle

At least two of the sides
have the same length.

Scalene Triangle

Each side is a
different length.

Right Triangle

A scalene or
isosceles triangle
with one right angle.

Ask Yourself

• Are any of the sides
the same length?

• Are any of the angles
right angles?

▶ **Guided Practice**

**Name each triangle. Triangles can have more than one
name. Use a ruler to help.**

1.   2.   3.   4.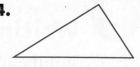

 Math Talk Are all triangles polygons? Are all
polygons triangles? Explain your reasoning.

▶ Practice and Problem Solving

Name each triangle. Triangles can have more than one name. Use a ruler.

5.

6.

7.

8.

Use the triangles at the right for Problems 9–10.

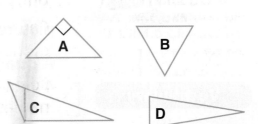

9. Which triangles appear to be isosceles?

10. Which triangles have at least one angle that appears to be greater than a right angle?

Solve.

11. Look at the equilateral triangles in the picture at the right. What do you know is true about their angles?

12. Justify Can a triangle have a right angle and be an isosceles triangle? Use a drawing to explain.

13. Explain Can a triangle have two sides that are parallel? Explain your reasoning.

14. Challenge Can an equilateral triangle also be a right triangle? Use a drawing to explain your answer.

✓ Spiral Review and Test Practice

Find each missing number. AF 1.5 page 152

15. $2 \times 0 \times 8 = 8 \times 2 \times \boxed{0}$

16. $2 \times 3 \times 2 = \boxed{2} \times 2 \times 3$

17. $5 \times 5 \times \boxed{5} = 5 \times 5 \times 5$

18. $\boxed{6} \times 1 \times 4 = 1 \times \boxed{4} \times 6$

Write the letter of the correct answer. KEY MG 2.3

19. At most, how many right angles can be in a triangle?

   A 0   **B** 1   **C** 2   **D** 4

Extra Practice See page 207, Set B.

CA Standards
KEY **MG 2.3** Identify attributes of quadrilaterals (e.g., parallel sides for the parallelogram, right angles for the rectangle, equal sides and right angles for the square).

Also NS 1.4, KEY NS 1.5, MG 2.0, KEY MG 2.1, MG 2.4, MR 2.0, MR 2.3, MR 2.4

Vocabulary

quadrilateral

parallelogram

rectangle

square

Quadrilaterals

Objective Identify, describe, and classify different four-sided figures.

▶ **Learn by Example**

The person who designed the Bateson Building used different quadrilaterals.

Which quadrilaterals do you see in the picture of the Bateson Building below?

A **quadrilateral** is a polygon with 4 sides and 4 angles. Some quadrilaterals have special names.

Quadrilateral

4 sides
4 angles

Rectangle

- 4 sides
- 4 right angles
- opposite sides are parallel

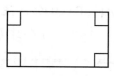 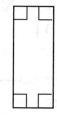

Square

- 4 equal sides
- 4 right angles
- opposite sides are parallel

Parallelogram

- 4 sides
- 4 angles
- opposite sides are parallel

  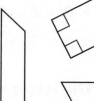

The Bateson Building in Sacramento

Tell whether the figure is a quadrilateral. If it has special names, write them.

Ask Yourself
- How many sides are there?
- Are there parallel sides or right angles?

1.

2.

3.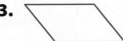

Write *true* or *false* for the statement.
Draw a picture to explain your answer.

4. A triangle is a quadrilateral.

5. A square has 2 pairs of parallel sides.

6. A rectangle is a parallelogram.

7. All quadrilaterals have 4 right angles.

 Math Talk Explain why a square is both a parallelogram and a rectangle.

Famous designer and architect Frank Lloyd Wright used geometric figures in this stained glass window.

► **Practice and Problem Solving**

Tell whether the figure is a quadrilateral. If it has special names, write them.

8.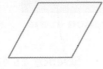

9.

10.

11.

12.

13.

14.

15.

16. Describe two different ways to sort the figures in Exercises 8–15 into two groups.

**Write *true* or *false* for the statement.
Draw a picture to explain your answer.**

17. Some polygons are quadrilaterals.

18. Some rectangles are squares.

19. All quadrilaterals are parallelograms.

20. **Challenge** No two sides of a triangle can be parallel.

 Science Link

Use the Fun Facts to help you solve the problems.

21. Look at the picture of the constellation Orion. Make a list of the polygons you see.

22. Draw an imaginary constellation. Include a parallelogram and a square.

23. There are 88 constellations named by scientists. Round this number to the nearest ten and the nearest hundred.

24. Some constellations were named as long ago as 2450 B.C. Write this year in expanded form.

Constellation

- Groups of stars that form patterns in the sky are called constellations.

- Constellations appear to move across the sky because the earth is rotating.

- Constellation forms stay the same from year to year.

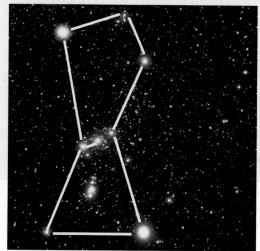

Orion is a familiar constellation in the winter sky.

Science ES 4.a

Spiral Review and Test Practice

Copy and complete. MG 1.4 page 172

25. 3 yd = _____ ft

26. 36 in. = _____ yd

27. 5,280 ft = _____ mi

Write the letter of the correct answer. KEY MG 2.3

28. A parallelogram MUST have
   A 4 right angles.
   B opposite sides that are parallel.
   C 4 equal sides.
   D 4 equal angles.

Extra Practice See page 207, Set C.

Make a Sculpture!

Ms. Adell is an artist. She uses aluminum and steel to make sculptures for parks and other public places.

Use the pictures to solve.

1. Ms. Adell built a red and white sculpture for North Street Park. She named the sculpture "All the Right Angles." Write the names of the polygons in the sculpture. If the shape has a special name, write it.

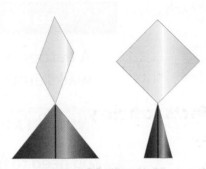

"All the Right Angles" from two viewpoints.

2. Ms. Adell built a blue and white sculpture for the police station. She named it "Badge of Courage." Are both figures polygons? Explain. Name the figures.

"Badge of Courage"

Solve.

3. Ms. Adell is building a new sculpture for the hospital. The base of the sculpture will have 4 right angles and opposite sides that are parallel. The sides are not all the same length. What shape is she going to use?

Sculptor at work

 **CA Standards**
KEY **MG 2.1**, KEY **MG 2.2**, KEY **MG 2.3**, MR 2.0, MR2.3, MR 2.4

CA Standards

KEY MG 2.2 Identify attributes of triangles (e.g., two equal sides for the isosceles triangle, three equal sides for the equilateral triangle, right angle for the right triangle).

MR 2.3 Use a variety of methods, such as words, numbers, symbols, charts, graphs, tables, diagrams, and models, to explain mathematical reasoning.

Also KEY NS 2.1, NS 2.8, MG 2.0, MR 1.1, MR 1.2, MR 2.0, MR 2.4, MR 3.0, MR 3.1, MR 3.2, MR 3.3

Materials
Inch ruler

Problem Solving Strategy
Draw a Picture

Objective Draw a picture to solve a problem.

> **Learn by Example**

A garden is shaped like an isosceles triangle. Kamala walks around the garden. How many feet does she walk?

UNDERSTAND

You need to find the distance around the garden.

- The garden is shaped like an isosceles triangle.
- The length of the two shorter sides is 72 feet.
- The length of the longest side is 95 feet.

PLAN

You can draw a picture to help you find the answer.

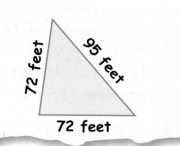

SOLVE

Add the lengths of the 3 sides.

Kamala walked 239 feet.

$$\begin{array}{r} 95 \\ 72 \\ + 72 \\ \hline 239 \end{array}$$

LOOK BACK

Estimate to see if your answer is reasonable.

▶ Guided Problem Solving

Solve using the Ask Yourself questions.

1. Claudio has a board that is 9 feet long. He cuts it into 9 pieces that are each 1 foot long. How many cuts does he make?

123 Math Talk Look back at Problem 1. How did drawing a picture help you to solve the problem?

▶ Independent Problem Solving

Solve. Explain why your answer makes sense.

2. Draw a square that is 1 inch on each side. Then draw a rectangle with a width of 1 inch and a length 3 times as long. How many squares will fit inside the rectangle?

3. **Multistep** Erin is using a piece of ribbon to make bows. Each bow uses 6 inches of ribbon. After making 5 bows, Erin has 5 inches of ribbon left. How long was the piece of ribbon Erin started with?

4. Stacy has 2 squares. Each square is 3 inches on a side. Can she put the squares together to make a rectangle? a scalene triangle? a parallelogram that is not a rectangle?

5. Chip made knots in a rope to make a swing. The knots divide the rope into 15 sections. He also made knots at each end of the rope. How many knots in all did Chip make?

6. **Challenge** Chandra has 2 right triangles. The sides that form the right angle measure 3 inches and 4 inches. The third side measures 5 inches. Can Chandra put the triangles together to form a rectangle? an isosceles triangle? a square?

7. **Create and Solve** Write a word problem that you could solve by drawing a picture.

Reading & Writing Math

Vocabulary

Polygons can be named by the number of sides.

Copy and complete the chart by writing the name of each polygon and the number of sides.

Polygons		
Polygon	Name	Number of sides
1.	hexagon	_____
2.	_____	_____
3.	quadrilateral	_____
4.	_____	_____
5.	_____	_____

Tell whether the shape belongs in the table. Explain.

6. a square _____

7. a circle _____

Writing Can you draw a polygon with 2 sides and 2 vertices? Explain your reasons.

Reading Look for this book in your library.

- *The Greedy Triangle*, by Marilyn Burns

CA Standards

MR 2.3 Use a variety of methods, such as words, numbers, symbols, charts, graphs, tables, diagrams, and models, to explain mathematical reasoning.

Also KEY MG 2.1

Standards-Based Extra Practice

Set A
KEY MG 2.1 page 192

Tell whether the figure is a polygon. If it is, write its name.

1.   2.   3.   4.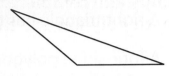

5. Draw a figure that is not a polygon. Explain why it is not a polygon.

Set B
KEY MG 2.2 page 198

Name the triangle. Write *equilateral, isosceles, right,* or *scalene*. Use a ruler to help you.

1.   2.   3. 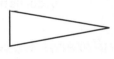   4.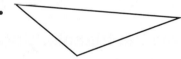

5. Suppose you draw a line connecting opposite corners of a sheet of paper. What kind of triangles would you have made? Explain.

Set C
KEY MG 2.3 page 200

Tell whether the figure is a quadrilateral. If it has special names, write them.

1. 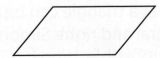   2.   3.   4.

Write *true* or *false* for the statement. Draw a picture to explain your answer.

5. All polygons are triangles.

6. All circles are polygons.

7. All squares are rectangles.

8. Some polygons are quadrilaterals.

Education Place
Visit www.eduplace.com/camap/
for more **Extra Practice**.

Chapter Review/Test

Vocabulary and Concepts

KEY **MG 2.1**, KEY **MG 2.2**, KEY **MG 2.3**

Choose the best term to complete each sentence.

Word Bank
right angle
quadrilateral

1. A right triangle has two acute angles and one _____.

2. A four-sided polygon is also called a _____.

Skills

KEY **MG 2.1**, KEY **MG 2.2**, KEY **MG 2.3**

Tell whether the figure is a polygon. If it is, write its name.

3.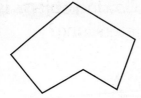

4.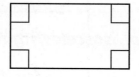

5.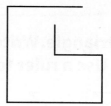

Name the triangle. Write *equilateral*, *isosceles*, *right*, or *scalene*.

6.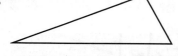

7.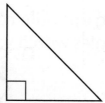

8.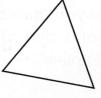

Problem Solving and Reasoning

MG 2.0, KEY **MG 2.1**, KEY **MG 2.2**, KEY **MG 2.3**
MR 1.1, MR 2.3

Solve.

9. Winston says that parallel line segments will form an acute angle. Do you agree or disagree? Explain.

10. Gloria says that a triangle can be both equilateral and right. Simon says that is impossible. Who is right? Explain.

Writing Math Explain the difference between a polygon and a quadrilateral. Give examples of each.

Spiral Review and Test Practice

1. There were 7812 visitors to the Ocean World exhibit and 5416 visitors to the Deep Space exhibit. How many more people visited Ocean World than visited Deep Space?

A 2296

B 2396

C 12,228

D 13,228

Test Tip
Find the key words that tell you what operation to use.

KEY **NS 2.1** page 78

2. If $5 \times 4 \times 10 = 200$, then what is $4 \times 10 \times 5$?

A 20

C 40

B 200

D 4105

AF **1.5** page 102

3. Mrs. Lyons bought 9 boxes of paper for her office. If each box cost $9, how much did Mrs. Lyons spend on paper?

A $1

B $18

C $81

D $90

KEY **NS 2.2** page 128

4. Hector is feeding cats for 5 families that each have 3 cats. If he feeds each cat 2 times a day, how many meals does he fix every day?

A 6

C 10

B 15

D 30

KEY **NS 2.2** page 106

5. Which of the following objects is about 3 centimeters long?

A

B

C

D

MG **1.1** page 176

6. Which of these is a pentagon?

A

C

B

D

KEY **MG 2.1** page 200

Perimeter and Area

KIDS ONLY

Check **What You Know**

Word Bank

Word Bank

length

rectangle

sides

triangle

Vocabulary and Concepts   KEY MG 2.1, MR 2.3

Choose the best word to complete each sentence. page 192

1. A _____ has three sides.

2. A rectangle and a square have the same number of _____.

3. The _____ and width of a square have the same measure.

Skills   NS 2.0

Find each sum. page 50

4. $2 + 3 + 3 + 2$

5. $8 + 7 + 6 + 4$

6. $6 + 8 + 6 + 2 + 4$

Find each difference. page 74

7. $\begin{array}{r} 24 \\ -18 \\ \hline \end{array}$

8. $\begin{array}{r} 14 \\ -9 \\ \hline \end{array}$

9. $\begin{array}{r} 35 \\ -24 \\ \hline \end{array}$

Problem Solving and Reasoning   KEY MG 2.1   page 200

10. Stefano drew a polygon with 4 straight sides. Name two figures he could have drawn.

Vocabulary

Visualize It!

perimeter

The distance around a plane figure.

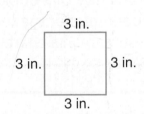

The perimeter of the figure is 12 in.

$3 \text{ in.} + 3 \text{ in.} + 3 \text{ in.} + 3 \text{ in.} = 12 \text{ in.}$

area

The number of square units needed to cover the figure.

square unit

A square used to measure area. Each side is one unit in **length**.

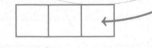

The area of the figure is 3 square units.

Language Tip

Some words are similar in Spanish and English.

English	Spanish
length	longitud
perimeter	perímetro

See **English-Spanish Glossary** pages 628–646.

Education Place Visit www.eduplace.com/camap/ for the **eGlossary** and **eGames**.

CA Standards MR 2.3 Use a variety of methods, such as words, numbers, symbols, charts, graphs, tables, diagrams, and models, to explain mathematical reasoning. **Also KEY MG 1.3**

Chapter 10   211

CA Standards

KEY MG 1.3 Find the perimeter of a polygon with integer sides.

MG 1.1 Choose the appropriate tools and units (metric and U.S.) and estimate and measure the length, liquid volume, and weight/ mass of given objects.

Also NS 2.0, MG 1.0, KEY MG 2.2, KEY MG 2.3, MR 1.1, MR 2.0, MR 2.3, MR 2.4

Vocabulary

perimeter

Materials
• String
• Inch ruler
• Centimeter ruler

Hands On
Explore Perimeter

Objective Estimate and measure the distance around a figure.

▶ **Explore**

The distance around a plane figure is called the **perimeter**.

Question How can you estimate and measure the perimeter of the cover of a book?

Perimeter of the Cover of a Book

	Estimate	Measurement
Number of Inches		
Number of Centimeters		

1 Trace around one face of a book on a piece of paper. Estimate the perimeter of the rectangle in inches. Record your estimate in a chart.

2 Run a string around the perimeter of the rectangle. Mark the spot where you end. Cut the string.

3 Measure the length of the string to the nearest inch. Record the number in your chart. What is the perimeter of the rectangle in inches?

4 Estimate. Then measure the length of the string to the nearest centimeter. Record the number in your chart. What is the perimeter of the rectangle in centimeters?

▶ **Extend**

Copy and complete the chart below.

- Trace a face of the object.
- Estimate. Then measure the perimeter of the object to the nearest inch.
- Estimate. Then measure the perimeter of the object to the nearest centimeter.

	Object	Estimate (in.)	Measurement (in.)	Estimate (cm)	Measurement (cm)
1.	cover of a notebook				
2.	cover of a storybook				
3.	desktop				
4.					
5.					

6. How did your estimates compare to your measurements?

7. **Compare** For each object, compare your measurements with those of other students in the class. Were your measurements all the same? Explain why or why not.

8. If the perimeter of a square is 16 inches, how long is each side?

9. **Challenge** If the perimeter of an equilateral triangle is 21 cm, how long is each side?

 Writing Math

Analyze If you drew three figures with the same perimeter, would they all have the same shape? Explain why or why not.

CA Standards

KEY MG 1.3 Find the perimeter of a polygon with integer sides.

MG 1.0 Students choose and use appropriate units and measurement tools to quantify the properties of objects.

Also NS 2.0, KEY NS 2.1, KEY MG 2.1, KEY MG 2.3, MR 2.0, MR 2.3, MR 2.4

Vocabulary

perimeter

length

width

Find Perimeter

Objective Find the perimeter of polygons.

▶ **Learn by Example**

The Cruz family is moving to a new neighborhood next week. Sam and his friends are making a welcome sign for the family. They plan to put yarn around the edge of the sign as a border.

The **length** of the sign is 32 inches. The **width** is 20 inches. How many inches of yarn do they need in all?

To solve this problem, you need to find the **perimeter**.

Welcome to the Neighborhood

32 in.

20 in.

Example

To find the perimeter, add the measurements of the sides.

$20 + 32 + 20 + 32 = 104$

The perimeter of the sign is 104 inches.

Solution: The friends need 104 inches of yarn.

Another Example

To find the perimeter of this octagon, add the measurements of the sides.

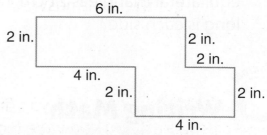

6 in.

2 in.   2 in.

2 in.

4 in.   2 in.

2 in.   2 in.

4 in.

$6 + 2 + 2 + 2 + 4 + 2 + 4 + 2 = 24$ inches

Solution: The perimeter is 24 inches.

Think

An octagon is a plane figure with 8 sides.

Ask Yourself
- What numbers do I add?
- How should I label my answer?

Find the perimeter of the figure.

1.
3 ft
2 ft | | 2 ft
3 ft

2.
5 in. ◇ 5 in.
5 in.   5 in.

3.
2 mi
3 mi   2 mi   6 mi
3 mi   2 mi   3 mi
5 mi

Guided Problem Solving

Use the questions to solve this problem.

4. Jim is watering his garden. The garden is the shape of a rectangle. The length of the garden is 8 feet. The width is 4 feet. What is the perimeter of Jim's garden?

   a. Understand How many sides are there? What do you need to find?

   b. Plan Draw a picture of the garden. Label the length of each side.

   c. Solve Add the lengths of the sides. Solve the problem.

      ____ + ____ + ____ + ____ = ◯ feet

   The perimeter of the garden is ◯ feet.

   d. Look Back Check your work by adding the four lengths in a different order. Did you get the same answer?

Think
Add the lengths of all the sides to find the perimeter.

 Math Talk Can you find the perimeter of a square if you know the length of one side? Why or why not? Explain.

Practice and Problem Solving

Find the perimeter of the figure.

5.

5 in.

2 in.   2 in.

3 in.   3 in.

6.

6 ft

7 ft   7 ft

10 ft

7.

7 mi

5 mi

9 mi

10 mi

8.

6 cm

6 cm   6 cm

 Science Link

A rectangular park is 24 meters long and 16 meters wide. The corners are 4 right angles.

9. List all the names that describe the shape of the park.

10. What is the perimeter of the park?

11. Challenge There is one California lilac shrub in each corner of the park and one every 8 meters on each side. How many shrubs are there?

Plant Adaptations

The California lilac's unique root system helps it to survive long periods of time with very little water.

Science LS 3.a

Spiral Review and Test Practice

Compare. Write >, <, or = for each ⬭. MG 1.4 page 178

12. 6 km ⬭ 60 m   **13.** 300 cm ⬭ 3 m   **14.** 9,000 m ⬭ 9 km

Write the letter of the correct answer. KEY MG 1.3

15. A rectangular garden is 20 m long and 10 m wide. What is the perimeter in meters?

A 30 meters   **B** 50 meters   **C** 60 meters   **D** 200 meters

Extra Practice See page 227, Set A.

Key Standards Review

Need Help?
See Key Standards Handbook.

Identify each kind of triangle. Write *equilateral, isosceles, right,* or *scalene*. Explain how you decided. KEY **MG 2.2**

     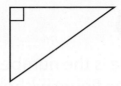

1.   2.   3.   4.

Name the figure that does NOT belong in each group. Explain how you decided. KEY **MG 2.1**

5.   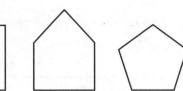   6.   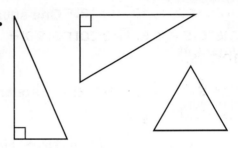

7.   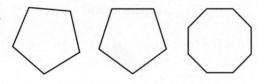   8.   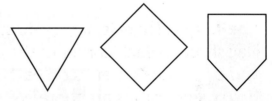

Challenge   Geometry and Measurement

Name that Length

Solve. KEY **MG 2.1**

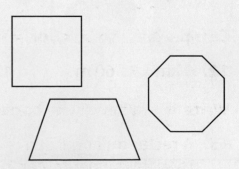

1. The perimeter of a quadrilateral is 36 inches. Three of the sides are 8 inches each. What is the length of the fourth side?

2. The perimeter of an octagon is 72 inches. The sides are of equal length. What is the length of one side?

CA Standards
KEY **MG 1.2** Estimate or determine the area and volume of solid figures by covering them with squares or by counting the number of cubes that would fill them.

Also MG 1.0, MR 2.3, MR 2.5

Vocabulary

area

square unit

Materials
Learning Tool 15 (Inch Grid Paper)

Hands On
Explore Area

Objective Estimate the number of square units that cover a figure.

▶ **Explore**

The **area** of a figure is the number of **square units** needed to cover the figure without overlapping.

One square unit

$\frac{1}{2}$ square unit

$\frac{1}{2}$ square unit

About $\frac{1}{2}$ square unit

Question How can you estimate the area of a figure?

Work with a partner. Estimate the area of the bottom of your partner's shoe.

1 Make an outline of the bottom of your partner's shoe on 1-inch grid paper.

2 Count the number of whole square units inside the outline of the shoe.

3 Count the partly-covered squares. Two partly-covered squares can be counted as one square unit.

4 Record the number of square units.

- About how many square units did you count?

- What is the area of the bottom of your partner's shoe?

▶ **Extend**

Estimate the area of the figure. Each ☐ = 1 square unit.

1.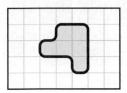

2.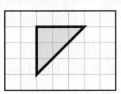

3.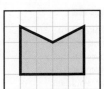

4.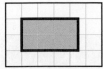

5.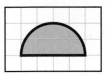

6.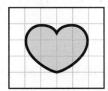

7.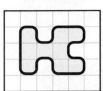

8.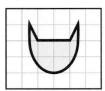

9.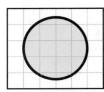

Use one-inch grid paper for Problems 10–12.

10. Trace around one of your hands on grid paper. About how many square units is your hand? Estimate the area.

11. **Explain** Look at Exercises 1 and 5. Is it easier to estimate the area of a rectangle or a heart?

12. **Challenge** Draw a pentagon with an area of about 10 square units.

 Writing Math

Compare What is the difference between *area* and *perimeter*?

LESSON 4

CA Standards
KEY **MG 1.2** Estimate or determine the area and volume of solid figures by covering them with squares or by counting the number of cubes that would fill them.

Also MG 1.0, KEY **MG 1.3**, KEY **MG 2.3**, MR 2.0, MR 2.3, MR 2.4

Vocabulary

area

Materials
• Scissors
• Learning Tool 11 (Centimeter Grid Paper)
• Learning Tool 30 (Dot Paper)

Find Area

Objective Find the area of a figure.

▶ Learn by Example

The Cruz family had a new tile floor put in their kitchen. Each of the tiles is square. What is the **area** of the entire floor?

To solve this problem, you can count the number of square tiles to find the area of the floor.

Example

Each tile or  = 1 square unit.

There are 24 square units.

Solution: The area of the floor is 24 square units.

Another Example

You can find the area of a figure on dot paper.

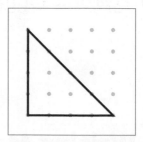

Each ☐ = 1 square unit.

Two $\frac{1}{2}$ squares can be counted as 1 square unit.

Solution: The area of the triangle is 8 square units.

▶ Guided Practice

**Find the area of the figure.
Label your answer in square units.**

Ask Yourself
- How do I find area?
- What do I do with the $\frac{1}{2}$ squares?
- Did I label my answer correctly?

Each ▢ or ◫ = 1 square unit.

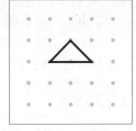

1.   **2.**   **3.**

Use grid paper for Problems 4–6.

4. Draw a square with an area of 25 square units.

5. Draw a rectangle with an area of 18 square units.

6. Draw any figure with an area of 13 square units.

(123) Math Talk Look at the triangle in Exercise 3. If two of these triangles were put together to form a square, what would be the area of the square? Explain.

▶ Practice and Problem Solving

Find the area of each figure. Label your answer in square units.

Each ▢ or ◫ = 1 square unit.

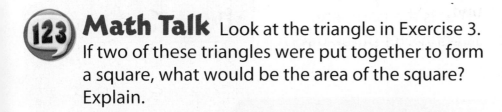

7.   **8.**   **9.**

Use grid paper for Problems 10–12.

10. Draw a square with an area of 16 square units.

11. Draw a rectangle with an area of 24 square units.

12. **What's Wrong?** Jill says that polygons with the same area will have the same perimeter. Use models to explain why Jill is wrong.

 Real World Data

Use the diagram for Problems 13–15.

13. The diagram shows the design of a tiled pool deck. What is the area of the deck?

14. Which has the greater area—the deck or the pool? How much greater?

15. **Challenge** Suppose each side of a square in the diagram is 1 foot. What is the perimeter of the pool? What is the perimeter of the deck?

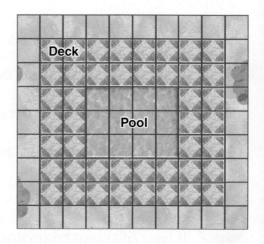

Spiral Review and Test Practice

Write the name of the polygon that tells the number of sides. KEY MG 2.1 page 192

16.
17.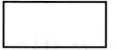
18.
19.

Write the letter of the correct answer. KEY MG 1.2

20. What is the area of this figure?

    A 4 square units
    B 6 square units
    C 12 square units
    D 8 square units

 = 1 square unit

Extra Practice See page 227, Set B.

Challenge

Three-Dimensional Figures

Making Boxes

Ann wants to make a box that will hold 8 cubes.
Below are 3 ways to arrange 8 cubes.

A 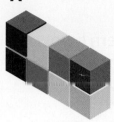   B    C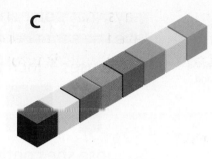

The drawings below show the sides of the boxes
needed to hold 8 cubes. Which box will take the
least cardboard?

A    B    C

Each box has a volume of 8 cubic units. Count to
find how many square units it takes to make the
faces of each box.

  A 28 square units   **B** 24 square units   **C** 34 square units

Box B takes the least cardboard.

**Using unit cubes, find two different ways to arrange
the number of cubes in Problems 1–3. Draw a sketch
of the box and the faces unfolded. Find the amount
of cardboard needed.**

  1. 9 cubes   **2.** 10 cubes   **3.** 16 cubes

  4. Look back at the examples. Find the
     perimeter of the lid of each box.
     Which lid has the greatest perimeter?

CA Standards
KEY MG 1.2, KEY MG 1.3

CA Standards

MR 1.1 Analyze problems by identifying relationships, distinguishing relevant from irrelevant information, sequencing and prioritizing information, and observing patterns.

AF 2.2 Extend and recognize a linear pattern by its rules (e.g., the number of legs on a given number of horses may be calculated by counting by 4s or by multiplying the number of horses by 4).

Also AF 2.0, KEY MG 1.2, KEY MG 1.3, MR 1.0, MR 2.0, MR 2.3, MR 2.4, MR 2.6, MR 3.0, MR 3.1, MR 3.2, MR 3.3

Materials
Grid paper

Think

A 1-inch tile measures 1 inch on each side.

Problem Solving Strategy
Find a Pattern

Objective Solve problems by finding patterns.

Jenna uses 1-inch tiles to make the pattern below.

Suppose she continues her pattern. What will be the perimeter of the seventh figure?

UNDERSTAND

The pattern shows figures made from tiles. Each figure has two more tiles than the one before it.

PLAN

The question asks about perimeter. You can use the pattern to find the perimeter of the seventh figure.

SOLVE

Find the perimeter of each of the first four figures.

| Perimeter: | 6 in. | 8 in. | 10 in. | 12 in. |

Continue the pattern for the next three figures.

Perimeter: 14 in.   16 in.   18 in.

The perimeter of the seventh figure will be 18 inches.

LOOK BACK

Does the solution answer the question?

Guided Problem Solving

Solve using the Ask Yourself questions.

Ask Yourself
- What is the pattern?
- How can I use the pattern to answer the question?

1. Trina made the pattern shown below. Each 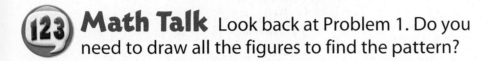 = 1 square unit.

Suppose she continues her pattern. What will be the area of the seventh figure in her pattern?

123 **Math Talk** Look back at Problem 1. Do you need to draw all the figures to find the pattern?

Independent Problem Solving

Solve. Explain why your answer makes sense.

2. The pattern was made with rectangles that are 3 inches long and 2 inches wide.

If the pattern is continued, what will be the perimeter of the fifth figure in the pattern?

3. Challenge The pattern at the right was made using 1-inch tiles.

If the pattern is continued, what will be the perimeter of the figure made using 29 tiles?

4. Create and Solve Use grid paper. Draw the first three figures in your pattern. Predict the area or perimeter of the sixth figure. Then continue your pattern and check your answer.

Reading & Writing Math

Vocabulary

When you find the distance around a figure, you find its **perimeter**. When you find how much surface a figure covers, you find its **area**.

You will need:

- a pencil
- a piece of paper or index card
- an inch ruler
- a centimeter ruler

What is the perimeter of your paper or card? Estimate, then measure. Record your answers in a table like this one.

	Estimate	Measure
inches ruler (0–2)	1.	2.
centimeters ruler (0–5)	3.	4.

Trace the square at the right. It is 1 square unit.

5. Find the area of your paper or card in square units.

Writing
What is the difference between perimeter and area? Use a drawing to explain your answer.

Reading
Check out this book in your library.

- *Spaghetti and Meatballs for All: A Mathematical Story*, by Marilyn Burns

CA Standards
MR 2.3 Use a variety of methods, such as words, numbers, symbols, charts, graphs, tables, diagrams, and models, to explain mathematical reasoning.

Also MG 1.0, KEY MG1.2, KEY MG1.3

Standards-Based Extra Practice

Set A ───────────────────────── KEY **MG 1.3** page 214

Find the perimeter of the figure.

1.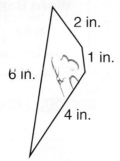
2 in.
1 in.
6 in.
4 in.

2.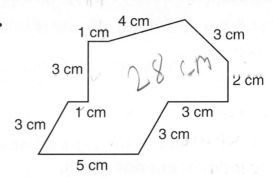
4 cm
1 cm
3 cm
3 cm
28 cm
2 cm
1 cm
3 cm
3 cm
3 cm
5 cm

3. The length of a side of an equilateral triangle is 5 inches. What is the perimeter?

Set B ───────────────────────── KEY **MG 1.2** page 220

Find the area of the figure.

Each ☐ = 1 square unit.

1.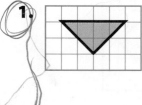

2.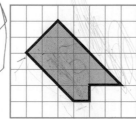

3.

Cut out squares from grid paper. Make shapes with the given area. Record your work on grid paper.

4. A triangle with an area of 16 square units.

5. A rectangle with an area of 15 square units.

6. Consider two rectangles: one is 6 units wide and 3 units long, and the other is 2 units wide and 9 units long. Do both rectangles have the same area? Explain.

Education Place
Visit www.eduplace.com/camap/
for more **Extra Practice**.

Chapter 10 Extra Practice **227**

Chapter Review/Test

Vocabulary and Concepts

KEY MG 1.3, KEY MG 1.2

Choose the best word to complete each sentence.

Word Bank
area
perimeter

1. The distance around a figure is called the _____.

2. The _____ measures the amount of space inside a figure.

Skills

KEY MG 1.3, KEY MG 1.2

Find the perimeter of the figure. Use a centimeter ruler if the side lengths are not given.

3.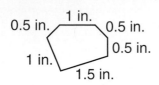
0.5 in.   1 in.   0.5 in.
0.5 in.
1 in.
1.5 in.

4.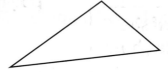

5.
1 in.
2 in.   1.5 in.
3 in.   1 in. 1 in.
1 in.
2 in. 1 in.   3 in.
2 in.

Estimate the area of the figure. Write your answers in square units. Each or ▢ = 1 square unit.

6.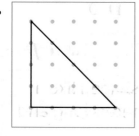

7.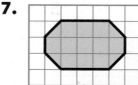

8.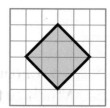

Problem Solving and Reasoning

KEY MG 1.3, KEY MG 1.2, MR 1.0, MR 2.3

Solve.

9. Cheryl's rectangular tile mosaic is 6 inches wide and 8 inches long. If each tile is 1 inch on each side, how many tiles did she use?

10. An equilateral triangle has a perimeter of 27 inches. What is the length of each side?

Writing Math Ariel draws two different shapes. Each has a perimeter of 30 inches. She says that their areas are equal because their perimeters are equal. Is she right or wrong? Explain using an example.

Spiral Review and Test Practice

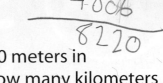

$+\ 3414$
4806
$\overline{8220}$

1. On Tuesday, 3414 people visited an amusement park. On Wednesday, 4806 people visited the park. About how many people visited the park on these two days?

   3210

A 6000   **C** 7000

B 8000   **D** 9000

NS 1.4 page 84

2. Trudy is making 4 bracelets. If she puts 8 beads on each bracelet, how many beads will she need?

A 4   **C** 12

B 32   **D** 36

KEY NS 2.2 page 110

3. Paco has 2046 marbles in his collection. Which of these equals 2046?

Test Tip
Will the place the zero represents be in your answer?

A $2000 + 400 + 60$

B $2000 + 40 + 6$

C $200 + 40 + 6$

D $2 + 4 + 6$

KEY NS 1.5 page 14

4. There are 1,000 meters in 1 kilometer. How many kilometers are in 4,000 meters?

A 4,000 km   **C** 1,000 km

B 40 km   **D** 4 km

MG 1.4 page 178

5. How many right angles are in this polygon?

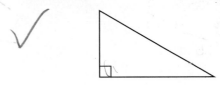

A 3   **C** 2

B 1   **D** 0

KEY MG 2.2 page 198

6. A parking lot is shaped like a rectangle 100 meters long and 50 meters wide.

What is the perimeter in meters of the parking lot?

A 150 m   **C** 200 m

B 300 m   **D** 5,000 m

KEY MG 1.3 page 214

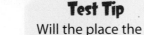

Education Place
Visit www.eduplace.com/camap/ for **Test-Taking Tips** and **Extra Practice**.

Chapter 10 Spiral Review and Test Practice **229**

Solids and Volume

This is a closeup view of the Chromatic Gate sculpture in Santa Barbara, CA.

Check What You Know

Vocabulary and Concepts   MG 2.0, MR 2.3
Choose the best term to complete each sentence.   pages 192, 212

1. The distance around a polygon is the _____.

2. A _____ is a polygon with 3 sides.

Skills   KEY MG 2.1

Use the list below. Write the name of each figure.   page 192

rectangle   pentagon   circle   octagon   square   hexagon

3.

4.

5.

6.

7.

8.

Problem Solving and Reasoning   KEY MG 2.1, KEY MG 2.2   page 192

9. Nolan made a polygon with three sides and two equal angles. What figure did he make?

Vocabulary

Visualize It!

Three-Dimensional Figures

cone

sphere

cube

square pyramid

rectangular prism

Language Tip

Some words are similar in Spanish and English.

English	Spanish
cone	cono
cylinder	cilindro
rectangular prism	prisma rectangular
cube	cubo

See **English-Spanish Glossary** pages 628–646.

Education Place Visit www.eduplace.com/camap/ for the **eGlossary** and **eGames**.

CA Standards **MR 2.3** Use a variety of methods, such as words, numbers, symbols, charts, graphs, tables, diagrams, and models, to explain mathematical reasoning. **Also MG 2.5**

Chapter 11   231

CA Standards

MG 2.5 Identify, describe, and classify common three-dimensional geometric objects (e.g., cube, rectangular solid, sphere, prism, pyramid, cone, cylinder).

MG 2.0 Students describe and compare the attributes of plane and solid geometric figures and use their understanding to show relationships and solve problems.

Also MR 1.1

Vocabulary

A **face** is a flat surface of a solid figure.

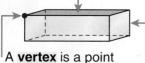

A **vertex** is a point where edges meet.

An **edge** is formed when two faces meet.

Materials

• Learning Tools 16, 17, 18, 19 (Rectangular Prism Net, Cube Net, Square Pyramid Net, Solid Figures Table)
• Scissors
• Tape

Hands On
Build Solids

Objective Build models to identify, describe, and classify rectangular prisms, cubes, and square pyramids.

▶ **Explore**

In Chapter 9, you learned about plane figures. In this lesson, you will make models of solid figures.

Look at the rectangular prism at the left. It has **faces**, **edges**, and **vertices**.

Question How can you use nets to learn about solid figures?

Use the Learning Tool to make a rectangular prism.

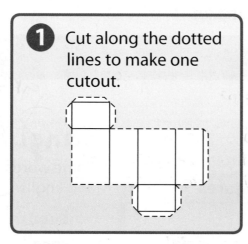

1 Cut along the dotted lines to make one cutout.

2 Fold along the solid lines to make a 3-dimensional figure.

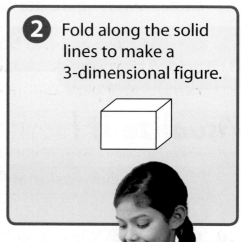

3 Tape the flaps to the sides. You made a rectangular prism.

Use the Learning Tools. Follow steps 1–3 to make a cube and a square pyramid.

▶ **Extend**

Name the solid figures that have the faces shown.

1. ☐△△△△
2. ☐☐☐☐☐☐
3. [figure of faces]

Complete Learning Tool 19. Use the models you made.

	Model	Shapes of Faces	Number of Faces	Number of Edges	Number of Vertices
4.	Rectangular prism				
5.	Cube				
6.	Square pyramid				

Solve.

7. Which solid figures in the table above have the same number of faces, edges, and vertices?

8. Drew made a wooden box shaped like a cube. He painted each face a different color. How many colors did he use?

9. Suppose you made several cubes and attached them by joining faces. Can you make a rectangular prism? Can you make a cube?

10. **Challenge** Ashley is holding a solid figure. It has fewer faces than a cube. One of its faces is a square. The other faces are all the same shape. Which solid figure is it?

Writing Math

Describe two ways to sort the solid figures you used for Exercises 4–6.

CA Standards

MG 2.5 Identify, describe, and classify common three-dimensional geometric objects (e.g., cube, rectangular solid, sphere, prism, pyramid, cone, cylinder).

MG 2.6 Identify common solid objects that are the components needed to make a more complex solid object.

Also MG 2.0, MR 2.3, MR 1.1

Vocabulary

rectangular prism

cube

sphere

cone

cylinder

square pyramid

Solid Figures

Objective Identify simple solid figures that make up complex solid figures.

▶ Learn by Example

The figures below are solid figures. They are 3-dimensional. They have height, width, and length.

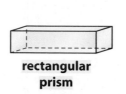

rectangular prism **cube** **sphere**

cone **cylinder** **square pyramid**

Complex Solid Figures

This figure is made up of a square pyramid and a cube.

This figure is made up of a cone and a cylinder.

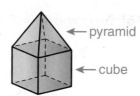 ← pyramid

← cube

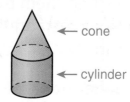 ← cone

← cylinder

Ask Yourself

Is the figure made up of more than one solid figure?

▶ Guided Practice

Name the solid figure or figures.

1.

2.

3.

Guided Problem Solving

Use the questions to solve this problem.

4. Josie made this sculpture for a local park. Name the solid figures in the sculpture. Sort them into 2 groups.

a. **Understand** What do you need to do?

b. **Plan** How will you sort the figures?

c. **Solve** Write the sorting rule. List the names of the figures in each group.

d. **Look Back** How many solid figures are in the picture? Did you include each of them in your list?

Hint
Think about how the faces are similar or different.

 Math Talk How are a cylinder and a cone alike? How are they different?

Practice and Problem Solving

Name the solid figure or figures that make up the object.

5.

6.

7.

Name the solid figure that the object looks like.

8.

9.

10.

11.

Solve.

12. **Reasoning** At the grocery store, Danielle bought items in the shape of a sphere, a cylinder, and a rectangular prism. Name three items she could have bought.

13. **Explain** A cube is a special kind of rectangular prism. What makes a cube different from other rectangular prisms?

History-Social Science Link

Solve.

14. Name all the plane figures you see in the picture.

15. Name all the solid figures you see in the picture.

16. The mint opened to turn gold from the California Gold Rush into coins. What solid figure is a coin shaped like?

17. The first mint building was made of bricks. What solid figure is a brick shaped like?

The San Francisco Mint

• The United States Mint in San Francisco opened in 1854 during the California Gold Rush.

• The famous stone building was used from 1874 to 1937.

History-Social Science 3.4.3

 Spiral Review and Test Practice

Copy and complete. MG 1.4 page 178

18.

Meters	1	2	3	4	5
Centimeters	100	200			

Write the letter of the correct answer. MG 2.5

19. Which object looks like a cylinder?

A   B   C   D

Extra Practice See page 248, Set B.

Key Standards Review

Need Help?
See Key Standards Handbook.

Copy and complete the sentence. Then use the triangles to answer the question. KEY **MG 2.2**

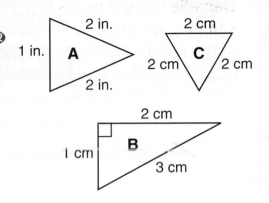

1. _____ triangles have at least 2 equal sides. Which triangle has 2 equal sides?

2. _____ triangles have exactly 1 right angle. Which triangle has exactly 1 right angle?

3. _____ triangles have 3 equal sides. Which triangle has 3 equal sides?

Use the figures to complete Exercises 4–7. Explain your answers. KEY **MG 2.1**

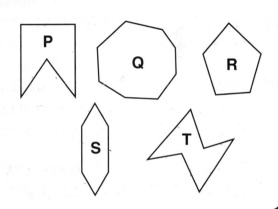

4. Which polygons are octagons?

5. Which polygons are hexagons?

6. Which polygons are pentagons?

7. Which polygons are triangles?

 **Logical Thinking**

Analogies

Look at the way the first pair of words is related. Choose the letter that shows a similar relationship for the second pair. MG 2.0

1. **Pyramid** is to **triangle** as **cube** is to ___.

   A triangle   **C** cone

   B square   **D** pyramid

2. **Quadrilateral** is to **4 sides** as **octagon** is to ___ **sides**.

   F 3   **H** 6

   G 5   **J** 8

CA Standards
KEY **MG 1.2** Estimate or determine the area and volume of solid figures by covering them with squares or by counting the number of cubes that would fill them.

MG 1.0 Students choose and use appropriate units and measurement tools to quantify the properties of objects.

Also MR 2.3

Vocabulary

volume

estimate

Materials
- Ones cubes
- Small box
- Various containers

Hands On
Explore Volume

Objective Estimate and determine the volume of a solid figure.

▶ **Explore**

The number of unit cubes that make up a solid figure is the **volume** of that figure.

Question How can you use ones cubes to **estimate** and measure the volume of a solid figure?

1 Estimate how many cubes it will take to fill the box. Record your estimate.

2 Fill the box with cubes so there are no gaps. Count the cubes as you fill the box. Record the number of cubes you used.

This is the volume of the box.

3 Estimate the volume of the solid figure shown to the left. Record.

Use cubes to build the same figure.

Record the volume of the figure.

The volume of a figure is the amount of space it takes up.

▶ **Extend**

Find containers in your classroom that are rectangular prisms. Copy and complete the table.

- Estimate how many cubes you will need to fill the container. Record your estimate.
- Fill the container with cubes. Record the number of cubes you used.

	Containers	Estimate	Volume
1.	Crayon Box		
2.			
3.			

Estimate the volume of the figure and record. Then build it with cubes. Write the number of cubes you used.

4.

5.

6.

7. Explain How is finding the area of a plane figure different from finding the volume of a container?

8. Challenge Use your cubes to create a figure that has a volume of 14 unit cubes. Build another figure with the same volume. Must the two figures have the same shape?

Writing Math

Analyze Do you think that the number of cubes used to fill a soup can is greater than or less than the actual volume for the can? Explain your answer.

CA Standards
KEY **MG 1.2** Estimate or determine the area and volume of solid figures by covering them with squares or by counting the number of cubes that would fill them.

MG 1.0 Students choose and use appropriate units and measurement tools to quantify the properties of objects.

Also MG 2.6, MR 2.3

Vocabulary

cubic unit

Materials
Ones cubes

Find Volume

Objective Find the volume of a solid figure.

▶ **Learn by Example**

This is a unit cube. It has a volume of 1 **cubic unit**. Volume is the number of cubic units that fill a solid figure.

To find the volume of a solid figure, count the cubic units that make up the solid figure.

1 cubic unit

Each edge has a length of 1 unit.

Example 1

Find the volume of the figure.

• How many layers of cubes are there?

• How many cubes are in each layer?

The volume is 8 cubic units.

Example 2

Find the volume of the figure.

• How many cubes are in the bottom layer?

• How many cubes are in the top layer?

The volume is 8 cubic units.

> Some cubes may be hidden. Don't forget to count these cubes.

Ask Yourself

• How can I find the volume of a solid?

• How many cubes are hidden?

▶ **Guided Practice**

Find the volume of the figure.

Each = 1 cubic unit.

1.

2.

Estimate the volume of the container in cubic units.

3.

4.

5.

 Math Talk Why can different solid figures both have a volume of 8 cubic units? Explain.

▶ Practice and Problem Solving

Find the volume of the figure.

6.

7.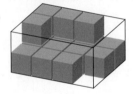

8.

Estimate the volume of the container in cubic units.

9.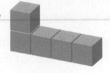

10.

11.

Use the diagram for Problems 12–13.

12. Look at the box on the right. What is the volume of the box in cubic units?

13. **Analyze** Suppose Mrs. Cruz only packs half of the box with cups. Would the volume of the box change? Explain.

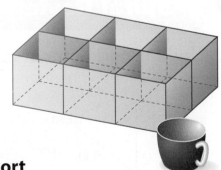

Write *true* or *false*. Draw or write an example to support your answer.

14. All solid figures with the same volume look the same.

15. If you know the length of one side of a square, you can find the area.

16. If you know the length and width of a rectangle, you can find the perimeter.

17. If you know the perimeter of a shape, you can draw the shape.

Use the figure at the right for Problems 18–19.

18. What is the volume of the figure at the right?

19. Challenge Is there a way to find the volume of the figure at the right without counting every unit cube? Explain your answer.

 Science Link

Solve.

Ice

20. What two solid figures make up the ice sculpture at the right?

21. An artist carved a block of ice that had a volume of 12 cubic units. Which figure has the same volume as the block of ice he used?

Each = 1 cubic unit.

- Ice sculptors join rectangular prisms to begin a sculpture.

- Each rectangular prism can weigh as much as 300 pounds, about the weight of a small motorcycle.

a.   **b.**

Science PS 1.e

 Spiral Review and Test Practice

Find the perimeter of the figure. KEY **MG 1.3** page 214

22.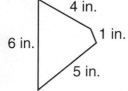
4 in.
6 in.
1 in.
5 in.

23.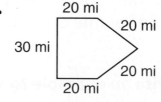
20 mi
20 mi
30 mi
20 mi
20 mi

24.
8 ft
8 ft   8 ft
8 ft   8 ft
8 ft

Write the letter of the correct answer. KEY **MG 1.2**

25. What is the volume of the rectangular prism?

A 9 cubic units   **C** 18 cubic units

B 10 cubic units   **D** 20 cubic units

Extra Practice See page 249, Set C.

Three's a Set!

Object of the Game Match a picture and the solids that make it.
Match 3 cards to make a set. The player with the most sets wins.

Materials
Learning Tool 74 (Complex Solid Objects)

Number of Players 2–3

How to Play

1 Shuffle the game cards and lay them face down in an array.

2 On your turn, turn three cards face up. If they match, take them and make a set. If they do not match, turn them face down again. But remember where you saw them!

3 Continue until all 5 sets have been made.

4 The player with the most matched sets wins the game.

CA Standards
MG 2.6 Identify common solid objects that are the components needed to make a more complex solid object.
Also MG 2.5

Education Place
Visit www.eduplace.com/camap/ for **Brain Teasers** and **eGames** to play.

CA Standards

MG 1.0 Students choose and use appropriate units and measurement tools to quantify the properties of objects.

MR 2.4 Express the solution clearly and logically by using the appropriate mathematical notation and terms and clear language; support solutions with evidence in both verbal and symbolic work.

Also NS 1.2, KEY NS 2.2, NS 2.8, KEY MG1.2, KEY MG1.3, MR 1.0, MR 1.1, MR 1.2, MR 2.0, MR 3.0, MR 3.1, MR 3.2, MR 3.3

Problem Solving Plan
Perimeter, Area, or Volume?

Objective Decide if you need to find perimeter, area, or volume to solve a problem.

▶ **Learn by Example**

Chris needs a tank for his pet iguana that has a floor area of at least 4 square units. Look at the diagrams below. Which tanks have enough floor area for Chris's iguana?

Tank A

Tank B   **Tank C**

1 unit

□ 1 unit

1 square unit
Each side has a length of 1 unit.

UNDERSTAND

You need to find which tanks have a floor area of at least 4 square units.

PLAN

Find the area of each tank.

Count the number of squares on the bottom of each tank. Compare your answer to 4 square units.

SOLVE

Tank A = 2 square units
Tank B = 6 square units
Tank C = 4 square units

So Tank B and Tank C have enough floor area.

LOOK BACK

Read the problem again. Did you answer the question asked?

▶ Guided Problem Solving

Solve using the Ask Yourself questions. Tell whether you found perimeter, area, or volume.

1. Jack needs a tank that has at least 4 cubic units of space. Is the tank shown big enough? Explain.

 Math Talk Explain the difference between perimeter, area, and volume.

▶ Independent Problem Solving

Solve. Explain why your answer makes sense. Tell whether you found perimeter, area, or volume.

2. Chris wants to put a border along the top of this iguana tank. How much border will he need to put around the tank?

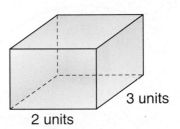

3 units

2 units

3. As his iguana grows, Chris will need a tank with 24 cubic units of space. Will this tank be large enough?

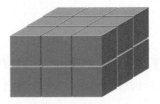

4. **Multistep** Mandy wants to put carpeting on the floor of her pet's doghouse shown below. Will $30 be enough to pay for the carpeting?

doghouse floor

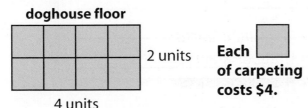

2 units

4 units

Each ▢ **of carpeting costs $4.**

5. **Challenge** Javier has a box that is 8 units high, 6 units wide, and 4 units long. How many cubes like this one can he fit in the box?

6. **Create and Solve** Write a problem that can be solved by finding perimeter, area, or volume. Include a drawing with your problem.

Vocabulary

Solid figures have special names.

Fill in the missing labels.

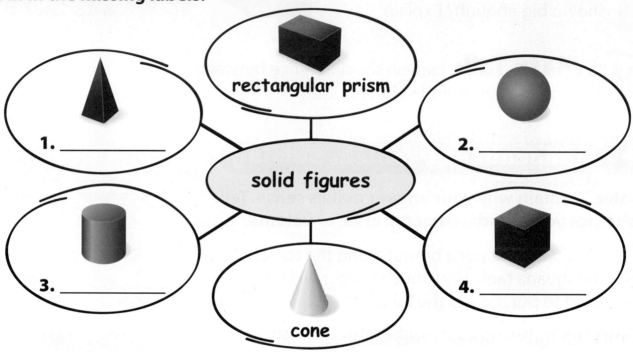

rectangular prism

solid figures

1. _____

2. _____

3. _____

cone

4. _____

Copy and complete the table. List which objects in the word map have faces, edges, and vertices.

5. Faces	6. Edges	7. Vertices
_____	_____	_____
_____	_____	_____
_____	_____	_____

Writing
Suppose you placed a cone on top of a cylinder. Describe this complex solid figure. Then name 2 real-world objects that look like it.

Reading
Look for this book in your library.

• *The Village of Round and Square Houses*, by Ann Grifalconi

CA Standards

MR 2.3 Use a variety of methods, such as words, numbers, symbols, charts, graphs, tables, diagrams, and models, to explain mathematical reasoning.

Also MG 2.5, MG 2.6

Standards-Based Extra Practice

Name the solid figure.

1.

2.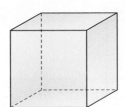

3.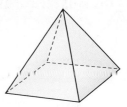

Copy and complete the table.

	Solid Figure	Shapes of Faces	Number of Faces	Number of Edges	Number of Vertices
4.	Rectangular prism				
5.	Cube				
6.	Square pyramid				

Name the figure you can make with the net.

7.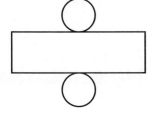

8.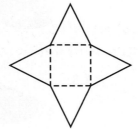

9.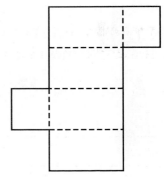

10. Sal says that the net in Exercise 9 makes a cube.
Do you agree? Explain.

Education Place
Visit www.eduplace.com/camap/
for more **Extra Practice**.

Chapter 11 Extra Practice   **247**

Standards-Based Extra Practice

Set B ———————————————————— **MG 2.5, MG 2.6** page 234

Name the solid figure or figures.

1.

2.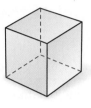

3.

4.

5.

6.

Name the solid figure that each object looks like.

7.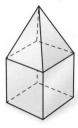

8.

9.

10.

11.

12.

13.

14.

15.

16.

17. Which solid figure has no faces and no vertices?

18. Which solid figure has all equal-size faces?

Standards-Based Extra Practice

Set C KEY **MG 1.2** page 240

Find the volume of each figure.

Label your answer in cubic units. Each = 1 cubic unit.

1.

2.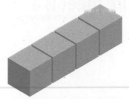

3.

4.

5.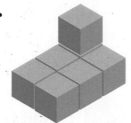

6.

Estimate the volume of each container in unit cubes.

7.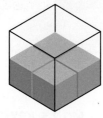

8.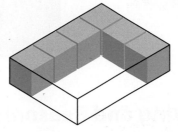

Solve.

9. Sue needs a box that can hold at least 8 cubic units for her hiking gear. Is the space inside this box big enough? Explain.

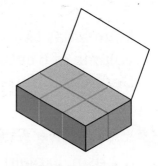

Education Place
Visit www.eduplace.com/camap/
for more **Extra Practice.**

Chapter 11 Extra Practice **249**

Chapter Review/Test

Vocabulary and Concepts ——————————————— MG 2.5

Choose the best term to complete each sentence.

1. A _____ has 6 square faces.

2. A point where the edges of a figure meet is a _____.

3. Volume is measured in _____.

> **Word Bank**
> vertex
> (vertices)
> cube
> cubic units

Skills ————————————————————— MG 2.5, KEY **MG 1.2**

Name the solid figure or figures.

4.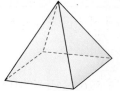

5.

6.

Find the volume of the figure. Each **= 1 cubic unit.**

7.

8.

9.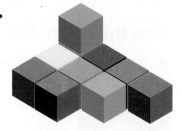

Problem Solving and Reasoning ——————————— MG 2.5, KEY **MG 1.2**

Solve.

10. Mandy has two rectangular boxes. Both boxes have a volume of 6 cubic units. The boxes are different shapes. Describe the shape of each box.

Writing Math A cube is a special kind of rectangular prism. Explain what is special about a cube.

Spiral Review and Test Practice

1. One side of a rectangle is 6 feet. Another side is 8 feet. What are the lengths of the other 2 sides of the rectangle?

> **Test Tip**
> Find the words that tell you what operation to use.

A 6 feet and 6 feet

B 6 feet and 8 feet

C 6 feet and 10 feet

D They could be any length.

KEY **MG 1.3** page 214

2. In January 2006, the population of Needles, California was 5681. The population of Big Bear Lake was 6182. How many more people lived in Big Bear Lake than in Needles?

A 501   **C** 1501

B 4176   **D** 11, 863

KEY **NS 2.1** page 78

3. Which of the following is used to find out how many inches are in 6 feet?

A 6 + 12   **C** 12 − 6

B 6 × 12   **D** 12 ÷ 6

MG 1.4 page 172

4. A square has 2 sides that are each 4 inches long. What are the lengths of the other 2 sides?

A 4 inches and 8 inches

B 6 inches and 8 inches

C 4 inches

D 8 inches

KEY **MG 2.3** page 200

5. What is the area of this figure?

 = 1 square unit

A 2 square units

B 4 square units

C 3 square units

D 5 square units

KEY **MG 1.2** page 220

6. Which figure is a cone?

A   **C**

B   **D**

MG 2.5 page 234

Education Place
Visit www.eduplace.com/camap/ for
Test-Taking Tips and **Extra Practice.**

Unit 4 Review/Test

Vocabulary and Concepts ─────────────────── MR 2.3 Chapters 8–11

Choose the best word to complete each sentence.

1. The distance from Los Angeles to Sacramento is measured in _____.

2. A point where two edges of a figure intersect is called a _____.

3. An _____ triangle has at least two equal sides.

4. The _____ is the distance around a figure.

Word Bank
perimeter
miles
vertex
area
isosceles

Skills ─────────────────── MG1.0, MG 1.1, KEY **MG 1.2** Chapter 8, Lessons 3–4

Choose the unit you would use to measure each.
Write *mm*, *cm*, *m*, or *km*.

5. thickness of your fingernails

6. length of a school bus

Tell whether the figure is a polygon. If it is, write its name. Chapter 9, Lesson 2

7.

8.

9.

Find the area of the figure. Each ☐ = 1 square unit. Chapter 10, Lesson 4

10.

11.

Find the volume. Each = 1 cubic unit. Chapter 11, Lesson 4

12.

13.

Problem Solving and Reasoning

MG 1.1, KEY **MG 1.3**, KEY **MG 2.2** Chapters 8–10

Solve.

14. Gina wants to find the length of her shoes in centimeters. What can she use as a estimate of a centimeter, the width of her fingernail, or the length of her thumb?

15. Richard jogged around a path that forms an equilateral triangle. One side of the triangle is 2 miles. How many miles did Richard jog?

BIG IDEA!

Writing Math Jack wants to know the perimeter, area, and volume of a box. Explain what each measures and what units he could use.

Performance Assessment

Math and Art Flyer

KEY **MG 1.3**, KEY **MG 2.1**, KEY **MG 2.2**, KEY **MG 2.3**, MR 1.0, MR 2.0, MG 2.5

Make a flyer for this month's library theme. The theme is Math and Art.

Task	Information You Need
Use the information at the right to create the flyer. Explain why you drew each shape.	The flyer should have a perimeter of 34 inches.
	The flyer should show at least 2 different triangles and 2 different quadrilaterals.
	The border on the flyer should include at least 3 solid figures.

Multiply by 9

A group of 9 requires tact, start with 10 and then subtract!

Ten take away 1 is easier than a group of 9! Look at Problem 1. Start with 10 groups of 5—it's easier. $10 \times 5 = 50$. To get 9, subtract one 5 to get 45.

1. $9 \times 5 = \boxed{50} - \boxed{5} = \boxed{45}$
  10×5 1×5

2. $9 \times 7 = \boxed{70} - \boxed{} = \boxed{}$
  10×7 1×7

3. $9 \times 6 = \boxed{} - \boxed{} = \boxed{}$
  10×6 1×6

4. $9 \times 10 = \boxed{} - \boxed{} = \boxed{}$
  10×10 1×10

Great work!

5. $9 \times 3 = \boxed{} - \boxed{} = \boxed{}$
  10×3 1×3

6. $9 \times 9 = \boxed{} - \boxed{} = \boxed{}$
  10×9 1×9

7. $9 \times 4 = \boxed{} - \boxed{} = \boxed{}$
  10×4 1×4

8. $9 \times 2 = \boxed{} - \boxed{} = \boxed{}$
  10×2 1×2

Doing Great!

Take It Further!
Now try doing all the steps in your head!

9. 9×8

10. 9×12

11. 9×20

12. 9×7

5

Division Facts

BIG IDEAS!

- You can find a division fact by thinking about a related multiplication fact.
- You can divide by making equal groups, drawing arrays, using repeated subtraction, and looking for patterns.

Songs and Games

Math Music Track 5: *15 Carrots*

eGames at
www.eduplace.com/camap/

Math Readers

Corey's Cookie Caper

The Homework Table

Lost!

Game

Let Me Count the Ways

Object of the Game Explore how to separate items into equal groups.

Materials
- 2 number cubes labeled 1–6
- Workmat 8
- ones blocks

Number of Players 2

How to Play

1 Player 1 rolls the number cubes. He or she then multiplies the 2 numbers rolled. The product is the number of ones blocks Player 1 will place in equal groups.

2 Player 1 places ones blocks on Workmat 8 to show the different ways to place them into equal groups. The player may choose to use two workmats.

3 Player 1 gets 1 point for each correct way the blocks are grouped. Player 1 then removes all of his or her blocks from the workmat.

4 Player 2 repeats Steps 1–3. The player who first earns a total of 20 points wins.

4 groups of 2

2 groups of 4

8 gro of

CA Standards
NS 2.0 Students calculate and solve problems involving addition, subtraction, multiplication, and division.

MR 2.3 Use a variety of methods, such as words, numbers, symbols, charts, graphs, tables, diagrams, and models, to explain mathematical reasoning.

Education Place
Visit www.eduplace.com/camap/ for **Brain Teasers** and **eGames** to play.

Reading To get the right answer to a mathematics problem, you need to make sure you understand the question. Here is an example.

Problem 1

Adam has a pack of 24 animal cards. He gives an equal number of cards to each of 6 friends. How many cards will each friend get?

    A 12

    B 6

    C 4

    D 2

Thinking Through the Problem

Think about the question. This question asks how many cards each friend will get.

Think about what you know. There are 24 cards to share with 6 friends. Each friend will get the same number of cards.

Think about what you don't know. You don't know how many cards Adam gives each friend.

The correct answer is **C**.

Writing Now it's your turn! Answer Problem 2. Then write about how you solve the problem, step by step.

Problem 2

Shaniqua has 56 photos that she is putting into a family album. She can fit 8 photos on each page. How many pages will she need?

    A 6

    B 7

    C 48

    D 64

> I always check to see if I answered the question that was asked.

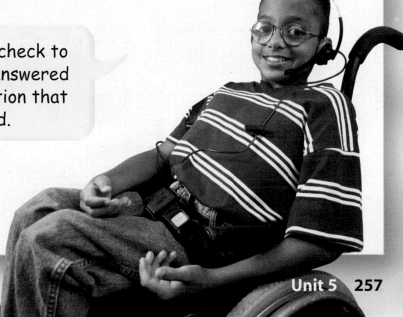

Division Concepts

Check What You Know

Vocabulary and Concepts NS 2.0, MR 2.3

Choose the best term to complete each sentence. page 142

Word Bank

array

equal groups

factor

multiply

product

1. In the number sentence $2 \times 4 = 8$, the 2 is a ____.

2. You can use repeated addition to help you ____.

3. An arrangement of objects or pictures in equal columns and rows is an ____.

Skills KEY NS 2.2

Write two multiplication sentences for each array. page 102

4. ●●●●●●
   ●●●●●●

5. ●●●●●
   ●●●●●
   ●●●●●
   ●●●●●

Multiply. page 144

6. 2×7 7. 2×6 8. 5×7 9. 5×8

Problem Solving and Reasoning NS 2.0, KEY NS 2.2

10. A pet shop has 4 cages of birds. There are 6 birds in each cage. How many birds does the pet shop have?

Vocabulary

Visualize It!

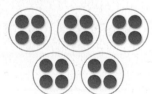

$$20 \div 5 = 4$$

The dots are **divided** equally into 5 groups.

divisor
the number you are dividing by

quotient
the answer

$$5\overline{)20} \quad \overset{4}{\phantom{5\overline{)20}}}$$

dividend
the number that is divided

Language Tip

Some words are similar in Spanish and English.

English	Spanish
dividend	dividendo
quotient	cociente
divisor	divisor
divide	dividir

See **English-Spanish Glossary** pages 628–646.

Education Place Visit www.eduplace.com/camap/ for the **eGlossary** and **eGames**.

CA Standards MR 2.3 Use a variety of methods, such as words, numbers, symbols, charts, graphs, tables, diagrams, and models, to explain mathematical reasoning. **Also NS 2.0**

LESSON 1

CA Standards

NS 2.0 Students calculate and solve problems involving addition, subtraction, multiplication, and division.

MR 2.3 Use a variety of methods, such as words, numbers, symbols, charts, graphs, tables, diagrams, and models, to explain mathematical reasoning.

Also MR 2.4

Vocabulary

divide

equal groups

division

Materials

- Counters
- Workmat 1
- Learning Tool 20 (Recording Sheet)

Hands On
Model Division

Objective Use models to explore two ways to think about division.

 **Explore**

When you **divide**, you separate items into **equal groups**.

Question How can you use counters and drawings to model **division**?

Suppose you have 18 counters and want to make 6 equal groups. How many counters are in each group?

1 Get 18 counters. Draw 6 circles on your Workmat.

2 Share 18 counters equally among the circles.

There are 3 counters in each circle.

3 Write the division sentence.

$$18 \div 6 = 3$$

number of counters   number of groups   number in each group

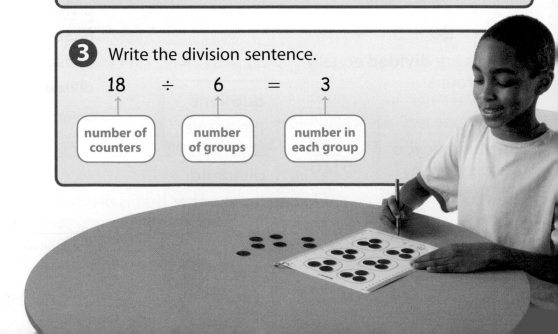

You can also divide to find the number of equal groups.
Suppose you have 18 counters and want to make groups
of 6. How many groups of 6 can you take out of 18?

1 Get 18 counters. Make as many
groups of 6 as you can.

2 Draw a circle around each group.

3 Write the division sentence.

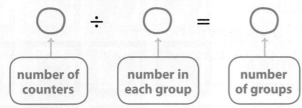

| number of counters | number in each group | number of groups |

▶ **Extend**

Divide. Make a drawing. Then complete the division sentence.

	Number of Counters	Number of Equal Groups	Number in Each Group	Drawing	Division Sentence
1.	9	3	■	⊙⊙⊙	9 ÷ 3 = ■
2.	14	2	■	⊛⊛	14 ÷ 2 = ■
3.	30	■	6	⊛⊛⊛⊛⊛	30 ÷ 6 = ■
4.	48	■	6	⊛⊛⊛⊛ ⊛⊛⊛⊛	48 ÷ 6 = ■

5. Challenge In how many ways can you divide
50 counters evenly? Explain.

Writing Math

Describe Describe two ways to divide 8 objects into
equal groups.

CA Standards

KEY NS 2.3 Use the inverse relationship of multiplication and division to compute and check results.

MR 3.2 Note the method of deriving the solution and demonstrate a conceptual understanding of the derivation by solving similar problems.

Also NS 2.0, MR 2.0, MR 2.3, MR 2.4

Vocabulary

inverse operations

dividend

divisor

quotient

Relate Division and Multiplication

Objective Use arrays to relate division and multiplication.

▶ **Learn by Example**

You can use arrays to understand how division and multiplication are related. Multiplication and division are **inverse operations**.

The 12 pictures of kittens form an array.

You know how to write a multiplication sentence for the array. You can also write the related division sentences.

Draw It	**Write It**

1 Multiply to find the number of pictures in all.

$$3 \quad \times \quad 4 \quad = \quad 12$$

number of rows	number in each row	number in all
(factor)	(factor)	(product)

2 Divide to find the number of pictures in each row.

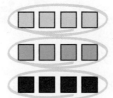

$$12 \quad \div \quad 3 \quad = \quad 4$$

number in all	number of rows	number in each row
(dividend)	**(divisor)**	**(quotient)**

3 Divide to find the number of rows.

$$12 \quad \div \quad 4 \quad = \quad 3$$

number in all	number in each row	number of rows
(dividend)	(divisor)	(quotient)

Draw an array for the multiplication sentence.
Then write two related division sentences.

1. $4 \times 6 = 24$ **2.** $4 \times 9 = 36$ **3.** $2 \times 10 = 20$

Ask Yourself
- How many rows are there?
- How many are in each row?
- How many are there in all?

Guided Problem Solving

Use the questions to solve this problem.

4. Ann has 15 photos of dogs. She wants to hang the photos on the wall in an array. If she makes 5 rows, how many pictures will be in each row?

  a. Understand What do you know? What do you want to find out?

  b. Plan Draw an array to help you. How many rows will there be?

  c. Solve Draw the array. Write the answer to the problem.

  d. Look Back Did you draw 15 squares in all? Did you draw 5 rows? Is there the same number of squares in each row?

 Math Talk How is the product in multiplication related to the dividend in division?

▶ **Practice and Problem Solving**

Use the array to complete the number sentences.

5. ✿✿✿✿✿✿✿

$1 \times \boxed{} = 7$

$7 \div \boxed{} = 7$

6. ♥♥♥
  ♥♥♥

$\boxed{} \times 3 = 6$

$\boxed{} \div 2 = 3$

7. ◆◆◆◆◆
  ◆◆◆◆◆

$\boxed{} \times 5 = 10$

$\boxed{} \div 2 = 5$

**Draw an array for the multiplication sentence.
Then write two related division sentences.**

8. $6 \times 3 = 18$ **9.** $3 \times 4 = 12$ **10.** $6 \times 1 = 6$

 Real World Data

Use the pictograph to solve Problems 11–14.

11. What symbol represents 1 report?

12. Each student in Mrs. Holly's class wrote one report. How many students are in Mrs. Holly's class?

13. How many more dog reports were written than cat reports?

14. Challenge Can Rick display the turtle reports in 3 equal rows? Explain.

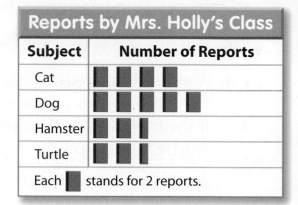

Subject	Number of Reports
Cat	▮ ▮ ▮ ▮
Dog	▮ ▮ ▮ ▮ ▮
Hamster	▮ ▮ ▮
Turtle	▮ ▮ ▮

Reports by Mrs. Holly's Class

Each ▮ stands for 2 reports.

 Spiral Review and Test Practice

Name the kind of triangle shown. Write *equilateral*, *isosceles*, or *right*. KEY MG 2.2 page 198

15. 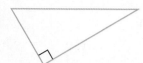   **16.**   **17.**

Write the letter of the correct answer. KEY NS 2.3

18. The figure below is a model for the multiplication sentence. Which division sentence is modeled by the same figure?

$3 \times 8 = 24$

A $3 \div 24 = 8$ **C** $8 \div 24 = 3$

B $24 \div 4 = 6$ **D** $24 \div 8 = 3$

Extra Practice See page 275, Set A.

Key Standards Review

Need Help?
See Key Standards Handbook.

Name the place of the underlined digit. Then tell its value. KEY **NS 1.3**

1. 8<u>4</u>8   **2.** <u>7</u>66   **3.** 4,0<u>8</u>2   **4.** <u>6</u>,918   **5.** <u>8</u>,531

Write each number in expanded notation. KEY **NS 1.5**

6. 687   **7.** 402   **8.** 3,789   **9.** 5,910   **10.** 8,002

Write the number in standard form. Read carefully. KEY **NS 1.3**

11. 5 in the hundreds place, 7 in the ones place, 6 in the tens place

12. 1 in the tens place, 4 in the hundreds place, 8 in the ones place

13. 5 in the thousands place, 2 in the hundreds place, 8 in the tens place, 0 in the ones place

Number Sense

Factor Trees   KEY **NS 2.2**

To find the factors of a number you can make a factor tree.

❶   24
       4   6

❷   24
     4   6
   2 × 2   2 × 3

Make a factor tree for each number. Continue until the bottom row includes only the factors 2, 3, or 5.

1. 8   **2.** 12   **3.** 16   **4.** 27   **5.** 30

CA Standards
KEY **NS 2.3** Use the inverse relationship of multiplication and division to compute and check results.
Also NS 2.0, MR 2.3

Vocabulary

repeated subtraction

Think

Count forward to multiply. Count back to divide.

Different Ways to Divide

Objective Use different strategies to divide.

▶ **Learn by Example**

You already know several division strategies. **Repeated subtraction** is another way to divide.

The pet store has 12 hamsters. If Kim wants to put 2 hamsters in each cage, how many cages will she need?

Different Ways to Divide

Way 1   Use repeated subtraction.

- Start at 12.

- Count back by 2s to 0.

0 1 2 3 4 5 6 7 8 9 10 11 12

- Count the number of 2s you subtracted.

You subtracted 2 six times. So $12 \div 2 = 6$.

Way 2   Make equal groups.

⬤⬤ ⬤⬤ ⬤⬤ ⬤⬤ ⬤⬤ ⬤⬤

There are 6 groups of 2. So $12 \div 2 = 6$.

Way 3   Make an array.

⬤⬤⬤⬤⬤⬤
⬤⬤⬤⬤⬤⬤

$12 \div 2 = 6$

Way 4   Use a related multiplication fact.

$12 \div 2 = \bigcirc$ Think: $2 \times \bigcirc = 12$ So $12 \div 2 = 6$.
$2 \times 6 = 12$

Solution: Kim will need 6 cages.

▶ Guided Practice

Find the quotient. Tell which way you used.

1. $6 \div 2 = \blacksquare$
2. $15 \div 3 = \blacksquare$
3. $8 \div 4 = \blacksquare$
4. $12 \div 3 = \blacksquare$
5. $10 \div 2 = \blacksquare$
6. $14 \div 2 = \blacksquare$

 Math Talk Which strategy is easiest for you to use? Explain.

Ask Yourself

How can a multiplication fact help me find the quotient?

▶ Practice and Problem Solving

Find the quotient. Tell which way you used.

7. $40 \div 10 = \blacksquare$
8. $30 \div 5 = \blacksquare$
9. $18 \div 2 = \blacksquare$
10. $10 \div 2 = \blacksquare$
11. $12 \div 4 = \blacksquare$
12. $60 \div 10 = \blacksquare$
13. $16 \div 2 = \blacksquare$
14. $20 \div 5 = \blacksquare$
15. $45 \div 5 = \blacksquare$
16. $35 \div 5 = \blacksquare$
17. $8 \div 2 = \blacksquare$
18. $70 \div 10 = \blacksquare$

Solve the problems below.

19. A store has 20 hamster cages on 4 shelves. There is an equal number of cages on each shelf. How many cages are on 1 shelf?

20. There are 8 hamsters. If Kyle feeds 2 pieces of lettuce to each hamster, how many pieces of lettuce does he need?

✓ Spiral Review and Test Practice

Tell whether the figure is a quadrilateral. If it has a special name, write it. KEY **MG 2.3** page 200

21.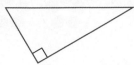

22.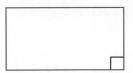

23.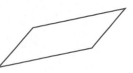

Write the letter of the correct answer. KEY **NS 2.3**

24. Which can you use to check $72 \div 9 = 8$?

   A $9 + 8 = \blacksquare$ **B** $9 - 8 = \blacksquare$ **C** $9 \times 8 = \blacksquare$ **D** $9 \div 8 = \blacksquare$

CA Standards

KEY **NS 2.3** Use the inverse relationship of multiplication and division to compute and check results.

MR 2.0 Students use strategies, skills, and concepts in finding solutions.

Also NS 2.0, MR 1.0, MR 2.3, MR 2.4

Practice Dividing by 2, 5, or 10

Objective Use different ways to divide by 2, 5, and 10.

▶ Learn by Example

There are 20 treats for the dogs in a training class. If each dog gets 5 treats, how many dogs are there in the class?

You can write 20 divided by 5 in two ways.

$20 \div 5 = \bigcirc$ or $5\overline{)20}$

Different Ways to Divide

Way 1 Use repeated subtraction.

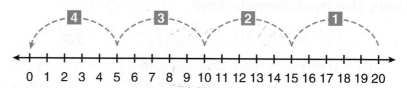

You subtracted 5 four times.

So $20 \div 5 = 4$ or $\dfrac{4}{5\overline{)20}}$

Way 2 Make equal groups.

There are 4 groups of 5.

So $20 \div 5 = 4$ or $\dfrac{4}{5\overline{)20}}$

Way 3 Make an array.

$20 \div 5 = 4$ or $\dfrac{4}{5\overline{)20}}$

Way 4 Use a related multiplication fact.

$20 \div 5 = \bigcirc$ $5 \times \bigcirc = 20$

$5 \times 4 = 20$ $5\overline{)20}$ ⁴

Solution: There are 4 dogs in the class.

▶ Guided Practice

Divide. Check by multiplying.

1. $6 \div 2$ **2.** $4 \div 2$ **3.** $10 \div 5$ **4.** $25 \div 5$

5. $20 \div 10$ **6.** $70 \div 10$ **7.** $2\overline{)14}$ **8.** $2\overline{)18}$

9. $5\overline{)35}$ **10.** $10\overline{)20}$ **11.** $10\overline{)40}$ **12.** $10\overline{)70}$

Ask Yourself
- Which division strategy will I use?
- Can I check my answer with multiplication?

Guided Problem Solving

Use the questions to solve this problem.

13. There are 30 dogs competing in a dog show. Each trainer takes care of 5 dogs. How many trainers take care of the 30 dogs?

a. **Understand** What do you know? What do you want to find out?

b. **Plan** Which strategy will you use?

c. **Solve** Use the strategy to solve the problem. Write the answer.

d. **Look Back** How can you use multiplication to check your answer? How can you solve the problem in a different way?

Other Strategies
- repeated subtraction
- equal groups
- arrays
- using a related fact

123 Math Talk How can you use multiplication to check that $40 \div 5 = 8$?

Practice and Problem Solving

Divide. Check by multiplying.

14. $20 \div 2$ **15.** $12 \div 2$ **16.** $8 \div 2$ **17.** $10 \div 2$ **18.** $16 \div 2$

19. $45 \div 5$ **20.** $15 \div 5$ **21.** $20 \div 5$ **22.** $30 \div 5$ **23.** $50 \div 5$

24. $90 \div 10$ **25.** $60 \div 10$ **26.** $20 \div 10$ **27.** $50 \div 10$ **28.** $80 \div 10$

29. $2\overline{)24}$ **30.** $5\overline{)40}$ **31.** $5\overline{)35}$ **32.** $10\overline{)30}$ **33.** $10\overline{)100}$

Science Link

Solve. Use the Fun Facts to solve Problem 34.

34. How many claws does a cat have in all?

35. Two cats together weigh 18 pounds. If both cats weigh the same, what is the weight of each cat?

36. Challenge Suzie's cat sleeps 20 hours a day. How many hours is her cat awake in one week?

Cats

- Cats usually weigh between 9 and 14 pounds.

- A cat can sleep about 12 to 20 hours a day, napping often for short periods of time.

- A cat has 4 claws on each of its rear paws and 5 claws on each of its front paws.

Science LS 3.e

 Spiral Review and Test Practice

Name the figure shown. MG 2.5 page 234

37.

38.

39.

Write the letter of the correct answer. KEY NS 2.3

40. Jill bought 60 bagels packed equally into 10 bags. Which number sentence shows how to find the number of bagels in each bag?

A $60 + 10$ **B** 60×10 **C** $60 - 10$ **D** $60 \div 10$

Extra Practice See page 275, Set C.

Lightning and Thunder

Have you ever noticed that during a thunder storm, first you see lightning, then you hear thunder?

You can use division to estimate how many miles away lightning is from where you are. First, you need to know the number of seconds between the flash of lightning and the crash of thunder. Then, you need to keep in mind that it takes five seconds for the round of thunder to travel one mile.

Sam saw lightning. Twenty seconds later he heard thunder. How many miles away was the lightning?

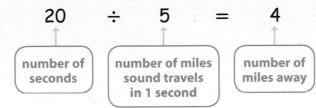

20 ÷ 5 = 4

number of seconds   number of miles sound travels in 1 second   number of miles away

The lightning was 4 miles away.

Each time shows the number of seconds between seeing lightning and hearing thunder. Estimate how many miles away the lightning is.

1. 10 seconds   **2.** 35 seconds

3. 15 seconds   **4.** 30 seconds

5. Burt says the lightning he saw is 9 miles away. About how many seconds later did he hear thunder?

This meteorologist studies lightning using a computer.

CA Standards
NS 2.0

San Diego, CA

CA Standards
MR 1.0, MR 1.1,
MR 1.2, MR 2.0,
NS 1.2, NS 2.0,
KEY **NS 2.1**, NS 2.8,
KEY **AF 1.1**, AF 2.0,
KEY **AF 2.1**, AF 2.2,
MG 1.4

Problem Solving

Objective Use skills and strategies to solve word problems.

Funani, an African River Hippo, swims with her baby.

At the San Diego Zoo, you can see and learn about animals from all over the world.

Solve. Tell which strategy or method you used.

Yards	4	1	
Feet			9

1. At the zoo, Pam kept track of how far a frog leaped. Copy and complete the table to see how far the frog jumped in feet and yards.

Hint

3 feet = 1 yard

2. **Multistep** Tembo, an elephant, weighs 9,900 lbs. Jabba and Funani are hippos. Jabba weighs 5,300 lbs. Funani weighs 3,500 lbs. Are the two hippos together heavier than Tembo?

3. Two adult gorillas and 3 baby gorillas were eating. Four gorillas were grooming. Which compares the number of gorillas eating to the number of gorillas grooming?

   A $2 + 3 > 4$ **B** $2 + 3 + 4 = 9$

4. Mark saw 2 bird nests and 6 eggs. There was an equal number of eggs in each nest. How many eggs were in each nest?

Gorilla at the San Diego Zoo

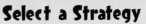

Problem Solving On Tests

Select a Strategy
- Estimate
- Choose the Operation
- Draw a Picture

1. There are 5000 tickets for a play. The box office sold 3286 tickets. How many tickets have not been sold?

A 3824 **C** 1714

B 2714 **D** 1614

KEY **NS 2.1** page 80

2. Chou used his calculator to find that $8 \times 12 \times 9 = 864$. What is the product of $9 \times 8 \times 12$?

A 72

B 96

C 108

D 864

> **Test Tip**
> What does the Commutative Property of Multiplication tell you?

AF **1.5** page 102

3. Paulo drew a picture of an object that is shaped like a cube. Which could be the object he drew?

A

B

C

D

MG **2.5** page 234

4. For 5 days in a row, Miquel puts 4 coins in each of 2 piggy banks. He writes this equation to show the number of coins.

$(5 \times 4) \times 2 = 40$.

Which expression is also equal to 40?

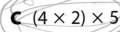

A $(5 \times 4) + 2$ **C** $(4 \times 2) \times 5$

B $2 \times (5 + 4)$ **D** $5 + (4 + 2)$

AF **1.5** page 152

5. There are 36 inches in 1 yard. Lydia's garden is 3 yards in length. How many inches is this?

A 12 inches   **C** 108 inches

B 36 inches   **D** 918 inches

MG **1.4** page 172

6. Bob has 50 toy cars. He wants to share them equally with 5 friends. How many toy cars will each friend get?

A 5   **B** 10   **C** 15   **D** 20

NS **2.0** page 268

Education Place
Visit www.eduplace.com/camap/ for
Test-Taking Tips and **Extra Practice**.

Reading & Writing **Math**

Vocabulary

When you **divide** you are separating items into **equal groups**. You have learned several **division** strategies. Solve this problem in 4 ways.

Josh has 30 toy cars. He puts them in small boxes. Five toy cars fit in each box. How many boxes does Josh need?

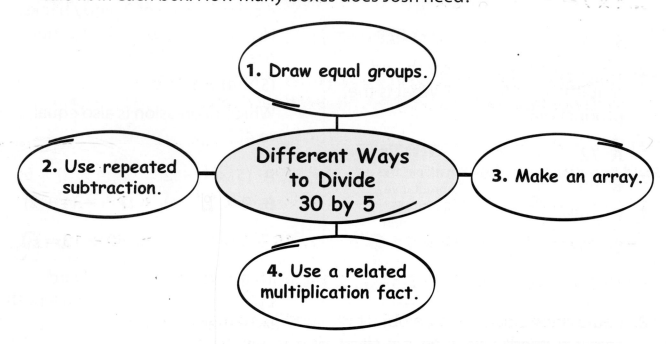

1. Draw equal groups.

2. Use repeated subtraction.

Different Ways to Divide 30 by 5

3. Make an array.

4. Use a related multiplication fact.

Read the list of words in the **Word Bank**. Find the word that best completes the sentence.

5. The answer in a division problem is called the _____.

6. The number that divides the dividend is called the _____.

7. The number that is divided is called the _____.

Word Bank
dividend
divisor
inverse relationship
missing factor
quotient

Writing Which division strategy do you like the best? Tell why.

Reading Check out this book in your library.

- *The Doorbell Rang*, by Pat Hutchins

CA Standards
MR 2.3 Use a variety of methods, such as words, numbers, symbols, charts, graphs, tables, diagrams, and models, to explain mathematical reasoning.

Also NS 2.0, KEY NS 2.3

Standards-Based Extra Practice

Set A ———————————————————————— KEY **NS 2.3** page 262

Draw an array for the multiplication sentence. Then write two related division sentences.

1. $8 \times 9 = 72$ **2.** $6 \times 5 = 30$ **3.** $10 \times 3 = 30$ **4.** $5 \times 8 = 40$

5. $4 \times 7 = 28$ **6.** $2 \times 9 = 18$ **7.** $6 \times 7 = 42$ **8.** $4 \times 2 = 8$

9. $5 \times 3 = 15$ **10.** $9 \times 6 = 54$ **11.** $3 \times 8 = 24$ **12.** $2 \times 7 = 14$

13. There are 27 people sitting in 3 equal rows. Write a division sentence to show how many people are in each row.

Set B ———————————————————————— NS **2.0** page 266

Find the quotient. Tell which strategy you used.

1. $14 \div 7 = $ ■   **2.** $45 \div 9 = $ ■   **3.** $16 \div 4 = $ ■   **4.** $27 \div 3 = $ ■

5. $42 \div 6 = $ ■   **6.** $12 \div 4 = $ ■   **7.** $15 \div 5 = $ ■   **8.** $40 \div 10 = $ ■

9. $16 \div 2 = $ ■   **10.** $24 \div 8 = $ ■   **11.** $10 \div 2 = $ ■

12. Lisa collects beads. She has 15 beads lined up to make a necklace. Every third bead is silver. How many silver beads are there in her necklace?

Set C ———————————————————————— KEY **NS 2.3** page 268

Divide. Check by multiplying.

1. $8 \div 2$ **2.** $10 \div 5$ **3.** $70 \div 10$ **4.** $45 \div 5$ **5.** $4 \div 2$

6. $30 \div 5$ **7.** $80 \div 10$ **8.** $18 \div 2$ **9.** $10 \div 2$ **10.** $40 \div 10$

11. $5 \overline{)5}$ **12.** $2 \overline{)12}$ **13.** $10 \overline{)60}$ **14.** $5 \overline{)40}$ **15.** $10 \overline{)100}$

16. $2 \overline{)18}$ **17.** $5 \overline{)35}$ **18.** $10 \overline{)20}$ **19.** $2 \overline{)20}$ **20.** $5 \overline{)15}$

21. Mrs. Johnston's class wants to give out 5 prizes each hour in a prize drawing. They have 35 prizes to give away. How many times can they have a drawing?

 Education Place
Visit www.eduplace.com/camap/
for more **Extra Practice.**

Chapter Review/Test

Vocabulary and Concepts ——————————————— NS 2.0

Choose the best term to complete each sentence.

Word Bank
~~equal groups~~
~~dividend~~
~~quotient~~

1. The answer to a division problem is the _dividend_.

2. When you divide, you can separate the items into _equal groups_.

3. The _quotient_ is the number that is being divided.

Skills ——————————————————————————————— KEY NS 2.3

Draw an array for the multiplication sentence. Then write two related division sentences.

4. $4 \times 3 = 12$

5. $7 \times 8 = 56$

6. $5 \times 10 = 50$

7. $6 \times 9 = 54$

Find the quotient. Tell which strategy you used.

8. $60 \div 4 = \blacksquare$

9. $24 \div 6 = \blacksquare$

10. $72 \div 9 = \blacksquare$

Divide. Check by multiplying.

11. $10\overline{)20}$

12. $5\overline{)45}$

13. $2\overline{)32}$

Problem Solving and Reasoning —————————————— KEY NS 2.3

Solve.

14. Theresa has 24 dolls in her collection. She wants to display them in equal groups on 3 shelves. How many dolls will be on each shelf?

15. Aimee has four puppies. Together the puppies weigh 60 pounds. If the puppies weigh the same, what is the weight of each puppy?

Writing Math Mark says that you can find the missing factor in $8 \times \blacksquare = 48$ by using division. Is he right? Why or why not?

Spiral Review and Test Practice

1. Look at the number sentence below.

$5005 - 7 = \square$

Which number will make the number sentence true?

A 4008   **C** 4098

B 4998   **D** 5012

KEY **NS 2.1** page 80

2. Which shapes make up this solid object?

A circle and square

B cube and square

C cylinder and cube

D cylinder and circle

MG **2.6** page 234

3. How many millimeters are in 8 centimeters?

A 800 mm

B 80 mm

C 118 mm

D 18 mm

MG **1.4** page 178

4. What is the volume of this figure?

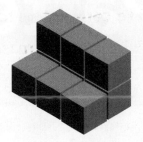

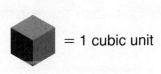 = 1 cubic unit

A 15 cubic units

B 9 cubic units

C 7 cubic units

D 6 cubic units

Test Tip
Remember to include the cubes you cannot see.

KEY **MG 1.2** page 240

5. The figure below is a model for the multiplication sentence.

$3 \times 9 = 27$

Which division sentence is modeled by the same figure?

A $9 \div 3 = 3$

B $18 \div 2 = 9$

C $27 \div 3 = 9$

D $18 \div 9 = 2$

Test Tip
Think of the relationship between multiplication and division.

KEY **NS 2.3** page 262

Education Place
Visit www.eduplace.com/camap/ for **Test-Taking Tips** and **Extra Practice**.

Division Patterns

Peruvian dolls for sale at Old Town Market in San Diego, CA.

Check What You Know

Vocabulary and Concepts NS 2.0, MR 2.3

Choose the best word to complete each sentence. page 262

1. In the number sentence $14 \div 2 = 7$, the 2 is the _____.

2. The answer in a division problem is called the _____.

3. In the number sentence $40 \div 5 = 8$, the _____ is 40.

Skills NS 2.0, KEY NS 2.3

Write a multiplication sentence and a division sentence for each array. page 262

4. ▲▲
   ▲▲

5. ▲▲▲▲▲▲
   ▲▲▲▲▲▲
   ▲▲▲▲▲▲

6. ▲▲▲▲▲▲▲▲
   ▲▲▲▲▲▲▲▲
   ▲▲▲▲▲▲▲▲

Divide. Chapter 12

7. $10 \div 5$

8. $15 \div 5$

9. $20 \div 4$

Problem Solving and Reasoning NS 2.0

10. Omar has 20 berries. He wants to put the same number of berries in each of 5 bowls. How many berries should he put in each bowl?

Vocabulary

Visualize It!

fact family

Related facts using the same numbers.

Fact Family for 2, 4, and 8	
▲▲ ▲▲ ▲▲ ▲▲ $4 \times 2 = 8$	▲▲▲▲ ▲▲▲▲ $2 \times 4 = 8$
(▲▲) (▲▲) $8 \div 2 = 4$	(▲)(▲)(▲)(▲) $8 \div 4 = 2$

Language Tips

The members of a family are related and share traits. In mathematics, the members of a **fact family** are related and share numbers.

Some words are similar in Spanish and English.

English	Spanish
family	familia

See **English-Spanish Glossary** pages 628–646.

CA Standards MR 2.3 Use a variety of methods, such as words, numbers, symbols, charts, graphs, tables, diagrams, and models, to explain mathematical reasoning. **Also KEY NS 2.3**

Chapter 13   279

LESSON 1

CA Standards
KEY NS 2.3 Use the inverse relationship of multiplication and division to compute and check results.
Also NS 2.0, MR 1.1, MR 2.3, MR 2.4

Vocabulary

multiple

Materials

- Learning Tool 12 (Multiplication Table)
- Learning Tool 22 (Recording Sheet)

Hands On
Use a Multiplication Table to Divide

Objective Use a multiplication table to understand how divisors, dividends, and quotients are related.

 **Explore**

Multiplication and division are inverse, or opposite, operations.

Question How can you use a multiplication table to help you divide?

---

1 Use the table to find $30 \div 5$.

column for 6 →

×	0	1	2	3	4	5	6	7	8	9	10
0	0	0	0	0	0	0	0	0	0	0	0
1	0	1	2	3	4	5	6	7	8	9	10
2	0	2	4	6	8	10	12	14	16	18	20
3	0	3	6	9	12	15	18	21	24	27	30
4	0	4	8	12	16	20	24	28	32	36	40
5	0	5	10	15	20	25	(30)	35	40	45	50
6	0	6	12	18	24	30	36	42	48	54	60
7	0	7	14	21	28	35	42	49	56	63	70
8	0	8	16	24	32	40	48	56	64	72	80
9	0	9	18	27	36	45	54	63	72	81	90
10	0	10	20	30	40	50	60	70	80	90	100

row for 5 →

5 is the divisor. Find the row marked 5.

All the numbers in this row are **multiples** of 5.

---

2 30 is the dividend. Move across the row for 5 to the square that shows 30.

3 Look at the number at the top of the column. 6 is the quotient.

$30 \div 5 = 6$

4 Use multiplication to check.

$6 \times 5 = 30$

▶ **Extend**

Copy and complete the chart.
Use the multiplication table to help you.

	Division	Divisor	Dividend	Quotient	Related Multiplication Facts
1.	$30 \div 5$	5	30	6	$5 \times 6 = 30$ $6 \times 5 = 30$
2.	$35 \div 7$				
3.	$56 \div 8$				
4.	$81 \div 9$				
5.	$36 \div 4$				
6.	$30 \div 3$				

Use the multiplication table to find the quotient.

7. $12 \div 2$ **8.** $9 \div 1$ **9.** $36 \div 4$ **10.** $18 \div 3$ **11.** $15 \div 5$

12. $28 \div 4$ **13.** $30 \div 6$ **14.** $28 \div 7$ **15.** $16 \div 8$ **16.** $27 \div 9$

17. Challenge If the dividend and the divisor are even numbers, is the quotient always an even number? Support your answer.

Writing Math

Explain How can you use a multiplication table to find $32 \div 4$?

CA Standards
KEY (NS 2.3) Use the inverse relationship of multiplication and division to compute and check results.

NS 2.0 Students calculate and solve problems involving addition, subtraction, multiplication, and division.

Also AF 1.2, AF 1.3, MR 2.0, MR 2.3, MR 2.4, MR 3.0, MR 3.3

Practice Dividing by 3 or 4

Objective Use different ways to divide by 3 and 4.

▶ **Learn by Example**

You can use the division strategies you already know to help you divide by 3 and 4.

Inez bakes sourdough bread. In the morning, she makes 15 loaves of fresh bread. She puts the same number of loaves into each of 3 bins. How many loaves are in each bin?

Think

Here are some other ways to divide by 3 and 4.

- Make equal groups.
- Make an array.
- Use a multiplication table.

Different Ways to Divide

Way 1   Use repeated subtraction.

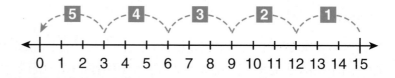

- Start at 15 on the number line.
- Count back by 3s to 0.
- Count the number of 3s you subtracted.

You subtracted five 3s.

So $15 \div 3 = 5$.

Way 2   Use a related multiplication fact.

$15 \div 3 = \bigcirc$

So $15 \div 3 = 5$.

Think:
$3 \times \bigcirc = 15$
$3 \times 5 = 15$

Solution: There are 5 loaves in each bin.

Divide. Use any strategy.

1. $9 \div 3$ **2.** $12 \div 4$ **3.** $4\overline{)36}$ **4.** $3\overline{)21}$

Ask Yourself
- What multiplication fact can help me?
- Can I make equal groups?

Guided Problem Solving

5. Inez puts 18 muffins onto 3 trays. There are the same number of muffins on each tray. How many muffins are on each tray?

     a. Understand What is the total number of muffins? How many trays are there?

     b. Plan Choose a division strategy.

     c. Solve Use the strategy you chose. Solve the problem. Write the answer.

     d. Look Back Solve the problem using a different strategy. Did you get the same answer?

6. Look back at Problem 5. If Inez divided 21 muffins equally on 3 trays, how many muffins would be on each tray?

123 **Math Talk** Pam divided 12 by 4 by dividing 12 by 2 and then dividing 6 by 2. Will this strategy always work for dividing by 4?

► **Practice and Problem Solving**

Divide. Use any strategy.

7. $40 \div 4$ **8.** $9 \div 3$ **9.** $32 \div 4$ **10.** $27 \div 3$ **11.** $30 \div 3$

12. $4\overline{)28}$ **13.** $4\overline{)24}$ **14.** $3\overline{)6}$ **15.** $4\overline{)16}$ **16.** $3\overline{)18}$

17. $3\overline{)15}$ **18.** $4\overline{)20}$ **19.** $4\overline{)36}$ **20.** $3\overline{)21}$ **21.** $4\overline{)12}$

Algebra Equations

Find the missing factor and quotient for the pair of facts.

22. $3 \times \blacksquare = 24$
$24 \div 3 = \blacksquare$

23. $4 \times \blacksquare = 36$
$36 \div 4 = \blacksquare$

24. $3 \times \blacksquare = 18$
$18 \div 3 = \blacksquare$

Write $>$, $<$, or $=$ for the ⬤.

25. $15 \div 3$ ⬤ $15 + 3$

26. 3×3 ⬤ $36 \div 4$

27. $28 \div 4$ ⬤ 2×5

Use $\div$ or $\times$ to complete the number sentence.

28. 4 ⬤ $3 = 6 \times 2$

29. $36 \div 4 = 3$ ⬤ 3

30. 2 ⬤ $4 = 24 \div 3$

 ## Real World Data

Use the graph for Problems 31–33.

31. The third grade is hosting breakfast. Students who brought muffins brought 4 muffins each. How many students brought muffins?

32. If 42 people come for the breakfast, can each person have either a roll or a bagel? Explain.

33. **Analyze** Four people cut the rolls in half. One person cut 6 rolls. Did each person cut the same number of rolls? Explain why or why not.

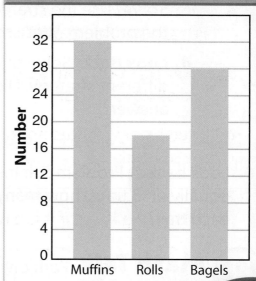

Foods Brought for Breakfast

Spiral Review and Test Practice

Compare. Write $>$, $<$, or $=$ for the ⬤. MG 1.4 page 172

34. 2 ft ⬤ 13 in.

35. 5,000 ft ⬤ 1 mi

36. 2 yd ⬤ 6 ft

Write the letter of the correct answer. KEY **NS 2.3**

37. How could Rachel check $36 \div 4 = 9$?

A $4 + 9 = \blacksquare$ **B** $9 - 4 = \blacksquare$ **C** $4 \times 9 = \blacksquare$ **D** $9 \div 4 = \blacksquare$

Extra Practice See page 295, Set A.

Key Standards Review

Need Help?
See Key Standards Handbook.

Solve. KEY **MG 2.3**

1. One side of a rectangle is 6 inches long. Another side is 4 inches long. How long are the two other sides of the rectangle?

2. Two opposite sides of a rectangle are each 5 inches long. What are the lengths of the other two sides of the rectangle?

3. How many right angles are in a square?

Use the words in the box. Write all the names that match each figure. KEY **MG 2.3**

4. Tom's figure has exactly 1 pair of parallel sides. What figure did Tom draw?

5. LaKeisha's polygon has 4 right angles and all equal sides.

6. Jared's polygon has opposite sides that are parallel.

7. What else do you need to know about Jared's polygon to know if it is a rectangle?

> quadrilateral
> parallelogram
> rectangle
> square

 Math Reasoning

Mystery Numbers

Use the clues to find the mystery number. NS 2.0, NS 2.8

1. If you divide the number by 5 and then you divide the answer by 2, you get 4. What is the mystery number?

2. If you divide the number by 9 and then you add 12, you get 20. What is the mystery number?

CA Standards

KEY **NS 2.3** Use the inverse relationship of multiplication and division to compute and check results.

AF 1.2 Solve problems involving numeric equations or inequalities.

Also NS 2.0, AF 1.0, AF 1.3, MR 1.1, MR 2.3, MR 2.4

Vocabulary

fact family

related facts

Fact Families

Objective Use fact families to show how multiplication and division are related.

▶ Learn by Example

A **fact family** is a group of equations that use the same numbers. Fact families show how multiplication and division are related.

How many ways can you describe the array of stickers? You can use the fact family for 3, 4, and 12.

Example

There are 4 rows of stickers. There are 3 stickers in each row. There are 12 stickers in all.

$$12 = 4 \times 3$$

total   number in each row   rows

$$12 = 3 \times 4$$

total   rows   number in each row

$$12 \div 4 = 3$$

total   number in each row   rows

$$12 \div 3 = 4$$

total   rows   number in each row

Another Example

The fact family for 4, 4, and 16 has only 2 **related facts** because the number of rows and the number in each row are the same.

$$4 \times 4 = 16 \qquad 16 \div 4 = 4$$

▶ Guided Practice

Copy and complete the fact family.

1. ○○○○ $3 \times 3 = 9$
   ○○○○ $9 \div 3 = \blacksquare$
   ○○○

2. ●●●● $2 \times 4 = 8$
   ●●●● $4 \times 2 = \blacksquare$
             $8 \div 4 = \blacksquare$
             $8 \div 2 = \blacksquare$

(123) Math Talk How are the products and dividends related in each fact family?

▶ Practice and Problem Solving

Copy and complete the fact family.

3. $1 \times 8 = 8$
   $8 \times \blacksquare = 8$
   $8 \div 1 = \blacksquare$
   $8 \bullet 8 = 1$

4. $5 \times 9 = 45$
   $9 \bullet 5 = 45$
   $\blacksquare \div 5 = 9$
   $45 \div 9 = \blacksquare$

5. $3 \times 10 = 30$
   $\blacksquare \times 3 = 30$
   $30 \bullet 3 = 10$
   $30 \div \blacksquare = 3$

6. $6 \times 5 = 30$
   $5 \bullet 6 = 30$
   $30 \div \blacksquare = 5$
   $\blacksquare \div 5 = 6$

Write a fact family for the set of numbers.

7. 2, 3, 6

8. 10, 2, 20

9. 8, 3, 24

10. 4, 9, 36

Solve.

11. **Right or Wrong?** Shelley says that $4 \times 8 = 32$ and $8 \div 4 = 2$ are in the same fact family. Do you agree? Explain your thinking.

12. **Challenge** Array A is 4 rows and 2 columns. Array B is 3 rows and 4 columns. Which array has the greater dividend in its fact family?

✓ Spiral Review and Test Practice

Write the related division equations. KEY **NS 2.3** page 262

13. $3 \times 6 = 18$

14. $7 \times 7 = 49$

15. $6 \times 5 = 30$

Write the letter of the correct answer. KEY **NS 2.3**

16. Which number sentence is part of the same fact family as $10 \div 2 = 5$?

    A $10 \times 2 = 20$ **B** $5 \times 2 = 10$ **C** $10 + 2 = 12$ **D** $10 \times 5 = 50$

CA Standards
KEY NS 2.3 Use
the inverse relationship of
multiplication and division to
compute and check results.

AF 1.2 Solve problems
involving numeric equations or
inequalities.

**Also NS 2.0, NS 2.8,
AF 1.3, AF 2.0,
KEY AF 2.1, MR 1.1,
MR 1.2, MR 2.0,
MR 2.3, MR 2.4**

Practice Dividing by 9

Objective Learn different ways to divide by 9.

▶ Learn by Example

You can use a related division fact
to help you solve a division problem.

Mr. Nakane has 36 paintings
to hang in 9 rooms at an art
gallery. He hangs the same
number of paintings in each
room. How many paintings
are hung in each room?

$36 \div 9 = \bigcirc$

Different Ways to Divide

Way 1 Use a related multiplication fact.

$9 \times \bigcirc = 36$

$9 \times 4 = 36$ So $36 \div 9 = 4$.

. . . .

Way 2 Use a related division fact.

$36 \div \bigcirc = 9$

$36 \div 4 = 9$ So $36 \div 9 = 4$.

Solution: Four paintings are hung in each room.

▶ Guided Practice

Ask Yourself

• What multiplication
fact can help me?

• What division fact
can help me?

Find the quotient.

1. $9\overline{)45}$ **2.** $9\overline{)63}$ **3.** $81 \div 9$ **4.** $18 \div 9$

 Math Talk Without dividing, how can you tell
that $45 \div 9$ is greater than $36 \div 9$?

Find the quotient.

5. $9\overline{)27}$ **6.** $9\overline{)9}$ **7.** $9\overline{)54}$ **8.** $4\overline{)36}$

9. $3\overline{)24}$ **10.** $5\overline{)30}$ **11.** $4\overline{)16}$ **12.** $63 \div 9$

13. $36 \div 9$ **14.** $72 \div 9$ **15.** $18 \div 3$ **16.** $90 \div 9$

Find the factor and quotient.

17. $9 \times \blacksquare = 36$
$36 \div 9 = \blacksquare$

18. $9 \times \blacksquare = 45$
$45 \div 9 = \blacksquare$

19. $9 \times \blacksquare = 18$
$18 \div 9 = \blacksquare$

20. $9 \times \blacksquare = 72$
$72 \div 9 = \blacksquare$

21. $9 \times \blacksquare = 81$
$81 \div 9 = \blacksquare$

22. $9 \times \blacksquare = 63$
$63 \div 9 = \blacksquare$

23. Mr. Nakane has 45 small stone carvings to display in a case. If he puts 9 carvings in each row, how many rows will he have?

24. Analyze Mr. Nakane has 40 small wood carvings. He wants to arrange them in one case, with an equal number of carvings in each row. How can he do it?

X Algebra Functions and Equations **Copy and complete the table.**

25.

Rule: _____ .	
Input	Output
45	5
18	2
36	4
26. ■	9
27. 9	■

28.

Rule: _____ .	
Input	Output
18	6
27	9
9	3
29. 15	■
30. 6	■

Write $+, -, \times,$ **or** $\div$ **for the** ⬭ **to make the number sentence true.**

31. $9 \times 3 = 27 \,⬭\, 0$ **32.** $5 \,⬭\, 5 = 5 + 20$ **33.** $2 \,⬭\, 1 = 16 \div 8$

Science Link

Solve.

34. Denisha's family has a regular car and a hybrid car. The regular car gets 25 miles per gallon of gas. The hybrid car gets twice as many miles per gallon. How many miles per gallon does the hybrid car get?

35. A car dealer ordered 63 new hybrid cars. He will display the cars in 9 equal rows. How many cars will be in each row?

36. **Challenge** Mr. Singh's hybrid car can travel 50 miles on one gallon of gasoline. If gasoline costs $3 per gallon, how much does it cost Mr. Singh to drive 200 miles?

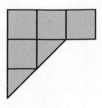

Science PS 1.b

 Spiral Review and Test Practice

Find the area of the figure. Label your answer in square units.

Each ☐ = **1 square unit.** KEY MG 1.2 page 220

37.

38.

39.

Write the letter of the correct answer. NS 2.0

40. Carmen planted 54 trees in 9 days. She planted the same number of trees each day. How many trees did Carmen plant each day?

    A 4   **B** 5   **C** 6   **D** 7

Extra Practice See page 295, Set C.

Shapes in Equations

Write the value of each shape. Use what facts you know about multiplication and division to solve. Copy and record your answers in the table below.

1. $4 \div \blacktriangle = \blacktriangle$

2. $16 \div \bullet = \bullet$

3. $25 \div \blacklozenge = \blacklozenge$

4. $36 \div \blacksquare = \blacksquare$

5. $\blacksquare \times \blacklozenge = \blacksquare\blacksquare$

6. $\blacksquare\blacksquare \div \bigstar = 3$

7. $\bigstar \times 3 = \blacksquare\blacksquare$

8. $\blacksquare\blacksquare \div \blacktriangle = 15$

9. $\bullet \times \blacklozenge = 20$

10. $\blacksquare\blacksquare \div \blacksquare = \blacklozenge$

11. $\blacktriangle \times \blacklozenge = \bigstar$

12. $\bigstar \div \blacktriangle = \blacklozenge$

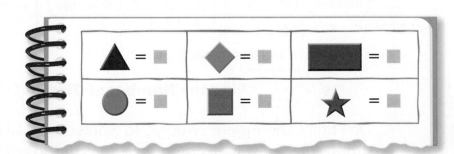

CA Standards
KEY NS 2.2,
KEY NS 2.3, AF 1.2

CA Standards

MR 2.4 Express the solution clearly and logically by using the appropriate mathematical notation and terms and clear language; support solutions with evidence in both verbal and symbolic work.

KEY NS 2.3 Use the inverse relationship of multiplication and division to compute and check results.

Also NS 2.0, NS 2.8, KEY AF 1.1, MR 1.0, MR 1.1, MR 1.2, MR 2.0, MR 2.3, MR 3.0, MR 3.1, MR 3.2, MR 3.3

Problem Solving Plan
Equal Groups Problems

Objective Solve problems about equal groups.

▶ **Learn Through Reasoning**

You will often have to solve problems about equal groups.

Find the Total

At the kennel Jo feeds dogs in groups of 6. On Monday, she fed 3 groups. How many dogs were at the kennel?

$$3 \quad \times \quad 6 \quad = \quad \bigcirc$$

| Number of groups | Number in each group | Total number |

There were 18 dogs at the kennel.

Find the Number in Each Group

On Tuesday, Jo walked 24 dogs in 4 equal groups. How many dogs were in each group?

Think: Multiplication and division are inverse operations.

$$24 \quad \div \quad 4 \quad = \quad \bigcirc \qquad \text{or} \qquad 4 \quad \times \quad \bigcirc \quad = \quad 24$$

| Total number | Number of groups | Number in each group | Number of groups | Number in each group | Total number |

There were 6 dogs in each group.

Find the Number of Groups

On Friday, there were 27 dogs. Jo worked with all the dogs in groups of 9. How many groups of dogs did Jo work with?

$$27 \quad \div \quad 9 \quad = \quad \bigcirc \qquad \text{or} \qquad \bigcirc \quad \times \quad 9 \quad = \quad 27$$

| Total number | Number in each group | Number of groups | Number of groups | Number in each group | Total number |

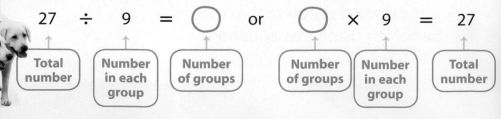

Jo worked with 3 groups of dogs.

► Guided Problem Solving

Solve using the Ask Yourself questions.

1. Dora jogs the same number of miles each week. In 2 weeks, she jogs a total of 18 miles. How many miles does she jog each week?

(123) **Math Talk** Look back at Problem 1. Tell the total, the number of groups, and the number in each group.

Ask Yourself
• Am I looking for a total, the number of groups, or the number in each group?
• What number sentence can I write?

► Independent Problem Solving

Solve. Explain why your answer makes sense.

2. A box of dog treats contains 15 treats. Don gives his dog 3 treats each day. How many days will the box of treats last?

3. Joy had a piece of rope that was 20 inches long. She cut the rope into 4 equal pieces. How long was each piece?

4. On Saturdays, Sarah offers free dance classes at a school. She gives 2 classes with a maximum of 10 people in each class. What is the greatest number of people that can attend a class on Saturday? How many people can attend over 3 Saturdays?

5. **Multistep** Jenna needs 9 pieces of fabric. She needs 4 pieces that are each 3 yards long and 5 pieces that are each 2 yards long. How many yards of fabric does she need?

6. **Challenge** Roger has 20 toy cars to display in equal sized-rows. What are all the different ways Roger can display the toy cars?

7. **Create and Solve** Write an equal groups word problem that can be solved using this equation.
$2 \times \boxed{} = 18$

Reading & Writing **Math**

Vocabulary

A **fact family** is a group of equations that use the same numbers. Fact families show how multiplication and division are related. Writing a number sentence to show **related facts** can help you solve a problem.

Read the two problems. Then answer the questions.

The clerk in Murphy's Sports Shop is organizing the tennis balls that are on sale. There are 6 balls in each package. She counts 9 packages. How many tennis balls are there?	A customer in Murphy's Sports Shop decides to buy the tennis balls that are on sale. He buys 9 packages and has 54 tennis balls. How many tennis balls were in each package?
1. Draw equal groups to show the problem and the solution.	**4. Draw equal groups** to show the problem and the solution.
2. Complete the sentence. 9 groups of 6 balls equals _____.	**5. Complete the sentence.** 54 balls in 9 equal groups equals _____ in each group.
3. Write the number sentence. _____	**6. Write the number sentence.** _____

7. Write four number sentences using these numbers: 6, 9, 54.

Writing Choose a fact family and write a multiplication word problem to go with it. Then write a division word problem using the same numbers.

Reading Look for this book in your library.

- *Math All Around: Patterns in Nature*, by Jennifer Rozines Roy and Gregory Roy

CA Standards
MR 2.3 Use a variety of methods, such as words, numbers, symbols, charts, graphs, tables, diagrams, and models, to explain mathematical reasoning.

Also NS 2.0, KEY NS 2.3

Standards-Based Extra Practice

Set A ───────────────────────────── NS 2.0 page 282

Divide. Use any strategy.

1. $20 \div 4 = 5$ **2.** $27 \div 3$ **3.** $24 \div 4$ **4.** $9 \div 3$ **5.** $8 \div 4$

6. $12 \div 3 = 4$ **7.** $32 \div 4$ **8.** $28 \div 4$ **9.** $6 \div 3$ **10.** $15 \div 3$

11. $4\overline{)16}$ **12.** $4\overline{)8}$ **13.** $3\overline{)24}$ **14.** $4\overline{)12}$ **15.** $3\overline{)30}$

Set B ───────────────────────────── KEY NS 2.3 page 286

Copy and complete the fact family.

1. $8 \times 4 = 32$
$4 \times 8 = \blacksquare$
$32 \div 8 = \blacksquare$
$32 \div 4 = \blacksquare$

2. $7 \times 6 = 42$
$6 \times 7 = 42$
$\blacksquare \div 7 = 6$
$42 \div \blacksquare = 7$

3. $5 \times 3 = 15$
$3 \bullet 5 = 15$
$\blacksquare \div 3 = 5$
$15 \div 5 = \blacksquare$

4. $2 \times 7 = 14$
$7 \times 2 = \blacksquare$
$14 \div \blacksquare = 7$
$14 \div \blacksquare = 2$

5. $4 \times 4 = 16$
$16 \bullet 4 = 4$

6. $4 \times 6 = 24$
$6 \times \blacksquare = 24$
$24 \div 4 = \blacksquare$
$\blacksquare \div 6 = 4$

7. $3 \times 10 = 30$
$\blacksquare \times 3 = 30$
$30 \div 10 = \blacksquare$
$\blacksquare \div 3 = 10$

8. $5 \times 9 = 45$
$9 \times \blacksquare = 45$
$45 \bullet 5 = 9$
$\blacksquare \div 9 = 5$

9. Jenna wants to arrange her shell collection in a display case. She has 45 shells. Write two ways she could display her shells in equal rows.

Set C ───────────────────────────── KEY NS 2.3 page 288

Find the quotient.

1. $9\overline{)81}$ **2.** $9\overline{)45}$ **3.** $9\overline{)90}$ **4.** $9\overline{)18}$ **5.** $9\overline{)63}$

Find the factor and the quotient.

6. $9 \times \blacksquare = 81$
$81 \div 9 = \blacksquare$

7. $9 \times \blacksquare = 45$
$45 \div 9 = \blacksquare$

8. $9 \times \blacksquare = 72$
$72 \div 9 = \blacksquare$

9. $9 \times \blacksquare = 36$
$36 \div 9 = \blacksquare$

10. John builds model cars. It takes him 9 hours to build one car. If he spends 45 hours a week building cars, how many cars can he make?

Education Place
Visit www.eduplace.com/camap/
for more **Extra Practice**.

Chapter Review/Test

Vocabulary and Concepts ———————————————— KEY NS 2.3

Choose the best term to complete each sentence.

> **Word Bank**
> multiples
> fact family

1. A group of equations that use the same numbers is called a _____.

2. The numbers 5, 10, 15, and 20 are all _____ of 5.

Skills ———————————————————————— KEY NS 2.3

Divide. Use any strategy.

3. $4\overline{)36}$ 4. $3\overline{)18}$ 5. $9\overline{)36}$ 6. $3\overline{)9}$ 7. $9\overline{)72}$ 8. $4\overline{)28}$

Copy and complete the fact family.

9. $7 \times 8 = 56$
   $8 \bigcirc 7 = 56$
   $56 \div 7 = \blacksquare$
   $\blacksquare \div 8 = 7$

10. $5 \times 5 = 25$
    $25 \div 5 = \blacksquare$

11. $3 \times 6 = 18$
    $6 \times \blacksquare = 18$
    $18 \div 3 = \blacksquare$
    $\blacksquare \div 6 = 3$

12. $4 \times 7 = 28$
    $7 \times 4 = \blacksquare$
    $28 \div \blacksquare = 7$
    $28 \bigcirc 7 = 4$

Find the factor and the quotient.

13. $9 \times \blacksquare = 63$
    $63 \div 9 = \blacksquare$

14. $\blacksquare \times 9 = 27$
    $27 \div 9 = \blacksquare$

15. $9 \times \blacksquare = 54$
    $54 \div 9 = \blacksquare$

16. $7 \times \blacksquare = 21$
    $21 \div \blacksquare = 7$

Problem Solving and Reasoning ———————— KEY NS 2.3, MR 1.2, MR 3.1

Solve. Show how to check your answer.

17. There are 72 trucks in a used car lot. If the manager displays 9 trucks in each row, how many rows of trucks will he have?

18. Angelica baked 27 muffins. If she gives 3 friends the same number of muffins, how many muffins does each friend get?

19. How can you use $48 \div 6 = 8$ to find $24 \div 6$?

20. Why is there only one related multiplication fact for $64 \div 8 = 8$?

Writing Math Lisa says that $6 \times 3 = 18$ and $6 \div 3 = 2$ are in the same fact family. Is she right? Explain.

Spiral Review and Test Practice

1. What measurement is missing on the equilateral triangle below?

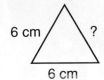

6 cm
?
6 cm

A 3 cm

B 4 cm

C 6 cm

D 9 cm

KEY **MG 2.2** page 198

2. 2403 + 1618 =

A 785

B 3011

C 3021

D 4021

> **Test Tip**
> Add in a different order to check your work.

KEY **NS 2.1** page 60

3. An equilateral triangle MUST have

A no equal sides

B 2 equal sides

C 3 equal sides

D 4 equal sides

KEY **MG 2.2** page 198

4. Which figure is a sphere?

A   **C**

B   **D**

MG **2.5** page 234

5. Six friends divided 30 baseball cards equally. How many cards did each friend receive?

A 5 cards   **C** 6 cards

B 25 cards   **D** 24 cards

KEY **NS 2.3** page 266

6. Madeline did this division problem.

$$28 \div 4 = 7$$

Which problem could she do to check her answer?

A $7 + 4 = \square$

B $7 - 4 = \square$

C $7 \times 4 = \square$

D $7 \div 4 = \square$

KEY **NS 2.3** page 282

Education Place
Visit www.eduplace.com/camap/ for **Test-Taking Tips** and **Extra Practice**.

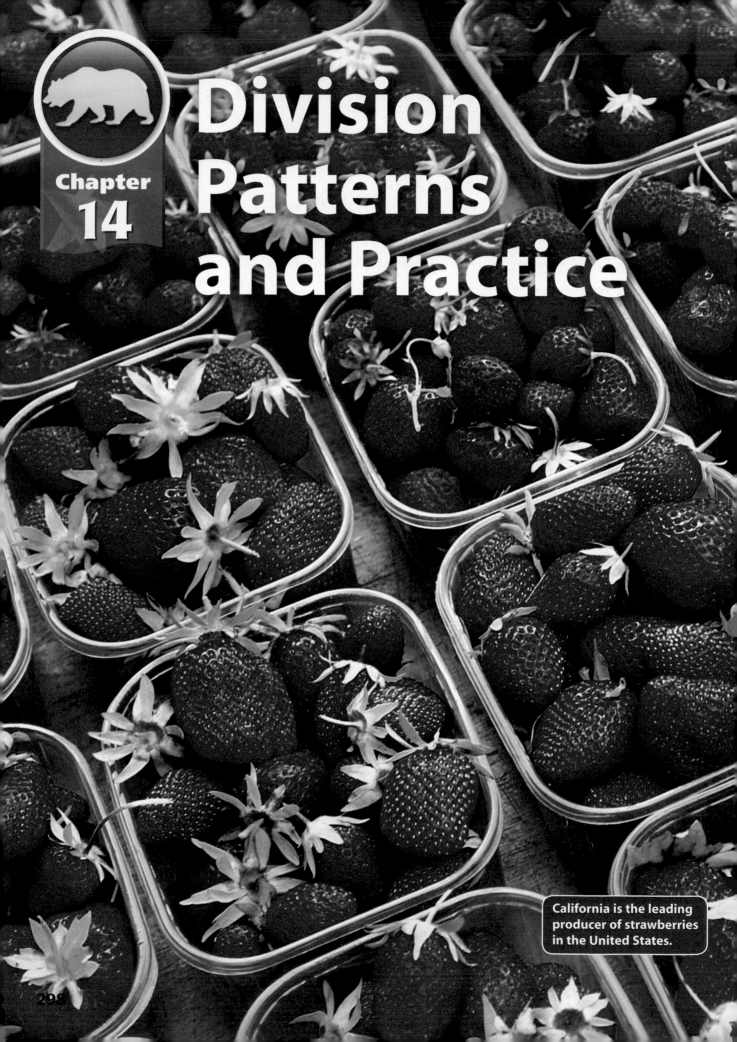

Division Patterns and Practice

California is the leading producer of strawberries in the United States.

Vocabulary and Concepts NS 2.0, MR 2.3
Choose the best term to complete each sentence. pages 262, 286

Word Bank

divide

fact family

inverse
 relationship

multiplication

related facts

1. A group of number sentences that use the same numbers is a ____.

2. You can use repeated subtraction to ____.

3. You can show ____ with an array.

Skills KEY NS 2.3
Write a division sentence that is related to each multiplication sentence. page 262

4. $6 \times 3 = 18$ **5.** $8 \times 7 = 56$ **6.** $9 \times 4 = 36$

Divide. page 266

7. $21 \div 3$ **8.** $81 \div 9$ **9.** $32 \div 4$

Problem Solving and Reasoning NS 2.0
10. Shaniqua put 24 flowers into 4 equal bunches. Joe put 24 flowers into 6 equal bunches. Who had the most flowers in each bunch?

Vocabulary

Visualize It !

You can model division.

The amusement park has 7 crazy cars. If 14 children can ride at one time, how many children can ride in each car?

Model It

Write It

$14 \div 7 = 2$

Two children can ride in each car.

Language Tip
Some words are similar in Spanish and English.

English	Spanish
divide	dividir
division	división
problem	problema

See **English-Spanish Glossary** pages 628–646.

Education Place Visit www.eduplace.com/camap/ for the **eGlossary** and **eGames**.

CA Standards MR 2.3 Use a variety of methods, such as words, numbers, symbols, charts, graphs, tables, diagrams, and models, to explain mathematical reasoning. **Also NS 2.0**

Chapter 14 299

CA Standards

NS 2.6 Understand the special properties of 0 and 1 in multiplication and division.

MR 3.0 Students move beyond a particular problem by generalizing to other situations.

Also MR 2.3

Materials
- Workmat 1
- Counters

Hands On
Division Rules

Objective Use special rules when you divide with 0 or 1.

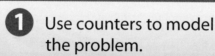 **Explore**

You already know the special rules for multiplying by 0 and 1. There are also special rules for dividing with 0 or 1.

Question How can you use counters to discover the division rules for 0 and 1?

Shelley has a total of 3 jade plants. She puts them into 3 equal groups. How many jade plants are in each group?

1 Use counters to model the problem.

2 Write the division sentence.

> When any number except 0 is divided by itself, the quotient is 1.

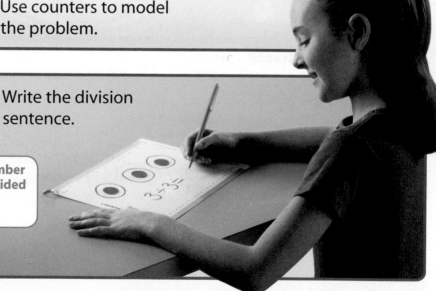

Solution: There is one jade plant in each group.

Suppose that Shelley puts 3 jade plants in 1 equal group. How many jade plants are in the group?

> When any number is divided by 1, the quotient is that number.

1 Use counters to model the problem.

2 Write the division sentence.

 $\bigcirc \div \bigcirc = \bigcirc$

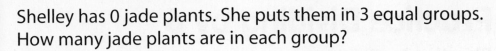

Shelley has 0 jade plants. She puts them in 3 equal groups. How many jade plants are in each group?

1 Use counters to model the problem.

2 Write the division sentence.

◯ ÷ ◯ = ◯

> When 0 is divided by any number except 0, the quotient is 0.

▶ **Extend**

Divide. Use the special rules.

1. 2 ÷ 1   **2.** 1 ÷ 1   **3.** 0 ÷ 9

4. 6 ÷ 6   **5.** 7 ÷ 7   **6.** 5 ÷ 1

Think

What is the rule for
- dividing by 1?
- dividing 0 by a number?
- dividing a number by itself?

Match the division sentence with the division rule that helps you solve it.

7. When any number except 0 is divided by itself, the quotient is 1.

8. When any number is divided by 1, the quotient is that number.

9. When 0 is divided by any number except 0, the quotient is 0.

a. $689 ÷ 1 = $ ▢

b. $2{,}385 ÷ 2{,}385 = $ ▢

c. $0 ÷ 5{,}288 = $ ▢

10. Analyze You cannot divide a number by 0. Use counters to explain why you cannot divide 3 by 0.

Write *true* or *false* for the equation.

11. 0 ÷ 5 = 0   **12.** 9 ÷ 1 = 9   **13.** 8 ÷ 8 = 0   **14.** 3 ÷ 3 = 1

Find the missing number.

15. 120 × ▢ = 120   **16.** 45 ÷ ▢ = 45   **17.** ▢ ÷ 235 = 0   **18.** 4,758 × 0 = ▢

Math Journal

Writing Math

Explain Draw a picture that shows 5 ÷ 1. Write the answer and explain how your picture shows the answer.

CA Standards
KEY NS 2.3 Use the inverse relationship of multiplication and division to compute and check results.

MR 2.4 Express the solution clearly and logically by using the appropriate mathematical notation and terms and clear language; support solutions with evidence in both verbal and symbolic work.

Also NS 2.0, MR 2.0

Practice Dividing by 6

Objective Apply division strategies when dividing by 6.

▶ Learn by Example

Using a related fact is a quick way to solve a division problem. You can use the division strategies you already know to divide by 6.

24 orange trees are planted in 6 rows. If each row has the same number of trees, how many trees are in each row?

$24 \div 6 = \bigcirc$

Different Ways to Divide

Way 1   Use a related multiplication fact.

$24 \div 6 = \bigcirc$

Think: $6 \times \bigcirc = 24$

$6 \times 4 = 24$

So $24 \div 6 = 4$

Way 2   Use a related division fact.

$24 \div 6 = \bigcirc$

Think: $24 \div \bigcirc = 6$

$24 \div 4 = 6$

So $24 \div 6 = 4$

Solution: There are 4 orange trees in each row.

Another Strategy
Use repeated subtraction.

Ask Yourself

- What related multiplication fact can help me?
- What related division fact can help me?

▶ Guided Practice

Divide. Use any strategy.

1. $6\overline{)36}$ **2.** $6\overline{)60}$ **3.** $6\overline{)42}$ **4.** $6\overline{)54}$

5. $6 \div 6$ **6.** $0 \div 6$ **7.** $12 \div 6$ **8.** $48 \div 6$

9. $18 \div 6$ **10.** $30 \div 6$ **11.** $60 \div 6$ **12.** $42 \div 6$

Guided Problem Solving

Use the questions to solve this problem.

13. Zoe picked 12 lilies. She wants to put the same number of lilies in 6 vases. How many lilies will she put in each vase?

   a. **Understand** How many lilies are there? How many vases does Zoe have?

   b. **Plan** What related division or multiplication fact can you use?

   c. **Solve** Use the related fact to solve the problem. Write the answer.

   There will be ◯ lilies in each vase.

   d. **Look Back** Draw a picture to show your answer is correct.

14. Zoe picks 18 more lilies. She wants to divide them equally among the 6 vases she has. How many lilies will there now be in each vase?

(123) **Math Talk** What related multiplication and division facts can you use to help you find $48 \div 6$?

Practice and Problem Solving

Divide. Use any strategy.

15. $6\overline{)18}$ 16. $6\overline{)6}$ 17. $6\overline{)24}$ 18. $6\overline{)42}$ 19. $6\overline{)30}$

20. $54 \div 6$ 21. $18 \div 6$ 22. $36 \div 6$ 23. $48 \div 6$ 24. $24 \div 6$

Solve.

25. George has 36 roses from his garden to divide equally among 6 friends. How many roses does he give each friend?

26. **Multistep** Donna gets one free plant for every 6 she buys. Donna wants 35 plants. How many plants does she need to buy?

History-Social Science Link

Solve.

27. Many communities hold parades in honor of Cesar Chavez. Jeff counted 24 balloons in this year's parade. The balloons were divided evenly among 6 people. How many balloons was each person holding?

28. Luisa counted 36 musicians in the parade. They were marching in 6 even rows. How many people were in each row?

29. **Multistep** Cesar Chavez Park in Berkeley is a popular place to fly kites. Suppose 6 families were flying kites on Saturday and 9 families were flying kites on Sunday. If each family had 3 kites, how many kites were at the park that weekend?

History-Social Science 3.4.6

Spiral Review and Test Practice

Tell whether the figure is a polygon. If it is, write its name. KEY **MG 2.1** page 192

30.

31.

32.

33.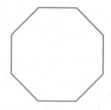

Write the letter of the correct answer. KEY **NS 2.3**

34. Which multiplication sentence can help you solve this problem?

$24 \div 6 = \blacksquare$

A $3 \times 8 = 24$ **B** $12 \times 2 = 24$ **C** $6 \times 4 = 24$ **D** $24 \times 1 = 24$

Extra Practice See page 315, Set A.

Key Standards Review

Need Help?
See Key Standards Handbook.

Find the area of the figure. Each = 1 square unit. **KEY MG 1.2**

1.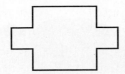

2.

3.

Find the volume of each figure. Each = 1 cubic unit. **KEY MG 1.2**

4.

5.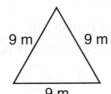

6.

Find the perimeter of the polygon. Show your work. **KEY MG 1.3**

7.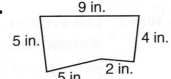
9 in.
5 in.
4 in.
5 in.
2 in.

8.
9 m   9 m
9 m

9.
4 ft
3 ft   3 ft
4 ft

Challenge   Number Sense

Missing Numbers

Fill in the blanks with the digits from 0–9. You may not use a digit more than once! **AF 1.2**

1. $4 \times \blacksquare = 3\blacksquare$

2. $3 \times \blacksquare = \blacksquare$

3. $3\blacksquare \div 6 = \blacksquare$

4. $7 \div \blacksquare = \blacksquare$

5. $2\blacksquare \div 4 = \blacksquare$

CA Standards
KEY **NS 2.3** Use
the inverse relationship of
multiplication and division to
compute and check results.
**Also NS 2.0, AF 1.3,
MR 2.0, MR 2.4**

Practice Dividing by 7

Objective Apply division strategies when dividing by 7.

▶ ## Learn by Example

You have learned to use division
strategies to divide by 6. You
can use the same strategies to
divide by 7.

> Stanley has 21 California
> poppies that he wants to
> plant in equal rows. If he puts
> 7 poppies in each row, how
> many rows will he plant?

$21 \div 7 = \bigcirc$

California Poppies

Different Ways to Divide

Way 1 Use a related multiplication fact.	**Way 2** Use a related division fact.
$21 \div 7 = \bigcirc$	$21 \div 7 = \bigcirc$
Think: $7 \times \bigcirc = 21$	Think: $21 \div \bigcirc = 7$
$7 \times 3 = 21$	$21 \div 3 = 7$
So $21 \div 7 = 3$	So $21 \div 7 = 3$

Solution: Stanley will plant 3 rows.

Another Strategy
Use repeated subtraction.

▶ ## Guided Practice

Ask Yourself
• What multiplication
fact can help me?
• What division fact
can help me?

Find the quotient.

1. $7\overline{)14}$ **2.** $7\overline{)49}$ **3.** $7\overline{)56}$ **4.** $7\overline{)28}$

5. $7 \div 7$ **6.** $70 \div 7$ **7.** $42 \div 7$ **8.** $35 \div 7$

 Math Talk What multiplication and division
facts can you use to find $63 \div 7$?

Find the quotient.

9. $7\overline{)28}$ **10.** $7\overline{)63}$ **11.** $7\overline{)35}$ **12.** $7\overline{)14}$ **13.** $7\overline{)42}$

14. $0 \div 7$ **15.** $21 \div 3$ **16.** $56 \div 7$ **17.** $7 \div 7$ **18.** $49 \div 7$

 Algebra Equations

Write +, −, ×, or ÷ for the ⬭**.**

19. 35 ⬭ $7 = 5$ **20.** 35 ⬭ $7 = 28$ **21.** 35 ⬭ $7 = 42$

22. 21 ⬭ $7 = 3$ **23.** 21 ⬭ $7 = 28$ **24.** 21 ⬭ $7 = 14$

Solve.

25. Measurement Andy was in California for 28 days. How many weeks was Andy in California?

26. Challenge Jake had 70 plants. He put them in 7 equal rows. How many plants were in each row? What other ways could Jake have arranged the plants in equal rows?

> **Hint**
> 7 days = 1 week

 Spiral Review and Test Practice

Find the volume of the figure. Each ⬛ **= 1 cubic unit.**

KEY **MG 1.2** page 240

27.    **28.**   **29.**

Write the letter of the correct answer. KEY **NS 2.3**

30. Lisa plants 56 rose bushes in 7 different colors. If she plants the same number of each color, how many of each color does she plant?

     A 7   **B** 8   **C** 9   **D** 10

CA Standards
KEY **NS 2.3** Use the inverse relationship of multiplication and division to compute and check results.

AF 1.2 Solve problems involving numeric equations or inequalities.

Also NS 2.0, KEY AF 1.1, AF 1.4, MG 1.4, MR 2.0, MR 2.4

Practice Dividing by 8

Objective Apply division strategies to practice division by 8.

▶ Learn by Example

Using a related fact is a good way to remember a new fact.

Cindy has 32 flowers and 8 vases. She wants to put the same number of flowers in each vase. How many flowers will be in each vase?

$32 \div 8 = \bigcirc$

Different Ways to Divide

Way 1 Use a related multiplication fact.	**Way 2** Use a related division fact.
$32 \div 8 = \bigcirc$	$32 \div 8 = \bigcirc$
Think: $8 \times \bigcirc = 32$	**Think:** $32 \div \bigcirc = 8$
$8 \times 4 = 32$	$32 \div 4 = 8$
So $32 \div 8 = 4$	So $32 \div 8 = 4$

Another Strategy
Use repeated subtraction.

Solution: There will be 4 flowers in each vase.

Ask Yourself

• What multiplication fact can help me?

• What related division fact can help me?

▶ Guided Practice

Find the quotient.

1. $8\overline{)8}$ **2.** $8\overline{)24}$ **3.** $8\overline{)48}$ **4.** $8\overline{)16}$

5. $0 \div 8$ **6.** $64 \div 8$ **7.** $56 \div 8$ **8.** $72 \div 8$

 Math Talk How can knowing $40 \div 8 = 5$ help you find $48 \div 8$?

Practice and Problem Solving

Find the quotient.

9. $8\overline{)32}$ **10.** $8\overline{)64}$ **11.** $8\overline{)0}$ **12.** $8\overline{)40}$

13. $8\overline{)72}$ **14.** $8\overline{)80}$ **15.** $8\overline{)56}$ **16.** $8\overline{)48}$

17. $8 \div 8$ **18.** $24 \div 8$ **19.** $32 \div 8$ **20.** $16 \div 8$

Algebra Equations and Functions
Find the missing number.

21. $42 \div 7 = \blacksquare$ **22.** $8 \times \blacksquare = 24$ **23.** $5 \times 7 = \blacksquare$ **24.** $36 \div \blacksquare = 6$

25. $49 \div \blacksquare = 7$ **26.** $40 \div \blacksquare = 5$ **27.** $20 \div 2 = \blacksquare$ **28.** $56 \div 8 = \blacksquare$

Complete the table. Write the rule.

29.

Rule: _____	
Days	**Weeks**
30. 7	$\blacksquare$
56	8
31. 70	$\blacksquare$
32. $\blacksquare$	2
33. 28	$\blacksquare$

34.

Rule: _____	
mm	**cm**
50	5
35. 20	$\blacksquare$
36. $\blacksquare$	9
37. $\blacksquare$	7
38. 10	$\blacksquare$

39.

Rule: _____	
Feet	**Yards**
24	8
40. $\blacksquare$	1
41. 12	$\blacksquare$
42. $\blacksquare$	10
43. 21	$\blacksquare$

Solve.

44. Flowers are sold in bunches of 8. If Tom buys 40 flowers in all, how many bunches will he buy?

45. Hana plants 64 rose bushes in 8 equal rows. How many rose bushes are in each row?

46. **Multistep** Darryl has 72 lilies. There are 3 lilies on each stem. If Darryl makes 8 bouquets, how many stems are in each bouquet?

47. Camila has a plant that is 80 millimeters tall. How many centimeters tall is her plant?

Science Link

Solve.

48. An orchid plant has 32 flowers. If there are 8 flowers on each stem, how many stems are there?

49. Some orchid flowers have 3 petals. How many petals are on a stem of 8 orchids?

50. The stream orchid can grow up to about 3 feet. About how many inches tall can a stream orchid grow?

51. A vanilla orchid vine can produce 20 flowers. Each flower will form 1 seed pod. How many vines would produce 100 pods?

52. Challenge The Sacramento Orchid Society is holding a workshop for its 300 members. If the tables in the room can hold 575 orchids, is there enough space for each member to bring 2 orchids? Explain why or why not.

Science LS 3.b

Spiral Review and Test Practice

Find the quotient. NS 2.0 page 282

53. 3)21   **54.** 4)32   **55.** 4)20   **56.** 3)12   **57.** 4)24

58. 3)24   **59.** 4)16   **60.** 3)15   **61.** 4)36   **62.** 3)27

Write the letter of the correct answer. NS 2.0

63. Inez shared 40 pretzels equally with 8 friends. How many pretzels did she give each friend?

   A 8   **B** 7   **C** 6   **D** 5

Extra Pra... ...ge 315, Set C.

Choosing the Operation Signs

Jenny, Lee, and Sandra played two games. In Hit 5, they "made" the number 5 by picking two or more of these numbers: 1, 3, 6, and 8. Then they used one or more of the operations (addition, subtraction, multiplication, and division) to make the number 5.

Here's how Jenny made the number 5	Here's how Lee made the number 5.	Here's how Sandra made the number 5.
She wrote:	He wrote:	She wrote:
$6 - 1 = 5$	$8 - 6 + 3 = 5$	$3 \times 8 \div 6 + 1 = 5$

Then Jenny, Lee, and Sandra played Hit 6. This time, they picked from the numbers 1, 3, 5, and 9 to make the number 6.

Write $+$, $-$, $\times$, or $\div$ in each ⬭ to complete each child's number sentence.

1. $5 \ \bigcirc \ 1 = 6$

2. $9 \ \bigcirc \ 3 = 6$

3. $3 \ \bigcirc \ 5 \ \bigcirc \ 9 = 6$

4. $3 \ \bigcirc \ 9 \ \bigcirc \ 5 \ \bigcirc \ 1 = 6$

5. $9 \ \bigcirc \ 1 \ \bigcirc \ 5 \ \bigcirc \ 3 = 6$

6. $3 \ \bigcirc \ 9 \ \bigcirc \ 1 \ \bigcirc \ 5 = 6$

7. What is the greatest number you can make by using each of the numbers 1, 3, and 4 once with any two operations?

CA Standards
KEY NS 2.2,
KEY NS 2.1, AF 1.3

CA Standards

MR 2.0 Students use strategies, skills, and concepts in finding solutions.

NS 2.0 Students calculate and solve problems involving addition, subtraction, multiplication, and division.

Also KEY NS 2.1 , NS 2.5, NS 2.8, MR 1.1, MR 1.2, MR 2.3, MR 2.4, MR 3.0, MR 3.1, MR 3.2

Problem Solving Strategy
Work Backward

Objective Solve problems by working backward.

▶ **Learn by Example**

Jordan's garden has 6 rows of peppers and 1 row of lettuce. He has a total of 53 plants. The row of lettuce has 5 plants.

There are an equal number of peppers in each row. How many peppers are in each row?

UNDERSTAND

The problem gives this information.

- There are 6 rows of peppers and 1 row of lettuce.
- The row of lettuce contains 5 plants.
- There are 53 plants in all.

PLAN

You can work backward to find the answer.

- First, subtract to find the number of peppers.
- Then, divide to find the number of peppers in each row.

SOLVE

Total number of plants ⟶ 53 plants − 5 lettuce = 48 peppers

Total number of peppers

48 peppers ÷ 6 rows = 8 peppers per row

There are 8 peppers in each row.

LOOK BACK

How can you check your answer?

▶ Guided Problem Solving

Solve using the Ask Yourself questions.

Ask Yourself
• Can I work backward to find the answer?
• What operations should I use?

1. Mrs. Finnegan bought turkey sandwiches and a bag of chips for her son and his six friends. Seven sandwiches and one bag of chips cost $46. If the bag of chips cost $4, what was the cost of each sandwich?

 Math Talk Look back at Problem 1. Explain how you knew what operations to use.

▶ Independent Problem Solving

Solve. Explain why your answer makes sense.

2. Mrs. Patel bought 8 tomato plants and 2 zucchini plants. She spent a total of $34. If each zucchini plant cost $5, what was the cost of each tomato plant?

3. Mr. Clark took 9 of his students to the zoo. The cost for 9 student tickets and 1 adult ticket was $65. If the adult ticket cost $11, what was the cost of each student ticket?

4. Mr. Marino cut a piece of wire into 4 equal pieces. He then cut 2 centimeters off of one piece to make a piece 6 centimeters long. How long was the original piece of wire?

5. Kareem is helping his father build a planter box. They cut a board into 6 equal pieces. Then they cut 4 inches off one of the pieces to make a piece 5 inches long. How long was the original board?

6. **Challenge** Last year, 36 students tried out for the basketball team. This number is 4 more than twice the number of students that tried out this year. How many students tried out for the team this year?

7. **Create and Solve** Write a word problem that can be solved by working backward, and requires more than one operation to solve it.

Vocabulary

Multiplication and division are inverse operations.

You can use a **related multiplication fact** or a **related division fact** to help you divide.

Find 21 ÷ 7.

1. Use a related multiplication fact.

2. Use a related division fact.

Look at the two arrays. Use the Word Bank to label each part of the problem.

> **Word Bank**
>
> **dividend**
>
> **divisor**
>
> **factor**
>
> **product**
>
> **quotient**

3. _____

4. _____

5. _____

$$6\overline{)48}\;\;8$$

6. _____

7. _____

8. _____

$$\begin{array}{r} 6 \\ \times\,8 \\ \hline 48 \end{array}$$

Writing How does knowing the product of 7×8 help you to find $56 \div 8$? Explain.

Reading Look for this book in your library.

- *The Great Divide: A Mathematical Marathon*, by Dayle Ann Dodds and Tracy Mitchell

> **CA Standards**
>
> **MR 2.3** Use a variety of methods, such as words, numbers, symbols, charts, graphs, tables, diagrams, and models, to explain mathematical reasoning.
>
> **Also NS 2.0, KEY NS 2.3**

Standards-Based Extra Practice

Set A ─────────────────────────────── NS 2.0 page 302

Divide. Use any strategy.

1. 6)30   2. 6)60   3. 6)18   4. 6)24   5. 6)48

6. 6)42   7. 6)12   8. 6)36   9. 6)54   10. 6)60

11. 36 ÷ 6   12. 12 ÷ 6   13. 18 ÷ 6   14. 30 ÷ 6

15. 54 ÷ 6   16. 60 ÷ 6   17. 6 ÷ 6   18. 42 ÷ 6

19. A chorus practiced for 10 minutes each day. They practiced for 60 minutes in all. For how many days did they practice?

Set B ─────────────────────────────── NS 2.0 page 306

Find the quotient.

1. 7)35   2. 7)56   3. 7)21   4. 7)28   5. 7)7

6. 7)42   7. 7)14   8. 7)49   9. 7)63   10. 7)70

11. 35 ÷ 7   12. 14 ÷ 7   13. 21 ÷ 7   14. 28 ÷ 7

15. 63 ÷ 7   16. 42 ÷ 7   17. 0 ÷ 7   18. 70 ÷ 7

19. Chen has 28 pretzels. She gave 7 students each an equal number of pretzels. How many pretzels did each student get?

Set C ─────────────────────────────── NS 2.0 page 308

Find the quotient.

1. 8)32   2. 8)56   3. 8)24   4. 8)80   5. 8)8

6. 8)40   7. 8)16   8. 8)48   9. 8)64   10. 8)72

11. 32 ÷ 8   12. 24 ÷ 8   13. 8 ÷ 8   14. 48 ÷ 8

15. Thirty-two students are in a dance class. They practice in groups of 8. How many groups are there?

Education Place
Visit www.eduplace.com/camap/
for more **Extra Practice**.

Chapter 14 Extra Practice   **315**

Chapter Review/Test

Vocabulary and Concepts ———————— NS 2.6, MR 2.3

Choose the best word to complete each sentence.

> **Word Bank**
> dividend
> divide
> quotient

1. When you _____ 28 by 7 you get 4.

2. 3 is the _____ of 24 ÷ 8.

3. The _____ and divisor are the same when the quotient is 1.

Skills ———————————————————— NS 2.5

Divide. Use any strategy.

4. $18 \div 6$ **5.** $24 \div 6$ **6.** $42 \div 6$ **7.** $36 \div 6$

Find the quotient.

8. $7\overline{)56}$ **9.** $7\overline{)28}$ **10.** $7\overline{)63}$ **11.** $7\overline{)49}$ **12.** $7\overline{)84}$

13. $32 \div 8$ **14.** $96 \div 8$ **15.** $56 \div 8$ **16.** $16 \div 8$

Problem Solving and Reasoning ———————— NS 2.5, MR 1.2, MR 3.1

Solve. Show how you checked your answer.

17. Ting is helping plant trees for Arbor Day. His group has 35 trees to plant in 7 different plots. If they plant an equal number of trees in each plot, how many trees will be in each plot?

18. Peggy and 14 friends are having a party. Peggy wants enough pizza so that they can have 2 slices each. If each pizza has 10 slices, how many pizzas does she need to buy?

19. Multistep Shana's father runs 4 times a week. He runs 2 miles each time. How many miles does Shana's father run in 3 weeks?

20. Tom is planting roses. He has 18 rose bushes. He wants to put them in 6 equal groups. How many bushes are in each group?

Writing Math Why is dividing by zero impossible?

Spiral Review and Test Practice

1. What number makes this number sentence true?

$6 \times 8 > 9 \times \square$

A 8   **C** 7

B 6   **D** 5

KEY **AF 1.2** page 148

---

2. Which number sentence represents this array?

A $5 \times 4 = 20$

B $5 \times 5 = 25$

C $5 \times 6 = 30$

D $6 \times 5 = 30$

> **Test Tip**
> Think about what the rows and columns in an array stand for.

KEY **NS 2.2** page 128

---

3. What is the area of this figure?

$\square$ = 1 square unit

A 2 square units **C** 4 square units

B 5 square units **D** 6 square units

KEY **MG 1.2** page 220

---

4. The Ferris wheel at a fair had ticket sales of $1,270. The carousel had ticket sales of $1,820. What were the total ticket sales to the nearest thousand dollars?

A $5,000   **C** $4,000

B $3,000   **D** $2,000

KEY **NS 1.4** page 84

---

5. Which number sentence is in the same fact family as $16 \div 2 = 8$?

A $2 \times 8 = 16$ **C** $16 - 8 = 8$

B $16 \times 2 = 32$ **D** $8 - 2 = 6$

KEY **NS 2.3** page 286

---

6. Which multiplication sentence can you use to check the answer to this problem?

$36 \div 6 = \square$

A $3 \times 12 = 36$

B $6 \times 6 = 36$

C $9 \times 4 = 36$

D $36 \times 1 = 36$

KEY **NS 2.3** page 302

Education Place
Visit www.eduplace.com/camap/ for **Test-Taking Tips** and **Extra Practice**.

Unit 5 Review/Test

Vocabulary and Concepts ———————————— MR 2.3 Chapters 12–14

Choose the best term to complete each sentence.

1. The _____ is the answer to a division problem.

2. When you separate the items into _____, you divide.

3. When you divide, the number you divide is called the _____.

> **Word Bank**
> multiples
> equal groups
> dividend
> quotient

Skills ———————————————— NS 2.0, KEY **NS 2.3** Chapters 12–14

**Draw an array for the multiplication sentence.
Then write two related division sentences.**

4. $3 \times 4 = 12$

5. $9 \times 8 = 72$

Divide. Check by multiplying.

6. $27 \div 3$

7. $32 \div 4$

8. $72 \div 8$

9. $5\overline{)40}$

10. $6\overline{)36}$

11. $4\overline{)16}$

12. $4\overline{)32}$

13. $3\overline{)21}$

14. $35 \div 7$

Copy and complete the fact family.   Chapter 13, Lesson 3

15. $9 \times 8 = 72$
    $8 \bullet 9 = 72$
    $72 \div 8 = \blacksquare$
    $\blacksquare \div 9 = 8$

16. $7 \times 7 = 49$
    $49 \div 7 = \blacksquare$

Find the factor and the quotient.   Chapter 13, Lesson 3

17. $6 \times \blacksquare = 42$
    $42 \div 6 = \blacksquare$

18. $\blacksquare \times 9 = 45$
    $45 \div 9 = \blacksquare$

Problem Solving and Reasoning

KEY NS 2.3, NS 2.0 Chapters 12–14

Solve.

19. Sarah has 36 photos from her visit to her grandma. She put them in an album, 4 to a page. How many pages did she fill?

20. Why is there only one related multiplication fact for $81 \div 9 = 9$?

BIG IDEA!

Writing Math How is division related to subtraction? How is division related to multiplication? How can an array show both multiplication and division?

Performance Assessment

Musical Chairs

NS 2.0, KEY NS 2.3, MR 1.0, MR 2.0

A music program will take place in Mr. Hale's room. He is setting up 24 chairs for the audience.

1. Each row should have the same number of chairs. What are some different ways he can arrange the chairs?

2. Suppose there is extra space left to walk down the middle of the rows of chairs. Each side of the space should have the same number of chairs. How many chairs should there be on each side?

Greg Tang's Go Fast, Go Far

Unit 5 Mental Math Strategies

Divide by 4

Divide by 4? This way's shorter.
Half of half, it's called a quarter!

Dividing in two steps is easier than dividing in one! Look at Problem 1. Dividing by 4 is the same as dividing by 2 twice. Divide 36 by 2 to get 18, then divide 18 by 2 to get 9.

1. 36 ÷ 4 → 18 → 9
　　　Divide　Divide
　　　36 by 2.　by 2.

2. 12 ÷ 4 → ■ → ■
　　　Divide　Divide
　　　12 by 2.　by 2.

3. 20 ÷ 4 → ■ → ■
　　　Divide　Divide
　　　20 by 2.　by 2.

4. 16 ÷ 4 → ■ → ■
　　　Divide　Divide
　　　16 by 2.　by 2.

Way to go! Nice job!

5. 80 ÷ 4 → ■ → ■
　　　Divide　Divide
　　　80 by 2.　by 2.

6. 28 ÷ 4 → ■ → ■
　　　Divide　Divide
　　　28 by 2.　by 2.

7. 100 ÷ 4 → ■ → ■
　　　Divide　Divide
　　　100 by 2.　by 2.

8. 40 ÷ 4 → ■ → ■
　　　Divide　Divide
　　　40 by 2.　by 2.

Take It Further!
Now try doing all the steps in your head!

9. 16 ÷ 4

10. 44 ÷ 4

11. 24 ÷ 4

12. 400 ÷ 4

Go Faster!

320

Fractions, Decimals, and Money

BIG IDEAS!

- Fractions that show the same part of a whole are equivalent.
- A decimal is another way to show a fraction.
- You can add and subtract fractions using fraction tiles.
- You can add and subtract money by lining up the digits by place value.

Songs and Games

 Math Music Track 6: *Block Fractions*

eGames at
www.eduplace.com/camap/

Math Readers

Game

Fraction Match

Object of the Game Solve fraction problems to form a row on a game board.

Materials
- 32 counters (16 per player)
- index cards

Number of Players 2

Set Up
For each picture, write a fraction on an index card that shows how much is colored. Place the cards face down in a pile.

How to Play

1 Player 1 turns over one card from the pile. He or she finds the picture that represents the fraction on the game board. Then Player 1 places a counter on that picture.

2 Player 2 repeats Step 1.

3 The first player who has four counters in a row—horizontal, vertical, or corner-to-corner—wins.

Game Board ▶

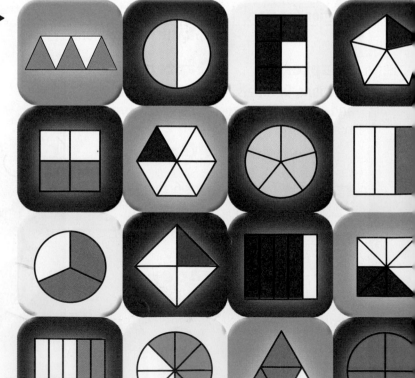

CA Standards

NS 3.1 Compare fractions represented by drawings or concrete materials to show equivalency and to add and subtract simple fractions in context (e.g., $\frac{1}{2}$ of a pizza is the same amount as $\frac{2}{4}$ of another pizza that is the same size; show that $\frac{3}{8}$ is larger than $\frac{1}{4}$).

Also MR 2.3

 Education Place
Visit www.eduplace.com/camap/ for **Brain Teasers** and **eGames** to play.

Reading

You use strategies to help you in reading. You also use strategies to help you solve problems. Read this problem:

A pizza is cut into 8 equal pieces. Four pieces have only cheese on them. Three pieces also have red pepper. One piece has olives. What fraction of the pizza has only cheese?

Before she solves the problem, Sue jots down problem-solving strategies that she knows.

Problem Solving Strategies

- Find a pattern.
- Guess and check.
- Draw a picture.
- Work backward.

> I know how many slices with cheese. I know how many slices in all. What can I do to find the fraction?

Writing

Copy Sue's list. Write other strategies you know. Then use one of the strategies to solve the problem.

Fraction Concepts

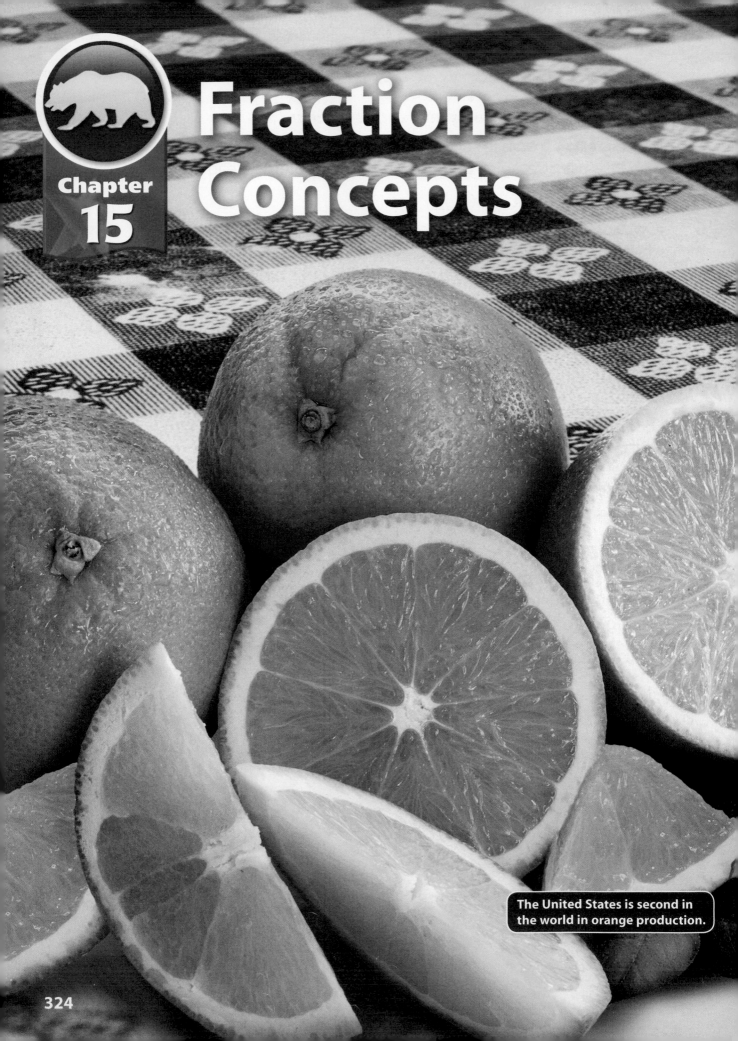

The United States is second in the world in orange production.

Vocabulary and Concepts   GRADE 2 KEY NS 4.2

Choose the best word to complete each sentence.

1. An apple cut into 2 equal parts has 2 ____.

2. Four ____ make one whole.

3. Parts of a whole are called ____.

Skills   GRADE 2 KEY NS 4.2

Write the fraction shown by the shaded part of the whole.

4.

5.

6.

7.

8.

9.

Problem Solving and Reasoning   GRADE 2 KEY NS 4.2

10. Dennis painted $\frac{1}{3}$ of the wall in his room. How much of the wall was left to paint?

Vocabulary

Visualize It!

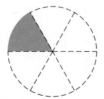

A **fraction** can name part of a set or a group.

$\frac{5}{9}$ of the balls are red.

$\frac{5}{9}$ ← numerator ← denominator

A **fraction** can name part of a whole.

$\frac{1}{6}$ of the circle is green.

$\frac{1}{6}$ ← numerator ← denominator

Language Tip

Some words are similar in Spanish and English.

English	Spanish
denominator	denominador
fraction	fracción
numerator	numerador

See **English-Spanish Glossary** pages 628–646.

Education Place Visit www.eduplace.com/camap/ for the **eGlossary** and **eGames**.

CA Standards

NS 3.0 Students understand the relationship between whole numbers, simple fractions, and decimals.
Also NS 3.1, MR 2.3, MR 2.4

Vocabulary

fraction

numerator

denominator

Materials
- Fraction tiles
- eManipulatives (optional)
  www.eduplace.com/camap/

Hands On
Model Fractions

Objective Model fractions that are less than, equal to, or greater than one whole.

▶ **Explore**

A **fraction** is a number used to describe part of a whole, a whole, or more than one whole.

Question How can you use fraction tiles to model fractions?

Rosa made this banner. It has 4 equal parts: 1 part blue, 1 part yellow, 2 parts red. What fraction of the banner is red?

1 Model the banner with fraction tiles.

Show one whole.

| 1 |

2 2 parts out of 4 equal parts are red.

Use two $\frac{1}{4}$ tiles to show the part of the banner that is red.

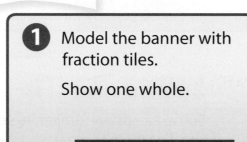

3 Record. Write a fraction.

numerator ⟶ $\frac{2}{4}$ ⟵ number of red parts
denominator ⟵ total number of equal parts

Read the fraction as "two fourths."

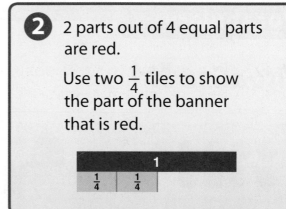

Solution: $\frac{2}{4}$ or $\frac{1}{2}$ of the banner is red.

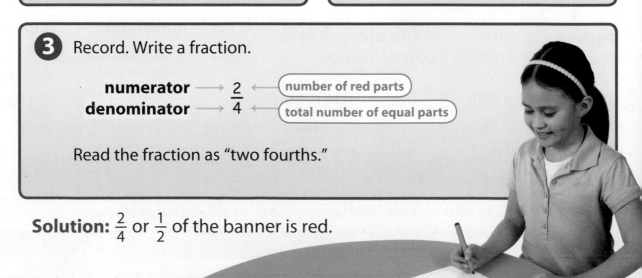

Other Examples

A. Model a fraction equal to 1 whole.

Model $\frac{8}{8}$.

1 Show one whole.

| 1 |

2 Place eight $\frac{1}{8}$ tiles under the whole.

$\frac{8}{8}$ is equal to 1 whole.

| 1 |
| $\frac{1}{8}$ $\frac{1}{8}$ $\frac{1}{8}$ $\frac{1}{8}$ $\frac{1}{8}$ $\frac{1}{8}$ $\frac{1}{8}$ $\frac{1}{8}$ |

3 Record. $\frac{8}{8} = 1$

B. Model a fraction greater than 1 whole.

Model $\frac{4}{3}$.

1 Show one whole.

| 1 |

2 Place four $\frac{1}{3}$ tiles under the whole.

$\frac{4}{3}$ is greater than 1 whole.

3 Record. $\frac{4}{3} > 1$

▶ **Extend**

Work with a partner to show the fractions with fraction tiles. Write <, =, or > for each ⬤.

1. $\frac{1}{4}$ ⬤ 1   **2.** $\frac{5}{8}$ ⬤ 1   **3.** $\frac{10}{10}$ ⬤ 1   **4.** $\frac{5}{12}$ ⬤ 1

5. $\frac{7}{5}$ ⬤ 1   **6.** $\frac{1}{2}$ ⬤ 1   **7.** $\frac{7}{6}$ ⬤ 1   **8.** $\frac{3}{3}$ ⬤ 1

9. $\frac{3}{2}$ ⬤ 1   **10.** $\frac{12}{12}$ ⬤ 1   **11.** $\frac{12}{8}$ ⬤ 1   **12.** $\frac{9}{9}$ ⬤ 1

13. two fourths ⬤ 1   **14.** five fifths ⬤ 1   **15.** four thirds ⬤ 1

> **Vocabulary Tip**
> Fractions equal to or greater than one whole are called **improper fractions**.

 Math Journal

Writing Math

Explain How can you tell by looking at a fraction if it is less than, equal to, or greater than one whole?

LESSON 2

CA Standards
NS 3.0 Students understand the relationship between whole numbers, simple fractions, and decimals.
Also MR 2.3, MR 2.4

Vocabulary

numerator

denominator

Fractions and Groups

Objective Use fractions to name parts of groups.

▶ **Learn by Example**

Ed is making a dinosaur with felt and buttons. What fraction of the buttons are blue?

You can use a fraction to name part of a group or set.

numerator ⟶ 7 ⟵ (number of blue buttons)
denominator ⟶ 12 ⟵ (total number of buttons)

Seven twelfths of the buttons are blue.

Ask Yourself

How do I decide what number to write as the numerator? the denominator?

▶ **Guided Practice**

Use the picture to solve.

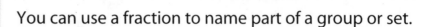

1. What fraction of the buttons have 4 holes?

2. What fraction of the buttons are red?

123 **Math Talk** Look at Ed's dinosaur again. What fraction of the buttons are red? Explain.

▶ **Practice and Problem Solving**

Write a fraction to name the part of the group that is round.

3.    4.    5.

Solve. Draw a picture to help you.

6. Geraldo has 8 different dinosaur pens. Five of those pens are green. What fraction of the pens are not green?

7. Ethan used 2 red, 3 white, and 3 blue buttons to make a button worm. What fraction of the buttons are blue?

8. **Right or Wrong?** Doris made a button worm with 3 green buttons and 2 red buttons. She says $\frac{2}{3}$ of the buttons are red. Is she right or wrong? Explain.

9. **Challenge** Claire has 8 beads. Four are red. One half of the beads that are not red are white. What fraction of Claire's beads are white?

 Real World Data

Use the table for Problems 10–13.

10. What fraction of the beads are red?

11. Which bead color is $\frac{2}{10}$ of the group?

12. What fraction of the beads are not blue?

13. Which bead color is $\frac{3}{10}$ of the group?

Bead Kit	
Color of Beads	**Number of Beads**
Red	3
Pink	3
Yellow	2
Purple	1
Blue	1

Spiral Review and Test Practice

Find the missing number. AF 1.2 pages 302, 306, 308

14. $32 \div \blacksquare = 4$ 15. $\blacksquare \div 7 = 6$ 16. $64 \div 8 = \blacksquare$ 17. $54 \div \blacksquare = 9$

Write the letter of the correct answer. NS 3.0

18. Lucy made button art from 3 orange buttons and 4 purple buttons. What fraction of the art is orange buttons?

  A $\frac{1}{3}$ B $\frac{3}{4}$ C $\frac{3}{7}$ D $\frac{4}{7}$

Extra Practice See page 341, Set A.

CA Standards

NS 3.1 Compare fractions represented by drawings or concrete materials to show equivalency and to add and subtract simple fractions in context (e.g., $\frac{1}{2}$ of a pizza is the same amount as $\frac{2}{4}$ of another pizza that is the same size; show that $\frac{3}{8}$ is larger than $\frac{1}{4}$).

MR 1.1 Analyze problems by identifying relationships, distinguishing relevant from irrelevant information, sequencing and prioritizing information, and observing patterns.

Also NS 3.0, MR 2.3, MR 2.4

Vocabulary

equivalent fractions

Materials
- Learning Tool 23 (Paper Circle)
- Crayons
- Scissors

Hands On
Model Equivalent Fractions

Objective Use different fractions to name the same amount.

▶ **Explore**

Fractions that name the same part of a whole are called **equivalent fractions**.

Question How can you use circle models to name equivalent fractions?

---

1 Work with a partner to model equivalent fractions. One person should:

- Fold a paper circle in half.
- Draw a line on the fold.
- Color one part of the circle.
- Record a fraction for the colored part.

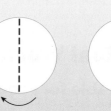

$\frac{1}{2}$

---

2 The other person should:

- Fold a paper circle in half. Fold it in half a second time. Then fold it in half again.
- Draw a line on each fold.
- Color 4 parts of the circle.
- Record a fraction for the colored part.

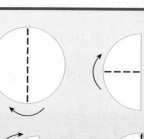

$\frac{4}{8}$

3 Compare the 2 circles.

The same amount is colored in each circle. $\frac{1}{2}$ and $\frac{4}{8}$ name the same amount. $\frac{1}{2}$ and $\frac{4}{8}$ are equivalent fractions.

So $\frac{1}{2} = \frac{4}{8}$.

▶ **Extend**

Write *equivalent* or *not equivalent* to describe the fractions in the pair.

1.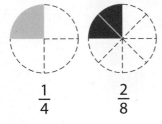

$\frac{1}{4}$ $\frac{2}{8}$

2.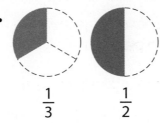

$\frac{1}{3}$ $\frac{1}{2}$

3.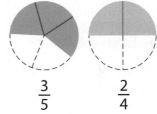

$\frac{3}{5}$ $\frac{2}{4}$

Use the circles to determine the equivalent fraction.

4.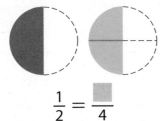

$\frac{1}{2} = \frac{\square}{4}$

5.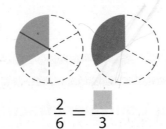

$\frac{2}{6} = \frac{\square}{3}$

6.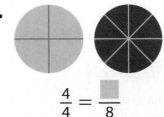

$\frac{4}{4} = \frac{\square}{8}$

7. Dave cut a circle into 6 equal pieces. He colored $\frac{1}{2}$ of the pieces purple and $\frac{1}{2}$ yellow. How many sixths were yellow?

8. Challenge Jessie made a potholder with 16 fabric squares. All but 4 squares are blue. Write two equivalent fractions for the part of the potholder that is not blue.

Writing Math

Analyze Describe how you can tell whether two fractions are equivalent.

CA Standards

NS 3.1 Compare fractions represented by drawings or concrete materials to show equivalency and to add and subtract simple fractions in context (e.g., $\frac{1}{2}$ of a pizza is the same amount as $\frac{2}{4}$ of another pizza that is the same size; show that $\frac{3}{8}$ is larger than $\frac{1}{4}$).

Also NS 3.0, MR 2.2, MR 2.4

Vocabulary

equivalent fractions

Find Equivalent Fractions

Objective Identify equivalent fractions.

▶ **Learn by Example**

Equivalent fractions name the same amount.

Look at the fraction tiles below.

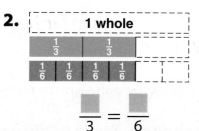

Use different fraction tiles to show fractions equivalent to $\frac{1}{2}$.

$$\frac{1}{2} = \frac{2}{4} = \frac{3}{6} = \frac{4}{8} = \frac{5}{10}$$

Ask Yourself

- How many equal parts are in each strip?
- How many parts are shaded?

▶ **Guided Practice**

Name the equivalent fractions shown.

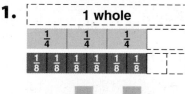

1. 1 whole

$$\frac{\square}{4} = \frac{\square}{8}$$

2. 1 whole

$$\frac{\square}{3} = \frac{\square}{6}$$

Write *equivalent* or *not equivalent* to describe the fractions.

3. $\frac{1}{4}$ and $\frac{3}{8}$ **4.** $\frac{1}{3}$ and $\frac{2}{6}$ **5.** $\frac{1}{2}$ and $\frac{3}{4}$

 Math Talk Are $\frac{2}{2}$, $\frac{4}{4}$, and $\frac{6}{6}$ equivalent fractions? Why or why not?

Name the equivalent fractions shown.

6.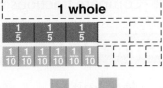

$$\frac{1}{2} = \frac{\blacksquare}{4}$$

7.

$$\frac{\blacksquare}{5} = \frac{\blacksquare}{10}$$

8.

$$\frac{5}{6} = \frac{\blacksquare}{\blacksquare}$$

**Look for a pattern in the equivalent fractions.
Then write two more equivalent fractions.**

9. $\frac{1}{2} = \frac{2}{4} = \frac{3}{6} = \frac{4}{8} = \frac{\blacksquare}{10} = \frac{\blacksquare}{12}$

10. $\frac{1}{3} = \frac{2}{6} = \frac{3}{9} = \frac{4}{12} = \frac{\blacksquare}{15} = \frac{\blacksquare}{18}$

11. $\frac{2}{3} = \frac{4}{6} = \frac{6}{9} = \frac{8}{12} = \frac{\blacksquare}{15} = \frac{\blacksquare}{18}$

12. $\frac{1}{10} = \frac{2}{20} = \frac{3}{30} = \frac{4}{40} = \frac{\blacksquare}{50} = \frac{\blacksquare}{60}$

 Real World Data

Use the table for Problems 13–15.

13. Which two students ran the same distance? Explain how you know.

14. **Explain** Tara said she ran farther than Kayla. Is she right?

15. **Analyze** Who ran farther than Kayla but not as far as Joe?

Distance Run	
Student	**Distance**
Sven	$\frac{3}{4}$ mile
Kayla	$\frac{4}{5}$ mile
Tara	$\frac{6}{8}$ mile
Larry	$\frac{9}{10}$ mile
Joe	$\frac{10}{10}$ mile

 Spiral Review and Test Practice

Find the quotient. NS 2.0 pages 268, 282, 288

16. $45 \div 5$

17. $81 \div 9$

18. $30 \div 3$

19. $16 \div 4$

Write the letter of the correct answer. NS 3.1

20. Which fraction is equivalent to $\frac{1}{3}$?

   A $\frac{2}{3}$ **B** $\frac{2}{6}$ **C** $\frac{3}{1}$ **D** $\frac{3}{6}$

LESSON 5

CA Standards

NS 3.1 Compare fractions represented by drawings or concrete materials to show equivalency and to add and subtract simple fractions in context (e.g., $\frac{1}{2}$ of a pizza is the same amount as $\frac{2}{4}$ of another pizza that is the same size; show that $\frac{3}{8}$ is larger than $\frac{1}{4}$).

Also NS 3.0, MG 2.5, MR 2.0, MR 2.3, MR 2.4

Materials
• Fraction tiles
• eManipulatives (optional)
   www.eduplace.com/camap/

Hands On
Compare Fractions

Objective Compare fractions with like and unlike denominators.

▶ **Learn With Manipulatives**

Dora's class knit scarves. Look at the scarves. Which scarf has more pink?

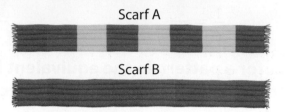

Scarf A

Scarf B

You can compare fractions that have the same denominator.

Compare $\frac{3}{8}$ and $\frac{4}{8}$.

Different Ways to Compare Fractions

Fractions with the Same Denominator

Way 1   Use fraction tiles.

$$\frac{3}{8} < \frac{4}{8}; \frac{4}{8} > \frac{3}{8}$$

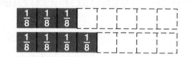

Way 2   Use a number line.

$$\frac{3}{8} < \frac{4}{8}; \frac{4}{8} > \frac{3}{8}$$

Solution: Scarf B has more pink.

Fractions with Different Denominators

Compare $\frac{1}{3}$ and $\frac{1}{2}$.

Way 1   Use fraction tiles.

$$\frac{1}{3} < \frac{1}{2}; \frac{1}{2} > \frac{1}{3}$$

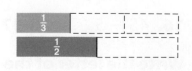

Way 2   Use a number line.

$$\frac{1}{3} < \frac{1}{2}; \frac{1}{2} > \frac{1}{3}$$

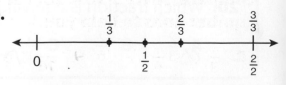

▶ Guided Practice

Compare. Write > or < for the .

1.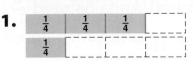

$$\frac{3}{4} \bigcirc \frac{1}{4}$$

2.

$$\frac{1}{4} \bigcirc \frac{1}{6}$$

Compare. Write > or < for the . Use fraction tiles or number lines to help you.

3. $\frac{1}{2} \bigcirc \frac{2}{2}$ **4.** $\frac{6}{8} \bigcirc \frac{3}{8}$ **5.** $\frac{5}{5} \bigcirc \frac{4}{5}$ **6.** $\frac{1}{3} \bigcirc \frac{1}{8}$

Guided Problem Solving

Use the questions to solve this problem.

7. Paul's scarf is $\frac{2}{5}$ yellow and Emily's scarf is $\frac{4}{5}$ yellow. If each scarf is the same size, whose scarf has more yellow?

  a. Understand Which two fractions do you need to compare?

  b. Plan What model can you use?

  c. Solve Use the method you chose.

  d. Look Back Draw a picture to show that your answer is correct.

123 Math Talk The circles are the same size. Which is greater, $\frac{1}{3}$ or $\frac{1}{4}$? How do you know?

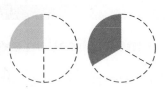

▶ Practice and Problem Solving

Compare. Write > or < for the . Use fraction tiles or number lines to help you.

8. $\frac{1}{3} \bigcirc \frac{1}{4}$ **9.** $\frac{7}{10} \bigcirc \frac{10}{10}$ **10.** $\frac{1}{3} \bigcirc \frac{2}{3}$ **11.** $\frac{7}{8} \bigcirc 1$

Solve.

12. **Analyze** Mia made a blanket that was $\frac{1}{4}$ red. Nadia made a blanket that was the same size but it was $\frac{1}{3}$ red. Whose blanket has less red?

13. **Challenge** Anita, Alex, and Sam painted a mural. Anita painted $\frac{4}{12}$, Alex painted $\frac{2}{12}$, and Sam painted $\frac{1}{2}$. Who painted the most?

 ## Science Link

Use the Fun Facts to help you solve the problems.

14. **a.** Red, orange, and yellow are called the warm colors. What fraction of the color spectrum are the warm colors?

    b. Green, blue, indigo, and violet are called the cool colors. What fraction of the color spectrum are the cool colors?

    c. Write an expression comparing the fraction of warm colors to the fraction of cool colors in the color spectrum.

15. **Challenge** Look at the solid figure in the picture. How many faces does it have? How many edges? How many vertices?

The Color Spectrum

- The 7 colors of the color spectrum are red, orange, yellow, green, blue, indigo, and violet.

- A prism separates light into the 7 colors of the color spectrum.

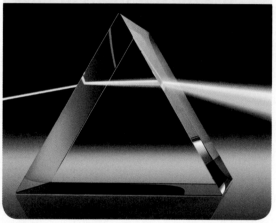

Science **PS 2.b**

 ## Spiral Review and Test Practice

Write a multiplication expression for each. AF 1.4 page 172

16. the number of feet in 2 yards

17. the number of feet in 9 yards

Write the letter of the correct answer. NS 3.1

18. Which fraction is greater than $\frac{1}{4}$?

   A $\frac{1}{2}$ **B** $\frac{1}{5}$ **C** $\frac{1}{6}$ **D** $\frac{1}{8}$

Extra Practice See page 341, Set C.

Key Standards Review

Need Help?
See Key Standards Handbook.

Use the array to write the number sentences. KEY **NS 2.3**

1.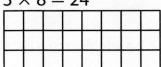

$2 \times \blacksquare = 12$
$12 \div \blacksquare = 2$

2.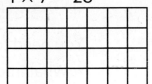

$3 \times \blacksquare = 21$
$21 \div \blacksquare = 3$

3.

$\blacksquare \times 6 = 24$
$24 \div \blacksquare = 6$

Write a division sentence that is modeled by the figure. KEY **NS 2.3**

4. $3 \times 8 = 24$

5. $4 \times 7 = 28$

Solve. Write a multiplication problem you can use to check the division. KEY **NS 2.3**

6. $72 \div 8 = \blacksquare$ **7.** $48 \div 6 = \blacksquare$ **8.** $63 \div 9 = \blacksquare$ **9.** $35 \div 7 = \blacksquare$

Number Sense

Make It True

Solve. NS 3.1

1. How many ways can you put the numbers 1, 2, 4, and 6 into the boxes to make a true statement? The fractions must be less than 1.

$$\frac{\blacksquare}{\blacksquare} < \frac{\blacksquare}{\blacksquare}$$

2. What fraction of the figure is shaded?

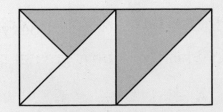

CA Standards

MR 1.1 Analyze problems by identifying relationships, distinguishing relevant from irrelevant information, sequencing and prioritizing information, and observing patterns.

NS 3.0 Students understand the relationship between whole numbers, simple fractions, and decimals.

Also MR 2.0, MR 2.3, MR 2.4, MR 3.0, MR 3.1, MR 3.2, MR 3.3

Problem Solving Plan
Too Much Information

Objective Find the information needed to solve a problem when too much information is given.

▶ Learn by Example

Janet made a bracelet using wooden beads. The bracelet has 7 brown beads and 5 white beads. Three of the white beads are smaller than the other beads. What fraction of the beads are brown?

UNDERSTAND

You need to find the fraction of the beads that are brown.

• What information is needed?

There are 7 brown beads and 5 white beads.

• What information is not needed?

Three white beads are smaller than the other beads.

PLAN

Find the total number of beads. Write a fraction to describe the portion of brown beads.

SOLVE

7 brown beads + 5 white beads = 12 beads in all

number of brown beads

total number of beads

$\frac{7}{12}$ of the beads are brown.

LOOK BACK

Does your answer make sense? How do you know?

Guided Problem Solving

Solve using the Ask Yourself questions. Tell what information is not needed to solve the problem.

1. A box of T-shirts contains 4 large, 3 medium, and 2 small shirts. Three of the T-shirts are white, and 6 are navy blue. What fraction of the T-shirts are size small?

 Math Talk Look back at the problem on page 338. Explain how you know that the information about the sizes of the white beads is not needed to solve the problem.

Independent Problem Solving

Solve. Tell what information is not needed to solve the problem.

2. Mr. Turner has 3 white shirts, 2 blue shirts, 1 pair of jeans, and 2 pairs of dress pants. What fraction of his shirts are blue?

3. Madison has 7 cousins. Three are girls. The rest are boys. Madison is older than 2 girls. What fraction of the girls are younger than Madison?

4. Jason has 2 dollar bills, 6 quarters, 3 dimes, and 1 nickel. What fraction of the coins are dimes?

5. There were 8 people waiting at a bus stop. Two of them were women, and the rest were men. Five of the people got on the first bus that came by. What fraction of the people were left at the bus stop after the first bus left?

6. **Challenge** Sally had 4 sheets of stickers. Each sheet had 5 stickers. $\frac{1}{4}$ of the stickers were red. If Sally used $\frac{1}{2}$ of the stickers, how many stickers does she have left?

7. **Create and Solve** Write and solve a word problem that contains information that is not needed.

Vocabulary

A **fraction** names part of a whole, or more than one whole.

Mrs. Johnson brought snacks for her scout troop.
What fraction of the fruits are oranges?

$\dfrac{2}{7}$

Two sevenths of the pieces of fruit are oranges.

Equivalent fractions name the same part of a whole.

Use the drawings to answer the questions.

 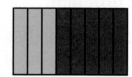

1. Are the red sections of the circles equivalent in size?

2. Write a number sentence to compare the fractions.

3. Are the red sections of the rectangles equivalent in size?

4. Write a number sentence to compare the fractions.

Writing Use one of the drawings on this page to explain what *numerator* and *denominator* mean. Write as if your reader had never heard of fractions!

Reading Look for this book in your library.

• *Fraction Fun*, by David Adler

CA Standards

MR 2.3 Use a variety of methods, such as words, numbers, symbols, charts, graphs, tables, diagrams, and models, to explain mathematical reasoning.
Also NS 3.1

Standards-Based Extra Practice

Set A ———————————————————————————————— NS 3.0 page 328

Write a fraction to name the part of the group that is round.

1.

2.

3.

4. Kirstie is making a pattern out of colored buttons. She has used 12 buttons. $\frac{3}{4}$ of the buttons are blue. How many are blue?

Set B ———————————————————————————————— NS 3.1 page 332

Are the fractions equivalent? Write *yes* or *no*.

1. $\frac{1}{4}$ and $\frac{2}{8}$

2. $\frac{1}{4}$ and $\frac{1}{3}$

3. $\frac{3}{6}$ and $\frac{1}{2}$

4. $\frac{3}{9}$ and $\frac{1}{3}$

5. $\frac{5}{6}$ and $\frac{6}{7}$

6. $\frac{1}{2}$ and $\frac{5}{10}$

Look for a pattern in the equivalent fractions. Then complete two more equivalent fractions in the pattern.

7. $\frac{1}{4} = \frac{2}{8} = \frac{3}{12} = \frac{4}{16} = \frac{\blacksquare}{20} = \frac{\blacksquare}{24}$

8. $\frac{2}{3} = \frac{4}{6} = \frac{6}{9} = \frac{8}{12} = \frac{\blacksquare}{15} = \frac{\blacksquare}{18}$

9. Brian and Martin both order small pizzas. Brian cuts his pizza into three equal pieces and eats two. Martin cuts his pizza into six equal pieces and eats four. Have they eaten the same amount of pizza? Explain.

Set C ———————————————————————————————— NS 3.1 page 334

Compare. Write $>$ or $<$ for the ■. Use fraction tiles or number lines to help you.

1. $\frac{3}{2}$ ■ $\frac{1}{2}$

2. $\frac{4}{6}$ ■ $\frac{3}{6}$

3. $\frac{8}{9}$ ■ $\frac{9}{9}$

4. $\frac{5}{2}$ ■ $\frac{2}{2}$

5. $\frac{7}{10}$ ■ $\frac{9}{10}$

6. $\frac{3}{8}$ ■ $\frac{5}{8}$

7. $\frac{5}{10}$ ■ $\frac{2}{10}$

8. $\frac{3}{4}$ ■ $\frac{7}{4}$

9. $\frac{1}{8}$ ■ $\frac{1}{3}$

10. $\frac{1}{3}$ ■ $\frac{1}{5}$

Education Place
Visit www.eduplace.com/camap/
for more **Extra Practice**.

Chapter Review/Test

Vocabulary and Concepts
MR 2.3

Choose the best word to complete each sentence.

1. The top number in a fraction is called the _____.

2. The _____ is the number of equal parts in the whole.

3. Two fractions showing the same amount are _____.

> **Word Bank**
> numerator
> denominator
> equivalent fractions

Skills
NS 3.0, NS 3.1

Write *equivalent* or *not equivalent* to describe the fractions.

4. $\frac{3}{6}$ and $\frac{1}{3}$ **5.** $\frac{2}{5}$ and $\frac{2}{10}$ **6.** $\frac{1}{2}$ and $\frac{3}{8}$ **7.** $\frac{6}{8}$ and $\frac{3}{4}$

Look for a pattern in the equivalent fractions. Then complete two more equivalent fractions in the pattern.

8. $\frac{2}{7} = \frac{4}{14} = \frac{6}{21} = \frac{8}{28} = \frac{\blacksquare}{35} = \frac{\blacksquare}{42}$ **9.** $\frac{1}{5} = \frac{2}{10} = \frac{3}{15} = \frac{4}{20} = \frac{\blacksquare}{25} = \frac{\blacksquare}{30}$

Compare. Write > or < for the ▨. Use fraction tiles or number lines to help you.

10. $\frac{1}{6}$ ▨ $\frac{1}{3}$ **11.** $\frac{8}{10}$ ▨ $\frac{7}{10}$ **12.** $\frac{9}{12}$ ▨ $\frac{11}{12}$ **13.** $\frac{1}{10}$ ▨ $\frac{1}{5}$

Problem Solving and Reasoning
NS 3.0

Solve. Explain how you can check your answer.

14. Rosa, Tyrone, and Rita designed a poster together. Rosa drew $\frac{2}{7}$, Tyrone drew $\frac{4}{7}$, and Rita drew $\frac{1}{7}$. Who drew the most?

15. Sheila made a bracelet with 6 blue beads, 6 purple beads, and 4 sparkle beads. What fraction of Shelia's beads are purple?

> **Writing Math** A baker has $\frac{1}{4}$ of a chocolate cake, $\frac{1}{2}$ of a lemon cake, and $\frac{3}{4}$ of a strawberry cake. Is the total amount of cake he has less than, equal to, or greater than one whole? Explain.

Spiral Review and Test Practice

1. Which number is 12 less than 600?

A 588

B 598

C 612

D 698

> **Test Tip**
> In this question, *less* means you should subtract.

KEY **NS 2.1** page 80

2. Aunt Mary sends letters to each of her nieces 2 times every month. The nieces live in 3 cities. She has 2 nieces in each city. How many letters does Aunt Mary send each month?

A 12

B 7

C 6

D 4

> **Test Tip**
> You need to do more than one step to solve some problems.

AF **1.5** page 152

3. There are 1,000 meters in 1 kilometer. How many meters are in 8 kilometers?

A 80 meters   **C** 800 meters

B 1,000 meters   **D** 8,000 meters

MG **1.4** page 178

4. Ella made 63 potholders in 9 days. She made the same number each day. How many potholders did Ella make each day?

A 4

B 5

C 7

D 9

KEY **NS 2.3** page 288

5. A designer is making a fountain with 49 bubblers. If the bubblers are in 7 equal rows, how many bubblers are in each row?

A 5

B 6

C 7

D 497

KEY **NS 2.2** page 306

6. Zack made punch with 3 pints of juice and 5 pints of water. What fraction of the punch is juice?

A $\frac{1}{3}$ **C** $\frac{3}{5}$

B $\frac{3}{8}$ **D** $\frac{5}{8}$

NS **3.0** page 328

 Education Place
Visit www.eduplace.com/camap/ for **Test-Taking Tips** and **Extra Practice**.

Chapter 15 Spiral Review and Test Practice   **343**

Vocabulary and Concepts GRADE 2 NS 4.0

Choose the best term to complete each sentence.

1. The bottom number of a fraction is the _____.

2. In the fraction $\frac{3}{7}$, the 3 is the _____.

3. The denominator shows how many _____ there are in the whole.

Skills GRADE 2 KEY NS 4.2

Write the fraction.

4. What fraction of the stars are red?

5. What fraction of the stars are green?

6. What fraction of the stars are *not* yellow?

Identify the fraction shown on the number line.

7. Point *A*   8. Point *B*

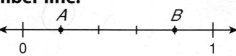

Problem Solving and Reasoning GRADE 2 KEY NS 4.3

9. Explain how $\frac{4}{4}$ and $\frac{6}{6}$ can both represent one whole.

Vocabulary

Visualize It!

You can add and subtract **fractions**.

When the denominators
are the same, add
the numerators.

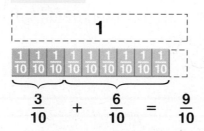

$$\frac{3}{10} + \frac{6}{10} = \frac{9}{10}$$

When the denominators
are the same, subtract
the numerators.

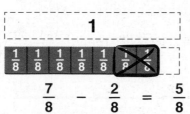

$$\frac{7}{8} - \frac{2}{8} = \frac{5}{8}$$

Language Tip

Some words are similar in Spanish
and English.

English	Spanish
fraction	fracción

See **English-Spanish Glossary** pages 628–646.

Education Place Visit www.eduplace.com/camap/ for the **eGlossary** and **eGames**.

CA Standards
KEY NS 3.2 Add and subtract simple fractions (e.g., determine that $\frac{1}{8} + \frac{3}{8}$ is the same as $\frac{1}{2}$).
MR 2.3 Use a variety of methods, such as words, numbers, symbols, charts, graphs, tables, diagrams, and models, to explain mathematical reasoning.
Also NS 3.1

Materials
• Fraction tiles
• eManipulatives (optional) www.eduplace.com/camap/

Hands On
Add and Subtract Fractions

Objective Use fraction tiles to model addition and subtraction of fractions with like denominators.

▶ **Explore**

You can use fraction tiles to add and subtract fractions.

Question How can you use fraction tiles to help you add and subtract fractions?

Sue and Dave bought a hero sandwich to share. The sandwich was cut into 6 equal pieces. Sue ate $\frac{2}{6}$ of the sandwich and Dave ate $\frac{3}{6}$ of the sandwich. What fraction of the sandwich did Sue and Dave eat together? Add $\frac{2}{6} + \frac{3}{6}$.

Fun Fact

The hero, which originated in Italy, is also known as a grinder, a hoagie, or a sub.

1 Start with the fraction tile for 1 whole.
Place two $\frac{1}{6}$ tiles below it.

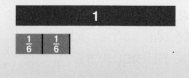

2 Add three $\frac{1}{6}$ tiles.
Write the number sentence.
$\frac{2}{6} + \frac{3}{6} = \frac{5}{6}$

Think
You show the fraction tile for 1 so that you can compare the sum or difference with one whole.

Solution: Sue and Dave ate $\frac{5}{6}$ of the hero sandwich together.

Dave gave Sue $\frac{7}{8}$ of a small pizza. Sue ate $\frac{4}{8}$ of the whole pizza. What fraction of the whole pizza was left?

Subtract $\frac{7}{8} - \frac{4}{8}$.

1 Start with the fraction tile for 1 whole.

Place seven $\frac{1}{8}$ tiles below it.

2 Subtract four $\frac{1}{8}$ tiles.

Write the number sentence.

$\frac{7}{8} - \frac{4}{8} = \frac{3}{8}$

Solution: $\frac{3}{8}$ of the whole pizza was left.

▶ Extend

Add. Use fraction tiles to help.

1. $\frac{3}{8} + \frac{4}{8}$

2. $\frac{2}{5} + \frac{3}{5}$

3. $\frac{4}{6} + \frac{3}{6}$

4. $\frac{1}{10} + \frac{5}{10}$

5. **Analyze** Look at your answers to Problems 1–4. Are any sums equal to 1? Are any sums greater than 1? If so, which ones?

Subtract. Use fraction tiles to help.

6. $\frac{2}{3} - \frac{1}{3}$

7. $\frac{8}{10} - \frac{3}{10}$

8. $\frac{4}{12} - \frac{1}{12}$

9. $\frac{8}{8} - \frac{3}{8}$

10. **Explain** How can you use what you know about adding or subtracting whole numbers to help you add or subtract fractions with like denominators?

Writing Math

Right or Wrong? Chris says that the sum of $\frac{1}{4}$ and $\frac{1}{4}$ is $\frac{2}{8}$.

What did Chris do wrong? Explain your thinking.

CA Standards
KEY NS 3.2 Add and subtract simple fractions (e.g., determine that $\frac{1}{8} + \frac{3}{8}$ is the same as $\frac{1}{2}$).

NS 3.1 Compare fractions represented by drawings or concrete materials to show equivalency and to add and subtract simple fractions in context (e.g., $\frac{1}{2}$ of a pizza is the same amount as $\frac{2}{4}$ of another pizza that is the same size; show that $\frac{3}{8}$ is larger than $\frac{1}{4}$).

Also AF 1.2, MR 2.6

Vocabulary

numerator

denominator

Add Fractions

Objective Add fractions with like denominators.

▶ Learn by Example

In this lesson you will learn to add fractions without models.

$\frac{3}{8}$ of the kite is yellow and $\frac{1}{8}$ is blue. Is the part that is either yellow or blue equal to $\frac{1}{2}$?

Fun Fact

The first kites were built in China about 3,000 years ago.

1 Start with three $\frac{1}{8}$ fraction tiles.

Add one $\frac{1}{8}$ tile.

$$\frac{3}{8} + \frac{1}{8} = \frac{4}{8}$$

When the **denominators** are the same, add the **numerators**.

2 Compare $\frac{4}{8}$ and $\frac{1}{2}$.

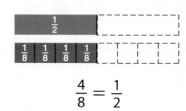

$$\frac{4}{8} = \frac{1}{2}$$

Solution: Yes, $\frac{1}{2}$ of the kite is yellow or blue.

▶ Guided Practice

Ask Yourself
• Are the denominators the same?
• Is the sum equal to 1?

Add.

1. $\frac{1}{3} + \frac{1}{3}$ **2.** $\frac{2}{8} + \frac{3}{8}$ **3.** $\frac{2}{4} + \frac{3}{4}$ **4.** $\frac{2}{6} + \frac{4}{6}$

Find the sum. Then find a fraction in the box that is equivalent to the sum.

$\boxed{\frac{1}{2} \quad \frac{1}{4} \quad \frac{1}{6}}$

5. $\frac{1}{8} + \frac{1}{8}$ **6.** $\frac{2}{10} + \frac{3}{10}$ **7.** $\frac{1}{12} + \frac{1}{12}$

Guided Problem Solving

Use the questions to solve this problem.

8. Look at the kite. Are the red or yellow parts together equal to $\frac{3}{4}$?

   a. **Understand** What fraction of the kite is red? What fraction of the kite is yellow?

   b. **Plan** Draw a picture to model this problem.

   c. **Solve** Write the addition sentence. Solve the problem.

   d. **Look Back** Look at the picture you made. Does your answer make sense?

 Math Talk How can you tell if the sum of two fractions is equal to one whole?

Practice and Problem Solving

Add.

9. $\frac{1}{10} + \frac{2}{10}$

10. $\frac{3}{5} + \frac{1}{5}$

11. $\frac{3}{6} + \frac{2}{6}$

12. $\frac{1}{4} + \frac{3}{4}$

Find the sum. Then find a fraction in the box that is equivalent to the sum.

$$\boxed{\frac{1}{2} \quad \frac{1}{5} \quad \frac{3}{4} \quad \frac{2}{3}}$$

13. $\frac{3}{8} + \frac{3}{8}$

14. $\frac{1}{10} + \frac{1}{10}$

15. $\frac{1}{4} + \frac{1}{4}$

16. $\frac{3}{6} + \frac{1}{6}$

X Algebra Variables
Find the value of ▨.

17. $\frac{1}{4} + \frac{\blacksquare}{4} = \frac{2}{4}$

18. $\frac{\blacksquare}{8} + \frac{1}{8} = \frac{6}{8}$

19. $\frac{4}{5} + \frac{\blacksquare}{5} = \frac{5}{5}$

20. $\frac{5}{9} + \frac{\blacksquare}{9} = \frac{8}{9}$

21. $\frac{\blacksquare}{6} + \frac{2}{6} = \frac{5}{6}$

22. $\frac{1}{5} + \frac{\blacksquare}{5} = \frac{3}{5}$

Solve the problems below.

23. Ji and Ruby are painting a fence. Ji paints $\frac{2}{8}$ of the fence, Ruby paints $\frac{3}{8}$. Together, did Ruby and Ji paint more than half the fence?

24. Explain Al eats $\frac{2}{6}$ of the cake, Sal eats $\frac{3}{6}$, and Hal eats $\frac{1}{6}$. Are there any pieces left? If so, how many? Explain how you know.

 Science Link

Solve each problem.

25. Some ostriches are raised on farms. $\frac{3}{8}$ of the ostriches on one farm are 9 feet tall or more. What fraction are less than 9 feet tall?

26. Use your inch ruler to measure the length of the ostrich egg in the picture to the nearest inch. The average ostrich egg is 3 times that length. How long is the average ostrich egg?

Fun Facts

Ostriches

- Ostriches are the largest and heaviest living birds.
- Ostriches have no teeth, so they swallow sand to help them grind up food.

Science LS 3.a

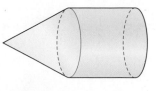 **Spiral Review and Test Practice**

What shapes make up the solid object? MG 2.6 page 234

27.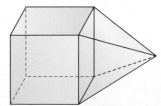

28.

29.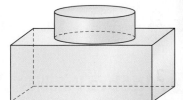

Write the letter of the correct answer. KEY NS 3.2

30. $\frac{2}{10} + \frac{3}{10} = \blacksquare$

   A $\frac{1}{4}$ **B** $\frac{10}{5}$ **C** $\frac{1}{2}$ **D** $\frac{5}{20}$

Extra Practice See page 361, Set A.

Key Standards Review

Need Help?
See Key Standards Handbook.

Find the perimeter of the polygon. Show your work. KEY MG 1.3

1.

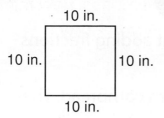

10 in.
10 in.   10 in.
10 in.

2.

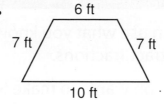

6 ft
7 ft   7 ft
10 ft

3.

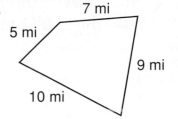

7 mi
5 mi
9 mi
10 mi

4.

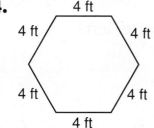

4 ft
4 ft   4 ft
4 ft   4 ft
4 ft

5.

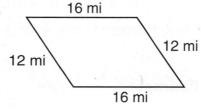

16 mi
12 mi   12 mi
16 mi

6.

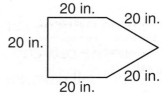

20 in.   20 in.
20 in.
20 in.   20 in.

Challenge   Number Sense

Fraction Sums

Match the expressions that have the same value. KEY NS 3.2

1. $\frac{3}{8} + \frac{1}{8}$ **A.** $\frac{3}{6} + \frac{3}{6}$

2. $\frac{2}{3} + \frac{1}{3}$ **B.** $\frac{3}{12} + \frac{6}{12}$

3. $\frac{2}{5} + \frac{1}{5}$ **C.** $\frac{1}{4} + \frac{1}{4}$

4. $\frac{1}{4} + \frac{2}{4}$ **D.** $\frac{4}{10} + \frac{2}{10}$

LESSON 3

CA Standards
KEY **NS 3.2** Add and subtract simple fractions (e.g., determine that $\frac{1}{8} + \frac{3}{8}$ is the same as $\frac{1}{2}$).

NS 3.1 Compare fractions represented by drawings or concrete materials to show equivalency and to add and subtract simple fractions in context (e.g., $\frac{1}{2}$ of a pizza is the same amount as $\frac{2}{4}$ of another pizza that is the same size; show that $\frac{3}{8}$ is larger than $\frac{1}{4}$).
Also MR 2.3

Subtract Fractions

Objective Subtract fractions with like denominators.

▶ **Learn by Example**

You can use what you know about adding fractions to subtract fractions.

Ramon wants to make Southern cornbread. The recipe says he needs $\frac{5}{8}$ of a stick of butter. Ramon has $\frac{7}{8}$ of a stick of butter. After he makes the bread, will Ramon have $\frac{1}{4}$ of a stick of butter left?

Think

When the denominators are the same, subtract the numerators.

Example 1

1 Start with seven $\frac{1}{8}$ fraction tiles.

Subtract five $\frac{1}{8}$ tiles.

$$\frac{7}{8} - \frac{5}{8} = \frac{2}{8}$$

2 Next, compare $\frac{2}{8}$ and $\frac{1}{4}$.

$$\frac{2}{8} = \frac{1}{4}$$

Solution: Yes, Ramon will have $\frac{1}{4}$ of a stick of butter left.

Example 2

Find $1 - \frac{4}{6}$.

1 Use like denominators.

Think: $\frac{6}{6} = 1$

2 Subtract four $\frac{1}{6}$ tiles.

$$\frac{6}{6} - \frac{4}{6} = \frac{2}{6}$$

So $1 - \frac{4}{6} = \frac{2}{6}$.

▶ Guided Practice

Subtract.

Ask Yourself
- Are the denominators the same?
- How many fraction tiles are left?

1.

$$\frac{2}{3} - \frac{1}{3} = \blacksquare$$

2.

$$\frac{5}{6} - \frac{3}{6} = \blacksquare$$

3. $\frac{2}{6} - \frac{1}{6}$

4. $\frac{7}{8} - \frac{2}{8}$

5. $1 - \frac{1}{9}$

123 Math Talk Look at Exercise 5. Why should you write 1 as $\frac{9}{9}$ before you subtract?

Hint
The denominator helps you write a fraction equivalent to 1.

▶ Practice and Problem Solving

Subtract.

6. $\frac{4}{5} - \frac{1}{5} = \blacksquare$

7. $\frac{1}{2} - \frac{1}{2} = \blacksquare$

8. $1 - \frac{2}{3}$

9. $\frac{4}{9} - \frac{3}{9}$

10. $\frac{6}{8} - \frac{1}{8}$

Solve the problem.

11. Justify Isaac says that $1 - \frac{4}{4}$ is 0. Lita says that the difference is $\frac{0}{4}$. Are they both correct? Explain.

12. Challenge The sum of two fractions is $\frac{7}{9}$. The difference is $\frac{3}{9}$. What are the two fractions?

Spiral Review and Test Practice

Write a fact family for the set of numbers. KEY NS 2.3 page 286

13. 4, 5, 20

14. 1, 8, 8

15. 3, 4, 12

Write the letter of the correct answer. KEY NS 3.2

16. $\frac{3}{5} - \frac{2}{5} = \blacksquare$

A $\frac{1}{25}$ **B** $\frac{1}{10}$ **C** $\frac{1}{0}$ **D** $\frac{1}{5}$

Extra Practice See page 361, Set B.

LESSON 4

CA Standards

MR 1.2 Determine when and how to break a problem into simpler parts.

KEY NS 3.2 Add and subtract simple fractions (e.g., determine that $\frac{1}{8} + \frac{3}{8}$ is the same as $\frac{1}{2}$).

Also MR 3.2

Practice Adding and Subtracting Fractions

Objective Add and subtract fractions with like denominators to solve multistep problems.

▶ Learn by Example

Anna cut a cake into 8 equal pieces. She placed $\frac{3}{8}$ of the cake on one plate and $\frac{2}{8}$ of the cake on another plate. How much of the cake was left?

To solve this problem, you need to break it into parts.

1 How much of the cake did Anna put on plates?

$$\frac{3}{8} + \frac{2}{8} = \frac{5}{8}$$

When the denominators are the same, add the numerators.

Anna put $\frac{5}{8}$ of the cake on plates.

2 How much of the cake was left?

$$1 - \frac{5}{8} = \bigcirc$$

$$\frac{8}{8} - \frac{5}{8} = \frac{3}{8}$$

When the denominators are the same, subtract the numerators.

Solution: $\frac{3}{8}$ of the cake was left.

Ask Yourself

- Are the denominators the same?
- Do I add or subtract?

▶ Guided Practice

Find the sum or difference. Then find a fraction in the box that is equivalent to the sum or difference.

$$\boxed{\frac{1}{2} \quad \frac{1}{3} \quad \frac{2}{3} \quad \frac{1}{4}}$$

1. $\frac{8}{8} - \frac{6}{8}$

2. $\frac{5}{6} - \frac{3}{6}$

3. $\frac{5}{12} + \frac{3}{12}$

354

Guided Problem Solving

Use the questions to solve this problem.

4. A sushi roll was divided into sixths. Leon ate $\frac{2}{6}$ of the roll. Taro ate $\frac{1}{6}$ of the roll. Lee ate $\frac{2}{6}$ of the roll. How much of the roll was left?

   a. **Understand** What do you need to find out?

   b. **Plan** What do you need to do first? What do you need to do next?

   c. **Solve** Write the equation.
      Leon, Taro, and Lee ate ◯ of the roll.
      There was ◯ of the roll left.

   d. **Look Back** Read the problem again. Does your answer make sense?

> **Think**
>
> The sushi roll is equal to 1 whole. It is divided into 6 equal pieces. I know the whole roll equals $\frac{6}{6}$.

5. Another sushi roll was divided into sixths. Leon ate $\frac{1}{6}$ of the roll. Taro ate $\frac{1}{6}$ of the roll. Lee ate $\frac{1}{6}$ of the roll. Was there exactly $\frac{1}{2}$ of the roll left?

(123) Math Talk Look at Exercise 3. How did you find a fraction in the box that was equivalent to the sum?

▶ Practice and Problem Solving

Add or subtract.

6. $\frac{11}{12} - \frac{6}{12}$

7. $\frac{1}{3} + \frac{1}{3}$

8. $\frac{10}{10} - \frac{1}{10}$

9. $\frac{2}{4} + \frac{1}{4}$

Find the sum or difference. Then find a fraction in the box that is equivalent to the sum or difference.

$$\boxed{\frac{1}{3} \quad \frac{1}{4} \quad \frac{2}{3} \quad \frac{1}{5}}$$

10. $\frac{8}{6} - \frac{6}{6}$

11. $\frac{10}{12} - \frac{2}{12}$

12. $\frac{1}{10} + \frac{1}{10}$

13. $\frac{5}{8} - \frac{3}{8}$

Solve the problem.

14. **Multistep** Sora ate $\frac{2}{10}$ of the lasagna. Her sister ate $\frac{3}{10}$ of the lasagna. Her father ate $\frac{4}{10}$ of the lasagna. How much of the lasagna is left?

15. **Explain** Flora and Jane each ate $\frac{1}{3}$ of a pizza. Is there more or less than $\frac{1}{2}$ of the pizza left?

 History-Social Science Link

Use the facts about the Statue of Liberty to solve each problem.

16. Saria climbed up the stairs and back down again. How many steps did she climb in all?

17. Maria climbs $\frac{5}{8}$ of steps to the crown then rests. What fraction of the steps are left to climb?

18. The Statue of Liberty was built in France. The statue was shipped in 350 pieces. It was packed in 214 crates. How many more pieces than crates were there?

19. How many inches long is the statue's mouth?

 Statue of Liberty

- There are 354 steps to the crown.
- The mouth is 3 feet wide.
- Lady Liberty was a gift from France in 1885.

The Statue of Liberty

History-Social Science 3.4.3

 Spiral Review and Test Practice

Draw a picture to compare the fractions. Write >, <, or =. NS 3.1 page 334

20. $\frac{3}{8}$ $\frac{1}{4}$ 21. $\frac{1}{2}$ ● $\frac{2}{4}$ 22. $\frac{1}{3}$ ● $\frac{2}{5}$

Write the letter of the correct answer. KEY NS 3.2

23. A loaf of bread was divided into eighths. Sally ate $\frac{1}{8}$ of the bread. Aida ate $\frac{1}{8}$ of the bread. Marco ate $\frac{1}{8}$ of the bread. How much of the bread was left?

A $\frac{7}{8}$ B $\frac{1}{8}$ C $\frac{5}{8}$ D $\frac{8}{8}$

Test Tip
How can you break the problem into parts?

 Extra Practice See page 361, Set C.

Use the table on the right to solve Problems 1–5.

1. How tall would a stack of 6 dimes be?

2. How much taller is a stack of 13 pennies than a stack of 4 nickels?

3. Use fraction tiles. Find how much taller a stack of 6 quarters would be compared to 4 nickels.

4. How tall would a stack of 8 nickels be?

5. How tall would a stack of 12 quarters be?

Stack of Coins	Height of Stack
6 quarters	$\frac{3}{8}$ inch
13 pennies	$\frac{3}{4}$ inch
4 nickels	$\frac{1}{4}$ inch
3 dimes	$\frac{1}{8}$ inch

Use the information in the table. How tall would the stack of coins be? Write the coins you used.

6. $1.80 in all

7. $0.43 in all

8. $0.40 in all

Solve.

9. What would be the value of a stack of nickels that is 1-inch tall?

CA Standards
KEY **NS 3.2**, KEY **NS 3.3**

LESSON 5

Field Trip...

San Francisco, CA

CA Standards
MR 1.0, MR 1.1,
MR 2.0, MR 2.6,
NS 2.0, KEY **NS 2.1**,
NS 3.0, KEY **NS 3.2**,
AF 1.0, KEY **AF 1.1**,
KEY **MG 1.3**

Problem Solving

Objective Use skills and strategies to solve word problems.

This mural is called *A Celebration of African and African American Artists*.

The African American Art and Culture Complex in San Francisco is a great place to learn about African American culture and history.

Solve. Tell which strategy or method you used.

1. **Analyze** There are 4 men and 4 women shown in the mural.

   a. What fraction of the people in the mural are men?

   b. What fraction of the people are women?

   c. Write an equation to show that the fraction of the people who are men plus the fraction of the people who are women is equal to 1.

2. The mural was made in 1993. How old is the mural now?

3. The perimeter of the mural is 352 feet.

   a. Look at the diagram of the mural. What is its width?

   b. Explain why you think your answer is reasonable.

Fun Facts

- The library at the complex has books on important people like Martin Luther King Jr.

- The complex has exhibits, plays, classes, and other activities.

length = 131 ft

Problem Solving On Tests

Select a Strategy
- Draw a Picture
- Estimate
- Choose the Operation
- Make a Table

1. A package of dog treats costs $3. How much will LeRoy pay for 8 packages of dog treats?

A $5   **B** $11   **C** $24   **D** $32

KEY **NS 3.3** page 132

2. Gerry biked a total of 8 kilometers. How many meters is this?

A 8000 meters

B 800 meters

C 80 meters

D 8 meters

Test Tip
There are 1,000 meters in 1 kilometer.

MG **1.4** page 178

3. Sammie has 54 baseball cards divided into 6 equal stacks. He says there are 9 cards in each stack because 54 ÷ 6 = 9. Which multiplication problem can he use to see if he is correct?

A 6 + 9 = 15   **C** 15 ÷ 3 = 5

B 9 − 6 = 3   **D** 6 × 9 = 54

KEY **NS 2.3** page 302

4. Dipak drew this figure. What is the area of his figure?

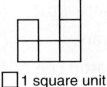
☐ 1 square unit

A 4 square units   **C** 6 square units

B 5 square units   **D** 7 square units

KEY **MG 1.2** page 220

5. Janet had $25. She bought a sweater for $12 and two pairs of socks for $3.00 each. How much money did Janet have left?

A $7

B $10

C $19

D $23

Test Tip
You need to do more than one step to solve this problem.

NS **2.8** page 134

6. A submarine sandwich was divided into ninths. Selena ate $\frac{1}{9}$, and her brother ate $\frac{2}{9}$. Their cousin ate $\frac{4}{9}$ of the sandwich. How much of the sandwich was left?

A $\frac{6}{9}$ **B** $\frac{4}{9}$ **C** $\frac{2}{9}$ **D** $\frac{1}{9}$

KEY **NS 3.2** page 352

7. Rita bought 48 hot-dog buns that were packed equally into 6 bags. Which number sentence shows how to find the number of hot-dog buns in each bag?

A 48 − 6 = ▨   **C** 48 + 6 = ▨

B 48 ÷ 6 = ▨   **D** 48 × 6 = ▨

KEY **AF 1.1** page 302

Education Place
Visit www.eduplace.com/camap/ for **Test-Taking Tips** and **Extra Practice**.

Chapter 16 Lesson 5   **359**

Reading & Writing

Vocabulary

You know how to add and subtract fractions with equal **denominators**. When the denominators are the same, you can add or subtract the **numerators**.

Leelee

Mary and Leelee bought a pizza to share. The pizza had 6 equal slices. Mary ate 2 slices. Leelee ate 3 slices.

1. How much of the pizza did they eat?

Mary and Leelee ate $\frac{5}{6}$ of the pizza. $\frac{2}{6} + \frac{3}{6} = $ ___

2. How much of the pizza was left?

One slice was left. $\frac{6}{6} - \frac{5}{6} = $ ___

Mary

Tara, Jorge, and Joey are painting a wall mural. The mural has 8 panels. Tara paints 4 panels. Jorge paints 3 panels. Joey paints 1 panel.

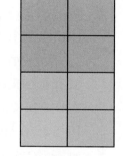

3. Write a fraction to show the part of the mural each person painted.

4. Is the part of the mural that Jorge and Joey painted equal to $\frac{1}{2}$?

Writing Is the sum of $\frac{3}{10}$ and $\frac{9}{10}$ greater than, less than, or equal to 1 whole? Explain your thinking.

Reading Check out this book in your library.

• *Mega-Fun Fractions*, by Marcia Miller and Martin Lee

CA Standards

MR 2.3 Use a variety of methods, such as words, numbers, symbols, charts, graphs, tables, diagrams, and models, to explain mathematical reasoning.

Also NS 3.0, NS 3.1, KEY NS 3.2

Standards-Based Extra Practice

Set A ———————————————————————— KEY **NS 3.2** page 348

Add.

1. $\frac{5}{8} + \frac{2}{8}$ **2.** $\frac{2}{7} + \frac{3}{7}$ **3.** $\frac{1}{2} + \frac{2}{2}$ **4.** $\frac{3}{12} + \frac{2}{12}$

Find the sum. Then find a fraction in the box that is equivalent to the sum.

5. $\frac{1}{10} + \frac{1}{10}$ **6.** $\frac{1}{8} + \frac{1}{8}$ **7.** $\frac{2}{6} + \frac{1}{6}$

$$\frac{1}{2} \quad \frac{3}{4}$$
$$\frac{1}{3} \quad \frac{1}{5} \quad \frac{1}{4}$$

8. Chad drew a square and divided it into 10 equal parts. He colored 2 parts. Write two equivalent fractions for the part that is colored.

Set B ———————————————————————— KEY **NS 3.2** page 352

Subtract.

1. $\frac{7}{8} - \frac{3}{8}$ **2.** $\frac{5}{9} - \frac{2}{9}$ **3.** $\frac{2}{2} - \frac{1}{2}$ **4.** $\frac{3}{4} - \frac{2}{4}$

5. $\frac{2}{3} - \frac{2}{3}$ **6.** $\frac{7}{7} - \frac{5}{7}$ **7.** $\frac{5}{6} - \frac{1}{6}$ **8.** $\frac{3}{5} - \frac{2}{5}$

9. Lou and Jan each ate $\frac{1}{4}$ of an apple. Is there more than, less than, or exactly $\frac{1}{2}$ of the apple left? Explain.

Set C ———————————————————————— KEY **NS 3.2** page 354

Add or Subtract.

1. $\frac{5}{6} + \frac{2}{6}$ **2.** $\frac{6}{8} - \frac{4}{8}$ **3.** $\frac{8}{11} - \frac{3}{11}$ **4.** $\frac{4}{5} - \frac{2}{5}$

Find the sum or difference. Then find a fraction in the box that is equivalent to the sum or difference.

5. $\frac{1}{8} + \frac{5}{8}$ **6.** $\frac{3}{6} + \frac{1}{6}$ **7.** $\frac{7}{8} - \frac{3}{8}$

$$\frac{2}{3} \quad \frac{1}{3}$$
$$\frac{3}{4} \quad \frac{1}{2} \quad \frac{2}{3}$$

Education Place
Visit www.eduplace.com/camap/
for more **Extra Practice**.

Chapter 16 Extra Practice   **361**

Chapter Review/Test

Vocabulary and Concepts ————————————— MR 2.3

Choose the best word to complete each sentence.

Word Bank
numerator
denominator

1. The top number in a fraction is called the _____.

2. The _____ represents how many equal parts the whole was split into.

Skills ————————————————————————————— KEY NS 3.2

Add.

3. $\frac{2}{9} + \frac{5}{9}$

4. $\frac{3}{8} + \frac{2}{8}$

5. $\frac{3}{5} + \frac{1}{5}$

6. $\frac{3}{6} + \frac{2}{6}$

Subtract.

7. $\frac{7}{8} - \frac{3}{8}$

8. $\frac{6}{9} - \frac{5}{9}$

9. $\frac{4}{5} - \frac{2}{5}$

10. $\frac{5}{7} - \frac{2}{7}$

Add or subtract.

11. $\frac{2}{10} + \frac{5}{10}$

12. $\frac{3}{4} - \frac{2}{4}$

13. $\frac{2}{7} + \frac{3}{7}$

14. $\frac{8}{12} - \frac{3}{12}$

Find the sum or difference. Then find a fraction in the box that is equivalent to the sum or difference.

15. $\frac{3}{8} + \frac{3}{8}$

16. $\frac{1}{4} + \frac{1}{4}$

17. $\frac{3}{6} + \frac{1}{6}$

18. $\frac{8}{10} - \frac{4}{10}$

$\frac{1}{2}$	$\frac{2}{5}$
$\frac{2}{3}$	$\frac{3}{4}$

Problem Solving and Reasoning ————————— KEY NS 3.2, MR 2.3, MR 2.4

Solve. Show how you checked the answer.

19. Ty needs $\frac{3}{4}$ cup of corn for one recipe and $\frac{1}{4}$ cup of corn for another. How much corn does he need?

20. Mica and Ali painted a room together. If Ali painted $\frac{2}{3}$ of the room, how much did Mica paint?

Writing Math Sim has $\frac{5}{4}$ cups of raisins. He needs $\frac{3}{4}$ cup for one recipe and $\frac{1}{4}$ cup for another. Does Sim have enough raisins? Explain.

Spiral Review and Test Practice

1. Ms. Gardner is making up baskets that each have 3 pieces of fruit. If Ms. Gardner makes up 8 baskets, how many pieces of fruit does she use?

A 11 **C** 16

B 24 **D** 30

KEY **NS 2.2** page 132

2. There are 36 inches in 1 yard. How many inches are in 4 yards?

A 12 inches

B 72 inches

C 108 inches

D 144 inches

MG **1.4** page 172

3. Which triangle appears to have exactly two equal sides?

A

C

B

D
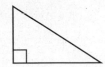

KEY **MG 2.2** page 198

4. Walter shared 48 balloons equally with 8 friends. How many balloons did Walter give each friend?

A 8 **C** 7

B 6 **D** 5

KEY **NS 2.3** page 308

5. The circle shows $\frac{1}{3}$ shaded.

Which fractional part of a circle below is equal to $\frac{1}{3}$?

Test Tip
Find a circle that has the same amount shaded as the given circle.

A

C

B

D

NS **3.1** page 330

Education Place
Visit www.eduplace.com/camap/ for
Test-Taking Tips and **Extra Practice**.

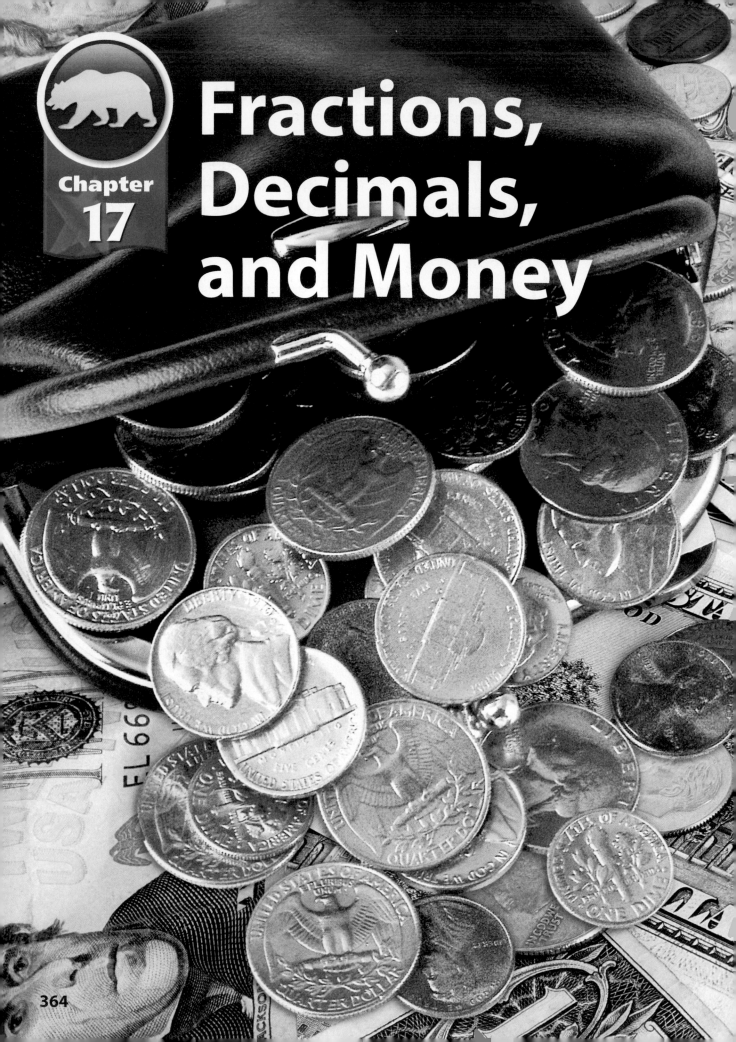

Chapter 17

Fractions, Decimals, and Money

Vocabulary and Concepts GRADE 2 NS 5.0

Choose the best word to complete each sentence.

1. A _____ has a value of 10¢.

2. One hundred cents is equal to one _____.

3. A _____ has a value of 1¢.

Skills GRADE 2 NS 5.0, KEY NS 5.2

Write the value of each coin.

4.   5.   6.   7.

Write each amount using a dollar sign and decimal point.

8. forty-one cents   9. twenty-three cents

Problem Solving and Reasoning GRADE 2 NS 5.0

10. How many dimes are in 1 dollar? how many quarters?

Vocabulary

Visualize It !

Twelve hundredths can be shown in more than one way.

$\dfrac{12}{100}$ of a dollar = $0.12

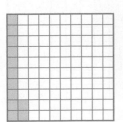 =

Language Tips

In everyday life, if something has *value* it is worth something. If groups of coins have the same *value*, they are worth the same amount of money.

Some words are similar in Spanish and English.

English	Spanish
value	**valor**

See **English-Spanish Glossary** pages 628–646.

 Education Place Visit www.eduplace.com/camap/ for the **eGlossary** and **eGames**.

CA Standards MR 2.3 Use a variety of methods, such as words, numbers, symbols, charts, graphs, tables, diagrams, and models, to explain mathematical reasoning. **Also NS 3.4**

Chapter 17 365

CA Standards

NS 3.0 Students understand the relationship between whole numbers, simple fractions, and decimals.

NS 3.1 Compare fractions represented by drawings or concrete materials to show equivalency and to add and subtract simple fractions in context (e.g., $\frac{1}{2}$ of a pizza is the same amount as $\frac{2}{4}$ of another pizza that is the same size; show that $\frac{3}{8}$ is larger than $\frac{1}{4}$).
Also MR 2.3, MR 2.4

Materials

• Workmat 7
• Workmat 8
• Learning Tools 24, 25 (Tenths and Hundredths Models)

Hands On
Tenths and Hundredths

Objective Use models to learn about tenths and hundredths.

▶ Explore

You already know that the denominator of a fraction tells the number of equal parts into which a whole is divided.

In this lesson you will model fractions that have a denominator of 10 or a denominator of 100.

Question How can you use models to show fractions with a denominator of 10 or 100?

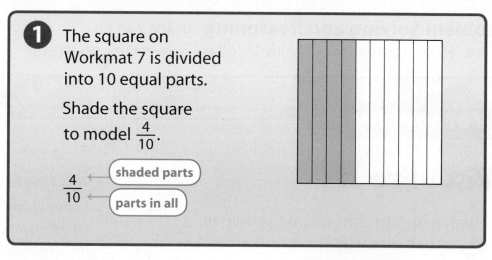

1 The square on Workmat 7 is divided into 10 equal parts.

Shade the square to model $\frac{4}{10}$.

$\frac{4}{10}$ ← shaded parts
  ← parts in all

Think

Start at the top left. Each column has 10 squares. Color 1 column at a time. You can count by 10s to help you.

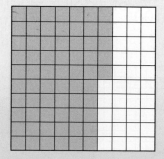

2 The square on Workmat 8 is divided into 100 equal parts.

Shade the square to model $\frac{65}{100}$.

$\frac{65}{100}$ ← shaded parts
  ← parts in all

▶ **Extend**

Use the Learning Tool for Tenths. Model the fraction.

1. $\frac{3}{10}$ 2. $\frac{5}{10}$

3. $\frac{9}{10}$ 4. $\frac{1}{10}$

Use the Learning Tool for Hundredths. Model the fraction.

5. $\frac{12}{100}$ 6. $\frac{47}{100}$

7. $\frac{90}{100}$ 8. $\frac{30}{100}$

9. Use the models you made in Problems 1–8 to find pairs of equivalent fractions.

$$\frac{9}{10} = \frac{\blacksquare}{100} \text{ and } \frac{\blacksquare}{10} = \frac{\blacksquare}{100}$$

Hint
Equivalent fractions name the same amount.

Use the Learning Tool for Hundredths. Model the fraction. Then, use the Learning Tool for Tenths to model an equivalent fraction for each.

10. $\frac{60}{100}$ 11. $\frac{50}{100}$ 12. $\frac{80}{100}$ 13. $\frac{20}{100}$

14. $\frac{30}{100}$ 15. $\frac{70}{100}$ 16. $\frac{10}{100}$ 17. $\frac{90}{100}$

18. **Analyze** Tell how you can make a fraction equivalent to $\frac{7}{10}$ without drawing a model.

19. **Challenge** What is another way to write $\frac{100}{100}$?

Writing Math

Right or Wrong? Esteban says that $\frac{5}{10}$ is equivalent to $\frac{5}{100}$. Explain why he is wrong.

LESSON 2

CA Standards

NS 3.0 Students understand the relationship between whole numbers, simple fractions, and decimals.

NS 3.4 Know and understand that fractions and decimals are two different representations of the same concept (e.g., 50 cents is $\frac{1}{2}$ of a dollar, 75 cents is $\frac{3}{4}$ of a dollar).

Also MR 2.3, MR 2.4

Vocabulary

decimal

decimal point(.)

tenths

Tenths

Objective Write fractions with denominators of 10 as decimals.

▶ Learn by Example

You can use what you know about fractions to learn about decimal numbers.

A **decimal** is a number that has one or more digits to the right of a **decimal point**.

The fence has 10 equal parts. What part of the fence is blue?

Different Ways to Show Parts of a Whole

Way 1 You can use a model.

Way 2 You can write a fraction.

$\frac{3}{10}$ ← blue parts
← parts in all

Way 3 You can write a **decimal**.

Write 0.3
Read three **tenths**

ONES		
ones	tenths	hundredths
0 .	3	

Decimal point

Ask Yourself

- How many equal parts are there?
- How many parts are shaded?

▶ Guided Practice

Write a fraction and a decimal for the shaded part.

1. 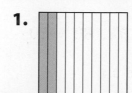 2.  3.

 Math Talk What does the 0 to the left of the decimal point tell you?

368

Write a fraction and a decimal for the shaded part.

4. 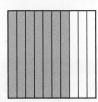   **5.**    **6.**    **7.**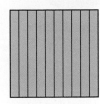

Write as a decimal.

8. $\frac{9}{10}$ **9.** $\frac{1}{10}$ **10.** $\frac{6}{10}$ **11.** $\frac{3}{10}$ **12.** $\frac{8}{10}$ **13.** $\frac{4}{10}$

14. one tenth   **15.** eight tenths   **16.** five tenths   **17.** two tenths

Write as a fraction.

18. 0.3   **19.** 0.5   **20.** 0.9   **21.** 0.6   **22.** 0.1   **23.** 0.2

24. nine tenths   **25.** six tenths   **26.** four tenths   **27.** seven tenths

Use the picture of a fence for Problems 28 and 29.

28. Write a decimal for the part of the fence that is not blue.

29. **Challenge** Suppose it took Simon 5 minutes to paint each board in the fence. How long would it take him to paint 0.6 of the fence?

 Spiral Review and Test Practice

Find the quotient. NS 2.0 page 268

30. 18 ÷ 2   **31.** 45 ÷ 5   **32.** 80 ÷ 10   **33.** 30 ÷ 5

Write the letter of the correct answer. NS 3.4

34. Dana shaded $\frac{3}{10}$ of a figure. Which decimal equals $\frac{3}{10}$?

 A 0.03   **B** 0.3   **C** 0.33   **D** 3.0

LESSON 3

CA Standards

NS 3.0 Students understand the relationship between whole numbers, simple fractions, and decimals.

NS 3.4 Know and understand that fractions and decimals are two different representations of the same concept (e.g., 50 cents is $\frac{1}{2}$ of a dollar, 75 cents is $\frac{3}{4}$ of a dollar).

Also MR 1.1, MR 2.0, MR 2.3, MR 2.4

Vocabulary

hundredths

Hundredths

Objective Write fractions with denominators of 100 as decimals.

▶ **Learn by Example**

A group of 100 students volunteered to help build a playground. They put their photos on a display.

On Monday there were 9 photos displayed. On Friday there were 81 photos.

What part of the display is filled with photos on each of the two days?

You can use decimal models to show each part.

Model It	**Write It**
Monday 0.09	$\frac{9}{100}$

	ONES		
	ones	tenths	hundredths
	0 .	**0**	**9**

Read nine **hundredths**

Friday 0.81	$\frac{81}{100}$

	ONES		
	ones	tenths	hundredths
	0 .	**8**	**1**

Read eighty-one hundredths

Solution: 0.09 of the display is filled on Monday.
0.81 of the display is filled on Friday.

Write a fraction and a decimal for the shaded part.

1.

2.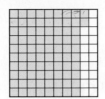

3.

Guided Problem Solving

Use the questions to solve this problem.

4. Mike is making this tile design with 100 tiles. Write a decimal to show the part of the design that is done.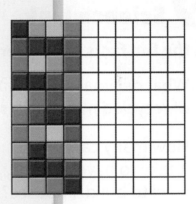

   a. **Understand** What do you know? What do you need to find out?

   b. **Plan** What fraction can you write?

   c. **Solve** Use the fraction to write a decimal.

   ○ of the design is done.

   d. **Look Back** What other fraction and decimal could you use to show the part of the design that is done?

123 Math Talk Do 0.50 and 0.5 represent the same amount? Explain.

► **Practice and Problem Solving**

Write a fraction and a decimal for the shaded part.

5.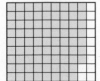

6.

7.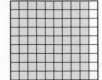

8.

Write as a decimal.

9. $\frac{78}{100}$
10. $\frac{5}{10}$
11. $\frac{4}{100}$
12. $\frac{63}{100}$
13. $\frac{9}{10}$
14. $\frac{12}{100}$

15. seven hundredths

16. six tenths

17. fifty-three hundredths

Solve.

18. Represent Draw models to show 0.9 and 0.09. Is 0.9 greater than 0.09? Explain why or why not.

19. Challenge Out of 100 people, 58 own dogs. The others own cats. What decimal represents the number of people who own cats?

Science Link

Use the fun facts to answer Problems 20–22.

20. What decimal represents the amount of recycled material in steel cans?

21. How many cars would it take to have enough steel to build 4 houses?

22. How many pounds of steel cans would 2 American families use in 1 year?

Fun Facts

Steel

• Steel is a very strong metal made from iron and a small amount of carbon.

• If you recycled steel from 6 cars, you'd have enough steel to build a house!

• The average American family uses 90 pounds of steel cans each year.

• $\frac{25}{100}$ of the material in a steel can is made from recycled materials.

Science PS 1.g

Spiral Review and Test Practice

Find the quotient. NS 2.0 page 288

23. $72 \div 9$
24. $45 \div 9$
25. $81 \div 9$
26. $36 \div 9$

Write the letter of the correct answer. NS 3.4

27. Monica shaded $\frac{23}{100}$ of a figure. Which decimal equals $\frac{23}{100}$?

A 0.023
B 0.23
C 2.30
D 23.0

Extra Practice See page 381, Set B.

Key Standards Review

Need Help?
See Key Standards Handbook.

Add or subtract. KEY NS 3.2

1. $\frac{1}{3} + \frac{2}{3}$ **2.** $\frac{4}{6} - \frac{3}{6}$ **3.** $\frac{3}{4} + \frac{1}{4}$ **4.** $\frac{3}{5} - \frac{2}{5}$

5. $\frac{7}{10} - \frac{2}{10}$ **6.** $\frac{2}{6} + \frac{4}{6}$ **7.** $\frac{6}{8} - \frac{3}{8}$ **8.** $\frac{3}{7} + \frac{2}{7}$

Solve. KEY NS 3.2

9. Lily put a stamp on $\frac{3}{6}$ of the postcards. Carl put a stamp on $\frac{1}{6}$ of the postcards. Len put a stamp on $\frac{1}{6}$ of the postcards. What fraction of the postcards still need stamps?

10. Tom, Ana, and Zeb are sharing a pizza that is cut into 8 equal pieces. Tom eats $\frac{2}{8}$ of the pizza. Ana eats $\frac{3}{8}$ of the pizza. Zeb eats $\frac{1}{8}$ of the pizza. How much of the pizza is left?

Subtract. Estimate to check your answer. KEY NS 2.1

11. $5,280 - 3,021$ **12.** $9,000 - 1,720$ **13.** $6,250 - 1,999$

14. $\begin{array}{r} 5,006 \\ -625 \end{array}$ **15.** $\begin{array}{r} 9,823 \\ -241 \end{array}$ **16.** $\begin{array}{r} 4,935 \\ -3,976 \end{array}$ **17.** $\begin{array}{r} 7,500 \\ -4,275 \end{array}$ **18.** $\begin{array}{r} 8,000 \\ -7,625 \end{array}$

Challenge
Number Sense

Fraction and Decimal Match

Match the expressions that have the same value. NS 3.0, KEY NS 3.2, NS 3.4

1. $\frac{3}{8} + \frac{1}{8}$ **A.** 0.60

2. $\frac{2}{3} + \frac{1}{3}$ **B.** 0.75

3. $\frac{4}{10} + \frac{2}{10}$ **C.** 1

4. $\frac{1}{4} + \frac{2}{4}$ **D.** 0.50

CA Standards

NS 3.4 Know and understand that fractions and decimals are two different representations of the same concept (e.g., 50 cents is $\frac{1}{2}$ of a dollar, 75 cents is $\frac{3}{4}$ of a dollar).

NS 3.0 Students understand the relationship between whole numbers, simple fractions, and decimals.

Also MR 2.0, MR 2.3, MR 2.4

Materials
• Coin set
• Learning Tool 26 (Recording Sheet)

Hands On
Relate Fractions, Decimals, and Money

Objective Relate money to fractions and decimals.

▶ **Learn With Manipulatives**

Question How can you use what you know about money to help you understand fractions and decimals?

Work with a partner. Use play money to see how different coins can be thought of as parts of a dollar.

1 Use pennies to show $1.

2 Write the value of 1 penny.   1¢

Hint
One hundred pennies have a value of 100¢.

3 Write the value of 1 penny as a fraction of a dollar. $\frac{1}{100}$

4 Write the value as a decimal. $0.01

Repeat the steps using a nickel, a dime, a quarter, and a half-dollar. Record your work in your table.

Name of Coin	Number of Cents	Fraction of a Dollar	Value as a Decimal
Penny	1¢	$\frac{1}{100}$	$0.01
Nickel			
Dime			
Quarter			
Half-Dollar			

▶ Guided Practice

Ask Yourself
What is the value of each set of coins?

Match the group of coins with the correct value.

1. $\frac{5}{100}$ of a dollar

2. $\frac{1}{2}$ of a dollar

3. $\frac{3}{10}$ of a dollar

4. $\frac{3}{4}$ of a dollar

A    B

C   D

▶ Practice and Problem Solving

Copy and complete the table. Use coins to help you.

	Coins	Number of Cents	Fraction of a Dollar	Value as a Decimal
5.	10 Pennies			$0.10
6.	8 dimes		$\frac{80}{100}$ or $\frac{8}{10}$	
7.	2 quarters	50¢		
8.	25 pennies			
9.	4 nickels			
10.	2 half-dollars			

Write the amount as a fraction of a dollar.

11. $0.15 = _____ of a dollar

12. $0.25 = _____ of a dollar

13. $0.75 = _____ of a dollar

14. $0.40 = _____ of a dollar

15. $1.00 = _____ of a dollar

16. $0.01 = _____ of a dollar

Solve.

17. Samantha has $\frac{7}{10}$ of a dollar. Alberto has $\frac{75}{100}$ of a dollar. Who has more money? Explain.

18. Right or Wrong? Ramona has 43 pennies. She says she has more than $\frac{4}{10}$ of a dollar. Is she correct? Explain.

19. Analyze Aaron wants to divide a dollar equally among 5 friends. Can he give each friend a quarter? Explain your thinking.

 Real World Data

Use the table to answer the question.

20. Which item costs $\frac{3}{4}$ of a dollar?

21. Which item costs $\frac{1}{2}$ of a dollar?

22. Write the cost of the box of crayons as a fraction of a dollar.

23. Write the cost of the soccer ball as a fraction of a dollar.

24. Challenge Taby has $\frac{3}{4}$ of a dollar. Does she have enough to buy a kite and a box of crayons? Explain.

Yard Sale Items

Baseball Hat	$0.75
Kite	$0.60
Book	$1.00
Jump rope	$0.50
Box of crayons	$0.25
Soccer ball	$0.99

 Spiral Review and Test Practice

Add or subtract. KEY NS 3.2 pages 348, 352, 354

25. $\frac{1}{4} + \frac{3}{4} = \blacksquare$ **26.** $\frac{2}{8} + \frac{5}{8} = \blacksquare$ **27.** $\frac{7}{12} - \frac{3}{12} = \blacksquare$ **28.** $\frac{7}{9} - \frac{5}{9} = \blacksquare$

Write the letter of the correct answer. NS 3.4

29. Which represents $0.50?

A $\frac{5}{100}$ of dollar   **B** $\frac{1}{4}$ of a dollar   **C** $\frac{1}{2}$ of a dollar   **D** $\frac{3}{4}$ of a dollar

Fractional Fish

Object of the Game Find pairs of cards that name the same amount.
Match 2 cards to make a pair. The first player to run out of cards wins.

Materials
Learning Tools 75, 76 (Fraction and Decimal Cards)

Number of Players 2–3

How to Play

1
- Shuffle the game cards and deal out 5 cards to each player.
- Place the remaining cards face down in a stack.

2
- On your turn, ask a player for a card. Remember, your goal is to match one of your own cards!
- If the player has the card, he or she must give it to you and you get to ask again.
- If the player does not have a matching card, you take the top card from the stack.

3 Each time you find a pair, place them face-up in front of you. If another player gets a card that matches, he or she can add to your stack.

4 The first player to run out of cards wins the game.

CA Standards

NS 3.0 Students understand the relationship between whole numbers, simple fractions, and decimals.

NS 3.4 Know and understand that fractions and decimals are two different representations of the same concept (e.g., 50 cents is $\frac{1}{2}$ of a dollar, 75 cents is $\frac{3}{4}$ of a dollar).

 Education Place
Visit www.eduplace.com/camap/ for **Brain Teasers** and **eGames** to play.

CA Standards

MR 3.1 Evaluate the reasonableness of the solution in the context of the original situation.

NS 3.4 Know and understand that fractions and decimals are two different representations of the same concept (e.g., 50 cents is $\frac{1}{2}$ of a dollar, 75 cents is $\frac{3}{4}$ of a dollar).

Also NS 3.0, MR 1.1, MR 2.0, MR 2.3, MR 2.4, MR 3.0, MR 3.2, MR 3.3

Problem Solving Plan
Reasonable Answers

Objective Decide whether an answer to a problem is reasonable.

> ▶ **Learn Through Reasoning**

After you have solved a problem, look back and decide whether the answer is reasonable.

Not Reasonable	
Ed has $\frac{3}{4}$ of a dollar. His mother gives him 25¢ more. How much does he have now? $\frac{3}{4}$ of a dollar ⟶ $\begin{array}{r} 75¢ \\ -\ 25¢ \\ \hline 50¢ \end{array}$ Is this answer reasonable?	This answer is **not reasonable**. Ed cannot have less money than he started with. You should add to find the answer. $\begin{array}{r} 75¢ \\ +\ 25¢ \\ \hline 100¢ = \$1.00 \end{array}$

Reasonable but Not Correct	
Mato has 90¢. He gives his brother 15¢. How much does he have now? $\begin{array}{r} 90¢ \\ -\ 15¢ \\ \hline 85¢ \end{array}$ Is this answer reasonable?	The answer is **reasonable**. It makes sense that Mato has less money than he started with. But, the answer is **not correct**. You need to regroup and then subtract. $\begin{array}{r} \overset{8\ 10}{9\cancel{0}¢} \\ -\ 15¢ \\ \hline 75¢ \end{array}$

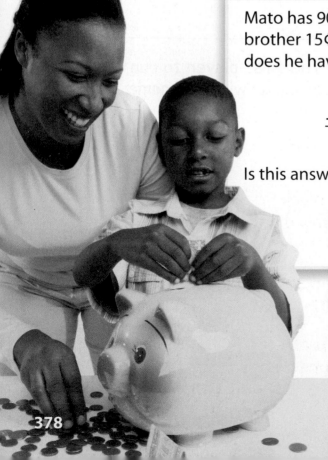

Reasonable and Correct

Carla has $\frac{1}{4}$ of a dollar. She finds 1 quarter. How much does she have now?

$$\frac{1}{4} \text{ of a dollar} \longrightarrow \begin{array}{r} 25¢ \\ + 25¢ \\ \hline 50¢ \end{array}$$

Is this answer reasonable?

The answer is **reasonable**. It makes sense that she has more money than she started with. The answer is **correct**.

▶ Guided Problem Solving

Tell whether the answer is reasonable. Then solve the problem and tell if the answer is correct.

1. Jason has 25¢. He earns $\frac{1}{2}$ of a dollar raking leaves. How much money does he have now? **75¢**

2. Inez has 50¢. Her sister has $\frac{1}{2}$ of a dollar. How much money do they have in all? **25¢**

Ask Yourself
• Is my answer reasonable?
• Is my answer correct?

123 Math Talk Look back at Problem 1. Explain how you decided if the answer was reasonable.

▶ Independent Problem Solving

Tell whether the answer is reasonable. Then solve the problem and tell if the answer is correct.

3. Jolon earns 50¢ an hour washing cars. Last week he washed cars for 4 hours. How much money did he earn last week? **$1.50**

4. **Challenge** Tom has 40¢. His sister gives him 30¢. How much money does he have now? **$0.07**

5. **Create and Solve** Write and solve a word problem about money. Tell why your answer is reasonable.

Reading & Writing Math

Vocabulary

A **decimal** is a number that has one or more digits to the right of a **decimal point**. The numbers to the right show parts of 1 whole.

When there are 10 equal parts, each part is called a **tenth**. When there are 100 equal parts, each part is called a **hundredth**.

Destiny is painting the stones in her mother's garden. There are 100 stones in all. She has painted 25 stones already. What part of the job has she done?

Different Ways to Show Parts of a Whole

1. You can use a model. Show 100 stones, 25 of them painted.

2. You can write a fraction.

$$\frac{\blacksquare}{100} \rightarrow \text{painted parts}$$
$$\phantom{\frac{\blacksquare}{100}} \rightarrow \text{parts in all}$$

3. You can write a decimal.

ones	tenths	hundredths
0 .	___	5

Writing
Destiny paints another 50 stones. What part of the job has she done *now*? (Remember she's already painted 25!) Write it as a fraction and as a decimal.

Reading
Look for this book in your library.

- *The Go-Around Dollar*, by Barbara Johnston Adams

CA Standards
MR 2.3 Use a variety of methods, such as words, numbers, symbols, charts, graphs, tables, diagrams, and models, to explain mathematical reasoning.
Also NS 3.0, NS 3.4

Standards-Based Extra Practice

Set A — NS 3.0, NS 3.4 page 368

Write as a decimal.

1. $\frac{8}{10}$ 2. $\frac{1}{10}$ 3. $\frac{6}{10}$ 4. $\frac{3}{10}$ 5. $\frac{9}{10}$

6. $\frac{4}{10}$ 7. $\frac{10}{10}$ 8. $\frac{7}{10}$ 9. $\frac{5}{10}$ 10. $\frac{2}{10}$

11. two tenths   12. nine tenths   13. five tenths   14. eight tenths

Write as a fraction.

15. 0.8   16. 0.3   17. 0.5   18. 0.1   19. 0.7

20. three tenths   21. one tenth   22. six tenths   23. four tenths

24. Mrs. Kent baked 10 bagels. She gave her neighbor 7 of the bagels and kept the rest for herself. Write a fraction and a decimal for the number of bagels she kept.

Set B — NS 3.0, NS 3.4 page 370

Write as a decimal.

1. $\frac{89}{100}$ 2. $\frac{15}{100}$ 3. $\frac{45}{100}$ 4. $\frac{36}{100}$ 5. $\frac{59}{100}$

6. seventeen hundredths   7. sixty-two hundredths   8. fifty-eight hundredths

Write as a fraction.

9. 0.38   10. 0.27   11. 0.07   12. 0.73   13. 0.59

14. four hundredths   15. seventy-seven hundredths   16. thirty-two hundredths

17. twenty-eight hundredths   18. ninety-six hundredths   19. fifty-one hundredths

20. In a survey, eighty-five out of 100 people said they liked fruit for a snack. What is $\frac{85}{100}$ written as a decimal?

Education Place
Visit www.eduplace.com/camap/
for more **Extra Practice**.

Chapter 17 Extra Practice   **381**

Chapter Review/Test

Vocabulary and Concepts ——————————— NS 3.0, NS 3.4

Choose the best word to complete each sentence.

> **Word Bank**
> tenths
> hundredths
> decimal point

1. In the number 0.6, the 6 is in the _____ place.

2. A _____ separates the whole number and the fraction of a number.

3. In the number 0.18, 8 is in the _____ place.

Skills ————————————————————— NS 3.0, NS 3.4

Write as a decimal.

4. $\frac{1}{10}$ 5. $\frac{6}{10}$ 6. $\frac{67}{100}$ 7. five tenths

Write as a fraction.

8. 0.5 9. 0.9 10. 0.09 11. eighty-eight hundredths

Problem Solving and Reasoning ———— NS 3.0, NS 3.4, MR 1.1, MR 3.1

Solve. Show how to check the answer.

12. Harish had $\frac{78}{100}$ of a dollar. What is the decimal that names the same amount?

13. Out of 100 children in a show, 26 dance. The rest of the children sing. What decimal represents the number of children who dance?

14. Suppose it takes Justin 10 minutes to decorate one tenth of a banner. How long will it take him to decorate seven tenths of the banner?

15. Ava has 1 quarter and 6 pennies. She says she has exactly $\frac{3}{10}$ of a dollar. Is she correct? Explain.

Writing Math Cassi says that 0.4 is equivalent to 0.04 because the value of 4 does not change when you add a zero. Is she right or wrong? How can you use fractions to check?

Spiral Review and Test Practice

1. A bus has 6 tires. If a company has to replace all the tires on 5 buses, how many tires is that?

A 30   **C** 24

B 11   **D** 1

KEY NS 2.2 page 148

2. What is the volume of this figure?

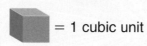 = 1 cubic unit

A 9 cubic units

B 4 cubic units

C 8 cubic units

D 1 cubic unit

> **Test Tip**
> Remember that you cannot see all the cubes.

KEY MG 1.2 page 240

3. There are 27 people lined up for a singing contest. The judges separate them into 9 equal groups. How many people are in each group?

A 243

B 36

C 18

D 3

NS 2.0 page 288

4. Which fraction is equal to $\frac{1}{5}$?

A $\frac{2}{5}$

B $\frac{2}{10}$

C $\frac{5}{1}$

D $\frac{5}{10}$

NS 3.0 page 332

5. $\frac{7}{9} - \frac{4}{9} =$

A $\frac{3}{81}$

B $\frac{3}{18}$

C $\frac{3}{0}$

D $\frac{3}{9}$

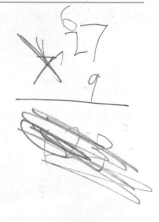

KEY NS 3.2 page 352

6. Mr. Moses painted $\frac{9}{10}$ of the steps to his back door. Which decimal equals $\frac{9}{10}$?

A 0.09

B 0.9

C 0.99

D 9.0

> **Test Tip**
> A denominator of ten means that the decimal place is tenths.

NS 3.4 page 368

Education Place
Visit www.eduplace.com/camap/ for **Test-Taking Tips** and **Extra Practice**.

Chapter 17 Spiral Review and Test Practice   **383**

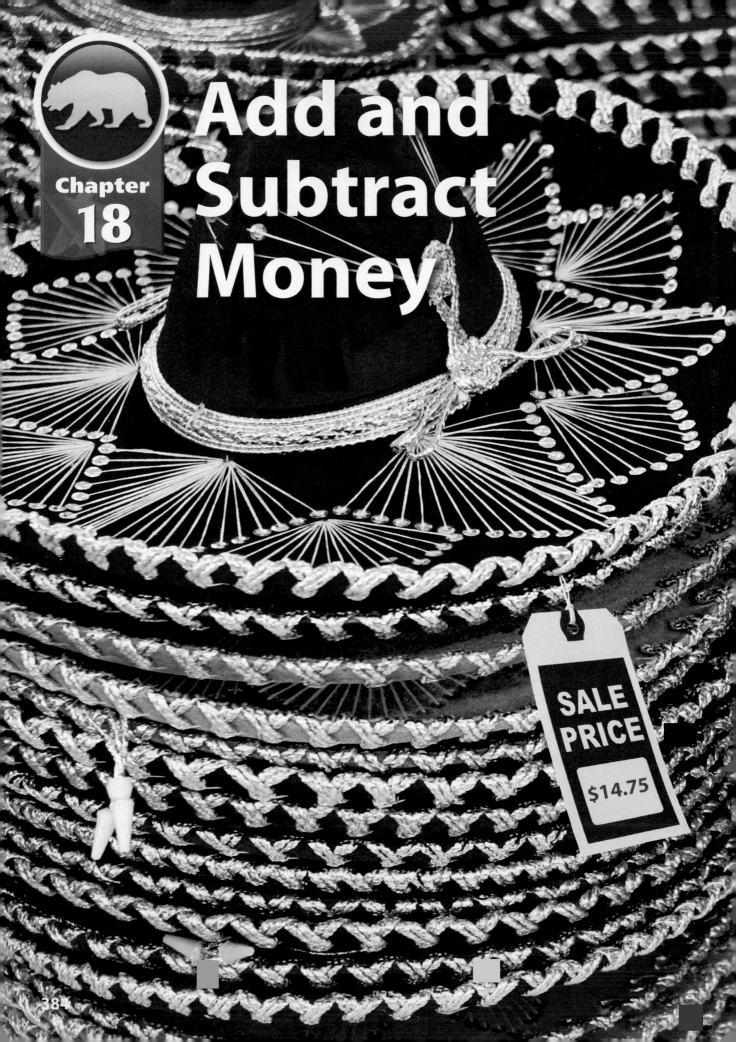

Add and Subtract Money

SALE
PRICE

$14.75

Vocabulary and Concepts NS 3.0, MR 2.3

Choose the best term to complete each sentence. pages 368, 374

1. One of the 10 equal parts of a whole or collection is a _____.

2. A _____ is another way to write fractions with denominators of 10, 100, and so on.

3. One hundredth of a dollar has a value of 1 _____.

Skills KEY NS 2.1

Add or Subtract. pages 56 and 74

4.	392	5.	406	6.	$735	7.	$912
	+ 527		− 215		+ 465		− 341

Write each amount using a decimal. GRADE 2 KEY NS 5.2

8. one dollar and forty-five cents   9. twenty-one cents

Problem Solving and Reasoning GRADE 2 KEY NS 5.1

10. Name three different sets of coins that you could use to buy a balloon that costs 75¢.

Vocabulary

Visualize It!

function rule

A rule that gives one value for each different amount.

function table

A table that matches each input value in a function with one output value.

Rule: Multiply by $3	
Amount (Input)	Cost (Output)
1	$3
2	$6
3	$9
4	$12

Language Tip

Some words are similar in Spanish and English.

English	Spanish
function	función

See **English-Spanish Glossary** pages 628–646.

Education Place Visit www.eduplace.com/camap/ for the **eGlossary** and **eGames**.

CA Standards MR 2.3 Use a variety of methods, such as words, numbers, symbols, charts, graphs, tables, diagrams, and models, to explain mathematical reasoning. **Also AF 2.0**

Chapter 18 385

CA Standards

KEY NS 3.3 Solve problems involving addition, subtraction, multiplication, and division of money amounts in decimal notation and multiply and divide money amounts in decimal notation by using whole-number multipliers and divisors.

MR 2.0 Students use strategies, skills, and concepts in finding solutions.

Also MR 2.2, MR 2.3, MR 2.4

Materials

- play money (dollar bills, dimes, pennies)
- eManipulatives (optional) www.eduplace.com/camap/

Hands On
Add and Subtract Money Amounts

Objective Model addition and subtraction with money.

 **Explore**

Use what you know about addition and subtraction of whole numbers to add and subtract money.

Question How can you use play money to add and subtract money amounts?

Sam bought a pair of scissors and a pen for school. How much did he spend in all?

$2.34

$5.50

$1.75

$1.29

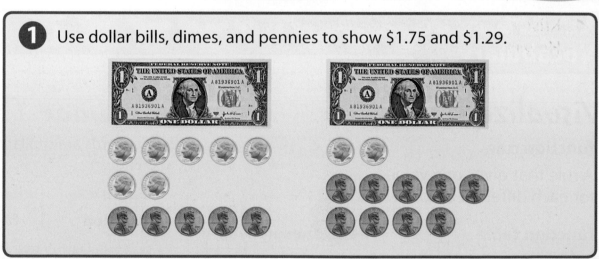

1 Use dollar bills, dimes, and pennies to show $1.75 and $1.29.

2 Add. Begin with the pennies.

Regroup 10 pennies as 1 dime.

3 Add the dimes.

Regroup 10 dimes as 1 dollar.

4 Add the dollars.

Count the money.

Solution: Sam spent $3.04 in all.

386

Phillip has $4.00. If he buys a pencil box, how much money will he have left?

1 Use dollar bills to show $4.00.

2 Subtract the pennies. ●

3 Subtract the dimes.

4 Subtract the dollars.
Count the money.

> **Hint**
> Regroup 1 dollar as 10 dimes, and 1 dime as 10 pennies.

▶ **Extend**

Use play money and the picture on page 386 to solve the problems.

1. Carlos bought a pen and a pencil box. How much did he spend in all?

2. How much more does a pencil box cost than a pair of scissors?

3. What is the total cost of 2 pens? 2 notebooks?

4. Kristen had $6.75. She bought a notebook. How much does she have left?

5. Create and Solve Write a word problem about money that can be solved using addition or subtraction. Solve the problem.

6. Challenge Is the cost of 3 pairs of scissors greater or less than the cost of 1 notebook? Explain.

Writing Math

Explain How is adding pennies, dimes, and dollars like adding ones, tens, and hundreds?

LESSON 2

CA Standards
KEY **NS 3.3** Solve problems involving addition, subtraction, multiplication, and division of money amounts in decimal notation and multiply and divide money amounts in decimal notation by using whole-number multipliers and divisors.

Also MR 2.0, MR 2.3

Materials
• play money (optional)
• eManipulatives (optional)
  www.eduplace.com/camap/

Hands On
Add Money Amounts

Objective Solve problems involving addition with money.

▶ **Learn With Manipulatives**

Adding money is like adding whole numbers.

Rosita bought a small poster for $2.85 and a key chain for $1.49. How much did she spend in all?

	Model It	**Write It**
1	Use dollar bills, dimes, and pennies to show $2.85 and $1.49.	Line up the decimal points. ↓ $2.85 + 1.49
2	Add the pennies. • There are 14 pennies. • Regroup the pennies as 4 pennies 1 dime.	¹ $2.85 + 1.49 4
3	Add the dimes. • There are 13 dimes. • Regroup the dimes as 1 dollar 3 dimes.	¹ ¹ $2.85 + 1.49 34
4	Add the dollars. There are 4 dollars.	Bring down the decimal point and the dollar sign. ¹ ¹ $2.85 + 1.49 $4.34

Solution: Rosita spent $4.34 in all.

▶ Guided Practice

Add.

1. $1.50 + $6.90

2. $18.84 + $21.59

3. $3.19 + $2.73

4. $1.52 + $0.64 + $5.17

 Math Talk Look back at Exercise 2. What did you need to regroup?

Ask Yourself
- Which digits should I add first?
- Do I need to regroup?
- Did I write the dollar sign and the decimal point in the answer?

▶ Practice and Problem Solving

Add.

5. $4.63 + $3.86

6. $64.08 + $27.38

7. $14.92 + $58.59

8. $2.46 + $3.14 + $5.48

9. $45.68 + $42.79

Real World Data

Use the menu to solve Problems 10–11.

10. Alejandro ordered pancakes, eggs, and juice for breakfast. What was the total cost of his meal?

11. **Challenge** Kim has $6.00. She wants pancakes, yogurt, and juice. Does she have enough money?

Rosie's Cafe
BREAKFAST MENU

EGGS $2.85
PANCAKES $3.50
MUFFIN $2.75
YOGURT $1.25
JUICE $1.10
MILK $0.99

✓ Spiral Review and Test Practice

Divide. NS 2.0 page 282

12. $20 \div 4$

13. $27 \div 3$

14. $18 \div 3$

15. $32 \div 4$

16. $21 \div 3$

Write the letter of the correct answer. KEY NS 3.3

17. At the gift shop, Lauren bought 2 postcards for $1.25 each and a bracelet for $6.75. What is the total cost of these 3 items?

   A $8.00   B $8.25   C $9.15   D $9.25

CA Standards

KEY NS 3.3 Solve problems involving addition, subtraction, multiplication, and division of money amounts in decimal notation and multiply and divide money amounts in decimal notation by using whole–number multipliers and divisors.

MR 3.2 Note the method of deriving the solution and demonstrate a conceptual understanding of the derivation by solving similar problems.

Also NS 2.8, MR 1.2, MR 2.0, MR 2.3, MR 2.4, MR 3.1

Subtract Money Amounts

Objective Solve problems involving subtraction with money.

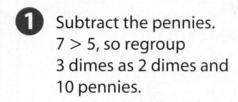

▶ Learn by Example

You can use what you know about subtracting whole numbers to subtract money.

Scott is trying to decide which toy to buy for his dog. How much more does the bone cost than the ball?

To compare two amounts, you can subtract.

$3.47

$6.35

Example 1

1 Subtract the pennies. 7 > 5, so regroup 3 dimes as 2 dimes and 10 pennies.

$$\begin{array}{r} \overset{2\,15}{\$6.3\cancel{5}} \\ -\ 3.47 \\ \hline 8 \end{array}$$

2 Subtract the dimes. 4 > 2, so regroup 6 dollars as 5 dollars and 10 dimes.

$$\begin{array}{r} \overset{12}{\overset{5\ \ 2\,15}{\$6.3\cancel{5}}} \\ -\ 3.47 \\ \hline 88 \end{array}$$

3 Subtract the dollars. Be sure to bring down the dollar sign and the decimal point.

$$\begin{array}{r} \overset{12}{\overset{5\ \ 2\,15}{\$6.3\cancel{5}}} \\ -\ 3.47 \\ \hline \$2.88 \end{array}$$

4 Use addition to check.

$$\begin{array}{r} \$6.35 \\ -\ 3.47 \\ \hline \$2.88 \end{array} \qquad \begin{array}{r} \$2.88 \\ +\ 3.47 \\ \hline \$6.35 \end{array}$$

Solution: The bone costs $2.88 more than the ball.

Example 2

1 $\overset{1\,10}{\$2\cancel{0}.00}$
$-\ 19.21$

There are no dollars, dimes, or pennies to subtract from, so regroup the ten dollars.

2 $\overset{9}{\underset{}{\$2\cancel{0}.00}}$ $\overset{1\,10\ 10}{}$
$-\ 19.21$

Regroup the dollars.

3 $\overset{9\quad 9}{\$2\cancel{0}.\cancel{0}0}$ $\overset{1\,10\ 10\,10}{}$
$-\ 19.21$

Regroup the dimes.

4 $\overset{9\quad 9}{\$2\cancel{0}.\cancel{0}0}$ $\overset{1\,10\ 10\,10}{}$
$-\ 19.21$
$\$0.79$

Subtract.

> ## Guided Practice

Subtract. Check by adding.

1. $8.10
     $-\ 3.60$

2. $4.53
     $-\ 1.86$

3. $20.00
     $-\ 7.14$

Ask Yourself

Which digits should I subtract first?

Guided Problem Solving

Use the questions to solve this problem.

4. Yoko bought a collar that cost $6.19 for her dog. She gave the store clerk $7.00. How much change should Yoko get back?

  a. Understand Think about your answer. Will it be more or less than $7.00?

  b. Plan Should you add or subtract?

  c. Solve Solve the problem. Write the answer.

  d. Look Back How do you know your answer makes sense?

Vocabulary Tip

Change is the money you get back when you give the cashier more than the cost of the items.

 Math Talk How are adding and subtracting money amounts like adding and subtracting whole numbers? How are they different?

Subtract. Check by adding.

5. $6.83
     − 3.52

6. $7.59
     − 2.96

7. $5.26
     − 2.48

8. $9.30
     − 3.97

9. $86.16
     − 21.72

10. $65.39
      − 49.85

11. $86.00
      − 48.43

12. $50.00
      − 18.36

13. $7.92 − $1.68

14. $87.64 − $45.65

15. $70.30 − $34.28

 Real World Data

Use the table to solve Problems 16–19.

16. How much more does **Brand B** cost than **Brand A**?

17. Simon bought a **Brand C** birdcage and a **Brand D** birdcage. What is the total cost of these 2 items?

18. Multistep Joan bought a **Brand A** birdcage. She gave the store clerk a $20 bill and a $5 bill. How much change should she get back?

19. Challenge Marla bought 2 birdcages. The total cost was $60.96. Which brands did she buy?

Cost of Birdcages

Brand	Cost
A	$23.40
B	$31.57
C	$32.75
D	$29.39

 Spiral Review and Test Practice

Write *equivalent* or *not equivalent*. NS 3.1 page 332

20. $\frac{1}{2}$ and $\frac{3}{6}$

21. $\frac{1}{2}$ and $\frac{5}{8}$

22. $\frac{1}{2}$ and $\frac{3}{4}$

23. $\frac{2}{5}$ and $\frac{4}{10}$

Write the letter of the correct answer. KEY NS 3.3

24. Alicia has $5.00 to buy a fish that costs $3.29. How much change will she get?

   A $1.71   **B** $2.71   **C** $2.29   **D** $8.29

Extra Practice See page 401, Set B.

Key Standards Review

Need Help?
See Key Standards Handbook.

Write the letter of all the figures that match the sorting rule. **KEY MG 2.1**

1. **Set A** Polygons
   Set B Not Polygons

2. **Set A** Quadrilaterals
   Set B Not Quadrilaterals

Write the name of the figures that match the clue. **KEY MG 2.3**

3. I have exactly two pairs of parallel sides.

4. I have all right angles.

5. I have all right angles and equal sides.

6. I have four sides.

> square
> rectangle
> parallelogram
> quadrilateral

 **Number Sense**

Lunch Time!

Use the price list and the clues to solve.
KEY NS 3.3

1. Todd paid with $10.00. He got 13 quarters and 3 nickels in change. What did Todd have for lunch?

2. Su paid with $5.00. She got 3 dimes and 4 nickels in change. What did Su have for lunch?

Sandwiches

Tuna Fish...............$3.25
Chicken Salad........$4.00
Ham and Cheese... $5.25

Drinks

Milk........................ $1.75
Lemonade..............$1.25
Orange Juice..........$1.35

CA Standards
KEY **AF 2.1** Solve simple problems involving a functional relationship between two quantities (e.g., find the total cost of multiple items given the cost per unit).

AF 2.0 Students represent simple functional relationships.

Also KEY NS 3.3, AF 2.2, MR 1.1, MR 2.0, MR 2.3, MR 2.4, MR 3.0, MR 3.2

Vocabulary

function

function table

function rule

Function Tables and Money

Objective Represent money relationships in a function table.

▶ **Learn by Example**

A **function** shows how two sets of numbers are related. Every input number has only one output number.

Chloe saves the same amount of money each week. She made a **function table** to show the total amount of money she has at the end of each week. How much money will Chloe have at the end of Week 4?

1 Find the relationship between the input and the output. Write the **function rule**.

Input (Number of Weeks)	Output (Total Amount Saved)
1	$7
2	$14
3	$21

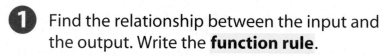

A function rule can use addition, subtraction, multiplication, or division.

$1 \times \$7 = \$7$

$2 \times \$7 = \$14$

$3 \times \$7 = \$21$

Chloe saves $7 each week.

The function rule is:
Multiply $7 by the number of weeks.

2 Use this relationship to solve the problem.

$4 \times \$7 = \$28$

Solution: Chloe will have $28 at the end of Week 4.

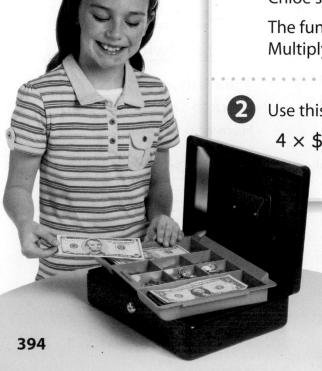

Find the function rule and complete the function table.

Ask Yourself

What operation do I use to get the output value?

Rule: _____

	Input	Output
1.	$4.00	
	$5.19	$7.69
2.	$6.50	
	$6.97	$9.47

Rule: _____

	Input (Number of T-shirts)	Output (Cost of T-shirts)
4.	1	
	2	$16
5.	3	

3. What would the output be if the input was $7.48?

6. How much would 5 T-shirts cost? 6 T-shirts? 8 T-shirts?

 Math Talk You are given a function table that was made using an addition or subtraction rule. How will you know which operation was used?

▶ **Practice and Problem Solving**

Find the function rule and complete the function table.

Rule: _____

	Input (Number of Sandwiches)	Output (Cost of Sandwiches)
	1	$4
7.	2	
	3	$12
8.	4	

9. How much would 5 sandwiches cost? 6 sandwiches? 10 sandwiches?

Rule: _____

Input	Output
10. $5.00	
$6.03	$4.03
11. $7.20	
$8.86	$6.86

12. What would the output be if the input was $9.08?

Science Link

Use the table to solve Problems 13–15.

The price of silver varies from day to day. The table shows the cost of silver on one day.

13. What is the function rule? How did you decide?

14. How much would 5 ounces of silver cost?

15. **Challenge** On another day one ounce of silver costs $11.80. Two ounces cost $23.60. Three ounces cost $35.40. How much would 4 ounces of silver cost?

Silver

- An element is a pure form of matter in which all the atoms are the same.
- Silver is an element.
- Each element has its own kind of atom.
- A pure silver ring is made up of silver atoms.

Input (Number of Ounces)	Output (Total Cost of Silver)
1	$9
2	$18
3	$27
4	$36

Science PS 1.i

Spiral Review and Test Practice

Write the fraction as a decimal. NS 3.4 pages 368, 370

16. $\frac{7}{10}$ **17.** $\frac{9}{10}$ **18.** $\frac{54}{100}$ **19.** $\frac{30}{100}$ **20.** $\frac{6}{100}$

Write the letter of the correct answer. KEY AF 2.1

21. One eraser costs 10¢. Two erasers cost 20¢. Three erasers cost 30¢. How much would 4 erasers cost?

A 30¢   **B** 40¢   **C** 50¢   **D** 60¢

Test Tip
You can write *20 cents* two ways: $0.20, or 20¢.

Extra Practice See page 401, Set C.

Make Change!

Mr. Jones is a cashier at a bookstore. It is his job to add up the price of each customer's purchase, collect money, and make change.

1. Sarah is thinking about getting a pet. She buys one book about hamsters for $8.65, and one book about guinea pigs for $11.56. What is the total cost of her purchase?

2. Mr. Jolly loves to read about the presidents of the United States. He buys a book about Grover Cleveland for $21.95, a book about John Adams for $16.75, and a book about Woodrow Wilson for $13.99. How much money does Mr. Jones need to collect from him?

3. **Multistep** Mrs. Tanaka is buying two books of poetry. A book by Shel Silverstein costs $12.95. Jack Prelutsky's poetry book costs $14.50. Mrs. Tanaka gives Mr. Jones $40.00. How much change will she get?

4. Jordan wants to buy two mystery books. They are $6.15 each. Jordan has $15.00. Does he have enough to buy both books? Explain.

CA Standards
KEY **NS 3.3**, MR 1.2, MR 2.0, MR 2.4

CA Standards

MR 2.4 Express the solution clearly and logically by using the appropriate mathematical notation and terms and clear language; support solutions with evidence in both verbal and symbolic work.

KEY AF 1.1 Represent relationships of quantities in the form of mathematical expressions, equations, or inequalities.

Also NS 2.8, KEY NS 3.3, AF 1.0, AF 1.2, MR 1.1, MR 1.2, MR 2.0, MR 2.3, MR 3.0, MR 3.1, MR 3.2

Problem Solving Strategy
Write a Number Sentence

Objective Write a number sentence to solve a problem.

▶ **Learn by Example**

Liz buys a hat for $3.75. She pays with a five dollar bill. How much change should Liz get?

UNDERSTAND

The problem gives this information.
- The hat costs $3.75.
- Liz gives the cashier $5.00.

PLAN

Write a number sentence to solve the problem.

SOLVE

- Decide which operation to use and write the number sentence.
- Use ◯ for the number you are trying to find.

$$\$5.00 \; - \; \$3.75 \; = \; \bigcirc$$

| amount paid | cost of hat | change |

or

$$\$3.75 \; + \; \bigcirc \; = \; \$5.00$$

| cost of hat | change | amount paid |

$5.00 - $3.75 = $1.25
Liz should get $1.25 in change.

LOOK BACK

Use addition to check your answer.

Think

No matter which number sentence you use, you subtract to solve the problem.

Guided Problem Solving

**Write a number sentence to solve this problem.
Use the Ask Yourself questions to help you.**

1. Tom has $4.00. He buys a bottle of juice for $2.25.
How much money does he have left?

123 **Math Talk** Can you write a different
number sentence to solve Problem 1?

Independent Problem Solving

**Write a number sentence to solve each problem. Explain
why your answer makes sense.**

2. Lily's mother gives her $6.25 to buy
a loaf of bread. The bread costs
$3.75. How much money does she
have left?

3. A burrito costs $5.27. A taco
costs $4.69. How much more
does a burrito cost than a taco?

4. Adam buys a newspaper for $1.39,
a comic book for $1.85, and a
magazine for $4.95. What is the
total cost of the three items?

5. Multistep The total cost for a
toothbrush, toothpaste, and dental
floss is $9.97. The toothpaste costs
$3.29 and the dental floss costs
$2.67. What is the cost of the
toothbrush?

6. Challenge Tarek buys some clothes.
He gives the cashier 2 twenty dollar
bills. He gets back $12.57 in change.
What is the cost of the clothes?

7. Create and Solve Write a word
problem that can be solved with
the equation $6.50 + ▭ = $20.00.

Vocabulary

You can use what you know about adding and subtracting whole numbers to add and subtract money amounts.

1. On the way home from school, Janine bought a bunch of bananas for $2.35. She gave the grocer a five-dollar bill. How much change should she get back?

$$\begin{array}{r} \$5.00 \\ -2.35 \\ \hline \end{array}$$

A **function table** shows how input numbers and output numbers are related. A **function rule** tells what to do to the input to get the output. You can use a function table to help you solve problems.

Janine wants to know how much it will cost her to buy 4 bunches of bananas. Complete the function chart to show how much the bananas will cost.

Input (Number of bunches)	Output (Total Cost)
1	$2.35
2. 2	
3. 3	
4. 4	

5. The **function rule** is: _____.

6. Four bunches of bananas will cost _____.

7. How much would 8 bunches of bananas cost?

Writing Make a function table that shows the total cost of 5 pens if each pen costs $1.25.

Reading Look for this book in your library.

- *Once Upon a Dime: A Math Adventure*, by Nancy Kelly Allen

CA Standards

MR 2.3 Use a variety of methods, such as words, numbers, symbols, charts, graphs, tables, diagrams, and models, to explain mathematical reasoning.

Also KEY **NS 3.3**, AF 2.0, KEY **AF 2.1**

Standards-Based Extra Practice

Set A ———————————————————————————————————— KEY **NS 3.3** page 388

Add.

1. $5.64
+ 3.96

2. $15.42
+ 17.31

3. $6.98
+ 8.64

4. $12.47
+ 10.75

5. $1.26 + $8.94 + $5.48   **6.** $8.34 + $1.36   **7.** $2.84 + $1.72

Set B ———————————————————————————————————— KEY **NS 3.3** page 390

Subtract.

1. $14.23
− 10.25

2. $9.64
− 7.88

3. $28.74
− 23.99

4. $34.31
− 5.56

5. $20.65 − $15.95   **6.** $8.35 − $4.71   **7.** $5.36 − $2.89

Set C ———————————————————————————————————— KEY **AF 2.1** page 394

Find the function rule and complete the function tables.

Rule: _____

	Input	Output
	$3.00	$2.25
1.	$4.50	
2.	$5.25	
3.	$6.30	
	$8.60	$7.85
4.	$9.10	
	$10.00	$9.25

5. What would the output be if the input was $7.26?

Rule: _____

	Input (Number of hats)	Output (Cost of hats)
	1	$6
6.	2	
	3	$18
7.	4	
8.	5	

9. How much would 6 hats cost? 8 hats? 10 hats?

Education Place
Visit www.eduplace.com/camap/ for more **Extra Practice**.

Chapter 18 Extra Practice   **401**

Chapter Review/Test

Vocabulary and Concepts ————————————————— MR 2.3

Choose the best word to complete each sentence.

> **Word Bank**
> function
> function table
> function rule

1. To show how input and output numbers are related, you can use a _____.

2. A _____ shows how two sets of numbers are related.

3. A _____ tells you what to do to the input to get the output.

Skills ——————————————————————————— KEY NS 3.3, KEY AF 2.1

Add or subtract.

4. $15.85 + $26.35   5. $2.39 + $1.65   6. $21.06 − $4.52

Complete the function table. Write the rule.

	Input	Output
7.	$3.65	
	$5.00	$6.50
8.	$7.23	
	$8.15	$9.65
9.	$9.00	

10. Rule: _____

	Input (Number of books)	Output (Cost of books)
	1	$4.25
11.	2	
	3	$12.75
12.	4	
	5	$21.25

13. Rule: _____

Problem Solving and Reasoning ———— KEY NS 3.3, KEY AF 2.1, MR 2.3, MR 2.4

Solve.

14. Esteban had $10.65. He bought a snack for $3.67. How much money did he have left?

15. One bagel costs $1.29. Two bagels cost $2.58. Three bagels cost $3.87. How much will 5 bagels cost?

Writing Math Jan had $8.50 and bought a snack for $4.25. She says she should have $12.75 now. Is she correct?

Spiral Review and Test Practice

1. A quadrilateral MUST have

   A 4 right angles.

> **Test Tip**
> Draw different kinds of quadrilaterals to help you understand this problem.

   B 4 equal angles.

   C 4 angles.

   D 4 sides the same length.

KEY **MG 2.3** page 200

2. What is the area of this figure?

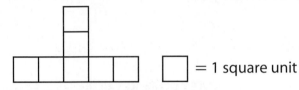 $= 1$ square unit

   A 7 square units

   B 4 square units

   C 5 square units

   D 1 square units

KEY **MG 1.2** page 220

3. Josh displayed 35 dinosaurs on 5 shelves. If each shelf held the same number of dinosaurs, how many were on each shelf?

   A 40   **C** 30

   B 7   **D** 5

KEY **NS 2.3** page 268

4. A garden is divided into thirds. Jill plants roses in $\frac{1}{3}$ of the garden. She plants daisies in $\frac{1}{3}$ of the garden. How much of the garden is left?

   A $\frac{1}{3}$ **C** $\frac{2}{3}$

   B $\frac{3}{3}$ **D** $\frac{3}{1}$

KEY **NS 3.2** page 354

5. Penny shaded $\frac{36}{100}$ of a figure. Which decimal equals $\frac{36}{100}$?

   A 0.036

   B 0.36

   C 3.60

   D 36.0

NS 3.4 page 370

6. William bought a hammer for $9.25 and 2 boxes of nails for $2.75 each. What is the total cost of these 3 items?

   A $3.75

   B $6.50

   C $12.00

   D $14.75

KEY **NS 3.3** page 388

Education Place
Visit www.eduplace.com/camap/ for
Test-Taking Tips and **Extra Practice**.

Unit 6 Review/Test

Vocabulary and Concepts ———————————— MR 2.3 Chapters 15–18

Choose the best word to complete each sentence.

> **Word Bank**
> function rule
> numerator
> function
> denominator
> decimal

1. In a fraction, the number above the fraction bar is the _____.

2. In a fraction, the _____ tells how many equal parts are in the whole or in the group.

3. A relationship between two sets of numbers is also called a _____.

4. The _____ tells you how to get the output when you know the input.

Skills ———————————— KEY **NS 3.2**, KEY **NS 3.3**, NS 3.4 Chapter 15

Look for a pattern in the equivalent fractions. Then complete three more equivalent fractions.

5. $\dfrac{1}{2} = \dfrac{2}{4} = \dfrac{3}{6} = \dfrac{\blacksquare}{8} = \dfrac{\blacksquare}{10} = \dfrac{\blacksquare}{12}$

6. $\dfrac{1}{5} = \dfrac{2}{10} = \dfrac{3}{15} = \dfrac{\blacksquare}{20} = \dfrac{\blacksquare}{25} = \dfrac{\blacksquare}{30}$

Compare. Write > or < for the ⬭.

7. $\dfrac{6}{12}$ ⬭ $\dfrac{5}{12}$
  8. $\dfrac{1}{4}$ ⬭ $\dfrac{1}{10}$
  9. $\dfrac{4}{8}$ ⬭ $\dfrac{9}{8}$
  10. $\dfrac{1}{2}$ ⬭ $\dfrac{1}{3}$

Add or subtract. Simplify if possible. Chapter 16, Lessons 2–4

11. $\dfrac{2}{8} + \dfrac{5}{8}$
  12. $\dfrac{5}{8} - \dfrac{4}{8}$
  13. $\dfrac{2}{12} + \dfrac{4}{12}$
  14. $\dfrac{7}{9} - \dfrac{4}{9}$

Write as a fraction or decimal. Chapter 17, Lessons 2–3

15. $\dfrac{3}{10}$
  16. five tenths
  17. 0.32
  18. eighteen hundredths

Add or subtract. Chapter 18, Lessons 1–3

19. $3.39 + $2.89
  20. $9.65 - $4.78
  21. $2.49 + $1.37

Problem Solving and Reasoning

NS 3.0, NS 3.1, KEY NS 3.2, KEY NS 3.3, NS 3.4, MR 1.0, MR 1.1, MR 2.0, MR 2.3 Chapters 15–18

Solve.

22. Sam counted 2 red, 4 blue, 1 white, and 1 black car on the parking lot. What fraction of the cars on the parking lot are red?

23. Gina has a quilt on her bed. $\frac{1}{12}$ is red, $\frac{7}{12}$ is pink, and the rest is white. What fraction of the quilt is white?

24. Lee bought a $12.11 book. She paid with a 10 dollar bill plus a 5 dollar bill. How much change did she get?

25. What set of coins are worth $\frac{1}{2}$ of a dollar?

BIG IDEA!

Writing Math What does a decimal point show? Explain how $0.25 is related to place value, fractions, and decimals.

Performance Assessment

Party Menu

NS 3.0, KEY NS 3.3, MR 1.0, MR 1.1, MR 2.3, MR 2.4, MR 2.6

Sam and his dad are planning a party. They want to order 6 different foods from Max's Restaurant. They don't want to spend more than $45.

MAX'S RESTAURANT

Chicken		Platters		Vegetarian	
Chicken Wings	$5.75	Nachos	$5.25	Cheese Sticks	$3.50
Chicken Fingers	$6.50	Cold Cuts	$7.25	Potato Salad	$3.25
Fried Chicken	$6.75	Shrimp	$6.50	Bean Salad	$7.95

Task	Information You Need
Use the menu and the information at the right. Which food should they choose? Explain your thinking.	One of the items should be a platter.
	$\frac{1}{2}$ of the items must be vegetarian.
	$\frac{1}{3}$ of the items should contain chicken.

Greg Tang's Go Fast, Go Far

Unit 6 Mental Math Strategies

Divide by 9

It's true 9 groups would be just fine, but better yet are groups of 9!

Look at Problem 1. Instead of dividing 27 into 9 groups, I divide 27 into groups of 9. Because $9 + 9 + 9$ or 3×9 is 27, the answer is 3!

1. $27 \div 9 \rightarrow \boxed{3} \times 9 = 27$
How many 9s?

2. $54 \div 9 \rightarrow \blacksquare \times 9 = 54$
How many 9s?

3. $36 \div 9 \rightarrow \blacksquare \times 9 = 36$
How many 9s?

4. $81 \div 9 \rightarrow \blacksquare \times 9 = 81$
How many 9s?

Great! Keep on moving!

5. $18 \div 9 \rightarrow \blacksquare \times 9 = 18$
How many 9s?

6. $90 \div 9 \rightarrow \blacksquare \times 9 = 90$
How many 9s?

7. $45 \div 9 \rightarrow \blacksquare \times 9 = 45$
How many 9s?

8. $99 \div 9 \rightarrow \blacksquare \times 9 = 99$
How many 9s?

Good For You!

Take It Further!
Now try doing all the steps in your head!

9. $63 \div 9$

10. $36 \div 9$

11. $72 \div 9$

12. $90 \div 9$

Multiply Greater Numbers

- You can use basic facts to estimate.
- You can multiply any multidigit number by a one-digit number by multiplying one digit at a time and regrouping.

Chapter 19
Multiply with Multiples of 10

Chapter 20
Multiply 2-Digit Numbers by 1-Digit Numbers

Chapter 21
Multiply 3- and 4-Digit Numbers

Songs and Games

Math Music Track 7: *The Factor Trees*

eGames at www.eduplace.com/camap/

Math Readers

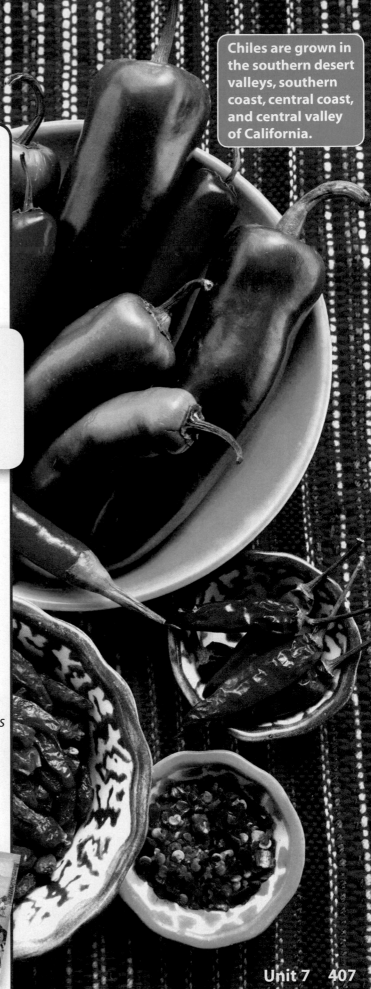

Game

Multiplication Shuffle

Object of the Game Find products and reach a total of 100 to win.

Materials
Learning Tool 39: Number Cards 0–10
Number of Players 2–3

Set Up
Place one set of 0–10 cards face down on the table in a pile.

How to Play

1 Player 1 takes two cards from the pile and finds the product of the numbers. The product is the number of points the player earns.

2 He or she returns the cards to the pile, and the cards are shuffled.

3 Each player repeats steps 1–3 in turn. Continue play by adding each product to the previous total.

4 If a player multiplies incorrectly, he or she must subtract 5 points from his or her score. The first player to reach 100 wins.

CA Standards
KEY **NS 2.2** Memorize to automaticity the multiplication table for numbers between 1 and 10.

Education Place
Visit www.eduplace.com/camap/ for **Brain Teasers** and **eGames** to play.

Reading When you read a story, you can look at the illustrations to help you visualize or picture what is happening. You can use pictures or models to help you visualize math.

Read the problem. Use the drawing to help you visualize multiplication.

Rosa and 4 friends each plant 20 tomato seeds in the class garden. How many seeds do the 5 children plant in all?

This drawing shows 5 groups of 20, or 100 seeds.

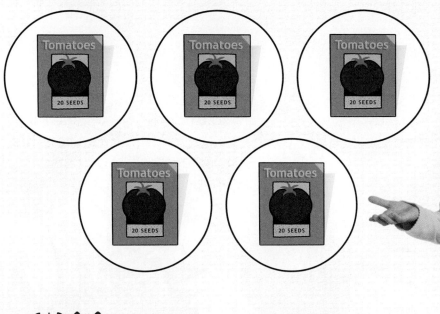

Writing Work with a partner. Use models to solve the problem that follows. Explain how using models helps you understand multiplication.

Tony plants 6 rows of tomato plants with 10 plants in each row. Tina plants 10 rows of tomato plants with 6 plants in each row. Who plants more tomatoes? Explain.

Multiply With Multiples of 10

California is one of eight states that grows sunflowers as a crop.

Vocabulary and Concepts NS 2.0, MR 2.3
Choose the best word to complete each sentence. page 100

1. A number that is multiplied is called a ____.

2. An answer that is close to the exact answer is an ____.

3. Objects arranged in rows and columns are an ____.

Skills NS 1.4
Round each number to the greatest place. page 30

4. 218 **5.** 45 **6.** 959

Problem Solving and Reasoning NS 2.0 page 84
7. Ricardo counted 346 students in the lunchroom. He counted 248 students in the auditorium. About how many more students were in the lunchroom than in the auditorium?

Vocabulary

Visualize It!

You can use basic facts and patterns to find a **product**.

$$3 \times 2 = 6$$
$$3 \times 20 = 60$$
$$3 \times 200 = 600$$
$$3 \times 2,000 = 6,000$$

- 10, 20, 30, and so on are **multiples** of 10.
- 100, 200, 300, and so on are multiples of 100.
- 1,000, 2,000, 3,000, and so on are multiples of 1,000.

Language Tip

Some words are similar in Spanish and English.

English	Spanish
product	producto
multiplication	multiplicación

See **English-Spanish Glossary** pages 628–646.

Education Place Visit www.eduplace.com/camap/ for the **eGlossary** and **eGames**.

CA Standards

KEY NS 2.4 Solve simple problems involving multiplication of multidigit numbers by one-digit numbers ($3{,}671 \times 3 =$ __).

MR 1.1 Analyze problems by identifying relationships, distinguishing relevant from irrelevant information, sequencing and prioritizing information, and observing patterns.

Also NS 2.0, AF 1.4, MG 1.4, MR 1.2, MR 2.3, MR 2.4, MR 3.3

Materials
- Workmat 1
- Base-ten blocks
- Learning Tools 27, 28, 29 (Hundreds Flats, Thousands Cubes, Recording Sheet)

Hands On
Multiplication Patterns with 10, 100, and 1,000

Objective Use basic facts to learn patterns in multiplication.

Personal robot assembly in California facility

▶ **Explore**

You can use patterns of zeros to help you multiply with 10, 100, and 1,000.

Question How can you use base-ten blocks to multiply with 10, 100, and 1,000?

Ted E. Electronics invented a robot to do chores. It takes the company 3 hours to build 1 robot. How many hours would it take to build 10 robots? 100 robots? 1,000 robots?

---

1 Use blocks to show 3×1.

Write the equation.

$3 \times 1 = 3$

---

2 Use blocks to show 3×10.

Write the equation.

$3 \times 1 = 3$

$3 \times 10 = 30$

---

3 Use blocks to show 3×100.

Write the equation.

---

4 Use blocks to show $3 \times 1{,}000$.

Write the equation.

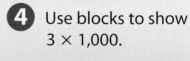

Solution: It will take 30 hours to build 10 robots, 300 hours to build 100 robots, and 3,000 hours to build 1,000 robots.

▶ **Extend**

Copy and complete the table. Fill in the missing number sentences in the table.

	Multiply by 1	Multiply by 10	Multiply by 100	Multiply by 1,000
	1 × 1 = 1	1 × 10 = 10	1 × 100 = 100	1 × 1,000 = 1,000
1.	2 × 1 = 2		2 × 100 = 200	
2.		3 × 10 = 30		3 × 1,000 = 3,000
3.		4 × 10 = 40	4 × 100 = 400	
4.				5 × 1,000 = 5,000
5.	6 × 1 = 6			
6.			7 × 100 = 700	
7.	8 × 1 = 8		8 × 100 = 800	
8.	9 × 1 = 9	9 × 10 = 90		

9. What patterns do you notice in the table?

Copy and complete the table.

10.

Meters	1	2		7		9	12
Centimeters			500		800		

11.

Kilometers	1	2		6		8	
Meters			4,000		7,000		9,000

Solve.

12. What is the product of 36 × 1? 36 × 10? 36 × 100?

13. What is the product of 46 × 1? 46 × 10? 46 × 100?

Writing Math

Generalize What rule can you write for multiplying by 10? by 100? by 1,000?

CA Standards

KEY NS 2.4 Solve simple problems involving multiplication of multidigit numbers by one-digit numbers (3,671 × 3 = __).

MR 1.1 Analyze problems by identifying relationships, distinguishing relevant from irrelevant information, sequencing and prioritizing information, and observing patterns.

Also NS 2.0, NS 2.8, MR 1.2, MR 2.3, MR 2.4

Vocabulary

10, 20, 30, and so on are **multiples** of 10.

100, 200, 300, and so on are multiples of 100.

Multiply with Multiples of 10, 100, or 1,000

Objective Use basic facts and patterns to multiply.

▶ Learn by Example

If Mrs. Smith makes 200 telephone sales calls a day, how many calls will she make in 4 days?

1 Use the basic fact.

$$4 \times 2 = 8$$

2 Then use a pattern of zeros.

10, 20, 30, 40, and so on, are multiples of 10.

100, 200, 300, 400, and so on, are multiples of 100.

Multiple of 10
$$4 \times 20 = 80$$
$$4 \times 200 = 800$$
Multiple of 100

Solution: Mrs. Smith will make 800 phone calls in 4 days.

Ask Yourself

- What basic fact can help me find the product?
- What pattern of zeros can help me?

▶ Guided Practice

Use a basic fact and patterns to find the product.

1. $3 \times 2 =$ ▮
$3 \times 20 =$ ▮
$3 \times 200 =$ ▮
$3 \times 2,000 =$ ▮

2. $4 \times 3 =$ ▮
$4 \times 30 =$ ▮
$4 \times 300 =$ ▮

3. $5 \times 6 =$ ▮
$5 \times 60 =$ ▮
$5 \times 600 =$ ▮

 Math Talk Use $4 \times 5 = 20$ to find 4×500. What can you predict about the product when there is a zero in the basic fact?

Use a basic fact and patterns to find the product.

4. $3 \times 3 = $
$3 \times 30 = $
$3 \times 300 = $
$3 \times 3,000 = $

5. $4 \times 4 = $
$4 \times 40 = $
$4 \times 400 = $

6. $8 \times 5 = $
$8 \times 50 = $
$8 \times 500 = $

7. 2×50

8. 6×600

9. $4 \times 2,000$

10. $1 \times 8,000$

Real World Data

Use the table for Problems 11–13.

11. Al needs to buy 10 bottles of glue for his new invention. How much will they cost altogether?

12. **Multistep** A new 8-story office building has 40 light bulbs installed on each floor. How much did it cost to install all the light bulbs?

13. Connie's mom bought 3 sheets of plywood and 100 nails to build her a dollhouse. How many dollars did she spend?

Item	Price
Light bulb	$2
Nail	5¢
Glue	60¢
Hammer	$10
Plywood	$10

Spiral Review and Test Practice

Write an equation or inequality to show the relationship. KEY **AF 1.1** page 52

14. Five plus three is equal to eight.

15. Six plus nine is less than seventeen.

16. Four times three is equal to seven plus five.

Write the letter of the correct answer. KEY **NS 2.4**

17. There are 1,000 meters in 1 kilometer. How many meters are in 6 kilometers?

   A 60 meters   **B** 600 meters   **C** 1,000 meters   **D** 6,000 meters

CA Standards
MR 2.5 Indicate the relative advantages of exact and approximate solutions to problems and give answers to a specified degree of accuracy.
Also NS 1.4, NS 2.0, KEY NS 2.4, NS 2.8, MG 2.5, MR 1.2, MR 2.3, MR 2.4, MR 2.5

Vocabulary

estimate

round

Estimate Products

Objective Round numbers to estimate products.

▶ **Learn by Example**

The head of the cafeteria at Wilson Elementary orders 285 cartons of milk each day. About how many cartons does she order in 5 days?

"About" suggests to **estimate**, or find an answer that is close to the exact answer. One way to estimate a product is to **round** and then multiply.

Example

1 Round 285 to the nearest hundred.
285 rounds to 300.

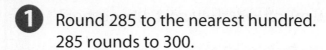

2 Multiply using the rounded number.

$$
\begin{array}{r} 285 \\ \times\ 5 \end{array} \quad \boxed{\text{rounds to}} \quad \begin{array}{r} 300 \\ \times\ 5 \\ \hline 1{,}500 \end{array}
$$

The actual answer is less than 1,500 because $5 \times 285 < 5 \times 300$.

So, 5×285 is *about* 1,500.

Solution: She orders *about* 1,500 cartons of milk in 5 days.

Other Examples

Estimate 7×53.

$$
\begin{array}{r} 53 \\ \times\ 7 \end{array} \quad \boxed{\text{rounds to}} \quad \begin{array}{r} 50 \\ \times\ 7 \\ \hline 350 \end{array}
$$

7×53 is *about* 350.

Estimate 6×35.

$$
\begin{array}{r} 35 \\ \times\ 6 \end{array} \quad \boxed{\text{rounds to}} \quad \begin{array}{r} 40 \\ \times\ 6 \\ \hline 240 \end{array}
$$

6×35 is *about* 240.

Estimate the product. Round the larger factor to its greatest place.

Ask Yourself
- Should I round to the nearest 10 or 100?
- Which basic multiplication fact will help me find the product?

1. 65
  × 2

2. 24
  × 7

3. 432
  × 3

4. 6 × 28

5. 9 × 93

6. 4 × 550

7. 47 × 5

8. 212 × 8

9. 372 × 2

Guided Problem Solving

Use the questions to solve this problem.

10. A supermarket sells 821 gallons of milk each week. About how many gallons of milk does it sell in 4 weeks?

a. **Understand** What information do you know?

b. **Plan** Is the problem asking for an exact amount or an estimate?

c. **Solve** Estimate the product. Write the answer.
821 rounded to the greatest place is ◯.
The supermarket sells about ◯ gallons of milk in 4 weeks.

d. **Look Back** Is your answer greater than or less than the actual amount? How do you know?

 Math Talk Look back at Exercise 1. How can you tell if the estimated product is greater than or less than the exact answer?

Estimate the product. Round the larger factor to its greatest place.

11. 42
   × 5

12. 85
   × 6

13. 385
   × 3

14. 223
   × 6

15. 615
   × 5

16. 5 × 24

17. 3 × 498

18. 127 × 8

19. 358 × 5

20. 13 × 8

 Science Link

Solve.

21. Look at the picture. Name the solid figure the glass looks like.

22. A dairy farm in Atwater produces 465 gallons of milk each day. About how many gallons does the farm produce in one week?

23. **Multistep** Mr. Lin's class drank 21 cartons of milk each day for 4 days. Ms. Colton's class drank 29 cartons of milk each day for 3 days. Estimate to find the class that drank more milk.

The Color of Milk

• When we look at milk, we see white.

• Some objects absorb all light and appear black.

• Milk reflects all colors, so it looks white.

Science PS 2.b

 Spiral Review and Test Practice

Find the sum or difference. KEY **NS 3.3** page 388, 390

24. $36.72
   + 19.58

25. $132.66
   − 83.29

26. $318.03
   + 169.28

27. $200.00
   − 149.99

Write the letter of the correct answer. KEY **NS 2.4**

28. Paul correctly estimated the cost for 5 tickets to the water park. His estimate is $100. Which could be the exact cost of each ticket?

   A $2   **B** $23   **C** $68   **D** $500

Extra Practice See page 423, Set B.

Key Standards Review

Need Help?
See Key Standards Handbook.

Use the price list to solve Problems 1–3. KEY NS 3.3

1. Liana bought a pencil, a notebook, and a marker set. What is the total cost of these 3 items?

pencil:	$0.35
notebook:	$2.29
marker set:	$4.79
drawing paper:	$5.29

2. Clare bought 2 packs of drawing paper and one pencil. What is the total cost of these 3 items?

3. Pete bought 2 notebooks. He paid with a $5 bill. How much change should he get?

Add or subtract. KEY NS 3.2

4. $\frac{2}{4} + \frac{1}{4}$

5. $\frac{2}{8} + \frac{6}{8}$

6. $\frac{4}{5} - \frac{3}{5}$

7. $\frac{7}{8} - \frac{7}{8}$

8. $\frac{3}{5} + \frac{4}{5}$

9. $\frac{11}{10} - \frac{1}{10}$

10. $\frac{2}{3} + \frac{2}{3}$

11. $\frac{2}{4} - \frac{1}{4}$

Challenge — Use Estimation

Estimate and Compare

Estimate and Compare. Write >, <, or = for each ⬭. KEY NS 2.4, AF 1.3

1. 6×40 ⬭ 4×60

2. 3×491 ⬭ 3×500

3. 10×68 ⬭ 100×68

4. 47×3 ⬭ 40×3

5. 7×52 ⬭ $(6 \times 52) + 52$

6. 16×27 ⬭ 20×27

7. 4×33 ⬭ 4×30

8. 8×30 ⬭ 80×3

9. $(8 \times 90) - 90$ ⬭ $(6 \times 90) + 90$

LESSON 4

Field Trip...

Saratoga, CA

CA Standards
MR 1.0, MR 1.1,
MR 1.2, MR 2.0,
MR 2.4, NS 2.0,
KEY NS 2.4, NS 3.0,
KEY NS 3.2

Problem Solving

Objective Use skills and strategies to solve word problems.

The Moon Bridge is set over a koi pond at the Hakone Gardens.

The Hakone Foundation takes care of the beautiful
Japanese gardens called the Gardens of Hakone.

Solve. Tell which strategy or method you used.

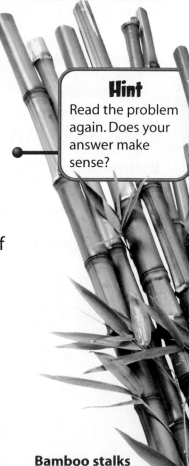

Hint
Read the problem
again. Does your
answer make
sense?

1. **Multistep** A bamboo stalk was cut into 10 pieces.
   Each of these pieces was cut into 3 parts. Each of
   these parts was 2 feet long. How long was the original
   bamboo stalk?

2. **Explain** A class visited the gardens. $\frac{1}{4}$ of the class
   went on Monday. $\frac{1}{4}$ of the class went on Tuesday. $\frac{2}{4}$ of
   the class went on Wednesday. Did $\frac{1}{2}$ of the class visit
   the gardens on Monday and Tuesday?

3. Chandra works 3 days a week at the gardens.
   a. If she drives to and from work each day, how many
      trips does she make in one week?
   b. The driving distance from her home to the gardens
      is 20 miles. How many miles does she drive to and
      from work in one week?

Bamboo stalks

Problem Solving On Tests

Select a Strategy
- Write an Equation
- Choose the Operation
- Estimate
- Draw a Picture

1. On Monday, John read 200 pages of his book. On Tuesday he read 200 pages, and on Wednesday he read 200 pages. How many pages did John read in all?

A 600 pages   **C** 6000 pages

B 60 pages   **D** 60,000 pages

KEY **NS 2.4** page 414

2. Carman drew a picture of an octagon. Which is Carman's picture?

A

C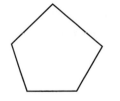

B

D

KEY **MG 2.1** page 192

3. Wally is making two kinds of muffins. One recipe needs $\frac{1}{5}$ cup of pecans. The other needs $\frac{2}{5}$ cup of walnuts. How many cups of nuts is this?

A $\frac{3}{5}$ **B** $\frac{2}{5}$ **C** $\frac{3}{10}$ **D** $\frac{2}{10}$

KEY **NS 3.2** page 348

4. A math poster shows this multiplication sentence and model.

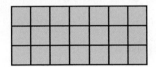

$$9 \times 3 = 27$$

Which division sentence is modeled by the same figure?

A $9 \div 3 = 3$ **C** $27 \div 9 = 3$

B $12 \div 3 = 4$ **D** $36 \div 3 = 12$

KEY **NS 2.3** page 262

5. Soo Ha drew this figure and shaded $\frac{3}{10}$ of it.

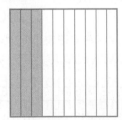

Which decimal equals $\frac{3}{10}$?

A 3.0   **B** 0.3   **C** 0.03   **D** 0.003

NS 3.4 page 368

Education Place
Visit www.eduplace.com/camap/ for **Test-Taking Tips** and **Extra Practice**.

Chapter 19 Lesson 4   **421**

Vocabulary

You can use basic facts and patterns to multiply with 10, 100, and 1,000.

Example 1

$7 \times 10 = 70$ $7 \times 100 = 700$ $7 \times 1{,}000 = 7{,}000$

1. Look at Example 1. Write a rule about multiplying by 10, 100, and 1,000.

Example 2

$6 \times 3 = 18$ $6 \times 30 = 180$ $6 \times 300 = 1{,}800$

2. Look at Example 2. Write a rule about multiplying by **multiples** of 10.

Example 3

$$\begin{array}{r} 28 \\ \times\,5 \\ \hline \end{array}$$ rounds to $$\begin{array}{r} 30 \\ \times\,5 \\ \hline 150 \end{array}$$ $$\begin{array}{r} 719 \\ \times\,7 \\ \hline \end{array}$$ rounds to $$\begin{array}{r} 700 \\ \times\ \ 7 \\ \hline 4{,}900 \end{array}$$

3. Look at Example 3. Explain how you can multiply a **rounded** number to **estimate** an answer.

Writing Write a multiplication sentence that uses a pattern of zeros to find the product.

Reading Check out this book in your library.

- *Great Estimations*, by Bruce Goldstone

CA Standards
MR 2.3 Use a variety of methods, such as words, numbers, symbols, charts, graphs, tables, diagrams, and models, to explain mathematical reasoning.
Also MR 1.1, KEY NS 2.4

Standards-Based Extra Practice

Set A ——————————————————————— KEY **NS 2.4** page 414

Use basic facts and patterns to find the product.

1. $2 \times 3 =$ ▢
$2 \times 30 =$ ▢
$2 \times 300 =$ ▢
$2 \times 3,000 =$ ▢

2. $3 \times 4 =$ ▢
$3 \times 40 =$ ▢
$3 \times 400 =$ ▢

3. $3 \times 5 =$ ▢
$3 \times 50 =$ ▢
$3 \times 500 =$ ▢

4. $7 \times 2 =$ ▢
$7 \times 20 =$ ▢
$7 \times 200 =$ ▢

5. Janet is making a snack tray for the school party. She bought 9 different items to put on the tray. She wants 40 of each item. How many items in all will she have on the tray?

Set B ——————————————————— KEY **NS 2.4**, AF 1.3, MR 2.5 page 416

Estimate the product. Round the larger factor to its greatest place then multiply.

1. 474
$\times\ 8$

2. 45
$\times\ 5$

3. 32
$\times\ 6$

4. 744
$\times\ 2$

5. 281
$\times\ 9$

6. 137
$\times\ 4$

7. 583
$\times\ 7$

8. 54
$\times\ 3$

9. 273
$\times\ 6$

10. 437
$\times\ 2$

11. 184×2 **12.** 114×6 **13.** 811×8 **14.** 347×4 **15.** 96×5

16. 287×5 **17.** 89×3 **18.** 874×1 **19.** 451×2 **20.** 456×7

21. Susan brings the water for the soccer team. There are 16 girls on the team. If each girl needs 3 bottles of water, estimate how many bottles Susan needs for the team.

Education Place
Visit www.eduplace.com/camap/
for more **Extra Practice.**

Chapter Review/Test

Vocabulary and Concepts ———————————— MR 2.3

Choose the best word to complete each sentence.

Word Bank
multiples
estimate
round

1. An answer that is close to the exact answer is called an _____.

2. One good way to estimate an answer to a multiplication problem is to _____ the greater factor and then multiply.

3. 10, 20, 30, and 40 are _____ of 10.

Skills ————————————— KEY NS 2.4, AF 1.3, MR 1.1, MR 2.2, MR 2.5

Use basic facts and patterns to find the product.

4. $3 \times 2 = $ ▢
$3 \times 20 = $ ▢
$3 \times 200 = $ ▢
$3 \times 2000 = $ ▢

5. $4 \times 6 = $ ▢
$4 \times 60 = $ ▢
$4 \times 600 = $ ▢
$4 \times 6000 = $ ▢

6. $7 \times 3 = $ ▢
$7 \times 30 = $ ▢
$7 \times 300 = $ ▢
$7 \times 3000 = $ ▢

7. $5 \times 2 = $ ▢
$5 \times 20 = $ ▢
$5 \times 200 = $ ▢
$5 \times 2000 = $ ▢

Round the larger factor to its greatest place. Estimate the product.

8. 5×62 **9.** 9×78 **10.** 3×546 **11.** 897×4

Compare. Write $>$, $<$, or $=$ for the ⬭.

12. 5×296 ⬭ 5×300 **13.** 6×400 ⬭ 6×427

Problem Solving and Reasoning ———— NS 1.4, KEY NS 2.4, MR 2.2, MR 2.3

Solve.

14. The local farmers' market sells 412 peaches a week. Estimate how many peaches they sell in 4 weeks.

15. Janice takes 932 photos a week. About how many photos will she take in 5 weeks?

Writing Math When you multiply 5×400, why are there 3 zeros in the product?

Spiral Review and Test Practice

1. Which number makes the number sentence true?

$(4 + 3) + 7 = 4 + (\square + 7)$

A 3

C 4

B 7

D 14

AF 1.0 page 54

2. Which is equal to $\frac{3}{4}$ of a dollar?

A $0.25

C $0.50

B $0.75

D $1.00

NS 3.4 page 374

3. Tanisha has $5.00 to buy a puzzle that costs $2.95. How much change should she get back?

A $2.05

C $3.05

B $4.15

D $7.95

KEY NS 3.3 page 390

4. Mrs. O'Brien knows that a case of cat food costs about $20. She wants to buy 3 cases of cat food. About how much will she spend?

A $6

C $60

B $20

D $80

KEY NS 2.4 page 416

5. Which of these is a polygon?

> **Test Tip**
> A polygon is a closed figure with at least 3 straight sides.

A ●————————●

B

C

D

KEY MG 2.1 page 192

6. The figure below is a model for the multiplication sentence $4 \times 7 = 28$.

Which division sentence is modeled by the same figure?

A $7 \div 28 = 4$ **C** $28 \div 2 = 14$

B $28 \div 4 = 7$ **D** $7 \times 4 = 28$

KEY NS 2.3 page 262

Education Place
Visit www.eduplace.com/camap/ for **Test-Taking Tips** and **Extra Practice**.

Chapter 19 Spiral Review and Test Practice   **425**

Chapter 20

Multiply 2-Digit Numbers by 1-Digit Numbers

The koosh ball was invented by a graduate of Stanford University in Palo Alto, CA.

Vocabulary and Concepts NS 2.0, MR 2.3

Choose the best word to complete each sentence. pages 102, 280

1. The answer in a multiplication problem is the ____.

2. 10, 20, 30, and 40 are ____ of 10.

3. In 3 × 8, 3 is a ____.

Skills KEY NS 2.4, KEY AF 1.1

Write a multiplication sentence for each. page 100

4. $9 + 9 + 9 + 9 + 9 = 45$ 5. $20 + 20 + 20 + 20 = 80$ 6. $50 + 50 + 50 = 150$

Find each product. page 414

7. 2×30

8. 3×20

9. 3×100

Problem Solving and Reasoning NS 2.0, KEY NS 2.4 page 414

10. Dave carried 4 boxes of books to the storeroom. There were 20 books in each box. How many books were there altogether?

Vocabulary

Visualize It!

multiply
To combine equal groups.

$$\begin{array}{r} 1 \\ 13 \\ \times\ 6 \\ \hline 78 \end{array}$$

You need to **regroup** 10 ones as 1 ten.

product
The result of multiplication

Language Tip

Some words are similar in Spanish and English.

English	Spanish
regroup	reagrupar
multiply	multiplicar

See **English-Spanish Glossary** pages 628–646.

 Education Place Visit www.eduplace.com/camap/ for the **eGlossary** and **eGames**.

CA Standards MR 2.3 Use a variety of methods, such as words, numbers, symbols, charts, graphs, tables, diagrams, and models, to explain mathematical reasoning. **Also KEY NS 2.4**

Chapter 20   427

CA Standards

KEY NS 2.4 Solve simple problems involving multiplication of multidigit numbers by one-digit numbers (3,671 × 3 = ___).

MR 2.3 Use a variety of methods, such as words, numbers, symbols, charts, graphs, tables, diagrams, and models, to explain mathematical reasoning.

Also NS 2.0, AF 1.0, AF 1.5, MR 2.4

Vocabulary

product

Materials

• Base-ten blocks

• eManipulatives (optional)
  www.eduplace.com/camap/

Hands On
Multiply 2-Digit Numbers

Objective Use base-ten blocks to multiply a 2-digit number by a 1-digit number without regrouping.

▶ Explore

You already know how to multiply 1-digit numbers. In this lesson, you will model multiplying a 2-digit number by a 1-digit number.

Question How can you use base-ten blocks to find the **product** of a 1-digit number and a 2-digit number?

Yo-yos were invented in China over 3,000 years ago. A store displays 23 yo-yos on each shelf. How many yo-yos are on 3 shelves?

1 Show 3 groups of 23.

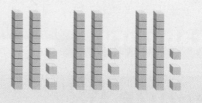

2 Find the total.

• There are 6 tens blocks in all.

• There are 9 ones blocks in all.

3 Record your answer.

$$\begin{array}{r} 23 \leftarrow \text{number in each group} \\ \times\ 3 \leftarrow \text{number of groups} \\ \hline 69 \end{array}$$

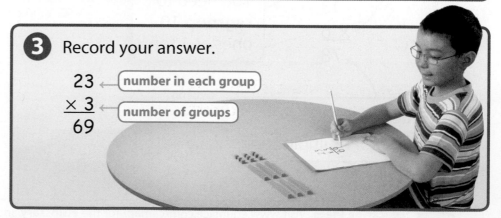

Solution: There are 69 yo-yos on 3 shelves.

Suppose there are 43 yo-yos on each of 2 shelves. How many yo-yos are there in all?

1 Use blocks to show 2 groups of 43. | **2** Find the total.

3 Record your answer.

▶ **Extend**

Tell what multiplication sentence is shown by the blocks.

1.

2.

Use base-ten blocks to help you find the product.

3. 4 × 22   **4.** 2 × 24   **5.** 2 × 13   **6.** 3 × 22

7. 3 × 33   **8.** 4 × 21   **9.** 3 × 31   **10.** 5 × 11

11. How much greater is the product of 4 × 22 than the product of 3 × 22?

12. Challenge How can you use the product of 4 × 12 to find the product of 5 × 12?

Math Journal

Writing Math

Connect Ben used blocks to show 3 × 11 and 11 × 3. He says the product is the same. Explain why he is correct.

3 × 11   11 × 3

CA Standards
KEY **NS 2.4** Solve simple problems involving multiplication of multidigit numbers by one-digit numbers (3,671 × 3 = ___).

Also NS 2.0, KEY NS 2.1, NS 2.6, NS 2.8, MG 1.4, MR 1.2, MR 2.0, MR 2.3, MR 2.4, MR 2.6

Multiply 2-Digit Numbers

Objective Multiply a 1-digit number by a 2-digit number without regrouping.

▶ **Learn by Example**

In Lesson 1, you modeled multiplying a 1-digit number by a 2-digit number. In this lesson, you will practice multiplication without base-ten blocks.

Every day many cars drive over the Golden Gate Bridge. A car has 4 tires. How many tires are there on 21 cars?

$21 \times 4 = \bigcirc$

Golden Gate Bridge, San Francisco, CA

1 Multiply the ones.

4×1 ones $= 4$ ones

$$\begin{array}{r} 21 \\ \times\ 4 \\ \hline 4 \end{array}$$

2 Multiply the tens.

4×2 tens $= 8$ tens

$$\begin{array}{r} 21 \\ \times\ 4 \\ \hline 84 \end{array}$$

Solution: There are 84 tires on 21 cars.

Ask Yourself

What do I multiply first?

▶ **Guided Practice**

Multiply.

1. $\begin{array}{r} 33 \\ \times 2 \\ \hline \end{array}$

2. $\begin{array}{r} 11 \\ \times 7 \\ \hline \end{array}$

3. $\begin{array}{r} 32 \\ \times 2 \\ \hline \end{array}$

4. $\begin{array}{r} 41 \\ \times 2 \\ \hline \end{array}$

5. $\begin{array}{r} 20 \\ \times 3 \\ \hline \end{array}$

6. $\begin{array}{r} 77 \\ \times 1 \\ \hline \end{array}$

7. $\begin{array}{r} 24 \\ \times 2 \\ \hline \end{array}$

8. $\begin{array}{r} 13 \\ \times 2 \\ \hline \end{array}$

Guided Problem Solving

Use the questions to solve this problem.

9. One week a bicycle shop in Solana Beach replaces both tires on 24 bicycles. How many tires does the shop replace in all?

   a. **Understand** How many bicycles are there? How many tires does each bicycle have?

   b. **Plan** Explain why you can use multiplication to solve the problem.

   c. **Solve** Write the equation.

   The bicycle shop repaired ◯ tires.

   d. **Look Back** Read the problem again. Does your answer make sense?

> **Think**
> You can multiply the factors in any order.

123 Math Talk Look back at Problem 9. How could you use addition to solve the problem?

Practice and Problem Solving

Multiply.

10. 12 × 2	**11.** 32 × 3	**12.** 52 × 0
13. 21 × 2	**14.** 22 × 2	**15.** 11 × 8
16. 67 × 1	**17.** 40 × 2	**18.** 13 × 3

19. 1×45 **20.** 31×2 **21.** 3×32 **22.** 72×0

> **Hint**
> Remember the special properties of 0 and 1 in multiplication.
> • $24 \times 0 = 0$
> • $24 \times 1 = 24$

Solve the problems below.

23. Sue is making 4 dozen tortillas. There are 12 tortillas in a dozen. How many tortillas does she make?

24. Kele's bicycle has tires that are 2 feet across. How many inches is this?

25. There are 3 rows of students in the school picture. Each row has 13 students. How many students are in the picture?

26. Challenge Lauren has 36 stickers in her sticker collection. Stickers come in packs of 12. How many packs of stickers did she buy to create her collection?

 Real World Data

Use the graph to solve Problems 27–29.

27. How many customers bought car tires?

28. How many customers bought pick-up truck tires?

29. Multistep How many customers in all bought tires that day?

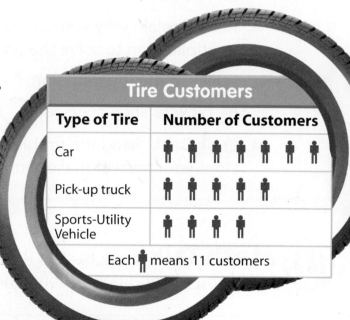

Tire Customers	
Type of Tire	**Number of Customers**
Car	👤👤👤👤👤👤👤
Pick-up truck	👤👤👤👤👤
Sports-Utility Vehicle	👤👤👤👤

Each 👤 means 11 customers

 Spiral Review and Test Practice

Write each amount as a fraction of a dollar. NS 3.4 page 374

30. $0.25 = _____ of a dollar

31. $0.50 = _____ of a dollar

32. $0.75 = _____ of a dollar

33. $1.00 = _____ of a dollar

Write the letter of the correct answer. KEY NS 2.4

34. A class went to the swimming pool in 3 buses. There were 31 students in each bus. How many students went to the swimming pool?

   A 34   **B** 62   **C** 91   **D** 93

Extra Practice See page 443, Set A.

Key Standards Review

Need Help?
See Key Standards Handbook.

Copy and complete the table. Then solve the problem. **KEY AF 2.1**

1.

Number of packs	1	2	3	4	5	6	7
Napkins	5	10					

Pat needs 28 napkins for a party. How many packs does he need to buy to have enough?

2.

Number of packs	1	2	3	4	5	6	7	8
Hot dogs	8	16	24					

Multistep Nehru invited 25 people to a picnic. He wants to have 2 hot dogs per person. How many packages of hot dogs does he need?

Challenge

Geometry

Multiply or Add? **KEY NS 2.4, KEY MG 1.3**

You can find the perimeter of polygons using different operations. If the sides of a polygon are equal, you can multiply.

Find the perimeter of each figure. If you can multiply to find the perimeter, write the multiplication sentence you can use.

1.
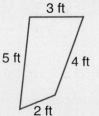
$\frac{4}{8}$ in.
$\frac{3}{8}$ in.
$\frac{5}{8}$ in.

2.
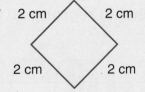
2 cm   2 cm
2 cm   2 cm

3.
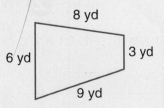
8 yd
6 yd   3 yd
9 yd

4.
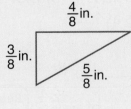
3 ft
5 ft   4 ft
2 ft

5.
6 in.
5 in.
7 in.   10 in.
11 in.

6.
11 ft
11 ft   11 ft
11 ft   11 ft
11 ft   11 ft
11 ft

CA Standards
KEY **NS 2.4** Solve simple problems involving multiplication of multidigit numbers by one-digit numbers (3,671 × 3 = ___).

MR 2.1 Use estimation to verify the reasonableness of calculated results.
Also NS 1.0, NS 1.4

Vocabulary

regroup

product

estimate

Materials
• Base-ten blocks
• eManipulatives (optional)
  www.eduplace.com/camap/

Hands On
Regroup in Multiplication

Objective Model multiplication of a 2-digit number by a 1-digit number with regrouping.

▶ **Explore**

Thomas A. Edison improved the way light bulbs worked so that they could be used in people's homes. Sandy is buying light bulbs for her office. The bulbs come in packs of 3. If she buys 24 packs, how many light bulbs does she buy in all?

Question How can you use base-ten blocks to multiply a 2-digit number by a 1-digit number with regrouping?

$24 \times 3 = \bigcirc$

1 Show 3 groups of 24.

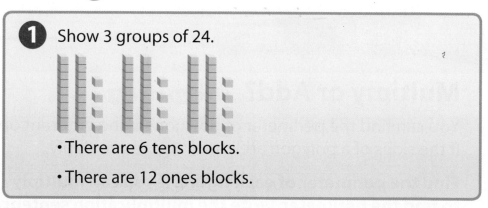

• There are 6 tens blocks.

• There are 12 ones blocks.

2 When the number of ones blocks is 10 or more, you need to **regroup** 10 ones as 1 ten.

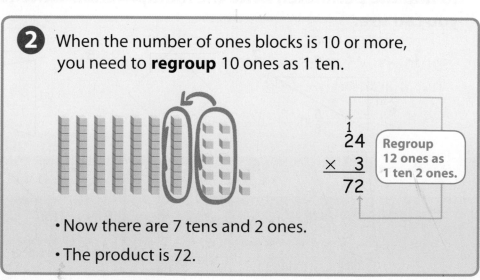

$$\begin{array}{r} \overset{1}{2}4 \\ \times\ \ 3 \\ \hline 72 \end{array}$$

Regroup 12 ones as 1 ten 2 ones.

• Now there are 7 tens and 2 ones.

• The product is 72.

Solution: Sandy buys 72 light bulbs in all.

Use estimation to see if your answer is reasonable.

1 Round the greater factor to the nearest 10.

$$\begin{array}{r} 24 \\ \times\ 3 \\ \hline \end{array}$$ **rounds to** $$\begin{array}{r} 20 \\ \times\ 3 \\ \hline \end{array}$$

2 Multiply

$$\begin{array}{r} 20 \\ \times\ 3 \\ \hline 60 \end{array}$$

3 Compare to your exact answer.

$$\begin{array}{r} 24 \\ \times\ 3 \\ \hline 72 \end{array}$$

- 24 rounds down to 20.
- So, the exact answer should be more than the estimate.
- 72 > 60
  My answer is reasonable.

▶ **Extend**

Use base-ten blocks to help you find the product. Then estimate to check your answer.

Hint
Remember. You can multiply the factors in any order.

1. 4 × 16 **2.** 3 × 26 **3.** 23 × 4 **4.** 2 × 27

5. 46 × 2 **6.** 25 × 3 **7.** 3 × 15 **8.** 2 × 38

9. 15 × 5 **10.** 4 × 24 **11.** 17 × 3 **12.** 2 × 18

13. Challenge Use your blocks to multiply 2 × 57. How is this exercise different from the other exercises above?

14. Nancy used base-ten blocks to show her solution to a multiplication problem. What is the missing number in her problem?

14 × ▨ = 56

Writing Math

Analyze Frank solved a multiplication problem. Then he estimated to check his answer. Explain why his estimate is greater than his solution.

Estimate to check.

$$\begin{array}{r} 38 \\ \times\ 2 \\ \hline 76 \end{array} \qquad \begin{array}{r} 40 \\ \times\ 2 \\ \hline 80 \end{array}$$

CA Standards

KEY NS 2.4 Solve simple problems involving multiplication of multidigit numbers by one-digit numbers (3,671 × 3 = ___).

MR 2.1 Use estimation to verify the reasonableness of calculated results.

Also NS 1.0, NS 1.4, NS 2.0, MR 2.0, MR 2.3, MR 2.4

Vocabulary

regroup

Regroup in Multiplication

Objective Multiply a 2-digit number by a 1-digit number with regrouping.

▶ Learn by Example

Suppose Manuel's father bought 14 copies each of 3 different books. How many books did he buy in all?

$3 \times 14 = \bigcirc$

Model It	Write It
1 Use blocks to show 3 groups of 14. 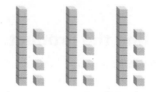	$\begin{array}{r} 14 \\ \times\ \ 3 \\ \hline \end{array}$
2 Multiply the ones. • 3×4 ones = 12 ones • Since there are more than 10 ones, **regroup**. • 12 ones = 1 ten and 2 ones 	$\begin{array}{r} \overset{1}{1}4 \\ \times\ \ 3 \\ \hline 2 \end{array}$ (12 ones) 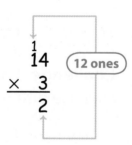
3 Multiply the tens. • 3×1 ten = 3 tens • Add the 1 regrouped ten. • 3 tens + 1 ten = 4 tens	$\begin{array}{r} \overset{1}{1}4 \\ \times\ \ 3 \\ \hline 42 \end{array}$ (4 tens) 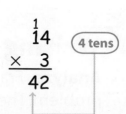

Solution: Manuel's father bought 42 books.

Another Example

Sometimes you have to regroup ones and tens.

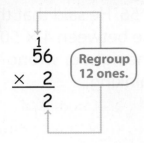

①
$$\overset{1}{56} \times 2 = 2$$
Regroup 12 ones.

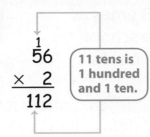

②
$$\overset{1}{56} \times 2 = 112$$
11 tens is 1 hundred and 1 ten.

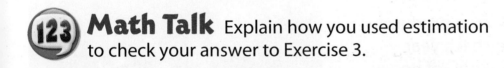

▶ Guided Practice

Find the product. Estimate to check.

1. 49
   × 2

2. 16
   × 4

3. 11
   × 6

4. 18
   × 5

5. 21×4

6. 5×14

7. 34×2

8. 45×2

9. 3×32

10. 27×3

Ask Yourself
- What do you need to multiply first?
- Do you need to regroup ones?
- Do you need to add any regrouped tens?

123 Math Talk Explain how you used estimation to check your answer to Exercise 3.

▶ Practice and Problem Solving

Find the product. Estimate to check.

11. 33
    × 3

12. 24
    × 4

13. 15
    × 5

14. 29
    × 3

15. 12
    × 4

16. 21
    × 4

17. 11
    × 0

18. 19
    × 4

19. 34
    × 2

20. 14
    × 8

21. 14
    × 5

22. 27
    × 3

23. 13
    × 4

24. 23
    × 4

25. 36
    × 2

26. 5×14

27. 3×28

28. 21×3

29. 2×27

30. 31×3

31. 1×43

32. 12×6

33. 5×26

Solve the problems below.

34. Mrs. Jones has 29 picture books in her classroom. There are 3 times as many picture books in the school library. How many picture books are in the school library?

35. **Right or Wrong?** Jerome multiplied 4×56. He said that the answer must be between 4×50 and 4×60. Is he right or wrong? Explain your thinking.

 ## Science Link

Solve the problems.

36. **Money** A beekeeper charges farmers $26 to rent a beehive. How much does he charge to rent 3 beehives?

37. Beehives are placed near cucumber crops for 30 days. Hives are placed near eggplant crops for twice as long. How long do beehives remain near eggplant crops?

38. Mrs. Franklin's honey crop produces 1,230 barrels of honey each year. Estimate how many barrels of honey her crop produces in 5 years.

Honeybees

- Honeybees spread pollen between flowers, helping the plants reproduce.
- They are an important part of agriculture in California.
- Many California crops require bee pollination.

Science LS 3.c

 ## Spiral Review and Test Practice

Estimate the product. NS 1.4, KEY NS 2.4 page 416

39. 7×12

40. 5×432

41. 23×3

42. 291×2

43. 2×39

44. 67×3

Write the letter of the correct answer. KEY NS 2.4

45. A train car has 16 wheels. How many wheels do 6 cars have?

A 10　　　　**B** 22　　　　**C** 66　　　　**D** 96

Extra Practice See page 443, Set B.

Multiplying in a Different Way

When people multiply, they often multiply the ones digit and then the tens digit.

Here's how you can multiply 29 × 4 in another way:

Think of 29 in expanded form. Now you have numbers that are easier to multiply.

$$29 \times 4 = (20 + 9) \times 4$$
$$= (20 \times 4) + (9 \times 4)$$
$$= 80 + 36$$
$$= 116$$

Try multiplying 29 × 4 in the way you have been taught before. Did you get the same answer?

Use the method above to complete the multiplication.

1. $17 \times 9 = (10 + \boxed{}) \times 9$
$= (10 \times 9) + (\boxed{} \times 9)$
$= 90 + \boxed{}$
$= \boxed{}$

2. $98 \times 7 = (\boxed{} + \boxed{}) \times 7$
$= (\boxed{} \times 7) + (\boxed{} \times 7)$
$= \boxed{} + \boxed{}$
$= \boxed{}$

Multiply using the method above.

3. 32 × 8

4. 69 × 5

5. 24 × 9

6. 48 × 8

7. 77 × 6

8. 36 × 9

CA Standards
KEY **NS 1.5**, KEY **NS 2.1**,
KEY **NS 2.4**, NS 2.8

CA Standards

KEY NS 2.4 Solve simple problems involving multiplication of multidigit numbers by one-digit numbers ($3,671 \times 3 =$ ___).

MR 2.2 Apply strategies and results from simpler problems to more complex problems.

Also NS 2.0, KEY NS 2.1, NS 2.8, MR 1.1, MR 1.2, MR 2.0, MR 2.3, MR 2.4, MR 3.0, MR 3.2, MR 3.3

Problem Solving Strategy
Use a Simpler Problem

Objective Use a simpler problem to solve a more complex one.

▶ **Learn by Example**

Michelle and her brother use a computer to do their homework. Michelle printed 48 reports during the school year. Tyrone printed 45 reports. Each report used 7 sheets of paper. How many pieces of paper were used in all?

UNDERSTAND

You need to find how many pieces of paper used in all.

- Michelle printed 48 reports.
- Tyrone printed 45 reports.
- Each report used 7 sheets of paper.

PLAN

You can use smaller numbers to help you decide how to solve the problem.

SOLVE

1 Choose easier numbers. What if Michelle printed 3 reports and Tyrone printed 2 reports.

Add.	Multiply.
3	5
+ 2	× 7
5	35

2 Solve the problem using the original numbers.

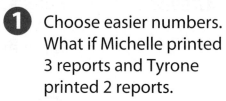

Add.	Multiply.
$\overset{1}{4}8$	$\overset{2}{9}3$
+ 45	× 7
93	651

651 sheets of paper are used in all.

LOOK BACK

Could you solve the problem by first using multiplication and then addition?

Guided Problem Solving

Solve using the Ask Yourself questions.

Ask Yourself
• Can I work with easier numbers?
• Does my answer make sense?

1. The regular price of a package of white paper is $28. A package of colored paper costs $35. If Mike buys 6 packages of white paper instead of the colored paper, how much money will he save?

123 Math Talk How can using small numbers in place of large numbers help you decide how to solve a problem?

Independent Problem Solving

Solve. Explain why your answer makes sense.

2. Every 2 hours, 98 people can ride a Ferris wheel. How many people can ride the Ferris wheel in 8 hours?

3. A Ferris wheel has 6 cars. Each car holds 4 people. Rides start every 10 minutes. How many people can ride in 60 minutes?

4. Another Ferris wheel can hold 72 people. There were 12 empty seats on the first ride and 19 on the second. How many people rode on the two rides?

5. One Ferris wheel measures about 85 yards around. Suppose you rode it 4 times and each ride took you around twice. How many yards did you travel?

6. **Challenge** One Ferris wheel has 24 cars that hold 6 people. Another has 52 cars that hold 4 people. In 5 rides, how many more people can ride on the 52-car Ferris wheel?

7. **Create and Solve** Write and solve a multistep problem with 3-digit numbers. Show how you can use simpler numbers to understand how to solve the problem.

Reading & Writing

Vocabulary

You can use base-ten blocks to model **regrouping** when multiplying a 2-digit number by a 1-digit number.

Georgia is buying gel pens to use as party favors. The pens come in packages of 12. If she buys 6 packages, how many pens does she buy in all?

Find the product. $6 \times 12 =$ ▪
Use models.

1. How many tens blocks are there?
2. How many ones blocks are there?
3. **Because there are more than ten ones, regroup.**
   12 ones = _____

Or multiply with regrouping.

4. Multiply the ones.
   2×6 ones = ◯ ones

5. Multiply the tens.
   6×1 ten = ◯ tens
   Then add the regrouped ten.

6. Record your work.

Georgia buys _____ pens in all.

Writing

Write a word problem of your own for the number sentence 3×16. Model it like the example above. Use regrouping to solve it.

Reading

Check out this book in your library.

• *The Best of Times*, by Greg Tang

CA Standards

MR 2.3 Use a variety of methods, such as words, numbers, symbols, charts, graphs, tables, diagrams, and models, to explain mathematical reasoning.

Also NS 2.0, KEY NS 2.4

Standards-Based Extra Practice

Set A ——————————————————————————————— KEY NS 2.4 page 430

Multiply.

1. 22
     × 4

2. 13
     × 2

3. 34
     × 2

4. 15
     × 1

5. 23
     × 5

6. 11
     × 7

7. 22
     × 4

8. 31
     × 3

9. 41
     × 2

10. 23
      × 3

11. 24 × 2   **12.** 13 × 3   **13.** 32 × 1   **14.** 14 × 2   **15.** 43 × 2

16. 18 × 0   **17.** 46 × 1   **18.** 15 × 5   **19.** 11 × 8   **20.** 12 × 2

21. The third grade class donated toys to a children's hospital. They donated 3 toys for each child. If there were 21 children, how many toys did they donate in all?

Set B ——————————————————————————————— KEY NS 2.4 page 436

Find the product.

1. 14
     × 5

2. 25
     × 3

3. 16
     × 4

4. 18
     × 2

5. 16
     × 6

6. 16
     × 5

7. 12
     × 6

8. 13
     × 5

9. 12
     × 8

10. 18
      × 3

11. 23 × 4   **12.** 12 × 7   **13.** 47 × 2   **14.** 14 × 5   **15.** 25 × 3

16. 17 × 5   **17.** 28 × 3   **18.** 39 × 2   **19.** 14 × 7   **20.** 19 × 2

21. Sam helped his dad plant sweet corn on their farm. They planted 7 rows with 13 plants in each row. How many plants did they plant in all?

Education Place
Visit www.eduplace.com/camap/
for more **Extra Practice.**

Chapter 20 Extra Practice   **443**

Chapter Review/Test

Vocabulary and Concepts ———————————————— MR 2.3

Choose the best word for each sentence.

Word Bank
product
regroup
estimate

1. You need to _____ when there are more than 10 ones.

2. When you round the greatest factor to the nearest ten and multiply, you are finding an _____ of the real answer.

3. The answer to a multiplication problem is called the _____.

Skills ———————————————————————— KEY NS 2.4

Multiply.

4.	5.	6.	7.	8.
12	11	24	31	32
× 5	× 8	× 2	× 3	× 4

9. 51 × 6   **10.** 13 × 2   **11.** 73 × 1   **12.** 92 × 4

13. 34 × 2   **14.** 29 × 2   **15.** 46 × 3   **16.** 38 × 5

Problem Solving and Reasoning ———————— KEY NS 2.4, NS 2.8, MR 1.2, MR 2.3

Solve.

17. **Estimate** The Finns rented a cabin on the lake. If a cabin costs $47 a night, about how much would they pay for a week?

18. Jerry changes tires at the local service station. If he changes 4 tires each on 22 cars, how many tires does he change in all?

19. Tulips cost $3 each and carnations cost $1 each. You have $48. How many carnations can you buy if you buy 15 tulips?

20. Kathryn checks out one whole shelf of books a month from the library. If there are 25 books on a shelf, how many books will she check out in 3 months?

Writing Math Ray estimates that the answer to 3 × 28 will be between 3 × 30 and 3 × 20. Is he right or wrong? Explain.

Spiral Review and Test Practice

1. What number makes this number sentence true?

$8 + 3 = 9 + \square$

> **Test Tip**
> How can you use subtraction to solve this problem?

A 20

C 11

B 3

D 2

AF 1.2 page 52

2. Only 8 people can go into a model ship each hour. What is the greatest number of people that can go into the ship in 8 hours?

A 72

C 64

B 56

D 16

KEY **NS 2.2** page 148

3. What is the volume of this figure?

 = 1 cubic unit

A 20 cubic units

B 15 cubic units

C 11 cubic units

D 3 cubic units

KEY **MG 1.2** page 240

4. Which fraction is equal to $\frac{1}{2}$?

A $\frac{3}{2}$

C $\frac{2}{1}$

B $\frac{2}{4}$

D $\frac{1}{4}$

NS 3.1 page 332

5. The table shows the cost of different numbers of cases of soup.

Number of Cases	Cost
1	$6
2	$12
3	$18

How much do 5 cases of soup cost?

A $24

C $30

B $36

D $42

KEY **AF 2.1** page 394

6. Sarah put 4 photos on every page of her album. There are 32 pages in the album. How many photos are in the album?

A 28

C 36

B 128

D 432

KEY **NS 2.4** page 430

Education Place
Visit www.eduplace.com/camap/ for **Test-Taking Tips** and **Extra Practice**.

Chapter 20 Spiral Review and Test Practice **445**

Multiply 3- and 4-Digit Numbers

Ladybugs are used to control harmful insects.

Word Bank

equal
 groups
product
regrouping
skip count

Vocabulary and Concepts NS 2.0, MR 2.3

Choose the best term to complete each sentence. page 100

1. In the problem $5 \times 34 = 170$, 170 is the _____.

2. Using place value to exchange equal amounts, is called _____.

3. You multiply _____ to get the product. You can also add _____ to get the sum.

Skills NS 2.0, KEY NS 2.4, KEY AF 1.1

Write a multiplication sentence for each. page 100

4. $25 + 25 + 25 + 25 = 100$　　　　**5.** $30 + 30 + 30 + 30 = 120$

6. $101 + 101 + 101 + 101 + 101 = 505$

Find each product. page 100

7. 2×300　　　　　　**8.** 325×2　　　　　　**9.** $6 \times 1,000$

Problem Solving and Reasoning NS 2.0, KEY NS 2.2 page 106

10. Clara put 10 stamps on each page of her stamp book. She used 10 pages. How many stamps did she use?

Vocabulary

Visualize It!

You can add or multiply to find 3 groups of 225.

$$225 + 225 + 225 = 675$$

sum
the result of addition

$$3 \times 225 = 675$$

multiply
to combine equal groups

product
the result of multiplication

Language Tip

Some words are similar in Spanish and English.

English	Spanish
sum	suma
product	producto
multiply	multiplicar

See **English-Spanish Glossary** pages 628–646.

Education Place Visit www.eduplace.com/camap/ for the **eGlossary** and **eGames**.

CA Standards

KEY **NS 2.4** Solve simple problems involving multiplication of multidigit numbers by one-digit numbers (3,671 × 3 = __).

Also NS 1.0, KEY **NS 1.3**, NS 2.0, MR 2.3, MR 2.4

Vocabulary

regroup

product

Materials
• Base-ten blocks
• Workmat 3
• eManipulatives (optional)
  www.eduplace.com/camap/

Hands On
Multiply Greater Numbers

Objective Model multiplication of a 3-digit number by a 1-digit number.

▶ Explore

In this lesson, you will learn how to multiply a 3-digit number by a 1-digit number.

Question How can you use base-ten blocks to model multiplying a 3-digit number by a 1-digit number?

Ernesto is making models of dragonflies. He has 2 bags of pipe cleaners. Each bag has 162 pipe cleaners. How many pipe cleaners does Ernesto have in all?

$$2 \times 162 = \bigcirc$$

1 Show 2 groups of 162.

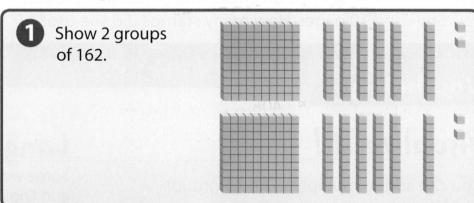

2 When the number of ones blocks or tens blocks is 10 or more, **regroup**.

Now there are 3 hundreds blocks, 2 tens blocks, and 4 ones blocks.

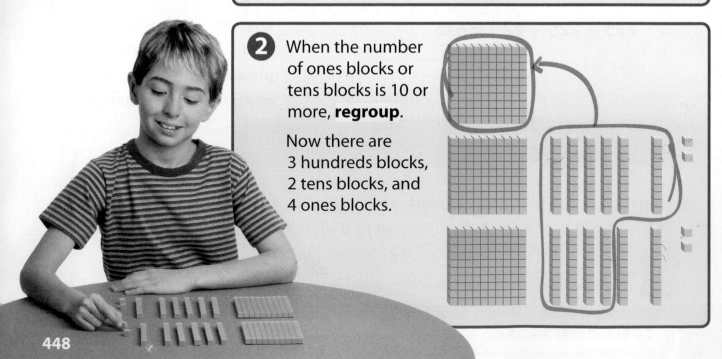

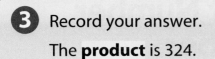

3 Record your answer.

The **product** is 324.

THOUSANDS			ONES		
hundred thousands	ten thousands	thousands	hundreds	tens	ones
			3	2	4

Solution: Ernesto has 324 pipe cleaners in all.

Find 3 × 215.

1 Show 3 groups of 215.

2 If the number of ones blocks or tens blocks is 10 or more, regroup.

3 Record your answer.

What is the product of 3 × 215?

▶ **Extend**

Work in groups. Use base-ten blocks to help you find the product.

1. 3 × 123

2. 4 × 182

3. 334 × 2

4. 5 × 117

5. 408 × 2

6. 7 × 101

> **Hint**
>
> Remember the Commutative Property of Multiplication.

Solve.

7. A dragonfly has 6 legs. How many legs do 112 dragonflies have in all?

8. Create and Solve Write a word problem about dragonflies that requires one regrouping.

9. Challenge A spider has 8 legs. How many legs do 125 spiders have?

Fun Facts

- Several kinds of red dragonflies live in Southern California.
- The Neon Skimmer gets its name from how it glows in the sun.

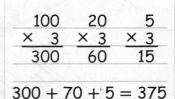

Writing Math

Explain Look at the way Dwight multiplied 125 × 3. Does this method work? Explain.

$$\begin{array}{ccc} 100 & 20 & 5 \\ \times\ 3 & \times\ 3 & \times\ 3 \\ \hline 300 & 60 & 15 \end{array}$$

$$300 + 70 + 5 = 375$$

CA Standards

KEY **NS 2.4** Solve simple problems involving multiplication of multidigit numbers by one-digit numbers (3,671 × 3 = __).

MR 2.1 Use estimation to verify the reasonableness of calculated results.

Also NS 2.0, KEY NS 2.1, NS 2.8, MR 1.2, MR 2.0, MR 2.2, MR 2.5, MR 2.6

Vocabulary

regroup

Multiply a 3-Digit Number by a 1-Digit Number

Objective Multiply a 3-digit number by a 1-digit number.

▶ **Learn by Example**

To multiply a 3-digit number, multiply the ones, then the tens, and then the hundreds.

A museum has 3 displays of insects. Each display has 126 insects. How many insects are displayed?

$3 \times 126 = \bigcirc$

1 Multiply the ones.

$3 \times 6 = 18$ ones

Regroup the 18 ones as 1 ten and 8 ones.

$$\begin{array}{r} \overset{1}{126} \\ \times \quad 3 \\ \hline 8 \end{array}$$

18 ones

2 Multiply the tens.

$3 \times 2 = 6$ tens

Add the 1 regrouped ten.

$6 + 1 = 7$ tens

$$\begin{array}{r} \overset{1}{126} \\ \times \quad 3 \\ \hline 78 \end{array}$$

7 tens

3 Multiply the hundreds.

$3 \times 1 = 3$ hundreds

$$\begin{array}{r} \overset{1}{126} \\ \times \quad 3 \\ \hline 378 \end{array}$$

7 tens

Think

- 126 rounds down to 100.
- The actual answer will be greater than the estimate.
- 378 > 300
- My answer is reasonable.

4 Is your answer reasonable? Estimate to check.

Round the larger factor to the nearest hundred.

126 rounds to 100 $3 \times 100 = 300$.

Solution: The museum has 378 insects on display.

▶ Guided Practice

Find the product. Estimate to check if your answer is reasonable.

Ask Yourself
- Do I need to regroup ones? tens?
- Is my answer reasonable?

1. 234 × 2	**2.** 218 × 4	**3.** 140 × 7	**4.** 121 × 5

Guided Problem Solving

Use the questions to solve this problem.

5. An art museum can give tours to 160 people every half-hour. How many people can tour the museum in 2 hours?

   a. Understand What information do I need to solve the problem?

   b. Plan How do you know the number of tours given in 2 hours?

   c. Solve Multiply the number of tours given in 2 hours by the number of people who can be in each tour.

   d. Look Back Estimate to check if your answer is reasonable.

 Math Talk How is multiplying 3-digit numbers like multiplying with 2-digit numbers? How is it different?

▶ Practice and Problem Solving

Find the product. Estimate to check if your answer is reasonable.

6. 202 × 4	**7.** 394 × 2	**8.** 107 × 6	**9.** 313 × 3	**10.** 116 × 2

11. 2 × 317   **12.** 4 × 132   **13.** 6 × 112   **14.** 7 × 114

Solve.

15. **Analyze** Estimate the product of 260 × 3. Then find the actual product and round it to the greatest place. What do you notice?

16. **Challenge** The centipede ride at the park has 64 seats. Each seat holds 2 people. How many people can ride in 4 rides?

 Science Link

Solve.

17. If a clothes washer uses 350 watts, how many watts will 2 clothes washers use?

18. If a ceiling fan uses 65 watts, how many watts will 3 ceiling fans use?

19. Miguel's stereo uses 120 watts. Sam's stereo uses 3 times as many. How many watts do the two stereos use together?

20. Al's stereo uses 400 watts. His radio uses 10 watts and his fan uses 175 watts. If Al runs the stereo, the radio, and the fan at the same time, how many watts will he use?

Electrical Energy

- Electrical energy is the energy of charged particles.
- The flow of charged particles is an electric current.
- The rate at which electrical energy is used is measured in watts.

Science PS 1.c, PS 1.d

 Spiral Review and Test Practice

Find the sum or difference. KEY **NS 3.2** pages 348, 352, 354

21. $\frac{3}{6} + \frac{2}{6}$ 22. $\frac{8}{9} - \frac{3}{9}$ 23. $\frac{7}{8} - \frac{6}{8}$ 24. $\frac{2}{5} + \frac{2}{5}$ 25. $\frac{2}{9} + \frac{5}{9}$

Write the letter of the correct answer. KEY **NS 2.4**

26. On Thursday, 173 people visited the museum. Three times as many people visited the museum on Friday than on Thursday. How many people visited on Friday?

   A 319   **B** 409   **C** 519   **D** 579

Extra Practice See page 463, Set A.

Key Standards Review

Need Help?
See Key Standards Handbook.

Multipy. Estimate to check. KEY NS 2.4

1. 25 × 7   **2.** 6 × 83   **3.** 39 × 7   **4.** 57 × 8

Write an equation or inequality to show each relationship. KEY AF 1.1

5. The difference between 12 and 4 is less than the sum of 1 and a number.

6. The sum of 8 and a number is greater than 3 times 4.

7. The product of 5 and a number is equal to the sum of 12 and 18.

Write =, −, ×, or ÷ for each ⬭ **to make the number sentence true.** AF 1.3

8. 20 ⬭ 5 = 4   **9.** 20 ⬭ 5 = 15   **10.** 20 ⬭ 5 = 25

11. 20 ⬭ 5 = 100   **12.** 36 ⬭ 6 = 30   **13.** 36 ⬭ 6 = 42

 Problem Solving

Case of the Missing Digits KEY NS 2.4

Detective Dibble is hot on the trail of the missing digits. His only clues are the numbers left behind. Help him find the missing digits.

1.
```
   1 ▨ ▨
 ×     2
 ─────────
   2 8 2
```

2.
```
     ▨
   ▨ 3
 ×     4
 ─────────
   5 ▨ 8
```

3.
```
       ▨
   2 ▨ 4
 ×     ▨
 ─────────
   6 4 2
```

4.
```
   2 ▨ ▨
 ×     5
 ─────────
 1,0 6 0
```

5.
```
 ▨ ▨ ▨
 ×     3
 ─────────
   7 5 6
```

6.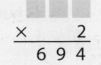
```
 ▨ ▨ ▨
 ×     2
 ─────────
   6 9 4
```

LESSON 3

CA Standards
KEY **NS 2.4** Solve
simple problems involving
multiplication of multidigit
numbers by one-digit numbers
$(3{,}671 \times 3 = \underline{})$.
**Also NS 2.0, MR 2.2,
MR 2.3, MR 2.4**

Regroup More than Once

Objective Multiply 3- and 4-digit numbers, regrouping
more than once.

▶ **Learn by Example**

No matter how large the numbers and how many
times you need to regroup, the rules for multiplication
are the same.

Ladybugs help protect plants from harmful insects.
Mr. Kahn buys ladybugs for his gardens. If there are
185 ladybugs in one order, how many ladybugs will
Mr. Kahn receive in five orders?

$5 \times 185 = \bigcirc$

1 Multiply the ones.

$5 \times 5 = 25$ ones

Regroup 25 ones as 2 tens 5 ones.

$$\begin{array}{r} \overset{2}{18}5 \\ \times\quad 5 \\ \hline 5 \end{array}$$ 25 ones

2 Multiply the tens.

$5 \times 8 = 40$ tens

Add the 2 regrouped tens.

$40 + 2 = 42$ tens

Regroup 42 tens as 4 hundreds 2 tens.

$$\begin{array}{r} \overset{4}{\overset{}{1}}\overset{2}{8}5 \\ \times\quad 5 \\ \hline 25 \end{array}$$ 42 tens

3 Multiply the hundreds.

$5 \times 1 = 5$ hundreds

Add the 4 regrouped hundreds.

$5 + 4 = 9$ hundreds

$$\begin{array}{r} \overset{4}{\overset{}{1}}\overset{2}{8}5 \\ \times\quad 5 \\ \hline 925 \end{array}$$ 9 hundreds

Solution: Mr. Kahn will receive 925 ladybugs.

454

Find the product. Regroup if needed.

1.	138	2.	2,267	3.	485	4.	543
	× 7		× 3		× 2		× 6

 Math Talk Look back at Exercise 4. How many times did you regroup? Explain the regroupings.

Find the product. Regroup if needed.

5.	137	6.	1,269	7.	487	8.	5,000	9.	238
	× 6		× 3		× 2		× 2		× 5

10. 436 × 2   **11.** 2,500 × 4   **12.** 788 × 3

Ask Yourself
• Do I need to regroup ones, tens, or hundreds?
• Do I need to add any regrouped numbers?

Spiral Review and Test Practice

Write the rule. Then complete the function table. KEY **NS 3.3**, KEY **AF 2.1** page 394

13.

Rule:	
Input	**Output**
14. $0.50	
15. $1.00	
16.	$2.50
17. $2.75	$4.00

18.

Rule:	
Input	**Output**
19. 1	
20. 2	$12
21. 3	
22. 4	

Write the letter of the correct answer. KEY **NS 2.4**

23. In May, Janet ordered 1215 pencils. She ordered four times as many pencils in June. How many pencils did she order in June?

A 1219   **B** 4840   **C** 4660   **D** 4860

CA Standards

KEY NS 3.3 Solve problems involving addition, subtraction, multiplication, and division of money amounts in decimal notation and multiply and divide money amounts in decimal notation by using whole-number multipliers and divisors.

KEY NS 2.4 Solve simple problems involving multiplication of multidigit numbers by one-digit numbers ($3,671 \times 3 = $ __).

Also NS 2.0, NS 2.8, AF 2.0, KEY **AF 2.1**, MR 1.2, MR 2.0, MR 2.5

Multiply Money

Objective Multiply money amounts to solve problems.

▶ Learn by Example

You can use what you know about multiplying whole numbers to multiply money.

Gina and her brother are saving money to buy an ant farm. Together they save $2.25 each week for three weeks. How much money have Gina and her brother saved?

$$\$2.25 \times 3 = \bigcirc$$

Example 1

1 Multiply as if you were multiplying whole numbers.

$$\begin{array}{r} \overset{1}{2}25 \\ \times\ \ \ 3 \\ \hline 675 \end{array}$$

2 Write the dollar sign and decimal point in the product.

$$\begin{array}{r} \overset{1}{2}.25 \\ \times\ \ \ 3 \\ \hline \$6.75 \end{array}$$

> Write the decimal point in the product in the same place as the decimal point is in the money amount.

Solution: Gina and her brother have saved $6.75.

Example 2

$$\$10.78 \times 4 = \bigcirc$$

1 Multiply as if you were multiplying whole numbers.

$$\begin{array}{r} \overset{3\,3}{10}78 \\ \times\ \ \ \ 4 \\ \hline 4312 \end{array}$$

2 Write the dollar sign and decimal point in the product.

$$\begin{array}{r} \overset{3\,3}{10}.78 \\ \times\ \ \ \ 4 \\ \hline \$43.12 \end{array}$$

Solution: $10.78 \times 4 = \$43.12$

Find the product. Regroup if necessary.

1. $3.24
   × 2

2. $30.99
   × 3

3. $3.89
   × 4

4. $22.55
   × 4

5. $1.48
   × 7

6. $2.25
   × 4

Ask Yourself
• Do I need to regroup?
• Where will I place the dollar sign and the decimal point in the product?

(123) **Math Talk** Which is a reasonable answer for 2 × $1.50: $300 or $3.00? Explain.

▶ **Practice and Problem Solving**

Find the product. Regroup if necessary.

7. $12.80
   × 7

8. $8.11
   × 3

9. $31.25
   × 3

10. $10.74
    × 4

11. $1.92
    × 3

12. $2.41
    × 4

13. $2.81
    × 4

14. $1.19
    × 6

15. 4 × $8.88

16. 6 × $9.55

17. 2 × $45.89

18. 5 × 11.33

19. 9 × $2.17

20. 8 × $7.29

21. 3 × $1.35

22. 6 × $2.51

Use the rule to complete the table.

Rule: Multiply by 2	
Input	Output
$6.25	$12.50
23. $4.49	
24. $5.35	
25.	$5.00

Rule: Multiply by $2.35	
Input	Output
1	$2.35
2	$4.70
26. 3	
27. 4	

Solve.

28. **Multistep** Ralph takes the bus to and from his aunt's house each day. A one-way bus ticket costs $1.25. How much does Ralph spend on the bus in one week?

29. **Challenge** Stella has $4.45. Dan has $0.50 less than Stella. Al has twice as much money as Dan. How much money does Al have?

 Real World Data

Use the data in the table to solve.

30. **Multistep** The Jefferson family is going to the Insect Zoo. There is 1 adult, 3 students, and 1 senior. What is their total cost for admission?

31. **Explain** Ann has $27. She wants to know if she has enough money to buy 3 adult tickets to the Insect Zoo. Does she need to find the exact amount or can she use an estimate?

32. **Multistep** Sam had $30. He bought 2 student tickets to the Insect Zoo. At the zoo, he bought a key chain for $2. How much money did Sam have left?

Admission to the INSECT ZOO	
Adult	$9.25
Seniors & Students	$6.50
Children under 5	FREE

 Spiral Review and Test Practice

Find the product. KEY NS 2.4 page 430

33. 33 × 2   34. 3 × 23   35. 12 × 4   36. 2 × 42

Write the letter of the correct answer. KEY NS 2.4, KEY NS 3.3

37. Mrs. Santos bought 7 hats. Each hat cost $6.43. What was the total cost of the hats?

   A $42.01   **B** $42.81   **C** $44.01   **D** $45.01

Extra Practice See page 463, Set C.

Estimation High and Low

When you estimate, you can find a high and a low estimate. The actual answer should be between the two estimates.

Carlo spent 3 hours at the Insect Zoo. Each hour, he saw 127 types of bugs on display. *About* how many types of bugs did Carlo see at the Insect Zoo?

The front digit in 127 is in the hundreds place.

Round up to the next hundred to get a high estimate.

$$
\begin{array}{r} 127 \\ \times\ \ 3 \\ \hline \end{array}
\qquad
\begin{array}{r} 200 \\ \times\ \ \ 3 \\ \hline 600 \end{array}
$$

Round down to the closest lesser hundred to get the low estimate.

$$
\begin{array}{r} 127 \\ \times\ \ 3 \\ \hline \end{array}
\qquad
\begin{array}{r} 100 \\ \times\ \ \ 3 \\ \hline 300 \end{array}
$$

Carlo saw between 300 and 600 types of bugs.

Estimate the product. Give a high and a low estimate.

1. $\begin{array}{r} 3{,}562 \\ \times\ \ \ \ 2 \\ \hline \end{array}$
2. $\begin{array}{r} 1{,}713 \\ \times\ \ \ \ 4 \\ \hline \end{array}$
3. $\begin{array}{r} 649 \\ \times\ \ 8 \\ \hline \end{array}$
4. $\begin{array}{r} 842 \\ \times\ \ 3 \\ \hline \end{array}$
5. $\begin{array}{r} 2{,}655 \\ \times\ \ \ \ 2 \\ \hline \end{array}$

Solve.

6. A photographer has 5 boxes of butterfly prints. Each box contains 237 prints. About how many butterfly prints does the photographer have in boxes?

CA Standards
NS 1.4, KEY NS 2.4,
NS 2.8

CA Standards

MR 2.3 Use a variety of methods, such as words, numbers, symbols, charts, graphs, tables, diagrams, and models, to explain mathematical reasoning.

KEY AF 2.1 Solve simple problems involving a functional relationship between two quantities (e.g., find the total cost of multiple items given the cost per unit).

Also NS 2.0, KEY NS 2.4, KEY NS 3.3, AF 2.0, MR 2.0, MR 2.1, MR 2.4, MR 3.0, MR 3.1, MR 3.2, MR 3.3

Problem Solving Strategy
Make a Table

Objective Use a table to solve a problem.

▶ **Learn by Example**

Ms. Jenkins uses larvae to control insects in her garden. One container of 1,000 eggs costs $8.90. Ms. Jenkins needs 4 containers of eggs. How much will the containers cost?

UNDERSTAND

The problem gives this information.

- Ms. Jenkins needs 4 containers of eggs.
- 1 container costs $8.90.

PLAN

You can make a table to solve this problem.

- The first column is the number of containers.
- The second column is the cost for some number of containers.

Number of Containers (Input)	Cost (Output)	
1	$8.90	
2	$17.80	← + $8.90
3	$26.70	← + $8.90
4		← + $8.90

Think: You can multiply the number of containers by $8.90 or add $8.90 for each additional container.

Lacewing eggs

SOLVE

Make the table.

The 4 containers will cost $35.60.

LOOK BACK

Use estimation to check if your answer is reasonable.

▶ Guided Problem Solving

Use the Ask Yourself questions and make a table to help you solve this problem.

1. Ellis has one type of plant in each section of his garden. He uses one container of eggs for every 3 sections of his garden. How many eggs will Ellis need for the 15 sections of his garden?

 Math Talk Look back at Problem 1. How does making a table help you solve the problem?

▶ Independent Problem Solving

Make a table to solve each problem. Explain why your answer makes sense.

2. Ralph read that one larva can eat 60 aphids per hour. How many aphids can it eat in 7 hours?

3. A brick wall has 156 bricks for every foot of wall. If a mason builds a 9-foot wall, how many bricks will he need?

4. Dana saves $14 one week. Each week after that Dana saves $6 more. How much money will Dana have at the end of four weeks?

5. Julie counted the number of people who attended the garden show. If 25 people came to the show every 30 minutes, how many people attended the show in 5 hours?

6. For the first hour of the garden show, every 15th person in line gets a free plant. Ninety people arrive in the first hour. How many free plants are given away?

7. **Challenge** Ms. Gleason's class completed a science unit on insects. The students are lining up their desks to show their projects. Each desk is 24 inches wide. If they line up 3 desks in a row, 4 desks in a row, and 5 desks in a row, how many inches long will each row be?

8. **Create and Solve** Write a problem that can be solved using a table. Make the table and solve the problem.

A lacewing larvae eats an aphid.

Reading & Writing Math

Vocabulary

When you multiply a 3-digit number you multiply the ones, the tens, and then the hundreds.

After the bake sale was over, the students counted the money. Ernesto counted the five-dollar bills. He had 143 five-dollar bills. How much money did Ernesto have?

Find the product. $5 \times 143 = \bigcirc$

1. Multiply the ones. $5 \times 3 = \bigcirc$
   Do you need to **regroup**?

2. Multiply the tens. $5 \times 4 =$
   Do you need to regroup?

3. Multiply the hundreds. $\bigcirc \times 1 =$
   Do you need to regroup?

4. Record your work.
$$
\begin{array}{r}
143 \\
\times 5 \\
\hline
\end{array}
$$

Ernesto has _____ dollars.

Writing Write a word problem that can be solved by multiplying a 3-digit number by a 1-digit number.

Reading Look for this book in your library.

• *A Grain of Rice*, by Helena C. Pittman

CA Standards
MR 2.3 Use a variety of methods, such as words, numbers, symbols, charts, graphs, tables, diagrams, and models, to explain mathematical reasoning.
Also NS 2.0, KEY NS 2.4

Standards-Based Extra Practice

Set A ──────────────────────────────── KEY **NS 2.4** page 450

Find the product. Estimate to check if your answer is reasonable.

1. 212 ✕ 3	**2.** 216 ✕ 3	**3.** 410 ✕ 2	**4.** 192 ✕ 3	**5.** 252 ✕ 3

6. 214 ✕ 4   **7.** 305 ✕ 3   **8.** 109 ✕ 3   **9.** 114 ✕ 4

10. Jamie's art club is making collages out of paper. Each person needs 115 small pieces of paper. There are 5 people in the class. How many pieces of paper are needed?

Set B ──────────────────────────────── KEY **NS 2.4** page 454

Find the product. Regroup if needed.

1. 248 ✕ 7	**2.** 1,126 ✕ 3	**3.** 637 ✕ 2	**4.** 1,562 ✕ 3	**5.** 2,215 ✕ 4

6. 2,500 ✕ 4   **7.** 1,659 ✕ 6   **8.** 2,553 ✕ 3   **9.** 789 ✕ 2

10. John was in a book-reading contest with 3 other contestants. All four of the readers had to read the same book, which was 1,972 pages long. How many pages had to be read in all?

Set C ──────────────────────────────── KEY **NS 3.3** page 456

Find the product. Regroup if necessary.

1. $13.16 ✕ 5	**2.** $4.24 ✕ 5	**3.** $11.91 ✕ 6	**4.** $2.39 ✕ 8	**5.** $31.46 ✕ 3

6. $27.41 ✕ 2   **7.** $11.55 ✕ 6   **8.** $7.42 ✕ 9   **9.** $48.25 ✕ 2

10. Cindy sells roses from her garden for $12.50 a dozen. She sold 3 dozen roses the first day. How much money did she make?

Education Place
Visit www.eduplace.com/camap/
for more **Extra Practice**.

Chapter Review/Test

Vocabulary and Concepts ———————————————— MR 2.3

Choose the best word to complete each sentence.

> **Word Bank**
> regroup
> product

1. When you multiply two numbers together, the answer is called the _____.

2. Sometimes you need to _____ ones as tens in order to multiply.

Skills ————————————————————————— KEY NS 2.4, KEY NS 3.3

Multiply. Estimate to check that your answer is reasonable.

3. 259×3 **4.** 112×4 **5.** 192×5 **6.** 457×2

Find the product. Regroup if needed.

7.	8.	9.	10.	11.
299 × 8	1,143 × 3	3,571 × 2	457 × 5	2,375 × 4

12.	13.	14.	15.	16.
$3.17 × 2	$13.82 × 5	$5.26 × 3	$8.44 × 7	$10.37 × 4

Problem Solving and Reasoning ———— KEY NS 2.4, NS 2.6, KEY NS 3.3, MR 2.3

Solve.

17. Harold owns a flock of sheep and needs to clean their hooves. If he has 236 sheep, and each sheep has 4 legs, how many hooves will he need to clean?

18. Chris is looking at an ant farm. There are 188 ants, and each ant has 6 legs. He estimates that there are 1,200 total legs. Is this a good estimate? Explain.

19. Nikki makes necklaces. She has red, purple, silver, and blue beads. If she has 2,435 of each color, how many beads does she have in all?

20. Edith went to the grocery store to buy 6 cakes for a party. If each cake costs $12.99, how much does she pay for all the cakes?

Writing Math Devon says that when you multiply any number by 1, the product is the number. Is he correct? Explain.

Spiral Review and Test Practice

1. Toni invited 3 friends to a game in the park. Those friends each invited 2 friends from school. Then, each friend from school invited 3 friends. How many friends is that in all?

A 8   **C** 9

B 15   **D** 27

NS 2.0 page 152

2. Which gives the exact length of the ladybug in millimeters?

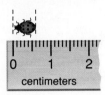

A 1 centimeter

B 9 millimeters

C 6 millimeters

D 4 millimeters

Test Tip
Each small mark on the ruler is a millimeter.

MG 1.1 page 176

3. A truck has 18 wheels. How many wheels do 5 trucks have?

A 90   **C** 50

B 23   **D** 13

KEY NS 2.4 page 436

4. Warren has $\frac{1}{4}$ dollar. How many cents is that?

A 75 cents   **C** 50 cents

B 25 cents   **D** 4 cents

NS 3.4 page 374

5. Which of these is an octagon?

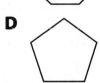

A   **C**

B   **D**

KEY MG 2.1 page 192

6. A bakery sold 182 muffins on Saturday. On Sunday, the bakery sold 2 times as many muffins as on Saturday. How many muffins did the bakery sell on Sunday?

A 264

B 364

C 384

D 546

Test Tip
Remember to keep track of regrouped digits.

KEY NS 2.4 page 450

Education Place
Visit www.eduplace.com/camap/ for **Test-Taking Tips** and **Extra Practice**.

Chapter 21 Spiral Review and Test Practice   **465**

Unit 7 Review/Test

Vocabulary and Concepts

Choose the best word to complete each sentence.

1. When you don't need the exact answer but only need to know about how much, you _____.

2. In multiplication, the answer is called the _____.

> **Word Bank**
> product
> estimate
> factor

Skills

Use basic facts and patterns to find the product.

3. $7 \times 7 =$ ■
   $7 \times 70 =$ ■
   $7 \times 700 =$ ■

4. $5 \times 9 =$ ■
   $5 \times 90 =$ ■
   $5 \times 900 =$ ■

Estimate the product. Round the larger factor to its greatest place then multiply.

5. 68×9

6. 546×3

Compare. Write >, <, or = for the ⬤.

7. 8×396 ⬤ 8×300

8. 7×300 ⬤ 7×307

Multiply.

9. $\begin{array}{r} 37 \\ \times\ 5 \\ \hline \end{array}$

10. $\begin{array}{r} 17 \\ \times\ 8 \\ \hline \end{array}$

11. $\begin{array}{r} 21 \\ \times\ 4 \\ \hline \end{array}$

12. $\begin{array}{r} 43 \\ \times\ 3 \\ \hline \end{array}$

13. $\begin{array}{r} 37 \\ \times\ 2 \\ \hline \end{array}$

Find the product. Estimate to check that your answer is reasonable.

14. 148×3

15. 157×4

16. 159×5

17. 497×2

Find the product. Regroup if necessary. Chapter 21, Lessons 3–4

18. $\begin{array}{r} \$4.95 \\ \times\ \ \ \ 8 \\ \hline \end{array}$

19. $\begin{array}{r} 301 \\ \times\ \ \ 6 \\ \hline \end{array}$

20. $\begin{array}{r} 207 \\ \times\ \ \ 9 \\ \hline \end{array}$

21. $\begin{array}{r} \$3.27 \\ \times\ \ \ \ 7 \\ \hline \end{array}$

Problem Solving and Reasoning

KEY **NS 2.4**, KEY **NS 3.3** Chapters 19–21

Solve.

22. Hillary drives 285 miles each week to and from work. Estimate how many miles Hillary drives in 4 weeks.

23. Mrs. Sanchez and her three daughters went on a trip. The plane fare is $97 per person. How much did they pay for airfare in all?

24. Saul counted 47 sea stars at the aquarium petting pool. Each sea star has 5 arms. How many arms is that in all?

25. Arvin bought 8 CDs. Each CD was $11.95. How much did Arvin pay for the CDs?

BIG IDEA!

Writing Math Jill has $35.00 to buy some books. She estimates that 8 × $4.25 is about $40.00. Explain how Jill might have arrived at her estimate.

Performance Assessment

Skateboards for Sale

KEY **NS 2.4**, KEY **NS 3.3**, MR 1.0, MR 1.1, MR 2.0

John helps his mom in the garden. He earns $3.00 each Monday and each Wednesday by raking. On Sundays, he earns $5.00 for pulling weeds.

$ 39.99

$ 59.99

$ 99.99

a. How much money does he earn in one week?

b. Estimate how many weeks it will take him to earn enough money to buy each of the skateboards.

c. John wants to buy the $59.99 skateboard for himself and the $39.99 skateboard for his sister. How many weeks does he need to work?

Greg Tang's Go Fast, Go Far

Unit 7 Mental Math Strategies

Multiply by 10

It's fast to multiply by 10, just add a zero at the end!

Look at Problem 1. The answer is just the number with a zero placed on the end! 10 groups of 5 equal 5 groups of 10, so I get 5 tens or 50.

1. $10 \times 5 = \boxed{5} \times \boxed{10} = \boxed{50}$ **2.** $10 \times 6 = \blacksquare \times \boxed{10} = \blacksquare$

3. $10 \times 9 = \blacksquare \times \blacksquare = \blacksquare$ **4.** $10 \times 7 = \blacksquare \times \blacksquare = \blacksquare$

Nice work! Keep on going!

5. $10 \times 8 = \blacksquare \times \blacksquare = \blacksquare$ **6.** $10 \times 10 = \blacksquare \times \blacksquare = \blacksquare$

7. $10 \times 2 = \blacksquare \times \blacksquare = \blacksquare$ **8.** $10 \times 4 = \blacksquare \times \blacksquare = \blacksquare$

Take It Further!
Now try doing all the steps in your head!

9. 10×7 **10.** 10×3

11. 10×1 **12.** 10×12

Good For You!

8

Data and Probability

BIG IDEAS!

- Line plots and bar graphs are good ways to show the results of probability experiments.
- You can do probability experiments and use the results to make predictions.

Chapter 22
Data and Graphs

Chapter 23
Probability

Songs and Games

Math Music Track 8: *A Balloon for You*

eGames at
www.eduplace.com/camap/

Math Readers

Take a Guess

Object of the Game Predict the outcome of a probability experiment.

Materials
- Transparent spinner
- Learning Tool 40: Spinner 1

Number of Players 2

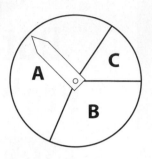

How to Play

1 Player 1 predicts which letter the spinner will land on.

2 Then Player 1 spins the spinner. If the prediction is correct, the player gets 1 point.

3 Player 2 repeats Steps 1 and 2.

4 Players continue to take turns predicting and spinning the spinner. The player with more points after 10 rounds is the winner.

CA Standards
SDAP 1.0 Students conduct simple probability experiments by determining the number of possible outcomes and make simple predictions.

KEY SDAP 1.2 Record the possible outcomes for a simple event (e.g., tossing a coin) and systematically keep track of the outcomes when the event is repeated many times.

Also SDAP 1.4

 Education Place
Visit www.eduplace.com/camap/ for **Brain Teasers** and **eGames** to play.

Reading Math When you read a story, you start at the top of the page, and you read to the bottom. When you read graphs or tables, you often have to look in more than one place and in more than one direction.

Sam surveyed his classmates about their favorite pet. The results are shown in the bar graph below. Use the checklist to preview the bar graph.

Find:
✓ the title
✓ two headings
✓ labels
✓ the number scale
✓ the bars

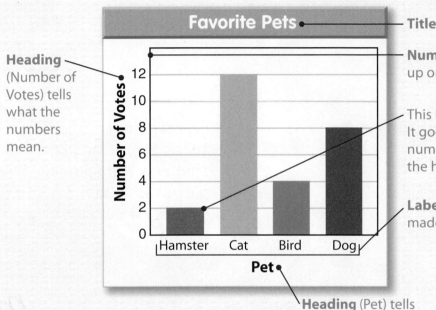

Title

Heading (Number of Votes) tells what the numbers mean.

Number scale goes up on this bar graph.

This bar is labeled "hamster." It goes up to the 2 on the number scale. That means that the hamster got two votes.

Labels tell which pets made the list

Heading (Pet) tells what the category is.

Writing Find a bar graph in Chapter 22. Locate the title, the headings, the labels, and the number scale. Then study the bars. Write about your findings.

Cats are our favorite pets.

Data and Graphs

Snowboarding in California's mountains is fast and exciting.

Vocabulary and Concepts GRADE 2 KEY SDAP 1.0
Choose the best term to complete each sentence.

Word Bank

bar graph

data

pictograph

survey

tally marks

1. You can take a _____ to find out which sport is most popular.

2. You can use _____ to keep track of votes.

3. A _____ uses symbols instead of tally marks.

Skills GRADE 2 SDAP 1.2
Write the number for each set of tally marks.

4. |||

5. ℍℍ |||

6. ℍℍ ℍℍ

Use the tally chart for Problems 7–9.

7. How many children chose baseball?

8. How many more children chose soccer than baseball?

9. Which is the most popular sport?

Favorite Sport	
soccer	ℍℍ ||||
basketball	||||
baseball	ℍℍ ||

Problem Solving and Reasoning GRADE 2 SDAP 1.4

10. How does making tally marks in groups of 5 help you count votes?

Vocabulary

Visualize It!

Two Ways to Show Data

Flowers Picked	
Roses	❁ ❁
Tulips	❁ ❁ ❁
Violets	❁
Each ❁ equals 5 flowers	

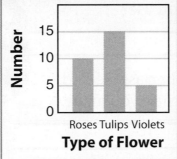

Flowers Picked

Number: 15, 10, 5, 0

Roses Tulips Violets
Type of Flower

pictograph

a graph that uses pictures to show **data**

bar graph

a graph that uses bars to show **data**, or information

Language Tip
Some words are similar in Spanish and English.

English	Spanish
graph	gráfica
bar	barra
data	datos

See **English-Spanish Glossary** pages 628–646.

Education Place Visit www.eduplace.com/camap/ for the **eGlossary** and **eGames**.

CA Standards MR 2.3 Use a variety of methods, such as words, numbers, symbols, charts, graphs, tables, diagrams, and models, to explain mathematical reasoning. **Also KEY** SDAP 1.3

Chapter 22   473

CA Standards

SDAP 1.4 Use the results of probability experiments to predict future events (e.g., use a line plot to predict the temperature forecast for the next day).

MR 2.3 Use a variety of methods, such as words, numbers, symbols, charts, graphs, tables, diagrams, and models, to explain mathematical reasoning.

Also KEY SDAP 1.3, MR 3.3

Vocabulary

data

Hands On
Organize Data

Objective Conduct a survey, summarize results, and predict future outcomes.

▶ **Explore**

One way to collect **data**, or information, is to conduct a survey. When you conduct a survey, you ask people a question and record their answers. You can use a tally chart to record answers.

Favorite Colors		
Color	**Tally**	**Number**
Red	☓☓☓☓☓	5
Blue	|||	3
Green	☓☓☓☓☓ ||	7
Purple	||||	4

The question for this survey was "Which of the colors listed do you like best?"

Question How can you conduct a survey and record results?

Work with a group to conduct a survey in your class.

1 Write a survey question that has three or four possible answers. Make a tally chart.

- What is the title of your tally chart?
- What headings did you use?

2 Conduct a survey in your class. Record the results in the tally chart you made.

3 Count the tally marks for each choice.

- Which choice has the greatest number of tallies?
- Which choice has the least number of tallies?

 **Extend**

Use the tally chart at the right for Problems 1–3.

1. How many students chose football?

2. How many more students chose football than baseball?

3. How many students chose either tennis or hockey?

Favorite Sport to Watch		
Sport	**Tally**	**Number**
Baseball	ЦН	5
Hockey	||	2
Tennis	|||	3
Football	ЦН ||	7

Record the information from the list using tallies in a tally chart. Then use your tally chart for Problems 4–7.

Our Favorite Sports

Sue	Skateboarding
Mary	Bicycling
Carlos	Skateboarding
Bob	Soccer
Kim	Soccer
Roger	Volleyball
Alyssa	Soccer
Cynthia	Bicycling
Rex	Soccer
Maggie	Bicycling

4. How many students were surveyed?

5. Which was the least preferred sport?

6. How many students chose either skateboarding or bicycling?

7. **Challenge** List the sports in order from the most preferred to the least preferred.

 Writing Math

Predict Look at the tally chart for Problems 1–3. If you asked 5 more students to choose a sport, do you think more students would choose hockey or choose football? Explain.

CA Standards
Prepares for
KEY **SDAP 1.3** Summarize and display the results of probability experiments in a clear and organized way (e.g., use a bar graph or a line plot).

SDAP 1.4 Use the results of probability experiments to predict future events (e.g., use a line plot to predict the temperature forecast for the next day).
Also MR 2.3, MR 3.3

Vocabulary

line plot

Line Plots

Objective Read and make line plots and make predictions from the data.

▶ **Learn by Example**

A **line plot** can show how often something happens.

The table at the right shows the number of games won by different teams. You can make a line plot to show the data.

Number of Games Won					
Lasers	2	Sparks	1	Wings	3
Bears	1	Falcons	1	Suns	4
Comets	5	Hawks	4	Foxes	1

① Use the chart title for the line plot title. Draw and label a scale.

- The smallest number in the chart is 1. Begin the scale at 1.

- The largest number in the chart is 5. So the scale goes from 1 to 5.

Number of Games Won

```
X
X
X           X
X   X   X   X   X
─────────────────
1   2   3   4   5
```

② Draw an X for each team that won that many games.

For example, draw 4 Xs above the 1 to show that 4 teams each won 1 game.

Ask Yourself

What do the Xs above the numbers stand for?

▶ **Guided Practice**

Use the line plot in Step 2 to solve Problems 1–2.

1. How many teams won exactly 4 games?

2. How many teams won more than 2 games?

Guided Problem Solving

Use the questions to solve this problem.

3. Use the data in the table to make a line plot.

Number of Goals Scored					
Dwight	1	Lian	1	Hamid	3
Joe	3	Asa	3	Jun	5
Ann	2	Bena	6	Tam	1
Steve	2	Emilio	3	Sue	5

a. **Understand** What is the least number of goals scored? What is the greatest number?

b. **Plan** How does knowing the greatest and least number of goals scored help label the number line?

c. **Solve** Draw and label the number line. Then draw an X above each number for each student that scored that many goals.

d. **Look Back** Does your line plot use all the information in the table?

Math Talk Look at the table on page 476. If the Comets played the Bears again, could you be sure which team would win? Explain.

Practice and Problem Solving

Use the data from the table to make a line plot that shows the same data. Then solve Problems 4–6.

4. What do the Xs on your line plot stand for?

5. How many players got more than 1 hit?

6. **Predict** Based on the data, which player is most likely to get a hit in the next game? Why?

Average Hits per Game	
Player	**Hits**
Sally	5
Max	4
Yoko	1
Amy	3
Edie	3

Real World Data

Use the line plot to solve Problems 7–9.

Bases Stolen Last Season

```
X
X                X
X    X    X    X
X    X    X    X              X
—————————————————————————————————
0    1    2    3    4    5
```

7. How many players stole exactly 3 bases?

8. How many players stole at least 1 base?

9. Predict If Sara asks the team how many bases they will steal this season, do you think the data will be exactly the same? Explain.

Spiral Review and Test Practice

Find each product. NS 2.0 pages 106, 110, 124

10. 8×5

11. 7×9

12. 10×10

13. 6×4

Write the letter of the correct answer. KEY SDAP 1.3

14. The chart shows how many baskets Amir and his friends made.

Amir	Marco	Denise	Kylie	Hiro
4	2	4	5	1

Which line plot can be made from these data?

A

Number of Baskets

```
                    X
X         X    X
X         X    X
X    X    X    X
X    X    X    X    X
—————————————————————
1    2    3    4    5
```

B

Number of Baskets

```
                         X
                    X    X
               X    X    X
          X    X    X    X
     X    X    X    X    X
—————————————————————————
1    2    3    4    5
```

C

Number of Baskets

```
                    X
X    X         X    X
—————————————————————
1    2    3    4    5
```

D

Number of Baskets

```
X    X              X    X
—————————————————————————
1    2    3    4    5
```

Extra Practice See page 491, Set A.

Key Standards Review

Need Help?
See Key Standards Handbook.

Add or subtract. KEY **NS 3.3**

1. $15.95
   + 0.64

2. $25.65
   + 1.25

3. $30.19
   + 2.39

4. $29.95
   + 12.49

5. $13.85
   + 46.89

6. $50.00
   − 29.95

7. $90.00
   − 35.49

8. $75.00
   − 69.05

9. $85.00
   − 81.34

10. $125.50
    − 79.95

Write a number sentence to show each relationship. KEY **AF 1.1**

11. The product of a number and 4 is less than the difference between 100 and 20.

12. The sum of 39 and a number is greater than the product of 7 and 9.

13. The difference between 9 and a number is equal to the difference between 18 and 12.

 **Math Reasoning**

Spinning Numbers SDAP 1.1

Robin spins one of the spinners below. The line plot shows the results of her experiment after 20 spins.

Which spinner did Robin most likely use?

A.

B.

C.

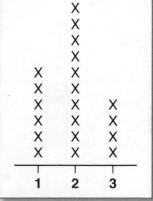

Spinner Results

LESSON 3

CA Standards
Prepares for
KEY SDAP 1.3 Summarize and display the results of probability experiments in a clear and organized way (e.g., use a bar graph or a line plot).

MR 2.0 Students use strategies, skills, and concepts in finding solutions.
Also MR 2.3

Hands On
Pictographs

Objective Use pictographs to show data and summarize results.

▶ Explore

Lucy conducted a survey. She asked her classmates, "Which California basketball team do you like the best?" The table shows the results.

Question How can you show the data on a pictograph?

Favorite Team	
Team	**Number**
Lakers	10
Monarchs	4
Sparks	8

Vocabulary

pictograph

Materials
Workmat 4

Hint

A **pictograph** uses pictures to represent data.

---

1 Use Workmat 4. Write a title and the name of each team.

Favorite Team	
Lakers	
Monarchs	
Sparks	

---

2 Decide what number to use for the key.

- The numbers in the table can all be divided by 2. Since the quotients are not too large, let each stand for 2 people.

Lakers	$10 \div 2 = 5$
Monarchs	$4 \div 2 = 2$
Sparks	$8 \div 2 = 4$

- The quotient is the number of to draw for each team.

---

3 Draw the correct number of for every 2 votes to complete the pictograph.

Favorite Team	
Lakers	♀ ♀ ♀ ♀ ♀
Monarchs	♀ ♀
Sparks	♀ ♀ ♀ ♀
Key: Each ♀ stands for 2 votes.	

Sometimes you have to use a fraction of a symbol to show the data.

There are 21 blue balloons, 18 green balloons, and 3 red balloons.

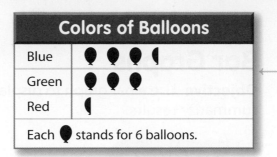

Colors of Balloons	
Blue	🎈🎈🎈🌙
Green	🎈🎈🎈
Red	🌙

Each 🎈 stands for 6 balloons.

Each picture stands for 6 balloons. So one half-picture stands for 3 balloons.

 **Extend**

1. Use the table to complete a pictograph.

Books Read	
Mom	4
Dad	8
Lucy	8
Billy	16

Books Read

Mom	
Dad	
Lucy	
Billy	

Each 📖 stands for 8 books.

Think

If 📖 stands for 8 books, how can I show 4 books?

2. **Summarize** Tell 2 things your pictograph shows.

Use the table at the right for Problems 3–5.

3. Use the table to make a pictograph. Use ☺ to stand for each vote.

4. **Summarize** Tell 2 things the pictograph shows about Favorite Things to Do.

5. **Challenge** Suppose each ☺ stands for 2 votes. How many ☺ would you need to draw for "Read a book"?

Favorite Things to Do	
See a movie	14
Read a book	10
Play Sports	18
Ride a bike	8

Writing Math

Explain Look back at Problem 3. How did you decide what number the picture in the key should be?

CA Standards
Prepares for
KEY SDAP 1.3 Summarize and display the results of probability experiments in a clear and organized way (e.g., use a bar graph or a line plot).

MR 2.3 Use a variety of methods, such as words, numbers, symbols, charts, graphs, tables, diagrams, and models, to explain mathematical reasoning.

Vocabulary

bar graph

Materials
Workmat 8 or Learning Tool 33 (10 × 10 Grid)

Hands On
Bar Graphs

Objective Use a bar graph to display data and summarize results.

▶ **Explore**

The Winter Olympics in 2002 took place in Salt Lake City, Utah. The table shows the number of medals won by four countries.

Question How can you make a **bar graph** to display data?

Medals Won	
Country	**Number of Medals**
Canada	17
Italy	12
France	11
China	8

1 Use Workmat 8 or a 10 × 10 grid. Write the title and label the side and the bottom of the graph.

2 Use a scale of 2 to show the number of medals. Start with 0. Complete the scale.

A "scale of 2" means that each horizontal line stands for 2 medals.

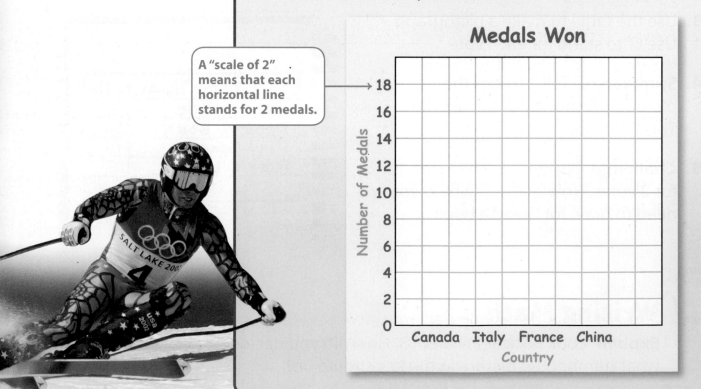

3 Draw the bars. Some of the bars may end halfway between two numbers because you used a scale of 2.

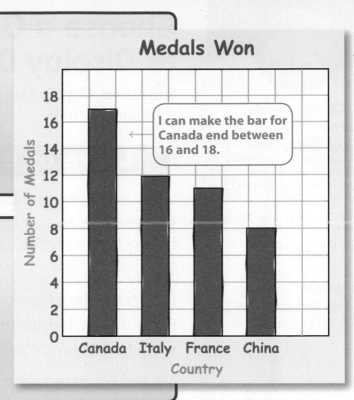

Medals Won

I can make the bar for Canada end between 16 and 18.

4 Look back at the table. Compare the bars of your graph to the data in the table.

▶ **Extend**

1. Make a vertical bar graph to show the data in the table.

2. **Summarize** Write a sentence that tells what the graph shows.

3. Write two questions you can answer using the data.

4. **Challenge** Use your vertical bar graph to make a horizontal bar graph of the same data.

Olympic Medals for Swimming

Country	Number of Medals
China	19
Greece	8
Denmark	6
Bulgaria	3

Writing Math

Explain Does displaying data on a horizontal bar graph instead of a vertical bar graph change the meaning of the data? Explain why or why not.

CA Standards
Prepares for

KEY SDAP 1.3 Summarize and display the results of probability experiments in a clear and organized way (e.g., use a bar graph or a line plot).

MR 1.0 Students make decisions about how to approach problems.

Also MR 2.0, MR 2.3

Materials
Workmat 8 or Learning Tool 33 (10 × 10 Grid)

Choose a Graph to Display Data

Objective Display data in different ways and summarize results.

▶ Learn by Example

You have learned different ways to collect and display data. In this lesson you will choose how to display a set of data.

A tally chart is a useful tool to use when collecting data from a survey or an experiment. Pictographs, bar graphs, and line plots are good ways to display data.

Miguel collected data about a Ping Pong Tournament in his school.

Tally Chart

Miguel made a tally chart as he counted the number of students who stayed for lunch on each day of the tournament.

Students that Stayed for Lunch		
Day	Tally	Number
Friday	⊮⊮ ⊮⊮ ⊮⊮	15
Saturday	⊮⊮ ⊮⊮ ⊮⊮ ⊮⊮	20
Sunday	⊮⊮ ⊮⊮ ⊮⊮ ⊮⊮	20

Pictograph

Miguel made a pictograph to show the number of students who played in the tournament.

A pictograph is a good way to compare data.

Tournament Players	
Third Graders	👤 👤 👤 👤 👤
Fourth Graders	👤 👤 👤 👤 ⸙
Fifth Graders	👤 👤 👤 👤 👤 👤
Each 👤 stands for 2 students.	

Bar Graph

Miguel made a bar graph to show the number of students who attended the tournament each year for three years.

A bar graph sometimes works better than a pictograph when the numbers are large and when you want to show an exact number.

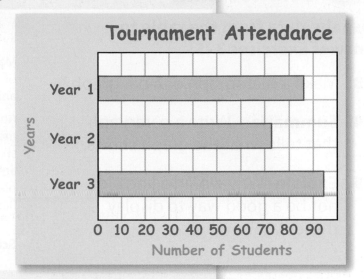

Tournament Attendance

Years

Year 1
Year 2
Year 3

0 10 20 30 40 50 60 70 80 90

Number of Students

Line Plot

Miguel made a line plot to show how often players scored 0, 1, 2, 3, or 4 points to win the game.

A line plot organizes data using a number line. It is a useful way to show how often something happens.

Number of Points Scored

```
                    X
                    X       X
            X       X       X
    X       X       X       X
_____
    0       1       2       3       4
```

▶ Guided Practice

Use the data from the tally chart on page 484.

1. Make a pictograph or a bar graph.

Ask Yourself
Did I include all the information from the tally chart?

(123) **Math Talk** Which way did you choose to display the data from the tally chart? Why did you choose that way?

▶ Practice and Problem Solving

Use the data from the pictograph on page 484.

2. **Summarize** Write a paragraph that tells what the pictograph shows.

Science Link

Use the data from the table to answer Exercises 3–5.

3. Make a pictograph or a bar graph.

4. **Summarize** Write a paragraph that tells what the graph shows.

5. **Explain** Why would a line plot not be a good way to display these data?

Animal Teeth

- Many animals have teeth, but the number of teeth is different depending on what the animal eats.

- Animals that eat meat have many sharp teeth and animals that eat plants have many flat teeth.

Animal	Teeth
Raccoon	40
Cat	30
Horse	44
Squirrel	22

Science **LS 3.a**

Spiral Review and Test Practice

Find each product. KEY **NS 2.4** pages 450, 454

6. 185 × 5

7. 237 × 9

8. 10 × 10

9. 11 × 11

Write the letter of the correct answer. KEY **SDAP 1.3**

10. Maria tossed a paper cup and recorded how it landed. The tally chart shows the results.

    Which graph shows these results?

right side up				
upside down			
on its side	⅋⅋⅋⅋⅋

A
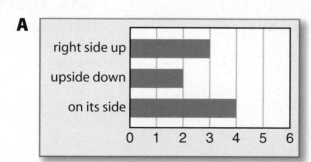

C
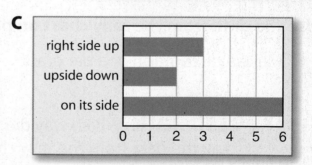

B
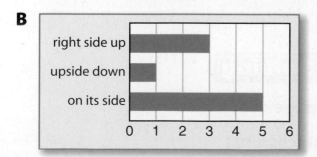

D
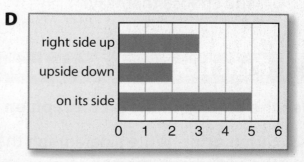

Extra Practice See page 491, Set D.

What Would You Buy?

Advertisers take surveys and study data so they can choose the best way to sell a product to consumers.

Ms. Smith is doing research to find the best way to sell a sports drink. She conducted a survey to find out which sports more people would like to see in an ad.

Use the table to solve.

1. How many people did Ms. Smith survey? How do you know?

2. Which were the two favorite sports?

3. Which two sports were chosen the least?

4. **Analyze** Based on the results of Ms. Smith's survey, which type of athlete is most likely to be used in the ad for the sports drink? Explain.

Sport	Tally	Number
Soccer	ЖЖ ЖЖ ЖЖ ЖЖ ЖЖ	25
Tennis	ЖЖ ЖЖ ЖЖ I	16
Football	ЖЖ ЖЖ ЖЖ IIII	19
Baseball	ЖЖ ЖЖ I	11
Basketball	ЖЖ ЖЖ ЖЖ I	16
Volleyball	ЖЖ ЖЖ III	13

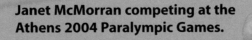

Janet McMorran competing at the Athens 2004 Paralympic Games.

CA Standards
SDAP 1.4, MR 2.0, MR 2.3, MR 2.4

CA Standards

MR 2.0 Students use strategies, skills, and concepts in finding solutions.

Prepares for KEY SDAP 1.3 Summarize and display the results of probability experiments in a clear and organized way (e.g., use a bar graph or a line plot).

Also NS 2.0, KEY NS 2.3, NS 2.8, MR 1.1, MR 1.2, MR 2.3, MR 2.4, MR 3.1, MR 3.3

Problem Solving Strategy
Use a Graph

Objective Find information in a graph to help you solve a problem.

▶ **Learn by Example**

Sometimes you need to get information from a graph in order to solve a problem.

Jack volunteers at a nature center. He is helping set up new tanks for the wood frogs. If he puts 3 wood frogs in each tank, how many tanks will he need?

Use the information in the bar graph to solve the problem.

The bar labeled "Wood Frog" ends halfway between 8 and 10. So the nature center has 9 wood frogs.

Wood Frog

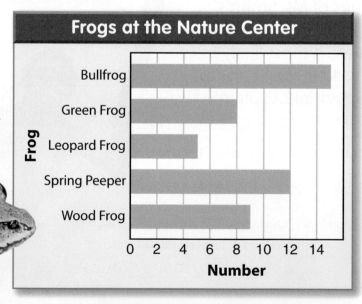

Frogs at the Nature Center

Divide the total number of wood frogs by 3.

$$9 \div 3 = 3$$

Solution: Jack will need 3 tanks.

Guided Problem Solving

Ask Yourself

What information do I need from the graph?

Use the line plot and the Ask Yourself question to solve each problem.

1. The Tigers play 5 other teams in the soccer league. If the Tigers played each of these teams the same number of times, how many times did they play each team? How do you know?

2. The Rockets scored 15 goals. Did the Tigers score more or fewer goals than the Rockets? Explain.

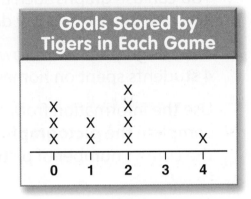

Goals Scored by Tigers in Each Game

```
                    X
    X               X
    X       X       X
    X       X       X               X
    +-------+-------+-------+-------+
    0       1       2       3       4
```

123 Math Talk Look back at Problem 1. How can you use multiplication to check your work?

▶ **Independent Problem Solving**

Use the pictograph to solve each problem. Explain why your answer makes sense.

3. **Multistep** A class is planning an exercise day. Which is a better choice for the exercise day activities?

   A swimming, running, and trampoline

   B bicycling, running, and soccer

4. **Challenge** The students who chose soccer and trampoline decide to break into groups of 3 to exercise together. How many groups of 3 will there be?

5. **Create and Solve** Write your own problem using information in the pictograph.

Favorite Ways to Exercise	
Bicycling	🚶 🚶 🚶 🚶
Running	🚶 🚶
Soccer	🚶 🚶 🚶
Swimming	🚶 🚶 🚶 🚶 🚶
Trampoline	🚶 🚶
Each 🚶 stands for 4 students	

Vocabulary

You can use graphs such as **bar graphs**, **pictographs**, and **line plots** to display data.

The bar graph below shows the number of minutes 4 students spent on homework in one week.

Use the information from the **bar graph** to copy and complete the **pictograph**. Start with the key. Then draw the correct number of pictures.

Bar Graph

Minutes Spent on Homework

Minutes Spent on Homework

	Dan	Joe	Ann	Ida

Students

Pictograph

Minutes Spent on Homework

Dan	
Joe	
Ann	
Ida	

Each ◯ stands for ▓ .

Writing Write 3 sentences to summarize the data in the pictograph you made.

Reading Look for this book in your library.

• *Tiger Math: Learning to Graph from a Baby Tiger*, by Ann Whitehead Nagda and Cindy Bickel

CA Standards
MR 2.3 Use a variety of methods, such as words, numbers, symbols, charts, graphs, tables, diagrams, and models, to explain mathematical reasoning.

Also KEY SDAP 1.3

Standards-Based Extra Practice

Set A ———————————————————— KEY SDAP 1.3 , SDAP 1.4 page 476

Use the line plot to answer the questions.

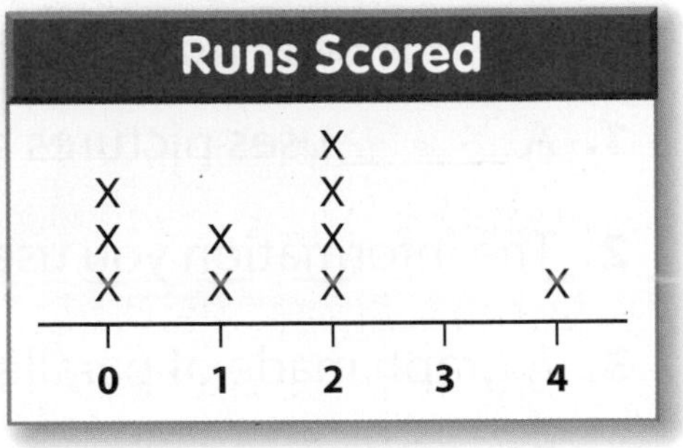

1. In how many games were 0 runs scored?

2. What was the greatest number of runs scored?

3. How many games were played?

4. If the team plays one more game, how many runs do you predict they will score? Explain.

Runs Scored

		X		
X		X		
X	X	X		
X	X	X		X
0	1	2	3	4

Set B ———————————————————— KEY SDAP 1.3 , MR 2.0 page 480

**Use the table to make a pictograph.
Use � to stand for 4 people.**

1. What is the title of your pictograph?

2. How many �
 did you use for *Play Sports*?

3. For which activities did you use half of a �
 ?

Favorite Activity

Activity	Students
Play Sports	12
Visit Friends	6
Make Crafts	10
Read a Book	8

Set C ———————————————————— KEY SDAP 1.3 , MR 2.3 page 482

Make a bar graph.

1. Use the table in Set B to make a bar graph.

2. What scale did you use?

Set D ———————————————————— KEY SDAP 1.3 , MR 1.0 page 484

Use the data to answer the questions.

1. Look at the line plot in Set A. Write 2 sentences that tell what the line plot shows.

2. Look at the line plot in Set B. Write 2 questions you can answer using the data.

Education Place
Visit www.eduplace.com/camap/
for more **Extra Practice**.

Chapter Review/Test

Vocabulary and Concepts

KEY **SDAP 1.3**, MR 2.3

Choose the best word to complete each sentence.

1. A _____ uses pictures to represent data.

2. The information you use to make a graph is called _____.

3. A graph made of parallel bars to compare data is called a _____.

4. A _____ uses a number line to show data.

Word Bank

data

line plot

pictograph

bar graph

Skills

KEY **SDAP 1.3**, MR 2.3

Use the line plot for Exercises 5–6.

Use the table for Exercises 7–8.

Number of Pets

```
              X
      X       X       X
      X       X       X               X
    ─────────────────────────────────────
      0       1       2       3       4
```

Lunch Count	
Food	**Students**
Pizza	7
Hamburger	5
Chicken	2

5. How many students have 4 pets?

6. What fraction of the students surveyed have no pets?

7. Draw a pictograph of the data.

8. Draw a bar graph of the data.

Problem Solving and Reasoning

KEY **SDAP 1.3**, MR 1.0, MR 2.3

Solve. Show how you checked your answer.

9. Write and answer a subtraction question using the data from the line plot.

10. Write and answer an addition question using the data from the table.

Writing Math Look at the pictograph and bar graph you made. How did you choose a key and a scale?

Spiral Review and Test Practice

1. Ms. Riley made 4 quilts for each of 4 school fundraisers. How many quilts did she make altogether?

A 1   **C** 8

B 16   **D** 20

KEY NS 2.2 page 128

2. Which object is a cone?

A

C
PAINT

B

D

MG 2.5 page 234

3. One balloon costs 8¢. Two balloons cost 16¢. Three balloons cost 24¢. If the cost of each balloon stays the same, how much will 4 balloons cost?

A 24¢

B 32¢

C 40¢

D 48¢

> **Test Tip**
> Which operation will you use to solve?

KEY AF 2.1 page 394

4. The table shows the number of goals the Wildcats scored during 10 games in one soccer season.

Goals	0	1	2	3	4
Games	1	?	4	?	1

Which line plot shows how many times the Wildcats scored each number of goals?

A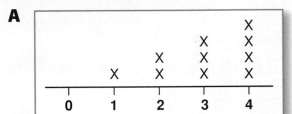

B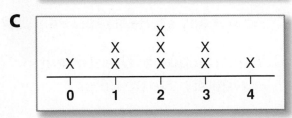

C

D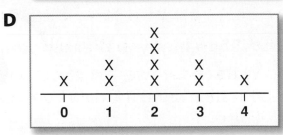

KEY SDAP 1.3 page 476

Probability

Word Bank

greater than

less than

sum

Vocabulary and Concepts   GRADE 2 KEY **NS 2.2**, KEY **NS 1.3**
Choose the best word to complete each sentence.

1. A bag has 3 black tiles and 7 white tiles. The _____ of the number of tiles is 10.

2. A bag has 5 green marbles and 2 blue tiles. Five is _____ 2.

Skills   GRADE 2 KEY **NS 4.2**, KEY **NS 5.1**
What fraction of the circle is blue?

3.   4.   5.   6.

Tell how many ways you can pay for a $0.65 pencil with

7. 6 dimes and 5 nickels.

8. 2 quarters, 3 nickels, and 11 pennies.

Problem Solving and Reasoning   GRADE 2 KEY **NS 1.3**

9. A bag has 3 black marbles, 9 red marbles, and 2 white marbles. Order the number of marbles of each color from greatest to least.

Vocabulary

Visualize It!

You can use words to describe the **probability** of an event.

What are the possible outcomes if you pick one tile from the bag?

- It is **likely** that you would pick a red tile.
- It is **unlikely** that you would pick a yellow tile.
- It is **impossible** that you would pick a green tile.

Language Tip

Some words are similar in Spanish and English.

English	Spanish
probability	**probabilidad**
equally	**igualmente**
impossible	**imposible**
predict	**predecir**

See **English-Spanish Glossary** pages 628–646.

 Education Place Visit www.eduplace.com/camap/ for the **eGlossary** and **eGames**.

CA Standards MR 2.3 Use a variety of methods, such as words, numbers, symbols, charts, graphs, tables, diagrams, and models, to explain mathematical reasoning. **Also SDAP 1.1**

Chapter 23   495

CA Standards
KEY SDAP 1.2 Record the possible outcomes for a simple event (e.g., tossing a coin) and systematically keep track of the outcomes when the event is repeated many times.

KEY SDAP 1.3 Summarize and display the results of probability experiments in a clear and organized way (e.g., use a bar graph or a line plot).
Also SDAP 1.0, MR 2.3

Vocabulary

probability

event

outcome

equally likely

Materials
- Penny or other coin
- Learning Tools 31, 32 (Spinner 2 and Spinner 3)
- Transparent spinner
- 2 number cubes labeled 1–6
- Crayons (red, yellow, and blue)

Hands On
Record Outcomes

Objective Record and display results of probability experiments.

▶ **Explore**

Probability describes how likely it is that an **event** will happen. Activities such as spinning a spinner and tossing a coin are used in probability experiments.

Question How can you record the results of probability experiments?

If you toss a coin, there are two possible **outcomes**, or results.

You are **equally likely** to get heads or tails. This means that heads and tails have the same probability.

Heads

Tails

1 Work with a partner. Make a table like the one on the right. Take turns tossing a coin 50 times.

Coin Toss Experiment		
Outcome	Tally	Number
Heads		
Tails		

2 Record a tally mark on your table for each outcome.

Record the total number of times each outcome occurred.

- How many times did the coin land heads up?

- How many times did the coin land tails up?

- Did heads land up about as often as tails?

► **Extend**

Use a spinner like the one shown. Spin 25 times. Record your results in a tally chart.

Spinner Experiment		
Outcome	Tally	Number
Blue		
Red		
Yellow		

1. How many possible outcomes are there for each spin? What are they?

2. Did the spinner land on each color an equal number of times?

Use a spinner like the one shown. Spin 25 times. Record your results in a bar graph.

3. Look at the bar graph you made. Can the bars above any of the colors show a number greater than 25? Explain why or why not.

Roll 2 number cubes labeled 1–6 100 times. Record the sum of the numbers from each roll on a line plot.

4. How many possible outcomes are there? What are they?

5. Challenge Which sum occurred most often? Why do you think this happened?

Writing Math

Analyze Review your results from the two spinner experiments. Are the results the same? Explain why or why not.

LESSON 2

CA Standards
SDAP 1.1 Identify whether common events are certain, likely, unlikely, or improbable.
Also SDAP 1.0, MR 1.0, MR 3.0, MR 3.2, MR 3.3

Vocabulary

certain

likely

unlikely

impossible

Probability

Objective Decide if an event is certain, likely, unlikely, or impossible.

▶ Learn by Example

You are able to describe the probability of an event with words like *certain*, *likely*, *unlikely*, or *impossible*.

Carla and Connor are playing a Grab Bag Game using blue and red cubes. What is the probability of picking a blue cube from each bag?

Bag A

The probability of picking a blue cube is **certain**.

Bag B

The probability of picking a blue cube is **likely**.

Bag C

The probability of picking a blue cube is **unlikely**.

Bag D

The probability of picking a blue cube is **impossible**.

Guided Practice

Look at the spinner. Write whether the event is *certain*, *likely*, *unlikely*, or *impossible*.

1. landing on orange
2. landing on red
3. landing on orange or blue
4. landing on blue
5. landing on white

Ask Yourself
- Which color covers more of the spinner?
- Which color covers less of the spinner?

Guided Problem Solving

Use the questions to solve this problem.

6. Draw a spinner on which it is likely you will land on blue, unlikely you will land on red, impossible you will land on purple, and certain you will land on blue or red.

   a. **Understand** How many colors will the spinner have? What will the colors be?

   b. **Plan** Which color should cover more of the spinner?

   c. **Solve** Draw the spinner.

   d. **Look Back** Read the problem again. Does your spinner match what the problem asked for?

7. Suppose you wanted to create a spinner on which it is certain you will land on purple. What would your spinner look like?

123 Math Talk Look at the spinner for Problems 1–5. Why is it possible, but unlikely, that the spinner will land on orange?

Draw and color a set of 6 cubes to represent the statements.

8. Picking a red cube is certain.

9. Picking a blue cube is impossible.

10. Picking a blue cube is likely.

11. Picking a red cube is possible, but unlikely.

 Science Link

Use the Fun Facts to answer Problems 12–14.

12. What is the probability that a block of ice will melt at 68°F (room temperature)?

13. What is the probability that water will freeze at 68°F?

14. What is the probability that water will boil at 68°F?

 **Fun Facts**

Water

- When water freezes, it changes from a liquid to a solid (ice).

- When ice is heated it melts, changing from a solid to a liquid. When more heat is added, it evaporates, turning it into a gas.

- The melting point of ice is 32°F.

- The boiling point of water is 212°F.

Science PS 1.e, PS 1.f

 Spiral Review and Test Practice

Find the product. KEY NS 2.4 page 436

15.   14
      × 7

16.   35
      × 2

17.   29
      × 3

18.   17
      × 5

Write the letter of the correct answer. SDAP 1.1

19. Robin put these 10 stickers on the table. She closed her eyes and picked one from the table. What is the probability that she picked a square?

A certain   **B** likely   **C** unlikely   **D** impossible

Extra Practice See pages 511, Set A.

Key Standards Review

Need Help?
See Key Standards Handbook.

Find the product. KEY **NS 2.4**

1. 252×4 **2.** 3×823 **3.** 739×5 **4.** 507×8

5. $\begin{array}{r} 325 \\ \times\ 8 \\ \hline \end{array}$ **6.** $\begin{array}{r} 672 \\ \times\ 6 \\ \hline \end{array}$ **7.** $\begin{array}{r} 719 \\ \times\ 9 \\ \hline \end{array}$ **8.** $\begin{array}{r} 445 \\ \times\ 5 \\ \hline \end{array}$ **9.** $\begin{array}{r} 539 \\ \times\ 4 \\ \hline \end{array}$ **10.** $\begin{array}{r} 828 \\ \times\ 3 \\ \hline \end{array}$

Write and solve an equation for each situation. KEY **AF 1.1**

11. Sharla has 12 boxes with 4 barrettes in each box. How many barrettes does Sharla have?

12. Sami has 36 toy dinosaurs. He puts 12 of them on a shelf. How many toy dinosaurs are not on the shelf?

13. Manuel gave 18 crackers to three friends. Each friend got the same number of crackers. How many crackers did each friend get?

14. Lela drove 59 miles on Monday, 65 miles on Tuesday, and 13 miles on Wednesday. How many miles did she drive on those three days?

   Probability

Likely Sums   SDAP 1.0

Suppose you roll two number cubes that are numbered 1–6. What is the most likely sum of the two numbers rolled? Make an organized list to find out.

LESSON 3

CA Standards
SDAP 1.4 Use the results of probability experiments to predict future events (e.g., use a line plot to predict the temperature forecast for the next day).

KEY SDAP 1.3 Summarize and display the results of probability experiments in a clear and organized way (e.g., use a bar graph or a line plot).
Also SDAP 1.0, SDAP 1.1, KEY SDAP 1.2, MR 3.3

Vocabulary

predict

outcome

Materials
- Paper bag
- Paper squares (10 red and 10 blue)
- 4 pennies

Hands On
Make Predictions

Objective Conduct probability experiments and predict outcomes.

▶ **Explore**

You can use data from a probability experiment to **predict** what is likely to happen if the experiment is repeated.

Question How can you use the results of experiments to predict **outcomes**?

1 Work with a partner. Place 10 red or blue paper squares into a bag. Use more of one color than the other. Exchange bags with your partner.

2 Pick a paper square from the bag without looking. Record the color of the paper in a tally chart. Replace the paper square and repeat this 24 more times.

Paper Square Experiment		
Outcome	Tally	Number
Red		
Blue		

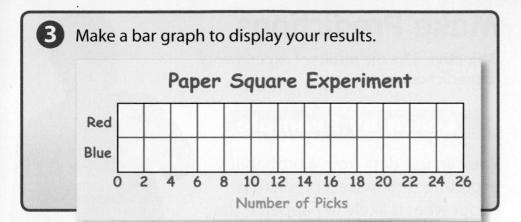

3 Make a bar graph to display your results.

Paper Square Experiment

Red

Blue

0 2 4 6 8 10 12 14 16 18 20 22 24 26

Number of Picks

4 Look at your graph. Try to predict what color paper you will pick next time.

▶ **Extend**

Toss 4 pennies at the same time. Record the number of heads you see. Repeat this 24 more times. Record the results of your experiment in a line plot.

1. Do you think it is likely or unlikely that if you tossed the 4 coins one more time, you would see 4 heads?

2. Suppose you tossed the 4 coins again, how many heads are you likely to see? Why?

Number of Heads Seen

0 1 2 3 4

3. If you tossed 5 pennies, would you be more likely to see heads or tails?

4. Suppose you tossed 8 pennies. Is it certain, likely, unlikely or impossible that you would see 2 heads and 6 tails?

Math Journal

Writing Math

Predict Suppose each letter of the word *California* is written on an identical card and put into a bag. If a person picks a card without looking, is the letter more likely to be a consonant or a vowel? Explain.

LESSON 4

CA Standards
SDAP 1.4 Use the results of probability experiments to predict future events (e.g., use a line plot to predict the temperature forecast for the next day).

KEY SDAP 1.3 Summarize and display the results of probability experiments in a clear and organized way (e.g., use a bar graph or a line plot).

Also SDAP 1.0, SDAP 1.1, MR 1.0, MR 2.0, MR 2.3

Make Predictions

Objective Use the results of experiments to predict outcomes.

Learn by Example

You can use data from a probability experiment to make a prediction about what is likely to happen if the experiment is repeated.

Example 1

Will has a bag of 10 marbles. Without looking, he drew from the bag 25 times and returned his pick each time. This tally chart shows the results of his experiments.

Picking a Marble From a Bag

Outcome	Tally	Number
Red	𝍸 𝍸 𝍸 𝍸 𝍷𝍷𝍷	23
Blue	𝍷𝍷	2

These results suggest the following:

- There are likely more red than blue marbles in the bag.
- It is unlikely there is a third color marble in the bag.

Example 2

This line plot shows the results of an experiment where Marcia tossed a number cube 20 times.

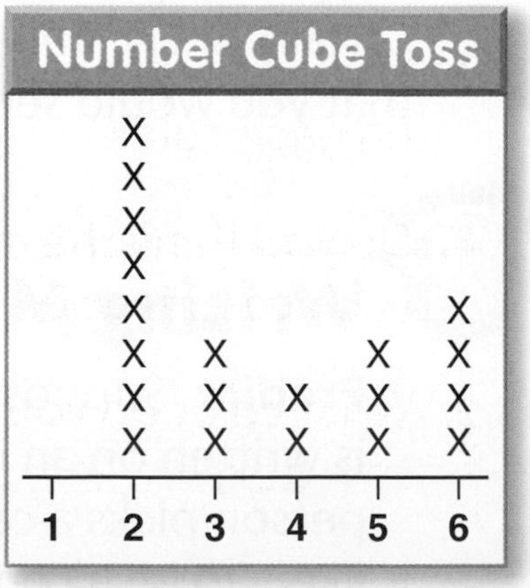

These results suggest the following:

- There may not be a 1 on the number cube.
- There may be two faces showing a 2 on the number cube.

▶ Guided Practice

The tally chart shows the results of Ricardo's experiment. Use the chart to answer the questions.

Picking Cubes From a Bag		
Outcome	**Tally**	**Number**
Yellow	卌 卌 卌	15
Green	卌 |||	8
Blue	||	2

Ask Yourself
- What color cube has the greatest number of tally marks?
- Are 15 yellow cubes about twice as much as 8 green cubes?

1. Suppose he picks another cube. What color is it most likely to be? Why?

2. Would you predict that there are about twice as many yellow cubes as green cubes in the bag? How do you know?

(123) Math Talk If there are 50 cubes in the bag above, how many of each color do you think there would be? How did you decide?

▶ Practice and Problem Solving

The bar graph shows the results of Catherine spinning a spinner 30 times. Use the graph to answer the questions.

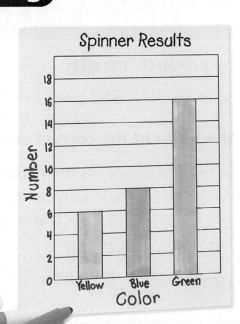

3. How many times did the spinner land on each color?

4. Do you think the chance of spinning each color is equally likely? Explain.

5. What color do you predict she will spin next?

6. Is it likely or unlikely that she will spin red next?

7. Represent Joe picks a marble and returns it. He does this 50 times. The results are 30 red, 10 blue, and 10 yellow. Make a pictograph to show the results of the experiment.

8. Look at the pictograph you made in Problem 7. If there are only 10 marbles in the bag, how many of each color are there likely to be?

9. Challenge A letter tile is made for each letter of the alphabet. If a person picks a tile without looking, is the letter more likely to be a consonant or a vowel? Explain.

 Real World Data

The line plot shows high temperatures in a city on May 10 for the past 20 years. Suppose tomorrow is May 10.

10. What is a likely prediction of the high temperature for tomorrow?

11. What is an unlikely prediction of the high temperature for tomorrow?

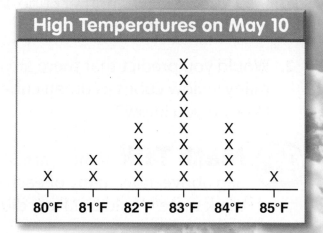

High Temperatures on May 10

| | 80°F | 81°F | 82°F | 83°F | 84°F | 85°F |

 Spiral Review and Test Practice

Find the product. KEY **NS 2.2** pages 106, 110

12. 5 × 7 **13.** 2 × 8 **14.** 10 × 9 **15.** 4 × 6

Write the letter of the correct answer. SDAP 1.4

16. The tally chart shows the results of spinning a spinner 20 times. If Sally spins the spinner one more time, which color is she most likely to spin?

    A blue   **C** red

    B green   **D** yellow

Spin Results	
Blue	卌
Red	||
Green	卌 ||||
Yellow	||||

Extra Practice See page 513, Set C.

At the Races

Object of the Game Predict which sum is more likely to come up. Choose a position and test your prediction. Record each play. The first player across the finish line wins the round.

Materials
- Two number cubes labeled 1–6
- Learning Tool 77 (Probability Game Board)

Number of Players 2–4

How to Play

1 Choose a number from 2–12 on the game board. Place a marker on your chosen number.

2
- On your turn, toss the number cubes and find the sum of the numbers.
- The player with that number advances one space on the game board.
- Record the toss.

3 The first player to cross the finish line wins.

4
- Before you play again, make a list of the outcomes. Which sums came up most often?
- How will you choose your place on the number line for the next game?

CA Standards

KEY SDAP 1.2 Record the possible outcomes for a simple event (e.g., tossing a coin) and systematically keep track of the outcomes when the event is repeated many times.

KEY SDAP 1.3 Summarize and display the results of probability experiments in a clear and organized way (e.g., use a bar graph or a line plot).

Also SDAP 1.0

Education Place
Visit www.eduplace.com/camap/ for **Brain Teasers** and **eGames** to play.

Field Trip...

Bodie, CA

CA Standards
MR 1.0, MR 1.1,
MR 2.0, NS 1.1,
NS 1.4, KEY NS 1.5,
KEY NS 3.3, SDAP 1.1

Problem Solving

Objective Use skills and strategies to solve word problems.

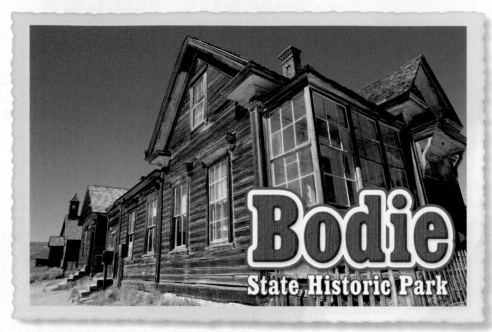

Deserted houses line the streets of Bodie.

Bodie grew into a gold-mining boomtown during the Gold Rush. Soon after, the town was deserted.

Solve. Use the table for Problems 1 and 2.

1. About how many people lived in Bodie in 1886? Write the number in expanded form and in word form.

2. If you walked around Bodie in 1879, would it be certain, likely, unlikely, or impossible to see someone else walking on the street?

History of Bodie	
1859	Bodie was founded.
1877	The Standard Mining Company struck gold.
1879	Bodie became a boomtown.
1881	Mining slowed down.
1886	Only about 1,500 people were left.
1940	Bodie began to fade into a ghost town.

3. When Bodie was booming, about 10,000 people lived there. If the exact number of people was rounded to the nearest thousand, could the exact number be 9,485? 10,050?

4. **Patterns** At one time, a room in Bodie cost $1.00 per night. How much would it cost to rent a room for 2 weeks? for 4 weeks? for 8 weeks?

Problem Solving On Tests

Select a Strategy
- Choose the Operation
- Draw a Picture
- Make a Table
- Make an Organized List

1. The figure shows the shape of a display in a museum. What is the perimeter of the display?

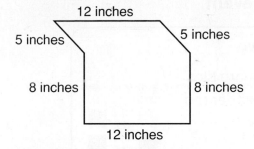

12 inches

5 inches   5 inches

8 inches   8 inches

12 inches

A 25 inches   **C** 50 inches

B 40 inches   **D** 62 inches

KEY **MG 1.3** page 214

2. Danny used pattern blocks to make this shape. Which angle is a right angle?

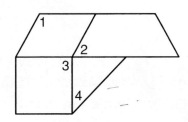

A 1   **B** 2   **C** 3   **D** 4

MG 2.4 page 190

3. In math class, Yuki shaded $\frac{1}{3}$ of a circle.

Which fractional part of a circle below is equal to $\frac{1}{3}$?

A   **C**

B   **D**

NS 3.1 page 332

4. Ellen put 7 triangles and 3 circles on the table. She closed her eyes and picked one. What is the probability she picked a triangle?

A certain   **C** unlikely

B likely   **D** impossible

SDAP 1.1 page 498

Reading & Writing Math

Vocabulary

You can use the words **certain**, **likely**, **unlikely**, or **impossible** to describe the **probability** of an **event**.

What You Have

- one bag

- many square tiles that are either red or yellow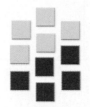

You can choose red or yellow tiles or both.

Pick Tiles

- You put 10 tiles in a bag.
- You will have one pick.
- You want the probability of picking a red tile to be *likely*.
- You want the probability of a yellow tile to be *unlikely*.

1. How many red tiles will you use?

2. How many yellow tiles?

3. Explain your reasoning.

Writing
Write a problem using tiles in which it would be *impossible* to pick a red tile. Write another problem using tiles in which it would be *certain* to pick a red tile.

Reading
Check out this book in your library.

- *Do You Wanna Bet? Your Chance to Find Out About Probability*, by Jean Cushman

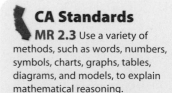

CA Standards

MR 2.3 Use a variety of methods, such as words, numbers, symbols, charts, graphs, tables, diagrams, and models, to explain mathematical reasoning.

Also SDAP 1.1

Standards-Based Extra Practice

Set A ———————————————————— SDAP 1.1 page 498

Look at the spinner. Write whether it is *certain*, *likely*, *unlikely*, or *impossible* to land on a blue section of each spinner.

1.

2.

3.

4.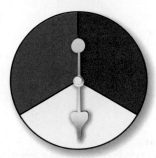

5.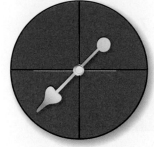

6.

Solve.

7. Draw a spinner on which it is impossible to land on red, likely to land on green, and unlikely to land on yellow.

8. How would you change your spinner so that you are certain to land on yellow?

Education Place
Visit www.eduplace.com/camap/ for more **Extra Practice**.

Chapter 23 Extra Practice **511**

Standards-Based Extra Practice

Solve.

1. A number cube is labeled 1–6. What are the possible outcomes?

2. Are the outcomes when tossing a number cube marked 1–6 equally likely? Why or why not?

3. A spinner has four equal sections: one red, two blue, and one yellow. What are the possible outcomes on one spin?

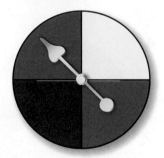

Sarah tossed two number cubes marked 1–6 and found the sum. She repeated this 25 times. Here are her results.

   2, 6, 7, 3, 6, 8, 5, 7, 6, 7, 6, 4, 10, 11, 7, 5, 4, 12, 2, 4, 8, 3, 6, 7, 2

5. Copy and complete the line plot to show Sarah's sums.

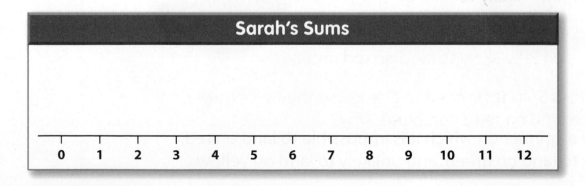

Sarah's Sums

0 1 2 3 4 5 6 7 8 9 10 11 12

6. Kyle said that it is impossible to toss a sum of 9 because Sarah did not get one in 25 tosses. Is Kyle right?

Standards-Based Extra Practice

Set C ── SDAP 1.4 page 504

Ricardo put some marbles in a bag. Some were red, some were green, and the rest were blue.

Sherry picked a marble, recorded the color, and put it back 20 times. The line plot shows the colors she picked.

1. If there are 40 marbles in the bag, how many of each color do you predict there are? Why?

2. On her next try, do you predict that Sherry will pick a green marble? Why?

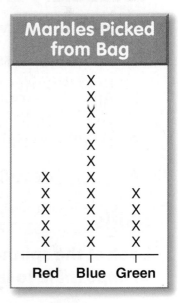

Use the spinners for Problems 3–5.

Spinner A

Spinner B

Spinner C

3. You and a friend are playing a game with Spinner A. Is the spinner more likely to land on red or blue? Why?

4. What color should be in the blank space on Spinner B so that it is equally likely to land on red or blue?

5. How does Spinner C need to change so that it is equally likely to land on red or on blue? Why?

Education Place
Visit www.eduplace.com/camap/
for more **Extra Practice**.

Chapter Review/Test

Vocabulary and Concepts

SDAP 1.1, MR 2.3

Choose the best word to complete each sentence.

> **Word Bank**
> outcomes
> equally likely
> probability
> impossible

1. When you toss a coin, heads or tails are _____ to occur.

2. An _____ outcome will never happen.

3. When you roll a number cube, there are 6 possible _____.

4. _____ describes how likely it is that an event will happen.

Skills

SDAP 1.1, KEY SDAP 1.3, SDAP 1.4

Look at the spinner. Write whether it is *certain*, *likely*, *unlikely*, or *impossible* to land on a blue section of each spinner.

5.

6.

7.

Use the bar graph for problems 8–9. The button is replaced after every pick.

8. Does the bar graph tell you how many buttons are in the bag? Explain.

9. What color button do you predict will be picked next? Explain.

Experiment Results

Bar graph — Number of Occurrences vs Buttons:
Red: 2, Blue: 5, Green: 1, Yellow: 2

Problem Solving and Reasoning

SDAP 1.0, MR 2.3

Solve.

10. Molly put 7 red, 3 green, 1 yellow, and 2 blue cubes in a bag. Which color cube is she least likely to pick? Why?

> **Writing Math** A spinner is divided into two unequal sections. Tell which section the spinner is more likely to land on.

Spiral Review and Test Practice

1. What is 2514 rounded to the nearest thousand?

A 3000　　**C** 2500

B 2510　　**D** 2000

NS 1.4 page 34

2. Anna compared the prices of two telephones. The table below shows the prices.

Brand	Cost
A	$23.95
B	$21.79

How much more does Brand *A* cost than Brand *B*?

A $1.16　　**C** $2.16

B $2.24　　**D** $2.26

KEY NS 3.3 page 390

3. Mr. Ortega bought 4 shirts. Each shirt cost $8.25. What was the total cost of the shirts?

A $3.30

B $32.00

C $32.80

D $33.00

> **Test Tip**
> Which operation will you use to solve?

KEY NS 3.3 page 456

4. Patty picked colored cubes out of a bag without looking. The results are shown in the tally chart below.

Color	Blue	Green	Red
Tally	|||	|||	₩₩

Which graph shows these results?

A
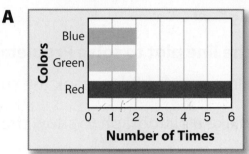

B
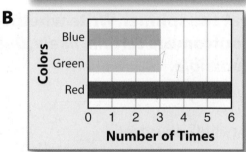

C
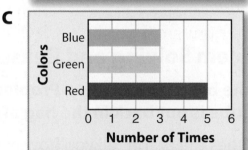

D
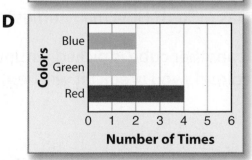

KEY SDAP 1.3 page 502

Education Place
Visit www.eduplace.com/camap/ for
Test-Taking Tips and **Extra Practice**.

Unit 8 Review/Test

Vocabulary and Concepts ———————————— MR 2.3 Chapters 22–23

Choose the best word to complete each sentence.

> **Word Bank**
> outcomes
> bar graph
> probability

1. The weatherman said the _____ of rain is likely.

2. When you toss a coin, there are 2 possible _____.

Skills ——————————— SDAP 1.1, KEY **SDAP 1.3**, MR 2.3 Chapter 22, Lessons 2–3

Use the line plot to solve Problems 3–4.

3. How many children took the survey?

4. Make a pictograph to show the data.

Number of Sisters

```
              X
              X         X
    X    X    X    X
    X    X    X    X    X
    X    X    X    X    X              X
  ┬────┬────┬────┬────┬────┬────┬
    0    1    2    3    4    5    6
```

Look at the spinner. Write whether each outcome is *certain*, *likely*, *unlikely*, or *impossible*. Chapter 23, Lesson 2

5. landing on yellow _____

6. landing on white _____

7. landing on one of the three colors red, yellow, or orange _____

Problem Solving and Reasoning ——————— KEY **SDAP 1.3**, SDAP 1.4 Chapter 23, Lessons 2–4

Use the bar graph to solve Problems 8–9. The cube is put back in the bag after every pick.

8. Does the graph tell you how many times a cube was picked? How many times?

9. If another cube is picked without looking, what color do you predict it will be? Explain.

Color of Cube Picked From a Bag

Solve.

10. Fiona put 5 red cubes, 2 green cubes, 1 yellow cube, and 5 blue cubes in a bag. She closed her eyes and picked a cube out of the bag. Which color cube is she most likely to pick? Why?

Writing Math Brad put 40 yellow, red, or blue cubes in a bag. If you pull a cube out of the bag it is impossible to pick blue, likely to pick red, and unlikely to pick yellow. How many of each color might Brad have put in the bag?

Performance Assessment

Lemonade Stand

KEY **SDAP 1.3**, SDAP 1.4, MR 1.0, MR 1.1, MR 2.0

Andrea has a lemonade stand. The graph shows the number of cups of lemonade she sold last week.

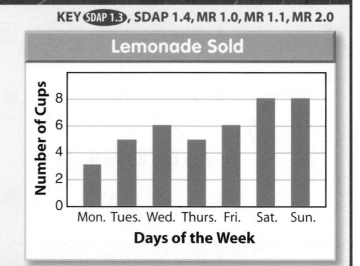

Task	Information You Need
Use the bar graph and the information at the right to decide how many bags of cups and canisters of lemonade powder Andrea should buy for next week.	Each bag contains 25 cups.
	When mixed with water, a canister of powder will make about 40 cups of lemonade.
	Next week is the last week Andrea will sell lemonade.

Multiply by 5

A group of 5 you'll find with ease.
Half of 10 is just a breeze!

A group of 5 is easier as half of 10!
Look at Problem 1. I want 5 groups
of 4. 10 × 4 = 40, so to get 5, I take
half, which makes 20.

1. 5 × 4 → half of $\boxed{40}$ = $\boxed{20}$
10 × 4

2. 5 × 8 → half of ▉ = ▉
10 × 8

3. 5 × 6 → half of ▉ = ▉
10 × 6

4. 5 × 10 → half of ▉ = ▉
10 × 10

Way to go! Keep it up!

5. 5 × 7 → half of ▉ = ▉
10 × 7

6. 5 × 16 → half of ▉ = ▉
10 × 16

7. 5 × 3 → half of ▉ = ▉
10 × 3

8. 5 × 14 → half of ▉ = ▉
10 × 14

Doing Great!

Take It Further!
Now try doing all the steps in your head!

9. 5 × 8

10. 5 × 12

11. 5 × 5

12. 5 × 20

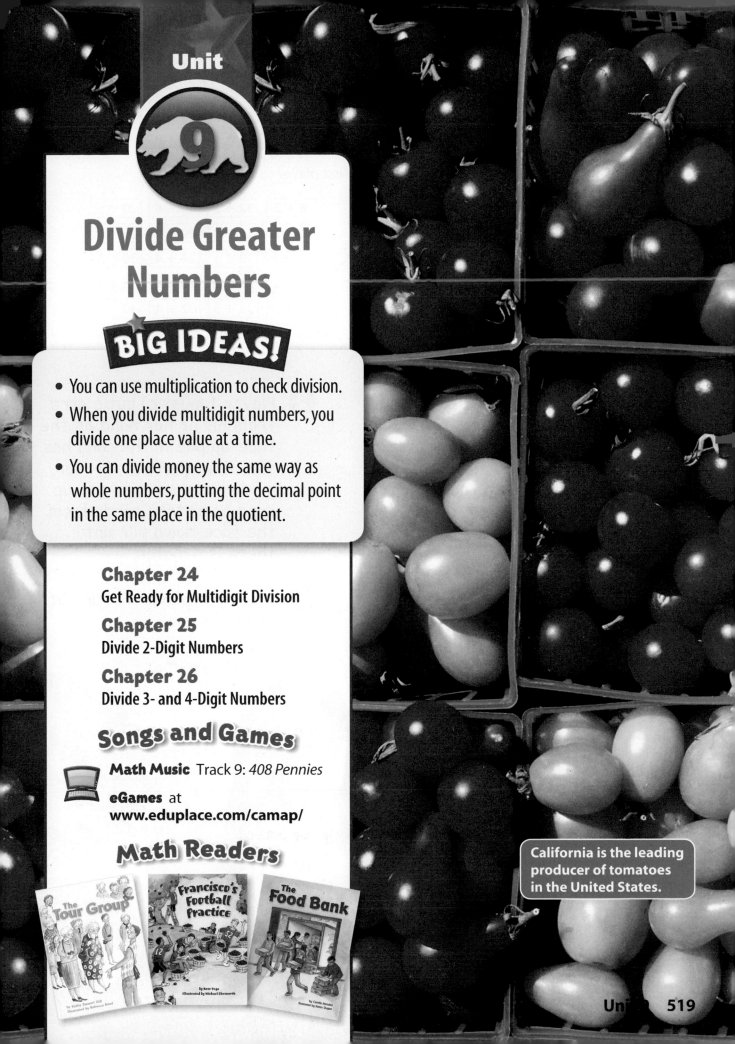

9

Divide Greater Numbers

BIG IDEAS!

- You can use multiplication to check division.
- When you divide multidigit numbers, you divide one place value at a time.
- You can divide money the same way as whole numbers, putting the decimal point in the same place in the quotient.

Chapter 24
Get Ready for Multidigit Division

Chapter 25
Divide 2-Digit Numbers

Chapter 26
Divide 3- and 4-Digit Numbers

Songs and Games

Math Music Track 9: *408 Pennies*

eGames at
www.eduplace.com/camap/

Math Readers

The Tour Group

Francisco's Football Practice

The Food Bank

California is the leading producer of tomatoes in the United States.

Game

Make a Match

Object of the Game Be the first player to use all your cards.

Materials
Learning Tool 41: Division Fact Cards

Set Up
Shuffle the division fact cards.

Number of Players 2

8 ÷ 2	12 ÷ 3	16 ÷ 4	20 ÷ 5
10 ÷ 2	15 ÷ 3	20 ÷ 4	25 ÷ 5
12 ÷ 2	18 ÷ 3	24 ÷ 4	30 ÷ 5
14 ÷ 2	21 ÷ 3	28 ÷ 4	35 ÷ 5
16 ÷ 2	24 ÷ 3	32 ÷ 4	40 ÷ 5
18 ÷ 2	27 ÷ 3	36 ÷ 4	45 ÷ 5

How to Play

1 Player 1 deals 5 fact cards to each player and places the remaining cards face down in a pile. The top card is turned over and placed face up next to the pile.

2 Player 1 must a) put a card from his or her hand on the face-up pile if the card has the same quotient, divisor, or dividend as the face-up card or b) take cards from the face-down pile until there is a match.

3 Players take turns repeating Step 2. If the face-down pile runs out, the cards below the top face-up card are shuffled to make a new face-down pile.

4 The first player to run out of cards wins.

CA Standards
NS 2.0 Students calculate and solve problems involving addition, subtraction, multiplication, and division.

Education Place
Visit www.eduplace.com/camap/ for
Brain Teasers and **eGames** to play.

Reading You can use a K-W-L chart to help you understand a reading selection. To help you solve a math problem, you can use a K-W-P-L chart. The chart shows important facts without extra information. Here is an example:

Admission to Nature Park is free on Sundays. On Mondays through Saturdays, tickets cost $4 for children and $8 for adults. Mrs. George paid $24 for tickets for herself and her children. How many children's tickets did Mrs. George buy?

What Do I Know?	What Do I Want to Know?	What is My Plan to Find Out?	What Did I Learn?
• Tickets cost $4 for children, $8 for adults • $24 spent for all tickets	• How many children go?	• Subtract to find how much is spent on child tickets. • Divide to find the number of children.	

$24 − $8 = $16
$16 ÷ $4 = 4
Mrs. George bought 4 children's tickets.

Writing Use the information in this K-W-P-L chart to write your own problem.

What Do I Know?	What Do I Want to Know?	What is My Plan to Find Out?	What Did I Learn?
• Tickets cost $3 for children, $5 for adults • $21 spent • There is at least 1 adult	• Who goes?		

Get Ready for Multidigit Division

A colorful float in the Tournament of Roses parade in Pasadena, CA

Vocabulary and Concepts NS 2.0, MR 2.3

Choose the best word to complete each sentence. page 262

1. In the division sentence 8 ÷ 2 = 4 , the _____ is 2.

2. In the division sentence 15 ÷ 3 = 5, the _____ is 15.

3. When you divide 12 by 3, the _____ is 4.

Skills NS 2.0

Write a division sentence for each array. page 260

4.

5.

6.

Write a division fact for each set of numbers. page 260

7. 4, 8, 32   **8.** 5, 9, 45   **9.** 6, 7, 42

Problem Solving and Reasoning NS 2.0

10. Mrs. Lee has 36 post cards to display on the bulletin board. She puts 9 post cards in each row. How many rows does she make?

Vocabulary

Visualize It!

You can make equal groups to help you solve division problems.

Mr. Pell has 17 goldfish. He wants to give 7 goldfish to each of his 2 children and keep the rest. How many goldfish will Mr. Pell keep?

Divide the 17 goldfish into 2 equal groups. How many goldfish are left over?

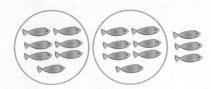

Mr. Pell will keep 3 goldfish.

Language Tip

Some words are similar in Spanish and English.

English	Spanish
division	división
problem	problema

See **English-Spanish Glossary** pages 628–646.

 Education Place Visit www.eduplace.com/camap/ for the **eGlossary** and **eGames**.

CA Standards
Prepares for NS 2.5
Solve division problems in which a multidigit number is evenly divided by a one-digit number (135 ÷ 5 = ___).

NS 2.0 Students calculate and solve problems involving addition, subtraction, multiplication, and division.

Also MR 2.2, MR 2.3, MR 2.4

Materials
- Counters
- Learning Tool 34 (Recording Sheet) (optional)
- eManipulatives www.eduplace.com/camap/ (optional)

Hands On
Equal Groups

Objective Use models to solve division problems that have some left over.

▶ **Explore**

You already know how to divide small numbers. Before you can divide greater numbers, it is important to know what to do when you divide and there are some left over.

At a book sale, 4 friends buy a box of 25 books. Each person wants the same number of books. What is the greatest number of books each person can take?

Question How can you use counters to model division with some left over?

Divide 25 counters into 4 equal groups. Put any leftover counters aside.

●●● ●●● ●●● ●●●
●●● ●●● ●●● ●●● ●

- There are 6 counters in each group.
- There is 1 counter left over.

Solution: Each person can have 6 books. There will be 1 book left over.

What if the 25 books were divided equally among 7 people?
What is the greatest number of books each person could take?

Divide 25 counters into 7 equal groups.
Put any leftover counters aside.

- How many counters are in each group?
- How many counters are left over?

▶ **Extend**

Use counters to complete the table.

	Division	Number (dividend)	Number of Equal Groups (divisor)	Number in Each Group (quotient)	Number Left Over
	4)25	25	4	6	1
1.	3)14				
2.	2)9				
3.	5)32				
4.	8)36				
5.	6)35				
6.	9)43				
7.	4)10				
8.	7)17				
9.	3)21				
10.	5)28				
11.	2)11				
12.	5)57				

13. Analyze Is the number left over always less than, equal to, or greater than the divisor?

Writing Math

Right or Wrong? Diane says that $16 \div 5 = 2$ with 6 left over. Is Diane right or wrong? Explain.

CA Standards
Prepares for NS 2.5
Solve division problems in which
a multidigit number is evenly
divided by a one-digit number
(135 ÷ 5 = ___).

NS 2.0 Students calculate and
solve problems involving addition,
subtraction, multiplication, and
division.

**Also MR 2.3, MR 3.0,
MR 3.1, MR 3.2**

Materials
• Counters
• Learning Tool 35 (Recording
  Sheet) (optional)
• eManipulatives
  www.eduplace.com/camap/
  (optional)

Hands On
Repeated Subtraction

Objective Use repeated subtraction to solve division
problems with some left over.

▶ **Learn With Manipulatives**

In this lesson, you will use
repeated subtraction to divide.

Nineteen police officers
are divided into groups
of 3. What is the greatest
number of groups that
can be made? How
many officers will
be left over?

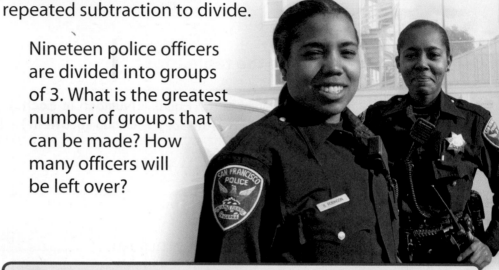

1 Use 19 counters. Remove
3 counters at a time until
you cannot remove a full
group of 3.

2 Record the subtraction.
Count how many groups
of 3 you removed.

• How many groups of
  3 counters did you
  remove?

• How many counters are
  left over?

	groups
19	
− 3 ⟶	1
16	
− 3 ⟶	2
13	
− 3 ⟶	3
10	
− 3 ⟶	4
7	
− 3 ⟶	5
4	
− 3 ⟶	6
1 ⟶	left over

Solution: Six groups can be made. There will be
1 officer left over.

▶ Guided Practice

Use counters and repeated subtraction to complete the table.

Ask Yourself
- How many counters are in each group?
- How many groups are there?
- How many counters are left over?

	Division	Number (dividend)	Number in Each Group (divisor)	Number of Equal Groups (quotient)	Number Left Over
1.	4)14				
2.	2)7				
3.	5)28				
4.	7)37				
5.	8)19				
6.	6)21				

Guided Problem Solving

Use the questions to solve this problem.

7. There are 30 officers in a parade. They ride in cars in groups of 4. The remaining officers ride on horseback. What is the greatest number of filled cars? How many officers are on horseback?

   a. Understand What are you asked to find?

   b. Plan What operation can you use to solve the problem?

   c. Solve Use the operation to solve.

     There are ◯ filled cars.

     There are ◯ officers on horseback.

   d. Look Back Does your answer make sense?

 Math Talk Look back at Problem 7. How did you know when you had the answer?

Practice and Problem Solving

Use counters and repeated subtraction to complete the table.

	Division	Number (dividend)	Number in Each Group (divisor)	Number of Equal Groups (quotient)	Number Left Over
8.	3)‾1‾1‾				
9.	2)‾1‾3‾				
10.	6)‾3‾2‾				
11.	8)‾3‾2‾				
12.	4)‾3‾5‾				

 History-Social Science Link

Solve.

13. Sean is a volunteer computer teacher. There are 26 people in his class. He divides them in as many groups of 4 as possible. The remaining people are in a smaller group. How many groups of 4 are there? How many people are in the smaller group?

14. Claire, an artist, volunteers at a senior center. One day, 36 seniors want to paint. If 6 people sit at each table, how many tables will they need?

Citizenship

Good citizens are people who do things to help make their community a better place.

History-Social Science 3.4.2

 Spiral Review and Test Practice

Find the product. KEY **NS 3.3** page 456

15. $3.35 × 2   **16.** $3.18 × 3   **17.** $2.83 × 4   **18.** $7.29 × 8

Write the letter of the correct answer. Prepares for NS 2.5

19. Jack has 27 muffins. He will give 8 to each of his 3 friends. How many muffins will be left?

   A 1   **B** 2   **C** 3   **D** 4

Extra Practice See page 537, Set A.

Key Standards Review

Need Help?
See Key Standards Handbook.

Write the letter of the expression, equation, or inequality that matches the statement. **KEY AF 1.1**

1. 12 plus a number is greater than 20.

2. A number is five times 15.

3. 20 is greater than a number plus 12.

4. The difference of 15 and 12 is greater than a number multiplied by zero.

5. Ten more than a number is equal to the sum of 15 and 12.

A ■ $= 5 \times 15$

B $20 >$ ■ $+ 12$

C $12 +$ ■ > 20

D $15 - 12 >$ ■ $\times 0$

E $10 +$ ■ $= 15 + 12$

Find the missing factor. **KEY NS 2.2**

6. $9 \times$ ■ $= 72$
7. ■ $\times 7 = 28$
8. $8 \times$ ■ $= 24$
9. ■ $\times 6 = 54$

10. $4 \times$ ■ $= 24$
11. ■ $\times 5 = 35$
12. $6 \times$ ■ $= 42$
13. ■ $\times 6 = 48$

14. $8 \times$ ■ $= 56$
15. ■ $\times 4 = 32$
16. $4 \times$ ■ $= 36$
17. ■ $\times 9 = 81$

Number Sense

Perimeter and Area Clues

Solve. Explain how you decided. NS 2.5, KEY MG 1.3, KEY MG 2.1, KEY MG 2.3

1. Harish says, "My polygon has a perimeter of 36 inches. All the sides are equal." What could his polygon be?

2. Mira says, "My polygon has an area of 24 square centimeters. It has opposite sides that are parallel. All the angles are right angles." What could her polygon be?

CA Standards

KEY **NS 2.3** Use the inverse relationship of multiplication and division to compute and check results.

Prepares for NS 2.5 Solve division problems in which a multidigit number is evenly divided by a one-digit number ($135 \div 5 = $ ___).

Also NS 2.0, NS 2.8, AF 1.5, MG 1.4, MR 1.2, MR 2.0, MR 2.3, MR 2.4

Materials
Learning Tool 36
(Recording Sheet)

Use Multiples

Objective Use multiplication facts to solve division problems with some left over.

▶ Learn by Example

In this lesson, you will use multiplication facts to solve division problems with some left over.

> The school band is getting ready to march in a parade. There will be 8 band members in each row. There are 35 members.

> What is the greatest number of full rows that can be made? How many band members will not be in a full row of 8?

① Find the number of groups of 8 in 35.

Think about multiplication facts for 8 or think about multiples of 8.

multiples of 8.

$1 \times 8 = 8$

$2 \times 8 = 16$

$3 \times 8 = 24$

$4 \times 8 = 32$ ← There are 4 groups of 8 in 35.

$5 \times 8 = 40$ ← There are *not* 5 groups of 8 in 35.

② Find how many are left over.

$35 - 32 = 3$.

There are 3 left over.

Solution: There can be 4 full rows.
Three band members will not be in a full row.

The University of California Marching Band

Complete the table.

	Division	What multiplication fact can you use?	Number of Equal Groups	Number Left Over
1.	3)19	6 × 3 = 18	6	1
2.	2)15			
3.	4)17			
4.	5)29			

(123) Math Talk How does knowing 2 × 7 = 14 help you solve 15 ÷ 7?

▶ **Practice and Problem Solving**

Complete the table.

	Division	What multiplication fact can you use?	Number of Equal Groups	Number Left Over
5.	7)29			
6.	9)41			
7.	6)29			
8.	5)12			
9.	2)17			
10.	3)23			
11.	4)21			
12.	8)19			
13.	6)7			
14.	3)10			
15.	5)11			

Solve.

16. Leon has 29 flags. He wants to put 3 flags on each float in a parade. What is the greatest number of floats he can decorate?

Science Link

Use the fun facts to solve Problems 17–19.

17. Campers tie their food to a branch that is 72 inches high. Is the food safe from a brown bear? Explain.

18. Multistep A scientist counts the heartbeats of Lola, a hibernating bear. She counts 19 heartbeats in 3 minutes. Is Lola's heartbeat faster or slower than the typical heartbeat of a hibernating bear?

19. Challenge Ralph and Juan want to find the total number of times a brown bear's heart beats each day while awake.

- Ralph multiplies $(40 \times 60) \times 24$.

- Juan multiplies $40 \times (60 \times 24)$.

Will they get the same answer? Explain.

Brown Bears

- Brown bears can tower up to 8 feet tall when standing upright.

- When a brown bear is awake, its heart beats about 40 times per minute.

- Bears hibernate spending the winter in a deep sleep. During hibernation, a bear's heart usually beats about 8 times per minute.

Science LS 3.a

Hint

Think about the properties of multiplication.

Spiral Review and Test Practice

Write whether the event is *certain, likely, unlikely,* or *impossible*. SDAP 1.1 page 498

20. Pick any pair of one-digit numbers and their sum is 13.

21. A dog will speak English.

Choose the letter of the correct answer. NS 2.5

22. Jeremy has 39 cards. He will give 7 to each of his 5 friends. How many cards will be left?

    A 1   **B** 2   **C** 3   **D** 4

Extra Practice See page 537, Set B.

Left Over Race

Object of the Game Practice division by playing this game with a partner. Try to be the first person to score 30 points.

Materials
- a number cube labeled 1 to 6
- Learning Tool 78
  (*Left Over Race* Game Board)

Number of Players 2

How to Play

1 The first player rolls the number cube. He or she then writes the number rolled in any empty ☐ on the game board.

2 The first player then names the quotient and number left over for that problem. The other player checks that the quotient and number left over are correct.

3 The number left over is the number of points scored. If there is no left-over, the player scores 10 points.

4 Players take turns, repeating Steps 1–3. The first player to reach a total of 30 points wins.

Share Your Thinking

What is the best strategy for placing a number?

CA Standards
Prepares for NS 2.5 Solve division problems in which a multidigit number is evenly divided by a one-digit number $(135 \div 5 = \underline{\hspace{1cm}})$.

Also MR 2.0

Education Place
Visit www.eduplace.com/camap/ for
Brain Teasers and **eGames** to play.

CA Standards

MR 2.4 Express the solution clearly and logically by using the appropriate mathematical notation and terms and clear language; support solutions with evidence in both verbal and symbolic work.

NS 2.7 Determine the unit cost when given the total cost and number of units.

Also **NS 2.0**, **NS 2.8**, KEY **AF 2.1**, **MR 1.0**, **MR 1.1**, **MR 1.2**, **MR 2.0**, **MR 2.3**, **MR 2.6**, **MR 3.1**, **MR 3.2**

Problem Solving Plan
Total Cost and Unit Cost

Objective Use total cost and unit cost to solve problems.

▶ **Learn Through Reasoning**

Total cost is the sum of prices for a set of items. When all the items are the same price, the cost of 1 item is the unit cost.

Find Total Cost

Mr. Mendez planted 5 plants in his backyard. Each plant cost $4. What was the total cost of the plants?

$$5 \quad \times \quad \$4 \quad = \quad \bigcirc$$

Number of items   Unit cost   Total cost

$5 \times \$4 = \$20$

The total cost of the plants was $20.

Find Unit Cost

Maria bought 6 calla lily plants for the town garden. All the plants were the same price. The total cost was $18. What was the unit cost of a calla lily plant?

$$\$18 \quad \div \quad 6 \quad = \quad \bigcirc$$

Total cost   Number of items   Unit cost

$\$18 \div 6 = \$3$

The unit cost of a calla lily plant was $3.

▶ Guided Problem Solving

Solve using the Ask Yourself questions.

1. Billy bought 4 flower pots. All the flower pots were the same price. The total cost was $32. How much did each flower pot cost?

   123 Math Talk Look back at Problem 1. Tell the total cost, the unit cost, and the number of items.

> **Ask Yourself**
> • Do I need to find the total cost or the unit cost?
> • Is my answer reasonable?

▶ Independent Problem Solving

Solve. Explain why your answer makes sense.

2. Megan bought 5 hoses to water the garden. All the hoses were the same price. The total cost was $45. How much money did each hose cost?

3. The total cost for 4 tomato plants is $24. Each plant is the same price. What is the unit cost?

4. One watering can costs $7. Two watering cans cost $14. Three watering cans cost $21. If the cost of each watering can remains the same, how much would 4 watering cans cost?

5. **Multistep** The total cost for 8 tulip bulbs is $16. Each tulip bulb is the same price. What is the cost of 5 tulip bulbs?

Use the price list for Problem 6.

6. **Challenge** Alonzo needs to buy mulch for his garden. There are 3 different brands to choose from. What brand is the least expensive?

7. **Create and Solve** Write a word problem that includes finding a unit cost.

MULCH
FOR SALE!
★
Brand A 3 bags for $15
Brand B 8 bags for $24
Brand C 5 bags for $20

Vocabulary

Sometimes when you **divide** whole numbers there are some **left over**.

Mrs. Ruiz reads her daughter Sarah 5 pages of a 32-page book each night. How long will it take to finish the book?

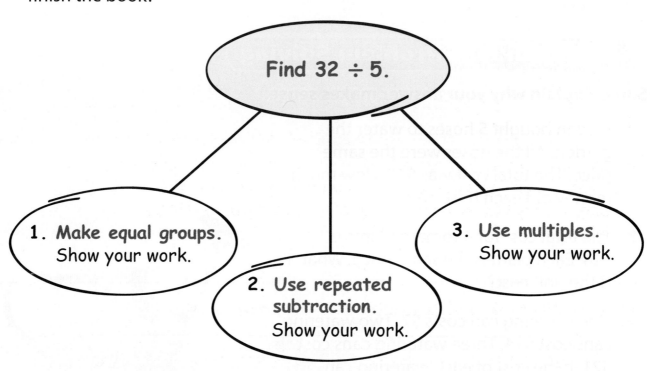

Find 32 ÷ 5.

1. **Make equal groups.** Show your work.

2. **Use repeated subtraction.** Show your work.

3. **Use multiples.** Show your work.

It will take 7 days to read the book. After _____ days 30 pages are read. There are _____ pages left over. These pages are read on the 7th day.

Writing
Sarah's mom says the book will take 5 nights to finish if she reads 7 pages each night. Is she right? Explain your answer.

Reading
Look for this book in your library.

• *Math Curse*, by Jon Scieszka

CA Standards
MR 2.3 Use a variety of methods, such as words, numbers, symbols, charts, graphs, tables, diagrams, and models, to explain mathematical reasoning.
Also Prepares for NS 2.5

Standards-Based Extra Practice

Set A ────────────────────────────────── NS 2.0 page 526

Copy and complete the table.

	Division	Number (dividend)	Number of Equal Groups (divisor)	Number in Each Group (quotient)	Number Left Over
1.	5)23̄				
2.	10)34̄				
3.	6)35̄				
4.	3)17̄				
5.	7)27̄				

6. Mrs. Cooley has 38 bags of clay to share among 7 students. Each student gets the same amount of clay. How many bags of clay will each student get? How many bags will be left over?

Set B ────────────────────────────────── KEY NS 2.3 page 530

Complete the table. Relate multiplication and division.

	Division	What multiplication fact can you use?	Number of Equal Groups	Number Left Over
1.	6)13̄			
2.	5)22̄			
3.	8)29̄			
4.	9)33̄			
5.	5)44̄			

6. 24 students want to make 6 game booths for the school carnival. How many students can work at each booth if the same number of students are at each booth? Show how to check your answer.

Education Place
Visit www.eduplace.com/camap/
for more **Extra Practice.**

Chapter 24 Extra Practice   **537**

Chapter Review/Test

Skills KEY **NS 2.3**, Prepares for NS 2.5

Copy and complete the table.

	Division	Number (dividend)	Number of Equal Groups (divisor)	Number in Each Group (quotient)	Number Left Over
1.	2)7̄				
2.	5)29̄				
3.	8)22̄				
4.	3)14̄				

Copy and complete the table.

	Division	What multiplication fact can you use?	Number of Equal Groups	Number Left Over
5.	4)34̄			
6.	7)33̄			
7.	2)23̄			
8.	5)38̄			

Problem Solving and Reasoning NS 2.0, MR 2.3, MR 2.6, Prepares for NS 2.5

Solve.

9. Mary wants to plant 3 rows of flowers in her garden. She has 20 packets of seeds. If she uses the same number of packets for each row, how many packets will she need for each row? Will she have any packets left over?

10. Adela made 35 sandwiches for a picnic. She put the same number of sandwiches in each of 7 baskets. How many sandwiches were in each basket? Are you finding equal groups or unequal groups? Explain.

Writing Math Meghan says that 17 ÷ 4 is 3 with 5 left over. Is she correct? Explain.

Spiral Review and Test Practice

1. Which of these is a pentagon?

A

C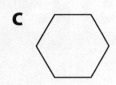

B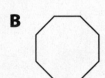

D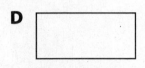

KEY MG 2.1 page 192

2. A carpenter cut a board into 8 equal pieces. She used $\frac{1}{8}$ of the pieces for the base of a birdhouse. She used $\frac{2}{8}$ of the pieces for the roof of the birdhouse. She used $\frac{4}{8}$ for the sides of the birdhouse. What fraction of the board was left?

A $\frac{1}{8}$ **C** $\frac{3}{8}$

B $\frac{5}{8}$ **D** $\frac{7}{8}$

KEY NS 3.2 page 354

3. The population of a town was 1146 twenty years ago. Now the population is 5 times that number. What is the population now?

A 5500   **C** 5530

B 5720   **D** 5730

KEY NS 2.4 page 454

4. Al picked cubes from a bag. He picked a black cube 7 times, a red cube 4 times, and a yellow cube 5 times. Which chart shows these results?

A

Cube Results	
Black	||||| ||
Red	|||||
Yellow	||||

B

Cube Results	
Black	||||| ||
Red	||||
Yellow	|||||

C

Cube Results	
Black	||||
Red	||||| ||
Yellow	|||||

D

Cube Results	
Black	|||||	
Red	|||||
Yellow	|||||

Test Tip

Do the results match the problem?

KEY SDAP 1.2 page 496

Education Place
Visit www.eduplace.com/camap/ for
Test-Taking Tips and **Extra Practice**.

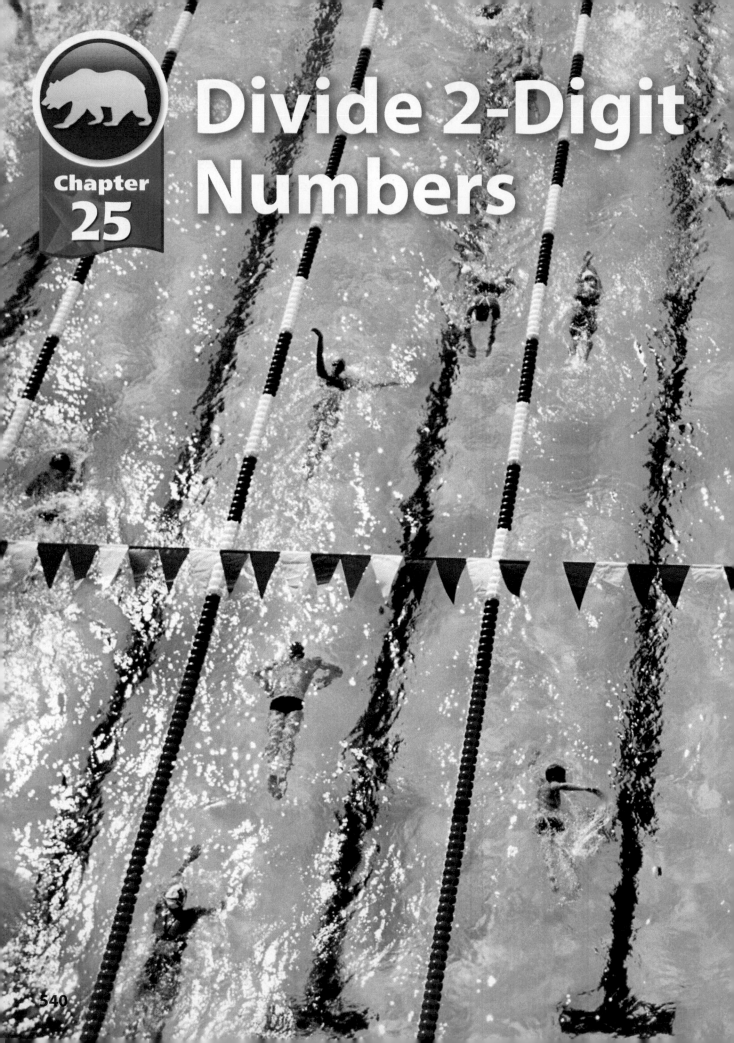

Divide 2-Digit Numbers

Chapter
25

Vocabulary and Concepts NS 2.0, MR 2.3 pages 262, 286
Choose the best term to complete each sentence.

1. In the division sentence $18 \div 6 = 3$, the 18 is the _____.

2. $3 \times 5 = 15$, and $15 \div 3 = 5$ are in the same _____.

3. In the number sentence $18 \div 6 = 3$, the _____ is 6.

Skills NS 2.0, KEY NS 2.3
Write the fact families. page 286

4. 3, 5, 15

5. 7, 49

6. 5, 9, 45

Divide. page 260

7. $4\overline{)24}$

8. $9\overline{)63}$

9. $4\overline{)28}$

Problem Solving and Reasoning NS 2.0

10. The 24 students in Pete's class are going on a field trip. They will ride in vans that carry 6 students each. How many vans will they need?

Vocabulary

Visualize It!

If you put 78 pencils into 6 equal groups, how many pencils will be in each group?

You can **divide** to find the answer. When you divide, you separate an amount into smaller equal groups.

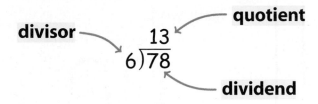

divisor — quotient

13
6)78

dividend

Language Tip

Some words are similar in Spanish and English.

English	Spanish
dividend	dividendo
quotient	cociente
divisor	divisor
divide	dividir

See **English-Spanish Glossary** pages 628–646.

Education Place Visit www.eduplace.com/camap/ for the **eGlossary** and **eGames**.

CA Standards MR 2.3 Use a variety of methods, such as words, numbers, symbols, charts, graphs, tables, diagrams, and models, to explain mathematical reasoning. **Also NS 2.5**

Chapter 25   541

CA Standards

NS 2.5 Solve division problems in which a multidigit number is evenly divided by a one-digit number (135 ÷ 5 = ___).
Also NS 2.0, MR 2.2, MR 2.3, MR 2.4

Materials
- Base-ten blocks
- Learning Tool 37 (Recording Sheet)
- Workmat 1
- eManipulatives (optional) www.eduplace.com/camap/

Hands On
Divide 2-Digit Numbers

Objective Model division of 2-digit numbers.

▶ **Explore**

You can use what you know about division facts to help you divide a 2-digit number by a 1-digit number.

Question How can you use base-ten blocks to divide 2-digit numbers?

For practice, 46 runners divide into 2 equal groups. How many runners are in each group?

$46 \div 2 = \bigcirc$

1 Use base-ten blocks to show 46.

2 Divide the tens blocks into 2 groups. Your groups must be
- equal in size.
- as large as possible.

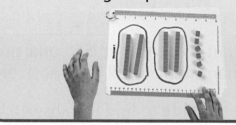

3 Divide the ones blocks into 2 equal groups. Put 3 in each group.

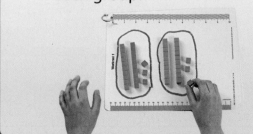

4 Draw a quick picture to show your work.

Solution: There are 23 runners in each group.

What if 39 runners divided into 3 equal groups?
How many runners would be in each group?

1 Use base-ten blocks to show 39.

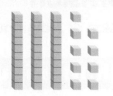

2 Divide the tens blocks into 3 equal groups. Your groups must be equal in size and as large as possible.

3 Divide the ones blocks into 3 equal groups. How many ones are in each group?

4 Draw a quick picture to show your work.

▶ **Extend**

Use blocks to complete the table.
Draw quick pictures to show your work.

	Number	Number of Equal Groups	Number in Each Group	Show the Division
1.	28	2	14	28 ÷ 2 = 14
2.	40	4		
3.	55	5		
4.	69	3		
5.	48	4		
6.	93	3		
7.	68	2		
8.	99	9		
9.	80		10	
10.	42		21	

Writing Math

Explain How can you use division facts to help you divide 84 by 2?

CA Standards

NS 2.5 Solve division problems in which a multidigit number is evenly divided by a one-digit number (135 ÷ 5 = ___).

MR 2.3 Use a variety of methods, such as words, numbers, symbols, charts, graphs, tables, diagrams, and models, to explain mathematical reasoning.

Also NS 2.0, NS 2.8, KEY AF 1.1, MR 1.2, MR 2.4, MR 3.0, MR 3.2, MR 3.3

Vocabulary

regroup

Materials
• Base-ten blocks
• Workmat 1
• eManipulatives (optional) www.eduplace.com/camap/

Think

You can show your work with a quick picture.

Hands On
Regroup in Division

Objective Model division of 2-digit numbers with regrouping.

▶ 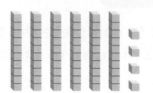 **Learn With Manipulatives**

Mr. Vega collects baseballs. He wants to divide 64 baseballs equally among his 4 children. How many baseballs will each child get?

$64 \div 4 = \bigcirc$

---

1 Use base-ten blocks to show 64.

2 Divide the 6 tens blocks into 4 equal groups.

3 **Regroup** the 2 left-over tens as 20 ones.
20 ones + 4 ones = 24 ones

4 Divide the 24 ones into 4 equal groups.

Solution: Each child gets 16 baseballs.

▶ Guided Practice

Divide. Use blocks to help you.
Draw a quick picture to show your work.

Ask Yourself
• Are any tens left over?
• Did I regroup the left-over tens as ones?

1. $57 \div 3$ **2.** $75 \div 5$ **3.** $58 \div 2$

4. $68 \div 4$ **5.** $84 \div 7$ **6.** $84 \div 6$

Guided Problem Solving

Use the questions to solve this problem.

7. One van can take 7 players from the school to the training center. There are 84 players. How many vans do they need?

a. **Understand** What do you know?

b. **Plan** Which operation should you use? Write a number sentence.

c. **Solve** Use base-ten blocks to help divide.

They need ◯ vans.

d. **Look Back** How can you use multiplication to check your answer?

8. Look back at Problem 7. How many vans would 91 players need?

(123) Math Talk How do you know when you need to regroup tens as ones when dividing greater numbers?

▶ Practice and Problem Solving

Divide. Use blocks to help you. Draw a quick picture to show your work.

9. $52 \div 2$ **10.** $56 \div 4$ **11.** $65 \div 5$ **12.** $51 \div 3$ **13.** $90 \div 6$

14. $85 \div 5$ **15.** $78 \div 6$ **16.** $48 \div 3$ **17.** $91 \div 7$ **18.** $92 \div 4$

Solve.

19. **Challenge** Sara baked 4 dozen muffins. She gave 3 to her grandmother. She wants to divide the rest equally among her 3 teammates. How many muffins will each teammate get?

 Science Link

Solve.

20. There are 70 calories in 2 ounces of canned tuna. How many calories are in each ounce?

21. There are 75 calories in an egg. How many calories are there in 2 eggs?

22. An ounce of roast beef has 55 calories. How many calories are there in 3 ounces?

Calories

- Chemical energy is energy stored in food, gasoline, and batteries.
- The energy we get from food is measured in calories.
- Calories give us the energy to move, stretch, and grow.
- Different foods store different amounts of energy.

Science PS 1.b

 Spiral Review and Test Practice

For a probability experiment, Sally tossed a coin and recorded heads or tails. Use her pictograph for Problems 23–25. KEY SDAP 1.3 page 496

23. How many times did the coin land on heads?

24. How many times did the coin land on tails?

25. How many times did Sally toss the coin?

Coin Toss Experiment	
Heads	🪙 🪙 🪙 🪙 🪙 🪙
Tails	🪙 🪙 🪙 🪙 🪙 🪙 🪙
Key: Each 🪙 = 2 tosses.	

Write the letter of the correct answer. NS 2.5

26. For dance practice, 72 students were divided equally into 3 different groups. How many students were in each group?

   A 23   **B** 24   **C** 25   **D** 26

Extra Practice See page 555, Set A.

Key Standards Review

Need Help?
See Key Standards Handbook.

The table shows the number of people at a pool during 5 days. Copy and complete the bar graph, using the data in the table. **Prepares for KEY SDAP 1.3**

1. How many bars does your graph have? Explain.

2. What scale did you choose?

3. How did you choose your scale?

4. Write a question about the data that you can answer using subtraction.

People at the Pool	
Day	Number
Monday	18
Tuesday	12
Wednesday	20
Thursday	15
Friday	22

People at the Pool

Monday

Tuesday

Wednesday

Thursday

Friday

Number

Geometry

Changing Shapes   KEY MG 2.1, KEY MG 1.3

A string is shaped into an octagon with sides of equal length. Each side of the octagon is 12 cm long. If the string is reshaped into a hexagon with sides of equal length, how long will each side be? Explain how you decided.

12 cm

CA Standards
NS 2.5 Solve division problems in which a multidigit number is evenly divided by a one-digit number (135 ÷ 5 = ___).

KEY NS 2.3 Use the inverse relationship of multiplication and division to compute and check results.

Also NS 2.0, NS 2.8, AF 1.3, KEY MG 1.3, KEY MG 2.2, KEY MG 2.3, MR 1.2, MR 2.3, MR 2.4

Divide 2-Digit Numbers

Objective Divide 2-digit numbers and check the quotients using multiplication.

▶ Learn by Example

Mina scored 78 points in all during 3 basketball games. If she scored the same number of points in each game, how many points did she score in the first game?

$$3\overline{)78}$$

Example 1

1 Divide 7 tens into 3 groups.

There are 2 tens in each group. There is 1 ten left over.

> Write 2 in the tens place.

$$
\begin{array}{r}
2 \\
3\overline{)78} \\
-6 \\
\hline
1
\end{array}
$$

> Multiply. 3 × 2 tens = 6 tens

Subtract. 7 − 6 = 1
Compare. 1 < 3

2 Regroup.

10 ones + 8 ones = 18 ones

$$
\begin{array}{r}
2 \\
3\overline{)78} \\
-6 \\
\hline
18
\end{array}
$$

> Bring down 8 ones.

3 Divide the 18 ones into 3 groups.

There are 6 ones in each group.

> Write 6 in the ones place.

$$
\begin{array}{r}
26 \\
3\overline{)78} \\
-6 \\
\hline
18 \\
-18 \\
\hline
0
\end{array}
$$

> Multiply. 3 × 6 ones = 18 ones

Subtract. 18 − 18 = 0
Compare. 0 < 3

Check

Multiply the quotient by the divisor.

$$
\begin{array}{r}
26 \\
\times 3 \\
\hline
78
\end{array}
$$

Solution: Mina scored 26 points in the first game.

Lisa Leslie of the Los Angeles Sparks

Other Examples

A
```
     34
  2)68
  - 6
    08  ← Sometimes there are
  - 08    no tens to regroup.
     0
```

B
```
     35
  2)70  ← Even though there is a zero
  - 6     here, remember to divide
    10    the tens that you regroup.
  - 10
     0
```

► Guided Practice

Find the quotient. Multiply to check your work.

1. 3)66

2. 2)38

3. 4)84

4. 46 ÷ 2

5. 68 ÷ 4

6. 70 ÷ 5

(123) Math Talk If you divide 32 by 2, do you have to regroup the tens? Explain how you know.

Ask Yourself
• When I divide the tens are there any tens left over?
• Do I need to regroup?

► Practice and Problem Solving

Find the quotient. Multiply to check your work.

7. 2)32

8. 5)50

9. 4)76

10. 8)96

11. 6)90

12. 2)48

13. 3)36

14. 6)78

15. 3)51

16. 8)88

17. 4)92

18. 3)39

19. 99 ÷ 9

20. 84 ÷ 7

21. 95 ÷ 5

22. 96 ÷ 8

23. 84 ÷ 4

24. 98 ÷ 7

25. 64 ÷ 2

26. 57 ÷ 3

𝑥 Algebra Equations

What sign makes the number sentence true?
Write +, −, ×, or ÷ for the ⬮.

27. 48 ⬮ 3 = 16

28. 24 ⬮ 4 = 96

29. 57 ⬮ 19 = 38

30. 1 ⬮ 45 = 45

31. 99 ⬮ 58 = 157

32. 72 ⬮ 9 = 8

Solve.

33. Kayla is a long distance runner. She runs 60 miles over 5 days. She runs the same distance each day. How far does she run each day?

34. **Multistep** In 3 days, Jay bikes 93 miles and runs 21 miles. He bikes the same distance each day and runs the same distance each day. How many more miles does he bike than run each day?

 Real World Data

The table shows the lengths of yarn Jocelyn has. Use the table for Problems 35–37.

Yarn Color	Length
Red	18 inches
Blue	24 inches
Green	36 inches

35. Jocelyn uses the blue yarn to make a square. What is the length of each side of the square?

36. Jocelyn uses the red yarn to make an equilateral triangle. What is the length of each side of the triangle?

37. **Challenge** Jocelyn uses the green yarn to make an isosceles triangle. Draw 2 different triangles Jocelyn could make and label the length of each side.

Think

• An isosceles triangle has 2 sides of equal length.

• An equilateral triangle has 3 sides of equal length.

 Spiral Review and Test Practice

Find the difference. KEY **NS 2.1** page 80

38.
$$\begin{array}{r} 500 \\ -\ 269 \end{array}$$

39.
$$\begin{array}{r} 3,014 \\ -\ 1,432 \end{array}$$

40.
$$\begin{array}{r} 7,709 \\ -\ 5,630 \end{array}$$

41.
$$\begin{array}{r} 803 \\ -\ 415 \end{array}$$

Write the letter of the correct answer. KEY **NS 2.3**

42. Sandra did this division problem: $425 \div 25 = 17$
Which equation could she use to check her answer?

A $25 + 17 = $

C $25 \times 17 = $

B $25 - 17 = $

D $25 \div 17 = $

Extra Practice See page 555, Set B.

Divisor Puzzle

Find three different paths to get to 60.

- Each path starts at a corner of the big triangle.
- Use the corner number as a divisor.
- Cross only sides of small triangles.
- Move to the next triangle only if its number can be divided by your divisor with none left over.

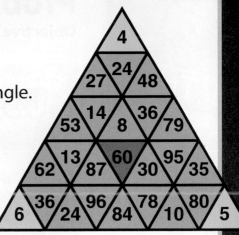

How are all of the divisors and the number 60 related?

Make your own Divisor Puzzle.

- Trace the triangle below. Record the start and end number .
- Make a path of numbers from 3 to 54. The numbers should be able to be divided by 3 with no left overs.
- Fill in the remaining triangles with numbers that cannot be divided evenly by 3.
- Trade puzzles with a friend. Find the path in your friend's puzzle.

CA Standards
NS 2.0, NS 2.5

Field Trip...

Chula Vista, CA

CA Standards
MR 1.0, MR 1.1,
MR 2.0, MR 2.1,
MR 2.2, MR 2.4,
NS 2.0, KEY NS 2.4,
KEY AF 1.1

Problem Solving
Objective Use skills and strategies to solve word problems.

U.S. OLYMPIC TRAINING CENTER

About 4,000 athletes train at the U.S. Olympic Training Center each year.

The Olympic Training Center in Chula Vista is a great place to watch Olympic athletes train.

Solve. Tell which strategy or method you used.

1. **Draw a Picture** Suppose 8 athletes tried out for the cycling team. If $\frac{1}{4}$ of them made the team, how many athletes made the team?

2. Suppose 96 athletes tried out for the cycling team. If $\frac{1}{4}$ of them made the team, how many athletes made the team?

3. **Explain** In the 2006 Winter Games, the torch relay lasted for 64 days. Is this more or less than 9 weeks?

4. Four buses arrive at the training center. There are 22 athletes in each bus.

    a. Write and solve an equation to show how many athletes there are in all.

    b. Use estimation to check if your answer is reasonable.

Hint
Look back at Problem 1. Use your picture to decide how to solve Problem 2.

Problem Solving On Tests

Select a Strategy
- Draw a Picture
- Guess and Check
- Choose the Operation
- Estimate

1. Ellis wrote these four descriptions of quadrilaterals. Which is true for a rectangle?

A Only two angles are right angles.

B There are no right angles.

C Each side has a different length.

D Opposite sides are parallel.

> **Test Tip**
> Draw a picture of the figure. Check each answer choice against your figure.

KEY **MG 2.3** page 200

2. Julia put 12 beans in a bag. Seven of the beans are black, three of the beans are white, and 2 of the beans are speckled.

Julia closed her eyes and took out a bean. What word best describes the probability that she took out a white bean?

A certain   **C** unlikely

B likely   **D** impossible

SDAP 1.1 page 498

3. Jake recorded the results of spinning a spinner 25 times.

Spin Results	
Red	~~IIII~~ III
Yellow	~~IIII~~ ~~IIII~~
Blue	~~IIII~~ II

Which shows the spins recorded on the tally chart?

A 8 red, 2 yellow, 7 blue

B 5 red, 10 yellow, 5 blue

C 8 red, 10 yellow, 7 blue

D 3 red, 0 yellow, 2 blue

KEY **SDAP 1.2** page 474

4. Joe has 36 postcards. He can fit 4 postcards on each page of his scrapbook. How many pages of his scrapbook will be filled?

A 9   **B** 6   **C** 3   **D** 4

NS 2.0 page 548

Education Place
Visit www.eduplace.com/camap/ for **Test-Taking Tips** and **Extra Practice**.

Reading & Writing Math

Vocabulary

Sometimes you need to **regroup** tens as ones to divide.

The principal is ordering 84 erasers. The erasers come in packages of 6. How many packages should she buy?

Use base-ten blocks to show 84.

- Divide the tens blocks into 6 equal groups.
- Regroup any remaining tens blocks as ones.
- Divide the ones blocks.
- Record your answer.

Find 84 ÷ 6.

- Divide with numbers to solve the problem.
- Record your work.

$$6\overline{)84}$$

The principal should buy _____ packages of erasers.

Writing
Write and solve a word problem of your own for the number sentence 65 ÷ 5.

Reading
Check out this book in your library.

- *Math Man*, by Teri Daniels

> **CA Standards**
> **MR 2.3** Use a variety of methods, such as words, numbers, symbols, charts, graphs, tables, diagrams, and models, to explain mathematical reasoning.
> **Also NS 2.5**

Standards-Based Extra Practice

Set A —————————————————————————— NS 2.5, MR 2.3 page 544

Divide. Use blocks to help you.

1. 45 ÷ 5	**2.** 96 ÷ 2	**3.** 64 ÷ 4	**4.** 76 ÷ 4	**5.** 48 ÷ 4
6. 22 ÷ 2	**7.** 72 ÷ 3	**8.** 95 ÷ 5	**9.** 81 ÷ 3	**10.** 56 ÷ 4
11. 35 ÷ 5	**12.** 72 ÷ 4	**13.** 56 ÷ 8	**14.** 85 ÷ 5	**15.** 75 ÷ 3
16. 45 ÷ 3	**17.** 63 ÷ 3	**18.** 84 ÷ 7	**19.** 92 ÷ 2	**20.** 54 ÷ 2

21. The marching band lined up for the half-time performance. They were split into 5 equal groups. There were 95 members in the band. How many band members were in each group?

Set B —————————————————————————— NS 2.5, KEY NS 2.3, AF 1.3 page 548

Find the quotient. Multiply to check your work.

1. 3)‾96	**2.** 4)‾44	**3.** 2)‾24	**4.** 6)‾90	**5.** 3)‾39
6. 2)‾58	**7.** 7)‾98	**8.** 5)‾55	**9.** 4)‾84	**10.** 2)‾68
11. 45 ÷ 3	**12.** 72 ÷ 6	**13.** 84 ÷ 4	**14.** 96 ÷ 3	**15.** 33 ÷ 3

What sign makes the number sentence true?
Write +, −, ×, or ÷ for the ⬤.

16. 45 ⬤ 1 = 45   **17.** 27 ⬤ 16 = 43

18. 55 ⬤ 5 = 11   **19.** 13 ⬤ 4 = 52

20. 61 ⬤ 35 = 96   **21.** 32 ⬤ 2 = 64

22. 72 ⬤ 48 = 24   **23.** 85 ⬤ 5 = 17

24. Marie has 84 streamers for a party. She asked 3 friends to help decorate. She divided the streamers evenly. How many streamers did each person get?

Education Place
Visit www.eduplace.com/camap/
for more **Extra Practice**.

Chapter 25 Extra Practice   **555**

Chapter Review/Test

Vocabulary and Concepts ———————————————— NS 2.5

Choose the best word to complete each sentence.

1. The total being divided in a division problem is the _____.

2. The _____ is the answer to a division problem.

3. The number by which a number is being divided is called the _____.

> **Word Bank**
> dividend
> quotient
> divisor

Skills ————————————————— KEY (NS 2.3), NS 2.5, AF 1.3, MR 2.3

Divide. Show how to check your work.

4. $52 \div 2$

5. $2\overline{)86}$

6. $3\overline{)69}$

7. $56 \div 4$

What sign makes the equation true? Write $+$, $-$, $\times$, or $\div$ for the ⬭.

8. $84 \;⬭\; 6 = 14$

9. $43 \;⬭\; 27 = 16$

10. $54 \;⬭\; 21 = 75$

11. $31 \;⬭\; 4 = 124$

Problem Solving and Reasoning ——————— NS 2.0, NS 2.5, MR 2.3

Solve.

12. The art teacher had 54 pieces of chalk for her students to use. If she gave an equal number to each of 3 groups, how many pieces of chalk would each group have?

13. Shaun has 28 daisies. He wants to divide them equally between his mother and grandmother. How many flowers would each receive?

14. Each car on the mini train can hold 6 people. There are 87 people. How many cars are needed for the people?

15. Mrs. Black had 86 stickers. If she gave each of her students 4 stickers, how many does she have left?

Writing Math If you divide 36 by 2, do you have to regroup the tens? Explain.

Spiral Review and Test Practice

1. What number can be multiplied by 1346 to give the answer 1346?

$$1346 \times \square = 1346$$

A 0 **C** 1

B 2 **D** 1346

NS 2.6 page 122

---

2. For a contest, 64 dancers were divided equally into 4 different groups. How many dancers were in each group?

A 12 **C** 8

B 31 **D** 16

NS 2.5 page 544

---

3. A painting is shaped like a rectangle that is 6 feet long and 4 feet wide.

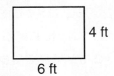

4 ft

6 ft

What is the perimeter of the painting?

A 10 feet **C** 16 feet

B 20 feet **D** 24 feet

KEY MG 1.3 page 214

4. Alex shaded $\frac{3}{10}$ of the figure.

Which decimal equals $\frac{3}{10}$?

A 0.03

B 0.3

C 0.10

D 3.0

> **Test Tip**
> The denominator, tenths, gives the name of the decimal place.

NS 3.4 page 368

---

5. Look at the four angles marked on the picture of a boat.

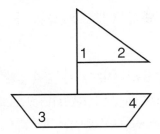

Which angle is greater than a right angle?

A angle 1

B angle 2

C angle 3

D angle 4

> **Test Tip**
> You can use a corner of a sheet of paper to check a right angle.

MG 2.4 page 190

Education Place
Visit www.eduplace.com/camap/ for
Test-Taking Tips and **Extra Practice**.

**Chapter
26**

Divide 3- and
4-Digit Numbers

The Golden Poppy is the official
state flower of California.

558

Vocabulary and Concepts NS 2.0, MR 2.3

Choose the best word to complete each sentence. page 262

1. You can use _____ to check a division problem.

2. The numbers 5, 10, and 15 are _____ of 5.

3. You can use _____ to check multiplication.

Skills NS 2.0, KEY NS 2.4

Find each product. page 428

4. 3×90

5. 5×42

6. 7×15

Find each quotient. page 260

7. $49 \div 7$

8. $24 \div 6$

9. $32 \div 4$

Problem Solving and Reasoning NS 2.0

10. Perry's collection has 64 model cars. He can fit 8 models in each box. How many boxes does he need?

Vocabulary

Visualize It !

You can use **multiplication** to check your answer to a **division** problem.

$$
\begin{array}{r}
15 \\
7\overline{)105} \\
-7 \\
\hline
35 \\
-35 \\
\hline
0
\end{array}
$$

Check

$$
\begin{array}{r}
15 \\
\times 7 \\
\hline
105
\end{array}
$$

You can multiply the quotient by the divisor to check your work.

Language Tip

Some words are similar in Spanish and English.

English	Spanish
multiplication	multiplicación
division	división

See **English-Spanish Glossary** pages 628–646.

Education Place Visit www.eduplace.com/camap/ for the **eGlossary** and **eGames**.

CA Standards MR 2.3 Use a variety of methods, such as words, numbers, symbols, charts, graphs, tables, diagrams, and models, to explain mathematical reasoning. **Also KEY NS 2.3**

Chapter 26   559

CA Standards

NS 2.5 Solve division problems in which a multidigit number is evenly divided by a one-digit number (135 ÷ 5 = ___).

MR 2.3 Use a variety of methods, such as words, numbers, symbols, charts, graphs, tables, diagrams, and models, to explain mathematical reasoning.

Also NS 2.0, KEY NS 2.3, **MR 2.4**

Materials

- Base-ten blocks
- Learning Tool 38 (Recording Sheet)
- eManipulatives (optional) www.eduplace.com/camap/

Hands On
Divide 3-Digit Numbers

Objective Model division of 3-digit numbers.

▶ **Explore**

Question How can you use base-ten blocks to divide 3-digit numbers?

Gina spent 2 days taking pictures of whales. She took 254 photos. If Gina took an equal number of photos each day, how many photos did she take each day?

254 ÷ 2 = ◯

1 Use base ten blocks to show 254.

2 Divide the hundreds blocks into 2 groups.

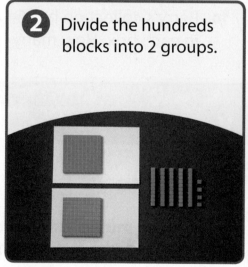

3 Divide the tens blocks into 2 equal groups. There are 2 tens in each group. There is 1 ten left over.

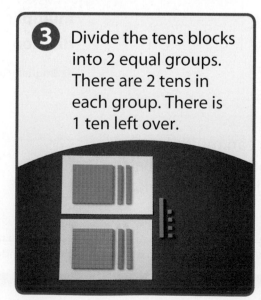

4 Regroup the 1 left-over ten as 10 ones.

10 ones + 4 ones = 14 ones

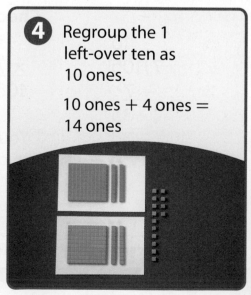

5 Divide the ones blocks into 2 equal groups.

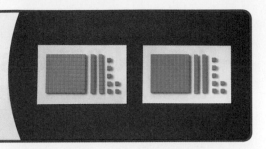

6 Draw a quick picture to show your work.

Solution: Gina took 127 photos each day.

 **Extend**

Use blocks to complete the table. Draw quick pictures to show your work.

	Number	Number of Equal Groups	Number in Each Group	Show the Division
1.	366	3	122	$366 \div 3 = 122$
2.	654	2		
3.	488	4		
4.	655	5		
5.	472	2		
6.	645	3		
7.	408		102	
8.	774		129	

9. Gina chose 242 of her whale photos to put in an album. If she puts 2 photos on each page, how many pages will she fill?

 Writing Math

Explain How can you use multiplication to check your answer to Exercise 2?

CA Standards
NS 2.5 Solve division problems in which a multidigit number is evenly divided by a one-digit number (135 ÷ 5 = ___).

MR 2.2 Apply strategies and results from simpler problems to more complex problems.

Also NS 2.0, KEY NS 2.3, NS 2.8, AF 1.0, AF 1.3, MR 1.2, MR 2.3

Divide 3- and 4-Digit Numbers

Objective Solve division problems with 3-digit and 4-digit dividends.

▶ **Learn by Example**

On Earth Day, 351 people helped clean up 3 parks. If they were divided equally, how many people helped clean each park?

Example 1

① Divide the hundreds.

$$\begin{array}{r} 1 \\ 3\overline{)351} \\ -\ 3 \\ \hline 0 \end{array}$$

Write 1 in the hundreds place.

Multiply. 3 × 1 hundred

Subtract. 3 − 3
Compare. 0 < 3

② Bring down the tens.

$$\begin{array}{r} 11 \\ 3\overline{)351} \\ -\ 3\downarrow \\ \hline 05 \\ -\ 3 \\ \hline 2 \end{array}$$

Write 1 in the tens place.

Bring down 5 tens.

Multiply. 3 × 1 ten

Subtract. 5 − 3
Compare. 2 < 3

③ Regroup leftover tens as ones.

$$\begin{array}{r} 11 \\ 3\overline{)351} \\ -\ 3 \\ \hline 05 \\ -\ 3 \\ \hline 21 \end{array}$$

Bring down 1 one. Regroup 2 tens 1 one as 21 ones.

④ Divide the ones.

$$\begin{array}{r} 117 \\ 3\overline{)351} \\ -\ 3 \\ \hline 05 \\ -\ 3 \\ \hline 21 \\ -\ 21 \\ \hline 0 \end{array}$$

Write 7 in the ones place.

Multiply. 3 × 7 ones

Subtract. 21 − 21
Compare. 0 < 3

Solution: 117 people helped clean each park.

Check

Multiply to check your work.

$$\begin{array}{r} 117 \\ \times\ 3 \\ \hline 351 \end{array}$$

Example 2

```
    3,368
2)6,736
  − 6↓
    0 7
    − 6↓
      1 3
    − 12↓
      16
    − 16
       0
```

The steps to divide are always the same no matter how large the dividend:

- Divide.
- Multiply.
- Subtract and compare.
- Bring down.

Check

```
    3,368
  ×     2
    6,736
```

▶ Guided Practice

Divide. Multiply to check.

1. 4)464

2. 3)852

3. 5)5,675

4. 856 ÷ 4

5. 794 ÷ 2

6. 8,748 ÷ 3

 Math Talk How is dividing a 2-digit number like dividing a 4-digit number? How is it different?

Ask Yourself

Do I need to regroup?

▶ Practice and Problem Solving

Divide. Multiply to check.

7. 5)595

8. 3)372

9. 3)642

10. 4)4,696

11. 648 ÷ 3

12. 837 ÷ 3

13. 8,748 ÷ 3

14. 5,476 ÷ 2

Solve.

15. There are 476 new recycling bins to be placed in 4 schools. Each school gets the same number of bins. How many bins will be placed in each school?

16. Challenge Three groups of students used 49 trash bags each. At the end of the day, 15 bags were left over. How many bags were there to start?

Algebra Equations

Find the sign that makes the equation true.
Write +, −, ×, or ÷ for the ▨.

17. 252 ▨ 2 = 126   **18.** 127 ▨ 3 = 381   **19.** 1,505 ▨ 938 = 567

20. 3,476 ▨ 1 = 3,476   **21.** 3,099 ▨ 1,457 = 4,556   **22.** 6,390 ▨ 5 = 1,278

 Science Link

Solve.

23. A coastal redwood tree is 370 feet tall. If Alex is 5 feet tall, how many times taller is the tree?

24. The distance around a Giant Sequoia trunk is 102 feet. If Mr. Wright spreads out his arms and measures from tip to tip, his armspan is 6 feet. How many of Mr. Wright's armspans are needed to circle around the tree's trunk?

Giant California Trees

- Redwood trees and Giant Sequoia trees are two of the world's largest trees.

- Redwood trees grow along the Pacific Coast where there is winter rain and summer fog. They need moisture all year.

- Giant Sequoias grow best on the west side of the Sierra Nevada where there are mild, wet winters and warm, dry summers.

General Sherman in Sequoia National Park

Science LS 3.b

Spiral Review and Test Practice

Multiply. KEY **NS 2.4** pages 450, 454

25.   327   **26.**   163   **27.**   237   **28.**   219
       × 3   × 5   × 4   × 6

Test Tip
You may be able to eliminate some choices because they are not reasonable.

Write the letter of the correct answer. NS 2.5

29. A farmer has 2434 apples to divide equally onto 2 trucks. How many apples will be on each truck?

   A 21   **B** 217   **C** 1217   **D** 1436

Extra Practice See page 575, Set A.

Key Standards Review

Need Help?
See Key Standards Handbook.

Use the spinner for Problems 1–5. KEY SDAP 1.2

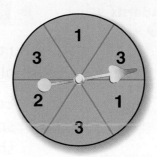

1. What are all the possible outcomes of spinning the spinner?

2. In 60 spins, which number is the spinner likely to land on *most* often? Why?

3. In 60 spins, which number is the spinner likely to land on *least* often? Why?

4. Is it *impossible*, *unlikely*, *likely*, or *certain* that the spinner will land on 4?

5. How would you change the spinner so it would be certain you would land on 2?

Number Sense

Division Wizard NS 2.5

You can use a simple rule to find out if 9 divides evenly into any number. Add the digits in the number. If you can divide that sum evenly by 9, then you can divide the number evenly by 9.

Use the numbers for Problems 1–2.

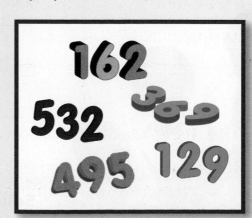

1. Which of these numbers are divisible by 9?

2. What number could you add to 129 to make it divisible by 9?

3. **True or false?** If 9 is a factor of a number, then 3 is also a factor of that number. Explain how you decided.

CA Standards

KEY NS 3.3 Solve problems involving addition, subtraction, multiplication, and division of money amounts in decimal notation and multiply and divide money amounts in decimal notation by using whole-number multipliers and divisors.

NS 2.7 Determine the unit cost when given the total cost and number of units.

Also NS 2.0, KEY NS 2.3, KEY AF 1.1, AF 1.2, MR 2.2, MR 2.3, MR 3.0, MR 3.3

Divide Money

Objective Divide amounts of money in decimal notation.

▶ **Learn by Example**

You can use what you know about dividing whole numbers to divide money amounts.

Ed, Bobby, Lori, and Joe have $5.88 to buy snacks at the Fall Festival. They want to share the money equally. How much will each friend receive?

$5.88 ÷ 4 = ◯

1 Divide the dollars.

$$\begin{array}{r} 1 \\ 4\overline{)\$5.88} \\ -\ 4 \\ \hline 1 \end{array}$$

Think: 1 × 4 dollars

2 Divide the dimes.

$$\begin{array}{r} 1\,4 \\ 4\overline{)\$5.88} \\ -\ 4 \\ \hline 1\,8 \\ -\ 1\,6 \\ \hline 2 \end{array}$$

Think: 4 × 4 dimes

3 Divide the pennies.

$$\begin{array}{r} 1\,4\,7 \\ 4\overline{)\$5.88} \\ -\ 4 \\ \hline 1\,8 \\ -\ 1\,6 \\ \hline 2\,8 \\ -\ 2\,8 \\ \hline 0 \end{array}$$

Think: 4 × 7 pennies

4 Write the dollar sign and the decimal point in the quotient.

$$\begin{array}{r} \$1.47 \\ 4\overline{)\$5.88} \end{array}$$

The decimal point separates the dollars and cents.

Check

Multiply to check your work.

$$\begin{array}{r} \$1.47 \\ \times\quad 4 \\ \hline \$5.88 \end{array}$$

Solution: Each friend will have $1.47 to spend.

Divide. Multiply to check.

1. $2\overline{)\$8.46}$ 2. $3\overline{)\$3.27}$ 3. $5\overline{)\$59.65}$

4. $\$10.26 \div 2$ 5. $\$6.81 \div 3$ 6. $\$9.56 \div 4$

Ask Yourself
· Do I need to regroup?
· Did I place the dollar sign and the decimal point in the quotient?

Guided Problem Solving

Use the questions to solve this problem.

7. Yuko buys 6 gourds for $9.00. Jeremy buys 1 gourd. If the price of each gourd is the same, how much does 1 gourd cost?

   a. **Understand** What do you need to find?

   b. **Plan** What operation will you use to solve the problem?

   c. **Solve** Write an equation to solve the problem.
   The cost of 1 gourd is $\bigcirc$.

   d. **Look Back** Use multiplication to check your work.

California Gourds

8. Look back at Problem 7. What is the cost of 2 gourds? What is the cost of 5 gourds?

123 Math Talk Look back at Exercise 3. Why was it important to write the decimal point in the answer?

► **Practice and Problem Solving**

Divide. Multiply to check.

9. $3\overline{)\$6.93}$ 10. $4\overline{)\$4.56}$ 11. $3\overline{)\$4.14}$ 12. $6\overline{)\$78.96}$ 13. $4\overline{)\$49.32}$

14. $\$9.50 \div 2$ 15. $\$4.83 \div 3$ 16. $\$88.88 \div 8$ 17. $\$75.20 \div 2$

Algebra Equations **Find the missing number.**

18. ▢ ÷ 3 = $1.21

19. $4.26 ÷ 2 = ▢

20. $2.12 = ▢ ÷ 4

21. ▢ = $5.55 ÷ 5

22. ▢ ÷ 2 = $3.24

23. ▢ ÷ 3 = $2.21

 Real World Data

Use the table for Problems 24–25.

24. What is the unit cost of an avocado?

25. Anja bought 5 pumpkins. She paid the unit cost for each pumpkin. How much did Anja spend on the pumpkins?

26. Challenge A loaf of pumpkin bread sells for $1.29. A box with 5 loaves of pumpkin bread costs $5.50. How much do you save if you buy a box of pumpkin bread instead of buying 5 individual loaves?

> **Vocabulary Tip**
> The **unit cost** is the cost for 1 item.

Fall Prices at the
DAVIS FARMERS' MARKET

APPLES	4 FOR $1.40
PUMPKINS	2 FOR $7.28
AVOCADOS	8 FOR $8.48

Spiral Review and Test Practice

Julian picked 1 marble from a bag without looking. He replaced the marble and repeated the experiment 19 more times. The bar graph shows the results. SDAP 1.4 page 504

Marble Experiment

yellow
red
blue

0 1 2 3 4 5 6 7 8 9 10

27. What color marble is Julian most likely to pick next?

28. What color marble is Julian least likely to pick next?

Write the letter of the correct answer. KEY **NS 3.3**, NS 2.7

29. A magazine costs $9.96 for 6 issues. What is the unit cost?

   A $1.11   **B** $1.16   **C** $1.66   **D** $59.76

Extra Practice See page 575, Set B.

Shop to Sell!

Mr. Martin is the store buyer for a gift shop. In a store, a buyer decides which items the store will sell. Some buyers also purchase items for the store to sell to its customers.

1. Mr. Martin bought 7 posters for $6.51. How much did each poster cost? How much would he have spent in all if he bought 3 more posters?

2. Mr. Martin bought 8 hats for $42.16. How much did each hat cost? How much would he have spent if he bought 9 hats? 5 hats?

3. **Multistep** Mr. Martin bought 6 white teddy bears for the shop. He paid $36.60. The shop sells them for $10.00 each. How much profit does the shop make on each bear?

4. Mr. Martin conducted a survey. He wanted to learn what type of new products the gift store should sell. Four hundred two people preferred wind-up toys. Four hundred twenty preferred board games. Which product should he buy for the store to sell?

5. **Challenge** Mr. Martin spent $53.24 on 4 board games. How much did each game cost? If the shop owner wants to make a profit of $5.50 on each game, how much should he charge for each game?

CA Standards
KEY **NS 3.3**, NS 2.7, NS 2.8, MR 1.0, MR 1.2

CA Standards
NS 2.5 Solve division problems in which a multidigit number is evenly divided by a one-digit number (135 ÷ 5).

KEY **NS 2.3** Use the inverse relationship of multiplication and division to compute and check results.

Also NS 2.0, NS 2.8, KEY NS 3.3, KEY MG 2.2, MR 2.3

Vocabulary

quotient

dividend

Place the First Digit

Objective Decide where to place the first digit in the quotient.

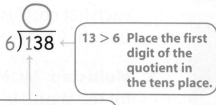 **Learn by Example**

Sometimes the **quotient** has fewer digits than the **dividend**. In this lesson, you will learn how to decide where to place the first digit in the quotient.

Example 1

1 Decide where to place the first digit in the quotient.

$$6\overline{)138}$$

? hundreds
Think 6)1 hundreds

13 > 6 Place the first digit of the quotient in the tens place.

1 < 6 There are not enough hundreds to divide.

2 Divide the tens.

$$6\overline{)138}$$ quotient 2
$$-12$$
$$1$$

? tens
Think 6)13 tens

Multiply. 6 × 2 tens

Subtract. 13 − 12. Compare. 1 < 6

3 Bring down the ones. Divide the ones.

$$6\overline{)138}$$ 23
$$-12$$
$$18$$
$$-18$$
$$0$$

? ones
Think 6)18 ones

Multiply. 6 × 3 ones

Subtract. 18 − 18. Compare. 0 < 6

Check
23
× 6
138

Think
The rules for placing the dollar sign and the decimal point do not change.

Other Examples

$$3\overline{)\$1.41}$$ $0.47
$$-12$$
$$021$$
$$-21$$
$$0$$

Check $0.47
× 3
$1.41

$$6\overline{)2,526}$$ 421
$$-24$$
$$12$$
$$-12$$
$$06$$
$$-6$$
$$0$$

Check 421
× 6
2,526

Guided Practice

Divide. Multiply to check.

1. 4⟌328   **2.** 2⟌$1.38   **3.** 4⟌3,348

Ask Yourself

Where should I write the first digit in the quotient?

123 Math Talk When you divide a 3-digit number by a 1-digit number, can you ever have a 1-digit quotient? Explain.

▶ **Practice and Problem Solving**

Divide. Multiply to check.

4. 3⟌$14.76   **5.** 5⟌620   **6.** 6⟌198   **7.** 2⟌$2.84

8. 5⟌320   **9.** 6⟌$5.52   **10.** 3⟌582   **11.** 3⟌2,598

12. 980 ÷ 5   **13.** 282 ÷ 6   **14.** $29.25 ÷ 3   **15.** 8,316 ÷ 2

16. Jane has 6 days to read a book that is 234 pages long. She wants to read the same number of pages each day. How many pages should she read each day?

17. Challenge Rachel and her 4 brothers are buying a book for $24.95 and a poster for $8.50. If they split the cost equally, how much will each person pay?

18. An equilateral triangle has a perimeter of 192 inches. How long is one side of the triangle?

Think

An equilateral triangle has 3 sides of equal length.

 Spiral Review and Test Practice

Divide and check. NS 2.5 page 548

19. 7⟌84   **20.** 5⟌75   **21.** 8⟌96   **22.** 3⟌84   **23.** 4⟌92

Write the letter of the correct answer. NS 2.5

24. A theater has 1,256 seats. There are 8 seats in each row. How many rows of seats are there?

   A 15   **B** 150   **C** 157   **D** 1157

Problem Solving Plan
Multistep Problems

Objective Solve problems that have more than one step.

▶ **Learn by Example**

What is the total cost of 3 notebooks, 3 pens, and 2 highlighters?

Back to School Supplies	
Notebooks	5 for $6.25
Pens	4 for $2.00
Highlighters	6 for $1.80

UNDERSTAND

The problem asks you to find the cost of a set of items. Before you begin you must find the cost of 1 item.

PLAN

It takes more than one step to solve this problem. Break the problem into parts.

- First, find the unit cost of each item.
- Then, find the total cost of each type of supply.
- Add the costs of all the supplies.

SOLVE

1 Find the unit cost of each item.

Unit cost of a notebook	$6.25 ÷ 5 = $1.25
Unit cost of a pen	$2.00 ÷ 4 = $0.50
Unit cost of a highlighter	$1.80 ÷ 6 = $0.30

2 Find the total cost of each type of supply.

3 notebooks	3 × $1.25 = $3.75
3 pens	3 × $0.50 = $1.50
2 highlighters	2 × $0.30 = $0.60

3 Add the costs of all of the supplies to find the total cost.

$3.75 + 1.50 + 0.60 = $5.85

LOOK BACK

Did you answer the question that was asked?

► Guided Problem Solving

Solve using the Ask Yourself questions.

1. A store sells 4 binders for $13.00 and 6 pencils for $3.54. What is the total cost of 1 binder and 2 pencils?

(123) Math Talk What is a good way to decide what you need to know before you can solve a problem?

► Independent Problem Solving

Solve. Explain why your answer makes sense.

2. A store sells pens for $1.25 each and magnets for $0.75 each. How much do 3 pens and 5 magnets cost in all?

3. On Monday, Mary bought 5 coconuts for $15. On Friday, she paid $20 for 10 coconuts. On which day was the unit cost for coconuts lower? Explain how you found your answer.

4. Kento checked the price of poster board at three stores. Where should Kento shop to get the best price?

Cost of Poster Board	
Store A	5 sheets for $1.25
Store B	4 sheets for $1.20
Store C	3 sheets for $0.99

5. A pair of socks costs $5.00 a pair. A package of 6 pairs costs $24. What is the difference in the unit price of the socks? How much do you save if you buy a package instead of 6 individual pairs?

6. **Challenge** Nelson buys 4 tickets to the homecoming football game. He gives the ticket seller $30 and gets $4.00 in change. How much does each ticket cost?

7. **Create and Solve** Write and solve a multistep problem. Use one of the price lists in the lesson or create your own price list.

Reading & Writing Math

Vocabulary

The **unit cost** is the cost for 1 item.

Read the problem and use the questions to solve.

At the supermarket, the sign says "Navel oranges—6 for 3 dollars! Mr. Waggoner doesn't want 6 oranges. He only wants one. How much will Mr. Waggoner pay for one orange?

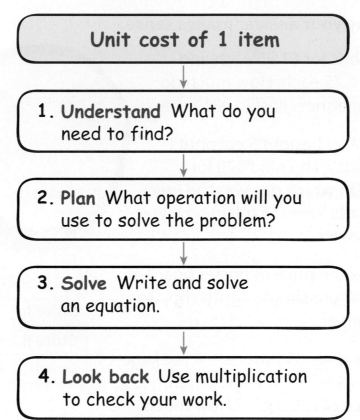

Unit cost of 1 item

1. **Understand** What do you need to find?

2. **Plan** What operation will you use to solve the problem?

3. **Solve** Write and solve an equation.

4. **Look back** Use multiplication to check your work.

Mr. Waggoner pays $_____ for each orange.

Writing Look back at the problem. How much would it cost Mr. Waggoner to buy 4 navel oranges? Explain your answer.

Reading Check out this book in your library.

• *The Number Devil: A Mathematical Adventure*, by Hans Magnus Enzensberger

CA Standards
MR 2.3 Use a variety of methods, such as words, numbers, symbols, charts, graphs, tables, diagrams, and models, to explain mathematical reasoning.

Also KEY NS 2.3, KEY NS 3.3, NS 2.7

Standards-Based Extra Practice

Set A
NS 2.5 page 562

Divide and check.

1. 3)651 **2.** 5)595 **3.** 2)6,948 **4.** 6)684

5. 8,946 ÷ 2 **6.** 9,422 ÷ 7 **7.** 476 ÷ 4 **8.** 1,865 ÷ 5

9. Suzie bought a 575-piece jigsaw puzzle. She invited four friends to help her do the puzzle. If 5 people each place the same number of pieces into the puzzle, how many pieces would each person place?

Set B
KEY NS 3.3, NS 2.7 page 566

Divide and check.

1. 4)$8.56 **2.** 6)$6.72 **3.** 3)$9.78 **4.** 2)$8.78

5. $3.48 ÷ 3 **6.** $4.92 ÷ 4 **7.** $9.68 ÷ 4 **8.** $12.54 ÷ 2

9. Apples were on sale for $2.98 for 2 pounds. Julie bought 1 pound. How much did Julie pay?

Set C
NS 2.5, KEY NS 3.3 page 570

Divide and check.

1. 5)$5.75 **2.** 2)138 **3.** 4)328 **4.** 6)264

5. 3)$4.41 **6.** 7)182 **7.** 9)378 **8.** 8)$3.92

9. 432 ÷ 6 **10.** 246 ÷ 3 **11.** $4.90 ÷ 5 **12.** 581 ÷ 7

13. 194 ÷ 2 **14.** $5.58 ÷ 9 **15.** 468 ÷ 4 **16.** 792 ÷ 8

17. A baker bakes the same number of loaves each day. If he makes 679 loaves in one week, how many loaves does he make each day?

Education Place
Visit www.eduplace.com/camap/
for more **Extra Practice**.

Chapter 26 Extra Practice **575**

Chapter Review/Test

Vocabulary and Concepts ———————————————— NS 2.5

Choose the best word to complete each sentence.

1. The number by which a number is being divided is called the _____.

2. The _____ is the total being divided in division.

3. The answer to a division problem is the _____.

> **Word Bank**
>
> quotient
> divisor
> dividend

Skills ———————————————— KEY **NS 2.3**, NS 2.5, KEY **NS 3.3**

Divide and check.

4. $575 \div 5$ 5. $3,579 \div 3$ 6. $452 \div 2$ 7. $9,460 \div 4$

8. $\$9.81 \div 3$ 9. $\$28.56 \div 6$ 10. $\$89.20 \div 4$ 11. $\$16.78 \div 2$

12. $6)\overline{\$10.44}$ 13. $4)\overline{4,456}$ 14. $4)\overline{\$1.68}$ 15. $3)\overline{477}$ 16. $2)\overline{122}$

Problem Solving and Reasoning ———————— NS 2.0, NS 2.5, KEY **NS 3.3**, MR 2.3

Solve.

17. Fremont is placing 318 new recycling bins in 3 districts of the city. Each district gets the same number of bins. How many bins will be placed in each section?

18. Mellie has 7 days to read a 294-page book. She wants to read the same number of pages each day. How many pages should she read each day?

19. The relay swim team has to swim a total of 315 laps. There are 9 swimmers. If each person swims the same distance, how many laps does each person swim?

20. James lives 858 miles from Los Angeles. He has 2 days to drive there, and he wants to drive the same number of miles each day. How many miles should he drive each day?

> **Writing Math** Max says that the quotient for $5)\overline{375}$ will have only 2 digits. Is he right or wrong? Explain.

Spiral Review and Test Practice

1. Which number can be multiplied by 697 to give the answer 0?

A 0   **B** 1   **C** 2   **D** 697

NS 2.6 page 122

2. One week, Kevin scored 2465 points on a game. The next week, he scored 3 times as many points. How many points did he score the second week?

A 7395   **C** 7295

B 7285   **D** 6285

KEY NS 2.4 page 454

3. Asia put 10 shape cards in this bag. She picked one card without looking.

What is the probability that the shape-card she chose was a circle?

A certain   **C** likely

B unlikely   **D** impossible

SDAP 1.1 page 498

4. Mr. Ortíz bought 7 cases of juice. The total cost was $98. How much money did each case of juice cost?

A $11   **C** $12

B $14   **D** $686

NS 2.7 page 534

5. Paula did this division problem.

$$84 \div 6 = 14$$

Which equation could she use to check her answer?

A $14 + 6 = \square$

B $14 - 6 = \square$

C $14 \times 6 = \square$

D $14 \div 6 = \square$

> **Test Tip**
> Remember that multiplication and division are related.

KEY NS 2.3 page 548

6. A landscaper has 125 rose bushes to divide equally into 5 gardens. How many rose bushes will be in each garden?

A 21   **C** 25

B 130   **D** 625

NS 2.5 page 562

Education Place
Visit www.eduplace.com/camap/ for
Test-Taking Tips and **Extra Practice.**   **Chapter 26** Spiral Review and Test Practice   **577**

Unit 9 Review/Test

Vocabulary and Concepts ———————————— MR 2.3 Chapters 24–26

Choose the best word to complete each sentence.

> **Word Bank**
> product
> divisor
> quotient
> dividend

1. In $12 \div 4 = 3$, 12 is the _____.

2. In $12 \div 4 = 3$, 4 is the _____.

3. In $12 \div 4 = 3$, 3 is the _____.

Skills ——————————— KEY **NS 2.3**, NS 2.5, KEY **NS 3.3**, Prepares for NS 2.5 Chapter 24, Lessons 2–3

Use counters to complete the table.

	Division	Number (dividend)	Number of Equal Groups (divisor)	Number in Each Group (quotient)	Number Left Over
4.	2)9				
5.	6)19				

Complete the table.

	Division	What multiplication fact can you use?	Number in Each Group (quotient)	Number Left Over
6.	4)31			
7.	7)59			

Find the quotient. Chapter 25, Lessons 2–3

8. 3)63   **9.** 7)84   **10.** 4)52   **11.** 6)78

Write $+$, $-$, $\times$, or $\div$ to make the number sentence true. NS 2.5, AF 1.3 Chapter 25, Lesson 3

12. 91 ⬤ 7 = 13   **13.** 37 ⬤ 2 = 74   **14.** 73 ⬤ 52 = 21

Divide and check. Chapters 26, Lessons 2–4

15. $4{,}788 \div 3$ **16.** $3{,}790 \div 2$ **17.** $\$99.40 \div 4$ **18.** $\$31.78 \div 7$

Problem Solving and Reasoning — NS 2.0, NS 2.5, MR 2.3 Chapters 24–26

Solve.

19. Mark has 27 quarters. He wants to trade them for dollar bills. How many dollar bills can he get? How many quarters will be left?

20. Anita has picked 168 flowers. She put them into 3 vases with the same number in each vase. How many flowers are in each vase?

Writing Math How is dividing $3\overline{)279}$ the same as dividing $3\overline{)\$2.79}$? How is it different?

Performance Assessment

The Spaghetti Fundraiser Problem — NS 2.0, KEY NS 2.4, NS 2.5, NS 2.8, MR 1.1, MR 1.2

Ms. Owens needs to decide how many of each shape table to use for the spaghetti fundraiser.

square table

rectangular table

circular table

Task	Information You Need
Use the information above and at the right. How many of each shape should she use? Explain your thinking.	There must be exactly 184 seats.
	There are 15 circular tables available.
	There are 12 rectangular tables available.
	There are 10 square tables available.

Greg Tang's Go Fast, Go Far

Unit 9 Mental Math Strategies

Divide by 2

> Divide a piece that's fast to do. Split the rest and add the two!

> When a number is hard to work with, just break it into easier pieces! Look at Problem 1. I think of 70 as 60 + 10. I divide 60 by 2 to get 30, and 10 by 2 to get 5. The answer is 30 + 5 = 35.

1. $70 \div 2 = \boxed{30} + \boxed{5} = \boxed{35}$
  $60 \div 2$ $10 \div 2$

2. $26 \div 2 = \blacksquare + \blacksquare = \blacksquare$
  $20 \div 2$ $6 \div 2$

3. $90 \div 2 = \blacksquare + \blacksquare = \blacksquare$
  $80 \div 2$ $10 \div 2$

4. $160 \div 2 = \blacksquare + \blacksquare = \blacksquare$
  $100 \div 2$ $60 \div 2$

Nice job! Now try some more!

5. $110 \div 2 = \blacksquare + \blacksquare = \blacksquare$
  $100 \div 2$ $10 \div 2$

6. $280 \div 2 = \blacksquare + \blacksquare = \blacksquare$
  $200 \div 2$ $80 \div 2$

7. $220 \div 2 = \blacksquare + \blacksquare = \blacksquare$
  $200 \div 2$ $20 \div 2$

8. $44 \div 2 = \blacksquare + \blacksquare = \blacksquare$
  $40 \div 2$ $4 \div 2$

Take It Further!
Now try doing all the steps in your head!

9. $42 \div 2$

10. $280 \div 2$

11. $86 \div 2$

12. $66 \div 2$

Go Faster!

Weight, Mass, and Capacity

BIG IDEAS!

- Weight, mass, and capacity can be estimated and measured using customary or metric units.
- You can multiply, divide, or use patterns to change from one unit to another unit.

Chapter 27
Customary Units

Chapter 28
Metric Units

Songs and Games

Math Music Track 10: *How Much?*

eGames at
www.eduplace.com/camap/

Math Readers

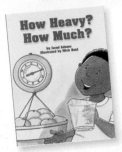

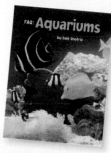

Orcas can be seen along the entire California coast.

Game

What's the Weight?

Object of the Game Correctly estimate the weight of classroom objects.

Materials
- balance scale
- box of crayons (or similar object)
- various classroom objects

Number of Players 2–3

How to Play

1 Each player finds 2 classroom objects that he or she estimates are lighter than the box of crayons, 2 objects that he or she estimates are about the same weight as the crayons, and 2 objects that he or she estimates are heavier than the crayons.

2 Players use the balance scale to check their predictions.

3 Each player gets 1 point for each correct choice.

4 After weighing the objects, the player with the most points wins.

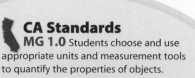

CA Standards
MG 1.0 Students choose and use appropriate units and measurement tools to quantify the properties of objects.

Education Place
Visit www.eduplace.com/camap/ for **Brain Teasers** and **eGames** to play.

Reading When you are doing homework, make use of nearby help. Check out the Glossary and Table of Measures at the back of the book.

In the next two chapters, you will be learning about measurement. You will read some words you know. You will see some new words.

Which of these words do you know?
Which should you look up in the Glossary?

Capacity	Weight	Mass
cup, pint, quart, gallon, liter, milliliter	ounce, pound	gram, kilogram

Writing Sometimes you may be able to use the Table of Measures to help you answer questions. Use the portion of the chart below to help you solve this problem.

Frank worked for one hour and 25 minutes. How many minutes did he work in all?

Units of Time
1 minute (min) = 60 seconds (s)
1 hour (hr) = 60 minutes
1 day (d) = 24 hours
1 week (wk) = 7 days
1 year (yr) = 12 months (mo)

I use the Glossary at the back of my book to check the meaning of words.

Customary Units

California farmers grow one fourth of all
the onions grown in the United States.

Vocabulary and Concepts   GRADE 2 KEY MG 1.3, MG 1.4

Choose the best word to complete each sentence.

1. There are 7 _____ in a week.

2. An _____ is a unit used to measure length.

3. There are 60 _____ in an hour.

Skills   GRADE 2 MG 1.0

Which holds more?

4. a cup or a pitcher

5. a pool or a lake

6. a bathtub or a bucket

Which is heavier?

7. a frying pan or a glove

8. a shoe or an eraser

9. a book or a desk

Problem Solving and Reasoning   GRADE 2 MG 1.0

10. Mai is lightest. Bill is heavier than Lee. Lee is heavier than Jo.
List the students in order from lightest to heaviest.

Vocabulary

Visualize It!

Capacity

The amount a container can hold.

1 gallon   =   16 cups

16 ounces   =   1 pound

Language Tips

Capacity means how much someone or something, like a machine or factory, can do or make. In mathematics, *capacity* is how much a container can hold.

Some words are similar in Spanish and English.

English	Spanish
capacity	capacidad
gallon	galón

See **English-Spanish Glossary** pages 628–646.

 Education Place Visit www.eduplace.com/camap/ for the **eGlossary** and **eGames**.

CA Standards

MG 1.1 Choose the appropriate tools and units (metric and U.S.) and estimate and measure the length, liquid volume, and weight/mass of given objects.

MG 1.4, Carry out simple unit conversions within a system of measurement (e.g., centimeters and meters, hours and minutes).

Also MG 1.0, MR 1.1, MR 2.3

Vocabulary

capacity

cup (c)

pint (pt)

quart (qt)

gallon (gal)

liquid volume

Materials

Cup, pint, quart, gallon containers

Hands On
Estimate and Measure Capacity

Objective Estimate and measure the amount a container can hold.

▶ **Explore**

Capacity, or **liquid volume**, is the amount a container can hold. In the customary system, **cup (c)**, **pint (pt)**, **quart (qt)**, and **gallon (gal)** are units for measuring capacity, or liquid volume.

Question How can you use different-sized containers and water to estimate and measure capacity?

1 Estimate how many cups are in a pint, a quart, and a gallon. Then check your estimates. Record your results in a table like the one shown.

Use the cup container to fill the pint container.
- How many cups are in a pint?

Use the cup container to fill the quart container.
- How many cups are in a quart?

Use the cup container to fill the gallon container.
- How many cups are in a gallon?

Capacity			
	Pint	Quart	Gallon
Cups			
Pints			
Quarts			

2 Estimate, and then check how many pints are in a quart and a gallon.

- How many pints are in a quart?
- How many pints are in a gallon?

3 Estimate, and then check how many quarts are in a gallon.

Use the quart container to fill the gallon container.

- How many quarts are in a gallon?

▶ **Extend**

Find the missing amount. Use your chart for help.

1. 1 gal = ▢ qt

2. 1 pt = ▢ c

3. 1 qt = ▢ pt

4. 2 c = ▢ pt

5. 8 pt = ▢ gal

6. 16 c = ▢ gal

7. 4 qt = ▢ gal

8. 1 gal = ▢ c

9. 1 gal = ▢ pt

10. 1 qt = ▢ c

11. 4 c = ▢ qt

12. 2 pt = ▢ qt

13. **Analyze** Suppose you pour 1 gallon of water into pint containers. Then you pour 1 gallon of water into quart containers. Would you use more pint containers or quart containers? Explain.

14. **Challenge** Suppose the largest measuring tool you have holds one cup. You need 2 quarts of broth to make soup. How many times would you fill the cup?

Writing Math

Explain Could these items have the same capacity? Explain. Then describe a way you could find out.

CA Standards

MG 1.1 Choose the appropriate tools and units (metric and U.S.) and estimate and measure the length, liquid volume, and weight/mass of given objects.

MG 1.0 Students choose and use appropriate units and measurement tools to quantify the properties of objects.

Also MG 1.4, MR 2.3

Customary Units of Capacity

Objective Choose the appropriate unit to measure capacity.

▶ Learn by Example

You can buy fresh California orange juice in one-pint, one-quart, and one-gallon containers. Cups, pints, quarts, and gallons are customary units of capacity.

Customary Units of Capacity	
1 pint = 2 cups	
1 quart = 2 pints	
1 gallon = 4 quarts	

You can use customary units to measure capacity.

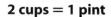

2 cups = 1 pint

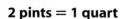

2 pints = 1 quart

4 quarts = 1 gallon

Ask Yourself

- Which is the smallest unit of measure? the largest?
- Can I use a larger unit for the container?

▶ Guided Practice

Choose the best unit to measure how much each container can hold. Write *cup*, *pint*, *quart*, or *gallon*.

1.

2.

3.

Guided Problem Solving

Use the questions to solve this problem.

4. Ann wants to have 12 one-cup servings of juice at her party. How many one-quart containers does Ann need to buy?

a. **Understand** What unit does Ann use to measure? What unit does she need?

b. **Plan** Make a diagram. Write a **C** for each cup.

c. **Solve** Circle groups of **C**s to show the number of pints. Then draw rectangles around the groups of **C**s to show the number of quarts. Write the answer.

d. **Look Back** Look at your diagram. Does it show that 2 cups = 1 pint and 2 pints = 1 quart?

 Math Talk Is a quart greater than or less than 5 cups? Explain.

▶ Practice and Problem Solving

Choose the best unit to measure how much each container can hold. Write *cup*, *pint*, *quart*, or *gallon*.

5.

6.

7.

Write in order from least capacity to greatest capacity.

8. 1 qt   3 c   1 pt

9. 1 gal   5 qt   6 pt

 Real World Data

Use the data in the table to help you solve Problems 10–11.

10. Ben wants to buy 3 pints of orange juice. How much will he pay?

11. Challenge Paula is bringing orange juice for her soccer team. She needs 1 gallon of juice. How much money will she save if she buys a gallon container instead of pint containers?

Price of Orange Juice	
Amount	**Price**
Pint	$0.79
Quart	$1.79
Gallon	$5.99

 Spiral Review and Test Practice

Use the information in the tally chart to make a bar graph. KEY **SDAP 1.3** page 482

12.

Spinner Experiment		
Outcome	**Tally**	**Number**
Red	III	3
Yellow	I	1
Blue	HHH I	6

Write the letter of the correct answer. MG 1.1

13. Which holds about 1 cup?

A    **B**    **C**    **D**

Extra Practice See page 603, Set A.

Key Standards Review

Need Help?
See Key Standards Handbook.

Use the price list for Problems 1–4. KEY **NS 3.3**

1. What is the cost of 1 scarf?

2. Cal bought 4 train whistles. How much did he spend?

3. Jack found the same train whistles for $3.85 each at the train station. Who got a better buy?

4. Barak had $20.00 and bought a hat. How much change should he get?

Souvenir Prices

HAT	$6.45
SCARF	4 FOR $8.48
TRAIN WHISTLE	2 FOR $7.28

Divide. KEY **NS 3.3**

5. $4)\overline{\$8.24}$

6. $5)\overline{\$5.75}$

7. $9)\overline{\$3.69}$

8. $6)\overline{\$4.92}$

9. $3)\overline{\$8.25}$

10. $\$10.00 \div 4$

11. $\$10.00 \div 5$

12. $\$10.00 \div 2$

13. $\$10.00 \div 8$

Challenge
Problem Solving

Missing Measurements

Pick a measurement from the box to complete each number sentence. You can use each measurement more than once. MG 1.4, AF 1.4

1. $2 \text{ ft} + \boxed{} = 1 \text{ yd}$

2. $11 \text{ in.} + \boxed{} = 1 \text{ ft}$

3. $22 \text{ in.} + \boxed{} + \boxed{} = 2 \text{ ft}$

4. $2 \text{ yd} - \boxed{} = 3 \text{ ft}$

5. $4 \text{ ft} + \boxed{} + \boxed{} = 2 \text{ yd}$

1 in.
12 in.
1 ft
1 yd

CA Standards

MG 1.1 Choose the appropriate tools and units (metric and U.S.) and estimate and measure the length, liquid volume, and weight/mass of given objects.

MG 1.0 Students choose and use appropriate units and measurement tools to quantify the properties of objects.

Also MR 2.3

Vocabulary

weight

ounce (oz)

pound (lb)

Materials
• Spring scale
• Small classroom objects to weigh

Hands On
Estimate and Measure Weight

Objective Estimate and measure the weight of objects.

▶ **Explore**

Weight is the measure of how heavy something is.

Pound (lb) and **ounce (oz)** are customary units used when measuring weight.

• Use ounces to measure things that are light.

• Use pounds to measure things that are heavy.

Customary Units of Weight
1 pound = 16 ounces

1 ounce (oz)

1 pound (lb)

Question How can you use a spring scale to measure weight?

① Find 3 objects in your classroom.

    • Choose one object that you think is less than 1 pound.

    • Choose one object that you think is about 1 pound.

    • Choose one object that you think is greater than 1 pound.

② Use the spring scale to check your estimates.

The object that weighs about 1 pound, also weighs about 16 ounces.

▶ **Extend**

Estimate the weight of the object. Write *more* or *less* than 1 pound.

1.

2.

3.

4.

5.

6.

7.

8.

Name an object that might have the given weight.

9. 1 lb

10. 8 oz

11. less than 1 oz

12. more than 1,000 lb

Choose the better estimate.

13. a pizza
  a. 2 lb   **b.** 2 oz

14. a banana
  a. 6 lb   **b.** 6 oz

15. a slice of cheese
  a. 1 lb   **b.** 1 oz

16. a wooden spoon
  a. 10 oz   **b.** 100 oz

17. a turkey
  a. 2 lb   **b.** 20 lb

18. a television set
  a. 20 oz   **b.** 20 lb

19. Estimate Estimate the weight of your textbook. Use the spring scale to check. How close was your estimate?

20. Challenge Choose an object in your classroom that you think weighs between 2 and 3 pounds. Use the spring scale to check.

 Math Journal

Writing Math

Explain Could a large object weigh less than a small object? Give an example.

CA Standards

MG 1.1 Choose the appropriate tools and units (metric and U.S.) and estimate and measure the length, liquid volume, and weight/mass of given objects.

MG 1.0 Students choose and use appropriate units and measurement tools to quantify the properties of objects.

Also MG 1.4, MR 2.3, MR 2.4

Customary Units of Weight

Objective Choose the appropriate unit to measure weight.

▶ Learn by Example

You can use customary units to measure weight.

Customary Units of Weight
1 pound = 16 ounces

Example 1

What unit would you use to measure the weight of a cookie?

A cookie is light. You would use *ounces* to measure its weight. A cookie weighs about 1 ounce.

Example 2

What unit would you use to measure the weight of a box of 16 cookies?

16 cookies weigh about 16 ounces. So, 16 cookies also weigh about 1 pound.

Using a larger unit can give you a number that is smaller and easier to work with. You would use *pounds* to measure a box of 16 cookies.

Ask Yourself

Do I need a small or large unit?

▶ Guided Practice

Choose the unit you would use to measure the weight. Write *ounce* or *pound*.

1.
2.
3.
4.

123 Math Talk How would you know if something that is measured in ounces weighs more than a pound?

▶ Practice and Problem Solving

**Choose the unit you would use to measure the weight.
Write *ounce* or *pound*.**

5.

6.

7.

Write in order from the least weight to the greatest weight.

8. 25 oz   50 oz   3 lb

9. $\frac{1}{2}$ lb   9 oz   7 oz

 Real World Data

**Mrs. Seaberg bought four boxes of
cookies. Use the table for Problems 10–12.**

10. Which box of cookies is heavier,
    pumpkin or blueberry? Explain.

11. Write the boxes of cookies in order
    from heaviest to lightest.

12. **Challenge** Suppose a box of
    lemon cookies weighs 20 ounces.
    Is it heavier or lighter than the
    box of apple cookies? How much
    heavier or lighter?

Country Bakery Cookies

Cookies	Weight
Apple	2 pounds
Chocolate	24 ounces
Pumpkin	8 ounces
Blueberry	1 pound

 Spiral Review and Test Practice

Find the product. **KEY** NS 2.4 page 450

13.   113
      × 7

14.   301
      × 2

15.   219
      × 4

16.   462
      × 2

Choose the letter of the correct answer. MG 1.1

17. Which object is heavier than a pound?

   A pen   **B** paper clip   **C** microwave oven   **D** postage stamp

CA Standards

AF 1.4 Express simple unit conversions in symbolic form (e.g., ____ inches = ____ feet × 12).

MG 1.4 Carry out simple unit conversions within a system of measurement (e.g., centimeters and meters, hours and minutes).

Also AF 1.0, AF 2.0, KEY AF 2.1, MG 1.0, KEY NS 2.4, NS 2.5, NS 2.8, MR 1.2, MR 2.0

Convert Customary Units and Units of Time

Objective Convert customary units and units of time.

▶ **Learn by Example**

In this lesson you will use multiplication and division to convert customary units and units of time.

> James made 60 cups of lemonade. How many pints is this?

Example 1

1 Show how the units are related.

$$1 \text{ pt} = 2 \text{ c}$$

Capacity
1 pint = 2 cups
1 quart = 2 pints
1 gallon = 4 quarts

2 Compare the units.

- When you change from larger units to smaller units, the number of units increases.

- When you change from smaller units to larger units, the number of units decreases.

1 pint   **1 cup**

3 Decide if you should multiply or divide.

Since cups are smaller and pints are larger, you divide.

$$60 \div 2 = 30$$

number of cups ⟶ 60

number of cups in 1 pint ⟶ 2

number of pints ⟶ 30

Solution: James made 30 pints of lemonade.

Leah worked 3 hours at the supermarket.
How many minutes is this?

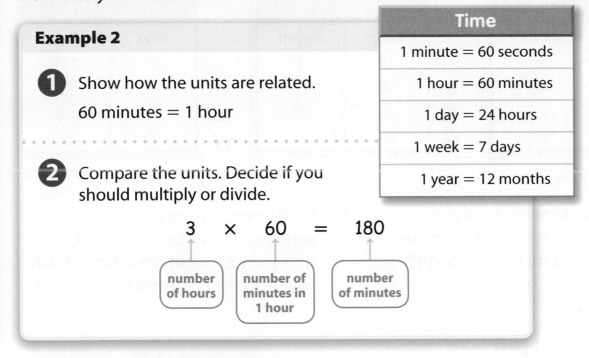

Example 2

1 Show how the units are related.

60 minutes = 1 hour

Time
1 minute = 60 seconds
1 hour = 60 minutes
1 day = 24 hours
1 week = 7 days
1 year = 12 months

2 Compare the units. Decide if you should multiply or divide.

$$3 \times 60 = 180$$

number of hours   number of minutes in 1 hour   number of minutes

Solution: Leah worked for 180 minutes.

▶ **Guided Practice**

Choose the expression you would use to convert the units. Then write the product or quotient.

1. the number of weeks in 21 days

    a. 21 × 7   **b.** 21 ÷ 7

2. the number of months in 6 years

    a. 6 × 12   **b.** 12 ÷ 6

Ask Yourself

• Which is the larger unit?

• Do I need to multiply or divide?

 Math Talk Write the units for measuring time in order from least to greatest.

▶ **Practice and Problem Solving**

Choose the expression you would use to convert the units. Then write the product or quotient.

3. the number of yards in 15 feet

    a. 15 × 3   **b.** 15 ÷ 3

4. the number of inches in 3 feet

    a. 3 × 12   **b.** 12 ÷ 3

Length
1 foot = 12 inches
1 yard = 3 feet
1 yard = 36 inches
1 mile = 5,280 feet

Complete the table.

Rule: Multiply by 16.	
Pounds	**Ounces**
6	96
1	▨
2	▨
10	▨

5. (row with 1)
6. (row with 2)
7. (row with 10)

Rule: Divide by 4.	
Quarts	**Gallons**
16	4
4	▨
44	▨
92	▨

8. (row with 4)
9. (row with 44)
10. (row with 92)

Rule: Multiply by 24.	
Days	**Hours**
6	144
1	▨
5	▨
10	▨

11. (row with 1)
12. (row with 5)
13. (row with 10)

Solve.

14. Hans has a rope that measures 7 ft in length. He needs 75 inches of rope. Does he have enough? How do you know?

15. Multistep Ari works at the supermarket 9 hours a week. He gets paid $7.00 an hour. How much will he make in 4 weeks?

Science Link

Solve.

16. It took 15 minutes for Annabel's ice cube to melt completely into water. How many seconds is this?

17. Lionel has 15 juice boxes. Each juice box contains 1 cup of juice. He wants to fill a gallon pitcher. Does Lionel have enough juice? Explain.

Liquids

- Some liquids are thin like water and juice.
- Some liquids are thick like paint and honey.
- If you freeze a liquid, it becomes a solid. If you heat a liquid, it becomes a gas.

Science PS 1.e

Spiral Review and Test Practice

Find the quotient. KEY NS 3.3, NS 2.5 pages 562, 566, 570

18. 6)$7.50

19. 5)395

20. 3)627

21. 6)$9.24

Write the letter of the correct answer. AF 1.4

22. Which of the following can be used to find how many feet are in 12 yards?

  A 3×12 **B** $12 \div 3$ **C** 36×12 **D** $12 \div 12$

Extra Practice See page 603, Set C.

Math Works!

Capacity

Some scientists work with sea animals. They study animals, plants, and other things that live in and around water. They often need to estimate capacity.

See if you have what it takes to work with sea animals. Choose the better estimate.

Whale Shark

1. Rhonda is a scientist. She needs to clean the shark tank. About how much water will it take to fill the tank when she is done?

    40 quarts or 40,000 gallons

2. Rhonda puts a special chemical in the turtle tank. The chemical bottle is about the same size as a shampoo bottle. About how much chemical does the bottle hold?

    1 pint or 1 gallon

3. Each dolphin eats one large pail of fish during the dolphin show. What is the capacity of that pail of fish?

    5 cups or 5 gallons

Solve.

Bottlenose Dolphin

4. **Multistep** The supply room at the aquarium has 100 gallons of chemicals for the fish tank. Each day 12 gallons of chemicals are poured into the tank. How many gallons are left at the end of the week?

CA Standards
MG 1.0, NS 2.8, MR 1.2

CA Standards

MR 2.4 Express the solution clearly and logically by using the appropriate mathematical notation and terms and clear language; support solutions with evidence in both verbal and symbolic work.

NS 2.7 Determine the unit cost when given the total cost and number of units.

Also NS 2.8, KEY NS3.3, KEY AF1.1, AF 1.4, KEY AF2.1, MG 1.4, MR 1.1, MR 1.2, MR 2.0, MR 2.3, MR 3.0, MR 3.1, MR 3.2, MR 3.3

Problem Solving Plan
Unit Costs

Objective Solve problems about unit costs.

▶ **Learn by Example**

Marley wants to compare the price of two brands of orange juice to find out which one is cheaper.

The units in the two costs are different. Before Marley can compare the prices, he needs to convert one of the unit costs.

Brand A
$5.12 per gallon

Brand B
$1.36 per quart

Think

4 quarts = 1 gallon

1 Find the unit cost per quart of **Brand A** orange juice.

There are 4 quarts in 1 gallon, so divide $5.12 by 4 to find the cost per quart.

The unit cost of **Brand A** is $1.28 per quart.

$$
\begin{array}{r}
\$1.28 \\
4\overline{)\$5.12} \\
-4 \\
\hline
11 \\
-8 \\
\hline
32 \\
-32 \\
\hline
0
\end{array}
$$

2 Compare the unit costs.

Brand A		Brand B
$1.28 per quart	<	$1.36 per quart

Solution: The unit cost per quart of **Brand A** is less than the unit cost per quart of **Brand B**. So, **Brand A** is cheaper.

> ## Guided Problem Solving

Solve using the Ask Yourself questions.

Ask Yourself
- What unit do I use for the unit cost?
- Do I need to convert units?

1. William and his family went to the Avocado Festival in Carpinteria. His mother bought a bag of 8 avocados for $5.20. What was the unit cost per avocado?

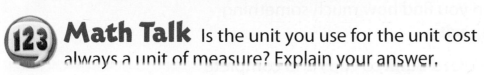 **Math Talk** Is the unit you use for the unit cost always a unit of measure? Explain your answer.

> ## Independent Problem Solving

Solve. Explain why your answer makes sense.

2. A box of 6 muffins costs $7.50. A box of 4 muffins costs $4.60. Which box has the lower unit cost?

3. A 1-pound box of spaghetti costs $1.28. A family-sized bag weighs 48 ounces and costs $3.90. Does the family-sized bag cost less per unit? Explain how you decided.

4. A bag of 10 apples costs $5.00, and a bag of 6 apples costs $2.88. Write an expression that compares the two unit costs. Which bag has the lower unit cost?

5. A package of 6 pencils costs $1.26. How much will 3 packages cost? If Dana needs 36 pencils, how much will they cost?

6. **Challenge** Jan makes charm bracelets. One catalog sells chains for $2.00 per foot. Another sells chains for 10¢ per inch. If Jan makes 4 bracelets that are 6 inches in length, how much will she save if she buys chains at the lower price?

7. **Create and Solve** Write and solve two word problems. In one, make the unit price a unit of measure, such as a pound or a foot. In the other, make the unit price an item, such as an apple or a toy car.

Vocabulary

When you find how long something is, you find its **length**. When you find how heavy something is, you find its **weight**. When you find how much something holds, you find its **capacity**.

Use the words in the **Word Bank** to copy and complete the table below.

Word Bank for Customary Measurements				
gallon	pound	pint	ounce	foot
yard	quart	inch	cup	

Capacity	Length	Weight
1. _____ 2. _____ 3. _____ 4. _____	5. _____ 6. _____ 7. _____	8. _____ 9. _____

Writing Look at the units of capacity you listed. Write that list in order by size from largest to smallest. Explain how you know you're right.

Reading Look for this book in your library.

• *Measuring Penny*, by Loreen Leedy

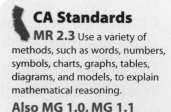

CA Standards

MR 2.3 Use a variety of methods, such as words, numbers, symbols, charts, graphs, tables, diagrams, and models, to explain mathematical reasoning.

Also MG 1.0, MG 1.1

Standards-Based Extra Practice

Set A ────────────────────────────── MG 1.1, MG 1.0 page 588

Choose the unit you would use to measure the capacity of each. Write *cup*, *pint*, *quart*, or *gallon*.

1.

2.

3.

4.

Choose the better estimate.

5. puppy's water bowl
   a. 1 gallon
   b. 1 pint

6. coffee mug
   a. 1 cup
   b. 10 cups

7. small flower pot
   a. 2 pints
   b. 20 pints

Set B ────────────────────────────── MG 1.1, MG 1.0 page 594

Choose the unit you would use to measure the weight of each. Write *ounce* or *pound*.

1.

2.

3.

4.

Write in order from the least weight to the greatest weight.

5. 8 oz   24 oz   1 lb

6. 34 oz   2 lbs   20 oz

7. $\frac{3}{4}$ lb   6 oz   18 oz

Set C ────────────────────────────── AF 1.4, MG 1.4 page 596

Choose the expression you would use to convert the units. Then write the product or quotient.

1. The number of months in 5 years
   a. 5 × 12
   b. 5 ÷ 12

2. The number of pints in 16 cups
   a. 2 × 16
   b. 16 ÷ 2

3. The number of seconds in 2 minutes
   a. 2 ÷ 60
   b. 2 × 60

 Education Place
Visit www.eduplace.com/camap/
for more **Extra Practice**.

Chapter 27 Extra Practice   **603**

Chapter Review/Test

Vocabulary and Concepts ───────────────── MG 1.0, MG 1.1

Choose the best word to complete each sentence.

> **Word Bank**
> capacity
> pound
> ounce
> weight

1. Two customary units used to measure weight are _____ and _____.

2. _____ is the amount a container can hold.

3. _____ tells how heavy something is.

Skills ───────────────── AF 1.4, MG 1.0, MG 1.1, MG 1.4

Choose the unit you would use to measure the capacity of each. Write *cup*, *pint*, *quart*, or *gallon*.

4. 　　　5. 　　　6.

Choose the expression you would use to convert the units. Then write the product or quotient.

7. the number of weeks in 28 days

   a. $28 \div 7$　　**b.** 28×7

8. the number of minutes in 2 hours

   a. $2 \div 60$　　**b.** 2×60

Problem Solving and Reasoning ─── MG 1.1, MG 1.0, MG 1.4, MR 1.2, MR 2.3, MR 3.1

Solve.

9. Serena needs 15 one-cup servings of punch. The punch comes in one-pint containers. How many containers will she have to buy?

10. Greta has a roll of paper that is 4 yards long. She needs 14 feet to wrap all her gifts. Does she have enough?

Writing Math How many ways can you measure your textbook? Which units would you use for each way?

Spiral Review and Test Practice

1. Joseph had $15. He paid $6 to get into a museum. Then he spent $5 on a dinosaur book. What amount of money did Joseph have left?

A $4   **C** $9

B $10   **D** $11

NS 2.0 page 134

2. The square shows $\frac{2}{5}$ shaded.

Which square also has $\frac{2}{5}$ shaded?

A   **C**

B   **D**

NS 3.1 page 330

3. Nell earned $5.15 running errands for her aunt. Her sister earned $3.20. How much more did Nell earn than her sister?

A $8.35   **C** $2.95

B $2.15   **D** $1.95

KEY NS 3.3 page 390

4. The tally chart shows the results of spinning a spinner 24 times. If Eric spins the spinner one more time, which color is he most likely to spin?

A blue

B green

C red

D yellow

Color	Number
Blue	IIII
Green	HHH I
Red	HHH I
Yellow	HHH III

SDAP 1.4 page 504

5. Which holds about 1 gallon?

Test Tip
First, eliminate answers you know are incorrect.

A   **C**

B    **D**

MG 1.1 page 588

Metric Units

Check What You Know

Vocabulary and Concepts MG 1.0, MR 2.3
Choose the best word to complete each sentence.

Word Bank

capacity

cups

ounces

weight

1. The greater a container's _____ , the more it holds.

2. There are 16 _____ in a pound.

3. There are 2 _____ in a pint.

Skills GRADE 2 MG 1.0

Which object is heavier?

4. a sock or a shoe

5. a book or a pen

6. a dog or a horse

Which object holds more?

7. a quart of milk or a teaspoon

8. a ladle or a pot

9. a water bottle or a bucket

Problem Solving and Reasoning MG 1.4

10. Carrie knows that a pitcher holds 1 gallon of juice. How many cups of juice will the pitcher hold?

Vocabulary

Visualize It!

Metric Measures of Mass
You can measure the mass of an egg in **grams**. 
You can measure the mass of a car in **kilograms**. 

Language Tips

You can use the prefix of words to help you understand their meanings. For example *cent* or *centi* refers to one hundred and *kil* or *kilo* refers to one thousand.

Some words are similar in Spanish and English.

English	Spanish
gram	gramo
kilogram	kilogramo

See **English-Spanish Glossary** pages 628–646.

 Education Place Visit www.eduplace.com/camap/ for the **eGlossary** and **eGames**.

CA Standards MR 2.3 Use a variety of methods, such as words, numbers, symbols, charts, graphs, tables, diagrams, and models, to explain mathematical reasoning. **Also MG 1.1**

Chapter 28   607

LESSON 1

CA Standards

MG 1.1 Choose the appropriate tools and units (metric and U.S.) and estimate and measure the length, liquid volume, and weight/mass of given objects.

Also MG 1.0, MG 1.4, MR 1.2, MR 2.3, MR 2.4

Vocabulary

liter (L)

milliliter (mL)

Materials
- Water
- 1-liter container
- Various other containers

This bottle holds 1 liter (1 L) of water.

This eyedropper contains 1 milliliter (1 mL) of liquid.

Hands On
Metric Units of Capacity

Objective Estimate and measure capacity in metric units.

▶ **Explore**

You already learned about customary units of capacity. The **liter (L)** and **milliliter (mL)** are metric units of capacity.

Metric Units of Capacity
1 liter = 1,000 milliliters

Work with a partner. Estimate and measure capacity using liters.

1 Choose 3 containers.
- One that you think holds less than 1 liter
- One that you think holds about 1 liter
- One that you think holds more than 1 liter

2 Use water and the 1-liter container to check your estimates.

3 Choose one of your containers. Does it hold more than, less than, or about 1,000 milliliters? Explain how you know.

▶ **Extend**

Choose the better estimate for the capacity of the container.

1.

3 L or 3 mL

2.

5 L or 5 mL

3.  Glue

14 L or 14 mL

4.

100 L or 100 mL

5.

20 L or 20 mL

6.

200 L or 200 mL

Choose the unit you would use to measure the capacity of the container. Write *mL* or *L*.

7. a bathtub

8. a spoon

9. a container of milk

10. a pail

11. a soup can

12. a drinking glass

13. a pond

14. a small vase

15. a watering can

16. Explain Would you need a larger container to hold 500 mL or to hold 1 L? Explain.

17. Challenge Nick poured 2,300 mL of apple juice into a pitcher. Then Rhea poured 3 L of cranberry juice into the same pitcher. How many milliliters of juice are in the pitcher now?

 Math Journal

Writing Math

Explain Why would you use liters instead of milliliters to measure the capacity of a kitchen sink?

LESSON 2

CA Standards

MG 1.1 Choose the appropriate tools and units (metric and U.S.) and estimate and measure the length, liquid volume, and weight/mass of given objects.

Also MG 1.0, MG 1.4, MR 2.0, MR 2.3, MR 2.4

Vocabulary

gram (g)

kilogram (kg)

mass

Materials
- balance scale
- 1-kilogram mass
- various classroom objects

Hands On
Metric Units of Mass

Objective Estimate and measure the mass of an object in metric units.

▶ **Explore**

Gram (g) and **kilogram (kg)** are metric units used to measure the **mass**, or amount of matter, in an object.

Metric Units of Mass
1 kilogram = 1,000 grams

You measure a shoelace or an egg in grams.

You measure a pair of sneakers or a car in kilograms.

Work with a partner to estimate and measure mass.

1 Choose 3 small objects in your classroom.
- One that you think is less than 1 kilogram
- One that you think is about 1 kilogram
- One that you think is more than 1 kilogram

2 Use the scale and 1-kilogram mass to check your estimates.

3 Choose one of your objects. Do you think it is more than, less than, or about 1,000 grams? Explain how you know.

► **Extend**

Choose the unit you would use to measure the mass of the object. Write *g* or *kg*.

1.

2.

3.

4. a canoe

5. a beach ball

6. a pair of goggles

Choose the better estimate.

7. pair of sunglasses
150 g or 2 kg

8. a horse
6 kg or 600 kg

9. a quarter
5 g or 500 g

10. a piece of chicken
500 g or 5 kg

11. a paper clip
1 g or 1 kg

12. a watermelon
40 g or 4 kg

 Real World Data

Use the table for Problems 13–15.

13. Is the mass of the delta kite greater or less than 1 kg? How much greater or less? Explain.

14. Four of Kyle's friends have box kites just like Kyle's. Will the total mass of all five kites be more or less than 1 kg? How do you know?

15. **Estimate** About how many diamond kites have a total mass of 1 kg?

Kyle's Kites	
Type of Kite	**Mass**
Box Kite	360 g
Delta Kite	150 g
Diamond Kite	210 g

 Writing Math

Explain Does a large object always have a greater mass than a small object? Give an example.

CA Standards

AF 1.4 Express simple unit conversions in symbolic form (e.g., ___ inches = ___ feet × 12).

Also AF 1.0, KEY AF 1.1, MG 1.0, MG 1.4, NS 2.0, MR 1.1, MR 1.2, MR 2.0

Convert Metric Units

Objective Use multiplication and division to convert between metric units.

▶ Learn by Example

In this lesson, you will use multiplication and division to convert metric units.

Metric Units	
Mass	1 kilogram = 1,000 grams
Capacity	1 liter = 1,000 milliliters
Length	1 meter = 100 centimeters 1 kilometer = 1,000 meters

Maneesh's pail can hold 2 liters of water. How many milliliters is this?

1 Show how the units are related.

1 L = 1,000 mL

2 Compare the units.

A milliliter is smaller than a liter, so the number of milliliters will be greater than the number of liters.

Think
Your answer will be greater than 2.

3 Decide if you should multiply or divide.

Since your answer is greater than 2, you multiply.

$$2 \times 1{,}000 = 2{,}000$$

number of liters — number of milliliters in 1 liter — number of milliliters

Solution: 2,000 mL is the same amount as 2 L.

▶ Guided Practice

Choose the expression you would use to convert the units. Then convert the units.

Ask Yourself
- Which unit is smaller?
- Which unit is larger?
- Do I multiply or divide?

1. the number of grams in 5 kilograms
   a. 5 × 1,000   **b.** 1,000 ÷ 5

Guided Problem Solving

Use the questions to solve this problem.

2. Micah is collecting shells. He has 3,000 grams of shells. How many kilograms is this?

   a. Understand What do you need to find?

   b. Plan Compare the units. Then decide if you need to multiply or divide.

   c. Solve Use the **Hint** to solve the problem.

   3,000 g is the same amount as ◯ kg.

   3,000 ÷ 1,000 = ▨
   1,000 × ▨ = 3,000
   1,000 × 3 = 3,000
   So, 3,000 ÷ 1,000 = 3

   Hint
   You can use multiplication to solve the problem.

   d. Look Back Explain why your answer makes sense.

 Math Talk Write a rule that gives you the number of grams when you know the number of kilograms.

▶ Practice and Problem Solving

Choose the expression you would use to convert the units. Then convert the units.

3. the number of centimeters in 15 meters
   a. 15 × 100   **b.** 100 ÷ 15

4. the number of kilograms in 9,000 grams
   a. 9,000 × 1,000   **b.** 9,000 ÷ 1,000

Solve. Show your work.

5. Mac has to bring 4 L of water to a beach picnic. He can only find 500 mL bottles at the store. How many bottles should Mac buy?

6. **Challenge** Gia puts 1 drop of medicine in her fish tank for every 5,000 mL of water. The tank holds 35 L of water. How many drops should she put in?

 Science Link

Use the Fun Facts to solve.

7. Sam, a California Sea Lion, stays under water for 3 minutes. How many seconds is this?

8. Write the expression you would use to find how many centimeters a Sea Lion can dive to find food.

9. A California Sea Lion can eat about 9 kg of food a day. How many kilograms would it eat in a week?

- California Sea Lions have large foreflippers that they move up and down to swim.
- California Sea Lions can dive 60 meters to find food.

Science LS 3.a

Spiral Review and Test Practice

Solve. MG 1.4 page 596

10. There are 16 ounces in a pound. How many ounces are in 4 pounds?

11. There are 4 quarts in a gallon. How many quarts are in 7 gallons?

Write the letter of the correct answer. AF 1.4

12. Which of the following can you use to find how many grams are in 4 kilograms?

   A 1,000 × 1   **B** 4 × 100   **C** 4 × 1,000   **D** 1,000 ÷ 4

Extra Practice See page 619, Set C.

Key Standards Review

Need Help?
See Key Standards Handbook.

Use the price list to solve Problems 1 and 2. KEY **NS 3.3**

1. Brina buys 1 shirt and 1 pair of shoes. She gives the clerk two $20 bills. What should her change be?

2. Jesse bought a t-shirt at a different sale where the same t-shirts were 4 for $32. Who got the better price?

HUGE SALE!

Shoes............. 2 pairs for $50
T-Shirts...................3 for $27

Use the table to solve Problems 3–5. KEY **AF 2.1**

3. Find the pattern. Then copy and complete the table.

Stamps	1	2	3	4	5	6
Cost	$0.42	$0.84	$1.26			

4. What is the cost of 8 stamps? Explain.

5. Kendra puts 3 stamps on one letter and 12 stamps on a package. What is the cost of Kendra's mail? Explain how you can check your answer.

 Measurement

Missing Units!

Pick two different measurement units to complete each number sentence. You may use each unit more than once. MG 1.4, AF 1.4

1. 36 ▨ = 1 ▨

2. 2,100 ▨ > 2 ▨

3. 19 ▨ < 2 ▨

4. 300 ▨ = 3 ▨

cm
in.   ft
m
km   yd

Problem Solving

Objective Use skills and strategies to solve word problems.

San Pedro, CA

CA Standards
MR 1.0, MR 2.0,
MR 2.5, MR 3.0,
MR 3.1, MR 3.3,
NS 2.0, KEY **NS 2.1**,
MG 1.0, MG 1.1

Pacific Gray Whales migrate along the Pacific Coast.

If you go whale watching with the Cabrillo Marine Aquarium,
you may see Pacific Gray Whales!

Solve. Tell which strategy or method you used.

1. Is 90 g or 900 kg a better estimate for the mass of a
baby whale?

2. The total mass of 2 baby whales is 2,100 kg. The mass
of one whale is 250 kg less than the mass of the other
whale. What is the mass of each whale?

> **Hint**
> Read the problem
> again. Does your
> answer make
> sense?

Use the price list for Problem 3.

3. Erica has $45. She wants to buy 4 books.

a. Does she need to find an exact amount or can she
use an estimate to find out if she has enough money?

b. Mato has $20. He wants to buy 2 posters. Does
he need to find an exact amount or can he use an
estimate to find out if he has enough money?

c. **Generalize** When is an estimate good enough if you
are trying to see if you have enough money?

*Whale Items
for Sale*

Book $12
Poster $9

Problem Solving On Tests

Select a Strategy
- Write an Equation
- Guess and Check
- Choose the Operation
- Estimate

1. Anna's dog weighs 9 kilograms. There are 1,000 grams in 1 kilogram. How many grams does Anna's dog weigh?

   A 900 g   **C** 9,000 g

   B 90 g   **D** 90,000 g

   MG 1.4 page 612

2. Remi wrote this number sentence.

   $4 \times 9 < 2 \times$ ▮

   Which number should she use to make the number sentence true?

   A 19

   B 18

   C 16

   D 17

   Test Tip
   Choose the answer you think is correct and check your pick.

   AF 1.2 page 124

3. Laura has this number sentence.

   72 ⬭ 8 = 9

   Which sign should she put in the box to make it true?

   A +   **C** ×

   B −   **D** ÷

   AF 1.3 page 308

4. Mrs. Sims paid $68 dollars for 4 small trees. Each tree had the same price. How much did each tree cost?

   A $17

   B $20

   C $62

   D $72

   Test Tip
   Use estimation to check your answer.

   NS 2.0 page 548

5. An outdoor theater can seat 1584 people in 6 equal sections. How many people can sit in each section?

   A 244   **C** 264

   B 246   **D** 266

   NS 2.5 page 562

Education Place
Visit www.eduplace.com/camap/ for
Test-Taking Tips and **Extra Practice**.

Chapter 28 Lesson 4   **617**

Reading & Writing **Math**

Vocabulary

When you find how long or tall something is, you find its **length**. When you find how much something holds you find its **capacity**. When you find how much matter something has, you find its **mass**.

Use the words in the **Word Bank** to copy and complete the table below.

Word Bank for Metric Measurements
centimeter   liter   meter   kilogram
gram   kilometer   milliliter

Capacity	Length	Mass
1. _____	3. _____	6. _____
2. _____	4. _____	7. _____
	5. _____	

Writing
Look at the units of mass you listed. Write them in order by size from smallest to largest. What is the relationship between these units of measurement?

Reading
Look for this book in your library.

- *Counting On Frank*, by Rod Clement

CA Standards
MR 2.3 Use a variety of methods, such as words, numbers, symbols, charts, graphs, tables, diagrams, and models, to explain mathematical reasoning.
Also MG 1.0, MG 1.1

Standards-Based Extra Practice

Set A ———————————————————————— **MG 1.1** page 608

Choose the better estimate for the capacity of the container.

1.

250 L or 250 mL

2.

150 L or 150 mL

3.

5 L or 5 mL

Set B ———————————————————————— **MG 1.1, MG 1.0** page 610

Choose the unit you would use to measure the mass of the object.

Write *g* or *kg*.

1.

2.

3.

Set C ———————————————————————— **AF 1.4, MG 1.4** page 612

Choose the expression you would use to convert the units. Then convert the units.

1. number of milliliters in 3 liters
   a. $3 \times 1{,}000$
   b. $1{,}000 \div 3$

2. number of meters in 5 kilometers
   a. $1{,}000 \div 5$
   b. $5 \times 1{,}000$

3. A basket of apples has a mass of 2 kg. Irene adds 570 g of apples to the basket. What is the mass, in grams, of the basket of apples now?

Education Place
Visit www.eduplace.com/camap/
for more **Extra Practice**.

Chapter 28 Extra Practice   **619**

Chapter Review/Test

Vocabulary and Concepts ───────────── MG 1.0, MG 1.1, MG 1.4

Choose the best word to complete each sentence.

1. A one liter bottle holds 1,000 _____.

2. _____ is the amount of matter in an object.

> **Word Bank**
>
> mass
>
> milliliters

Skills ───────────── AF 1.4, MG 1.0, MG 1.1, MG 1.4

Choose the better estimate for the capacity of the container.

3.

1 L or 10 L

4.

100 L or 100 mL

5.

50 mL or 50 L

Choose the unit you would use to measure the mass of the real world object. Write *g* or *kg*.

6. a car

7. a baseball

Choose the expression you would use to convert the units. Then write the product or quotient.

8. number of liters in 3,000 milliliters

    a. $3 \times 1{,}000$ **b.** $3{,}000 \div 1{,}000$

9. number of meters in 800 centimeters

    a. $800 \div 100$ **b.** 800×100

Problem Solving and Reasoning ───────────── MG 1.1, MG 1.4, MR 2.3

Solve.

10. Deirdre has 2,000 milliliters of water. Which container will hold all of her water, a teacup or a pitcher? Explain.

Writing Math Andy says you multiply to find the number of kilograms in 2,000 grams. Is he right? Explain.

Spiral Review and Test Practice

1. What is the area of the figure?

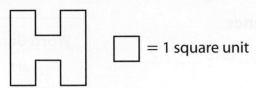 ☐ = 1 square unit

A 16 square units

B 5 square units

C 7 square units

D 3 square units

KEY **MG 1.2** page 220

2. Which sign goes in the box to make the number sentence true?

$63 \square 9 = 7$

Test Tip
Check your answer by using the sign to solve the equation.

A +   **C** −

B ×   **D** ÷

AF **1.3** page 288

3. What item costs $\frac{1}{2}$ dollar?

	Item	Price
A	Card	$1.25
B	Sticker	$0.50
C	Snack Bar	$0.75
D	Tote Bag	$2.50

NS **3.4** page 374

4. A theater has 315 seats. There are 9 seats in each row. How many rows are there?

A 31   **C** 35

B 306   **D** 2835

NS **2.5** page 570

5. Which of the following objects is heavier than 1 pound?

A
cat

C
feathers

B
flowers

D
insect

MG **1.1** page 592

6. Which number goes in the box to make the number sentence true?

$\square$ millimeters = 3 meters

A 3,000   **C** 1,000

B 3   **D** $\frac{1}{3}$

AF **1.4** page 612

Education Place
Visit www.eduplace.com/camap/ for **Test-Taking Tips** and **Extra Practice**.

Unit 10 Review/Test

Vocabulary and Concepts ———————————— MR 2.3 Chapters 27–28

Choose the best word to complete each sentence.

1. Two units used to measure weight are _____ and _____.

2. A _____ is larger than a pint, but smaller than a gallon.

3. _____ is the amount of matter in an object.

Word Bank

quart

weight

mass

ounce

pound

Skills ———————————— AF 1.4, MG 1.0, MG 1.1, MG 1.4 Chapter 27, Lesson 1

Choose the unit you would use to measure the capacity of each. Write *cup, pint, quart,* or *gallon*.

4.

5.

Choose the expression you use to convert the units. Then convert. Chapter 27, Lesson 4; Chapter 28, Lesson 3

6. The number of ounces in 4 pounds.

    a. $16 \div 4$ **b.** 4×16

7. The number of milliliters in 4 liters

    a. $1,000 \div 4$ **b.** $1,000 \times 4$

Choose the unit you would use to measure the capacity of each. Write *mL* or *L*. Chapter 28, Lesson 1

8. an eyedropper   **9.** a car gas tank   **10.** a sink

Choose the unit you would use to measure the mass of the object. Write *g* or *kg*. Chapter 28, Lesson 2

11. a person   **12.** a coin   **13.** a grape

Problem Solving and Reasoning ———— AF 1.4, MG 1.4 Chapters 27–28

Solve.

14. Sally needs 32 one-cup servings of juice for her party. How many one-quart containers of juice does Sally need?

15. Victor does yard work for 3 hours each day. How many hours does he work in 2 weeks?

BIG IDEA!

Writing Math How do you convert feet to inches? How do you convert meters to centimeters. Which is easier? Why?

Performance Assessment

Measurement Day MG 1.0, MG 1.1, MR 1.0, MR 2.0

Marcy looked around the classroom. She chose a water pitcher. She said that she could find the height of the pitcher, the mass of the pitcher, and how much water it holds.

| Object | Metric Units | | |
	Height or Length	Mass	Capacity

Task	Information You Need
Look around your classroom. Copy and complete the table for two different objects.	Find the height or length of each object.
	Estimate the mass and the capacity of each object.
	Label your measurements with the correct metric units.

Divide by 6

> The answer can be quick to see, divide by 2 and then by 3!

> Dividing in steps is easier than doing everything all at once. Look at Problem 1. First, I divide 42 by 2 to get 21, then I divide 21 by 3 to get 7.

1. $42 \div 6 \rightarrow \boxed{21} \rightarrow \boxed{7}$
Divide   Divide
42 by 2.   by 3.

2. $18 \div 6 \rightarrow \blacksquare \rightarrow \blacksquare$
Divide   Divide
18 by 2.   by 3.

3. $24 \div 6 \rightarrow \blacksquare \rightarrow \blacksquare$
Divide   Divide
24 by 2.   by 3.

4. $60 \div 6 \rightarrow \blacksquare \rightarrow \blacksquare$
Divide   Divide
60 by 2.   by 3.

Nice work! Now try these!

5. $30 \div 6 \rightarrow \blacksquare \rightarrow \blacksquare$
Divide   Divide
30 by 2.   by 3.

6. $48 \div 6 \rightarrow \blacksquare \rightarrow \blacksquare$
Divide   Divide
48 by 2.   by 3.

7. $66 \div 6 \rightarrow \blacksquare \rightarrow \blacksquare$
Divide   Divide
66 by 2.   by 3.

8. $120 \div 6 \rightarrow \blacksquare \rightarrow \blacksquare$
Divide   Divide
120 by 2.   by 3.

Take It Further!
Now try doing all the steps in your head!

9. $36 \div 6$

10. $72 \div 6$

624

Looking Ahead

THIS YEAR I learned to ...

Number Sense

- use place value to compare, order, and round whole numbers;
- find the sum or difference of whole numbers;
- multiply and divide using multiplication facts for 1 through 10;
- add and subtract simple fractions; and
- solve problems using money amounts in decimal notation.

Write the value of the underlined digit.

1. 5<u>8</u>9   **2.** 1,<u>3</u>74   **3.** 4,<u>0</u>89   **4.** <u>2</u>,561

 KEY **NS 1.3**

Algebra and Functions

- show relationships between quantities;
- solve problems involving functional relationships.

Copy and complete the table.

5. How much do 4 movie tickets cost?

Rule: Multiply by $6	
Movie Ticket	Cost
1	$6
2	$12
3	$18
4	

 KEY **AF 2.1**

Measurement and Geometry

- identify, describe, and classify polygons;
- identify attributes of triangles and quadrilaterals;
- find the perimeter of a polygon; and
- estimate or determine area and volume.

Identify each figure.

6.

7.

8.

9.

KEY **MG 2.1**, KEY **MG 2.2**, KEY **MG 2.3**

Statistics, Data Analysis, and Probability

- record the possible outcomes for a simple event; and
- display results of probability experiments in an organized way, such as a line plot or bar graph.

10. **You pick a block from this bag. What are the possible outcomes?**

11. **Use the data in the line plot to make a bar graph.**

Number Rolled on Number Cube					
X		X		X	X
X	X	X	X	X	X
X	X	X	X	X	X
1	2	3	4	5	6

KEY **SDAP 1.2**, KEY **SDAP 1.3**

NEXT YEAR I will learn more about...

- place value of larger numbers;
- computing with larger numbers;
- simple fractions and decimals; and
- the relationship between plane and solid geometric figures.

I can use the Review/Preview worksheets to get ready for next year.

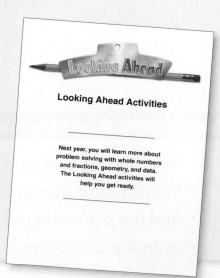

Looking Ahead

Looking Ahead Activities

Next year, you will learn more about problem solving with whole numbers and fractions, geometry, and data. The Looking Ahead activities will help you get ready.

Table of Measures

Metric

Length

1 meter (m) = 100 centimeters (cm)
1 centimeter = 10 millimeters (mm)
1 kilometer (km) = 1,000 meters

Capacity

1 liter (L) = 1,000 milliliters (mL)

Mass/Weight

1 kilogram (kg) = 1,000 grams (g)

Customary

Length

1 foot (ft) = 12 inches (in.)
1 yard (yd) = 36 inches
1 yard = 3 feet
1 mile (mi) = 5,280 feet

Capacity

1 pint (pt) = 2 cups (c)
1 quart (qt) = 2 pints
1 gallon (gal) = 4 quarts

Mass/Weight

1 pound (lb) = 16 ounces (oz)

Time

1 year = 365 days (d)
1 year = 12 months (mo)
1 year = 52 weeks (wk)
1 week = 7 days
1 day = 24 hours (h)
1 hour = 60 minutes (min)
1 minute = 60 seconds (s)

California English-Spanish

Glossary

A

addend A number to be added in an addition expression or number sentence

Example: $5 + 6 = 11$

addends

sumando Número que se suma en una expresión de suma o enunciado numérico

addition An operation that shows the joining of two or more numbers or quantities to form a new number called the sum

suma Operación que muestra la unión de dos o más números o cantidades para formar un número nuevo llamado la suma

angle A figure formed by two rays with the same endpoint

ángulo Una figura formada por dos semirrectas con el mismo origen

area The number of square units in a region

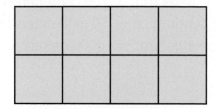

Area = 8 square units

área El número de unidades cuadradas en una región

array An arrangement of objects or pictures in equal columns and rows

matriz Un arreglo de objetos, dibujos o números en columnas y filas

Associative Property of Addition (Also called the Grouping Property of Addition.) The property that states that the way in which addends are grouped does not change the sum
Example: (2 + 3) + 4 = 2 + (3 + 4)

Propiedad asociativa de la suma (También llamada Propiedad de agrupación de la suma). Propiedad que establece que la manera en que se agrupan los sumandos no cambia la suma
Ejemplo: (2 + 3) + 4 = 2 + (3 + 4)

Associative Property of Multiplication (Also called the Grouping Property of Multiplication.) The property which states that the way in which factors are grouped does not change the product
Example: (5 x 4) x 3 = 5 x (4 x 3)

Propiedad asociativa de la multiplicación (También llamada Propiedad de agrupación de la multiplicación). Propiedad que establece que la manera en que se agrupan los factores no cambia el producto
Ejemplo: (5 x 4) x 3 = 5 x (4 x 3)

B

bar graph A graph that uses bars to show data

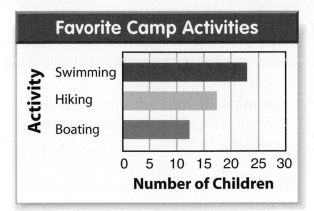

gráfica de barras Gráfica que usa barras para mostrar datos

C

capacity The amount a container can hold

capacidad Cantidad que puede contener un recipiente

Celsius (°C) The metric unit used to measure temperature

Celsius (°C) Unidad métrica usada para medir temperatura

centimeter (cm) A metric unit used to measure length. 100 centimeters = 1 meter

centímetro (cm) Unidad métrica usada para medir longitud. 100 centímetros = 1 metro

certain In probability, a prediction that implies something will definitely happen

seguro En probabilidad, una predicción que implica que algo definitivamente sucederá

change The amount of money returned when what is given is more than what is due

cambio Cantidad de dinero devuelta cuando lo que se da es más que lo que se debe

circle A two-dimensional figure where each part is the same distance from the center

círculo Figura de dos dimensiones en la que cada parte está a la misma distancia del centro

column A vertical group of entries in a table or an array

columna Un grupo vertical de entradas en una tabla o una matriz

Commutative Property of Addition (Also called the Order Property of Addition.) The property that states that the order of addends does not change the sum
Example: $6 + 7 = 7 + 6$

Propiedad conmutativa de la suma (También llamada Propiedad de orden de la suma). Propiedad que establece que el orden de los sumandos no cambia la suma
Ejemplo: $6 + 7 = 7 + 6$

Commutative Property of Multiplication (Also called the Order Property of Multiplication.) The property that states that the order of factors does not change the product
Example: $4 \times 3 = 3 \times 4$

Propiedad conmutativa de la multiplicación (También llamada Propiedad de orden de la multiplicación). Propiedad que establece que el orden de los factores no cambia el producto
Ejemplo: $4 \times 3 = 3 \times 4$

compare Examine the value of numbers to find if they are greater than, less than, or equal to one another

comparar Examinar el valor de un número para hallar si es mayor, menor o igual que otro

compatible numbers Numbers that are easy to compute mentally

números compatibles Números que son fáciles de calcular mentalmente

cone A three-dimensional figure with one circular flat surface, one curved surface, and a vertex

cono Figura de tres dimensiones con una superficie plana circular, una superficie curva y un vértice

cube A three-dimensional figure that has six square faces of equal size

cubo Figura de tres dimensiones que tiene seis caras cuadradas del mismo tamaño

cubic unit A unit for measuring volume. A cube with sides one unit long.

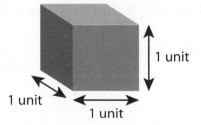

1 unit

1 unit

1 unit

unidad cúbica Unidad que se usa para medir el volumen. Cubo con lados que miden una unidad de largo.

cup (c) A customary unit used to measure capacity. 1 cup = 8 ounces

taza (tz) Unidad usual que se usa para medir capacidad. 1 taza = 8 onzas

customary measurement system A system of measurement that uses inches and feet to measure length, cups and gallons to measure capacity, and ounces and pounds to measure weight.

sistema inglés (usual) Sistema de medida que usa pulgadas y pies para medir longitud, tazas y galones para medir capacidad y onzas y libras para medir peso.

cylinder A three-dimensional figure with two identical, circular faces and one curved surface

cilindro Figura de tres dimensiones que tiene dos caras circulares idénticas y una superficie curva

data A set of numbers or pieces of information

datos Conjunto de números o información

decimal A number with one or more digits to the right of a decimal point. Examples: 0.5, 0.06, and 12.679 are decimals.

decimal Un número con uno o más dígitos a la derecha del punto decimal. Ejemplos: 0.5, 0.06 y 12.679 son decimales.

decimal point (.) The point separating the parts from the wholes in a number

punto decimal (.) Punto que separa las partes de los enteros en un número

denominator The number below the bar in a fraction. The denominator names the total number of equal parts.

Example: $\dfrac{1}{5}$ ← denominator

denominador Número que está debajo de la barra de una fracción. El denominador indica el número total de partes iguales.

difference The result of subtraction

Example: $10 - 7 = 3$

↑
difference

diferencia Resultado de una resta

digit Any of the symbols 0, 1, 2, 3, 4, 5, 6, 7, 8, 9 in the base-ten numeration system

dígito Cualquiera de los símbolos 0, 1, 2, 3, 4, 5, 6, 7, 8, 9 del sistema de numeración de base diez

divide To separate an amount into smaller, equal groups in order to find the number of groups or the number in each group

dividir Separar una cantidad en grupos más pequeños e iguales para hallar el número de grupos o el número que hay en cada grupo

dividend The number being divided in division. In the number sentence $30 \div 5 = 6$, the dividend is 30.

Examples: $32 \div 4 = 8$

$4 \overline{)32}^{\,8}$

↑ dividend   ↑ dividend

dividendo Número que se divide en una división. En el enunciado numérico $30 \div 5 = 6$, el dividendo es 30.

division An operation that shows the separation of a number or quantity (the dividend) into equal parts

división Operación que muestra la separación de un número o cantidad (el dividendo) en partes iguales

divisor The number that divides the dividend in division. In the number sentence $30 \div 5 = 6$, the divisor is 5.

Examples: $32 \div 4 = 8$

$4 \overline{)32}^{\,8}$

↑ divisor   ↑ divisor

divisor Número entre el cual se divide al dividendo en una división. En el enunciado numérico $30 \div 5 = 6$, el divisor es 5.

dollar sign A symbol ($) written to show that a number represents dollars

signo de dólar Un símbolo ($) escrito para mostrar que un número representa dólares

double Twice an amount

doble Dos veces una cantidad

edge The line segment where the faces of a three-dimensional figure meet

← edge

arista Segmento de recta donde se encuentran las caras de una figura de tres dimensiones

equal groups Groups that have the same number of items

grupos iguales Grupos que tienen el mismo número de objetos

equal shares Amounts that have the same value

partes iguales Cantidades que tienen el mismo valor

equal sign (=) The symbol that shows that two expressions have the same value

signo de igual (=) Símbolo que muestra que dos expresiones tienen el mismo valor

equality A number sentence with an equal sign that shows that two expressions have the same value. It is also called an equation.

igualdad Enunciado numérico con un signo de igual que muestra que dos expresiones tienen el mismo valor. También es llamada ecuación.

equally likely Having the same probability of happening

igualmente probable Que tiene la misma probabilidad de suceder

equation A mathematical sentence with an equal sign that shows that two expressions have the same value. It is also called an equality.

ecuación Enunciado matemático con un signo de igual que muestra que dos expresiones tienen el mismo valor. También es llamada igualdad.

equilateral triangle A triangle that has three equal sides

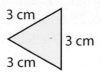

3 cm
3 cm
3 cm

triángulo equilátero Triángulo que tiene tres lados iguales

equivalent fractions Fractions that name the same part of a whole or collection

Example: $\frac{2}{3}$ and $\frac{10}{15}$ are equivalent fractions

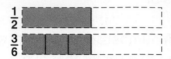

fracciones equivalentes Fracciones que indican la misma parte de un entero o grupo

Ejemplo: $\frac{2}{3}$ y $\frac{10}{15}$ son fracciones equivalentes

estimate A number close to an exact amount; to find about how many

estimación; estimar Número cercano a una cantidad exacta; hallar una cantidad aproximada

event In probability, an outcome of an experiment

suceso En probabilidad, resultado de un experimento

expanded form A way to write a number that shows the value of each digit. 25,040 in expanded form is 20,000 + 5,000 + 40.

notación extendida Manera de escribir un número que muestra el valor de cada dígito. 25,040 en forma extendida es 20,000 + 5,000 + 40.

expression A number or group of numbers with operation symbols

Examples: $6 + 4$; 6×4; $6 - 4$; $4 \div 2$; 10

expresión Número o grupo de números con símbolos de operaciones

face A flat surface of a three-dimensional figure

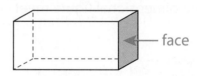

cara Superficie plana de una figura de tres dimensiones

fact family Related facts that use the same numbers with inverse operations. A fact family for 2, 4, and 6:

$2 + 4 = 6 \qquad 4 + 2 = 6$
$6 - 4 = 2 \qquad 6 - 2 = 4$

A fact family for 3, 5, and 15:

$3 \times 5 = 15 \qquad 5 \times 3 = 15$
$15 \div 5 = 3 \qquad 15 \div 3 = 5$

familia de operaciones Operaciones relacionadas que usan los mismos números con operaciones inversas. Familia de operaciones para 2, 4 y 6:

$2 + 4 = 6 \qquad 4 + 2 = 6$
$6 - 4 = 2 \qquad 6 - 2 = 4$

Familia de operaciones para 3, 5 y 15:

$3 \times 5 = 15 \qquad 5 \times 3 = 15$
$15 \div 5 = 3 \qquad 15 \div 3 = 5$

factor A number that can be multiplied to obtain a given product. For example, in the equation 3 x 5 = 15, 3 and 5 are the factors.

$$4 \times 5 = 20$$

factor   factor

factor Número que puede ser multiplicado por otro para obtener un producto dado. Por ejemplo, en la ecuación 3 x 5 = 15, 3 y 5 son los factores.

Fahrenheit (°F) The customary unit used to measure temperature

Fahrenheit (°F) Unidad usual que se usa para medir temperatura

foot (ft) A customary unit used to measure length. 1 foot = 12 inches

pie Unidad usual que se usa para medir longitud. 1 pie = 12 pulgadas

fraction A way of expressing a part of a whole, a whole, or more than one whole. $\frac{1}{2}$, $\frac{4}{4}$, and $\frac{6}{5}$ are fractions.

fracción Manera de expresar una parte de un entero, un entero o más de un entero. $\frac{1}{2}$, $\frac{4}{4}$ y $\frac{6}{5}$ son fracciones.

function rule A rule that gives exactly one output value for each input value

regla de función Regla que da exactamente un valor de salida por cada valor de entrada

function table A table of ordered pairs that follows a rule and matches an output to an input

tabla de función Tabla de pares ordenados que sigue una regla y empareja una salida con una entrada

gallon (gal) A customary unit used to measure capacity. 1 gallon = 4 quarts

galón (gal) Unidad usual que se usa para medir capacidad. 1 galón = 4 cuartos

gram (g) A metric unit used to measure mass. 1,000 grams = 1 kilogram

gramo (g) Unidad métrica que se usa para medir masa.
1,000 gramos = 1 kilogramo

greater than (>) The symbol used to compare two numbers
Example: 5 > 4 means 5 is greater than 4.

mayor que (>) Símbolo que se usa para comparar dos números
Ejemplo: 5 > 4 significa que 5 es mayor que 4.

H

hexagon A polygon having 6 sides and 6 vertices

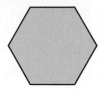

hexágono Polígono que tiene 6 lados y 6 vértices

hour A unit of time equal to 60 minutes

hora Unidad de tiempo que equivale a 60 minutos

hundreds

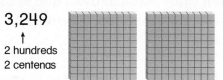

3,249
↑
2 hundreds
2 centenas

centenas

hundredths One or more of one hundred equal parts of a whole

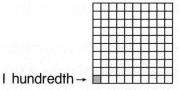

I hundredth →

centésimas Una o más partes de cien partes iguales de un entero

I

Identity Property of Addition (Also called the Zero Property.) The property that states that the sum of any number and zero is that number

Propiedad de identidad de la suma (También llamada Propiedad cero.) Propiedad que establece que la suma de cualquier número y cero es ese mismo número

Identity Property of Multiplication The property that states that the product of any number and 1 is that number

Propiedad de identidad de la multiplicación Propiedad que establece que el producto de cualquier número y 1 es ese mismo número

impossible An event that cannot happen is an impossible event

imposible Un suceso que no puede ocurrir es un suceso imposible

improper fraction A fraction that is greater than or equal to 1. The numerator in an improper fraction is greater than or equal to the denominator.
Examples: $\frac{5}{5}$ and $\frac{8}{7}$ are improper fractions.

fracción impropia Una fracción que es mayor que ó igual a 1. El numerador en una fracción impropia es mayor que ó igual al denominador.
Ejemplos: $\frac{5}{5}$ y $\frac{8}{7}$ son fracciones impropias.

inch (in.) A customary unit used to measure length. 12 inches = 1 foot

pulgada (pulg) Unidad usual que se usa para medir longitud. 12 pulgadas = 1 pie

inequality A sentence that contains > (is greater than) or < (is less than)
Examples: 8 > 2, 5 < 6

desigualdad Enunciado que contiene > (es mayor que) ó < (es menor que)
Ejemplos: 8 > 2, 5 < 6

intersecting lines Lines that cross each other at a common point

rectas secantes Líneas que se entrecruzan en un punto común

inverse operations Opposite operations. Addition and subtraction are inverse operations. Multiplication and division are inverse operations.

operaciones inversas Operaciones opuestas. La suma y la resta son operaciones inversas. La multiplicación y la división son operaciones inversas.

isosceles triangle A triangle that has two equal sides

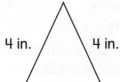

4 in.   4 in.

triángulo isósceles
Triángulo que tiene dos lados iguales

K

key A key tells what each symbol represents on a map or graph

clave Una clave indica qué representa cada símbolo en un mapa o una gráfica

kilogram (kg) A metric unit used to measure mass. 1 kilogram = 1,000 grams

kilogramo (kg) Unidad métrica que se usa para medir masa. 1 kilogramo = 1,000 gramos.

kilometer (km) A metric unit used to measure length. 1 kilometer = 1,000 meters

kilómetro (km) Unidad métrica que se usa para medir longitud. 1 kilómetro = 1,000 metros

L

length The dimension that tells how long something is

longitud Dimensión que indica cuán largo es algo

less than (<) The symbol used to compare two numbers. 4 < 5 means four is less than five.

menor que (<) Símbolo usado para comparar dos números. 4 < 5 significa cuatro es menor que cinco.

likely In probability, a prediction that implies something probably will happen

probable En probabilidad, una predicción que implica que algo probablemente sucederá

line A continuous straight path that goes on forever in opposite directions

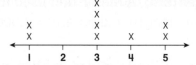

recta Línea continua que va hacia el infinito en ambas direcciones

line plot A diagram that organizes data above a number line

```
                X
                X
    X           X           X
    X           X     X     X
  ┬─────┬─────┬─────┬─────┬
    1     2     3     4     5
```

diagrama de puntos Diagrama que organiza datos sobre una recta numérica

line segment Part of a line. A line segment has two endpoints.

●━━━━━━━━━━━●

segmento de recta Parte de una recta. Un segmento de recta tiene dos orígenes.

liquid volume See *capacity*.
volumen líquido Ver *capacidad*.

liter (L) A metric unit used to measure capacity. 1 liter = 1,000 milliliters

litro (L) Unidad métrica que se usa para medir capacidad. 1 litro = 1,000 mililitros

mass The amount of matter in an object. Often it is measured using grams or kilograms.

masa Cantidad de materia en un objeto. Se mide frecuentemente en gramos o kilogramos.

meter (m) A metric unit used to measure length. 1 meter = 100 centimeters

metro (m) Unidad métrica que se usa para medir longitud. 1 metro = 100 centímetros

metric system A system of measurement that uses meters to measure length, liters to measure capacity, and kilograms to measure mass

sistema métrico Sistema de medida que usa metros para medir longitud, litros para medir capacidad y kilogramos para medir masa

mile (mi) A customary unit used to measure length. 1 mile = 5,280 feet

milla (mi) Unidad usual que se usa para medir longitud. 1 milla = 5,280 pies

milliliter (mL) A metric unit used to measure capacity. 1,000 milliliters = 1 liter

mililitro (mL) Unidad métrica que se usa para medir capacidad. 1,000 mililitros = 1 litro

millimeter (mm) A metric unit used to measure length. 1,000 millimeters = 1 meter

milímetro (mm) Unidad métrica que se usa para medir longitud. 1,000 milímetros = 1 metro

minute A unit of time equal to 60 seconds

minuto Unidad de tiempo igual a 60 segundos

missing addend The unknown addend when one addend and the sum are known

sumando que falta Sumando desconocido cuando un sumando y la suma se conocen

missing factor The unknown factor when one factor and the product are known

factor que falta Factor desconocido cuando un factor y el producto se conocen

multiple A number that is the product of the given number and a number. For example, 12 is a multiple of 4, because 3 x 4 = 12.

múltiplo Número que es el producto de un número dado y un número. Por ejemplo, 12 es múltiplo de 4, porque 3 x 4 = 12.

multiplication An operation on two numbers that gives a product

multiplicación Operación de dos números que resulta en un producto

multiply An operation to determine the total amount in a given number of equal groups

multiplicar Operación que determina la cantidad total en un número dado de grupos iguales

not equal to (≠) The symbol that shows that two expressions do not have the same value

no es igual a (≠) Símbolo que muestra que dos expresiones no tienen el mismo valor

numerator The number above the bar in a fraction

Example: $\dfrac{1}{5}$ ← numerator

numerador Número que se encuentra encima de la barra en una fracción

octagon A polygon with eight sides

octágono Un polígono de ocho lados

ones

$$3,249$$

↑
9 ones
9 unidades

unidades

order (numbers) Arrange numbers from greatest to least or least to greatest

ordenar (números) Agrupar números de mayor a menor o de menor a mayor

ounce (oz) A customary unit used to measure weight. 16 ounces = 1 pound

onza (oz) Unidad usual que se usa para medir peso. 16 onzas = 1 libra

outcome A result in a probability experiment. In tossing a coin, there are two possible outcomes, heads or tails.

resultado Consecuencia de un experimento de probabilidad. Al lanzar una moneda, los dos resultados posibles son cara y cruz.

parallel lines Lines that do not intersect. They are the same distance apart everywhere.

rectas paralelas Rectas que no se intersecan. Tienen la misma distancia de separación en cualquiera de sus puntos.

parallel line segments Line segments that are part of parallel lines

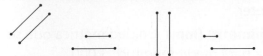

segmentos de recta paralelos Segmentos de recta que forman parte de rectas paralelas

parallelogram A quadrilateral in which both pairs of opposite sides are parallel

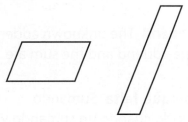

paralelogramo Cuadrilátero en el que ambos pares de lados opuestos son paralelos

pentagon A polygon with five sides

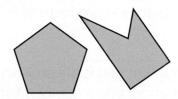

pentágono Polígono con cinco lados

perimeter The distance around a figure. Example: The perimeter of this rectangle is 20 inches.

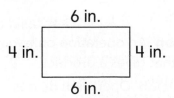
6 in.

4 in.   4 in.

6 in.

perímetro Distancia alrededor de una figura.
Ejemplo: El perímetro de este rectángulo es de 20 pulgadas.

perpendicular lines Lines that intersect at right angles

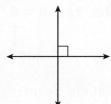

rectas perpendiculares Rectas que se intersecan formando ángulos rectos

pictograph A graph that represents data with pictures

Fish in Eric's Tank	
Guppies	🐟 🐟
Mollies	🐟 🐟 🐟 🐟 🐟
Neons	🐟 🐟 🐟
Each 🐟 stands for 5 fish.	

pictografía Gráfica que representa datos con dibujos

pint (pt) A customary unit used to measure capacity. 2 pints = 1 quart

pinta (pt) Unidad usual que se usa para medir capacidad. 2 pintas = 1 cuarto

place value The number assigned to each place in a number written in standard form. In 346, the digit 3 is in the hundreds place.

valor de posición Número asignado a cada posición en un número escrito en forma normal. En 346, el dígito 3 está en el lugar de las centenas.

plane figure A geometric figure that lies in one plane

figura plana Figura geométrica que se encuentra en un plano

polygon A simple closed plane figure made up of three or more line segments

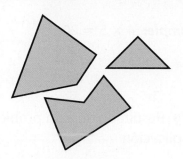

polígono Figura plana simple y cerrada, formada por 3 ó más segmentos de recta

pound (lb) A customary unit used to measure weight. 1 pound = 16 ounces

libra (lb) Unidad usual que se usa para medir peso. 1 libra = 16 onzas

predict To make a guess about the chance that an event will occur

predecir Estimar sobre la probabilidad de que un suceso ocurra

prism A solid figure that has two parallel congruent bases and parallelograms for faces

prisma Cuerpo geométrico que tiene dos bases paralelas congruentes y paralelogramos por caras

probability The chance of an event occurring

probabilidad Posibilidad de que ocurra un suceso

product The answer to a multiplication problem

Example: $4 \times 5 = 20$

product

producto Resultado de a un problema de multiplicación

pyramid A solid figure whose base can be any polygon and whose faces are triangles with a common vertex

pirámide Cuerpo geométrico cuya base puede ser cualquier polígono y cuyas caras son triángulos con un vértice común

quadrilateral A polygon with four sides

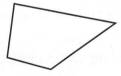

cuadrilátero Polígono con cuatro lados

quart (qt) A customary unit used to measure capacity. 4 quarts = 1 gallon

cuarto de galón Unidad usual que se usa para medir capacidad. 4 cuartos = 1 galón

quotient The answer to a division problem

Example: $32 \div 4 = 8$

quotient

cociente Resultado de un problema de división

ray A part of a line that has one endpoint and goes on forever in one direction

semirrecta Parte de una recta que tiene un origen y se extiende de manera infinita en una dirección

rectangle A polygon with opposite sides parallel and four right angles

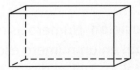

rectángulo Polígono de lados opuestos paralelos y cuatro ángulos rectos

rectangular prism A solid figure whose faces all are rectangular

prisma geométrico rectangular Cuerpo geométrico cuyas caras son todas rectangulares

regroup To use place value to exchange equal amounts when renaming a number

reagrupar Usar valor de posición para intercambiar cantidades iguales al convertir un número

related facts Facts that are in the same fact family. See *fact family*.

operaciones relacionadas Operaciones que pertenencen a la misma familia de operaciones. Ver familia de operaciones.

repeated addition The same addend is used again and again

suma repetida El mismo sumando es usado una y otra vez

repeated subtraction The same number is subtracted again and again

resta repetida El mismo número es restado una y otra vez

right angle An angle that measures 90°

ángulo recto Ángulo que mide 90°

right triangle A triangle with one right angle

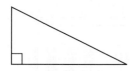

triángulo rectángulo Triángulo con un ángulo recto

round To find about how many or how much by expressing a number to the nearest ten, hundred, thousand, and so on

redondear Hallar una cantidad aproximando el número a la decena, centena, millar más cercanos

row A horizontal group of cells in a table

fila Grupo horizontal de celdas en una tabla

scalene triangle A triangle with sides of all different lengths

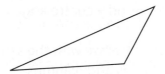

triángulo escaleno Triángulo con lados de longitudes diferentes

second A unit of time. There are 60 seconds in a minute.

segundo Unidad de tiempo. Un minuto tiene 60 segundos.

side (of a polygon) One of the line segments that make up a polygon

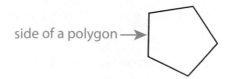

side of a polygon →

lado (de un polígono) Uno de los segmentos de recta que conforman un polígono

solid figure A figure that has three dimensions

cuerpo geométrico Una figura que tiene tres dimensiones

sphere A solid figure that is shaped like a round ball

esfera Cuerpo geométrico que tiene forma de pelota redonda

square A rectangle with four sides of equal length and four right angles

cuadrado Rectángulo con cuatro lados de igual longitud y cuatro ángulos rectos

square array An array with the same number of rows and columns

matriz cuadrada Matriz que tiene el mismo número de filas y de columnas

square number The product of a whole number multiplied by itself

número al cuadrado El producto de un número entero multiplicado por sí mismo

square pyramid A pyramid with a square base and four triangular faces

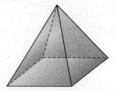

pirámide cuadrangular Pirámide cuya base es cuadrada que tiene cuatro caras triangulares

square unit A square with sides one unit long

unidad cuadrada Cuadrado con lados que miden una unidad de largo

standard form A way to write a number by using only digits. 25,040 is a number in standard form.

forma normal Manera de escribir un número, usando sólo dígitos. 25,040 es un número en forma normal.

subtraction An operation performed on two numbers to obtain a difference

resta Operación realizada en dos números para obtener una diferencia

sum The answer to an addition problem

Example: $5 + 8 = 13$
↑
sum

suma Resultado de un problema de suma

tally chart A chart that uses tally marks to record data

tablero de conteo Un tablero que usa marcas de conteo para registrar datos

tens

3,249
↑
4 tens
4 decends

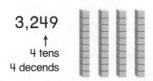

decenas

tenths One or more of ten equal parts of a whole

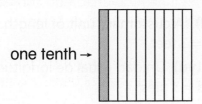

one tenth →

décimas Una o más de diez partes iguales de un entero

thousand Ten hundreds

millar Diez centenas

thousands

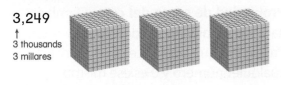

3,249
↑
3 thousands
3 millares

millares

thousandths One or more of a thousand equal parts of a whole

milésimas Una o más de mil partes iguales de un entero

three-dimensional Having length, width, and height

tridimensional Que tiene longitud, ancho y altura

triangle A polygon with three sides

triángulo Polígono con tres lados

two-dimensional Having length and width

bidimensional Que tiene longitud y ancho

 U

unit cost The cost of one item

unidad de costo El costo de un objeto

unit fraction A fraction whose numerator is 1. Example: 1/3 is a unit fraction.

unidad fraccionaria Fracción cuyo numerador es 1. Ejemplo: 1/3 es una unidad fraccionaria.

unlikely In probability, a prediction that implies something probably won't happen

improbable En probabilidad, una predicción que implica que algo probablemente no ocurrirá

V

vertex (vertices) of a polygon A point common to two sides of a polygon

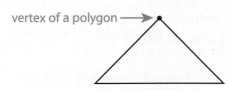

vertex of a polygon ⟶

vértice(s) de un polígono Punto común de dos lados de un polígono

vertex (vertices) of a prism A point common to the edges of a prism

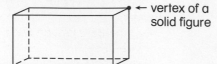

← vertex of a solid figure

vértice(s) de un prisma Punto común de las aristas de un prisma

volume The number of cubic units that fit inside a solid figure

volumen Número de unidades cúbicas que encajan dentro de un cuerpo geométrico

weight The measure of how heavy something is

peso La medida de cuán pesado es algo

whole number Any of the numbers 0, 1, 2, 3, 4, 5, and so on

número entero Cualquiera de los números 0, 1, 2, 3, 4, 5, y demás

width A dimension; The measure of how big something is from side to side

ancho Dimensión; la medida de cuán grande es algo de lado a lado

word form The form of a number that is written using words. 25,040 in word form is twenty-five thousand, forty.

forma verbal La forma de un número que es escrito usando palabras. 25,040 en forma verbal es veiticinco mil cuarenta.

yard (yd) A customary unit of length.
1 yard = 3 feet

yarda (yd) Unidad usual de longitud.
1 yarda = 3 pies

Zero Property of Addition (Also called Identity Property.) The property that states that the sum of any number and 0 is that number

Propiedad de suma del cero (También llamada Propiedad de identidad.) Propiedad que establece que la suma de cualquier número y 0 es ese mismo número

Zero Property of Multiplication The property that states that any number multiplied by zero is equal to zero

Propiedad de multiplicación del cero Propiedad que establece que cualquier número multiplicado por cero es igual a cero

Index

A

Activities, *see* Investigations and Challenges; Hands On lessons; Math Centers; Vocabulary

Addend
defined, 56–58
missing, 53, 54–55

Addition
calculating, 52–53, 54–55, 56–57, 58, 60–61, 62, 64–65, 84–85, 214–215, 216
column form, 56–58
estimate sums, 84–85, 86–87
four-digit and greater addends, 60–61, 84–85
inverse relationship to subtraction, 52–53, 54–55, 398–399
modeling, 50–51, 346–347, 348–349, 352, 386–387, 388–389
of fractions, 346–347, 348–349, 350, 354–356, 358
of greater numbers, 60–61
of money amounts in decimal notation, 386–387, 388–389, 395, 398–399
properties of, 54–55, 149
regrouping in, 50–51, 56–58, 60–61, 76
repeated, 100–101, 106–107, 144, 148
three or more addends, 56–57
three-digit numbers, 50–51
to solve problems, 52–53, 54–55, 56–58, 60–62, 64–65, 84–85, 214–216, 224
with regrouping, 50–51, 56–58, 60–61, 76
Zero Property of, 54–55

Addition sentences, 57, 62, 76, 214–215, 389, 395

Algebra, *see also* Functions; Properties
division sentences, 398–399
equations, 9, 52, 53, 57, 64, 100, 106, 111, 124, 132, 273, 284, 286–287, 288–289, 293, 301, 307, 308–309, 355, 358, 398–399, 412, 415, 421, 431, 549–550, 552, 564, 567–568

equations (continued), 617
inequalities, 52–53
input/output table, 597–598, 612–614
number sentences, 52–53, 54–55, 100, 124, 132, 152–153, 260–261, 262–263, 264, 266–267, 268–270, 282–284, 346–347, 348–350, 352–353, 354–356, 428–429, 489, 534–535
properties, 54–55, 102–104, 122–123, 106–107, 144–146, 149, 152–154, 430–431, 532
recognize patterns, 18–19
symbols, 562, 564

Algorithms, *see also* Addition; Division; Multiplication; Subtraction
division, 266–267
multiplication, 100–101
standard, 56–57, 60–61, 74–75, 78–79

Analyze problems
identifying relationships, 190–191, 196–197, 232–233, 234–235, 286–287, 330–331, 370–371, 398–399, 534–535, 600–601
observing patterns, 18–19, 104, 124, 143, 144–145, 148, 224–225, 280–281, 354–356, 392, 415
relevant and irrelevant information, 18, 338–339, 412–413

Angles
comparing, 190–191, 199
greater than, less than right angles, 190–191, 199
right, 190–191, 196–197, 198–199, 200–202, 204–205

Approximate solutions, 86–87, 416–417, 418, 608–609, 616

Area
contrasting to perimeter, 219, 222, 244–245
determining, 218–219, 220–222, 225, 244–245
estimating, 218–219
explore, 218–219

modeling, 218–219

Arrays
Commutative Property and, 102–104
division and, 262–264, 266–267
multiplication and, 102–103, 106, 128–129, 144, 148, 154, 170–171, 262–264
square numbers and, 128–129

Assessment, *see also* Spiral Review and Test Practice
chapter spiral review, 23, 41, 69, 91, 119, 139, 161, 187, 209, 229, 251, 277, 297, 317, 343, 363, 383, 403, 425, 445, 465, 493, 515, 539, 557, 577, 605, 621
chapter test, 22, 40, 68, 90, 118, 138, 160, 186, 208, 228, 250, 276, 296, 316, 342, 362, 382, 402, 424, 444, 464, 492, 514, 538, 556, 576, 604, 620
performance assessment, 43, 93, 163, 253, 319, 405, 467, 517, 579, 623
unit test, 42–43, 92–93, 162–163, 252–253, 318–319, 404–405, 466–467, 516–517, 578–579, 622–623

Associative Property
of addition, 54–55
of multiplication, 152–154, 430, 532

B

Background, *See* Math background

Bar graph, *see also* Daily Routines, Statistics, Data Analysis, and Probability
making, 482–483, 485–486
using, 194–195, 284, 482–483, 488–489

Base-ten blocks, modeling with, 6, 26, 50, 72, 73, 74, 412, 428–429, 430, 434–435, 448–449, 542–543, 544, 560

Basic facts
division, 282–284, 288–290, 302–304, 306–307, 308–310

collect and represent in tables, graphs, lists, diagrams, 12, 76, 104, 212–213, 214–215, 233, 239, 375–376, 394–396, 476–478, 485, 496–497, 503, 505–506, 525, 526–528, 531, 543, 561

compare, 28, 35, 474–475, 476–478, 486

making displays, 480–481, 482–483, 484–485, 502–503, 504 506

organizing, 101, 171, 281, 474–475

recording, 171, 281, 413, 480–481, 496–497

using, 12, 76, 104, 212–213, 214–215, 233, 239, 329, 375–376, 392, 394–396, 476–478, 480–481, 485, 496–497, 503, 505–506, 508, 525, 526–528, 531, 543, 550, 561, 568, 572–573, 590, 595, 611

Decimal point, 368, 370–372

Decimals

adding and subtracting, with money, 386–387, 388–389, 390–392

fractions and, 368–369, 370–371, 374–376

model, 366–367, 368–369, 370–372

money and, 374–376, 386–387, 388–389, 390–392

place the decimal point, 368, 370–372

place value, 368, 370–372

tenths and hundredths, 366–367, 368–369, 370–372

whole numbers and, 266

Denominator, 326–327, 328–329, 346–347, 348–350, 352–353

Difference, *See* Subtraction

Different ways

to divide, 266–267, 268–269, 270, 282–283, 284, 302, 306, 308

to multiply, 106–107, 144, 148

Distinguish relevant from irrelevant information, 18, 338–339, 412–413

Dividend, 260–261, 570–571

Divisibility rules, 565

Division

across zeros, 300–301

algorithm, 266–267

arrays, 262–264, 266–267

checking by multiplication, 269, 292–293, 548–549, 562–563, 566–568

fact families, 260–261, 262–264, 266–267, 268–270, 286–287, 288–289, 292–293, 302–304, 306–307, 308–310, 312–313, 527–528, 530–531

for converting units, 596–598, 612–614

in different ways, 266–267, 268–270, 282–284, 302, 306, 308

inverse relationship to multiplication, 280–281, 282–284, 286–287, 292–293, 302, 306, 308

modeling, 262–264, 266–267, 292–293, 542–543, 544–545, 560–561

of three- and four-digit numbers, 560–561, 562–564, 566–568, 570–571

of two-digit numbers, 542–543, 544–545, 548–549

practice, 302–303, 306–307, 308–309

regrouping in, 544–546, 548–550, 566–568, 570

relationship to multiplication, 262–263, 266–267, 268–270, 280–281, 288–289, 292–293, 530–532

rules for, 300–301

to solve problems, 260–261, 262–263, 266–267, 268–270, 286–287, 292–293, 302–304, 306–307, 308–310, 312–313, 526–528, 530–532

with money amounts in decimal notation, 534–535, 566–568

with remainders, 524–525, 526–528, 530–532

Division facts

fact families, 260–261, 262–264, 266–267, 268–270, 286–287, 288–289, 292–293, 302–304, 306–307, 308–310, 312–313, 527–528, 530–531

strategies, 268–270, 282–284, 288–290, 302–304, 306–307, 308–310

with multiplication table, 280–281

Division sentences, *See* Number Sentences, 149, 264, 284, 396, 488–489, 550

Draw a Picture, strategy, 204–205

Edge, 232–233, 234–235, 336

Equal groups problems, 260–261, 262–264, 524–525, 526–528

Equal parts, 326–327

Equality, *see* Equations

Equally likely events, 496–497, 498–500, 502–503, 504–506

Equations, 9, 52, 53, 57, 64, 100, 106, 111, 124, 132, 273, 284, 286–287, 288–289, 293, 301, 307, 308–309, 355, 358, 398–399, 412, 415, 421, 431, 549–550, 552, 564, 567–568, 617

Equilateral triangles, 198–199

Equivalent fractions

modeling, 330–331, 332–333

on a number line, 334–336

Estimate and measure, 238–239, 240–242

Estimation, 30, 31, 32, 35, 84, 85, 86, 87, 115, 126, 130, 146, 170–171, 172–173, 176–177, 178–180, 182, 204, 212–213, 218–219, 220, 238–239, 240–241, 273, 359, 416–418, 421, 434–435, 436–438, 450–452, 458, 460, 552, 586–588, 592–594, 608–609, 610–611, 616–617

area, 218–219

capacity, 586–587, 608–609

differences, 84–85, 86–87

exact or approximate solutions, 86–87, 416–418, 608–609

for comparing, 417

length, 170–171, 176–177, 212–213

money amounts, 86–87, 460–461

numbers, 30–31

perimeter, 212–213

products, 416–417, 434, 437, 450–451, 460–461

sums and differences, 84–85, 86–87

Index

Credits

PHOTOGRAPHY

1 ©Visions of America, LLC/Alamy bckgd **4-5** ©STScI/NASA/Corbis spread **6** ©S.T. Yiap Images/Alamy cr **8** ©NASA cr **10** ©NASA cr **16** ©NASA cr **17** ©Michael J. Doolittle / The Image Works cr **17** ©NASA Jet Propulsion Laboratory b **19** © Axel Hess / Alamy c **24-5** ©Anton J. Geisser/age fotostock spread **29** © Scott Montgomery/Stone/Getty Images cr **30** ©Mark Oristano 2005 bl **31** ©Morton Beebe/CORBIS cr **32** ©Chris George/Alamy cr **34** ©Sara Krulwich/The New York Times/Redux bl **36** ©Miroslav Tolimir/Shutterstock Inc. br **36** ©Bonnie Kamin/PhotoEdit Inc. inset **36** ©Mark Gibson Photography tr **45** ©Patricia Danna/Animals Animals/Earth Scenes bckgd **48-9** ©Shin Yoshino/Minden Pictures. spread **48-9** ©Cyril Laubscher/Dorling Kindersley spread **50** ©Chip Henderson/Index Stock tr **53** ©Galen Rowell/CORBIS c **56** ©Jeremiah Easter cr **57** ©AUSTIN J. STEVENS/Animals Animals - Earth Scenes cr **58** ©Rick & Nora Bowers/Alamy cr **60** ©G. Ronald Austing/Photo Researchers, Inc. cl **62** ©Momatiuk Eastcott/Corbis tr **63** ©Garry Adams/Index Stock Imagery cr **63** ©Yan Ke/Shutterstock Inc. b **63** © Andrew Linscott / Alamy c **64** ©Thomas Shjarback/Alamy tr **70-1** ©Chad Ehlers/Alamy bckgd **73** ©Hongwu Wang/Shutterstock Inc. br **74** ©Barbara Jablonska/Shutterstock, Inc. b **78** © Charles O'Rear/CORBIS bl **80** ©SUNNYphotography.com/Alamy cr **83** ©Idealink Photography/Alamy cr **83** ©Art Kowalsky/Alamy b **85** ©Mark Gibson Photography cr **93** ©bluestocking/Shutterstock br **95** ©Photodisc/Getty Images bckgd **98-9** ©Hemera Technologies/AbleStock.com/Jupiterimages bckgd **104** ©pixelman/Shutterstock cr **104** ©Bill Frische/Shutterstock tl **104** ©Avner Richard/Shutterstock cl **104** ©Antonio Ovejero Diaz/Shutterstock bc **104** ©Ljupco Smokovski/Shutterstock c **104** ©Ljupco Smokovski/Shutterstock tc **104** ©Popovici Ioan/Shutterstock c **107** ©Lawrence Manning/Corbis cr **107** ©Royalty Free/C Squared Studios/Photodisc Green/Getty Images br **108** ©Frank Vetere/Alamy cr **109** ©Buddy Mays/CORBIS **109** ©George D. Lepp/CORBIS b **111** ©David Young-Wolff/Photo Edit — All rights reserved. cr **114** © Richard Cummins/CORBIS tr **114** ©Royalty Free/Masterfile br **120-1** ©age fotostock/SuperStock spread **125** ©Natalia Bratslavsky/Shutterstock br **125** © George D. Lepp/CORBIS cr **129** © Ted Pink / Alamy tr **130** ©Lightphase Photography/Shutterstock c **132** © Blend Images / Alamy bl **133** ©Galen Rowell/CORBIS cr **134** ©Frans Lanting/Minden bl **134** ©Tina Rencelj/Shutterstock cl **140-1** ©Steve Hamblin/Alamy spread **145** ©Visions of America, LLC/Alamy br **146** ©Richard Cummins/CORBIS cr **151** ©D. Hurst/Alamy **152** ©Daniel Gilbey - My portfolio/Shutterstock Inc. cr **154** ©Royalty Free/Tanya Constantine/Photodisc Red/Getty Images cr **155** ©Richard Cummins/CORBIS b **155** ©Danita Delimont/Alamy cr **156** ©Andrea Chu/Taxi/Getty Images bl **157** ©Bristol City Museum/naturepl.com cl **157** ©Naturfoto Honal/CORBIS cr **165** ©Greg Vaughn/The Image Bank/Getty Images bckgd **168-9** ©Robert Harding Photography/PunchStock spread **167** ©AM Corporation / Alamy bl **168-9** ©Robert Harding Photography/PunchStock **169** ©Sergio Pitamitz/Corbis bl **169** ©Miguel Salmeron/The Image Bank/Getty Images b **169** ©Ismael Montero Verdu/Shutterstock t **171** © Mick Broughton / Alamy cr **172** ©Royalty Free/Corbis b **174** ©Emilia Stasiak/ShutterstoCk Inc. cr **176** ©Martin Cerny/Shutterstock Inc. c **178** ©Thinkstock/Corbis br **178** ©Jeff Greenberg/Index Stock Imagery cr **179** ©Patrick Eden/Alamy cr **180** © Randy Faris/Corbis cr **181** ©Jon Arnold Images/Alamy b **182** ©Danita Delimont/Alamy tr **182** ©Thinkstock/Corbis br **188-9** ©Ben Luxmoore/Arcaid/Corbis spread **192** © David Pollack/CORBIS tr **198** ©Lincoln Russell/Stock Boston, Inc./PictureQuest **199** ©Mark E. Gibson r **200** ©Kevin Matthews/ArtificeImages bl **201** © Farrell Grehan/CORBIS tr **202** ©Photo Network /Alamy cr **203** ©Greg Pease/Stone/Getty Images bl **204** © Skyscan Photolibrary / Alamy bl **205** © RubberBall / Alamy br **210-1** ©age fotostock/SuperStock spread **215** © Mika/zefa/Corbis cr **216** ©picturedimensions/Alamy cr **224** ©Jenny Horne/Shutterstock t **230-1** ©Steve Hamblin/Alamy spread **235** ©Dynamic Graphics Group/IT Stock Free/Alamy l **235** J. Norman Reid/Shutterstock c **235** Rebecca Photography/Shutterstock cr **236** ©Shubroto Chattopadhyay/Index Stock cr **242** ©FocusJapan/Alamy cr **244** ©Asterisco.org/Corbis bl **248** ©Ernst Wrba/Alamy bl **248** ©Charles Smith/Corbis br **248** ©Jakub Cejpek/Shutterstock **255** ©Stuart Westmorland/Corbis bckgd **257** © James W. Porter/CORBIS br **258-9** ©Jerry Shulman/SuperStock spread **258-9** ©PhotoSpin spread **262** ©PhotoDisc / Getty Images cr **266** ©Dennie Cody/Taxi/Getty Images bl **266** ©imagebroker/Alamy tr **266** ©Eric Isselee/Shutterstock tr **266** ©BananaStock/Alamy bl **268** ©Klein & Hubert/Bios/Peter Arnold, Inc. tr **269** ©Royalty Free/Sean Murphy/Riser/Getty Images cr **270** © Lew Robertson/Corbis cr **271** ©Joe Raedle/Getty Images News/Getty Images bl **271** ©Warren Faidley/Corbis b **272** ©Handout/Reuters/Corbis San Diego, California, United States tr **272** © Carl & Ann Purcell/CORBIS br **278-9** ©Kavita Favelle/Alamy spread **282** ©Royalty-Free/Corbis tr **283** ©Marie-Louise Avery/Alamy cr **284** ©Royalty Free/John A Rizzo/Photodisc Green/Getty Images cr **286** ©Angela Hill/Shutterstock r **286** ©Stacey Bates/Shutterstock cr **286** ©Claudia Steininger/Shutterstock cl **286** ©Johann Helgason/Shutterstock l **288** ©AP Images/Roland Weihrauch tr **290** ©Motoring Picture Library / Alamy cr **291** © Richard Cummins/CORBIS bckgd **292** © Frank Gaglione/Riser/Getty Images bl **293** © A. Inden/zefa/Corbis br **298-9** ©Bryan Peterson/Corbis spread **300** ©Linda Matlow/Pix Int'l./Alamy tc **302** © Owaki - Kulla/CORBIS tr **303** ©Ariel Skelley/CORBIS tr **304** ©AP Images/Alan Greth cr **306** ©Craig Tuttle/CORBIS cr **307** Denise Kappa/Shutterstock cr **310** ©Frans Lanting/Corbis cr **312** ©John Robertson/Alamy b **313** © SHOTFILE / Alamy br **321** ©DAJ/Alamy bckgd **324-5** ©Micheal Rosenfeld/Photographer's Choice/Getty Images. spread **324-5** ©Dan Hallman/Photonica/Getty Images spread **329** ©Dóri O'Connell/Shutterstock cr **333** ©Bob Daemmrich/Photo Edit cr **335** ©Tim Garcha/zefa/Corbis cr **336** ©Matthias Kulka/zefa/Corbis cr **338** ©Sean Justice/Photonica/Getty Images bl **340** ©newo/Shutterstock tc **340** ©Jakub Cejpek/Shutterstock tr **340** ©Radu Razvan/Shutterstock bc **344-5** ©Paul Poplis/FoodPix/Jupierimages spread **349** ©Don Smetzer/Stone/Getty Images cr **350** ©Sandro Vannini/CORBIS cr **350** ©Royalty Free/Siede Preis/Photodisc Green/Getty Images c **357** ©D. Hurst/Alamy cr **357** © Judith Collins / Alamy bckgd **358** ©James Prigoff and Robin Dunitz tr **358** © Flip Schulke/CORBIS br **360** © Burke/Triolo Productions/Brand X/Corbis tr **364-5** ©D. Hurst/Alamy spread

496 ©HMCo./Michael Indresano cr

542 cl **542** cr **542** ©HMCo./Susan Vicente bl

335 ©Tim Garcha/zefa/Corbis cr

609 Dave Starrett Photography cl

2 br **218** bl **232** b **326** br **352** bl **374** bl **408** br **412** bl **470** br **474** br **496** br **582** br **592** bl **610** Ed-Imaging br

3 br **6** br **12** cr **13** tr **18** bl **19** br **26** cr **46** br **47** br **72** bl **96** br **97** br **100** bl **100** cr **106** l **110** tr **122** br **142** cr **153** tr **166** br **167** br **170** br **171** bc **190** bl **196** c **197** t **213** br **219** br **233** cr **238** cr **238** br **238** cl **243** bl **256** br **260** br **263** cr **300** bc **308** tr **309** br **323** br **330** br **339** br **346** c **351** c **351** br **354** cl **355** tr **367** tr **370** tr **377** bl **386** cl **387** br **388** cl **390** tr **394** bl **409** br **418** cr **428** br **448** bl **471** br **481** br **481** c **499** cr **507** bl **520** br **521** br **524** br **560** tl **560** tr **560** bl **560** br **561** tc **572** bl **583** br **587** br **608** Ray Boudreau Photography br

Stock Photography

KSH1(b) Photodisc/PunchStock.

ILLUSTRATION

64 Bart Vallecoccia **84** Karen Minot cl **86** Andy Levine bl **87** Andy Levine tc **130** Wendy Smith cr **183** Dorian Melton tl **193** Theresa Sakno cr **235** Theresa Sakno tr **273** Dorian Melton bl **326** Ken Hansen tr **334** Nathan Jarvis tr **348** Claudia Davila tr **349** Claudia Davila tr **368** Claudia Davila tr **371** Theresa Sakno cr **372** Theresa Sakno c **376** Marek Jagucki cr **389** Marek Jagucki cr **405** Michael Cho **409** Chris Reed c **415** Robert Prince cr **432** John Kurtz cr **458** Dave Klug cr **535** Chris Reed br **568** Marek Jagucki cr **588** Ken Batelman c **590** John Kurtz tc **595** Claudia Davila cr **605** Dorian Melton br **611** Ken Hansen cr **621** Dorian Melton cr

Credits